Communication
Research ASKING QUESTIONS,

FINDING ANSWERS

SECOND EDITION

Joann Keyton

University of Kansas

Higher Education

Boston   Burr Ridge, IL   Dubuque, IA   Madison, WI   New York   San Francisco   St. Louis
Bangkok   Bogotá   Caracas   Kuala Lumpur   Lisbon   London   Madrid   Mexico City
Milan   Montreal   New Delhi   Santiago   Seoul   Singapore   Sydney   Taipei   Toronto

 **Higher Education**

COMMUNICATION RESEARCH: ASKING QUESTIONS, FINDING ANSWERS

Published by McGraw-Hill, a business unit of The McGraw-Hill Companies, Inc., 1221 Avenue of the Americas, New York, NY, 10020. Copyright © 2006, 2001 by The McGraw-Hill Companies, Inc. All rights reserved. No part of this publication may be reproduced or distributed in any form or by any means, or stored in a database or retrieval system, without the prior written consent of The McGraw-Hill Companies, Inc., including, but not limited to, in any network or other electronic storage or transmission, or broadcast for distance learning.

Some ancillaries, including electronic and print components, may not be available to customers outside the United States.

This book is printed on acid-free paper.

1 2 3 4 5 6 7 8 9 0 DOC/DOC 0 9 8 7 6 5

ISBN 0-07-304950-6

Editor in Chief: *Emily Barrosse*
Publisher: *Phillip A. Butcher*
Executive Editor: *Nannette Giles*
Associate Developmental Editor: *Joshua F. Hawkins*
Senior Marketing Manager: *Leslie Oberhuber*
Managing Editor: *Jean Dal Porto*
Project Manager: *Emily Hatteberg*
Art Director: *Jeanne Schreiber*
Associate Designer: *Srdjan Savanovic*
Cover Designer: *Jennifer McQueen*
Cover Credit: *© Corbis*
Senior Media Project Manager: *Nancy Garcia*
Production Supervisor: *Janean A. Utley*
Composition: *9.5/12 Palatino by International Typesetting and Composition*
Printing: *PMS Black, 45 # New Era Matte, R.R. Donnelley and Sons, Inc./Crawfordsville, IN.*

Library of Congress Cataloging-in-Publication Data

Keyton, Joann
    Communication research : asking questions, finding answers / Joanne Keyton.—2nd ed.
      p. cm.
    Includes bibliographical references and index.
    ISBN 0-07-304950-6 (alk. paper)
    1. Communication—Research. I. Title.
P91.3.K49 2006
302.2′072—dc22
                                       2005041592

www.mhhe.com

CONTENTS

CHAPTER 4   Introduction to Qualitative Research   58

APPENDIXES

PREFACE

This book began 12 years ago when I was forced to think about research methods in a new way. Approached by an organization to help them assess their human resources policy and training, I was overwhelmed by the task of identifying the problems and discovering and developing practical, yet theoretically based solutions. I eagerly agreed to help the organization because their problem—how to create a workplace in which respect and dignity were the core values—was an opportunity to test my skills and abilities as a researcher. I knew that I first needed to develop content expertise. After conducting library and electronic database searches, I realized that the information I obtained was incomplete and at times conflicting. Yet, this information allowed me to develop an initial response that included policy, training, and reporting procedures. I could have stopped there, presented the information to the organization, and considered myself done with the task. Yet, conducting research within the organization was a unique research opportunity, allowing me to both contribute to the organizational communication literature base and create a more tailored response for the organization.

Moving further into this process, I conducted focus groups with employees at all levels to gain insight into their personal experiences in the organization. Policy and training would not be as effective if they did not address the needs of employees and management. Data from the focus groups revealed that employees identified a few managers whom they believed to be effective in dealing with employee issues. I conducted field interviews with these individuals. Data from those interviews revealed that inconsistencies among the organization's current policies, training, and reporting procedures were a significant problem. Next, I conducted a content analysis of the organization's policies to examine how the organization defined and formalized the relationship between managers and employees.

Again, I could have stopped there, presented the information to the organization, and considered myself done with the task. But a new research opportunity presented itself—to test employee and management acceptance of the policy and training I proposed. After designing and conducting survey and experimental studies, I was able to tailor the messages the organization wanted to send in a way that was acceptable to and understandable by employees.

The point to this story is that research is a process. In some cases, library research from the vast store of communication literature may answer our research questions. In other cases, researchers must design studies to collect quantitative or qualitative data that, when analyzed, will answer those questions. Too many times, I hear students describe research as dull and boring with little relevance to their lives. But, when the research process is designed to answer questions about communication issues that are important to students, it provides them with a new perspective. Rather than considering research a boring and laborious chore, they recognize that research is the most effective means for answering meaningful questions in their lives.

The other point to my story is that far too often, I hear students and professors make claims such as "I'm a quantitative researcher" or "I'm an ethnographer." In reality, researchers must have a broad understanding and appreciation of all methodologies—quantitative and qualitative—in order to conduct their research effectively. The second edition of this book continues to emphasize three important points:

1. All research starts with an initial research question or problem.

2. Research is a process in which the researcher makes important decisions at crucial points about what to do and how to do it. This is in contrast to viewing research simply as a series of steps to be completed.

3. To answer the varied nature of questions about communication, one must be familiar with both quantitative and qualitative methodologies.

Communication Research: Asking Questions, Finding Answers covers basic research issues and processes for both quantitative and qualitative approaches appropriate for communication students with no previous research methods experience. The text's guiding principle is that methodological choices are made from one's research questions or hypotheses. This avoids the pitfall in which students learn one methodology or one methodological skill and then force that method to answer all types of questions.

FEATURES

The primary purpose of this textbook is to introduce students to communication research methods by meeting two objectives. The first objective is to help students become better consumers of the communication research literature by emphasizing effective methods for finding, consuming, and analyzing communication research. This objective is important because students are resident consumers of the communication literature through their participation in other content- or context-specific communication courses. The second objective is to provide a path for students who wish to develop and conduct research projects. To those ends, this book provides coverage of the entire research process: how one conceptualizes a research idea, turns it into an interesting and researchable question, selects a methodology, conducts the study, and writes up the study's findings. I believe that students who can effectively navigate, select, and use the communication research literature can become effective researchers, and, reciprocally, that students engaged in communication research will be able to more effectively use the existing research literature. Regardless of the role in which

students use their research knowledge, they must be able to read and understand the communication research literature.

This book provides several features to help students succeed in both roles. First, numerous examples are drawn from published research to provide clear direction on *what this process or step looks like*. These examples, 150 of which are new to the second edition, are drawn from recent journal articles, which are available in most university and college libraries. Using examples from the breadth of the discipline (for example, persuasion, interpersonal, group, organizational, mass communication, and public relations) lessens the ambiguity between information presented in the book and students' understanding and potential application of the information.

Second, the book incorporates two kinds of boxes, placed throughout the chapters that alert students to the nuances of the research process. The first, *Design Check*, alerts students to the practical and logistical issues that student researchers should consider when designing a study. These are the same issues that students should ask of the research studies they read, because how these issues are addressed by researchers influences study outcomes and data interpretations. The second type of box, *An Ethical Issue*, alerts students to issues of research ethics and integrity. Not only must researchers balance practical and logistical issues, they must do so while addressing ethical issues that occur when *people* and their communication artifacts are used as the basis of research.

Third, the book is based on active pedagogy and the philosophy that students learn best by doing. *Chapter Checklists* begin each chapter to highlight for students the essential learning objectives for each chapter. The objectives help students make discrete distinctions about the research process and give students a standard for what they should be able to demonstrate after reading and studying chapter material. *Try This!* boxes are placed throughout the chapters to engage students in short research activities that can be used in the classroom with individuals or groups, or as short homework assignments. End-of-chapter summaries have been developed as point-by-point summaries of information presented in the chapter. Stated simply, these factual statements can help direct students' study of the material and be used as a stimulus to extract students' understanding and application of the material. Key terms are boldfaced within the text and listed at the end of chapter. Key term definitions can be found in the glossary at the end of the book.

Fourth, the book presents a balance of quantitative and qualitative research because the communication research literature embraces both social scientific approaches. The second edition provides an improved focus on qualitative research: it has its own introductory chapter, two research design and one data analysis chapters, and a chapter devoted to the writing and reporting of qualitative data.

Finally, the book focuses on students. It is written for them—to their level of knowledge and understanding about human communication, the communication research literature, and the relative research processes. My goal in writing the chapters was to explain the research steps and identify the steps researchers take in developing and conducting communication research. With study and instruction, students should be able to use this material and integrate it with what they know and are familiar with from their other communication courses to accomplish two objectives: 1) to be more analytical and make more sophisticated interpretations of the communication research they read, and 2) to design and conduct basic quantitative and qualitative research studies.

ORGANIZATION

The book is divided into four sections. In the first section, Research Basics, students are introduced to the research process, its basic principles, both quantitative and qualitative research, and research ethics before specific methodological techniques are addressed. This organization emphasizes that research is a process, not just one type of method or research skill. Chapters 1 and 2 are introductory to research in general and are neutral with respect to methodology. The issues raised in these initial chapters are issues that both quantitative and

qualitative researchers must address. Then Chapters 3 and 4 provide introductions to both quantitative and qualitative methodologies. This arrangement encourages students to consider both methodologies and to gain a foundation in each before proceeding to detailed information in subsequent chapters on how specific methods within each work. Chapter 5 is devoted to issues of research ethics—issues students must consider regardless of which methodology they choose.

The second section of the book, Quantitative Communication Research, provides detailed coverage on how research is conducted with quantitative methodologies. Chapters 6 through 9 explain measurement concepts, sampling procedures, hypothesis testing, and experimental, quasi-experimental, descriptive, and survey research designs. Chapters 10 through 12 explain descriptive statistics and statistical tests of differences and relationships, with a special emphasis on interpreting the results of these tests. Chapter 13 explores two quantitative methods for analyzing text and message content. Chapters in the third section, Qualitative Communication Research, focus on qualitative research design and present detailed information on field interviewing, focus groups, narratives, and ethnography as qualitative methods of data collection. A chapter is devoted to analyzing qualitative data collected with these methods.

The fourth section of the book, Reading and Writing Research Reports, provides separate chapters for concluding the research process. These chapters demystify this stage of the research process for students, whether they are reading the research literature or ready to write a research report. Researchers relying on tradition and customary practices are able and adept consumers of the research literature. Alternately, students confront the research literature with little understanding of how and why finished research reports look the way they do. By having access to this *insider* information, students will be able to prepare their final projects in the traditions of the discipline as well as be able to better decode the research literature.

In talking with colleagues who also teach research methods, I have found that instructors differ greatly in their treatment of statistical concepts.

To accommodate these differences in pedagogical style, this book presents the conceptual foundation of each test supported with examples of the test from the research literature. Each test is discussed from the point of view of a student who finds this test in the literature. Questions used to develop these chapters include: How should I read the results of any particular test? How do I connect these results to the research questions and hypotheses the authors proposed? Alternately, for those students who wish to design and conduct quantitative research projects, the statistical formulas (with worked examples as models for each test) appear in an appendix.

TEACHING SUPPLEMENTS

A detailed instructor's manual available on an Instructor's Resource CD-ROM and on the Instructor Center website accompanies the book. This manual includes sample syllabi, teaching tips, chapter and course assignments, exercises for each chapter, and a test bank. This manual also includes worksheets for each chapter. Typically one or two pages in length, worksheets can be used as a homework or in-class assignment for students to review their knowledge and understanding about the material presented. Question types include objective (for example, fill in the blank), comprehension (for example, explain how academic research differs from proprietary research), and behavioral (for example, given a set of variables the student is asked to write research questions and hypotheses). For those chapters that cover statistics or the analysis and interpretation of qualitative data, additional worksheets are available, which provide students with the opportunity to work several examples from raw data through to interpretation.

Finally, the book's website, www.mhhe.com/keyton2, includes PowerPoint outlines for each chapter; URLs for websites that support or provide additional material presented in the chapters; and online review tests, a glossary, crossword puzzles, and flashcards for students to use in reviewing the material. The Instructor Center includes the Instructor's Manual, PowerPoint slides, and links to support materials.

ACKNOWLEDGMENTS

In writing this book, I have benefited from the generosity of researchers, scientists, and scholars from many disciplines around the world. Unlike many other bodies of knowledge, the web has become a cornucopia of information about research methods and statistics. When contacted by email, these colleagues were both prompt and generous.

I have also benefited from the many undergraduate students in my research methods course who continued to say that they did not understand after I had explained a concept or technique. Their questioning and my inability to always provide them an appropriate and acceptable answer provided the motivation for this text.

This second edition has benefited from the many instructors and students who have emailed me with questions or issues they would like me to address or explain further. I appreciate this feedback-in-progress and much of it has been incorporated here.

I also thank the scholars who reviewed this text during its development for the encouragement and wisdom they extended. Reviewers for the first edition were Julie Burke, Bowling Green State University; Mark Callister, Western Illinois University; Risa Dickson, CSU–San Bernardino; Laurel Heatherington, Boise State University; Peter Jorgenson, Western Illinois University; Gerianne Merrigan, San Francisco State University; David Schrader, Oklahoma State University; Tim Sellnow, North Dakota State University; Tom Socha, Old Dominion University; Mike Stephenson, University of Missouri; Paige Turner, St. Louis University; Michelle Violanti, University of Tennessee; Richard West, University of Southern Maine; Bryan Whaley, University of San Francisco; Gust Yep, San Francisco State University; Walter Zakahi, New Mexico State University.

Reviewers for the second edition were: Osabuohien P. Amienyi, Arkansas State University; James Kiwanuka-Tondo, North Carolina State University; Charles Roberts, East Tennessee State University; Laurel Traynowicz, Boise State University; Melinda Villagran, University of Texas at San Antonio.

Thanks to the McGraw-Hill team, led by executive editor Nanette Giles. Others on this team included Joshua Hawkins, developmental editor; Emily Hatteberg, project manager; Srdjan Savanovic, designer; Leslie Oberhuber, marketing manager; and Nancy Garcia, media project manager. They helped me produce the finished product.

In the first edition, I thanked my colleagues—Tommy Darwin, Steve Rhodes, and Pradeep Sopory. For this second edition, I'd like to add Ron Warren, Debbie Ford, and Tracy Russo. Each of these six people have enriched and challenged my role as researcher.

I would also like to thank the many undergraduate and graduate students who have worked with me at the University of Kansas and the University of Memphis on research projects and who have worked through research issues (and challenged me) in methodology classes.

For me, methodology is the best teaching assignment I can have.

Thank you to my friends—Bob, Randy, Christie, Sherry, Joanne and Tom, Pat and Jay, Linda, Liz and Kim, Allison, Amy, Stephanie, Kelby, and Bill. I appreciate your friendship and support. Again, fs, thanks for your special friendship. The completion of this book is another reason to enjoy two of the finer things in life.

Thank you Maggie and Sally for always reminding me what my *real* job is: to let the dogs in, let the dogs out, let the dogs in, let the dogs out. . . .

I am not one to dedicate things. But, Jeff—this book is for you. As a student, you would not allow me to let you down. As a friend, you have not let me down. Your invaluable lessons, both professional and personal, helped me write this text. Thanks for your continual support and encouragement. My love always.

CHAPTER ONE

Introduction to Research in Communication

Chapter Checklist

After reading this chapter, you should be able to:

1. Identify instances in which you could use or conduct communication research as a student, use or conduct communication research as a professional, and use the results of communication research in your personal life.

2. Explain the goals of research.

3. Explain the relationship of research and theory.

4. Explain communication research as a social science.

5. Describe how communication research from a social science perspective is different from other forms of communication research and other forms of social science research.

6. Differentiate among the characteristics of science.

7. Distinguish between research question and hypothesis.

8. Explain the law of the hammer.

9. Describe the differences among questions of fact, variable relations, value, and policy.

10. Identify questions about communication that you believe are worth pursuing.

As a student in a research methods course, you have two roles. In one role, you are a consumer of communication research. You read summaries of research in your textbooks. In some courses, your instructors may require you to read and analyze research articles published in the discipline's journals.

In the other role, you are a researcher collecting and interpreting data to answer research questions and hypotheses. These activities may be part of the course for which you are reading this book, an independent study, an upper-division course, or your senior project. The information in this book can help you succeed in both roles. But before you identify yourself with either or both roles, turn your attention to answering the question "What is research?"

WHAT IS RESEARCH?

In its most basic form, *research* is the process of asking questions and finding answers. You have likely conducted research of your own even if it wasn't in the formal sense. For example, as you chose which college or university to attend, you asked questions of students, faculty, and staff at the various institutions you were considering. You might also have looked for answers to your questions on webpages for the different colleges and universities or used the survey results from *U.S. News & World Report,* which ranks America's colleges and universities. As you made choices about your major, you read the college bulletin, talked to students and an advisor, and perhaps even talked to professionals in the field you believed you wanted to pursue. In these activities, you sought answers to your questions. Which school is best for me? Which school has the type of student experience I am looking for? Which schools are affordable? What is the annual income of alumni with my major? What kinds of career opportunities can I expect? By asking these questions, you were taking on the role of detective as you tracked down the information needed to make a decision.

Not only were you asking questions and seeking answers, but more than likely you were also relying on the results of research performed by others, on the detective work of others. It would be impossible for you to answer your set of questions without such input. For example, for the question "What is the annual income of alumni with my major?" it would not be realistic for you to survey graduates in your major field to discover their annual income. More likely you relied on a survey conducted by a professional association, an alumni association, or a fraternity or sorority. You used the reported results of their work to answer your question. Although someone else was doing the research, you still needed to evaluate the efficacy of their research to gauge its usefulness in answering the question.

You are also familiar with other types of research. *USA Today* profiles the results of research each day. You have heard the results of medical research reported in the news. During political campaigns, the results of preference polls are reported in the news and archived on news organization webpages. And, no doubt, you have heard the results of research on underage drinking and drug use. If you work, your company may have conducted research on the preferences of its customers or the quality of its products.

The point here is that research is all around us, often presented in ways that we would not recognize as research. Thus, **research,** as we will study it, is the discovery of answers to questions through the application of scientific and systematic procedures. Given this basic definition of research, you can see that you probably come into contact with several different forms of research on a daily basis. You probably also use the results of research in making both personal and professional decisions.

The specific focus of this text is communication research—that is, quantitative or qualitative research conducted by communication scholars about communication phenomena. The focus is also on research conducted from a social science perspective, which is distinct from rhetorical research and also distinct from critical research. Yet, distinctions among these three perspectives—social science, rhetorical, and critical—are not always clear (Craig, 1993), and scholars working from the other perspectives do use some methods more commonly associated with social science research. **Social science research** is conducted through the use of scientific and systematic methods, and it is based on the assumption that research can uncover patterns in the lives of people. When patterns of communication behavior are confirmed or discovered, scholars develop useful theories of communication that speak to the regularity of communication (Bostrom, 2003).

The research techniques and methods presented in this book are used to study the communication behavior of humans and the communication artifacts that people leave behind. Although some people think of social science research as objective research, communication scholars use both quantitative (more objective) and qualitative (more subjective) methods—sometimes separately and sometimes in combination with one another. Both types of methods are **empirical**, meaning that both methods are based on observations or experiences of communication. Both types are needed as it is unlikely that quantitative or qualitative methods alone can provide complete answers to the many questions we have about communication behavior.

Your Relationship With Research

As discussed earlier, your relationship to this material can be conceptualized in two ways—as that of a researcher or as that of a consumer of research. You may take on the researcher role as a student, as an employee, or as a consultant. It is likely that the class for which you are reading this book will develop and conduct a research project as part of a class assignment. You may also decide that the process of research is interesting enough that you plan to continue your education in graduate school, where you will receive additional instruction in research methodology. You might even decide to become a professor and spend much of your professional time as a researcher, finding answers to questions that interest you and matter to others.

After you graduate, you might find yourself in a professional position where research is part of your regularly assigned job responsibilities. Positions in marketing and advertising, as well as jobs in political, organizational, and legal communication, are just a few in which research plays a central role in decision making. Even though their organizational title may not be "researcher," many employees at the managerial or executive level are responsible for collecting and analyzing data to help organizations and employees make more effective and efficient decisions. But are these examples of communication research? They could be. Some organizations conduct surveys or focus groups to discover the degree of effectiveness of their internal communication practices. Media organizations regularly use surveys or focus groups to discover if informational, advertising, or promotional messages are being received as intended.

You could become a consultant and conduct **proprietary research,** research that is commissioned by an individual or organization for its own use. Organizations use consultants to evaluate their internal communication systems and operational effectiveness. Political figures also commission proprietary research to discover how they are doing in the polls and which of their central messages are having the most impact on potential voters. Marketing and advertising research is almost always proprietary. Even though the results of proprietary research are private and intended only for the use of whoever pays for the research, the researcher uses the same procedures and practices used in conducting scholarly or academic research.

Your relationship with research can also be conceptualized as that of a consumer. You consume the research of others when you read scholarly books and journals. You also consume research when you see or hear personally or professionally interesting information presented in the media, and use information about goods and services marketed to you. You might trust some sources more than others—or be more cautious—if you knew how the data were collected and analyzed.

Right now, your role as a consumer of research is more immediate than your current or potential role as a researcher. Your status as student forces you into the consumer role as you collect information in the library or from the World Wide Web to complete class assignments.

Is Communication Public or Private?

In general, what ethical issues do you believe are raised when researchers study the communication behavior of others? About what communication situations would you feel comfortable answering questions? In what situations would you feel comfortable having a researcher observe you? Are there some communication contexts that should remain the private domain of participants, closed to researchers' inquiries? What about intimate communication between significant others in the privacy of their bedroom? What about the communication of parent to child when discipline is required? What about communication that occurs among coworkers as they discuss ways to ridicule their boss? How would you respond if a communication researcher asked you questions about your communication behavior during these events? What arguments could you develop both for and against communication scholars conducting research about such events? Should some communication behaviors or contexts be off limits to communication researchers?

Your ability to evaluate the information you collect has a direct impact on your ability to learn and prepare assignments. Moreover, the media bombard us daily with information that has been accumulated through research. Even if you later become a professional researcher or academic, you will never be able to ignore your status as a consumer of research.

In both instances, your relationship with research requires that you assume the role of detective. As a researcher, you are the primary detective seeking answers to questions, fitting pieces of the puzzle together, and interpreting what you find to make conclusions and recommendations. As a consumer, you must still be a detective sorting through the data others have provided. In this role you still need to distinguish good information from bad, test assumptions and conclusions drawn by others, and analyze the extent to which the research process others used fits your needs and situation. In this case, your job as a detective is to determine if the information you are using is misleading or misinterpreted from its original form.

It is easy to feel overwhelmed or intimidated by the particular vocabulary and traditions of research. But if you approach learning about research as a detective would approach finding information, you are likely to discover that formal research is an extension of the types of informal asking and answering of questions that you have done all your life. After reading this chapter, you should be able to identify how research acts as an influence on your life and in your decision making. Throughout the rest of this chapter and throughout the book as well, specific examples of communication research will be highlighted as we explore how research is conducted—that is, how research is planned and carried out and how data are collected, analyzed, and reported. The goals of the book are to provide you with the basic skills of a researcher and to enhance your ability to be a better critic of the research reported by others.

SCHOLARLY RESEARCH

With this introduction to research in general, we will turn our attention to the formal and systematic method of scholarly research. Researchers, or scientists, who have been trained in research methods and procedures (generally as doctoral students) conduct research. These scholars formalize their questions into research questions or hypotheses, which provide the scope and direction of the research project as well as guide the researcher in selecting quantitative or qualitative methods to answer the questions. The questions or hypotheses direct what data the researcher collects. Once the data are collected, the researcher or research team analyzes the data to draw conclusions about the hypotheses or answer the research questions.

But the process is not complete. Scholarly, or academic, research is also public and available to consumers. However, the process of making it public is certainly different than it is for research conducted by a polling organization, for instance. Scholarly researchers describe what they have done in a paper that is submitted to a conference for presentation or to a journal or book for publication. Other experts in the field review the paper. This review serves as a test. Have the authors used the best methodology to answer their questions or hypotheses? Have the authors explained the results thoroughly and logically? Are there critical flaws in the research process that jeopardize the results? The papers that make it through the review process are then presented at a conference or published in an academic journal or book. This is where the results become consumable.

Pick up a text that is assigned reading for one of your other communication courses. You will find many references to research within the chapters. As an example, the following passage is from my text *Communication and Organizational Culture: A Key to Understanding Work Experiences* (Keyton, 2005):

> From any one position in the organization, it may look like the culture is consistently singular. However, it is more typical for organizations to structure themselves into networks based on tasks, relationships, information, and functions with organizational members identifying with, and belonging to, more than one network (Kuhn & Nelson, 2002).

The reference to the authors Kuhn and Nelson is called an in-text citation. If you turned to the references listed at the back of the text, you would find the publication information so you could look up the 2002 journal article written by Kuhn and Nelson. As the author of the text, I relied on the research of Kuhn and Nelson. As the reader of this passage, you are also a consumer and could verify my interpretation of their work by going to the original source.

Goals of Research

Accumulating knowledge through research is a continuous process. One research study cannot answer all the questions about any one issue or topic. This facet of learning—building on the research of others—is central to any academic discipline. Thus, the primary goal of research is to describe communication phenomena as well as discover and explain the relationships among them. Continuing with the example just given, discovery occurred when Kuhn and Nelson conducted research using both quantitative and qualitative methodologies to uncover how employees identified with their organization, and how those identifications resulted in communication networks. These scholars first built a case for their research question by drawing on the published research of other scholars. With the data they collected, they were able to describe employees' locations in their communication networks and their degree of organizational identification. Finally, they provided an explanation of the relationship between employees' organizational identification and their location in communication networks that followed logically from their arguments and the data. Thus, to put it more formally, research is the process of discovery and explanation.

The research process, if approached systematically, can have one of four results: It allows the researcher to describe behavior, determine causes of behavior, predict behavior, or explain behavior. *Describing behavior* entails describing outcomes, processes, or ways in which variables (another name for the concepts we study) are related to one another. The following example illustrates a research project that enabled a researcher to describe behavior.

Despite the number of contexts in which social support is given and received, detailed descriptions of the ways in which social support is enacted were missing. Using conversations from a peer-to-peer telephone counseling service, Pudlinski (2003) was able to develop three categories to describe the ways in which social support is constructed. Across a dataset of 366 responses from 44 calls, he discovered three common patterns in the ways support providers displayed social support: summarizing or minimizing the caller's problem (e.g., "I see what you're saying"), providing or seeking solutions (e.g., "What kind of a job do you think you'll apply for?"), and supporting a caller's report (e.g., "That's good"). Pudlinski's detailed descriptions of social support suggest that these messages are comprised of greater variety and complexity than generally thought.

Determining the cause or causes of behavior is of interest to communication scholars because knowing the cause of something allows scholars to later plan interventions or develop training to increase the effectiveness of communication. Keyton, Ferguson, and Rhodes (2001) wanted to determine which variables had greater effect on employees' perceptions that their organization lived up to its stated zero tolerance sexual harassment policy. Would constructs in the interaction environment (e.g., respondent sex, being a target of sexual harassment, being treated fairly by coworkers and supervisors) influence how respondents characterized the sexual nature of the organization's environment, and influence their perceptions of how well the organization lived up to its policy? Or, would organizational remedies, such as receiving sexual harassment training and retaining knowledge from that training, be more influential? Using the responses of 252 employees, the research team tested the influence of the interaction environment factors against the set of organizational remedy factors. Contrary to the presumption of the organization's executives, organizational remedies were not related to employees' perceptions about the organization's zero tolerance sexual harassment policy. The study's findings did support, however, that factors in the interaction environment caused two different employee reactions. First, male employees, employees who had been victims of sexual harassment, and employees who believed they were not being fairly treated by their coworkers perceived the organization's environment as sexualized and that the organization did not live up to its stated policy. Second, and alternately, employees who believed they were being fairly treated by their supervisors perceived that the organization's policy was being upheld.

If researchers can describe communication events and identify their causes, then they can turn to *predicting behavior*. If behaviors are predictable, then we can anticipate what will happen in the future. In turn, this knowledge can help us make better decisions. For example, Schneider, Lang, Shin, and Bradley (2004) wanted to determine if adding a story or narrative to justify game players' actions in violent video games would influence their game-playing experiences. This research team wondered if the addition of a story-based justification of killing to save the world would influence game players differently than the weaker narrative structure found in violent video games in which the story unfolds by moving to the next level of the game. Based on the research literature, the research team hypothesized that video game players would identify with characters and their goals to a greater extent when a story is present than when a story is not present. Experienced video game players participated in an experiment designed to test this prediction. Findings demonstrated that, yes, video game players more strongly identified with characters and their goals when a story was present. Thus, the research team's prediction was supported suggesting that violent video games with stories justifying violent acts may desensitize game players to violent behavior.

Going beyond describing, determining causes, and predicting, *explaining behavior* means understanding why a behavior occurs. For example, if researchers were able to determine how and why health campaigns work, more effective campaigns would ultimately result in a healthier society that spends less money on health care. But finding such an explanation is difficult and often requires a series of sophisticated research projects. Working from a well-developed and validated theoretical basis is another way to develop explanations for communication behavior. For example, A. J. Roberto, Meyer, Boster, and H. L. Roberto (2003) surveyed 488 junior high students about four aggressive behaviors: watching a fight, telling friends about a fight that is going to happen, insulting others, and fighting. For each of the aggressive behaviors except fighting, the explanatory model provided by the theory of reasoned action (i.e., the best determinant of actual behavior is behavioral intention) explained students' participation in aggressive behaviors. That is: students' attitudes about a behavior created behavioral intention, which, in turn, caused their participation in that behavior.

These four outcomes—description, determination of causes, prediction, and explanation—are closely related. New knowledge in one area will affect how questions are asked and answered in another.

Research and Theory

When researchers discover that one explanation about the relationship between phenomena occurs regularly, a theory can be constructed. Although many definitions exist for the term *theory*, in general, a **theory** is a related set of ideas that explains how or why something happens. In other words, a theory provides a way for thinking about and seeing the world (Deetz, 1992). More formally, a theory is a set of interrelated concepts, definitions, and propositions that presents a systematic view of phenomena. A theory specifies the relationships among the concepts with the objective of explaining and predicting the phenomena being studied (Kerlinger, 1986). As a result, theory helps us understand or make sense of the world around us. Of course, communication theories can help us understand our own communication behaviors as well as the communication behaviors of others (Miller & Nicholson, 1976).

With respect to communication, a theory is one or more propositions about people's communication behavior that enables a communicator to figure out how to communicate with particular individuals or in a given situation. The term *theory*, however, does not have one precise meaning. Rather, different definitions of the term are used because they promote different approaches to research (Craig, 1999; Miller & Nicholson, 1976). The best research is driven by theory, validates a theory, further explains a theory, challenges an existing theory, or aids in the creation of theory. Theoretically driven research is built on the results of previous researchers, and it provides a foundation for subsequent researchers. Theory cannot be formulated, tested, and verified

in one research study. Rather, theory is developed and tested over time. What we come to know as "the theory" to explain some phenomenon is the result of many research studies and the efforts of many researchers.

Cushman (1998, p. 9) points out that "human communication is one of the most creative, flexible, and thus anti-theoretic processes in which human beings engage." Why? The complexity of communicating in multiple cultures with multiple, and sometimes conflicting, social goals provides the opportunity for multiple individual interpretations. Moreover, communication occurs in multiple languages with different sets of rules and practices. According to Cushman, this variability is one important reason communication scholars must look for the mechanisms or constructs that are constant regardless of the language used to communicate. Thus, communication researchers who are part of a community of scholars and scientists take on the task of using systematic procedures and scientific principles to conduct research about how and why humans communicate as they do.

COMMUNICATION AS A SOCIAL SCIENCE

There are many methods of discovery and explanation, or many ways to solve problems. A rich variety of methods is available to communication researchers. This text will introduce you to both **quantitative methods** (generally speaking, research that relies on numerical measurement) and **qualitative methods** (generally speaking, research in which the researcher is the primary observer or data collector). Both methods are part of the social science research tradition as practiced in the communication discipline and reported in communication and related-discipline journals and scholarly books. Both quantitative and qualitative methods of research are empirical; that is, both methodologies are based on or are derived from experiences with observable phenomena. This is the critical element of research. Both quantitative and qualitative methodologies can observe and describe human communication. And both can help researchers in explaining or interpreting what was observed.

The study of communication from a social science perspective uses quantitative or qualitative methods to look for patterns of messages or communication behaviors. These patterns can be based on observations or measurements across cases or on the in-depth observations from one case over time. Either way, the data must be empirical; that is, the data must be able to be verified through observations or experiences.

How does the study of communication as a social science differ from humanistic and critical studies of communication? The study of communication from a rhetorical perspective focuses on how language is used to persuade in a particular case (for example, language use in a specific speech by a specific person or other one-time event from which a text can be drawn or developed). In addition to the rhetorical event itself, an analysis would include the historical, cultural, and social contexts surrounding it.

From a critical perspective, the emphasis is on the broader social structure that provides the context for understanding the inequality and oppression that can occur with communication practices and structures. (For example, what structures exist in our society that control or dominate the dissemination of new media technology?) Although some critical scholars will use some of the qualitative methods described in this book, the focus of their research is aligned more with broad societal issues than with the narrow questions asked by social scientists.

How does the study of communication differ from the study of other social sciences? Generally, the social sciences are defined as those areas of scientific exploration that focus on the study of human behavior. Psychology, sociology, and political science are other fields in the social sciences. As social scientist, the communication scholar focuses on symbols used to construct messages, messages, the effects of messages, and their meanings.

The social sciences are different from the natural sciences in that the social scientists focus on the study of human behavior. Problems that are significant for study in the social sciences involve several important variables, and untangling

the effects of one variable from another is difficult. Moreover, the social sciences recognize that the researcher is a human instrument with biases and subjective interpretations that can affect the individuals or processes under investigation. Finally, seldom can an entire system of human behavior (for example, an entire organizational communication system) be observed. Even if it could be, human systems are always subject to new influences; thus, what is being observed is dynamic. As a result of these differences, the study of human behavior is difficult to isolate and control even if the examination is done in the laboratory setting.

One last point is that social science research is contextually and culturally bound. Research is contextualized first by the number and type of people participating and by the type of communication being investigated. Second, research is contextualized by where the investigation occurs—in the lab or in the field. Third, research is contextualized by the culture in which it occurs. Researchers and participants bring cultural norms and values to what they do and how they communicate. All of these contextual and cultural factors influence the research investigation, the data produced, and the interpretation of results.

The Scientific Approach

So how do communication researchers incorporate scientific characteristics into the process of conducting research? Generally, research follows procedural traditions that have been tested, validated, confirmed, and accepted by social scientists of many disciplines over time. The research process has five general steps (Kerlinger, 1986).

First, researchers start with a question that interests them. A question may arise from their personal experiences or from experiences that have been reported to them by others. Or a question may arise from reading the scholarly or consumer literature. In other words, some question, or curiosity, is not explained or inadequately explained. A question may also be stated as a problem. In either form, the researcher cannot continue the research process without identifying and specifying the question or problem. For example, my own curiosity about why sexual harassment continues to occur in organizations despite clear societal and organizational signals that a perpetrator faces employment, legal, and even financial consequences for sexually harassing another employee caused me to pursue this area as a topic of research.

Second, the researcher uses the question or problem to formulate a **hypothesis,** or a tentative, educated guess or proposition about the relationship between two or more variables. Oftentimes, hypotheses take the form of statements like "If x occurs, then y will follow" or "As x increases, so will y." With respect to our sexual harassment research, we used previous scholarship to help direct our inquiry. One of our hypotheses proposed that participants who identified themselves as targets of sexual harassment would identify more verbal and nonverbal cues as harassment (Keyton & Rhodes, 1999).

If the researcher cannot formulate a tentative proposition after reviewing the existing literature, then a research question is developed. A **research question** asks what the tentative relationship among variables might be or asks about the state or nature of some communication phenomenon. For example, we used the research question "Will there be a relationship between ethical ideology and the ability to accurately distinguish between verbal and nonverbal behaviors that have been shown to be associated with flirting and sexual harassment?" (Keyton & Rhodes, 1997, p. 135). Although numerous studies had been published on both ethical ideology and sexual harassment, no study had explored the relationship between these two issues. Thus, we posed a question to help us determine if a relationship occurred. We could not propose what type of relationship would exist.

In the third step, which is often underemphasized, the researcher uses reason and experience to think through the hypotheses or research questions that are developed. A researcher might ask, "Do the research questions and hypotheses I've generated capture the essence of the problem?" or "Are there other variables that affect the relationship between the two variables I've identified?"

This step of reasoning, or thinking through, may, in fact, change the research agenda. It may broaden the nature and scope of research, or it

may more narrowly focus the researcher's inquiry. By taking this step in refining and formulating the research question or hypothesis, researchers discover the most significant issue that can be addressed given their initial questions or problems. By using the experience we gained in developing sexual harassment training for organizations and by searching the literature, we discovered that one of our proposed hypotheses ("participants who identified themselves as targets of sexual harassment would identify more verbal and nonverbal cues as harassment") would not adequately explain why some employees view behaviors as sexual harassment and others do not. In other words, an employee's perceptions of sexual harassment would not simply turn on whether she or he had been sexually harassed. As a result, we tested three other explanations.

Fourth, the researcher designs and conducts the observation, measurement, or experiment. Although each variable or element identified in the research question or hypothesis must be observed or measured, it is actually the relationship between them that is assessed. Fifth, the data are analyzed and interpreted in reference to the question or hypothesis posed in step 2 and refined in step 3.

Thus, the social scientific approach to communication research starts with a problem, a question, or an idea as the researcher identifies a barrier or gap in knowledge. Then, the research question or hypothesis is formulated. Once developed, the research question or hypothesis is revisited and refined. Only then can the methodology be designed and carried out. The results that are obtained are interpreted and fed back into our knowledge of the original problem. As a result, the problem is resolved, completely or partially, or new questions arise. Recognize that the five steps described are not necessarily discrete. One step blends into another. Work in one step may require the researcher to go back and revise what was previously completed.

Characteristics of Science

In pursuing these five steps of the research process, researchers can select from a variety of quantitative and qualitative methods. Although individual methods vary in the extent to which they encompass the following 12 characteristics, over time these characteristics have distinguished scholarly research from everyday, or informal, ways of knowing (Andersen, 1989; Bostrom, 2003; Katzer, Cook, & Crouch, 1978; Kerlinger, 1986). These characteristics are not unique to the study of communication. Rather, scientists of all disciplines have accepted them. Thus, the tradition of science rests with these 12 characteristics:

1. *Scientific research must be based on evidence.* Even experts can disagree. That is why evidence, or data, is paramount to the research process. Further, scientific research is based on the principle of empiricism. This means that careful and systematic observation must occur. What is observed and measured—the data—serves as the evidence researchers use in making their claims.

2. *Scientific research is testable.* This means that the proposition, research question, or hypothesis must be able to be probed or investigated with some quantitative or qualitative methodology. If the proposition cannot be tested or challenged in a research study, then only speculations about the validity of the claim can be made.

3. *Researchers must explore all possible explanations in an effort to demonstrate that their proposition cannot be disproved.* If a proposition can be shown to be false, then, logically, it cannot be true, or valid. If the proposition and its explanation hold up over time, scientists come to accept the finding as true or real, until shown otherwise.

4. *The results of a research study are replicable, or repeatable.* Ideally, different researchers in different settings and with different participants should conduct replication studies—studies that repeat the same procedures. The results of any one study could be wrong for many reasons. Repeating the same or a very similar study many times and obtaining the same or very similar results ensures that the finding is real and can be counted on.

5. *In order for replication to occur, research must be part of the public record.* This is why communication scholars publish their work in academic journals and scholarly books. Scholars typically are not paid for these publications, but their work is supported through their universities and sometimes by government agencies and other funding organizations. As part of the public record, libraries have copies of these journals and books so you can scrutinize what researchers did and how they did it. Scientific study is available to other researchers and the general public. It is not private, or proprietary, research conducted for the exclusive use of those who paid for the research to be done. Because scientific research is part of the public record, scholars build onto as well as challenge each other's work. All published research includes a section describing the methods by which the data were collected and interpreted. This allows others to evaluate the methods used for potential weaknesses and to replicate the study for further validation.

6. *Because scientific research is part of the public record, it is also self-correcting.* This characteristic means that the scholars who conducted the original study as well as the scholars who replicate or challenge studies are continually improving the methods by which they observe or measure the phenomenon of interest. Improving on the methods is one way to develop a greater understanding and more detailed explanations.

7. *Scientific research relies on measurement and observation.* Researchers can measure your communication apprehension, for example, by asking you to fill out a questionnaire. Or, they can observe your apprehension by counting the number of times you lose your place when you are speaking and have to refer to your notes. When something is not directly observable, researchers develop (and rely upon) other methods (such as questionnaires) to capture participants' attitudes, perceptions, and beliefs.

8. *Scientific research recognizes the possibility of error and attempts to control it.* When things are measured or observed, we expect that some error will occur. For example, errors occur when a researcher does not see the participant lose her place while speaking because his attention is distracted by loud music playing in another room or when a mistake is made in transferring data from the coding sheet to the spreadsheet. Error can occur in many places in the research process. Quantitative research limits and accounts for

error through the use of systematic procedures and statistics. Qualitative research accounts for error by providing detailed description to allow the reader to draw his or her own conclusions and interpretations. Most procedures have been standardized over time and across disciplines. Such formality in procedure acts as a form of control to help the researcher eliminate error, bias, and other explanations for the result found. Despite these control mechanisms, it is impossible to eliminate all bias and error in conducting research. Recognizing that bias and error can occur, researchers must take every precaution in helping to minimize it.

9. *Scientific objectivity requires the researcher to minimize personal bias and distortion.* Despite the passion for their topic and the time devoted to the project, researchers cannot be so committed to their own point of view and expectations that they fail to see other explanations when they appear. In essence, the objectivity of science distinguishes it from conclusions based solely on opinion. Too frequently, objectivity is associated only with quantitative research, and subjectivity is associated only with qualitative research. In reality, all researchers regardless of method must demonstrate objectivity in conducting research. Even though qualitative research is more subjective due to the greater intimacy of the researcher–participant relationship, scholars doing this type of research must be able to describe their role in the research process, and this act requires a certain amount of objectivity. Alternately, statistics must be selected and statistical findings must be interpreted—both subjective decisions. The point here is not to quibble over the alignment of objectivity/subjectivity to quantitative/qualitative method. Rather, it is to introduce the concept of scientific objectivity as practiced by all researchers regardless of which methodology they choose.

10. *Science by its nature rests on an attitude of skepticism.* By their nature, researchers are suspicious; they do not rely on what appears to be obvious or on common sense. Within the social science research tradition, researchers rely on data compiled from quantitative and qualitative methodologies to answer their questions and support their claims. This element of skepticism is what allows, even encourages, researchers to put their assumptions through a process of testing or verification.

11. *Scientific research has an interest in the generalizability of findings, or the extension of the findings to similar situations or to similar people.* In quantitative research, findings are more externally valid if they apply to a range of cases, people, places, or times. In other words, are the results of studies that use traditional college-age students as research participants applicable to nontraditional college-age students? What about teenagers? Or retired adults? All studies have limitations, but by using discipline-accepted procedures, researchers can help strengthen the generalizability of their results. In qualitative research, findings are typically less generalizable because they are more case-specific. However, the generalizability of qualitative results can also be strengthened as a researcher spends greater lengths of time observing research participants or observes participants at more than one point in the day.

12. *The final characteristic of science is its* **heuristic** *nature.* This means that research findings lead to more questions. At the conclusion of most journal articles, scholars identify new questions that surface from their findings. The ability of a finding to suggest additional questions or new methods of conducting the research is its heuristic ability. The ultimate objective of science should be to lead scientists to future discoveries and investigations.

Methodological Extremes

This introductory chapter is a good place to also introduce you to a methodological extreme that you should be aware of as you learn about research methodology (Bouma & Atkinson, 1995): the temptation to become a specialist in one method, known as the law of the hammer.

A child given a hammer for the first time is likely to run around the house and hammer anything and everything. From the child's viewpoint hammering is fun, even if hammering on Mother's new table is neither desirable nor appropriate (at least from the mother's point of view). The child hammers because it is new and novel.

Unfortunately, this same phenomenon can exist when students begin to learn research methods (see Cappella, 1977; Janesick, 1994). With each new technique, there is the tendency to believe that this particular method can answer any question. However, think of the method (or hammer) as a tool and recognize that there are appropriate tools for different purposes. Using the tool metaphor, hammers are good for pounding in nails, but screwdrivers are better for twisting in screws. Saws are good for cutting things in two but are ineffective for affixing something with a nail or a screw! The point here is that the substantive content of the research question or hypothesis drives the selection of the methodological tool (Hackman, 1992; Janesick, 2000).

Methods are useful or effective only to the degree that they help the researcher answer a specific question or explore a specific hypothesis. In fact, the answers produced through any method of investigation are influenced by the specific methodological technique used in the investigation (Clark, 1990). So, if you let the method drive the research questions you ask or the hypotheses you test, then your results are more likely to be tied to the method you selected than to represent a valid response to the question or test of the hypothesis. No one research method can answer all questions. Although you will find that you are drawn to some methods more naturally than others, you will develop stronger skills, both as a researcher and as a consumer of research, if you develop skills collecting and interpreting data from a variety of methodological techniques.

WHAT KINDS OF QUESTIONS DO COMMUNICATION SCHOLARS ASK?

Among the variety of questions that can be asked about communication are both important questions and trivial ones (Miller & Nicholson, 1976). How do researchers determine the significance of a question? There are three criteria: personal interest, social importance, and theoretical significance.

"Any question that interests or perplexes a person is personally significant" (Miller & Nicholson, p. 49). Questions that interest me include (1) How do children learn to communicate in groups? (2) Why do some employees persist in sexually harassing other employees given the individual, relational, professional, financial, and legal consequences that are likely to result? (3) To what extent does the relational development among group members affect the task effectiveness of a group? Some of the studies my colleagues and I have conducted in these areas are used as examples in this book.

What questions interest you? They are probably related to your personal or professional life. Your interests may be idiosyncratic, not coinciding with the interests of others. This demonstrates why the second criterion of social importance is valuable and necessary. Because communication is a social activity, significant questions are those that have a general social import (Miller & Nicholson, 1976). For example, "What media campaigns would decrease the likelihood that children try drugs and alcohol?" or "What negotiation strategies work best in resolving international differences?" Finding the answers to questions like these could have a powerful impact on our lives. Questions that drive research do not have to relate to all members of society. But we should ask who would be affected by the answer. If enough people are affected by or could use the answer to the question, then the question has social importance.

The third criterion is theoretical significance. Questions that further the construction of communication theories are significant (Miller & Nicholson, 1976) because they deepen our understanding and explanation of communication behavior. When these questions are posed and answered by research, we gain new knowledge.

Keeping these three criteria in mind can help us respond to the "So what?" question. Many times, people read research reports and have difficulty finding any significance or utility for the findings. If your research project is driven by personal interest, has societal significance, and helps further theory—and if these issues are described in the research report—then the "So what?" has been answered.

The Nature of the Questions

As you read the communication research literature, you will notice four different types of questions (Stacks & Salwen, 1996). The first type, **questions of fact,** provides definitions for phenomena in which we are interested. Whereas you may believe that all definitional issues have been addressed, remember that new communication situations and environments and changing societal values create new areas to explore and define. As a question of fact, Olson and Golish (2002) asked what topics of conflict are associated with the use of aggression in romantic relationships. In this study, the researchers wanted to discover the topics aggressive couples argue about. Some individuals reported as few as one topic; others reported as many as seven topics of argument in their romantic relationships. Analysis of these incidents resulted in nine categories of argument. Another example of communication research that asks questions of fact is a study that examined how individuals used email to communicate in romantic relationships at work (Hovick, Meyers, & Timmerman, 2003). Participants in the study responded to an online survey allowing the research team to answer how frequently partners in workplace romances used email to communicate at work, and to what extent organizational policies and procedures shaped their use of that medium. The descriptions provided by both studies move the phenomena from the abstract realm into the specific. Without defining phenomena of interest, it would be impossible to ask other types of questions.

After the "what" has been adequately defined, researchers generally turn to questions of relationships. These **questions of variable relations** examine if, how, and the degree to which phenomena are related. For example, Metzger and Flanagin (2002) asked how age, education, sex, and internet experience related to a relative instrumental orientation for using new media. The researchers measured college students' instrumental (i.e., intentional, selective, goal-driven) and ritualized (i.e., habitual, passing time) use of four new media. To create the relative score, the mean scores for instrumental and ritualized technology use were compared. This score was then assessed to

see if it differed according to student ages, education levels, sex, and internet experience. By doing so, the researchers could describe the relationship between relative instrumental orientation and the four other variables. In this case, only age was related to relative instrumental orientation. Older users used new media more instrumentally than did younger users.

By understanding how variables are related, we have a greater understanding of our world and the role of communication behavior in it. Most important, questions of variable relations help the community of communication scholars build and develop theory.

Questions of value, the third type, ask for individuals' subjective evaluations of issues and phenomena. Questions of value examine the aesthetic or normative features of communication, asking, for example, how good, right, or appropriate a communication phenomenon or practice is. Questions of value are inherent in a study that explored how temporary employees identified with the organizations in which they were currently working (Gossett, 2002). This study challenged the presumed value of organizations wanting their employees to form strong attachments to them. The results revealed that organizations that hire temporary workers may want to limit rather than promote the identification of these employees, as doing so enables organizational leaders to avoid including them in decision-making processes as well as relieve leaders of being responsible for temporary workers' welfare.

Questions of policy are the fourth type. Communication researchers seldom test policy issues directly, but the results of research studies are often used to recommend a course of action. Cai, Gantz, Schwartz, and Wang (2003) examined how online marketers complied with provisions of the Children's Online Privacy Protection Act. Of 162 websites analyzed, only four fully complied with the law. The researchers suggest two types of policy implications: (1) parents and schools can educate children about online privacy, and (2) the Federal Trade Commission should continue to disseminate information about the law to online marketers and actively enforce it.

As you can see, communication research varies widely in its subject matter. Some research

TRY THIS!   **Evaluating Communication Questions**

For each of the questions listed, evaluate your personal interest in the question and the question's social importance. Use the table to capture your evaluations. Rate your personal interest on a scale of 1 to 5, with 1 being "little or no personal interest" and 5 being "high personal interest." Rate social importance on a scale of 1 to 5 with 1 being "little or no social importance" and 5 being "high social importance."

Preliminary Research Question	Personal Interest	Social Importance
What do [medical] students' accounts of socialization experiences reveal about their ideological positioning during pre-clinical years of medical education? (FROM Harter & Krone, 2001)		
What topics of conflict are associated with the use of aggression in romantic couples? (FROM Olson & Golish, 2002)		
What proportion of websites for children requires parental permission for children to participate in activities? (FROM Cai et al., 2003)		
What are the processes that silence or encourage employees' discussion of organizational mistreatment? (FROM Meares, Oetzel, Torres, Derkacs, & Ginossar, 2004)		
How do people with disabilities communicatively manage solicited and unsolicited instrumental assistance in interactions with nondisabled others in early phrases of relationships? (FROM Braithwaite & Eckstein, 2003)		
What counts as excellent family communication and how are such standards associated with family satisfaction? (FROM Caughlin, 2003)		

Compare your evaluations with those of other students. How are your evaluations similar or different? What other questions about communication do you believe merit researchers' attention?

---

has implications for the development of communication theory, some has more practical application, and some contributes to both theory and practice. But all research starts with a basic question about communication that needs an answer, and all research uses some form of scientific and systematic research methodology in providing those answers.

SUMMARY

1. Research is asking questions and finding answers.

2. Scholarly research is the discovery of answers to questions through the application of scientific and systematic procedures.

3. Academic research follows accepted norms and procedures that have been adopted by scholars from many disciplines.

4. In the process of scientific discovery and explanation, four outcomes are sought: describing behavior, determining causes of behavior, predicting behavior, and explaining behavior.

5. The best research is that which is driven by theory, validates a theory, further explains a theory, challenges an existing theory, or aids in the creation of theory.

6. As a social science, communication researchers use both quantitative and qualitative methods.

7. The study of communication from a social science perspective looks for patterns across cases and focuses on symbols used to construct messages, messages, the effects of messages, and their meanings.

8. Communication scholars start with an interesting question and then formulate a formal research question or hypothesis.

9. Questions suitable for communication research are those for which the researcher has a personal interest, one that is of social importance, and one that has or can help develop theoretical significance.

10. A hypothesis is a tentative, educated guess or proposition about the relationship between two or more variables.

11. A formal research question asks what the tentative relationship among variables might be, or asks about the state or nature of some communication phenomenon.

12. Research is judged to be scientific by 12 characteristics: its empirical nature, its ability to be tested, the extent to which it can be falsified or disproved, the ability to replicate or repeat findings, the public nature of findings, its self-correcting nature, the ability to measure or observe the phenomenon of interest, the ability to minimize error through the control of procedures, its level of objectivity, the skepticism it raises, the generalizability of findings, and its heuristic nature.

13. Adopting a methodology and using it without regard to its appropriateness or effectiveness in answering the research question or hypothesis is known as the law of the hammer.

14. Questions suitable for communication research may be questions of fact, questions of variable relations, questions of value, or questions of policy.

KEY TERMS

empirical

heuristic

hypothesis

proprietary research

qualitative methods

quantitative methods

questions of fact

questions of policy

questions of value

questions of variable relations

research

research question

social science research

theory

CHAPTER TWO

The Research Process: Getting Started

Chapter Checklist

After reading this chapter, you should be able to:

1. Explain why the research process starts with identifying the research problem.

2. Develop a preliminary question from a topic or issue.

3. Explain why a preliminary question is superior to a topic in conducting library research.

4. Evaluate preliminary questions for their completeness and clarity.

5. Conduct a basic and detailed library search.

6. Identify and use communication discipline indexes and databases.

7. Adjust your preliminary question based on what you have found in the library search.

8. Glean the basic ideas from reading the abstract, literature review, and discussion sections of a research article.

9. Track a citation back to its original source.

10. Effectively summarize and report what you have found in the library.

11. Describe what a theory is and its role in communication research.

As a student researcher, you might find it difficult to make the transition from learning about research to finding the appropriate research literature to becoming part of the academic conversation about research. This chapter will help you identify ways of "getting into" the research conversation. After reading this chapter, you should be more comfortable and effective in conducting library research for your own research project and for assignments in other courses. Much of what you will find in the library will be related to the theories researchers use to describe, predict, and explain communication behavior. This chapter will also describe what theory is and how it is developed through the research process.

THE RESEARCH PROCESS MODEL

In Chapter 1, I introduced the metaphor of researcher as detective. Like detectives, researchers are seeking answers to questions. There are two possibilities regarding the information they need. First, an answer may already exist, but that information is not known to the researcher. In this case, library research usually provides the answer. Second, an answer is neither known nor available. In this case, the researcher must develop and conduct research to uncover an answer. In either case, finding an answer depends on the researcher's detective skills, or the ability to search and track down information that fits his or her needs.

The model for conducting research is similar to the plan a detective would follow in conducting an investigation. There are rules to be followed and multiple paths that can be taken according to the questions asked. Once started, the research process or investigation proceeds logically and steadily. Working from what you already know and understand, your primary objective as detective or researcher is to find information that answers the questions. Yet, there are obstacles and pitfalls along the way that may keep you from accomplishing your goal. You must be vigilant and pay attention throughout because your ability to respond to the changing environment presented to you is really the key issue and determines whether you

are successful in answering your question. Just as detectives conduct their investigations within the letter of the law, researchers conduct their investigations according to the traditions of scholarly research.

If you were trying to explain how a detective conducts an investigation to someone who was unfamiliar with the process, you might, in general, say that detectives seek answers to unanswered questions, assess the situation presented them, and then identify the procedures that are most likely to answer the questions presented by the situation. In the ideal situation, when the investigation was over, the questions would be answered. But detectives would not be able to explain in advance exactly how to find the answer to any one question because they would not be able to predict which clues they would uncover and which they would not. Certainly, an experienced detective has developed strategies that can help with the investigation. As a researcher, you can rely on scholarly standards, traditions, and norms to help you answer your question. Yet, in neither case would your strategies or predictions be certain.

There are two models—or strategies—that can provide a general explanation of what the research process is about, how one conducts research, and what one expects to be able to conclude at the end. Take a look at the first research model, presented in Figure 2.1, to see how the deductive research process is structured. Notice how the model is circular and cyclical. Each of the steps must occur for the research process to be complete. In this case, after identifying the research problem, the detective or researcher begins with a theory and then gathers evidence, or data, to assess whether the theory is correct. This type of research process is **deductive** because the researcher is moving from a known or assumed position supported by a theory to the particulars of the data.

After entering the research process where it begins—"Identify the research problem"—the researcher uses theory to guide the investigation. Next, based upon theory and research findings, the researcher formulates the research question or hypothesis. Continuing on from there, the researcher then selects the research methods that

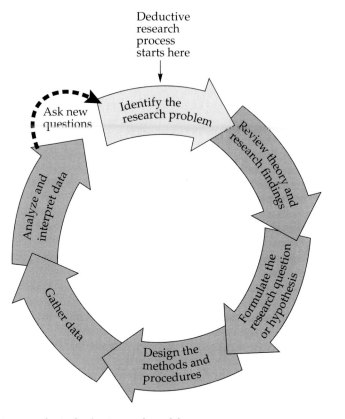

Deductive
research
process
starts here

Ask new
questions

Identify the
research problem

Review theory and
research findings

Analyze and
interpret data

Formulate the
research question
or hypothesis

Gather data

Design the
methods and
procedures

FIGURE 2.1 The Deductive Research Model

will help in answering the questions or hypotheses. Then data are gathered and interpreted. Although the researcher will be able to answer the initial questions at this point, the research process is not necessarily complete.

Recall that research is prized for its heuristic characteristic. If research has heuristic significance and values building on the work of others, answering one question should lead to other questions for which answers are needed. Thus, as answers are developed from the interpretation of data, the research process starts over again with a new question.

Alternately, a detective suspends judgment in beginning his or her detective work and develops a plan for gathering data that is framed around the foundation of a research question (Figure 2.2).

After the data are gathered and examined, theories are developed in response to what the data reveal. This type of research process is **inductive** because the researcher is moving from the specifics of the data to the more general explanation of theory. Once again, the research process is complete, but only temporarily. Reports of these findings are likely to encourage researchers to identify new research topics and start the process again.

Regardless of where one enters the research process, all of the steps are linked together. The steps are not independent activities but rather are interdependent. At times, researchers believe they have completed a step and proceed to the next—only to find that they do not have the most effective foundation from which to proceed. And so they must go back and work through the

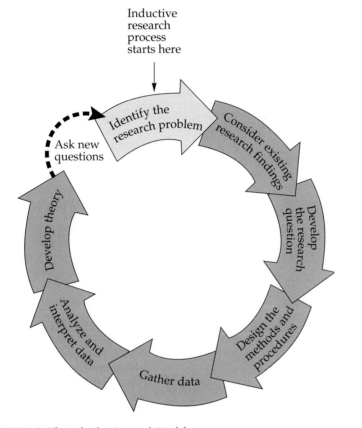

Inductive
research
process
starts here

Identify the research problem

Consider existing research findings

Develop the research question

Design the methods and procedures

Gather data

Analyze and interpret data

Develop theory

Ask new questions

FIGURE 2.2 The Inductive Research Model

preceding step again. As you will discover in the class for which you are reading this book, research is not evaluated solely on its outcomes. Rather, the process that leads to the outcome, or research result, is equally important.

Whether a researcher uses the deductive or inductive process, the first research activity is to identify the research problem or topic. This process of identification is the focus of the next section of this chapter. Formulating the problem into a research question or hypothesis formalizes the research as social science. Research conducted according to the deductive model, which typically relies on quantitative methods, is described in greater detail in Chapter 3. Research conducted according to the inductive model, which typically relies on qualitative methods, is described in greater detail in Chapter 4. Throughout the research process, researchers must be concerned with issues of ethics and integrity. Communication research is conducted on, with, or through others. Thus, the communication researcher must seriously consider and evaluate the integrity of the research proposed. Moreover, the research must balance the scientific needs of the researchers (as well as society's need for knowledge) with the physical, psychological, and emotional needs of those who participate in the research. These issues are addressed in Chapter 5. But, for now, we need to discover how researchers identify the communication problem or topic of interest.

IDENTIFYING THE RESEARCH PROBLEM

Remember that research is the process of asking questions and finding answers. Just as a detective must survey the crime scene to get an idea of where to begin, you must identify a topic or an issue as a focus for the project and the questions that will follow. Identifying the research problem is always the first activity in the research process.

Formulating Research Ideas

If you cannot think of a topic or problem, let your daily experiences guide you. What happened today to you, or in front of you, that illuminated a communication dilemma, problem, or question? What are your family, friends, and colleagues complaining or talking about? If you did not have to work, what would you do with your time and your money? Answering questions like these can help you think of a topic or problem. Often we tend to think that the daily problems of living we experience are unique to us. In reality, individual experiences may differ in some ways, but generally they are connected to and mirror the experiences of others. Thus, consider whatever problems you are facing as a good source for research ideas.

Still unsure about a topic or problem to pursue? A good way to survey contemporary problems and issues is to check what topics were on the front page of today's newspaper or presented on the radio or television. All of the major news outlets—*The New York Times* (http://www.nytimes.com), *USA Today* (http://www.usatoday.com), ABC News (http://www.abcnews.go.com), CBS News (http://cbsnews.com), NBC News (http://www.msnbc.com), CNN (http://www.cnn.com), and others—have webpages that are updated daily, sometimes hourly.

Turning Topics Into Preliminary Questions

With the topic identified, you can begin to frame preliminary questions, which will help you search through library holdings and electronic databases. The preliminary question is not the final research question you will see in both the deductive and inductive models. The research question is more formal, the foundation for the research project. The preliminary question is still important, however, because it can certainly lead you to the formal research question or research hypothesis. Remember to frame the preliminary question before you use library resources so that you can organize the time you spend there.

How does your topic lead to preliminary questions? Let's say you are interested in the impact of divorce on children's ability to communicate their feelings. Closer examination shows that there are two topics here: The first is impact of divorce; the second is children's abilities to express their feelings. You could do library research on each topic separately, but doing so might not lead you to the answer. By formulating your interest in this topic into a preliminary question, "How does divorce affect children's ability to communicate feelings?" you are more likely to seek resources that can answer your question or that will help you determine that the question has not been adequately answered.

But take another look at that question. What does the question assume? The question asks "how" divorce impacts children's abilities. A better first step would be to find out *if* divorce affects children's ability to communicate. Thus, "Does divorce affect children's ability to communicate feelings?" will be a better place to start, for it keeps you from falsely assuming that divorce does impact children in this way. Formulating the question this way specifies your interest, which can keep you from spending unproductive time in the library or at your computer.

As another example, you might recognize that the team leader of your shift at work has difficulty in organizing and conducting meetings. You wonder if there is anything you can do as a team member to help. In this case, questions could be "Are leaders the only team members responsible for how meetings are conducted?" "In what ways can a team member maintain the role of team member and help the leader conduct more effective meetings?" or "What risks do team members take when they help facilitate meetings?" Now look at these questions for the assumptions that are embedded within them. In the first, you are asking about the basic assumption of who is responsible for conducting team meetings. But notice in the second and third questions that the answer to the first question is assumed.

Rephrasing the topic as a preliminary question is the first step in seeking answers. Phrasing your question helps define your research area and narrow your search. Most important, questions help you uncover the links between concepts and help you identify assumptions you have made. And, as questions frequently do, they lead to more questions. If you end up with several questions, try to order them into a list of which questions must be addressed first, second, and so on. Or if questions in one area suggest questions in another area, try to draw a diagram of the relationship of the questions to one another. Regardless of how you identified your topic or problem, remember to formulate it into a question that focuses on communication. For example, a local news item on the prevalence of sexual harassment in your county government might end up as "In what ways does organizational culture promote or inhibit the occurrence of sexual harassment?"

Take a look at the examples of topics and problems in the Try This! box "Developing Initial Questions to Guide the Research Process." When you have finished revising a few of the examples listed, do the same to topics and problems that interest you.

Evaluating Your Questions

Once you have developed your preliminary question, it's time for evaluation. Use these questions to make a final assessment before you spend time searching the literature:

1. Is the question clearly stated?
2. Do others agree about the clarity of the question?
3. Have you asked only one question? Not two, three, or four?
4. What is the communication orientation of the question? In other words, what communication practice, policy, rule, procedure, or consequence is being investigated? Is your focus on symbols, messages, or meanings?
5. Is the question phrased in such a way that it is not biased toward a particular answer or solution?
6. Is there some way to observe or measure the communication phenomenon of interest?
7. Can you research this question given the limitations of time and resources?
8. Who would be interested in the answer to the question?
9. How could those who are interested use the information?

Once you are satisfied that you are asking the preliminary question in the most effective way and that the question is appropriate for communication research, you are ready to go to the library or use online library resources.

USING LIBRARY AND DATABASE RESOURCES

Armed with preliminary questions, you are now ready to visit the library and use online library resources. Which is the better place to start? It depends on what is available to you and your style of working (for example, the hours the library is available, your degree of computer literacy). Although working on a computer from home certainly has advantages, working in the library has advantages as well. Until all library documents are available online and in full-text format, you may find only titles and abstracts on electronic databases. When you work in the library you can actually put your hands on the books and articles referenced online. You can read the material to see if it fits your needs. Perhaps most important, you can ask a librarian for help.

Library Resources

The library can be an overwhelming place. Where should you start? The library contains books, scholarly journals, magazines, newspapers, audio-visual materials, and more. Generally, your search strategy as a communication student should produce scholarly articles published in academic

TRY THIS!   **Developing Initial Questions to Guide the Research Process**

Read the example given in the table for the topic of internet chat rooms. Notice how the general topic or problem is stated as a preliminary question. Then the question is analyzed for any underlying assumptions. For example, the sample question assumes that all people have access to the internet, use chat rooms on the internet, and can explain why they use chat rooms. With these assumptions uncovered, the preliminary question should be restated so that it is more specific. Use the topics and problems listed below to develop the preliminary questions to start the research process.

Topic or Problem	State as Preliminary Question(s)	Examine Question(s) for Assumptions	Restate Preliminary Question(s)
Internet chat rooms	How do people use internet chat rooms?	All people have access to the internet. All people who use the internet use chat rooms. People will be able to explain why they use chat rooms.	Do web users who use chat rooms report about their chat-room interaction as they would a face-to-face conversation?
Parents talking with their children about guns and violence			
Careers for communication graduates			
Talking with superiors at work			

journals; scholarly books written by one or multiple authors; or edited collections with a series of chapters written by different authors.

Journals are edited and published by scholarly professional associations, universities, or publishing houses dedicated to scholarly work. Scholars submit their manuscripts to a journal. The journal editor sends the manuscript out for review to at least two reviewers who do not know the identity of the author. This process allows reviewers to give their honest and critical feedback about the manuscript. After this review, the editor makes a decision about revision and publication. Oftentimes, journal articles are published only after an extensive review and revision process. In addition, most journals have a very high rejection rate, generally 80–90%. As a result, journal articles are regarded as quality research written by knowledgeable experts. Some of the journals specific to the discipline of communication that publish social science research include

Communication Education

Communication Monographs

Communication Research

Communication Quarterly

Communication Reports

Communication Research Reports

Communication Studies

Communication Theory

Health Communication

Howard Journal of Communications

Human Communication Research

Journal of Applied Communication Research

Journal of Broadcasting & Electronic Media

Journal of Communication

Journal of Computer-Mediated Communication

Journal of Social and Personal Relationships

Journal of the International Listening Association

Journalism & Mass Communication Quarterly

Public Relations Review

Qualitative Research Reports in Communication

Research on Language and Social Interaction

Southern Communication Journal

Western Journal of Communication

Women's Studies in Communication

Of course, there are other journals in the communication discipline as well as journals that are multidisciplinary (such as *Journal of Contemporary Etlmography, Management Communication Quarterly, Small Group Research*). Finally, journals in other disciplines (for example, management, psychology, and sociology) do publish research of interest to communication scholars. In some cases, the research of communication scholars can be found there as well. Check with your instructor or librarian to identify the journals that can be found in your library and that will satisfy your needs during your literature search.

Library Search Strategies

There are a variety of search strategies, and over time you are likely to develop one that works best for you. Try the search strategy described here. It is structured as a general-to-specific search, and it makes use of keywords rather than subject terms. Keywords provide a broader net for capturing the materials you seek. You may find some modifications necessary according to the availability of materials. If your library does not have one of the reference databases listed, ask a librarian for replacement suggestions. Start with a basic search to see what you can find.

Basic Library Search

Step 1: Identify the key terms in your question. For example, in the question "Does divorce affect children's ability to communicate feelings?" the key terms are *divorce* and *children*. But also try *adolescents* and *teenagers* as alternative key terms.

Step 2: Using the keywords search function of your university's catalog holdings, search separately for each term identified in step 1. As you peruse these listings, notice additional terms or phrases other researchers use to refer to your topic. Does one author's name consistently appear? Do any journals in your library include one of your search words in its title? This step helps you gain familiarity with the broad literature that supports your question.

Step 3: Again using the keywords search function of your university's catalog holdings, search for the keywords together (for example, *divorce children*). For some university databases, you may need to insert *AND* between the two keywords (for example, *divorce AND children*). This step narrows your search and examines the specific relationship in which you are interested.

Step 4: Examine some of the resources steps 2 and 3 have uncovered. By looking through these resources you may find alternative keywords (for example, *kids* instead of *children*) that could assist your search. If a journal is uncovered in steps 2 and 3, be sure to check out several issues; an article that interests you might appear in one issue and not another. One way to do this easily is to go to the last issue of each volume. Most journals list the table of contents for the entire volume at the back of the last issue for that volume. For a journal with four issues per volume check issue 4 of any volume to find the comprehensive index. If you find a helpful book, check the stacks for books on either side of the one you are looking for. Similar books are shelved together.

Step 5: Using your original or revised set of keywords, check your library for at least one of the following databases designed specifically for the communication discipline: (1) Communication & Mass Media Complete; an online database that indexes and provides full text for hundreds of journals across the speech communication and mass media disciplines. (2) ComAbstracts; an online database that indexes a broad spectrum of articles and books in the communication field. It can be searched by word, phrase, or author. (3) *Communication Abstracts;* this hard-copy source provides the abstracts of journal articles a organized according to subfields within the communication discipline.

Step 6: Using your original or revised set of keywords, check the online database Expanded Academic Index. If your search so far has led you to specific

authors, check this database for their names as well.

Step 7: Stop and examine what you have found. Read through the abstracts of the journal articles you found; then read the discussion section. Read the foreword or introduction and first chapter of each book. Check the list of references at the end of the articles and books. Could any of the sources listed there be helpful to you?

Step 8: With the information you found, are you able to answer your question? Remember from the beginning of this chapter that for some questions you ask, the answer is available, though unknown to you. This process of library research is designed to make that answer known. If you are able to answer your question to your satisfaction, you can stop searching. If not, your question needs to be revised, and you need to do some additional basic database searching.

Answering the following questions can help determine if you have enough information or if you need to continue on with a detailed search. Your library search has been adequate if you are satisfied with your answers to the following questions:

1. How much has been written on your topic?

2. How recent or relevant is the material?

3. Has some critical event occurred or societal value changed that could challenge the interpretation of the answers to the questions asked?

4. Who has done the most work on your topic?

5. Where has research on the topic been published?

6. What aspects of the topic received the most attention?

7. What questions about the topic have been answered?

8. What aspects of the topic have been ignored?

9. Are there reasons to replicate, or repeat, studies that have been conclusive?

10. What other topics have you found related to your primary topic?

If you cannot answer these questions, your basic library search is incomplete. You may need to once again revise your preliminary question. Taking the search steps in the detailed library search is likely to help you answer your question. This stage must be conducted in the library. If you are unfamiliar with any of the reference materials listed, do not hesitate to ask a librarian for assistance.

Detailed Library Search

Step 1: Check to see if your library carries *Communication Yearbook.* This annual series is an edited collection of literature reviews and topical critiques. You will have to check the table of contents of each *Yearbook.* If you find a chapter that helps you, be sure to review the resources in the reference section.

Step 2: Check to see if your library has a handbook related to your area of research. Handbooks are focused on one context of communication and provide extensive reviews and critiques of literature, theories, and methods in a particular area (examples are *Handbook of Family Communication, Handbook of Communication and Aging Research, Handbook of Political Communication Research, Handbook of Interpersonal Communication,* and *Handbook of New Media*). To find which handbooks your library carries, use the words *handbook* and *communication* as keywords in your university's catalog database. If you find a chapter that helps you, be sure to review the resources in the reference section.

Step 3: Check the online database Web of Science, which includes the Social Sciences Citation Index. This database is one of the most comprehensive indexes of scholarly research. You will be most effective searching for your keywords in this multidisciplinary database with the help of a reference librarian. In our example, you would check for *divorce* and *children* or any other pairings of words your basic search uncovered.

Step 4: Stop and examine what you have found. Read through the abstracts of each journal article or chapter you found, and then read the discussion section. Read the foreword or introduction and first chapter of each book. Check the list of references at the end of the articles or chapters. Could any of the sources listed there be helpful to you? Are you able to answer your question? Should your question be revised based upon what you have found? At this point, you have reached another decision point. If you can answer your question to your satisfaction, your search is over. If you cannot satisfactorily answer your question, or if you found conflicting answers in your search, you can write your question in its final form: You are ready to develop your research project.

If you have searched thoroughly and diligently, you are likely to have uncovered the materials you need to answer your question or to develop your research project. Remember, however, that it is nearly impossible to find all of the available literature. Finding everything is not a prerequisite for most undergraduate research projects. But you should have information available from a variety of authors, from a variety of publication outlets, and from sources published over time. Analyze your resources for their breadth and depth of coverage.

As you review the literature you have found, take good notes and copy or print all of the relevant pages. Check out the table of contents as well as subject and author indexes of books. Identify books that are helpful by noting the authors' names, complete book title, year of publication, place of publication, publisher, and call number. Identify journal articles that are helpful by noting the authors' names, complete article title,

---

TRY THIS!   **Searching the Research Literature . . .**

1. Using the keywords *media* and *ethics,* perform a basic search as described above. Using the information you obtain, what questions can you develop? What recommendations would you make before performing a detailed search?

2. Your question is "What nonverbal behaviors demonstrate confidence in public speaking?" What keywords would you use in your basic search? Conduct this search and report on your findings.

3. In your basic search for references on communication problems in marriages, you have found that Mary Anne Fitzpatrick is the author of several studies. How do you interpret this information? How would you use this information in your detailed search?

---

year of publication, complete journal title, volume number, and page numbers of the journal article. You will need all of this information to develop a reference list if you cite the material in your research project. If you download an article or photocopy a journal article, print or copy the entire article, including the reference pages. Saving money by not copying these pages may be a mistake if you decide later that you want to check out a reference listed in the text of the article.

Other Reference and Database Resources

Your library is an important source of reference works and databases. Some are directly relevant for searching the communication literature. Others can help you identify literature from related disciplines, such as psychology, sociology, and management. If you have completed the basic and detailed searches and still are in need of additional literature, check out the databases listed below. Given electronic access, most libraries have moved to electronic databases. Check with your library to see which of these other common references and databases are available for your use.

Reference or Database	Coverage
ABI/Inform	Business and management journals
ERIC	Education journals and convention papers
Periodical Abstracts	Social science journals
PsychINFO	Psychology and select related disciplines
Sociological Abstracts	Sociology and related disciplines

Getting Resources From the Web

There are a variety of uses for the World Wide Web as you conduct your search of the literature. First, you can use any search engine or metasearch engine to enter your keywords or key phrases to see what is on the web. You might find the homepages of authors who wrote the articles, books, and book chapters you have collected in your library searches. You might also find survey or poll results related to your topic archived on the webpages of news organizations. Even threads of discussions from newsgroups or web discussion groups can appear in these searches.

When you look at these resources, be sure to examine both the date and author, or sponsor, of the material or webpage. Because anyone can post information to the web, you must take responsibility for evaluating the validity and utility of the information.

Adjusting the Question

As you work through the search strategies, don't hesitate to adjust your preliminary question. As you discover new information, you will develop a more sophisticated appreciation and

*DESIGN
CHECK*

Reader Beware

"Reader beware! The information posted on this website is not factual." It would be great if websites came with such warnings. But they do not. It is up to you as a consumer to sort through what web information has utility for your research project. The easiest way to evaluate web-based information is to use common sense. Simply put, does the information make sense? Or do the information and claims seem farfetched? Can you identify the sponsor of the website? Are claims and information documented?

Use the following questions to guide you in evaluating information from webpages (Dochartaigh, 2002):

1. Is it clear who is responsible for material on the webpage? An individual? An institution? Is there information for you to evaluate the author's or organization's authority?

2. If a source is quoted or paraphrased on the webpage, is information about that source provided so you can independently verify the accuracy of the information?

3. Are biases and affiliations clearly stated on the webpage?

4. Is advertising clearly labeled as such?

5. Are opinions labeled as such? Or, are they disguised as an article or a report?

6. Is there a posting date for the website? Is there a date for when the webpage, or any of the material on the webpage, was updated or revised?

Anyone can produce a website. This means that you must carefully assess what is presented. A website can present research that appears to be scholarly. But unless the site includes citations and identifies the author and his or her qualifications, it may be very difficult to gauge the authenticity or validity of the material.

understanding of the problem. Incorporate the information you read into your preliminary question. In particular, did your search uncover theories that can help you make sense of your question? Are there several theories that could provide the basis for competing claims or solutions to your preliminary question? As you find new sources and information in the library, it is likely that your preliminary question will become more narrowly focused. Keep a list of all resources that you are using. You will use these again as you develop your research project and as you write up your research report.

It is time to stop adjusting the preliminary research question when two conditions are satisfied. First, you should be comfortable that your question

is specific enough to be interesting. Second, you should be comfortable with the quality and quantity of resources you can use to help you answer your question. At this point, it is time to move on to analyzing the resources you have collected.

READING SCHOLARLY ARTICLES AND BOOKS

Once you have collected the articles and books, there is still plenty of work to accomplish. How do you make sense of a large body of material, particularly when conclusions among them conflict? The first step is to evaluate the quality of the research. Conducting research is difficult and

AN ETHICAL
ISSUE

Using the Ideas of Others

A detective relies on information and clues provided by others. So does a good researcher. It would be impossible for one researcher to develop, document, and validate everything one needed to know about a subject or topic. In research, then, we must rely on the ideas and conclusions drawn by others. Anytime you use the work of others, you must provide a citation indicating in the text of your paper what idea you are using and whose idea it was. This is called an in-text citation. There are two types. The first is the citation for a direct quotation. In this case, you indicate with quotation marks the exact words you copied from the original work and provide the page number in addition to the author's last name and the year of the publication. This way anyone who reads your paper can locate the exact source.

Reel and Thompson (2004) conducted a three-phase study to investigate interpersonal strategies of negotiating condom use. On page 102 of their article, they use the following direct quote in-text citation.

> In addition, Brown and Levinson (1987) tied the notion of face directly to "mention of taboo topics, including those that are inappropriate" (p. 670).

The second type of in-text citation is for situations in which you have summarized or paraphrased the ideas or conclusions of others. This in-text citation is documented with the author's last name and year of publication. An example of an indirect in-text citation from the same article on page 100 is

> Regarding condom negotiation, feelings of embarrassment are especially strong in men (Cline & McKenzie, 1994); in particular, men are especially likely to feel that suggesting condom use will diminish the chances of sexual intercourse (Bryan, Aiden, & West, 1999).

A complete list of your references is provided at the end of your paper. This enables the reader to locate the source of any in-text citation you used. Most social science researchers use the citation and reference style of the American Psychological Association, which is the style used in this book. Check with your instructor to see which style you should use.

---

complex; and, as a result, some research is of higher quality than others.

Here are some recommendations for evaluating the quality of research. First, look at the body of literature you have collected. Are there one or two authors whose names appear over and over? If so, start your reading there. Researchers tend to work on lines, or streams, of research. This means that scholars become known for conducting research on certain topics. If the names of one or two scholars don't stand out, organize your literature by publication date. To get a historical overview, read from the older literature through to the newer

literature. Another way to start is to begin with an article or chapter that reviews or summarizes a particular line of research. *Communication Yearbook* is a particularly good source for this type of literature review. These sources are likely to provide you with the cumulative efforts of many researchers over a period of time.

Identifying Primary Ideas and Conclusions

Starting with the abstract is always a good place to find the primary ideas presented in an article or chapter. The abstract should describe what

*DESIGN
CHECK*

Evaluating the Literature You Found

As you can see, the research process starts with your identification of a research topic and your search of the research literature. You will use the articles and chapters that you find in the literature review for your study. Communication research is indexed on several different databases, so if you are not finding what you need be sure to ask your reference librarian for help. As you search the literature, be sure that you are collecting studies that are published in communication journals or are authored by communication scholars. Scholars in many disciplines study communication, but the most complete and thoughtful focus on communication is published by communication scholars.

the study was about, give a very brief description of how the study was completed, and provide a short description of the results.

Next, read the problem statement, which is usually part of the literature review or precedes the literature review. It identifies the research objectives. Although the exact research questions or hypotheses may not be presented here, the problem statement generally suggests them. The problem statement answers the question "Why did the researchers conduct this study?" Generally, reading this section will help you decide if the article or research report will be helpful to you.

In the literature review the authors present the literature that supports their formal research questions and hypotheses. Read the research questions and hypotheses carefully as the results or conclusions from the study are tied directly to them. For now, skim the methods and results section, and then move on to the discussion section. What did the scholars find? What were the answers to the research questions? Did they confirm or not confirm the hypotheses they proposed? Remember that the conclusion to the investigation is found in the discussion section. When a research question or hypothesis is presented in the literature review, it is still tentative.

Tracking Others' References

As you read the articles, books, and chapters, you will find in-text citations. This documentation device provides information within parentheses for the research work cited by the author. Each in-text

citation will include the authors' last names, year of publication, and the page number if material is quoted word for word. To track down this citation, turn to the reference list at the end of the article, book, or chapter. This is labeled with the heading "References," "Bibliography," or "Works Cited." For each citation you will find a complete bibliographic entry—all of the information necessary for you to find the article, book, or book chapter. Look at the "References" section at the end of this book for an example.

Why would you want to track down the articles, books, and book chapters that other authors have used? There are several reasons. First, these published works are part of an ongoing scholarly conversation. Something briefly mentioned in one article might lead you to another article that could provide valuable background information for you. Second, you may have missed this source in your library search. Tracking down the references used by others gives you the opportunity to fill in the gaps of your literature search. Third, authors draw conclusions about the work of others and then base their arguments on those conclusions. If you are not familiar with the literature, you have to take the authors' conclusions for granted. Rather than relying on their evaluative biases, you could track down the reference, read it, and draw your own conclusions.

Summarizing What You Have Found

Now that you have searched the literature, you have references from several sources. There are many ways in which to organize what you found.

One method is to arrange the material using major and minor points as primary and secondary headings, much like a traditional outline. A second method would be to arrange the findings in chronological order, usually working from the oldest to the most recent. This is particularly helpful if you want to demonstrate how a question was answered or how a topic developed over time. A third method is to ask a series of questions and respond with what you found for each question. In this case, working from the broadest question to the narrowest question is recommended. A final method for organizing your material is to work from general to specific (a deductive approach), or build from the specific to the general (an inductive approach). An effective way to conclude a written report on what you found is to generate new questions that take you in a different, but related, direction.

Whatever approach you take to summarizing what you found in your literature search, the primary question should be—"Have I answered my question?" If you have, you will need to think creatively about how to replicate, extend, or challenge those conclusions as the basis for a research project. If your search has been thorough but your question still has not been answered, you are ready to move forward with a research project. In either instance, considering the role of theory is your next step.

THE ROLE OF THEORY IN RESEARCH

Research revolves around theory. Thus, the journal articles and book chapters you find in the library use research as a basis for developing or challenging theory. *Theory* is a "set of interrelated propositions that present a systematic view of phenomena with the purpose of explaining and predicting the phenomena" (Lustig, 1986, p. 451). Although some researchers—particularly qualitative researchers—would disagree that all theories need to predict, at a minimum theories should describe and explain communication phenomena. Theory would be invalid or have little utility for the practice of communication if it could not be used to describe, predict, or explain.

Research is necessary to validate theory. Generally, quantitative research starts with a theory. Then researchers conduct a research study to demonstrate if a theory holds true for a set of data. If it does not, then the theory is altered or discarded. In this theory–research link, theory is the map by which the researchers conduct their studies. As described earlier, this type of research relies on *deductive* thinking or reasoning in that theory presumes what will result and the research verifies those claims. Theory directs the researcher in developing hypotheses and questions and in selecting the method for testing them.

Research is also necessary to develop theory. Generally, qualitative researchers start with a research question and use their findings to both answer the question and contribute to theory development. In this theory–research link, the theory, or map, is drawn from the experiences uncovered by the research. This type of research relies on *inductive* thinking or reasoning in that theory, or generalization, is derived from the cases explored.

As you can see, research and theory are necessary complements to one another. Theorizing is important to research in two additional ways (Brooks, 1970). First, researchers cannot observe the entire universe. Rather, researchers must select a subset of phenomena to be observed. Theory directs researchers' attention to particular communication patterns, functions, themes, processes, and so on. Second, theory helps "integrate data which otherwise would remain mere collections of facts" (Brooks, p. 4). This issue returns us to the definition of theory given earlier. In a theory, research findings are integrated into a system of description, prediction, and perhaps explanation that help us answer questions of "What?" "Why?" "How?" and sometimes "What if?"

Developing Theory

We engage in informal theorizing when we try to make sense of the past, operate effectively in the present, or anticipate events in the future (Lustig, 1986). Although theorizing is a common and fundamental human activity practiced every day, formal theorizing as a scientific process is quite different. There are six basic steps to formal theory building (Lustig). Each is described below.

In step 1, the researcher describes an event or observation that needs understanding. The event must be observable, interesting, important, and remarkable to come to the attention of the researcher or someone else who desires an understanding of it. This first step begins to identify the "what." In step 2, the researcher creates an explanation for the event. Although anyone can create an explanation, it is the scientist's job to formalize and test explanations. In this step the answer to "Why?" begins to be formulated.

In step 3, the researcher moves from the specific event or observation to a more generalized form. In other words, if the event of interest is family decision making around the dinner table, the researcher could move to the more generalized communication event of decision making or the more generalized communication event of family interaction. A decision must be made concerning which type of communication event is more interesting and intriguing to investigate. By moving to a more abstract level, the researcher can now look for similar events to see if the answer to "Why?" developed in step 2 is also suitable for explaining these other, different but similar, events. Instead of focusing on one specific interaction event, the researcher must develop answers suitable for a class of similar events. This characteristic of theory moves it from an informal to a formal level. Although you are comfortable with the way informal theorizing describes and explains events that happen in your daily life, you would not be comfortable applying others' informal theories to the events that you experience. Thus, the scientist's job is to discover the commonalities among events that allow them to be classified and then to develop and test theories that describe and explain all events belonging to a class. Thus, a theory of decision making should apply to many people's experiences of decision making, not just one's own.

In step 4, the researcher begins to derive predictions from the explanation developed in step 3. To do this, the researcher asks, "What else would be true, or observable, if the explanation was correct?" Continuing with our family decision-making example, the researcher could make several propositions that are testable. Examine Table 2.1 to see the progression from step 1 through step 4.

TABLE 2.1 Theory Development—Steps 1 Through 4

	Task	*Example*
Step 1	Describe event or observation	Family members (2 adults, 2 children) eat dinner and discuss their daily activities. Father introduces family activity for weekend, which generates considerable discussion from children. Although the discussion initially has both positive and negative points introduced, eventually the children agree that they do not want to pursue the weekend activity suggested.
Step 2	Create explanation for event	Explanation 1: Children are likely to reject ideas presented by parents during dinnertime discussions. Explanation 2: Parents introduce ideas for family dinnertime discussion to obtain family members' preferences.
Step 3	Move from specific to more generalized form	General form 1: Children's rejection or acceptance of parental input. General form 2: Parents desire input from other family members.
Step 4	Derive predictions from explanations	Focus 1: Children are likely to reject ideas presented by parents. Focus 2: Parents will seek input about family matters from other family members.

TRY THIS!   **Finding Theory in Journal Articles**

Find two or three journal articles for a communication topic that interests you. Carefully read the literature review of each article. Does the author identify by name the theory or theories that are providing the foundation for the research study? Does the author point to a description, cause, prediction, or explanation as the reason for conducting the research? If so, this is likely the theoretical basis of the study. Next, read the discussion and implication sections of the articles. In this part of the journal article, authors will discuss the implications of the study as a challenge to the theory or as further development or expansion of the theory.

Now, in step 5, the researcher must select a focus and test the proposed theory. Most communication observations are complex enough to support multiple attempts at theory building. The researcher must develop a plan for and collect data that can test the predictions.

Step 6 of the theory-building process uses the obtained data to confirm, revise, expand, generalize, or abandon the proposition tested (Lustig, 1986). Notice that collecting the data in step 5 is distinct from interpreting the data in step 6. If the results are consistent with the proposition, the theoretical framework is confirmed for the time being. If the results are not consistent with the proposition, the discrepancy must be explained by critically examining the methodological process or by reworking the theoretical framework. If the theoretical framework is revised or if two alternative and competing explanations are present, the theory-building process starts again. If methodological problems are identified, the researcher repeats steps 5 and 6 using different and improved methodological procedures.

Even after these six steps, the theory-building process is not complete or final. Theory is developed over time, and this theory-building process is repeated many times as different scholars test theoretical propositions in their research. Both quantitative and qualitative research contribute to theory development.

Theories are developed and tested incrementally. After a basic theoretical notion is presented as a proposition in the scholarly literature, scholars develop studies to test the propositions. This is possible because the results of scholarly research are presented in a public forum. Theory is confirmed only after many studies, usually conducted by different scholars with different methodologies, achieve similar results. Even at that point, theories are still considered tentative. A theory that was at one time believed to be valid can be questioned in the future. For example, new technologies can create new opportunities and circumstances for communication. Thus, theories of how and why interpersonal relationships develop over time may need to be reexamined in light of the extent to which these technologies are used in developing relationships.

Theory–Research Link

To the extent that a community of scholars accepts research findings and can agree on the theoretical propositions, theory has been achieved. But all theory should be judged by some aspect of utility (Lustig, 1986). The knowledge gained from the process of theory-building should be used "to suggest new questions that are worth answering, develop more accurate theories about human communication, communicate more effectively, teach others to communicate more effectively, create better human relationships, and improve the cultures and the environments within which we all live" (Lustig, p. 457). When the utility criterion is added as a test of the theory-building process, you can see not only that the theory–research relationship is reciprocal, but also that it is grounded in the practical issues of human communication.

In fact, theory is used four ways in the research process (Hoover & Donovan, 1995). First, theory provides patterns for interpreting data. Without working from or toward theory, research could produce results without an organizing framework. Second, theory links one study to another, helping to provide a continual conversation about our understanding of communication phenomena. Third, theory provides a framework for understanding how concepts and issues are important or significant in our interactions. For example, theorizing about communication apprehension and then conducting studies to validate those expectations helped researchers uncover the role apprehension plays in nearly every communication event in which we participate. Fourth, theory helps us interpret the larger meaning of research findings. For example, reading about how observers react to an apprehensive individual may cause you to monitor and manage your own apprehensiveness when speaking in public.

Scientific inquiry is a process of developing and testing theory. So there are direct relationships among questions asked, data observed, and theory development (Littlejohn, 1999; Miller & Nicholson, 1976). Quantitative research generally uses theory to develop questions to direct data collection. Examine the deductive and inductive research models (see Figures 2.1 and 2.2). See how theory drives quantitative research? Alternately, in qualitative methodology, observations tend to drive theory development. However, the selection of any particular quantitative or qualitative methodology does not guarantee that a study will result in theoretical development. Rather, a study must be designed to illuminate and examine underlying principles and propositions (Shapiro, 2002). Only then can its findings contribute to theoretical development.

Also recognize that the process of inquiry is not always linear, nor does one process of inquiry dominate all quantitative research or all qualitative research. The point here is that meaningful inquiry either drives theory or is theory-driven.

Also worth mentioning is that theory cannot be developed or challenged in one study. Recall that science can be characterized by its replicable and self-correcting nature. Multiple studies are needed to replicate findings just as multiple studies are needed to challenge and alter existing theory.

CONTINUING WITH THE RESEARCH PROCESS

If your assignment was to develop a preliminary question for a research project, your work has just started. Generally, there is little value in repeating the work of others if you agree with their conclusions and find no major faults in how they conducted the research. However, there is value in replication when the original study is dated, when societal values and practices surrounding the issue have changed or are changing, or when you find a flaw in the study that makes you question the results. For example, societal values about many adult relationships (such as marriage, living together, divorce, single parenting, adoption) have changed significantly within the past 20 years. Research in these areas may be necessary to see if the conclusions drawn in the past about communication in these relationships are relevant now.

As you read and sort the literature you found, you might find that scholars disagree. Or you might find that research conclusions have been drawn about most, but not all, of the issues surrounding your topic. If scholars disagree, you could develop a research study to examine the disagreement. If some, but not all, issues are answered, you could develop and conduct the study that fills in this gap. Remember that one of the characteristics of science is that it is heuristic. This means that conclusions, or answers to questions, help identify new questions to be answered.

Having identified your research topic, searched the literature, and developed a preliminary question, you are now ready to develop a formal research question or research hypothesis. The information you gained from your library search will provide direction in this next research step. These activities will be explored in greater detail in Chapters 3 and 4.

SUMMARY

1. Researchers seek answers to questions.

2. Library research can reveal if the answer to your question is available, but not known to you.

3. If the answer is neither known nor available, then research must be conducted to uncover the answer.

4. Research can be a deductive or an inductive process.

5. The steps of the deductive process are identifying the research problem, reviewing existing theory, formulating a research question or hypothesis, designing the methods and procedures, gathering data, and analyzing and interpreting data.

6. The steps of the inductive research process are identifying the research problem, considering existing research findings, developing the research question, designing the methods and procedures, gathering data, analyzing and interpreting data, and developing a theoretical explanation.

7. Both the deductive and inductive research processes are circular and cyclical as the final step, asking new questions, starts the research process once again.

8. The first step in both the deductive and inductive research processes—identifying the research problem—consists of identifying the topic or issue, turning the topic into a preliminary question or set of questions, conducting a library search, and adjusting the question, if necessary.

9. Evaluate your preliminary questions for their underlying assumptions, completeness, and clarity prior to conducting the library search.

10. Use either the basic or detailed search strategy to find scholarly articles published in academic journals or scholarly books.

11. When you find an article or book that may be helpful, take notes and document all of the citation information.

12. Your preliminary question may require adjustment as you discover new information.

13. The abstract states the primary ideas presented in an article or chapter.

14. The literature review usually concludes with the researchers' research questions and hypotheses.

15. The discussion section includes the answers to the questions the authors raised.

16. Using what you found in the library search, organize your material by major and minor points, in chronological order, by answering a series of questions, or from the general to the specific or from specific to general.

17. Theory is developed and tested through research.

KEY TERMS

deductive	inductive

CHAPTER THREE

Introduction to Quantitative Research

Chapter Checklist

After reading this chapter, you should be able to:

1. Describe quantitative research and its assumptions

2. Identify examples of quantitative research.

3. Explain analytic deduction.

4. Explain the five-component model for quantitative research.

5. Explain the role of hypotheses in quantitative research.

6. Assess the effectiveness of hypotheses in quantitative research.

7. Explain why research questions are used in quantitative research.

8. Distinguish among concepts, conceptual schemes, constructs, variables, and operationalizations.

9. Identify independent and dependent variables in hypotheses.

10. Explain the relationship between independent and dependent variables in hypotheses.

11. Explain the advantages and disadvantages of quantitative research.

12. Describe issues of reliability and validity that must be addressed in quantitative research.

When you think of research, you are likely to think of a laboratory experiment, which is what has traditionally been associated with scientific research. In communication research, lab experiments are only one of a variety of quantitative methods from which a researcher can choose.

This chapter provides a basic introduction to quantitative communication research. You will discover how quantitative methods rely on the identification of variables and the development of testable hypotheses and questions. Without these elements, quantitative research could not be conducted. Moreover, you will discover that the way in which the research question or hypothesis is written will actually help the researcher in selecting the research method. But do not conclude that quantitative research can answer all of our questions about human communication behavior. Some questions are better answered by qualitative research methods, which are introduced in Chapter 4.

WHAT IS QUANTITATIVE RESEARCH?

As the label implies, the unit of analysis in quantitative research is quantity (Anderson, 1996). Researchers use measurement and observation to represent communication phenomena as amounts, frequencies, degrees, values, or intensity. Once phenomena are quantified, researchers compare or relate them using descriptive or inferential statistics. By using traditional quantitative approaches and statistical techniques, researchers bring greater precision and, as a result, some would argue, greater objectivity to the study of communication phenomena. A few examples will demonstrate the variety of quantitative research methods available to communication researchers.

Examples of Quantitative Research

Memorable messages are those messages from others that are remembered for long periods of time and perceived by receivers to have a major influence on their behavior choices. Given the prevalence of those messages, Ellis and Smith (2004) wanted to investigate how individuals use such messages to assess behaviors that exceed their own expectations and behaviors that fail to meet their expectations.

The researchers asked undergraduate students to keep a journal for 5 days to record both types of behaviors. They also asked students to describe a memorable message that came to mind as they assessed the behaviors they recorded. Ellis and Smith (2004) coded the behaviors described in the journal entries that exceeded and failed to meet participants' expectations into the following categories: unlawful activity; moral activity; personal choices; substance abuse; aggressive behavior; inconsiderate and rude behavior; calm, considerate, kind, and helpful behavior; and miscellaneous. The researchers also coded the memorable messages, which fell into 12 general categories: the ten commandments; the golden rule; be kind, patient, and loyal to others; respect elders; be responsible; live a healthy life; do your best and work hard; obey the law; enjoy yourself and your life; love your family; take time for God; and miscellaneous.

Results from the study indicated that behaviors that failed to meet their expectations were more frequently about personal choices and that behaviors that exceeded their expectations were more frequently described as calm, considerate, kind, and helpful behavior. Participants reported using memorable messages about kindness, loyalty, and patience to assess both negative and positive behavior choices. This type of memorable message was most often given by participants' mothers. However, the frequency with which a kindness, loyalty, and patience memorable message was used to assess a positive behavior was 55.3%, whereas the frequency with which a kindness, loyalty, and patience memorable message was used to assess a negative behavior was 28.8%.

How were quantitative methods used in this study of memorable messages? To answer their research questions, the research team counted frequencies within categories to determine which types of positive and negative behaviors were reported, which types of memorable messages were used to assess behavior, and who delivered the memorable messages. Counting frequencies is one type of quantitative method used in

---

AN ETHICAL ISSUE

Giving Your Children Permission to Participate in a Research Study

To collect data from participants, researchers must ask for and gain the consent of participants. In addition to gaining participants' consent, researchers need the consent of a parent or guardian before individuals under the age of 18 can participate in an academically sponsored research project. If you were the parents of a 13-year-old girl, would you give your daughter permission to participate in a research project on dating? Drinking? Drug use? Why would some parents object to their daughter's participation? Is there any way the researcher could overcome these objections? What are the potential benefits of having teenagers participate in research projects like these?

---

communication research. By interpreting the frequencies, the research team members were able to focus on the way messages sent by valued or significant sources affected participants' assessment of their own behavior. The findings underscore that participants recalled a memorable message nearly every time they assessed their own behaviors—demonstrating the power of such messages in our lives.

Another quantitative research study relied on traditional paper-and-pencil questionnaires to examine the relationship between viewing television news coverage of the September 11, 2001 attacks and perceptions of violence, negative emotions, and personal relationships with individuals outside the United States. Six weeks after the attacks, Lett, DiPietro, and Johnson (2004) surveyed students to gauge how many hours of television news they had viewed before and after the attacks, to obtain students' estimates of violence initiated by individuals from outside the United States, and to measure their emotional states relative to the attacks and their perceptions of Islamic individuals including peers.

How were surveys used to create quantitative data? A series of items for each variable was used to measure students' perceptions. Summing students' responses across the items for each variable created scores, or numerical equivalents of the variables, that could be used in statistical tests. The research team discovered that stronger personal negative emotions were related to more hours of television news viewing and more negative

perceptions of Islamic peers. Alternately, students who watched more television news coverage had less negative perceptions of Islamic individuals than did those who watched less television news. The research team concluded that television viewing has different influences on personal and societal level judgments. Using surveys, or questionnaires, is a very popular quantitative method. Chapter 9 explores this topic.

Communication researchers also use experimentation to capture quantitative information about communication issues. To study how fear appeals concerning breast cancer could be used to motivate women to conduct self-exams, Roskos-Ewoldsen, Yu, and Rhodes (2004) randomly assigned female undergraduates to one of four conditions of an experiment. Some women heard a message that stressed the risks of breast cancer regardless of age and offered that self-exams were an effective method of early detection. The second group heard a message that stressed the same risks but offered that breast self-exams were difficult to do and not very effective at cancer detection. The third group heard a message that stressed that breast cancer occurred more frequently in older women and repeated the message that self-exams were effective at early detection. The final group also heard the message indicating that breast cancer was more likely for older women, but their efficacy message indicated that breast self-exams were difficult to do and not effective at cancer detection.

The research team measured participants' like or dislike of *breast cancer* and *breast self-exams* when the phrases appeared on a computer screen. Finally, participants responded to questionnaires so researchers could measure their attitudes toward breast cancer and their behavioral intention toward breast self-exams, as well as their defensive reactions to the fear appeal messages. By assigning the women to four different conditions, the researchers could determine if the different message combinations influenced women's responses to the fear appeal messages and their behavioral intention toward breast self-exam.

In another experimental design, Arpan and Pompper (2003) tested if journalists' stories differed according to how journalists heard of an organizational crisis: from the organization or from another party. In a simulated crisis—one in which an organization accidentally allowed a toxic chemical to spill from its factory into a river—half of the print and broadcast journalists read a scenario in which the journalists learned of the crisis directly from the organization; the other half read a scenario in which the journalists learned of the crisis from a police scanner. All other aspects of the conditions were the same. After reading the story, a subset of participants were asked to write a news story lead using the information from their condition. Then participants responded to questionnaires so the research team could measure three variables: journalists' interest in pursuing the story, perceptions of organizational credibility, and interest in the story.

Next, the researchers used a computer program to analyze the news story leads. Findings from this analysis and participants' responses to the questionnaires indicated that how journalists learned of the story influenced their perceptions of the organization's credibility. Only one aspect of the experiment (i.e., who broke the story) differed. Thus, any differences in journalists' responses could be attributed to the difference in how journalists learned of the organizational crisis. More important, the news story leads did not differ based on how journalists learned of the story.

These are just four examples of ways in which communication researchers used quantitative methods. One element underlying these examples that may not be apparent to you, but that

needs discussion, is the pattern of reasoning used by these researchers. We examine that next.

Deductive Reasoning

Quantitative research relies primarily on deductive reasoning (Hawes, 1975). This means that the researchers select a theory, or theories, as the basis of the propositions that are tested in the study. In this case, the logic flows from the generalized (the theory) to the specific (the research conclusion). In general, the researcher hopes that the research process supports, or verifies, what the theory proposes to be true.

If the data and results do not support hypotheses derived from the theory, then the researcher looks for an alternate explanation. Perhaps the theory, as it was developed, is deficient or incomplete. Therefore, the results must be faulty because they are a direct result of testing the theory. Or the methods or procedures followed could be faulty. In this case, the researcher develops a new manner in which to test the theoretical propositions and tries again.

A Model for Conceptualizing Quantitative Research

The deductive research model presented in Chapter 2 is a general overview of the research process: It gives the basic steps and can be applied to most quantitative research projects. But with both quantitative research and qualitative research (see Chapter 4), more specialized models are needed to guide us through selecting and developing the research plan for a specific study. The model for conceptualizing quantitative research shown in Figure 3.1 is the model that will guide us now.

Starting at the top left of the model, the first component is the research purpose. Because the researcher is familiar with the research literature and has developed some questions about communication issues, she or he begins with an overall purpose or objective. For example, I am interested in how a dysfunctional group member can take over a group's interaction to the point that the ineffective member replaces the task as

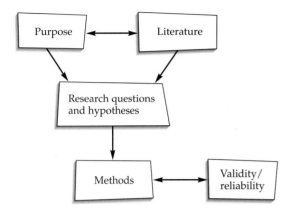

FIGURE 3.1 A Conceptual Model for Quantitative Research

the focus of the group. So my research purpose is to study that communication phenomenon.

Notice that the purpose component alone does not drive the model. The traditions of social science require that researchers use literature as a basis for their research. So my desire to study dysfunctional group members is framed within the context of the research literature and the contexts of real groups that I have observed experiencing this phenomenon. I take information (and motivation) from my original purpose, the research literature, and my experiences with groups. Balancing what I know as an academic and what I know as a group facilitator leads me to the research questions or research hypotheses that will guide my study and selection of quantitative methods.

Research questions and research hypotheses are central to the quantitative research process. No quantitative study can be done without one or a combination of these. This third component dominates the quantitative research methods process. Later in this chapter we will explore these in greater detail. But, for now, recognize that without one or several research questions or research hypotheses, there is nothing to direct or define the research process; therefore, I could not continue with my research project regardless of my motivation or objective.

The fourth component of the quantitative research model is the selection of the research methods for the project. Generally, quantitative researchers ask questions about differences and relationships. In other words, how are communication phenomena different? Or how are communication phenomena related? Either of these two forms is acceptable, but they require different types of statistical approaches. If I want to study the difference between dysfunctional members and functional, or effective, members, then I choose a quantitative method that will help me examine and illuminate those differences. If I want to study how the dysfunctional member influences the group's decision making and conflict management, I would choose a method that illuminates the relationships among the degrees of dysfunctional, decision-making, and conflict management behaviors.

Looking at some specific examples will help you distinguish between instances in which differences are the focus of the research and instances in which relationships between variables are the focus. Think about your interaction with your significant other and your interaction with your supervisor. First, think about how the two relationships are different. Look at Table 3.1 to see what I mean.

In comparing the interaction with a significant other to the interaction with a supervisor, it is easy to identify several variables on which there will be differences (for example, status, motivation, and level of intimacy). Notice how a difference can be extreme, as in the status and motivation examples. Also notice how the differences may be more moderate, as in the level of intimacy of the conversation. In each of these cases, the researcher would quantitatively measure status, motivation, and level of intimacy for each participant twice—once for each relationship type. Then the researcher would compare the scores for interaction with the significant other to the scores for interaction with the supervisor to see if a difference existed.

Now how could these two types of interactions be related to one another? Examine Table 3.2 to find these examples.

In looking for how interaction in the two relational types is related or similar, the researcher

TABLE 3.1 Looking for Differences Between Two Types of Interaction

Variables of Potential Differences Between the Two Relational Types	Interaction With Significant Other	Interaction With Supervisor
Relative status of other person in the relationship	I consider this person to be *my equal* in terms of power and status.	Due to the organizational hierarchy, this person has *more power and status* in the organization than I do.
Motivation for relationship	We are friends. I *voluntarily* developed this relationship.	I was assigned to my supervisor's work unit. This relationship *is not voluntary*.
Level of intimacy in conversations	We *share personal information* with one another.	I do *share some personal information* with my supervisor, especially when we eat lunch together.

TABLE 3.2 Looking for Relationships Between Two Types of Interaction

Potential Relationships Between the Two Relational Types	Interaction With Significant Other	Interaction With Supervisor
Number of conflicts	I *frequently* have conflicts with my significant other.	I *frequently* have conflicts with my supervisor.
Degree of satisfaction with interaction	I am *very satisfied* with my interaction with my significant other.	I am *not satisfied* with my interaction with my supervisor.
Frequency of interaction	My significant other and I *talk very frequently*.	I *talk* to my supervisor *only when necessary*.

would again obtain a quantitative measurement of number of conflicts, degree of satisfaction, and frequency of interaction for each relational type. Then the researcher would examine the pairs of scores to see how they relate to one another. Notice how the scores may be very similar, or highly related, as with the number of conflicts. Or the scores can be related, but in opposite directions, as with satisfaction with interaction and frequency of interaction.

Thus, we can look for the differences between these two relational types, or we can look for ways in which interaction in the two relational types is related. The point here is that almost any communication phenomenon can be examined for its differences to a similar communication phenomenon, or a communication phenomenon can be examined for how it relates to a similar communication phenomenon. Can you think of other elements that may differ or be related with respect to relationships with significant others and supervisors?

Returning to my example of dysfunctional group members, if I focus on differences, I might look for ways in which functional and dysfunctional group members deal with conflict, facilitate the group's decision making, or challenge the group's leadership. If I focus on ways in which these two types of group members are related, I might want to focus on the degree to which each type of group member possesses communication competence, or how similar the types of group members are in their communication style. To highlight differences, one set of statistical techniques is used. To highlight relationships, another set is chosen. These statistical techniques are covered in Chapters 11 and 12.

Notice that the final component of the quantitative research model is connected only to the methods component and that the connection is reciprocal (see Figure 3.1). This last component is an examination of the validity and reliability of the data collected through the method selected. Usually the researcher will make methodological choices and then assess those choices for their impact on *validity*—how truthful the data will be—and *reliability*—how consistent the data will be. These issues must be addressed before the research is undertaken and any data collected, for there is little opportunity to adjust the research method once the project is started. One of the assumptions of quantitative methods is that all participants are treated similarly; procedures or process should not change as you discover errors or lapses in your planning.

Once the researcher has addressed each of these five components, he or she moves through the quantitative research process in a linear fashion. Once the methods are designed, the researcher selects participants, collects and analyzes data, and then writes the research report. As demonstrated in Figure 2.1, findings from the current study are used to extend or challenge the current state of theory. New questions are formulated and the research process begins again. For now, though, we need to return to and examine in detail each step in conceptualizing the research project, as these steps provide the foundation for quantitative research projects.

CREATING THE FOUNDATION FOR QUANTITATIVE RESEARCH

After identifying the research problem and turning that topic into a preliminary question or questions, as described in Chapter 2, researchers

must further specify the concepts identified in their question. These conceptual definitions are based on theoretical information or past research studies. Generally, researchers build on the work of others and use existing concepts and definitions unless they are inadequate or inappropriate (Katzer et al., 1978).

As described in Chapter 2, communication researchers start with a preliminary question. That question asks about the differences or relationships between concepts. A **concept** represents a number of individual, but related things. It is an abstract way of thinking that helps us group together those things that are similar to one another and, at the same time, distinguish them from dissimilar other things. A concept can be an object, an event, a relationship, or a process. Examples of concepts include a faulty argument, an effective public speaker, a conflict between spouses, leadership, underrepresentation of minorities on prime-time television shows, and so on. Even though they are intended to represent a class of things that have common characteristics, a concept does not have a fixed or precise meaning or definition (de Vaus, 2001). With respect to the research literature, concepts are generally introduced early in the literature review with a general description.

In some cases, a set of concepts can be connected together to form a **conceptual scheme.** For example, a researcher could identify ways in which consequence is demonstrated in prime-time television dramas (for example, characters admit guilt and take responsibility, deny responsibility, assign responsibility to others, and so on). Individually, each concept describes a unique process. But as a group, the concepts still retain common characteristics. Together, they form a conceptual scheme that specifies and clarifies the relationships among them (Kibler, 1970).

The theoretical definition of a concept is a **construct.** Concepts can become constructs only when they are linked to other concepts. The linking between and among concepts is part of the theoretical definition. To be used in a research study, however, a construct must also be assigned an observable property, or a way for a researcher to observe or measure it. Obviously, a construct could be observed or measured in many different ways. Thus, researchers use the term **variable** to identify the theoretical construct as it is presented in research questions and hypotheses, and the term **operationalization** to denote how the variable is observed and measured. See Figure 3.2 for a visualization of how concepts, constructs, variables, and operationalizations are related to one another in the research process. Sections on identifying and operationalizing variables are presented later in this chapter.

It is important to note that both concepts and constructs are arbitrary creations of researchers (Kibler, 1970). As a result, in reading many research reports about the same topic, you are likely to find considerable variation in how scholars describe concepts and constructs. Generally, researchers describe the theoretical foundation of a study in the literature review. This is where concepts and constructs are introduced. Then, in the hypotheses and research questions, constructs are further defined as variables. Operationalizations of each variable are presented in the methods section of written research reports.

Variables are the elements of interest to researchers. Finding new descriptions, explanations, or predictions for variables is the primary motivator for conducting scholarly research. To better understand how variables are used in the research process, we need to consider hypotheses and research questions.

RESEARCH HYPOTHESES FOR QUANTITATIVE RESEARCH

Scholars rely on hypotheses to direct their quantitative inquiry. A hypothesis is an educated guess, or a presumption, that is based on a scholar's review of the research literature. It describes a logical explanation of the relationship between two or more variables. To be tested through research, the consequences of the hypothesis must be observable. In fact, the researcher designs the research study to test the relationships described in the hypothesis.

For example, the following hypothesis describes a relationship between patients' perceptions of physicians' communication characteristics

(Richmond, Smith, Heisel, & McCroskey, 2002, p. 209).

> Hypothesis: Assertiveness and responsiveness are positively correlated with patient satisfaction.

In this study, the researchers examined how patients viewed the communication behaviors of their physicians. The hypothesis proposes what the relationships will be. According to the hypothesis, when patients have high evaluations of their physicians' assertiveness they will also be satisfied with the quality of medical care they receive. Likewise, when patients have high evaluations of their physicians' responsiveness they will be satisfied with the quality of medical care they receive. A hypothesis *states* the nature of the relationship between variables. This is different from phrasing the relationship as a research question, which would ask *what* the relationship would be.

As another example, the following hypothesis predicts how strangers will communicate when they are getting to know one another through computer-mediated communication like instant messaging and how that differs from strangers getting acquainted through face-to-face interactions (Tidwell & Walther, 2002, p. 325).

> H: CMC interactants engage in deeper self-disclosures than do FtF counterparts.

Obviously, people choose how much personal information to disclose when meeting a stranger. The hypothesis addresses whether the channel through which that meeting occurs influences our behavior. Based upon the literature, the researchers hypothesized that computer instant messaging would provide a more conducive forum for such disclosures because interactants move more quickly into the conversation without having to engage in less personal conversation that is typical in the initiation of face-to-face interactions. In this hypothesis, the researchers predicted through which channel strangers would make deeper self-disclosures. In contrast, a research question would be posed as, "Will strangers make deeper self-disclosures through CMC interactions or through FtF interactions?"

Researchers choose hypotheses over research questions when the results of previous

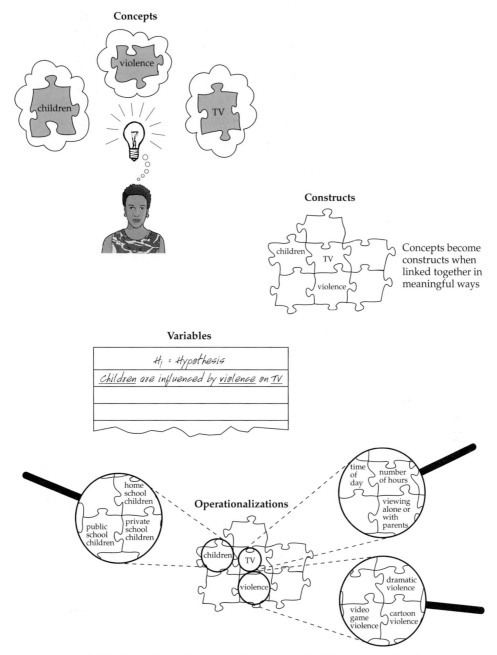

FIGURE 3.2 *Moving From Concepts to Constructs to Variables to Operationalizations*

research allow them to make predictions of research outcomes. For example, Holbert, Benoit, Hansen, and Wen (2002) wanted to examine whether earlier findings about the influence of political advertisements from a presidential debate could be confirmed in a subsequent presidential political campaign. Thus, they hypothesized (p. 300):

> H: The general pattern of results concerning the influence of political advertisement recall, television news use, and newspaper use on voter issue knowledge and salience in 1992 found by Brians and Wattenberg (1996) will replicate using 1996 ANES [American National Elections Study] data.

Why would the same relationships be tested again? Recall that science is characterized by replicability. Thus, a finding at one point in time should occur again. If the results once again verify the hypothesis, replication will be achieved and the result confirmed. As a consequence, there will be greater confidence in the findings (Boster, 2002).

Directional Hypotheses

Return to the hypothesis about self-disclosure when strangers meet. In this case the researchers expect to demonstrate that strangers who meet over instant messaging will make deeper self-disclosures than strangers meeting in face-to-face interactions. Because the hypothesis explicitly states through which channel strangers will provide greater self-disclosure, the hypothesis is directional. Thus, a **directional hypothesis** is a precise statement indicating the nature and direction of the relationship or difference between the variables.

Nondirectional Hypotheses

A nondirectional hypothesis is less explicit. Continuing with the same example, a nondirectional hypothesis could be

> H: There will be a difference in the depth of self-disclosures between interactants who meet over computer instant messaging and interactants who meet in face-to-face interactions.

The **nondirectional hypothesis** states that a difference will occur but does not state the direction of the difference. Instant messaging and face-to-face are two categories of the *media channel* variable examined in the study. The nondirectional hypothesis indicates that there will be a difference in the depth of self-disclosure between the two categories, but does not predict through which channel interactants will make deeper self-disclosures. Some researchers judge directional hypotheses to be more sophisticated than nondirectional hypotheses because they more explicitly state what differences will be found. Both types of hypotheses are found in the communication research literature.

Assessing Hypotheses

The following criteria can help you assess the clarity and utility of hypotheses (Hoover & Donovan, 1995; Pyrczak & Bruce, 2000). The first criterion asks evaluative questions about wording, such as, Is the hypothesis simply stated? Is the hypothesis stated as a single sentence? Are at least two variables identified?

The second criterion focuses on the variables in the hypothesis. Are the variables clearly specified? Can the variables be measured by techniques you know how to use? If not, you will need to learn the appropriate measurement or observation method or ask someone to help you with this aspect of the study.

A third criterion for assessing hypotheses is to examine how the relationships between variables are stated. Are the relationships precise? A good way to test this is to explain a hypothesis to someone who is unfamiliar with research methods. If you can describe it to someone else, the relationship in the hypothesis is likely to be precise enough to use in a research study.

The fourth criterion asks if the hypothesis is testable. In other words, can the differences or relationship between the variables be observed or demonstrated in some way? This criterion is crucial to conducting the research study. The method, or the way in which the study is conducted, must match the hypothesis. Evaluating hypotheses is important because they guide how the research project is developed and structured.

Null Hypotheses

Although a scholar spends time developing research hypotheses from the published literature, these are not directly tested. Rather, the statistical test is performed on the **null hypothesis,** or the implicit complementary statement to the research hypothesis. In using the statistical test, the researcher hopes to reject the null hypothesis and, in effect, validate the alternative, or the research hypothesis. A null hypothesis states that no relationship, except one due to chance, exists between the variables. As you can see, the null hypothesis is in direct opposition to the research hypothesis. According to the traditions of science, the null hypothesis must be assumed to be true until support for the research hypothesis can be demonstrated.

Although it is highly unlikely that you would see a null hypothesis presented in scholarly work, it is helpful to think through what the null hypothesis would be. As an example, refer back to the research hypothesis about self-disclosure when strangers meet. The research hypothesis was presented as

> H: CMC interactants engage in deeper self-disclosures than do FtF counterparts.

The null hypothesis could be written as

> H_0: CMC interactants will not engage in deeper self-disclosures than do FtF counterparts.

It could also be written in one of the following ways:

> H_0: Depth of self-disclosure will not vary between CMC interactants and FtF counterparts.

> H_0: There will be no difference in depth of self-disclosure between CMC interactants and FtF counterparts.

Notice that the symbol H indicates the research hypothesis and the symbol H_0 indicates the null hypothesis. In some journals, you may also see the symbols H_1 or H_{alt} to indicate the research hypothesis.

Research Traditions in the Use of Hypotheses

You should be aware of several traditions regarding the use of hypotheses (Kibler, 1970). The first is that hypotheses are always tentative. Even when support for a hypothesis is found, support is never considered absolute. Knowledge is developed over time, and the continual efforts of researchers contribute to the development of theory as they seek to confirm or disconfirm hypotheses. Thus, one study cannot absolutely confirm or disconfirm any relationship or difference between or among variables.

Researchers honor the second tradition when they present the research hypothesis. Although not explicitly stated in a journal article, the null hypothesis is assumed to be in direct opposition to the research hypothesis. The research hypothesis, the one the researcher wants to confirm, states the way in which the variables are different or the way in which the variables are related to one another. Alternately, the null hypothesis, even when not given, implies that there is no difference between the variables or that the variables are not related in any way. In nearly every case, the research, or alternative, hypothesis is the focus of a research project.

RESEARCH QUESTIONS IN QUANTITATIVE RESEARCH

Why would a researcher ask a research question instead of stating an educated guess with a hypothesis? There are several occasions when asking a research question has more utility. The first occasion is when little is known about a communication phenomenon. For example, some communication phenomena—particularly those linked to the use of media or technology—enter the mainstream faster than researchers can study their effects. As a result, Campbell and Russo (2003) had few research studies on which to base research hypotheses when they explored how social influence shaped individuals' perceptions and uses of mobile phones. Although there had been studies that looked at mobile phone use and the perceptions of users, there were few studies upon which to develop hypotheses regarding how individuals negotiate or learn rules for mobile phone use. Thus, the research team proposed the following research question:

> RQ: How are perceptions and uses of mobile phones socially constructed in the context of daily interactions?

Another opportunity for researchers to use research questions arises when several explanations could exist for the proposed relationship. For instance, Bartoo and Sias (2004) offered two competing and untested explanations about the information load from supervisor to employee and both parties' communication apprehension. One explanation is that employees supervised by individuals with high communication apprehension will experience information underload because the supervisor provides little information to the employee. Alternately, and from the other point of view, an employee with high communication apprehension might perceive any information from a supervisor as anxiety-inducing resulting in information overload. Thus, Bartoo and Sias asked, "How are supervisor CA [communication apprehension] and employee CA related to information load employees report from their supervisors?" A research question makes more sense in this instance as previous research could not help the researcher make an educated and informed guess about the relationship between the two variables. In both of these cases, the research question is an opportunity for the researcher to describe communication phenomena. Research questions are primarily tools of descriptive research.

TYPES OF VARIABLES

In hypotheses and research questions for quantitative studies, researchers make the object of their study more explicit by further specifying a construct as a variable. A *variable* is an element that is specifically identified in the research hypotheses or questions. The literature review may describe several related concepts and constructs, whereas the hypotheses and research questions identify a more limited set of variables to be explored.

The study of communication from a social science perspective borrows heavily from the traditional science disciplines. As a result, quantitative research relies on the study of variables. In social science, variables are the properties or characteristics of people or things that vary in quality or magnitude from person to person or object to object (Miller & Nicholson, 1976).

Simply, to be a variable, the element must vary. In other words, the variable must have two or more levels. For example, sex is a variable as it varies between male and female. Leadership can be a variable, as leaders can be described as autocratic or democratic. Communication apprehension, like other constructs measured by questionnaires, is a variable: Individuals' scores can have many levels, ranging between a potential minimum and maximum score.

Communication phenomena or communication-related phenomena do not always take on the role of variables in communication research. For example, even though sex varies, it cannot be a variable if the researcher studies only the leadership abilities of women. Leadership ability would be a variable; sex would not. In another example, leadership style cannot be a variable if the researcher examines only ways in which democratic leaders encourage group members to participate. In this case, encouragement of group member participation would be a variable; democratic leadership style would not. Something can be identified as a variable only if it fluctuates in the research study (Kibler, 1970). This can be confusing because not every concept that can vary and act as a variable does so in every research study.

Some variables are easy to view and count. They are tangible and observable. For example, it is easy to identify and count what type and how many hand gestures a person makes while arguing. Alternately, it may not be possible to directly view some variables. In these cases, researchers develop constructs to represent properties that control other events. For example, communication competence is a construct that was developed by communication scholars to represent perceptions of effectiveness and appropriateness of interaction. There is indirect evidence that this construct exists (after all, most people have ideas about what constitutes communication competence), but the construct itself is invisible. Communication researchers willingly accept constructs because they are able to demonstrate differing effects produced by variables. For example, competent communicators produce different effects on their receivers than incompetent communicators do. Similarly, it is impossible to see an attitude about violence on television. But a researcher can see the behavioral effects of your attitude when you report liking shows with violent content or when you change the channel to avoid watching such programming.

Whether they are tangible or constructed, when they are included in research questions or hypotheses, variables must also be identified as independent or dependent. Simply, the independent variable is presumed to have an effect on or cause a change in the dependent variable. The sections that follow describe how the two types of variable are used in research and explain the nature of the relationships between and among variables. In quantitative research, the researcher will usually specify which variables are independent and which are dependent.

Independent Variables

Variables manipulated by the researcher are called **independent variables.** Presumably, the manipulation, or variation, of this variable is the cause of change in other variables. Technically, the term *independent variable* is reserved for experimental studies (see Chapter 8) in which the researcher has control over its manipulation. In some research reports, independent variables are referred to as **antecedent variables, experimental variables, treatment variables,** and **causal variables.**

The independent variable is manipulated because the researcher wants to assess if different levels or values of the variable result in some relationship with another observed phenomenon, or the dependent variable. If the effect or relationship occurs, then the researcher presumes that the independent variable caused the change in the dependent variable.

For example, Floyd and Ray (2003) examined how acoustic intensity, or energy, influences perceptions of affection. In videotaped conversations, individuals were instructed to either "act like you really like your partner" or "act like you really dislike your partner" (p. 63). Obviously, the researchers' instruction was meant to manipulate how individuals communicated with their partners.

There are some cases, however, in which the researcher cannot directly control manipulation of the independent variable. In those instances, the term **predictor variable** is preferred and should be used in descriptive research designs (for example, survey research). Researchers are still interested in the predictor variable's effect on other variables, but distinguishing between the two terms helps remind us of this key difference.

Traditionally, the independent variable is manipulated in the context of an experiment to produce a change in the dependent variable. If all communication research were conducted as experiments, then we could end our explanation of independent variables here. However, communication researchers use experimental, quasi-experimental, and descriptive research designs (each of these is explained in detail in Chapter 8). While experimental research designs use researcher manipulation of the independent variable, quasi-experimental research does not. In these cases, the researcher relies on natural variation in the independent variable to produce different effects on the dependent variable. A few examples will help make this issue clearer.

In a study of how immigrants are socialized into American culture, Erbert, Perez, and Gareis (2003) used country of origin and sex as independent variables in their statistical tests. Obviously, the research team could not alter or change these aspects of the study's participants. Thus, these two variables varied naturally and the research team used information participants provided to code them as being from one of four world regions (i.e., Americas, Asia, Europe, or Middle East) and as female or male. Thus, both country of origin and sex had two or more levels and could be used as independent variables.

In a study of how people maintain romantic relationships (Dainton, 2003), relational equity was used as an independent variable. During the data collection procedures, the participants responded to questionnaire items that allowed the researcher to determine if participants perceived they were in equitable romantic relationships, or in romantic relationships in which they were benefiting more or less than their partner. Thus, the researcher used the natural variation in participants' reports of their relational equity to create this independent variable for the study.

DESIGN
CHECK

What Is Sex? What Is Gender?

Many quantitative communication studies use sex and gender interchangeably as an independent variable. Unfortunately, many authors do not give their operationalization of this variable. When sex or gender is not operationalized, it is probably safe to assume that the researcher had participants self-report their biological sex—male or female. Of course, biological sex is not the same as one's gender or psychological orientation to sex—for example, feminine, masculine, or androgynous. There is a difference in being female and being feminine. This confusion has become even greater because some editors and publishers have requested that the more politically correct term *gender* be substituted for the more traditional term *sex*. If sex or gender is not operationalized, read the methods section carefully to determine if participants self-reported this information, if researchers assumed this information about participants, or if participants responded to a measuring instrument. If in doubt, use the terms as they are used by the authors of the published research reports.

As you can see, it is better to describe the independent variable as the variable that alters or changes the dependent variable. The researcher does not always manipulate it. In many cases, variation in the independent variable occurs naturally as a characteristic of the population under study. Any change or difference in the independent variable is the presumed cause of a change in the dependent variable if an experimental method is used. Causality is weakened if the researcher does not directly manipulate the independent variable, but it would be impractical to conduct all of communication research from this experimental framework. Generally speaking, however, the independent variable is the variable a researcher predicts from, while the dependent variable is the one the researcher predicts to (Kibler, 1970).

Dependent Variables

Even though the independent, or predictor, variable causes the change, the dependent variable is of primary interest to the researcher, who is trying to describe, explain, predict, or control changes in it. The **dependent variable** is influenced or changed by the independent variable. Sometimes in descriptive research designs, the terms **criterion variable** and **outcome variable** identify the dependent variable. Regardless of what it is called, logically a researcher cannot have a dependent variable without an independent variable and vice versa.

Changes in the dependent variable are a consequence of changes in the values or levels of the independent variable. In a study of how students' use of background media influences students' performance on homework assignments, one hypothesis stated (Pool, Koolstra, & van der Voort, 2003, p. 77):

H: A soap opera will lead to stronger distraction effects than music videos when memorization assignments are involved.

In this case, the independent variable is type of televised background media with two levels: (1) eight episodes of a soap opera or (2) 50 music videos. But, the researchers are interested only in the televised background media variable to the degree to which it explains differences in the dependent variable—combined scores on memorization tasks. The dependent variable consisted of students' scores based on their abilities to identify 15 countries on an unmarked map, recall the names of capitals of seven of the countries, give responses to factual knowledge questions about a country's history, and recall the translation of 17 English words into Dutch or Dutch words into English. The combined scores for these tasks represented the dependent variable. Thus, the dependent variable is the variable the researcher is trying to explain in a research project (Kibler, 1970).

The Relationship Between Independent and Dependent Variables

In quantitative research, independent and dependent variables rely on each other. A researcher cannot specify independent variables without specifying dependent variables and vice versa. Variables are identified as independent and dependent to establish the presumed relationship between them.

How many independent and dependent variables can a researcher specify? That depends on the nature or complexity of what the researcher wants to explain. Most important, however, the number of independent and dependent variables dictates which statistical test will be used. We will review these distinctions in Chapters 11 and 12 as the most common statistical tests are described and explained. But, for now, analyzing a hypothesis from a research report will help you understand the nature of the relationship between independent and dependent variables.

Sparks, Pellechia, and Irvine (1998) wanted to study how television news affects viewers'

beliefs about UFOs (unidentified flying objects). They argued that although many people believe that the mass media play a role in misleading people so that they accept paranormal events like UFOs, little research has provided evidence to substantiate that claim. Thus, this research team designed an experiment to test the possible impact of news reports about UFOs on subsequent UFO beliefs. Their hypothesis was

> H: Subjects who view a high credibility, one-sided news report that supports the existence of UFOs will, subsequently, express greater belief in the existence of UFOs than will subjects who view a two-sided news report from the same program.

As a student, of course, you hope that the authors of the research report clearly identify which variables are independent and which variables are dependent. This is not always the case. Even if it is, you should be able to read the research article and verify the independent and dependent variables. One way to do so is to look for what changes or varies in the hypothesis statement. Examine Table 3.3. By comparing each mention of each element, we can determine the variables and then assign them as independent or dependent.

The authors made no distinction between the two mentions of "subjects" in the hypothesis, so "subjects" is not a variable. Likewise, there is no

TABLE 3.3 Determining Variables From the Elements of a Hypothesis

First Mention of Element	Second Mention of Element	Type of Comparison	Type of Variable
Subjects	Subjects	No distinction	—
View	View	No distinction	—
High credibility	—	No alternative given	—
One-sided news report	Two-sided news report	Explicit comparison	Independent variable
Supports the existence of UFOs	—	No alternative given	—
Greater belief in UFOs	(Less belief in UFOs)	Implied comparison	Dependent variable

distinction in the use of "view." Thus, viewing is not a variable.

The use of "high credibility" could imply a comparison to low credibility. But the researchers do not offer an alternative to "high credibility." Thus, it does not appear that the researchers are using the credibility of news reports as a variable. This is also apparent in the author's use of "supports the existence of UFOs."

Now notice the last entry in the table; reread the hypothesis. The authors explicitly state that viewers of the one-sided news report will express greater belief in UFOs. Also notice their use of the word "than." This word usage and sentence construction implies that the viewers of the one-sided news report will differ from viewers of the two-sided news report. Thus, the authors have implied a variable—belief in UFOs.

The second type of comparison is when differences are explicitly stated. The authors make a clear and explicit distinction between one-sided and two-sided news reports. So type of news report (one-sided or two-sided) must be a variable.

Which variable is the independent variable and which variable is the dependent variable? We could assume from the way the hypothesis is written that the authors use type of news report as the independent variable because they suspect that the variation in this element will cause a change in viewers' beliefs in UFOs, the dependent variable. However, it is always a good idea to read the methodology section of the research report to confirm your identification of variables and assignment of variables as independent and dependent, and to see exactly how the researchers measured or observed their variables.

Intervening and Confounding Variables

Besides independent and dependent variables, there is also the special case of the intervening, or mediating, variable. An **intervening variable** is an element that is presumed to explain or provide a link between other variables. In other words, a relationship between two variables can be explained only if the third variable is present and accounted for. Intervening variables can become important links in developing theoretical explanations.

For example, to examine the relationship between values and value-relevance relative to messages about values, Hullett (2002) measured participants' attitudes toward using personality criteria to choose dating partners, the extent to which they valued a partner who was loving, and the value-relevance—or the extent to which people perceive their attitudes as useful in attaining desire valued states—of their attitudes. Next, participants were given a message designed to counter the attitude about using personality characteristics to choose romantic partners. The findings demonstrated that message relevance was an intervening variable. If the value of choosing a romantic partner based on personality criteria was relevant, then the message was perceived as relevant and further influenced participants' perceptions of the message's quality, and ultimately, participants' attitude change.

Another special case is the **confounding variable.** A variable that confuses or obscures the effect of the independent variable on the dependent variable is said to confound the relationship. When a confounding variable is present, it is often difficult to isolate the effects of independent variables. Although a researcher carefully designs a study, no study is perfect and not all influential factors can be controlled. The researcher intends that the research design identifies and controls for the most influential variables as independent variables. Still, other influences can occur; these are the confounding variables. Lee's (2004) examination of visual representation in computer-mediated communication is a good example of how the researcher can control for confounding variables by carefully designing the experiment.

OPERATIONALIZING VARIABLES

Whether variables are used as independent or dependent variables in hypotheses or questions, researchers must take one additional step in order to actually use the variables in a quantitative study. Each variable must be operationalized, or observed or measured in a specified way. Most variables can be operationalized in multiple ways. That is why an operationalization specifies

TRY THIS!   **Identifying Independent and Dependent Variables**

Following the process shown in Table 3.3, identify the independent and dependent variables for each hypothesis below.

Hypothesis	Independent Variable	Dependent Variable
Customers' loyal behavioral intentions toward professional service providers will be predicted by their satisfaction with their most recent experience with the providers. (FROM Ford, 2003)	Customers' satisfaction with most recent experience with the professional service provider.	Customers' loyal behavior intentions toward professional service provider.
In addition to structural components, [on-air] promos' content components will significantly affect the ratings of promoted comedies. (FROM Eastman, Newton, & Bolls, 2003)		
Teacher expressions of anger early in the semester will be perceived as less normative or appropriate than anger expressed later in the semester. (FROM McPherson, Kearney, & Plax, 2003)		
More positive perceptions of communication experiences with grandparents will be related to be more positive attitudes toward older adults. (FROM Soliz & Harwood, 2003)		

the concrete steps or processes for creating and measuring the variable. The operationalization is specific enough that others reading the description of the operationalization in the research report can follow it (Miller & Nicholson, 1976).

Researchers use three criteria for selecting among available operationalizations. First, which operationalization is practical and useful

in their study? Second, can a justifiable argument be developed for this operationalization? Third, does the operationalization selected coincide with the conceptual definition?

A good example of the specificity needed for operationalizations is demonstrated in a study that examined the influence of message design strategies on changes in attitude and use of marijuana (Harrington et al., 2003). The first hypothesis of the study stated:

> H₁: Compared to low sensation value anti-marijuana messages, high sensation value anti-marijuana messages will lead to greater attitude, behavioral intention, and behavior change.

Although the research team identifies the variables in the hypothesis, there is not enough information to replicate the research study. What are low sensation value and high sensation value messages? How do you measure attitude, behavioral intention, and behavior change?

In the methods section of their study, the research team specifically defined, or operationalized, these variables. To create the high sensation and low sensation value messages, the research team reviewed public service announcements (PSAs) currently being shown on television. Identifying those that were high and low sensation, the research team then used focus groups to verify their characterizations. With this information, the team created high sensation value PSAs that featured high intensity, loud and driving music, quick and multiple edits, unusual camera angles, and extreme close-ups. Alternately, low sensation value PSAs featured slower paced music, fewer edits, more typical camera angles, and no extreme close-ups. Thus, the authors clearly described what constitutes a high sensation and low sensation value message and explained specifically how those messages were created.

The researchers also explained how they operationalized each of the other three variables—attitude change, behavioral intention change, and behavior change. Attitudes toward marijuana use were measured with questionnaire items from a study done as an evaluation of a national drug abuse campaign. Behavioral intention toward using marijuana was measured with this and similar items, "How likely is it that you will use _____ in the next 30 days?" Marijuana use behavior was measured with items that asked if participants had used marijuana in the past 30 days, the past year, or at any time during their lifetime. For each variable the research team provided examples of the items and indicated the direction of the desired change (i.e., should watching a PSA result in a higher or lower score).

Thus, different terms are used as the researcher moves between conceptual, theoretical, and empirical stages. Occasionally, you will notice that the terms are used interchangeably. But, technically, as the terms move from concept through construct through variable to operationalization, each provides a different level of specificity.

When you read scholarly journal articles using quantitative methods, you will read about concepts and constructs in the literature review. In this section, the researchers may even present conflicting definitions of the concept of interest. When researchers present their research questions and hypotheses, they will become more specific and treat the concepts and constructs as variables. In the methods section of the journal article, researchers will be precise and provide the operationalization—how the variable will be observed and measured—of each variable.

Both researchers and consumers of research benefit when there is specificity about what is being studied (Miller & Nicholson, 1976). If terms are defined explicitly in operationalizations, then it is more difficult for the researcher to draw conclusions beyond the boundaries established. Another advantage is that findings of studies that use the same or similar operationalizations can be compared. When an operationalization is accepted as a standardized way of measuring or observing, there are two consequences. First, preciseness is achieved, which allows our understanding of the communication phenomenon to be enhanced, and this enhancement supports theory development. Second, operationalizations allow other researchers to replicate the research to verify or challenge findings.

MAKING THE CASE FOR QUANTITATIVE RESEARCH

For many of the other social sciences and for a long period of time in communication, researchers conducting their research from the social science perspective relied primarily on quantitative research methods. Traditionally, experimental forms were preferred to other methods in which variables are

TRY THIS!

Operationalizing Variables

Communication researchers are often interested in studying concepts that are abstract in nature. For example, to study how couples in love communicate and then compare that to how couples not in love communicate, we would first have to describe what love is and then operationalize it. Review the examples below; which operationalization do you like best? What is problematic with the two operationalizations below? What operationalizations can you develop? Are there other descriptions of love more to central communication?

Description of Love	Operationalization of Love
When two people hold hands in front of others	The number of times a couple hold hands for longer than one minute in public.
When two people tell their friends and relatives that they are in love	The degree of vocal intensity in telling friends and relatives that they love the other person. The number of reasons given when telling friends and family that they love the other person.
When two people independently feel attracted to each other and decide not to date others	
When two people in a committed relationship do unexpected tasks for each other	

quantified (for example, surveys). But, today, communication researchers choose from a variety of quantitative *and* qualitative methods. Which method should be chosen is one of the decisions the researcher must make. By answering the question "What do I want to know in this study?" clearly and completely, the researcher can select the appropriate methodology. Reviewing the advantages and limitations of quantitative research will help you determine what types of questions are best answered by quantitative methods.

Advantages of Quantitative Research

The advantages of using quantitative research methods are obvious. First, quantitative methods used in communication research follow the tradition and history of quantitative methods in other disciplines. Thus, the use of quantitative methods implies a certain amount of rigor in the research process. By quantifying and measuring communication phenomena, communication researchers are using the same research language as researchers with whom they share interests. Sharing a research tradition could, for example, strengthen the relationship with communication researchers who study organizational communication and with researchers from the management discipline. Likewise, many communication researchers who study interpersonal issues would share a research tradition with psychologists who focus on individuals and their relationships.

A second advantage of quantitative research comes from the use of numbers and statistics. By quantifying communication concepts and using statistical procedures for evaluating differences and relationships, researchers are able to be very precise and exact in their comparisons. This is especially important in the study of microelements of communication. Quantifying abstract concepts provides researchers a way to isolate variables and gain knowledge about concepts that would otherwise remain hidden.

Third, because we can quantify communication phenomena, we can make comparisons, and those comparisons can be made among a large group of participants. As a result, researchers can generalize their findings to other individuals who have the same characteristics as those in the research project.

Limitations of Quantitative Research

Of course, with advantages come limitations. And, as is often true, limitations stem from the same sources as the advantages. Because quantitative research can focus on microelements of communication phenomena, this type of research generally does not lend itself to capturing the complexity or depth of communication over time. The restriction of focusing on just a few variables at a time makes it more difficult for researchers to examine the entirety of the communication process.

Likewise, quantitative research fails to capture communication phenomena that cannot be replicated or simulated in a controlled research environment. Although researchers can use quantitative methods in the field, all participants must be subjected to the same research procedures and stimuli. As a result, questions about a communication phenomenon that occurs spontaneously or sporadically are not as well suited to quantitative methods.

Issues of Reliability and Validity

All research, regardless of the method, hopes to be both reliable and valid. **Reliability** is achieved when researchers are consistent in their use of data collection procedures and when participants react similarly to them. Reliability also means that other researchers using the same measure in another project with comparable participants would get similar results (Hoover & Donovan, 1995).

But reliability is only part of evaluating a quantitative research method. **Validity** is achieved when the measurement does what it is intended to do (Hoover & Donovan, 1995). Validity is related to truth. Thus, within scientific reasoning, the better the technique is at uncovering the reality of the concept, the more valid it is. If a questionnaire presumably testing your degree of communication competence asks you to respond to an item about your ability to handle conflict, the item would be valid if you and other people in general believe that handling conflict effectively is, in fact, evidence of communication competence.

Reliability and validity are related. Both are evaluations of the utility of a measuring device. When reliability and validity are achieved, the data are free from systematic errors (Selltiz, Jahoda, Deutsch, & Cook, 1959). This is why quantitative researchers must carefully consider reliability and validity in the planning stages of their research project. But doing so is not enough. At the end of data collection, one of the first analytical steps quantitative researchers perform is to assess the reliability and validity of their data. Without reliable and valid measurement, the results of the study, which rely on how the data are collected, are suspect. More detailed information on how to assess reliability and validity can be found in Chapter 6.

Threats to Reliability and Validity

Any measuring device can be faulty—whether the device is a questionnaire or a researcher categorizing and counting the number of times you use "Ms. Wright" while talking to your boss. Communication research is especially vulnerable to threats to reliability and validity because it measures complex communication phenomena. Let's examine different types of threats to reliability and validity (Selltiz et al., 1959).

First, reliability and validity are threatened if the measuring device cannot make fine distinctions. To what degree can the measuring device capture specificity or exactness? In measuring a person's orientation, or relationship, to organizations, can the measure of organizational orientation (McCroskey, Richmond, Johnson, & Smith, 2004) really distinguish among individuals who have a strong affinity for organizations, those who do not care much about organizations, and those who cannot adapt to organizations well? Second, reliability and validity are threatened if the measuring device cannot capture how people differ. Not only must the organizational orientation measure make distinctions among the three different orientations a person can have to organizations, but it must also provide information about how individuals with those orientations communicate in organizations.

A third threat is present when researchers attempt to measure something that is irrelevant or unknown to the respondent. Anyone can respond to a questionnaire; but if the respondent does not understand the questions or if the respondent is asked to give responses for something for which he or she has no reference, then the measurement is faulty. This is especially true of opinions and attitudes, which are often part of quantitative communication research. Simply, it would not make sense to ask an unmarried and never-married respondent to answer questions about communication satisfaction with a marital partner.

Finally, the complexity of human communication behavior can threaten reliability and validity. Can any measuring instrument really capture the phenomenon? For example, if two researchers are measuring the length of a building and they disagree, together they can remeasure the building. Their individual measures can be verified by each other or a third party. But how can someone verify your organizational orientation? Asking you to respond again to the questionnaire may produce different results, depending on the number and types of interactions you have had

in organizations since you last answered the questionnaire or depending on a change in your motivation or necessity to be employed. Someone else cannot independently verify your organizational orientation—only you can provide that information. Moreover, what if your organizational orientation is not represented by the three orientations captured by this questionnaire?

As you can see, quantifying communication phenomena provides some difficulties and creates consequences for the validity and reliability of the research. Although researchers want to capture variation across the participants in the research project, the variation should be representative of the true differences among individuals and not result from measurement errors (Selltiz et al., 1959).

Besides the variation that researchers want to capture, there are many other possible sources of variation (Selltiz et al., 1959). Unless these variations are intended to be examined as part of the research design, when they are present, the following must be considered as threats to reliability and validity:

1. Variation due to factors not measured in the research study. For example, you want to measure effects of personality on conflict management strategy choice. A researcher would have to check the research literature to determine if personality is the best choice of independent variable. Rather than personality, could it be that our experiences with conflict help mold our preferences?

2. Variation or differences due to personal factors, such as mood, fatigue, health, time of day, and so on. How would these factors affect your choice of conflict management strategy?

3. Variation or differences due to situational factors. Would your choice of conflict management strategy be different at school, at work, at home?

4. Variation due to differences in how the research project is administered. Different researchers may use different communication styles in working with research participants. Would you respond differently to a researcher who appears to be bored than you would respond to a researcher who appears enthusiastic?

5. Variation due to the number of items included in the measuring device. Asking only one question about each of the conflict management styles would not be the same as asking several questions about each style. Multiple items are required to capture the breadth and complexity of most communication phenomena.

6. Variation due to unclear measuring device. As an assistant to a faculty researcher, you are asked to observe students giving speeches and count the number of times students use incomplete sentences. In one speech, the speaker gives an incomplete sentence but before moving on to the next sentence catches the error and restates the incomplete sentence as a full one. Do you count this or not?

7. Variation affected by mechanical or procedural issues. In a research experiment, you are asked to recall your last conflict with your relational partner and write out what you said to him or her. As you recall the conflict incident, you recognize that the conflict was a lengthy one lasting for about 20 minutes. But the researcher left only 3 inches of space on the questionnaire for you to describe what you said. Not knowing what to do, you select the most important things you said and leave out the rest.

8. Variation due to the statistical processing of the data. For example, the computer program may be written in such a way as to count your score twice. Or the person who enters your data in the computer pushes "4" every time you have responded with a "5."

Obviously, you want to capture and test variation in your research project. But this type of variation is planned for and identified in your hypotheses and research questions. Other variation is problematic. Look again at the model for quantitative research in Figure 3.1. Notice that selection of methods must be balanced with issues of reliability and validity. That is why researchers using quantitative methods must carefully consider and evaluate their research design, or their procedures and methods, before data are collected. Capturing variation beyond the variation the researchers want to capture is measurement error, which produces threats to reliability and validity.

SUMMARY

1. Quantitative research relies on the use of numbers as a way of observing and measuring communication phenomena.

2. Researchers bring objectivity to the study of communication through the use of traditional quantitative approaches and statistical techniques.

3. Quantitative research relies on deductive reasoning.

4. The primary objective of quantitative research is to test propositions developed from theory.

5. The quantitative research model includes five components: research purpose, literature foundation, research questions and research hypotheses, research methods, and validity and reliability.

6. Quantitative research requires that every phenomenon studied be conceptualized and then explicitly defined. Researchers work from concepts to constructs to variables to operationalizations in providing the degree of objective specificity needed to examine communication phenomena.

7. Operationalizations are the specific way in which researchers observe and measure variables in quantitative research.

8. Quantitative research typically relies on the use of hypotheses to drive the research process.

9. Hypotheses should be simply stated, have variables and their relationships clearly specified, and be testable.

10. Although researchers develop research hypotheses, the null hypothesis is actually the focus of the statistical test.

11. A hypothesis includes both independent and dependent variables.

12. Researchers can also use research questions as a foundation for their quantitative research. Research questions are appropriate to use when there is little known about a communication phenomenon or when previous results are inconclusive.

13. Advantages of quantitative research include a certain degree of rigor, objectivity achieved through the use of numbers and statistics, and ability to make comparisons among a large group of participants.

14. Limitations of quantitative research include difficulty in capturing the complexity or depth of communication over time, and the inability to capture communication phenomenon that cannot be replicated or simulated in a controlled environment.

15. Quantitative research must address threats to reliability and validity, including using imprecise measures of variables, attempting to measure something that is unknown or irrelevant to participants, and difficulty in capturing the complexity of human interaction.

KEY TERMS

antecedent variable
causal variable
concept
conceptual scheme
confounding variable
construct
criterion variable
dependent variable
directional hypothesis
experimental variable
independent variable
intervening variable
nondirectional hypothesis
null hypothesis
operationalization
outcome variable
predictor variable
reliability
treatment variable
validity
variable

CHAPTER FOUR

Introduction to Qualitative Research

Chapter Checklist

After reading this chapter, you should be able to:

1. Describe qualitative research and its assumptions.

2. Identify examples of qualitative research.

3. Explain inductive analysis.

4. Explain the qualitative research model.

5. Describe issues of credibility that must be addressed in qualitative research.

6. Explain the role of a research question in qualitative research.

7. Assess the effectiveness of research questions in qualitative research.

8. Describe different ways meaning is derived from data in qualitative research.

9. Distinguish among the different levels of data in qualitative research.

10. Explain the advantages and disadvantages of qualitative research.

11. Understand the key differences and similarities between quantitative and qualitative research.

12. Explain how to choose between quantitative and qualitative methodologies.

Communication researchers use a variety of research methods available to them because any one method cannot answer all questions about communication behavior. Why? Communication researchers recognize that human interaction is more complex and intricate than can be captured in the lab or quantified with measuring devices. Qualitative research methods, therefore, are more effective in capturing the complexity of communication phenomena, especially communication processes that unfold over time, and this quality is what draws researchers to these methods. Moreover, qualitative methods are sensitive to the social construction of meaning (Lindlof, 1991). In qualitative methods, researchers emphasize the communication environment of interactants, allowing researchers to explore everyday social phenomena in a way quantitative methods do not allow.

WHAT IS QUALITATIVE RESEARCH?

Qualitative research preserves the form and content of human interaction. These preservations, often in the form of text, are analyzed for their qualities but not subjected to mathematical transformations, as is the case with quantitative research (Lindlof & Taylor, 2002). Rather, qualitative research methods emphasize empirical, inductive, and interpretive approaches applied to interaction within a specific context.

This means that qualitative researchers are interested in the whole of the phenomenon, regardless of how complex or messy it gets. In direct opposition to quantitative research, qualitative researchers do not convert their observations or participants' observations into numerical form, nor do they separate out or isolate part of the interaction from the whole. Qualitative methodologies described in this book include participant observation, interviews, focus groups, narrative analysis, and ethnography. Other forms of qualitative research are used to study communication phenomena, but those listed are some of the most common.

Sometimes qualitative methods are referred to as naturalistic research, ethnography, field research, or participant observation, although the term *qualitative research* is preferred by communication scholars and is the broadest and most inclusive term (Lindlof & Taylor, 2002). Regardless of how it is labeled, qualitative research uses discourse (Anderson, 1996) as its data. In qualitative research, the **discourse,** or naturally occurring talk or gestures, is captured in a variety of forms and remains as it occurs. It is never transformed to numerical equivalents.

Qualitative research aims for **subjectivity** rather than objectivity. This means that researchers use interpretive research processes to make the subject of the interpretation meaningful (Anderson, 1996). This definition differs from the definition of the term *subjective* as meaning "individual" or "idiosyncratic." Rather, the qualitative researcher uses both data collection and analytic techniques from which research claims can be tested. In the strictest sense, the qualitative research tradition rejects the objectivity and absolute truth that is sought in quantitative methods and accepts that multiple interpretations are possible. In practice, however, both subjectivity and objectivity are matters of degree. For qualitative researchers, subjectivity is primary.

Subjectivity is favored over objectivity in qualitative research because researchers using qualitative methods have a strong concern for the context in which the interaction occurs. The qualitative researcher takes a more subjective frame in the research process because he or she must rely on research participants for their understanding of the research context. More precisely, qualitative researchers favor subjectivity because they are interested in exploring **inter-subjectivity,** or the social accomplishment of how people co-construct and co-experience the interaction of social life and their rules for doing so (Gubrium & Holstein, 2000).

Although differing in techniques for collecting the data, qualitative methods share certain characteristics (Denzin & Lincoln, 2000; Eisner, 1991; Lindlof & Taylor, 2002). First, qualitative methodologies have a theoretical interest in how people understand and interpret communication processes. Second, each of the methodologies is concerned with the study of communication as socially situated human action and artifacts. This means that qualitative research is conducted in the field as opposed to simulated or lab environments. It also means that qualitative researchers use interpretive lenses to capture and explore how social experience is created and how communicators develop and derive meanings from those experiences. Third, each method uses human investigators as the primary research instrument. This means that the researcher can capture rich descriptions of the interaction field and capture interactants' points of view more intimately. Finally, all qualitative methodologies rely on textual, usually written, forms for coding data and presenting results to participants and other audiences.

As a result of these characteristics, qualitative research reports have an inherently different quality than quantitative research reports. Qualitative reports rely heavily on the use of expressive language and, as the author allows, participants' voices.

In most quantitative research, the focus tends to be on causality. What causes a communicator to use a particular communication strategy? What causes one communication strategy to work better than another? Although there are certainly advantages to this type of research, causality may be achieved at the expense of understanding and explanation. Alternately, qualitative research replaces the concept of causality with that of **mutual simultaneous shaping** (Lincoln & Guba, 1985). From this perspective,

> everything influences everything else, in the here and now. Many elements are implicated in any given action, and each element interacts with all of the others in ways that change them all while simultaneously resulting in something that we, as outside observers, label as outcomes or effects. (p. 151)

With so much going on at once, identifying specific causality is difficult, if not impossible. As a result, qualitative researchers who discover causal relationships acknowledge the holistic frame in which cause and effect occurs and do not attempt to single out one variable that causes another (Figure 4.1).

Many qualitative researchers argue that interaction has no directionality (Lincoln & Guba, 1985) and maintain an emphasis on processes and

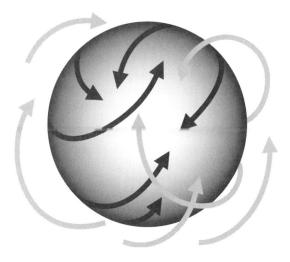

FIGURE 4.1 Mutual Simultaneous Shaping Acknowledges That All Elements Have Causal Influence

meanings (Denzin & Lincoln, 1994). Likewise, they see no need to identify outcomes of actions. Qualitative researchers argue that events are mutually shaped by other events and that dissecting events into parts for study, as is done in quantitative research, is inappropriate. Thus, the strength of qualitative research is that it captures the complexity of the interaction event because it does not artificially limit observation to one or a few aspects or components.

As a result, researchers using qualitative methods search for plausible explanations based on what is observed. At the same time, qualitative researchers acknowledge that the particular web or pattern of interactions observed may never occur again in that same way. So explanations are unique in that they represent how the interaction was enacted and influenced in this particular case.

Examples of Qualitative Research

Qualitative research is particularly useful for studying sensitive topics. For example, French (2003) interviewed women who had reported being raped to determine how women talk about their acquaintance rape, and how they frame, or evaluate, that experience. The researcher posted flyers at a rape crisis center and a college campus inviting women who had been sexually assaulted by acquaintances to participate in her study.

Data were collected from interviews that lasted between 45 and 60 minutes. The researcher used seven open-ended questions to encourage and allow the participants to describe the sexual assault in their own words. Subsequent questions focused on issues of blame and what, if any, negative or positive changes women had experienced subsequent to the assault. The interviews were audiotaped with the consent of participants, transcribed, and verified for accuracy.

In analyzing the data, French found that paradox emerged as a significant issue in their sense-making processes. After all, these women were talking about situations in which they anticipated respectful behavior from their male acquaintances. Participants reported that they struggled to find a way to frame their experience; some even described their own behavior as confusing and paradoxical. French discovered that the framing strategies the women used were similar to those in a study about sexual harassment, suggesting that women experiencing violence speak in similar voices.

As a second example of qualitative research, Ellingson (2003) used qualitative data collection techniques—ethnographic field notes, transcribed meetings, and interviews—to investigate the communication processes among medical team members. When you visit the doctor, you are focused on your interaction with the doctor and other medical personnel. Have you ever wondered how they were talking about you? Collaborative multidisciplinary health care teams are used increasingly to provide comprehensive diagnoses and treatment of patients, especially in the field of geriatric oncology.

Ellingson focused on what health care team members talked about when they were in areas of the clinic where patients could not hear their conversations. Her analysis of the data revealed that not only were team members talking about the patient by sharing information and their informal impressions but they were also managing their workload and their resources, building

relationships with one another, training students, handling both personal and professional interruptions, and working on the formal reports and recordkeeping prevalent in the health care industry.

Thus, by moving beyond the more traditional research context of health care team meetings and patient–physician interactions, the researcher was able to identify the crucial role of informal communication in the formation and maintenance of the team and its ability to effectively treat patients. Moreover, Ellingson discovered that the "team" more accurately could be described as a series of dyads and triads of team members in which disciplinary and professional lines became blurred.

As a third example of qualitative research, Leonardi (2003) used focus groups to discover how first-generation, working-class Latinos who reside permanently in the United States perceived and used new communication technologies. The researcher was particularly interested in exploring if, and how, their use of cell phones, computers, and the internet were influenced by their Latino cultural values. Leonardi conducted seven focus groups, each lasting about an hour and a half. The sessions were conducted in Spanish, audiorecorded, transcribed, and translated from Spanish into English.

Paying close attention to comments and stories that revealed participants' perceived purposes for technology use, as well as the benefits and hindrances of technology, Leonardi found that this group of participants did not view the three technologies similarly. Rather, cell phones were viewed as a medium that promoted their cultural communication value of close interpersonal contact; alternately, computers and the internet were viewed as impeding that value. By using portions of both the Spanish language transcript and the English language translation as evidence in the article, Leonardi allows us to follow his analysis and verify his claims.

Each of these qualitative studies asks different research questions, focuses on different communication contexts, and uses different qualitative methods. But the common thread to the three—and qualitative research in general—is the way in which researchers conceptualize what counts

TRY THIS!

Identifying Contexts for Qualitative Research

Qualitative methods are very useful in answering questions about communication contexts that are difficult to replicate in the lab or other controlled environments. Often the biggest advantage of qualitative methods is that the researcher can go into interaction contexts or capture interaction from contexts that would otherwise not be accessible. In the table below, after the examples given, identify five other communication contexts and the respective research question you believe deserves the attention of communication researchers.

Interaction Context	*Research Question*
Family reunions	How do distant relatives reestablish connections and relationships with one another during family reunion activities?
Employee dining room	In what ways do employees use informal lunchtime conversations to release work stress?
Police–community member interaction during community policing activities	How is communication characterized when police interact with community members from cultures different from their own?

as data. In all three examples, researchers captured or observed the interaction they were interested in studying. In all cases the researchers were immersed in the interaction context, either by being there or by obtaining detailed records of the interaction. The communication environments were real, the participants were natural actors in these settings, and, most important, the communication consequences to the participants were real. This is the hallmark of qualitative research methods. Just as some researchers who use quantitative methods would hold experimental research as the ideal against which other quantitative research is measured, these three elements represent the ideal against which qualitative research is measured.

Inductive Analysis

Qualitative methods rest on inductive reasoning, moving from the specific to the general. **Inductive analysis** is the reasoning used by qualitative researchers to discover and develop theories as they emerge from the data.

This process of analysis has several steps (Janesick, 2000; Lindlof & Taylor, 2002). First, the researcher becomes intimately familiar with the field of interaction and observes firsthand the interaction of participants in an effort to grasp its implicit meaning. After being immersed in the setting or in the data, the researcher needs to allow time to think and become aware of the nuance of the communication and its meaning in the setting. Being immersed allows the researcher to create better descriptions of what is occurring. Thus, taking time to complete more observations, or reading and rereading through the data allows the researcher to become intimately familiar with the setting, the interactants, their communication, and potential interpretations. But, the process of inductive analysis does not stop with description.

As the researcher becomes more familiar with the setting or data, a process of analysis and interpretation begins as the researcher tests alternative and tentative explanations. More formally, there are several methods for analyzing qualitative data. All include comparing and contrasting data for themes and patterns. Several of

these will be explained in detail in Chapter 16. As the data are being analyzed, the researcher begins to synthesize and bring together pieces into a whole. This allows the researcher to make tentative and plausible statements of the phenomenon being studied. Inductive analysis continues as the qualitative researcher begins to write the research document. For most qualitative researchers, the process of writing is where knowledge claims are solidified. Thus, the researcher moves from specifics of the data (i.e., transcripts, observations) to identification of patterns and themes to general conclusions.

A Model for Qualitative Research

Qualitative research requires forethought and planning, just as quantitative research does, although the process is slightly different. The model of qualitative research design presented in Figure 4.2 demonstrates how the stages of the qualitative research process are interdependent, emergent, cyclical, and, at times, unpredictable (Lindlof & Taylor, 2002; Maxwell, 1996).

Conducting qualitative research is not linear, as it cannot be planned out in its entirety before entering the field. Because the researcher enters an existing interaction context, the researcher cannot control it the way a quantitative researcher can control what happens in a laboratory experiment. However, that does not mean that the researcher enters the field unprepared.

The circle in Figure 4.2 identifies the activities the researcher should undertake in preparing for a qualitative research project. Most qualitative researchers are motivated to conduct an investigation because they have experienced a situation that the research literature does not adequately address. As the researcher begins to establish the phenomenon and context of interest, he or she should turn to the existing research literature. Searching the literature for studies about the phenomenon and studies about the context will help prepare the researcher to make the most of his or her time in the field.

The researcher must be able to identify the tentative goals of the study. Not only does the researcher have to address the academic research audience, but he or she should also address the

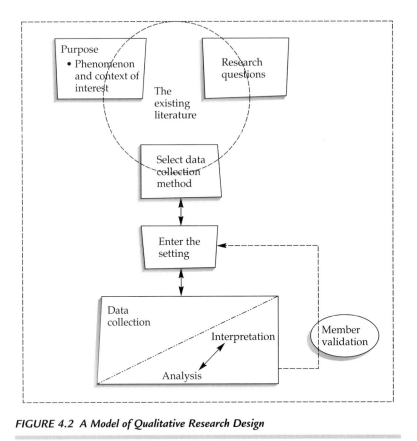

FIGURE 4.2 A Model of Qualitative Research Design

concerns of communicators. The first question—What communication practices or processes will be illuminated? helps provide the academic focus. The second question—For whom will the results be beneficial?—helps provide the practical focus. Because researchers using qualitative methods are entering or assessing natural communication and, in some cases, entering the lives of research participants, they must be able to answer the question "What is the most effective argument for pursuing this particular research project?"

Next, the researcher must develop tentative research questions. This component should not be overlooked simply because the research is qualitative. Research questions can be developed to help uncover greater understanding of or to determine what is not known about the communication

phenomenon. If a study requires multiple questions, these need to be articulated in such a way that the relationships among them are clear.

Likewise, the researcher turns to the existing literature to address the theories, previous findings, and conceptual frameworks that are related to the phenomenon of interest. Researchers will need to respond to the following questions: What do your personal experiences reveal about this phenomenon? Is there a theory to work from? Or will your study help develop a theoretical perspective on your phenomenon?

With these steps initiated, the researcher selects a data collection method or set of methods. This part of the process is at the bottom of the circle in Figure 4.2 to suggest that the method does not lead the inquiry. Just as with a quantitative research project and as suggested in earlier chapters, the method should be selected because it is the most appropriate for investigating the communication phenomenon of interest and for its ability to answer the research question. Here, there are some practical issues. What qualitative research skills do you, as a researcher, possess? What skills can be learned or enhanced? Finally, the researcher must be able to give an answer to the question "What qualitative techniques and approaches are appropriate for answering the research questions and can be effectively used in *this specific communication environment?*" Both parts of this question must be satisfied. Besides identifying the methods for collecting the data, the researcher should plan the method of data analysis. This decision must be made before the data are collected.

Now the researcher is ready to enter the setting—after securing the permission and consent of participants, if this is required. Although data collection is now the primary activity, the researcher needs to remain flexible. Once in the setting, the researcher may recognize that the planned research design and selected method are not the most effective or appropriate. Thus, adjustments may be made. The two-way arrows between method and setting and between setting and data collection emphasize the need for flexibility.

Once in the setting, the researcher begins data collection; that is the primary activity. However, analyzing and interpreting data can begin as soon as data are collected, or shortly thereafter. As mentioned earlier in this chapter, data collection is closely followed by data analysis and interpretation. In some cases, for example in interview and focus group research, all of the data may be collected before data analysis begins. In other cases, particularly when the researcher is making observations in the field, data analysis will begin while the researcher is still collecting data. In either case, making tentative and plausible statements of the phenomenon being studied gives the researcher the opportunity to expand or restrict questions that are being asked or observations that are being made. The long dashed line separating data collection from analysis and interpretation indicates this relationship. The two processes

can be separate activities, or they may become integrated activities. This type of continuous comparison is common in qualitative research methods and may suggest that the researcher make adjustments to what is being asked or observed.

There is a process to qualitative research with a beginning, middle, and end. But the process is cyclical, not linear. Thus, the researcher is likely to revisit some steps in the process and reconsider some decisions "until the researcher 'gets it right'" (Lindlof & Taylor, 2002, p. 67).

Issues of Credibility in Qualitative Research

The criteria of reliability and validity were developed for quantitative research methodologies, and applying them to qualitative research is difficult (Janesick, 2000). Still, qualitative researchers need to assure others of the quality of their interpretations. Rather than ask whether the data and interpretation are reliable and valid, qualitative researchers focus on the issue of **credibility,** or the extent to which interpretations can be validated as true, correct, and dependable (Lindlof & Taylor, 2002).

Credibility is essential to qualitative research findings because the process of qualitative research could result in multiple interpretations (Lindlof & Taylor, 2002). From the qualitative framework this is not a problem. In fact, many qualitative researchers doubt whether a "reality" exists (Altheide & Johnson, 1994). Recall, that subjectivity and intersubjectivity are primary in qualitative research as contrasted to the objective focus of quantitative research. Thus, researchers design their projects and then analyze and interpret their data to create "plausible, insightful and/or useful" interpretations (Lindlof & Taylor, 2002, p. 240). Triangulation and member validation are two ways qualitative researchers enhance the credibility of their findings.

Researchers use **triangulation,** or the use of several kinds of methods or data, to bring credibility to their findings. In an ideal world, you would choose the method that would absolutely answer your research question. However, alternative explanations will exist regardless of which research method you choose (Denzin, 1970a).

Thus, researchers use triangulation to overcome this inherent flaw in the research process. There are several ways in which communication scholars can triangulate their findings (Denzin, 1978; Janesick, 1994). The first method of triangulation common to qualitative research is **data triangulation.** By using a variety of data sources in one study, researchers are more confident about their findings and conclusions. For example, in a study of stability and trust in assembly plants in Mexico owned by U.S. companies, Lindsley (1999) used three qualitative methods to generate three types of data. Gathering data from interviews, nonparticipant observation, and analysis of organizational publications, she was able to develop multifaceted descriptions of communication behavior from both U.S. and Mexican perspectives.

A second method of triangulation common to qualitative research is **investigator triangulation.** When several different researchers or evaluators participate in the research, researchers have greater confidence in their findings because no result is dependent on one person's observations or interpretations. Qualitative methods frequently use multiple observers or coders to reduce the subjective bias that can be introduced when only one researcher acts as the observer and data collector. For example, eight communication students worked as a team of observers and data collectors in an ethnographic study of an entertainment center. Working together in the same communication environment, they were able to observe more interactions as well as consider the interaction from more perspectives than any one researcher could have done (Communication Studies 298, 1997).

Finally, **interdisciplinary triangulation** is possible when researchers from a variety of disciplines work together on a research project. Interdisciplinary triangulation is becoming more popular as communication researchers enter into highly specialized interaction environments. For example, two communication scholars teamed with a physician to examine how physician–patient interaction was influenced by the presence of a third person, an intern or resident

(Pomerantz, Fehr, & Ende, 1997). The research team represented both communication and medical expertise, creating greater ecological validity for their analysis. By working together as a team, researchers can question one another's biases and perspectives to find the most effective way to study and then analyze the phenomenon of interest.

Thus, triangulation through the use of multiple sources of data or multiple investigators from the same or different disciplines is used to dispel doubts about the reality of a finding and enhance the credibility of the qualitative research process (Lindlof & Taylor, 2002). Let's turn now to member validation.

Member validation, or **member check,** is the process of taking the research findings back to individuals from whom data were collected or were observed. For example, Lesch (1994) explains how she addressed the credibility of her findings in her study of a witch coven: "These two [coven members] also read the final report, corrected factual errors about the group's history, and offered their impressions about the accuracy of my descriptions and interpretations. Later, the rest of the group read the report; all members said they felt it represented their experiences accurately" (p. 61). Offering this information early in the research report encourages readers to more fully accept Lesch's descriptions and analyses of the interaction.

In this case, the researcher checked her findings directly with the research participants she observed. However, some member checks can be conducted with individuals who are knowledgeable about the context in which the study was conducted but did not participate in the project (Janesick, 2000). For example, if you were unable to validate your findings with the teacher and teacher's aide from an observation study in a second-grade classroom you could review your findings with other second-grade teachers. Having individuals who are intimately familiar with the generalized context (i.e., a second-grade classroom) review your findings may generate questions to uncover assumptions that the teacher who participated in the project might overlook.

CONCEPTUALIZING RESEARCH QUESTIONS FOR QUALITATIVE RESEARCH

The model of qualitative research provides an overview of what researchers encounter and must consider in designing and conducting qualitative research. Because research questions are central to the qualitative approach, let's return our attention there.

Typically, researchers use the published literature to develop formal research questions to guide their studies. Recall, from Chapter 2, the theory–research link presented for qualitative research. Although an overall research question guides the design of the study, theory is situated in the qualitative research process differently than it is in quantitative research. In qualitative research, theory development occurs during data analysis—at the end of the research process. In contrast, quantitative methods use data analysis to test the theory presented at the beginning of the project.

Because of these differences, research questions for qualitative research are broadly stated and generally nondirectional. For example, Martin (2004, p. 153) asked:

RQ: How do middle management women use conversational humor to negotiate paradoxes of organizational life?

Also typical are Apker's (2002) research questions:

RQ_1: How do nurse managers define their roles?

RQ_2: What role stressors do nurse managers experience?

RQ_3: How do nurse managers cope with role stress?

The use of research questions accomplishes two objectives simultaneously. First, the research question provides the researcher with a focus. At the same time, the generalized nature of the research question allows the researcher considerable latitude in following interesting paths that appear only as the researcher collects the data. Thus, many qualitative studies are structured around an overall research question.

Most qualitative research questions focus on some specific interaction context. As a result, the research questions are specific to a type of communication and specific communicators. Good examples of this type of qualitative research question are found in a study of one Alcoholics Anonymous group (Witmer, 1997):

RQ_1: What local and global influences contribute to the Friendship Group culture?

RQ_2: What is the nature of the Friendship Group culture as constituted by structures of signification, legitimation, and domination?

RQ_3: Upon what rules and resources do Friendship Group members draw to facilitate personal recovery?

Assessing Research Questions

Typically, qualitative research questions start with *how* or *what.* By using these openings, researchers can pose questions to discover, explain or seek to understand, explore a process, or describe the experiences of participants (Creswell, 1994). All of these objectives are particularly well suited to qualitative research. Notice that each of the research questions given in the examples begins with *what* or *how.*

Although not always the case, research questions developed for qualitative studies usually use nondirectional wording. Words such as *affect, influence, impact, determine, cause,* and *relate* all have a directional orientation (Creswell, 1994). Although qualitative research is not designed to develop causal explanations, it can be used in studies looking for causes. Rather than asking "To what extent did variable X cause variable Y?" qualitative researchers develop research questions that ask how X plays a role in causing Y (Maxwell, 1996).

If possible, research questions should reference the research site (Creswell, 1994). Qualitative research is conducted on specific interaction with specific interactants in a specific context. Thus, results from such a study are less generalizable to other interactions, other interactants, or other contexts. By identifying contextual elements in your research question, you remind the reader and yourself of this issue.

DESIGN
CHECK

What If Research Questions Are Not Presented?

Whereas quantitative research follows fairly strict traditions, authors of qualitative research have more flexibility in how they approach what they study and how they report their findings. In writing qualitative research reports, many authors will explicitly state the research question that provides the focus for the study. However, you will read some that do not. When this is the case, you must look for the implied research questions. Generally, you can find these in two places. The implicit question may be placed in the opening paragraphs of the article, or it may be at the end of the literature review just before the section in which the researcher explains the method and analytical process for the study. If you are still having trouble identifying the research question, read the conclusion or implications section at the end of the research report. With that information you should be able to work backward to develop the question that framed the researcher's study.

What kinds are questions are best answered with qualitative research methods? Qualitative methods can be effectively used when researchers ask questions about (1) a specific type of interaction, (2) how meaning is developed and shared by a specific set of interactants in a specific interaction context, (3) naturally occurring issues that would be difficult or unethical to replicate in experimental conditions, (4) unanticipated phenomena and influences, (5) communication processes that occur over time, and (6) a particular communication context and the influences of the context on the interactants (Erickson, 1986; Maxwell, 1996).

In asking these types of questions, qualitative research brings the "invisibility of everyday life" (Erickson, 1986, p. 121) to the surface. Sometimes interaction events that are familiar escape our assessment and analysis. Qualitative methods can bring an enhanced level of detail to familiar interaction events. Such detail allows researchers to examine message construction and the ways in which messages create meanings for individuals in intimate ways.

Thus, a researcher must plan for intensive study of the interaction, be especially complete in recording observations and taking notes, and be willing to spend considerable time in reflection to develop an appropriate analysis. Although qualitative methods focus the researcher's attention on common interaction events, the researcher must carefully scrutinize these events for their significance as well as consider the various points of view of the interactants or participants (Erickson, 1986).

WHAT COUNTS AS DATA IN QUALITATIVE RESEARCH?

What counts as data, or evidence, in qualitative research is a much more difficult matter than in quantitative research because anything that the researcher could observe or capture could count as data. Often the initial question that guides the development of the qualitative research project will broadly identify the phenomena the researcher wants to examine. But in qualitative research, the researcher seldom identifies variables or creates operationalizations before entering the research field. How, then, can the researcher construct meaning or develop interpretations of what he or she heard and saw? Two issues—the construction of meaning and the level of data representation—can help researchers determine what counts as data in qualitative research studies.

Interpreting Meaning

There are three ways in which researchers interpret meaning in qualitative research (Potter, 1996). The first is **researcher construction.** From

TABLE 4.1 Evidence at Three Levels

Microlevel Evidence	Midlevel Evidence	Macrolevel Evidence
Direct quotations from one person	Interaction patterns	Organizational norms
Answers to specific questions in an interview	Conversational structures	Cultural values
Diaries, memos, letters	Leadership behaviors	Rituals
A book	Genres of television shows	Cultural values demonstrated through a variety of sources
A television show	A body of work	All television shows

his or her personal, subjective position or perspective on the experience, the researcher develops an interpretation. Thus, evidence is fully the construction of the researcher. This would be the position a researcher would have to take if he or she were unable to communicate directly with the research participants. In some studies, the researcher takes on the role of the strict observer and does not interact with participants in their interaction environment. Thus, in analyzing the data, such researchers are forced to rely upon their interpretation of what happened and why. As a result, the researchers write the qualitative research report using their perceptions and insights.

The second method of interpretation is **subjective valuing.** This interpretation of meaning relies on a mix of both objective and subjective elements. Subjective valuing acknowledges that there are tangible artifacts, or objective sources of meaning. However, the researcher must make some interpretation of these objective elements. As a result, the researcher's subjectivity is introduced into the interpretation of meaning. With this type of meaning construction, the researcher would mix his or her interpretations with interpretations received directly from participants.

The third interpretation of meaning, **contingent accuracy,** relies on tangible artifacts, which are believed to be accurate representations of the phenomenon. This is the most objective of the three positions. However, some subjectivity is introduced when the researcher selects some elements over others to use as evidence. Well-trained researchers are capable of making the best selections; little interpretation is required. Thus, if direct quotes from research participants are available and the researcher selects the ones that require the least additional interpretation, then contingent accuracy has been achieved.

Level of Evidence

Evidence, or data, in qualitative research can range, for example, from the one-word quotation of an employee to the lengthy storylike description of an organization's culture. Microlevel evidence can be identified and stand on its own. Macrolevel evidence is broad-scale and many similar data belong to the same classification. Midlevel data, obviously, are somewhere between the two extremes. Examine Table 4.1 for examples of evidence at the three different levels (Potter, 1996).

Whereas quantitative methods rely on comparisons among data at the same level of analysis, qualitative methods are not as restrictive. Some qualitative studies will focus on the same level of evidence, or unit of analysis, throughout the study. In other qualitative studies, researchers will integrate levels of evidence in order to answer the research question.

MAKING THE CASE FOR QUALITATIVE RESEARCH

Qualitative research is widely known and accepted in the study of communication. Although the communication journals still publish more quantitative than qualitative research, qualitative research is being selected for publication more frequently, and some journals prefer qualitative research. Some qualitative research is reported in too much depth to be reported in a journal article or even in a series of journal articles. As a result, many qualitative research studies are reported as a book or as book chapters. Regardless of where it is found in the scholarly literature, qualitative research provides an intimate view of human communication.

Advantages of Qualitative Research

What advantages does qualitative research enjoy? First, the researcher documents what is going on in a way that individuals participating in the interaction event may not be able to see. Some communication features or functions are often taken for granted by those who use them. A researcher can uncover such phenomena by carefully planned observation. Second, qualitative research can provide information about those who cannot or will not speak for themselves. For example, babies, young children, and older adults cannot respond to questionnaires or surveys and are unlikely participants in laboratory experiments. But qualitative researchers can enter their communication environment and discover how communication functions for them. Qualitative researchers can also enter the communication environments of those who are deviant or hostile to participating in the research process. Finally, qualitative research can supplement information obtained from quantitative methodologies (Foster, 1996).

Limitations of Qualitative Research

As with any research method, qualitative research has limitations. The communication environment must be accessible to researchers. Thus, some communication environments (for example, parents talking with their children about sex) may be off-limits to researchers. Another limitation occurs because people being observed can consciously, or sometimes unconsciously, change their behavior as a result of being observed. Thus, what the qualitative researcher sees and hears may not occur when the researcher is not there. A third limitation is that all observations are filtered through the interpretive lens of the researcher. Finally, qualitative research is often more time consuming than quantitative methods. Thus, the researcher may attempt to limit observations to times and situations that are comfortable as well as convenient or may limit observing to when something is expected "to happen." As a result, the representativeness of the observations may be in question.

Threats to Credibility in Qualitative Research

A primary threat to the credibility of a qualitative research study is inaccuracy or incompleteness of the data (Maxwell, 1996). Audio- and videotaping largely resolve this problem. But what if it would be difficult or impossible to make such recordings? Then your field notes must be as complete and accurate as possible. Techniques for taking notes and other methods of qualitative data collection are described in detail in Chapter 14.

A second threat to your study is a problem of interpretation. Using yourself as the data collection instrument in qualitative methodologies requires that you carefully consider whose interpretation is being imposed upon the data. Is the interpretation your understanding? Or does the interpretation represent the perspective of the people you studied? You can counter this threat by carefully listening for your subjects' interpretation of the interaction. Viewing the interaction from the perspective of those you study can overcome this threat to validity. In some cases you will be able to verify your interpretation with the interactants, and it is always a good practice to do so if the situation allows.

Depending on yourself as both data collector and interpreter requires attention to the way in which you treat similar and different cases. Are two similar instances of communication behavior—from observations of different people or from the same person at different times—interpreted differently or similarly? If different interpretations are created, on what basis can you justify the differences?

A third threat in qualitative research is the threat to theoretical validity (Maxwell, 1996) that can occur if you do not pay attention to data that fail to fit the explanation or interpretation you are developing. These data cannot simply be dismissed. Rather, they must be considered and analyzed.

Finally, qualitative researchers must always be sensitive to selection bias and reactivity bias (Maxwell, 1996). Selection bias occurs when data stand out to the researcher. To counter this bias, the researcher must always be asking, "Why do these data stand out or seem unique to me?" Perhaps the data are really unique and should be captured for analysis. Or is it possible that the observed phenomena mirror an extreme example in the researcher's own life, and he is reacting to it because it has personal relevance for him?

Reactivity bias is the influence of the researcher on the interaction setting or the interaction among participants. In most qualitative studies, participants will know that you are the researcher and that you are there to observe them or to ask them questions. It is unlikely that anything you do or say will eliminate this bias completely. However, you should try to minimize this bias by monitoring your interactions and activities.

How can these biases be overcome? Using methods of triangulation, discussed earlier in this chapter, will certainly help. Researchers should get feedback from those who were observed if at all possible. If multiple researchers conduct observations, they should regularly check with one another about their interpretations. In some cases, training observers might be necessary.

COMPARING QUANTITATIVE AND QUALITATIVE RESEARCH

At this point, you have been introduced to both quantitative and qualitative methodologies. We could stop and have a serious debate about which one is better or which one produces better knowledge about how and why humans communicate the way they do. More productive, I believe, is to examine their key differences and similarities. Quantitative methodology is not inherently better than qualitative methodology, and vice versa. Simply, each has advantages and limitations. Recall from earlier chapters that a method should

be selected because it will help the researcher answer his or her questions. We will visit this issue again at the end of this chapter.

Key Differences in Quantitative and Qualitative Research

There are several key differences between the two research perspectives (Denzin & Lincoln, 2000; Potter, 1996). The first key difference is probably obvious. Quantitative research uses numbers to represent and summarize data. Qualitative research uses numbers only as a descriptive property.

For example, in a quantitative study of communication apprehension, numbers could be used in several ways. They could represent the score on the questionnaire that captures your perceptions of how apprehensive you are. Your score could be combined with the scores of others as a representation of apprehensiveness for participants in the study. Then that number could be used in several different types of statistical calculations to argue in support of the research questions or hypotheses. Alternately, in a qualitative research study of communication apprehension, the researcher would rely on detailed textual descriptions of how your face turned red, the way in which you gripped the speaker's podium, and how you stammered through the speech, ending with "Tha-a-a-a-at's all, folks."

The second key difference revolves around how participants are selected to be studied. Whereas quantitative studies can use individuals who are convenient to the researcher, most quantitative studies use some type of random or probability selection (see Chapter 7). This means that participants are selected without any regard to their identity beyond the characteristics that interested the researcher about all potential participants in the first place. Alternately, qualitative research studies individuals who are selected purposely. These individuals are observed or interviewed because they are specific actors in specific interaction contexts. As a result, qualitative research is interested in capturing and interpreting an individual's point of view—something that cannot be achieved with quantitative methodologies.

The third key difference is the issue of contextuality. Quantitative research removes some level of contextuality from the study. Laboratory studies may simulate certain interaction environments—but they are not that environment. On the other hand, qualitative research is deeply contextualized. The whole point is to capture the interaction in the context in which it occurs—naturally.

Fourth is the location of the argument. Quantitative research relies on formal logic as established in the tradition of statistical analysis. Thus, the basis of a researcher's argument would depend on whether or not a statistical test achieved significance. Chapter 7 describes this concept. Qualitative research relies on the interpretation of the researcher—an interpretation that is much closer to the actual communication event.

The location of the argument results in a fifth key difference. Quantitative methods presume that there is an interaction reality that can be measured, tested, and interpreted. This is in direct contrast to qualitative methods that presume multiple realities exist in social interaction. Thus, rather than focus on the deductive strategies and the cause-and-effect ideal of quantitative research, qualitative methods are inductive and strive to answer questions about how communication creates and provides meaning for our social experiences.

Key Similarities in Quantitative and Qualitative Research

Although quantitative and qualitative research methods are inherently different, there are also two key similarities. Both types of research rely on empirical evidence—that is, evidence that is external to the researcher (Potter, 1996). Although the quantitative researcher relies on numerical representation of communication phenomena and the qualitative researcher relies on what he or she sees and hears as data, the researcher has something to point to outside of him- or herself. Both researchers can say, "See, these are my data. This is what they signify."

The second key similarity is that both methods provide useful information for describing, understanding, and explaining human communication behavior. Our picture of communication would be incomplete without both.

Table 4.2 summarizes the advantages and limitations of quantitative and qualitative methodologies (Erickson, 1986; Mason, 1993). Using the

TABLE 4.2 Comparison of Quantitative and Qualitative Research Methods

	Quantitative Methodologies	*Qualitative Methodologies*
Advantages	Useful for isolating variables to examine their relationships	Strong for understanding meanings people use and attach to behavior
	Data are collected in the same way from all subjects, allowing for comparisons across participants	Provide opportunity for examining interaction unavailable in simulated environments
	Researcher controls interaction setting, limiting exposure to extraneous variables	Place interactants at center of inquiry
	Useful for replication and validation	Useful for discovering new phenomena
Disadvantages	Overly focused approach may cause researcher to miss key element or influence	Seldom used for testing predictions
	Weak for understanding people's interpretations	Require expanded commitment of time and resources from researcher
	Weak for discovering new phenomena	Difficult to generalize findings

AN ETHICAL ISSUE

Is Anything Off-Limits?

Communication researchers are especially interested in sexual harassment because communication is the medium for the inappropriate act as well as a medium for resisting it. Moreover, organizations communicate to their employees about sexual harassment through their sexual harassment training programs, policies, and procedures. Communication researchers have captured the narratives (qualitative) and perceptions (quantitative) of those who have been harassed. But researchers have not been able to document firsthand actual occurrences of sexual harassment. Why? Even when researchers spend considerable periods of time within an organization, some types of interaction are performed out of the researcher's view. This is the case with sexual harassment. Researchers can identify symptoms of a sexually harassing culture and other evidence that harassment has occurred (for example, negative attitudes toward women, victims' self-reports). But, generally, researchers will not see the actual harassment. How does this affect the researcher's attempt to study sexual harassment? Will this create any ethical dilemmas? How much verification does a researcher need or should a researcher seek when an employee describes a sexually harassing incident? Can you think of other interaction situations similar to this?

table, you can create a comparison of the two methodological perspectives. Recall that the perspectives are different—each has specific advantages and disadvantages that guide method selection after the research hypothesis or research question is developed.

Which Do I Choose?

Recall that the first step of the research process described in Chapter 2 is identifying the research topic or problem. This step actually begins with the researcher developing preliminary questions. By answering the question "What do I want to know in this study?" clearly and completely, researchers can then continue with either the inductive or deductive model and eventually make selections about appropriate methodology. Thus, to make a methodological choice, researchers should carefully assess which method will maximize the amount of useful data to answer their question (Mason, 1993).

As research questions or hypotheses become complex, you may find that a combination of quantitative and qualitative methodologies would be most effective in testing the hypothesis or answering your research question (Brannen, 2004).

SUMMARY

1. Qualitative research methods are sensitive to the social construction of meaning and they explore social phenomena through an emphasis on empirical, inductive, and interpretive approaches.

2. Qualitative methods aim for subjectivity and intersubjectivity.

3. Qualitative methods are characterized by the following: a theoretical interest in how humans interpret and derive meaning from communication practices, concern with socially situated interaction, reliance on the researcher as the data collection instrument, and reliance on textual data.

4. Qualitative research recognizes that everything in the communication environment influences everything else and generally does not seek to ascertain causality.

5. Qualitative research uses inductive reasoning, which requires the researcher to become intimately familiar with the field of interaction.

6. The qualitative research process is comprised of processes that are interdependent and cyclical.

7. Triangulation and member checks help establish credibility in qualitative research findings.

8. Research questions guide qualitative research projects.

9. The concept of data is broadly defined in qualitative research.

10. Researchers assess data for the way in which meaning is constructed and the level of the evidence.

11. Advantages of qualitative research include being able to study communication features or functions taken for granted, collect information about those who cannot or will not participate in more traditional quantitative research designs, and enter the communication environments of those who are deviant or hostile.

12. Limitations of qualitative research include difficulty in accessing or gaining entry to the desired communication environment, participants changing their normal behavior due to the presence of the researcher, and having the researcher being the sole interpretive lens of the interaction.

13. There are key differences, as well as similarities, between quantitative and qualitative research.

KEY TERMS

contingent accuracy

credibility

data triangulation

discourse

inductive analysis

interdisciplinary triangulation

intersubjectivity

investigator triangulation

member check

member validation

mutual simultaneous shaping

researcher construction

subjective valuing

subjectivity

triangulation

CHAPTER FIVE

Research Ethics

Chapter Checklist

After reading this chapter, you should be able to:

1. Address potential ethical issues during the design phase of the research project.

2. Explain how your research project minimizes risk and enhances benefits to participants.

3. Find alternative research procedures to avoid physical or psychological harm to participants.

4. Design a research project that demonstrates beneficence, respect for persons, and justice.

5. Follow procedures and guidelines required by your university's institutional review board.

6. Determine the content for and write an informed consent form that is understandable for participants.

7. Use deception and confederates only if other alternatives are unavailable, and only if these practices do not cause undue harm for participants.

8. Devise data collection procedures that maintain participants' confidentiality and anonymity.

9. Understand any risks associated with videotaping and audiotaping participants' interactions.

10. Provide an adequate debriefing for research participants.

11. Ensure the accuracy of data and findings.

12. Write a research report that does not plagiarize the work of others.

13. Write a description of research participants in such a way as to conceal their identities.

This chapter explores issues of ethics and integrity associated with the research process. Researchers, even student researchers, have a responsibility to conduct their investigations and report their findings without harming research participants and without misrepresenting the results. As a consumer of research, you should be aware of the ethical principles that guide researchers in the development, execution, and reporting of research studies. Knowing this information will help you identify where ethical breaches could occur and influence a study's findings.

Over the past 20 years, various standards and guidelines have been developed in specific scientific fields, particularly to guide researchers who use participants, oftentimes called human subjects, in their studies. While the National Communication Association (NCA) has developed a Code of Professional Responsibilities for the Communication Scholar/Teacher (see their research guidelines in the box An Ethical Issue: Professional Association Guidelines for Conducting Research), communication researchers generally follow or adapt the more specific ethical guidelines of research adhered to by psychologists or sociologists. Additionally, most universities require their researchers—faculty and students—to adhere to guidelines of ethical research promoted by the National Institutes of Health whether or not the research project is funded by that agency.

It is the researcher's responsibility not only to adhere to the guidelines but also to be familiar with the most recent developments. Ethical standards change in response to changes in scientific practices; for example, changes are required because of the increased use of technology to collect data, and in response to new locations for collecting data, such as the internet. Ethical standards have also changed due to research misconduct. Whereas many people are familiar with ethical problems that have occurred in medical research, a survey has documented ethical problems in the social sciences as well (Swazey, Anderson, & Lewis, 1993). As a result of these problems and other concerns about the privacy of medical information, the Health Insurance Portability and Accountability Act (HIPAA) guidelines were established by the U.S. Department of Health and Human Services to provide comprehensive federal protection for the privacy of personal health information. Thus, communication research that addresses any health-related issue or context may be subject to HIPAA guidelines as well as more general research guidelines from the Office for Human Research Protections (OHRP), a unit of the U.S. Department of Health and Human Services. Communication research on other topics is generally required to follow the OHRP guidelines that have been adopted by universities and funding agencies. The website URLs for these guidelines and others of interest to communication researchers are listed on the website for this book.

This chapter will introduce you to the fundamental concerns of research ethics. But it cannot act as a substitute for guidelines imposed at your university. Before you collect any data, quantitative or qualitative, be sure to check with your professor to determine which guidelines you must follow. Ethical considerations specific to your research project must be deliberated in the design phase of your research project. This is necessary to create a research environment in which participants will provide valid data (Sieber, 1998).

ETHICAL QUESTIONS IN PLANNING RESEARCH

Without question, all of the ethical issues of conducting and reporting research are the responsibility of the researcher. Researchers must have integrity and be honest and fair in interacting and working with research participants. Additionally, researchers must be concerned with how their research topic and procedures could create physical or psychological harm to participants.

The researcher has two broad ethical responsibilities (Kvale, 1996). First, the researcher has a scientific responsibility. This means that researchers are responsible to their profession and discipline. Guidelines developed and prescribed by the researcher's sponsor (for example, department, university, professional association, or funding agency) must be followed. Further, researchers have a responsibility for developing and conducting research projects that will yield knowledge worth knowing. Adhering to this responsibility ensures that participants' time and energy are not wasted or abused. Second, researchers must consider the ethical issues that arise from their relationships with research participants. Regardless of how close or distant those relationships are, researchers must assess the extent to which the nature of the researcher–participant relationship is affecting the collection, interpretation, and reporting of data.

At the beginning of any research project, the researcher must consider the basic questions of ethics just described. Although general ethical principles guide the researcher, ethical issues must be considered specific to the design of the study (how data will be collected) and by the nature of the study (for example, what is being studied and with which participants). All researchers should ask and answer the following questions about their research designs (Kvale, 1996; Sieber, 1992):

1. What are the benefits of this study? How can the study contribute to understanding communication? Will the contributions of the study be primarily for participants? For others similar to the participants? Or for people in general?

2. How will the consent of participants to participate in the study be gained? Should consent be given orally or in writing? Who should give the consent? Is the participant capable of doing so? If not, who is? How much information about the study needs to be given in advance? What information can be given afterward?

3. How can the confidentiality and anonymity of research participants be handled? Is there a way to disguise participants' identity? Who will have access to the data?

4. Are the participants appropriate to the purpose of the study? Are they representative of the population that is to benefit from the research?

5. What potential harm—physical or psychological—could come to the participants as a result of the study?

6. What are the consequences of the study for participants? Will potential harm be outweighed by expected benefits? Will reporting or publishing the outcomes of the study create risk or harm for participants?

7. How will the researcher's role affect the study?

8. Is the research design valid or credible? Does it take into account relevant theory, methods, and prior findings?

9. Is the researcher capable of carrying out the procedures in a valid manner?

The answers to these questions will affect how the researcher assesses the developing design and conducts the research study.

Because research participants are people, special attention is paid to how they are treated. In 1991, seventeen federal departments and agencies adopted a set of regulations, known as the *Belmont Report* (National Commission for the Protection of Human Subjects of Biomedical and Behavioral Research, 1979). Three ethical principles—beneficence, respect for persons, and justice—were identified in this report to guide researchers in designing the aspects of the research process that directly affect or involve research participants. These principles not only guide this aspect of research design but must also be simultaneously upheld.

Beneficence means that the well-being of participants is protected. The researcher must protect the participant from harm as well as meet the obligation to maximize possible benefits while minimizing possible harms. How does this work? Ideally, the outcomes of your research would provide immediate benefits for those who participated and longer term benefits for individuals like those who participated while at the same time minimizing risk for participants. You can justify a research project that does not provide immediate benefits for those who agree to participate in your study if the longer term benefits improve knowledge or aid in the development of more effective procedures or treatments. In other words, the long-term benefits outweigh the minimal risk participants might encounter.

The balance between risks and benefits must favor the benefits gained. Before research is

AN ETHICAL ISSUE

Professional Association Guidelines for Conducting Research

Communication research takes many forms, and ethical principles have been established for both quantitative and qualitative research methodologies. Quantitative research has traditionally been evaluated with the research guidelines Ethical Principles and Code of Conduct of the American Psychological Association (APA). For those using qualitative methodologies, the research guidelines of the American Anthropological Association (AAA) and the American Sociological Association (ASA) will be pertinent. For those who conduct research on or through the internet, the ethical guidelines of the Association of Internet Researchers (AOIR) will be useful. The URLs for these research guidelines and others can be found on the website for this text.

Regardless of method, however, the National Communication Association's (NCA) Code of Professional Responsibilities for the Communication Scholar/Teacher presents five guidelines that should inform all communication research activities.

1. Integrity: The goal is to generate knowledge about communicative phenomena in which both the scholarly community and the public can have a high level of confidence.

2. Confidentiality: Researchers and those engaged in creative activity should uphold the confidentiality and autonomy of participants as set forth in informed consent documents sanctioned by an institution's *use of human subjects* protocols.

3. Professional responsibility: Professional responsibility requires that communication researchers know and comply with the legal and institutional guidelines covering their work. They do not use the work of others as their own, plagiarizing others' ideas or language or appropriating the work of others for which one serves as a reviewer. Criticism of another's language, ideas, or logic is a legitimate part of scholarly research, but communication researchers avoid *ad hominem*

conducted, researchers should identify risks—emotional, physical, professional, or psychological—and benefits to participants. It is easy for researchers caught up in designing their research study to assume that their method of data collection will not present any risks for participants. One way to avoid this assumption is to talk with people who are similar to the potential pool of participants about their comfort level with the data collection method planned. You may not mind answering a set of questions, but others can provide insight into how a set of questions or observations may be too uncomfortable, personal, or revealing—too much of an imposition.

In every case, benefits to participants must outweigh the risks. Saying that knowledge will be gained is not an adequate benefit. Rather, researchers should explain specifically how the knowledge gained from the research study poses benefits to the participants or to similar individuals.

Respect for persons involves two separate principles: (1) treating individuals as capable of making decisions and (2) protecting those who are not capable of making their own decisions (National Commission, 1979). Researchers should treat participants as if they are capable of deliberating about personal goals and capable of determining their own actions. In other words, the researcher should refrain from making choices for participants. The research process should be described and explained, and then the attacks. Avoiding personal attacks does not mean that critics or reviewers refrain from commenting directly and honestly on the work of others, however. Communication researchers share credit appropriately and recognize the contributions of others to the finished work. They also decide through mutual consultation whether authors should be added or deleted from the finished product.

4. Honesty and openness: Responsibility to others entails honesty and openness. Thus, communication researchers:

   - Obtain informed consent to conduct the research, where appropriate to do so.
   - Avoid deception as part of the research process, unless the use of deception has been approved in advance by an appropriate review body.
   - Provide adequate citations when available and relevant in research reports to support theoretical claims and justify research procedures.
   - Disclose results of the research, regardless of whether those results support the researcher's expectations or hypotheses.
   - Do not falsify data or publish misleading interpretations of events or of results.
   - Report all financial support for the research and any financial relationship that the researcher has with the persons or entities being researched, so that readers may judge the potential influence of financial support on the research results.
   - Accurately reveal assumptions made in advancing specific interpretations of historical events.

5. Social responsibility: Likewise, the value of social responsibility mandates that communication researchers who work with human subjects honor their commitments to their subjects, and those who work with communities honor their commitments to the communities they research.

participant should make a choice about volunteering to participate. Unfortunately, the heavy-handed demeanor of some researchers leaves the impression that participants have no choice but to participate. When a researcher communicates with research participants this way, the researcher is being disrespectful.

Another issue of respect arises when individuals are not capable of self-determination. Usually, these individuals are those who are sick or disabled or those whose circumstances restrict their opportunity to deliberate freely. Thus, respect for the immature and the incapacitated is evident when the researcher refrains from placing these individuals in the position where they would be asked to make choices about research participation.

Justice is really an issue of fairness (National Commission, 1979). Ideally, all participants would be treated equally. In the past, however, research in disciplines other than communication has violated this criterion by creating risks for participants and, later, using the research results to generate benefits for those not involved in the research study. Thus, justice was not upheld because the benefits were withheld from research participants who took the risk of participating. Sometimes it is difficult to treat all participants equally, especially if the goal of research is to explore differences between and among groups of people (for example, differences between supervisors and subordinates or differences between males and females). But justice and equal treatment should always be the researcher's goal.

This type of inequality can also surface in communication research when training is offered to one group of participants and not another before the outcome measures are collected. At the conclusion of the study, the researcher should offer the same training to those who were initially denied it. Hopf, Ayres, Ayres, and Baker (1995) provided this type of justice in their study of public speaking apprehension. In this study, participants who were apprehensive about public speaking, as identified by their self-report scores, were contacted and asked to participate in a study. In two of the conditions, participants were assigned to workshops to receive some type of intervention for public speaking apprehension, a method for reducing anxiety about communicating. Participants assigned to the third condition were the control group and did not participate in any workshop activities. However, after all data were collected, participants in the control condition were given the opportunity to enroll in a workshop for apprehension reduction.

But the issue of justice raises a larger issue. In selecting individuals to participate in a study, a researcher must carefully examine why he or she made those population and sample choices. The researcher should ask, "Am I systematically selecting one group of people because they are (1) easily available, (2) in a position making it difficult for them to deny participating in the research, or (3) in a position in which they can be manipulated into participating?" Ideally, research participants are selected because they have characteristics relevant to the theoretical or practical issue being examined.

Although the three principles—beneficence, respect for persons, and justice—guide the development of the research design with respect to the use of research participants, they do not prescribe a specific set of ethical rules for researchers to follow. Each research situation is unique, causing unique applications of the three principles. At times, these principles may even be in conflict with one another (Vanderpool, 1996). The researcher's goal, however, is to design a research study that upholds these principles to the fullest degree possible.

As you can see, how the researcher treats or interacts with research participants is a significant element of research ethics. As a result, researcher integrity and the rights of participants in research studies are closely intertwined. These issues are so central to academic research that formalized procedures have been established to ensure both. Universities and funding agencies sponsor most academic research, and they require that research conducted under their sponsorship follow guidelines for informing participants of their rights and the potential risks of participating in research studies. These formal procedures require the researcher to gain permission to conduct research before any aspect of the research is conducted. In most universities and colleges, the institutional review board reviews the research proposal and grants the researcher approval to conduct the research.

Institutional Review Board

Federal agencies that sponsor research (for example, the National Institutes of Health, the National Science Foundation) require that universities have a formal process in place for considering the soundness and reasonableness of research proposals. These formal considerations are usually conducted by groups typically identified as **institutional review boards (IRBs)** or **human subjects review committees;** universities require their faculty and students to develop and submit a research proposal for the board's or committee's approval before any data are collected. Policies and procedures differ among universities, but if you intend to use the data collected to prepare a paper for distribution to any audience other than your professor or if there is any possibility you will do so in the future, approval is probably needed.

The primary role of such university groups is to determine if the rights and welfare of research participants are adequately protected (Sieber, 1992). By examining a research protocol or proposal before the researcher starts a project, an institutional review board can ensure that the research project adheres to both sound ethical and scientific or systematic principles. After its review, the board or committee can take one of several actions: (1) the research proposal can be approved and the researcher conducts the

AN ETHICAL ISSUE

Do Research Participants Have Any Ethical Responsibilities?

In terms of designing a research study, the burden of ethical treatment of participants is the responsibility of the researcher—after all, the researcher is in control of the data collection process. But you may be wondering, do participants bear any ethical responsibilities? We would hope that research participants would be truthful in providing data and that they would answer our questions completely and honestly. Some people fear or detest research studies and, as a result, provide answers or behave in a way that essentially undermines the research process. One of the reasons ethical principles for research have been established is to strengthen the relationships between researchers and participants. Researchers hope that if participants feel that they have been treated respectfully, they will reciprocate with truthful and complete answers and will try to behave characteristically (rather than modifying their normal behavior because they are being observed). Do you agree that providing truthful and complete answers and behaving characteristically are the ethical responsibilities of participants? Are there other ethical responsibilities for which participants should be responsible?

research as proposed; (2) the committee or board can request the researcher to change some aspect of the research proposal and resubmit the proposal for approval; (3) the research proposal can be denied or not approved.

Each university or college has its own procedures for submitting a research protocol for review. Generally, however, the following items are required in submitting a research protocol proposal:

- The research questions or research hypotheses
- Relevant literature to provide a foundation for the research project
- A description of how participants will be recruited and selected, and a copy of the intended informed consent form
- A description of research methods and procedures (for example, copies of questionnaires, measuring instruments, instructions or stimuli given to participants, interview schedules)
- A statement of how benefit is maximized and risk is minimized
- A statement of how subjects' anonymity and confidentiality will be protected
- A description of the investigator's background and education

Once your research protocol is approved, it carries legal implications. The protocol must reflect what you will actually do. You must follow the procedures detailed in your proposal. Even minor changes to your procedures will require a separate approval (Sieber, 1998).

Must all researchers adhere to these responsibilities? Yes, if the researcher will require interaction with other people to collect his or her data. Universities require that researchers, including student researchers, seek approval for their study before any data are collected. If you are conducting a study with the intention of presenting your conclusions in a paper at a professional meeting or convention, or submitting your conclusions in a manuscript for consideration for publication, you must seek approval of your institution's review board.

Informed Consent

Following a form agreed upon by federal agencies, researchers must give research participants **informed consent.** This means that a potential participant agrees to participate in the research project after he or she has been given some basic information about the research process. Of course, a person's consent to participate in a research

---

DESIGN CHECK   **Do You Need Informed Consent for Your Research Project?**

The Office of Human Research Protections of the U.S. Department of Health and Human Services provides an internet site (http://www.hhs.gov/ohrp/ humansubjects/guidance/decisioncharts.htm) that can help guide you in deciding if you need to provide your research participants with informed consent. Most universities follow these standards, but you should also check your university's rules and procedures. Your university's institutional review board is likely to post information about informed consent and research compliance on your school's website. Check to see if you can find it.

---

study must be given voluntarily. No one should be coerced into participating in research against his or her will or better judgment. In other words, participants cannot be threatened or forced into participating.

Informed consent creates obligations and responsibilities for the researcher. To gain a potential participant's informed consent, the researcher must provide certain information in writing to participants (Sieber, 1992). This information includes

- Identification of the principal researcher and sponsoring organization
- Description of the overall purpose of the investigation
- Main features of the research process including a description of what data will be collected
- The expected duration of participation
- Any possible risks to and benefits for research participants
- An explanation of how confidentiality and anonymity will be ensured or the limits to such assurances
- Any physical or psychological harms that might occur for participants and any compensation or treatment that is available
- A statement of whether deception is to be used; if so, the participant should be told that not all details of the research can be revealed until later, but that a full explanation will be given then

- The name and contact information for the principal investigator to whom questions about the research can be directed
- Indication that participation is voluntary
- Indication that a participant can discontinue participation at any time during the research process
- Indication that refusal to participate or to continue to participate will not result in a penalty
- Indication that the participant should keep a copy of the consent form

Not only must these details about the research process be provided, but the consent form should also be written in a manner that participants can easily understand. Thus, the consent form should be written in everyday language rather than scientific language. Finally, a copy of the consent statement should be given to each participant. An example of an informed consent form is shown in Figure 5.1. Whatever form your university or college follows, informed consent should be clear, friendly, and respectful of participants. It should also be an accurate representation of what participants will experience.

The concept of informed consent implies that the researcher knows what the possible effects of conducting the research are before the research is conducted (Eisner, 1991). This is more easily accommodated in quantitative research than in qualitative research. For example, a researcher using unstructured interviews to explore a relatively new research topic would find it quite

AN ETHICAL ISSUE

Would You Participate?

Imagine that one way you can receive extra credit for a communication course is to volunteer to participate in one of three research projects. The first is a study examining how strangers interact. When you sign up for the project, you are told to meet at a certain time and date at the information desk of your university's library. The second research project is described as a study of how relational partners talk about difficult topics. When you sign up for the project, you are asked to bring your relational partner (significant other, wife, husband) with you to the research session. The third project is a study of how people react in embarrassing situations. When you sign up, you are told that you will not be embarrassed, but that you will participate in interaction where embarrassment occurs. For each of these three studies, what information would need to be included in the informed consent for you to agree to participate? Would you be willing to withdraw from a study after it had already started? If yes, what would activate such a response in you?

difficult to develop a complete and comprehensive interviewing guide. The exploratory nature of the study precludes complete planning. Additionally, in such situations, the researcher is unable to predict how participants will answer. Thus, there is no way he or she can identify all of the probing and clarification questions that will be needed to conduct the study before the interviews begin. Still, the researcher must design as much of the research project as possible, develop a proposal, and request a review by the IRB.

How does the researcher know that any participant consents? In most cases of communication research, participants can simply refuse to participate. In other words, they can hang up the phone on a telephone survey. Or if data are being collected in person, a potential participant can turn and walk away from the research room or refuse to answer an interviewer's questions. Thus, a participant's behavior—for example, answering interview questions or filling out a survey—indicates consent.

For most communication research projects, informed consent is adequate. The research protocol is reviewed with participants, they are given a copy, and their participation implies their consent. In cases where the institutional review board requires participant-signed informed consent, participants read and sign one copy of the written consent form, return it to the researcher, and keep a copy for themselves. In extremely risky research, the institutional research board may even require that a witness sign the consent form as well. Signed consent forms create a paper trail of the identities of those who participated in your study. Recognize the difference between the two. For informed consent, participants receive all of the information they need to make a decision about participating, based on the written information you provide them. For participant-signed informed consent, participants receive the same information, but they must all sign a copy of the informed consent and return it to you, the researcher. When this is the case, you should keep the consent forms separate from any data collected. In either case, however, you may even want to read the consent form out loud as potential participants follow along.

Recall that one of the ethical principles for conducting research is respect for persons and that some types of research participants may not be able to speak for themselves. This is the case with minor children. In no case can the researcher rely upon the consent of a child to participate in a research project. Rather, the parents or guardian of each child must agree that the child can participate in the research project. If you want to collect data from children in a school environment, you should

State Systems Leadership Initiative Study

INTRODUCTION

The Department of Communication Studies at the University of Kansas supports the practice of protection for human subjects participating in research. The following information is provided for you to decide whether you wish to participate in the present study. You may refuse to sign this form and not participate in this study. You should be aware that even if you agree to participate, you are free to withdraw at any time. If you do withdraw from this study, it will not affect your relationship with this unit, the services it may provide to you, or the University of Kansas.

PURPOSE OF THE STUDY

The purpose of this study is to answer three questions. They are:

1. To what extent, and in what ways, does the State of Kansas agencies and departments engage in collaborative activities that support the vision that Kansas will be the best state in the nation in which to raise a child?
2. What are the facilitative and inhibiting processes and factors of that collaboration?
3. In what ways does the State Systems Leadership Initiative support current and future collaboration?

PROCEDURES

Data will be collected in three ways throughout your participation in the State Systems Leadership Initiative. One, you will be asked to complete a paper-and-pencil questionnaire (a) before the August 19 leadership training session, (b) after the October leadership training session, and (c) after the completion of the series of training sessions in December or January. Time to complete the questionnaires is estimated at 15–20 minutes for each data collection point. The questionnaires will be emailed to you as attachments. Two, the researcher and other members of the research team will observe your participation in the leadership training sessions. Three, you will be asked to participate in an interview after the series of leadership training sessions are completed. Interviews are expected to last approximately 30 minutes and will be audiotaped with your permission.

RISKS

No risks are anticipated. Data about *individuals* will not be shared with other participants of the leadership training sessions, nor will data about individuals be shared with other State of Kansas employees, or employees or consultants of the Kansas Health Foundation. However, periodically throughout the training sessions and at the conclusion of activities, *aggregate* information about the participants in the State Systems Leadership Initiative will be shared with the employees and consultants of the Kansas Health Foundation as part of the evaluation of the State Systems Leadership Initiative project.

BENEFITS

One of the goals of the Kansas Health Foundation is to enhance the statewide systems of services to improve the health of children in Kansas. Thus, answering the questionnaires will provide some direct benefits to you as you perform periodic self-assessments. Data at the aggregate level should be beneficial to the Kansas Health Foundation as they work to enhance or build relationships among and between state agencies that impact, or have the potential to impact, the health of children in Kansas.

PAYMENT TO PARTICIPANTS

Participants will not be paid.

INFORMATION TO BE COLLECTED

Survey data will be collected from you three times during your participation in the State Systems Leadership Initiative. You will be asked to respond to questions about the frequency and nature of your communication with other participants in the training sessions and your communication with individuals in other State of Kansas departments and agencies. You will be asked to complete the questionnaire and return it to the researcher. To assist in the interpretation of data collected, personal and organizational demographic information will be requested. In addition, the researcher and her

---

FIGURE 5.1 Example of Informed Consent Form

assistants will collect observational data about you as you participate in the training sessions. Interviews will be conducted after the completion of the training sessions to gather your perceptions about the training and collaborative practices between State of Kansas departments and agencies.

The information collected from you will be used by Joann Keyton and other members of the research team for scholarly articles and be reported to the Kansas Health Foundation.

In both the articles and reports, your name or personal identity will not be associated in any way with the information collected from you or about you. In these instances, the researcher will use a pseudonym instead of your name. The researchers will not share information about you with anyone not specified above unless required by law or unless you give additional written permission.

Permission granted on this date to use and disclose your information remains in effect indefinitely. By signing this form you give permission for the use and disclosure of your information for purposes of this study at any time in the future.

REFUSAL TO SIGN CONSENT AND AUTHORIZATION
You are not required to sign this Consent and Authorization form and you may refuse to do so without affecting your right to any services you are receiving or may receive from the University of Kansas or to participate in any programs or events of the University of Kansas. However, if you refuse to sign, you cannot participate in this study.

CANCELING THIS CONSENT AND AUTHORIZATION
You may withdraw your consent to participate in this study at any time. You also have the right to cancel your permission to use and disclose information collected about you, in writing, at any time, by sending your written request to: Joann Keyton, Dept. of Communication Studies, The University of Kansas, 1440 Jayhawk Blvd., Room 102 Bailey, Lawrence, KS 66045-7574. If you cancel permission to use your information, the researchers will stop collecting additional information from you. However, the research team may use and disclose information that was gathered before they received your cancellation, as described above.

PARTICIPANT CERTIFICATION
I have read this Consent and Authorization form. I have had the opportunity to ask, and I have received answers to, any questions I had regarding the study and the use and disclosure of information about me for the study. I understand that if I have any additional questions about my rights as a research participant, I may call 785-864-7429 or write the Human Subjects Committee Lawrence Campus (HSCL), University of Kansas, 2385 Irving Hill Road, Lawrence, Kansas 66045-7563, email dhann@ku.edu.

I agree to take part in this study as a research participant. I further agree to the uses and disclosures of my information as described above.

_____   _____
Type/Print Participant's Name   Date

_____
Participant's Signature

Researcher Contact Information:
Joann Keyton
Principal Investigator
Dept. of Communication Studies
1440 Jayhawk Blvd., Room 102 Bailey
University of Kansas
Lawrence, KS 66045-7574
785-864-9880
jkeyton@ku.edu

FIGURE 5.1 *(continued)*

also get approval for your project from your university's institutional review board and then obtain permission for conducting the research from the superintendent of schools, the principal of the particular school, the teacher or teachers of the children you want to use, and the children's parents or guardians.

The committee that reviews research proposals for your university or college will prescribe the type of consent required for your research project. Be careful, however. Even if written, or signed, consent is not needed, a participant's informed consent is still required. A researcher cannot forgo this step in the research process.

Informed Consent and Quantitative Research
Traditionally, quantitative communication research conducted in the lab or in field experiments has been associated with informed consent. Quantitative research requires considerable planning. As a result, the consent form is able to describe the exact procedures the participant will encounter. For example, in Dixon and Linz's (1997) study of rap music, participants were told that they might be asked to listen to sexually explicit lyrics, although not all participants were assigned to listen to that type of music. Participants were also told that they could withdraw from the experiment at any time, and one participant did.

Informed Consent and Qualitative Research
How do these standards and traditions apply to qualitative research? Unfortunately, there are no easy answers (Punch, 1994). In some qualitative research settings—for example, watching how teenagers interact as fans of the X Games—asking fans to agree to informed consent would disrupt the naturalness of the interaction. Thus, in these types of public and naturally occurring settings, asking for participants' informed consent would not only disrupt the interaction but would also divulge the identity of the researcher and expose the research purpose—all of which has the potential for stopping the interaction the researcher is interested in observing.

Thus, the questions "Is the interaction occurring naturally in a public setting?" and "Will my interaction with participants in that setting create negative consequences for any of the participants

being observed?" can serve as guidelines for qualitative researchers in considering the necessity of asking for participants' informed consent. If the answer is "yes" to the first question and "no" or "minimal consequences" to the second, then it is likely that the researcher will not need to adhere to the protocol of informed consent. If the answer to the first question is "in some ways" or "no," and acknowledgeable effects can be discerned, then the researcher must follow the principles of informed consent.

For example, interviewing is a form of qualitative research. The researcher may seek and conduct interviews at the library, so the interaction is public, but it is not naturally occurring. The researcher is significantly influential in and purposely directing the interaction. Thus, informed consent is needed. Alternately, a qualitative researcher wants to examine how patients approach the nurses' station in an emergency medical center and ask for help. This interaction is public—everyone in the waiting room has the opportunity to see and hear the interaction—and it is naturally occurring. The researcher is not involved in staging the interaction in any way. But this is an interesting case. Even though the interaction is public, interaction in an emergency medical center may be sensitive, and personal health information is revealed. Researchers should be sensitive to private interaction even when it occurs in public spaces. For example, a couple saying good-bye to each other at an airport should be regarded as acting in a private setting, even though the interaction occurs in public (Sieber, 1992). So what is a researcher to do?

Despite the public nature of the interaction you want to observe or your opinion about whether or not informed consent is necessary, it is always wise to take the most prudent course of action. For each research project—quantitative or qualitative—develop a research proposal to be reviewed by your university's IRB. This committee will guide you as to when informed consent is needed and, when it is, as to what type of informed consent is required.

Indeed, Lindlof and Taylor (2002) see applying for IRB approval as an expected and necessary aspect of qualitative research design. Completing the IRB proposal and approval process will

Private or Public?

The internet has created a form of electronic communication that is somewhere between written text and spoken communication (Sharf, 1999). As a result, current ethical guidelines may not address some of the ethical issues resulting from the use of internet-based data (such as written discussion resulting from chat rooms, email, bulletin boards, and listservs). Researchers using internet-based data must address the dichotomy between private and public domain. In fact, researchers must acknowledge that many of these data are produced in private situations within a larger, public context (Elgesem, 1996). Markham (2004) reminds us that some people who communicate in the public space of the internet can be angered by intruding researchers or prefer not to be studied. For research purposes, what is legal may not be ethical (Sharf, 1999). Because changes in technology and societal acceptance of technology can change fairly quickly, a researcher who wants to collect internet-based data should seek the advice of his or her university's institutional review board early in the design phase of the project. Reviewing the recommendations on ethical decision making and internet research from the Association of Internet Researchers (http://www.aoir.org) will help you make decisions about your research design and help you in describing your research project in your IRB proposal.

strengthen your thinking about and planning for interacting with or observing people in the field. Admittedly there are special challenges in qualitative research, such as balancing the protection of participant identity against the need to describe unique features and people in the setting. The process can be to your benefit if you view it as a "critical reading of a study's ethical orientation" (p. 91).

ETHICAL ISSUES IN CONDUCTING RESEARCH

Ethical issues must first be considered in the design and development phase of research. But ethical decisions made in the design phase must be carried out. Six areas of ethical concern—use of deception, use of confederates, the possibility of physical or psychological harm, confidentiality and anonymity, video- and audiotaping, and debriefing participants—affect the interaction between research participants and researcher. Each of these can contribute to or detract from developing positive relationships with research participants.

Intentional Deception

When experimentation is the primary method of data collection, deceptive scenarios or practices are often used. Actually, the broad use of intentional deception, particularly in social psychology, caused federal granting agencies to establish guidelines and ask universities to establish human subjects committees to monitor research in which people participate.

With **deception** researchers purposely mislead participants. Deception should be used only if there is no other way to collect the data and the deception does not harm participants. Deception is used when it is necessary for participants to be ignorant of the purpose of a study so that they can respond spontaneously (Littlejohn, 1991). Communication scholars regularly practice this type of deception. Deception might also be used to obtain data about interactions that occur with very low frequencies.

Researchers who use deception must be sure that it is justified, that the results are expected to have significant scientific, educational, or applied value. Additionally, researchers must give sufficient explanation about the deception as soon as is feasible (Fisher & Fryberg, 1994). Even in these conditions, however, it is never advisable to deceive participants if there would be significant physical risk and discomfort or if the deception would cause participants to undergo unpleasant or negative psychological experiences.

Recall that a major question of informed consent is how much information should be given to research participants and when. If full information is given about the research design and the purpose of the research, procedures that require deception cannot be used. Generally, however, institutional review boards will allow researchers to conceal some aspects of their studies if participants are debriefed and given all the information at the end of their involvement.

Researchers can underestimate as well as overestimate the effects of their techniques. Thus, a good source of information about the potential use of deception in research can come from potential research participants (Fisher & Fryberg, 1994). If you plan to use deceptive techniques, consider discussing them with persons who are similar to those who will be participants in your research project. Specifically, prospective participants can help you determine (1) if some significant aspect of the research procedure is harmful or negative, (2) if knowing some significant aspect of the research would deter their willingness to participate, and (3) the degree of explanation needed after the use of deception.

If you are thinking about using deception in a quantitative study, use it with caution. Answering the following questions will help you determine if your decision to use deceptive practices is justified. Will the deceptive practice cause the data collected to be invalid? Are there other equally effective ways to collect data? Of course, if deceptive practices are used, participants should be informed of this in their debriefing.

Researchers should consider alternatives to the use of deception. In some cases, the same information could be collected through role-playing, observing interaction in its natural settings, or using participant self-reports. However, deceptive practices can also create ethical problems when researchers use qualitative data collection methods.

For example, the extent to which participants in a qualitative study know that the researcher is, in fact, a researcher and that he or she is conducting research on them is an issue of deception. Chapter 14 describes four different types of researcher participation in qualitative research. The role of the strict participant—in which the researcher fully functions as a member of the scene but does not reveal this role to others—is deceptive. Is it ethical? This question can be answered only by examining the entirety of the research design. If the interaction is public and individuals in the interaction scene are accustomed to outsiders visiting, then it is doubtful that a question of ethics and integrity would arise. However, if a researcher joins a group for the express purpose of investigating the communication within that environment and has no other reason or motivation for being there, then an ethical question is raised. This type of research design would need a strong justification and the expected benefits would need to be substantial for an IRB to approve it.

Using Confederates

One type of deceptive practice is for the researcher to use a **confederate,** or someone who pretends to also be participating in the research project but is really helping the researcher. The use of confederates is a type of deceptive practice because research participants do not know that someone is playing the confederate role. In most cases, confederates are used when the researcher needs to create a certain type of interaction context or to provide a certain type of interaction to which an unknowing research participant responds.

To better understand how consuming alcohol can affect communication behavior and perceptions of self-esteem, Monahan and Lannutti (2000) used male undergraduate confederates with similar physical attractiveness and personalities to interact with female undergraduates recruited for their experiment. After a careful health screening to ensure that they could safely drink alcohol, female participants were randomly assigned to an alcohol consumption or sober condition.

After taking a breathalyzer test, the male confederate was introduced into the setting and also given a breathalyzer test in such a way that the test, but not the results, could be seen. Next, the confederates, as previously instructed by the research team, engaged in typical informal conversation with the female participant before beginning to flirt with her. The conversations lasted 10 minutes. Although the confederates did not drink during the experiment, they were instructed to answer that they had been drinking if asked by the female participants; moreover, the confederates were lead to believe that all female participants had been drinking. The female participants were not aware that their conversational partners were confederates until the debriefing. The use of confederates was necessary to create the stimuli conditions for the experiment.

Confederates can also be recruited from participants who agree to participate in a research study. Wanting to examine how people explain their failures, researchers recruited students for a study with the condition that they had to bring along a friend or sign up to be paired with a stranger (Manusov, Trees, Reddick, Rowe, & Easley, 1998). When the dyad came to the research site, the person standing on the left was assigned the confederate role by the researcher, although the researcher did not provide the dyad that information at this point. The individuals were separated and taken to different rooms. While the participant in the confederate role was given instructions to get the partner to discuss a failure event, the unknowing partner completed a questionnaire.

Once the confederate was clear about his or her interaction goal, both individuals were brought to a room where they were asked to talk for 10 minutes while being videotaped. Remember that in the role of confederate one member of the dyad was responsible for bringing up the topic of a failure event and getting the partner to discuss it. After the interaction task was completed, the partners were separated once again to fill out questionnaires. After that phase of the data collection, the unknowing partner was debriefed and told that the researchers were interested in the way people offered accounts or explanations for their failures and that the interaction partner had been asked to play the role of the confederate. Participants were further told that the confederates were supposed to get their unknowing partner to talk about a failure, unless the partner offered it without encouragement.

Without using one of the research partners in the role of confederate to encourage the other partner to talk about a failure, this topic may have never occurred in the limited time the interaction was being videotaped. After debriefing, participants in the study did not seem overly concerned with this deceptive practice, because they perceived that talking about failures was commonplace (V. Manusov, personal communication, January 26, 2000). In this case, deception was necessary to create the interaction condition the researchers were interested in studying. Recognize that the deceptive practice did not create any unusual harm for the unknowing partner, who still had control over which failure was discussed and how much detail was given.

Physical and Psychological Harm

Some research has the potential to harm participants. Whether the harm is physical or psychological, harm should always be minimized to the greatest extent possible. In communication research, it is unlikely that research participants would face many instances of physical harm. Researchers in the communication discipline do not engage in the type of invasive procedures more commonly found in medical research. Infrequently, however, communication researchers do take physiological measurements from participants to test how individuals respond to different stimuli. Generally, these are restricted to routine measurements of participants' heart rate, skin temperature, and pulse rate (for example, see Schneider et al., 2004). Of course, these procedures must be explained to participants as part of the informed consent procedure.

Communication research can create psychological harm when researchers venture into sensitive topics like abortion, the use of animals in laboratory research, or the sexual explicitness of music videos. The sensitive content of such studies seems obvious. Psychological harm can also occur for participants when they are asked to role-play interactions that are uncomfortable or are not normal for them or when they are asked to relive distressing or painful experiences through interviews or focus groups or even in self-report surveys. Such research experiences can create negative reactions with long-term effects (Sapsford & Abbott, 1996).

Researchers also need to realize that even seemingly innocuous topics (for example, talking about a relationship) or generally accepted research procedures (for example, responding to a questionnaire) could cause psychological harm for some participants.

It is doubtful that you would design your research project to include a topic or procedure you find distasteful. But we make attribution errors when we assume that research participants would not find the topic or procedure distasteful either. To help overcome our biases, it is a useful practice to ask at least 10 individuals who are like the people you expect to participate if they would agree to participate in and complete the research experience. Use their feedback to guide you in redesigning the research project to minimize any harm and to guide you in the type of explanations participants are likely to require as part of the informed consent. Some risks are inherent anytime humans participate in research, and we should never assume that our research topics or procedures are immune to this element.

Upholding Anonymity and Confidentiality

In scholarly research, anonymity and confidentiality are two types of protection given to participants. **Anonymity** means that names and other pieces of information that can identify participants are never attached to the data and sometimes are never known to the researcher. In fact, in many quantitative studies, the researcher has no idea who the participants are. Researchers do not ask participants to reveal information that would aid the researcher in identifying and finding them in the future. For example, in collecting data, a researcher should never ask for

the participant's social security number as a way to keep track of data.

For most quantitative studies, you can create some type of personal identification number to link data together over time. Rather than randomly assigning numbers to participants, it is better to create some other unique number that is easily remembered by participants. For example, have participants take the middle two-digit sequence of their social security number and use it as a prefix for their birth date. For a participant with the social security number 492-58-0429 and the birth date of April 24, the unique identification number would be 580424.

However, even with a unique identification number, some participants will be hesitant to respond to all of the demographic questions for fear that supplying this information will make it easy to trace their responses back to them. Employees, in particular, are sensitive to providing too much information. For example, you ask employees to identify their race or ethnicity and sex, as well as identify whether they are an hourly employee or salaried manager. If there is only one Black female manager, she may be particularly hesitant to provide the researcher with three pieces of data that could potentially identify her and her responses. Even if the information is not used to identify her, the participant may have the perception that the data could be used to do so, causing her to be less than truthful as she responds to the questionnaire. Whereas some demographic information generally is useful to collect, be careful of asking for more demographic information than you really need.

Protecting anonymity in qualitative studies that use interviewing, focus groups, and some participant-observation methods is difficult. In many of these cases, you would need to know the identity of participants to set up the interviews, focus groups, or observation periods. Or there may be some instances in which knowing who the participants are is important for interpreting and understanding the data they provide. However, even though you may know the full identity of a participant, you can protect her identity in your notes and in your research report by referring to her as Female #1 or in some other way that does not reveal her true identity.

TRY THIS!   **What Would You Include?**

Imagine that you want to collect data about other communication researchers, including their motivations for conducting and publishing research as well as information about their family backgrounds that you believe had an influence on their careers. What information about the research participants would you include in your research report? Their name? Age? Sex? Race or ethnicity? Marital, family, or relational status? Their parents' marital status or educational level? Number of siblings? First-born, middle child, or last-born status? Name of their university? Their communication research and teaching specialties? Be able to explain each of your choices. Would your choices to reveal or conceal participant identity differ if you were one of the research participants? Why or why not?

If you are taking notes on a focus group, it will probably be more convenient to do so using participants' names. But when you write up the results of the focus group, you will probably want to change the names. One way to do this is to pick any letter of the alphabet—for example, *R*. Assign the first person that speaks a same-sex name beginning with *R*, such as Roger. Assign the next person who speaks a same-sex name beginning with the next letter of the alphabet—for example, Saundra—and so on. If the ethnicity of participants is important to your study, assign names from the same ethnic group as well. If you use this method, readers of your research report will be able to clearly distinguish among the different participants' comments, and you have provided participants with anonymity. Table 5.1 demonstrates this type of name-change procedure.

Confidentiality is related to privacy. In the research process, **confidentiality** means that any information the participant provides is controlled in such a way that others do not have access to it. For example, the data from students participating in a research project are never given to their professors. The data from employees are never given to their supervisors. The data from children are never given to their parents. In each of these cases, results from all participants may be summarized and distributed as a research report, but in no case should the data provided by any one person be released to anyone except the participant. Providing confidentiality for participants is respectful and protects

TABLE 5.1 One Method for Ensuring Participant Anonymity

Speaker Sequence	Real Name	Name in Written Research Report
First speaker, male	Ted	Roger
Second speaker, female	Amy	Saundra
Third speaker, female	Shamieka	Tamithra
Fourth speaker, male	Melvin	Cal
Fifth speaker, female	Jamila	Vanessa

their dignity. The researcher who provides confidentiality is attempting to ensure that no harm or embarrassment will come to participants.

Recognize that data may be a participant's responses to a questionnaire, an audiotape or videotape of a participant interacting with another person, or your notes from an interview. Confidentiality needs to be expressly addressed in each research situation. Any materials or data you collect from participants should be carefully stored out of sight of others and away from the data collection site. In no instance should you deliver a participant's data to a parent, teacher, colleague, or relative.

Videotaping and Audiotaping Participants

Much communication research focuses on the interaction between or among people. Videotaping and audiotaping are good tools for providing researchers with accurate accounts of these processes. But videotaping and audiotaping raise special ethical concerns. First, research participants should be taped only if the researcher has told them what is to be recorded and how. Second, participants' consent to be taped must be specifically obtained through informed or written consent. Third, videotape and audiotape records must be treated like any other data. A videotape or audiotape record is not anonymous. Thus, maintaining the confidentiality of such data is paramount.

One study of patient communication skills illustrates these principles (McGee & Cegala, 1998). Patients with appointments who met the selection criteria for the study were contacted by phone prior to their appointments. The research procedures, including information about videotaping and audiotaping, were described to them. Once patients agreed to participate, their physicians were contacted to obtain their permission to record the doctor–patient meetings. When patients arrived at the doctor's office, they were once again briefed about the study procedures and asked to sign a consent form. Patients were also told that they could choose not to participate.

For those who agreed to participate in the study, data collection occurred in one of two examination rooms equipped with videotaping and audio-recording equipment. The equipment was unobtrusively placed but visible to both patient and doctor. Especially important in this interaction setting, the video camera and examination table were intentionally placed so the video camera could not capture the patient on the examining table. Thus, the patient's visual privacy was maintained even though verbal interaction with the doctor could still be audiotaped. At the conclusion of the project, the research team maintained the video- and audiotapes, honoring its original agreement with patients about privacy (Cegala, personal communication, January 31, 2000).

Debriefing Participants

Debriefing is the opportunity for the researcher to interact with participants immediately following the research activity. Generally, the researcher explains the purpose of the study and what he or she hopes to find. Any information that was withheld from participants before the research activity began can be shared at this time.

Debriefing can accomplish several other objectives as well (Sieber, 1992). First, this informal interaction is a good opportunity for researchers to obtain participants' observations on taking part in the research project. Information obtained here may help the researcher better interpret the results. Second, debriefing gives participants an opportunity to ask questions and express their reactions to participating in the research.

If your research deals with sensitive matters, then each participant should be debriefed separately. Likewise, if several different types of people participated in the research—for example, parents, teachers, and children—then separate debriefings may need to be held, a different one for each type of research participant. In general, your debriefing should include the purpose of the study, a description of the condition individuals participated in, what is known about the problem and the hypotheses tested or questions asked, and why the study is important. In some cases, you may even want to provide participants with a brief written description, including resources for their follow-up. Regardless of the information provided or the form of debriefing, this step should be a positive one for participants. If negative or difficult information must be conveyed, the researcher should consider providing participants with remedies such as counseling assistance or referrals, reading materials, or personal follow-up.

In some cases as a part of the debriefing, the researcher can promise that the findings of the research project will be made available to participants. Some researchers write a one-page summary of the results and distribute this to participants. Organizational communication researchers often promise to deliver a report of the research results as an incentive for executives to permit entry into the organization. If this is the case, be sure to specify how and when the findings will be delivered and give assurances that all findings will mask the identities of participants.

If delivering research results to participants is difficult or impossible, the researcher could provide a brief summary of the relevant literature and the rationale for the research questions or hypotheses. Prepared in advance, this type of summary sheet could be handed to participants at the conclusion of the study as part of the debriefing to satisfy their curiosity and needs (Sieber, 1994).

ETHICAL ISSUES IN REPORTING RESEARCH

Whether the report of a research study is presented to an instructor as a class paper or submitted to a communication conference or for publication, two long-standing ethical principles are adhered to by scholars in all disciplines. The first principle is ensuring accuracy of the information presented. The second principle is protecting intellectual property rights. A third principle, a carryover from ethical issues that surface in conducting the research, is protecting the identities of individuals.

Ensuring Accuracy

The principle of accuracy is fairly broad. Not only must you present the data accurately, but in addition data cannot be modified or adjusted in any way to better support a hypothesis or research question. Likewise, you cannot omit any data or results that are difficult to interpret or whose interpretation calls other results into question.

To be accurate in reporting your data, you must have been accurate throughout the research process. One way to increase the accuracy of your reporting is to document every step in the research process—from designing and developing your study, to collecting the data, to the methods used to interpret the data. Complex research projects can take months or even years to complete. Thus, relying on memory for details of the research process may not be adequate.

Once your research report is written, you are responsible for checking the manuscript for errors caused in typing or editing. When these aspects of accuracy are achieved, your results should be verifiable by others using the same data or be repeatable with data and procedures similar to those you used.

Avoiding Plagiarism

Researchers protect intellectual rights and avoid plagiarism in three ways. First, researchers must indicate with quotation marks when they use the exact words of others. Moreover, researchers must give complete citation and reference information for each of these occurrences. Second, citation and reference information must also be given when summarizing or paraphrasing the work of others. Even though the exact words of other researchers may not be used, those researchers deserve to be recognized when their ideas are used. Third, complete citation and reference information must be given when mentioning or making reference to the ideas or significant contributions of others. In any of these cases, it is not permissible to present the work of authors as one's own. Take a look at an example of each of these cases.

Dixon and Linz (1997) studied how listeners make judgments about the offensiveness of sexually explicit lyrics in rap music. Here are three excerpts from their journal article, each one providing an example of the cases described above.

The first example demonstrates how Dixon and Linz directly quote the work of other scholars. A reader is alerted to the fact that these three sentences were written by Dyson, rather than Dixon and Linz, because quotation marks identify the quoted passage:

> "At their best, rappers shape the tortuous twists of urban fate into lyrical elegies. They represent lives swallowed by too little love or opportunity. They represent themselves and their peers with aggrandizing anthems that boast of their ingenuity and luck in surviving" (Dyson, 1996, p. 177).

The second example demonstrates how Dixon and Linz summarize or paraphrase the

Ethics in Proprietary Research

Many of you will graduate and take jobs in industry rather than pursue academic careers. How would the ethical issues discussed in this chapter be relevant for research conducted in your organization for your organization? This type of research, called proprietary research, is quite common. In these instances, results are shared only with members of the organization that conducted or outsourced the survey; results are not disseminated to a wider audience. For example, many organizations ask employees to fill out surveys as a way of assessing organizational culture and climate or tracking employee satisfaction. Organizations also have confederates interact with their customer service representatives to determine the level and quality of assistance they provide. Finally, many organizations conduct research with customers to assess corporate image or to determine customers' satisfaction with their products or services. Which ethical principles do you believe should be upheld in these situations? Why?

work of other scholars. A reader knows that these are not the exact words of Hooks because quotation marks are not used.

> According to Hooks (1992) rap music is a form of male expression that provides a public voice for discarded young Black men, although it has led to the expression of unacceptable levels of sexism.

Finally, in the third example, Dixon and Linz are calling readers' attention to the research on rap music that precedes their study:

> There has been little research on listeners' perceptions of rap music and how these perceptions are related to the components of obscenity law. Only a handful of studies have examined listeners' responses to sexually explicit music in general, and rap music in particular (Hansen, 1995; Johnson, Jackson, & Gatto, 1995; Zillmann, Aust, Hoffman, Love, Ordman, Pope, & Siegler, 1995).

In using these techniques, Dixon and Linz have avoided representing the work of others as their own. Because the citation information is provided in the text for these cases, the reader can turn to the reference section of the manuscript or article and find the complete reference for any work—and then go to the library and find the original information. See Chapters

17 and 18 for more information about citation and reference styles.

Protecting the Identities of Participants

Earlier in this chapter, we discussed ways to protect and conceal participants' identities. Generally, participant identity is not an issue in quantitative research reports because a single participant is not the focus or interest of the research study. Rather, the report is about the findings of a group of people described by their demographic characteristics. For example, most researchers report the number of participants, their age, sex, and any other demographic characteristics important to the study. Seldom would a reader be able to identify exactly who participated. If the researcher reports on participants' organizational affiliation, the name of the participating organization is generally changed or referred to only generically.

Protecting the identities of participants in qualitative research can be more difficult. When identities must be concealed, the advice given earlier about changing names can be applied to the writing of the research report. In other cases, only partial concealment is necessary or preferred.

For example, in Lange's (1990) case study research on Earth First!—a radical environmental group—he changed informants' names, but not those of national leaders who were already publicly visible and associated with the movement. Garner (1999) partially concealed the identities of women who willingly participated in her qualitative web-based study and revealed information about their childhood and their reading habits as young girls and teenagers. In the journal article, Garner describes the group's demographic characteristics in general terms by giving their age, race, nationality, occupation, and relational status. When Garner specifically quotes women, she uses a real name if the woman requested that she do so. But she does not differentiate these women from those who preferred that their names be changed. Thus, with the use of identifiers like "Sue, 42, writer" or "Cathy, 47, professor," and the vastness of the web, it is unlikely that anyone reading the journal article could associate a designation with any specific person.

SUMMARY

1. Issues of ethics and integrity are an integral part of the research process and must be explored as the research project is designed and developed.

2. Researchers have three broad responsibilities: a scientific responsibility, a responsibility for developing and conducting research that will yield knowledge worth knowing, and a responsibility for verifying or validating the data they collect.

3. Three principles—beneficence, respect for persons, and justice—must be simultaneously upheld.

4. Universities and colleges have institutional review boards, or human subjects committees, that review the research proposals of both professors and students to determine if the rights and welfare of research participants are being adequately protected.

5. Obtaining informed consent, or a research participants' agreement to participate in the research project, is almost always required.

6. Informed consent contains information about the research procedures, including any possible risks and benefits.

7. Informed consent should be written in language participants can easily understand, and each participant should receive a copy.

8. Researchers use deception to purposely mislead participants when it is necessary for participants to be naive about the purpose of a study, or when telling participants all of the information beforehand would trigger unnatural responses.

9. Upholding confidentiality and anonymity of research participants during the collection of data is another ethical principle to which researchers must subscribe.

10. Videotaping and audiotaping participants as part of research procedures can be done only with their express knowledge and consent.

11. Debriefing gives researchers the opportunity to provide participants with additional knowledge about the research topic or procedure, especially when deception is used.

12. The ethical issues of ensuring accuracy, protecting intellectual property rights, and protecting the identities of individuals in research reports are researcher responsibilities.

KEY TERMS

anonymity

beneficence

confederate

confidentiality

debriefing

deception

human subjects review committee

informed consent

institutional review board (IRB)

justice

respect for persons

CHAPTER SIX

Measurement

Chapter Checklist

After reading this chapter, you should be able to:

1. Understand that measurement is a process.

2. Understand the principle that numbers have no inherent meaning until the researcher assigns or imposes meaning.

3. Develop categories for nominal data that are mutually exclusive, exhaustive, and equivalent.

4. Distinguish among the three types of continuous level data—ordinal, interval, and ratio—and use them appropriately.

5. Develop effective and appropriate Likert-type scales.

6. Understand the basic principles of validity and reliability and how they affect research results.

7. Understand the relationship between validity and reliability.

8. Consider research design issues that may threaten validity and reliability.

9. Collect, report, and interpret data accurately, ethically, and responsibly.

10. Question the measurement procedures and data interpretations reported by researchers.

Research relies on measurement and observation. Measurement is most often associated with quantitative methodologies, and observation is most often associated with qualitative methodologies. Much of this chapter is geared toward measurement as used in quantitative methodologies. Whether or not you plan to do such research, you should have a basic understanding of the concepts presented in this chapter because much of what is known about communication phenomena has been discovered through measurement and quantitative methodologies.

Measurement is a useful process because it aids researchers in identifying and presenting information about communication behavior. It is the link between the conceptual and the empirical. Using measurement principles, researchers can take widely varying phenomena and reduce them to compact descriptions we identify as variables (Judd & McClelland, 1998).

MEASUREMENT PRINCIPLES

You are familiar with using numbers to measure something in order to describe its value, intensity, depth, length, width, distance, and so on. In research, a measurement is simply a descriptive device. Measurement also allows us to evaluate what is described. Even though measurement provides these two functions, the numbers used to measure something have no value until we give meaning to them. For example, the number 99 could be your score on a recent test, in which case, you would be proud of your accomplishment if 100 points were possible. But how would you feel about a score of 99 if 200 points were possible? You see, the value we assign numbers is not inherent in the numbers. Rather, the value comes from the meaning we assign or impose, and much of this is done arbitrarily. The goal of this chapter is to help you become comfortable with the way in which numbers are used in research to account for or substitute for the observation of communication concepts and phenomena.

Although numbers are central to measurement, it may be more useful to think of **measurement** as a process that includes everything the researcher does to arrive at the numerica

estimates. Thus, measurement includes the measuring device or instrument, how the device or instrument is used, and the skill of the person using the device or instrument, as well as the attribute or characteristic being measured (Katzer, Cook, & Crouch, 1978). Each of these can affect the number obtained by the researcher. Measurement can also be the process of assigning a person, event, or thing to a particular category (Sirkin, 1995). In this way a researcher measures something by describing or identifying it.

Regardless of the type, measurement needs to be accurate because it is the foundation of statistical analyses and the subsequent interpretations made by the researcher. If measurement of a communication phenomenon is flawed, everything that flows from it is flawed as well (Emmert, 1989).

Why measure communication phenomena? When we measure something, we are describing it in some standardized form. Recall from Chapter 3 the discussion about operationalizing variables. Choosing a way to measure something standardizes how the variable is perceived, treated, and handled and, in essence, provides the operationalization of the variable. When variables are operationalized, or standardized, they can be used in three types of comparisons (Figure 6.1).

The first type entails comparing many measurements of the same variable. The second type of comparison is especially important to researchers because science is a process of extension and replication. When researchers use the same or similar methods of measurement, the results of one study can be compared to the results of another study. The third type of comparison allows researchers to make more distinct discriminations among elements that might appear to be similar. In making these three types of comparisons, measurement allows researchers to use mathematical techniques to verify the existence of some phenomenon as well as give evidence to the existence of relationships among communication phenomena (Kaplan, 1964).

Figure 6.1 shows a practical example of how researchers use measurement to make three different comparisons. At some point, almost everyone has experienced communication apprehension, or anxiety in interacting with others. The first

			Apprehension category	PRCA score
1st	**Comparisons among individuals**	Kale	high	78
		Dennis	low	56
		Halley	high	79
		Che Su	low	50
2nd	**Comparisons among studies using the same measure**	In one study (Beatty & Andriate, 1985), researchers gave participants three administrations of communication apprehension with mean scores of 68.05, 67.77, and 69.6, respectively, compared to the mean score of 65.60 of over 25,000 participants.		
3rd	**Comparisons among similar measures**	Scott and Rockwell (1997) compared the scores of 178 participants on communication apprehension, writing apprehension, and computer anxiety.		

FIGURE 6.1 Measurement Allows Three Types of Comparisons

type of comparison—comparing many measurements of the same variable—can occur in two ways. On the most basic level, we could identify people as having or not having communication apprehension. In making these identifications, we have assigned individuals to one of two categories—those who are communicatively apprehensive and those who are not. This is the most basic level of measurement. With that information, we would have two groups of people but not know very much about any differences between the two groups or differences among those within each group.

At this first level, we could also make comparisons among many individuals on this variable by using the Personal Report of Communication Apprehension, or the PRCA (McCroskey, Beatty, Kearney, & Plax, 1985). Individuals could answer

its 24 questions (see Appendix A for the complete questionnaire and response set), and we could calculate their score of communication apprehension. We could compare the scores of these individuals because this instrument is one way to standardize the measurement of communication apprehension. We could even identify a score that becomes the point for distinguishing between the two groups—those who are communicatively apprehensive and those who are not. Or we could use participants' scores to find subtle variations within groups.

In moving to the second type of comparison, we can compare our results to the results of other researchers who have used the PRCA. We could identify the journal articles that address communication apprehension and report PRCA scores. We could compare our participants' average score to the average scores from similar or different populations.

Communication apprehension is one of the most widely researched communication variables. But it is still only one way to measure participants' predisposition to communication avoidance. So in the third type of comparison, we could compare participants' scores on the PRCA with their scores on the Communication Anxiety Inventory (Booth-Butterfield & Gould, 1986) or the Unwillingness-to-Communicate Scale (Burgoon, 1976). These are other measuring instruments for related variables, and research studies have explored the relationships and differences among these three measures.

LEVELS OF MEASUREMENT IN COMMUNICATION RESEARCH

Communication research relies on researchers using measurement and observation to collect and organize data. Generally, researchers refer to two types of measurement—discrete and continuous. Each produces a different kind of data. How data are collected determines their use in statistical analyses, which are discussed in later chapters.

Perhaps the best way to think of data is that they can represent the name or the value of something. If data only name, or identify, what is being measured, then data are discrete. This level of data is referred to as categorical, or nominal, data. If data represent the value of elements, then they are referred to as continuous level data. Ordinal, interval, and ratio are three levels of continuous level data. Both discrete and continuous level data are regularly collected and reported in communication research.

Discrete Data

Some observations and measurements are discrete. In this case, data represent the presence or absence of some characteristic. All of the elements with the same characteristic belong to one category; elements with another characteristic belong to another category. This allows the researcher to group similar elements together and, at the same time, to identify these elements as distinct from others. Known as **nominal data,** or

categorical data, discrete data describe the presence or absence of some characteristic or attribute. In other words, the data give a name to the characteristic without any regard to the value of the characteristic. Sex, political affiliation, class level, and employment status are just a few examples of variables that are measured on the categorical level. The characteristic is present or absent because there is no practical way to express partial presence of the characteristic.

For example, you are male or female. Your political affiliation can be described as Democrat, Independent, or Republican. Your class level is freshman, sophomore, junior, or senior. You are a part-time or full-time employee or do not work. Even if a research study wanted to further specify your employment status, the researcher would use additional categories to describe that characteristic. For example, the employment status categories just given could be expanded to include

- Not employed, not looking for work
- Not employed, looking for work
- Working at a temporary job until a full-time permanent job becomes available
- Part-time employee working less than 10 hours a week
- Part-time employee working more than 10 hours a week, but less than 35 hours a week
- Full-time employee working 40 hours a week

Notice here that a variable (e.g., employment status) is represented by several categories like the six just listed. For example, the variable political affiliation is comprised of the categories of Democrat, Independent, and Republican. Likewise, class level is the variable, and its categories are freshman, sophomore, junior, and senior. It is important to remember that within each variable, the different categories reflect different *types* of political affiliation or class rank, not differing *amounts* of political affiliation or class rank. Categorizing people relies on the assumption that participants identified by a particular category are similar and have the same attributes.

Another aspect of categorical data is that the category levels within a particular variable possess

TABLE 6.1 Nominal Variables and Their Categories in Physician–Patient Study

Sex	Illness/Injury	Occupation	Payment Method	Race
Female	Abdominal disorder	Blue collar	Commercial insurance	African American
Male	Central nervous system disorder	Retired	Government	Caucasian
	Laceration	Student/child	None	Hispanic
	Medical problem	Unemployed		
	Orthopedic	White collar		
	Respiratory			

SOURCE: Schneider and Beaubien (1996).

no inherent value. Any value imposed on the categories is arbitrary. To avoid biasing responses or to avoid the appearance of a preferred response, researchers frequently arrange categories alphabetically. For example, eye color would be arranged as "black, blue, brown, green, hazel." Some categorical data, such as class level, follow a logical ordering. In this case, it would make sense to list the categories of class level as "freshman, sophomore, junior, senior" rather than in the alphabetical order of "freshman, junior, senior, sophomore." It is generally accepted that you must be a freshman before achieving sophomore standing, and you must be a junior before achieving senior standing. But recognize that in a particular case, being a freshman may be valued more than being a senior. The value ascribed is arbitrary. Thus, in some cases, societal standards and practices provide guidance in how categorical data are presented to research participants. If no such standard is present or appropriate, then alphabetical listing of categories is preferred. Remember, however, that the ordering of the categories imposes no particular value on any category.

Depending on your familiarity with some nominal variables, you may believe it is easy to identify a nominal variable and its representative categories. Be careful. In data collection, each participant should be identified by only one category of each variable. Thus, where we collect data and from whom can have a major impact on

the selection of nominal variables and their representative categories. For instance, Schneider and Beaubien (1996) investigated interactions between physicians and their patients. To describe the patients, these authors used five nominal variables: sex, illness/injury, occupation, payment method, and race. The categories for each variable are shown in Table 6.1. The health facility at which Schneider and Beaubien conducted their study was located in the Midwest. What categories would need to be changed or expanded if the health facility were located in San Diego? Seattle? New York? Miami?

To be both a valid (truthful) and reliable (consistent) measurement, the categories of a nominal variable need to be representative of the people involved. Therefore, categories must be **mutually exclusive;** people should not be able to identify themselves in more than one category. Categories also need to be **exhaustive,** representing the variety of characteristics of the people involved. At the same time, categories must also be **equivalent,** or equal to one another. Finally, a nominal variable must have at least two categories. Otherwise, differentiation is not possible. When these conditions are met, nominal data help researchers classify participants into membership categories. Using the patient descriptors in Table 6.1, we might expect that doctors would interact differently with an unemployed Caucasian female who has no insurance when she comes to

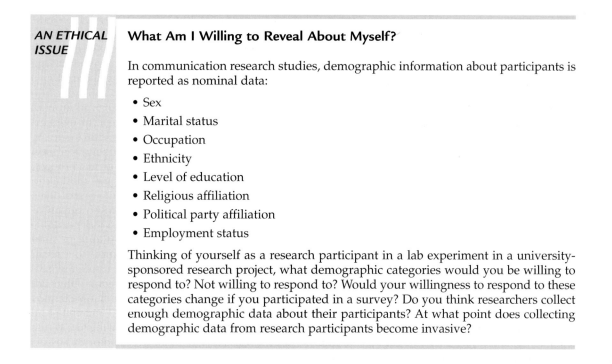

What Am I Willing to Reveal About Myself?

In communication research studies, demographic information about participants is reported as nominal data:

- Sex
- Marital status
- Occupation
- Ethnicity
- Level of education
- Religious affiliation
- Political party affiliation
- Employment status

Thinking of yourself as a research participant in a lab experiment in a university-sponsored research project, what demographic categories would you be willing to respond to? Not willing to respond to? Would your willingness to respond to these categories change if you participated in a survey? Do you think researchers collect enough demographic data about their participants? At what point does collecting demographic data from research participants become invasive?

the doctor with a minor medical problem than with an employed and insured Hispanic male who comes to the doctor with an orthopedic problem that prevents him from working his factory job.

Continuous Level Data

In contrast to discrete data, other variables take on or assume a quantity, intensity, or magnitude. Values can differ in degree, amount, or frequency, and these differences can be ordered on a continuum. These are known as **continuous level data,** or **quantitative data.** A person's score on a questionnaire is continuous level data because a score can range from some minimum to a maximum quantity. We can demonstrate this concept with the PRCA, introduced earlier in the chapter. Here are an item and the response scale from the PRCA:

I dislike participating in group discussions.

strongly agree	agree	undecided	disagree	strongly disagree
1	2	3	4	5

A research participant would use the same response scale to answer each of the PRCA's 24 items. His or her score could range from the minimum possible score to the maximum possible score, with any intermediate position possible. Thus, the data are continuous.

Sometimes, researchers create continuous data by simply counting some element to establish its level or degree of presence or absence. For example, Allen and Caillouet (1994) studied impression management strategies in one organization's written and spoken discourse to external audiences. The research team examined 799 statements from transcripts, press releases, articles, and brochures and categorized them by type of impression management strategy. By counting the number of instances in which each strategy was used, they found that the organization most frequently used ingratiation and completely avoided apology. The data are continuous because the number of impression management strategies within any category varied from as few as none to as many as 653.

Continuous level data also exist when a research participant is asked to rank-order items, for example, the radio stations to which he or she listens. Of a list of 5 FM radio stations in a specific market, the participant would give the radio station to which he listens most the rank of 1, the radio station to which he listens next most often a rank of 2, and so on. Thus, the data are continuous because each radio station could receive a rank of 1, 5, or anywhere in between.

There are three types of continuous level data—ordinal, interval, and ratio. They differ in terms of their properties and their abilities to be used in mathematical operations and statistical tests. Each one is more sophisticated than its predecessor because it contains more information about the phenomenon of interest. Each will be discussed in detail in the sections that follow.

Ordinal Data *Ordinal* means "in order." **Ordinal data** are data measured by ranking elements in logical order from high to low or low to high. Ordering suggests that there is some sequence to the value of data. Yet, this sequencing of data can occur without precise measurement and without knowing to what degree data are lower or higher than one another.

There are three important things to remember about ordinal data. First, ranking positions are only relative to the other ranking positions in that group. As a result, even a participant who has low preferences for all the choices presented will rank one of the low-preference choices as having the highest ranking. Second, the distance between ranked elements is uneven and often unknown. Third, because ordinal data consist of relative rankings, zero cannot exist.

Many times, ordinal measurement is used to make comparison judgments among a set of related topics, things, or issues. Ordinal data, or ranking information, can also be used to demonstrate the relative status or importance of each item in a group of related items. For example, in a study of the way in which emotions can affect information accessibility and information preference, Nabi (2003) asked participants in an experiment to evaluate 10 types of information they would like to have about drunk driving or gun violence. Participants were instructed to rank

order the 10 items from 1 to 10, using 1 to indicate the information they most wanted to receive about the topic. They were also asked to rank order 10 policy initiatives about drunk driving or gun violence, with 1 indicating the initiative they would most like to see enacted.

In another example, Peterson (1997) sent mail surveys to personnel interviewers of business organizations. The interviewers were asked to identify the five most prevalent communication inadequacies they observe among interviewees. Based on frequency of response, the highest ranking communication inadequacy was eye contact, followed by topic relevance, response organization, listening skills, and response clarity.

Ordinal data are not frequently used in communication research. The lack of precision in differentiating among what elements ranks first, second, and so on is problematic. Although there are no hard and fast rules, ordinal data can be treated as continuous data and used in some statistical tests if many rank positions are available. If not, ordinal data are best treated as categorical data.

Interval Data **Interval data** are data measured based on specific numerical scores or values. When using interval data, we can identify which participants scored highest and lowest, and we can determine the exact difference between and among scores. The distance between any two adjacent, or contiguous, data points is called an **interval,** and intervals are assumed to be equal. For example, for the set of scores 50, 60, 70, and 90, the distance between 50 and 60 is 10 units, the same as the distance between 60 and 70. That 10-unit difference is half the 20-unit distance between 70 and 90, or between 50 and 70.

Potential scores	50	60	70	80	90
Actual scores	x	x	x		x

A second important element of interval data is the acknowledgment of zero. Although this zero is arbitrary, these two properties allow us to use interval data in mathematical operations. In fact, in some interval data, particularly data from questionnaires, it would be impossible to obtain a zero score. For example, return to the Personal Report of Communication Apprehension (PRCA) in Appendix A. This 24-item questionnaire is used to evaluate the degree of communication apprehension individuals feel in four common communication settings. Respondents are instructed to use one of five numerical responses as an answer for each question or item. If a respondent strongly agrees with an item, then the "1" response is circled; if a respondent strongly disagrees with an item, then the "5" response is circled. Thus, an individual's score could range from a minimum of 24 to a maximum of 120. Recognize that it is not possible to produce a score of zero. The lowest score available is 24 (24 items × 1, the lowest possible response), which in this case would be interpreted to mean that the individual has very little communication apprehension. Technically, it would be inappropriate to interpret such a score as representing no communication apprehension. The highest score available is 120 (24 items × 5, the highest possible response).

As is typical of questionnaire and survey data, an individual's responses across the items on a questionnaire are totaled for a score. Then that score and all other scores are averaged to provide a mean score to represent the sample as a whole.

LIKERT-TYPE SCALES   One type of interval scale measurement that is widely used in communication research is the Likert, or **Likert-type, scale.** Research participants are given a statement and then asked to respond by indicating the degree to which they agree or disagree with the statement. Typically, the response set is like the following:

strongly disagree	disagree	undecided	agree	strongly agree
1	2	3	4	5

The wording can vary considerably, but the responses must be balanced at the ends of the continuum. In this example, "strongly disagree" offsets "strongly agree." It would be inappropriate to balance "strongly disagree" with "agree," or to balance "strongly disagree" with "strongly approve." Most Likert-type scales are 5-point scales, although 7-point scales can be used. This type of measurement is widely used to capture responses about attitudes, beliefs, and perceptions. In some cases, one Likert-type item will represent a variable. More typically, though, a series of Likert-type items will represent a variable. You will find a more complete description of Likert-type scales and their uses in survey research and questionnaires in Chapter 9.

SEMANTIC DIFFERENTIAL SCALES   Another interval measurement is the **semantic differential scale** (Osgood, Suci, & Tannenbaum, 1957). Using a stimulus statement, participants are asked to locate the meaning they ascribe to a stimulus. The response scale is anchored by two opposites, usually bipolar adjectives. As an example, Jones and Guerrero (2001) used five 7-point semantic differential scales to capture the degree to which an individual displays verbal person centeredness, or the degree to which the person verbally expresses empathy and validates the feelings of someone who is distressed. In this study, semantic differential scales were used to distinguish among self-centered versus other-centered, invalidates versus validates, judges versus empathizes, disregards versus acknowledges, and unconcerned versus concerned. As an example, a semantic differential scale would look like this:

Judges ___ ___ ___ ___ ___ ___ ___ *Empathizes*

You would be instructed to place an X in the spot that best represents your perception of the stimuli or target. In this case, if you believe the person judges others, you would place an X on one of the lines between the middle and that anchor of the scale; if you believe the person empathizes with others, you would place an X between the middle and that anchor of the scale. The middle space is considered neutral. Notice how the scales do not include descriptors for the intermediate positions. Only the poles of the continuum are anchored, and the anchors must be complete and logical opposites.

As with the Likert-type scales, semantic differential measurement can be used in a series

TRY THIS!   **Changing Levels of Measurement**

Some variables can be observed or measured in several different ways. Using the table below, review the example given for communication competence and then develop four levels of measurement for some aspect of intercultural communication competence.

Level	Communication Competence	Intercultural Communication Competence
Nominal	Identify a behavior that causes others to remark that you communicate competently (for example, you express disagreement tactfully). If another person agrees that you exhibit this behavior, you are competent; if you do not exhibit this behavior, you are incompetent. Use this yes–no decision to categorize yourself as competent.	
Ordinal	In your classroom group, select the five members who are best at expressing disagreement tactfully. Rank these five people; the person most competent at this communication task receives the number 1 ranking.	
Interval	Create a statement for which a Likert-type response scale can be used. For example, I can express disagreement tactfully. Response set = strongly agree (5), agree (4), undecided (3), disagree (2), strongly disagree (1).	
Ratio	During a classroom group meeting, count the number of times each member expresses disagreement in a tactful way.	

to represent a variable. To calculate the score, the researcher assigns a numerical value to each position on the semantic differential scale. The spaces would be assigned the values 1 through 7. In this case, the pole of the continuum labeled "Empathizes" would be marked as "7" because empathy is a characteristic of an individual who displays verbal person centeredness.

Sometimes, semantic differential scales include the numerical values of the response set. Using the earlier example, the scale would look like this:

Judges _1_ _2_ _3_ _4_ _5_ _6_ _7_ *Empathizes*

When the response set is configured this way, participants are instructed to indicate their response by circling one of the numbers.

DESIGN CHECK

Questioning Measurement Techniques

Measuring communication phenomena gives the appearance that the identity or value provided by the measurement is fixed, or static; when the identity or value provided is conceptualized this way, it is easy to think of it as being accurate. However, the identity or value is only as good as the measuring device. For example, a questionnaire requests that you check a category describing your ethnicity or race. Being of mixed racial heritage, what do you do? Check one racial category over another? Check both? Check none? In the same questionnaire, you are asked to respond to 20 statements about your most significant interpersonal relationship. By providing a likert-type response set for each question, the researcher presumes that you think of your interpersonal relationship in a standardized way (for example, "strongly agree," "agree," "undecided," "disagree," "strongly disagree"). But as you read the stimulus statements, you find that you strongly agree to the first item and agree even more strongly to the second. What do you do? Circle "strongly agree" in response to both? Change your response to the first item to "agree" so you can "strongly agree" to the second? How differently do you perceive the space between "strongly agree" and "agree"? Most research participants are unaware of researchers' assumptions about measurement techniques. Is it possible that participants who lack this knowledge will respond differently than participants who understand these assumptions?

Ratio Data   Finally, **ratio data** are similar to interval data except that zero is absolute. This means not only that intervals between data points are equal, but also that if the score is zero, there is a complete lack of this variable. Ratio measurement is not common in communication research. When used, it provides a measurement of the degree to which something actually exists. For example, in a study of patient–doctor interaction, researchers counted the number of questions patients asked their physicians (McGee & Cegala, 1998). Some patients asked no questions, which would be a true zero on the variable "asking questions." Of course, other patients asked many. Results from the study demonstrated that patients trained in information seeking averaged 12.10 questions, whereas the average for untrained patients was 3.90.

Another way in which communication researchers use ratio measurement would be to capture the length of interaction by audio- or video-recording the conversation. Noting the length of the conversation in minutes and seconds would be a ratio measurement as time has equal intervals and a true zero.

ISSUES OF VALIDITY AND RELIABILITY

Regardless of the type of observation or measurement you use, a measurement is not worthwhile unless it measures a dimension worth measuring (Simon, 1969). With respect to conducting communication research this means that you are measuring the characteristics required by your research questions and hypotheses. Researchers do not measure anything and everything just because they can.

The scientific process also requires that researchers provide valid and reliable measurements. In general, validity speaks to the truthfulness or accuracy of the measurement, and reliability speaks to the consistency or stability of the measurement. Measurements that are not valid or reliable are incapable of helping researchers answer research questions or confirm hypotheses. Thus, measurement validity and reliability are central to the research process. Each of these is explored in detail and in relation to the other.

Validity

Data obtained through measurements that are not valid are worthless data. Measurement has **validity** to the extent that it measures what you want it to measure and not something else (Katzer et al., 1978). Many of the variables studied by communication researchers cannot be directly observed. Instead they are inferred from behaviors that are observable (Carmines & Zeller, 1979). Because we often cannot be absolutely certain that measuring devices capture what was intended and only what was intended, validity is a matter of degree. These types of issues are known as **internal validity** because the accuracy of conclusions drawn from the data depends upon how the research is designed and the data collected. Thus, internal validity addresses the relationship between the concept being measured and the process for measuring it (Carmines & Zeller).

Another way to think of validity is as a test of true differences. A measurement is valid to the extent that differences in scores reflect true differences among individuals. If a measurement is ambiguous or unclear, then any differences produced by it are due to error, not to the true differences it seeks to measure (Selltiz et al., 1959).

Let's look at an example. Many high school and college students participate in public speaking contests. What is a valid measure of public speaking ability? Is it how long students can speak without referring to their notes? Is it how long they can speak without vocal interrupters (*ahh, umm, aaah*)? Or could it be how many people in the audience are persuaded by their presentation? Each of these measures could be valid for selecting the most competent public speaker. Notice, however, that each measures only one aspect of public speaking competence. Which one of these do you believe will make the greatest distinction between a competent public speaker and an incompetent one? Would combining the various measurements be more valid? If we combine

the three measurements, should they be equally represented in a composite, or should the measures be weighted in some way? As you can see, anytime something is measured, questions of validity should be raised. There are several different types of validity: face, content, criterion-related, concurrent, predictive, and construct. Each is described in the sections that follow.

Face Validity   A measure is said to have **face validity** if the items reference the construct we want to measure. We can use the Personal Report of Communication Apprehension, or the PRCA-24 (McCroskey et al., 1985; see Appendix A), as an example. The PRCA-24 is a 24-item questionnaire that measures communication apprehension, or the predisposition to avoid communication or suffer anxious feelings, across four contexts (public speaking, small group, meeting, and interpersonal encounters). Thus, in the PRCA, phrases like "nervous and tense" or, alternately, "calm and relaxed" are used to describe interaction. On the face of it—by just reading the items of the PRCA-24—it is clear to most individuals who respond to the items and researchers who have experience and expertise in that area that the instrument is measuring some aspect of apprehension as it would be associated with communicating.

In essence, face validity exists if the measurement looks and feels as if it will capture the construct we want to measure. Although face validity is the easiest to establish, most researchers would agree that it is the weakest type of validity. Frequently, researchers constructing questionnaires assert that they believe the measuring instrument has face validity. In other words, they believe that the questionnaire effectively captures what they want to measure. Face validity can be strengthened when researchers use experts in the content area of the measuring instrument to assess its viability in capturing the construct of interest.

Content Validity   The degree to which the items in the measuring device represent the full range of characteristics or attitudes associated with the construct of interest is a measurement's **content validity.** In other words, the measuring items are representative of all of the items potentially available. Using the PRCA, content validity is achieved if its 24 items represent the complete range of verbal and nonverbal behaviors associated with communication apprehension. Although the PRCA was designed to capture perceptions of communication apprehension in four contexts—groups, meetings, dyads, and public speaking—for a moment, focus on this list of items for public speaking situations (McCroskey et al., 1985):

- I have no fear of giving a speech.
- Certain parts of my body feel very tense and rigid while I am giving a speech.
- I feel relaxed while giving a speech.
- My thoughts become confused and jumbled when I am giving a speech.
- I face the prospect of giving a speech with confidence.
- While giving a speech I get so nervous, I forget facts I really know.

Notice how the six items represent a range of public speaking behaviors. Some items address a person's apprehension or anxiety before the speaking event; others address apprehension during the speech. Some items address a person's attitudes; others address physical behaviors. Content validity is achieved when the measurement covers the universe of possibilities. Can you think of other elements of communication apprehension in the public speaking context?

Criterion-Related Validity   Another type of validity, **criterion-related validity,** is achieved when one measurement can be linked to some other external measurement. Criterion-related validity can be achieved through two procedures—predictive validity and concurrent validity.

For the moment, assume that your research team wanted to develop a new measurement for communication apprehension, one that measured the apprehension workshop leaders and trainers might feel in those situations. You would want scores from your new apprehension measure to be consistent with participant scores on the PRCA. Why? Because the PRCA is an established and accepted measurement of communication apprehension. Collecting data from workshop leaders and trainers on both measuring instruments at the same time (just before a workshop or training session), or concurrently, is one way to demonstrate criterion-related validity. If participants' scores from the two measurements are highly related, or correlated, **concurrent validity** has been achieved. More information about correlation is provided in Chapter 12. Demonstrating that the new measuring instrument and the established measuring instrument—both measuring the same or similar things—are related is one way to establish the validity of your new measurement.

Another way to achieve criterion-related validity is through **predictive validity.** This type of validity is often the most central concern because communication researchers want to be certain that participants' responses to a questionnaire will, in fact, predict their communication behavior. For example, the PRCA-24 is most often used as a self-report questionnaire, meaning that individuals fill it out about themselves. So the question becomes, if someone has a high apprehension score on the public speaking component of the PRCA-24, do they in fact act apprehensive when giving a public speech? Research (Beatty, 1987, 1988; Beatty & Andriate, 1985; Beatty, Balfantz, & Kuwabara, 1989; Beatty & Friedland, 1990) has shown that, yes, in fact, that is the case. Thus, the PRCA-24 has predictive validity on its public speaking component because those who have high public speaking apprehension scores also demonstrate observable anxiety in that context.

There is another way to demonstrate predictive validity. In the study of a different communication construct and setting, Fairhurst (1993) wanted to establish the predictive validity of how conversation patterns distinguished among female leaders' use of personal and positional resources to influence subordinates' performance. To do this, Fairhurst collected two types of data—leaders' self-reports on a Leader-Member Exchange questionnaire and taped routine conversations between leaders and one of their subordinates. Fairhurst's primary interest was to establish how female leaders accomplished and displayed influence in social interaction.

According to the Leader-Member Exchange theory, differences should be evident among leaders who maintain and sustain high, medium, or low levels of influence with their subordinates.

Thus, the first step in assessing predictive validity was to examine the transcripts for patterns of leader influence. Twelve patterns were identified to distinguish how the leaders used aligning, accommodating, and polarizing behavior to influence their subordinates. Differing uses of these behaviors identified the type of leader–member exchange present in the leader–subordinate relationship. Of the 14 leader–subordinate conversations examined, 11 were consistent with the leaders' self-report scores on the questionnaire. Thus, Fairhurst could claim that her method of measurement did in fact predict leaders' use of influence according to the Leader-Member Exchange theory. Thus, the measurement captured the performance, and predictive validity was achieved.

Construct **Validity**   Researchers rely on **construct validity** to assure themselves that they are measuring the core concept that was intended to be measured and not something else. Often, researchers use a different measure of the same or similar phenomena to establish construct validity. Construct validity rests on the arguments and supporting evidence, provided they are consistent with theoretical expectations (de Vaus, 2001).

Look at how Rogan and Hammer (1994) assessed construct validity in their study of facework, or the presentation of self-image, in crisis negotiations (for example, police officers negotiating with a suicidal individual, an armed man holding his children hostage). Using transcripts of three crisis negotiations as their dataset, the authors identified speaking turns as the unit of analysis; there were 1,814 units across three incidents. Using the research literature as a foundation, the authors created a model of nine facework behaviors and trained research assistants to code the transcripts.

After this coding was complete, the authors turned to a study by Lim and Bowers (1991) that provided a coding scheme for face-supporting and non-face-supporting messages similar to the valence (threat, honor) dimension of the Rogan and Hammer coding scheme. Rogan and Hammer trained assistants to code the same 1,814 units according to the Lim and Bowers scheme. The coders achieved high levels of agreement between the two coding schemes, indicating support for the construct validity of the valence dimension of their coding scheme. Thus, construct validity is theoretically based, as one measurement is related in a theoretically meaningful way (Emmert, 1989) to another meaningful measurement.

Another example of how construct validity is tested and established is demonstrated in a study of employee empowerment (Chiles & Zorn, 1995). The research team searched the literature and did not find an appropriate instrument to measure employees' self-perceptions of empowerment, so they developed their own questionnaire. This made it necessary for them to assess the instrument's ability to capture what they intended it to measure. To establish construct validity, the research team compared participants' scores on their empowerment questionnaire to an established self-efficacy instrument. Assuming that feelings of empowerment would be influenced by factors of self-efficacy, the research team presumed that scores from the two instruments should be related. The authors did, indeed, find a relationship, allowing them to support their assumption and begin to establish the construct validity of their empowerment instrument.

Validity captures the essence of something. Moving closer to capturing the reality or true nature of the phenomenon being studied improves validity. Thus, validity is developed over time. When a measurement is valid, it is truthful or accurate. As you can see, it would be difficult to accept a measurement without a sense of its validity.

Reliability

The **reliability** of a measurement is its degree of stability, trustworthiness, and dependability. If a measuring device varies randomly, there will be greater error, and reliability will be lower. *Consistency* is another word often used to describe reliability. A reliable measure is one that is consistent, that gives very similar results each time it is used. Should reliable measuring devices always produce the same results? That outcome is highly unlikely because some degree of bias or error is always present.

As a result, reliability is expressed as a matter of degree. Rather than use phrases like "completely reliable" and "not reliable at all," researchers use the **reliability coefficient,** a number between zero and one, to express how reliable their measures are. The closer the reliability coefficient is to 1.00, the greater the degree of reliability. The closer the reliability coefficient is to 0, the less the degree of reliability. What is reliable enough?

Generally, communication researchers agree that a reliability coefficient of .70 or above is acceptable. Notice that this is the commonly accepted standard. It is not an absolute. If the construct is easy to measure, as communication apprehension is, then a reliability coefficient of .80 or greater is expected. On the other hand, if a construct is difficult to capture, and thus measure, then a lower reliability coefficient could be acceptable. Generally, this is the case with concepts that are more abstract. There are three primary types of reliability—internal reliability, test–retest reliability, and split-half reliability. We will look at each.

Internal Reliability Many measuring instruments have multiple interval level items to test one construct or variable. For example, the PRCA-24 described earlier has 24 items. Each item has been written to measure one aspect of a person's communication apprehension. The degree to which the 24 items invoke the same response from the person responding to the questionnaire is its degree of **internal reliability.** The PRCA has internal reliability if you would respond similarly to each of the items that ask about being nervous and tense.

It is highly unlikely that using any questionnaire will result in perfect reliability. Bias and error can occur in many ways and affect participants' abilities to respond in the same way to similar questions. First, the question or item itself may be ambiguously worded or may contain a word with which participants are unfamiliar. Second, the participant's experience or frame of mind may cause him or her to interpret the question differently than you intended. Third, where and how the participant fills out the questionnaire can affect the responses given. Perhaps the participant feels rushed because of late arrival at the session, or perhaps the room in which data are collected is cold and not well lighted. Environmental effects like these can alter a participant's responses.

Regardless of its source, imprecision weakens the reliability of a measurement.

Fourth, a participant's mood can be a big factor in the responses given. The participant may have had a particularly bad day or have plans for a birthday celebration after participating in your project. Extreme emotions, positive or negative, are likely to alter a participant's responses. Fifth, the participant's interaction with the researcher can affect how honestly the participant will respond to a questionnaire. Although this interaction is usually procedural and lasts only a few minutes, it can be a major factor in how a participant responds. In instances where several members of a research team interact with participants, variation in their manner and style of communication can result in variation in participants' responses. Finally, the participant's familiarity with the questionnaire can affect the consistency of responses. If participants have responded to the PRCA-24 several times as part of a class assignment, they may believe they are familiar with the items and not read them or the directions carefully.

How many of these factors will influence participants' responses to your questionnaire will vary with each person and each situation. But you should be able to see why it is unlikely that any measuring instrument would achieve perfect reliability. Simply put, there are a variety of sources of bias and error. As the researcher, you should try to control as many of these sources as possible. Pretesting the measuring instrument is under your control. You can also control some aspects of the research environment, including how you interact with participants when they enter the research setting. But it is unlikely that you will reduce all error and bias.

Researchers should calculate the internal reliability of any measuring instrument that includes multiple items. How can you calculate internal reliability? Statistical software programs (such as SAS, SPSS) can compute the internal reliability coefficient for a series of items across all respondents. This test is often referred to as **Cronbach's alpha** (Cronbach, 1951), internal reliability, or internal consistency. The statistic it produces is the coefficient alpha. The alpha for each variable is reported in the methods or results section of a research report. Recall that researchers generally agree that a coefficient alpha of .70 or greater is sufficient for establishing the internal reliability of a measuring instrument. If the internal reliability of a measuring instrument is not sufficient, the variable may have to be dropped from further analyses.

Ideally, coefficient alpha should be calculated and reported for each variable operationalized with a multiple-item instrument. For example, in a pretest–posttest experimental comparison, Morgan, Miller, and Arasaratnam (2002) examined the influence of a workplace campaign to result in more positive attitudes toward organ donation, stronger behavioral intent to sign an organ donor card, greater rates of signed donor cards, and the willingness to talk to family members about the decision to donate organs. In the study, the research team used five continuous level variables and reported these internal reliabilities using Cronbach's coefficient alpha:

- Attitude toward organ donation: .88
- Altruism: .87
- Subjective norm: .61
- Intent to sign organ donor card: .89
- Willingness to discuss organ donation with family members: .89

The internal reliability for four of the variables meets or exceeds the generally accepted standard of .70, indicating that the internal reliability of each measuring instrument is sufficient to include in other analyses. However, the research team labels the alpha for subjective norm as "modest," indicating to readers that interpretations made using this variable should be made cautiously.

RELIABILITY BETWEEN CODERS   Consistency in measurement is also an issue when two or more researchers, or coders, code elements into nominal categories. This technique, known as content coding, is discussed in greater detail in Chapter 13. You will find the formulas for calculating the reliability between coders in Appendix B. A brief introduction to content coding and the necessity for calculating the reliability between coders is provided here. Although some research studies rely only on content coding, other studies include content coding as part of an overall research design.

When there are several raters or evaluators, as in the following doctor–patient study, the measure of reliability is known as **interrater reliability, interrater agreement,** or **intercoder reliability.** This type of reliability should be reported when two or more coders assign communication behaviors to categories or when two or more raters evaluate some communication act on a scale or index.

Interrater reliability must be calculated for two types of content coding decisions (Cappella, 1987). The first is **unitizing reliability,** or the degree to which two or more observers agree that communication action has taken place and can identify the action in the stream of interaction (Krippendorff, 2004). In other words, do the coders agree on what is to be coded? Once units are agreed upon, then coders have to categorize, or discriminate among them by assigning each unit to one of the available categories. Thus, **categorizing reliability** is the second type. Unitizing reliability captures the degree to which coders consistently identify what is to be coded. Categorizing reliability captures the degree to which multiple coders make similar distinctions in assigning data to categories.

For example, in a study of the doctor–patient interaction (McGee & Cegala, 1998), it was necessary to identify patient information-seeking behavior. In the first pass through the videotaped interaction, the researchers had to identify each time the patient asked a direct or indirect question. Agreement on these decisions, made by two coders, would be the basis of the unitizing reliability calculation, or .84. In communication research, this level of coder reliability is generally acceptable.

In the next step, the researchers wanted to identify the question type and question content. Using a randomly selected 20% of the transcripts, two coders independently coded the questions for type and content. The research team calculated **Cohen's kappa,** a measure of interrater reliability for categorical data. Just like Cronbach's alpha, this reliability measure ranges from perfect agreement (1.0) to agreement that is no better than would be expected by chance (0.0). For the coding of question type, Cohen's kappa was .93; for content codes, .88. Because an acceptable level of coding reliability was established, the rest of the questions were coded.

Another example of intercoder reliability is demonstrated in Mastro and Stern's (2003) examination of racial and ethnic minority portrayals in television advertisements. The researchers recorded prime-time television programming across six networks for 3 weeks to capture 2,880 commercials. Among others, the commercials were coded by four coders for product type being advertised, the context or location of the character in the commercial, the characters' relationships to the product, and the characters' primary behaviors. **Scott's *pi*** (Holsti, 1969) was used to calculate intercoder reliability. The coders had complete agreement about the product types being advertised and the settings (i.e., work, home, other indoors, and outdoors). Their intercoder agreement, or reliability, for the character's relationship to the product (i.e., endorsing the product, other, or both) was .92; reliability for the coding of characters' primary behaviors (i.e., work, domestic, recreation, other) was .83.

With the current emphasis on written or visual texts and the ease with which interaction can be audio- or videotaped, one additional step may be needed before the unitizing and categorizing steps already discussed. When continuous streams of interaction are to be coded and the unit of analysis is theoretically driven (for example, violent scenes in film, topics of conversation, conflict episodes) rather than natural (for example, words, sentences, questions), coders must first identify whether the interaction called for by the unit of analysis exists (Krippendorff, 2004). Once that coding decision is made, then coders can continue with unitizing decisions of where and when the interaction starts and stops and categorizing decisions of how to code the interaction. Interrater reliability should be computed for each of these decision points. More information about unitizing and categorizing reliability and content coding as a research method is located in Chapter 13.

Test–Retest Reliability Communication is an interaction process, and over time the interaction or our perceptions of it can change. Thus, many researchers design their studies to capture measurements at different points in time—sometimes to demonstrate the stability of a measuring instrument. **Test–retest reliability** calculates the relationship, or correlation (see Chapter 12), between scores at two administrations of the same test, or measurement, to the same participants. As with other reliability scores, 1.0 would indicate that the same participants evaluated the stimulus the second time exactly as they did the first time. Alternately, a score of 0.0 would indicate that the two measurements were no better than chance.

In a study of how students perceive the organizational image of their university, Treadwell and Harrison (1994) needed a measurement of the extent to which students attended to three specific campus media (a current events publication, the student newspaper, and campus bulletin boards). A group of students were tested 7 to 10 days apart. The test–retest reliabilities for the three media were .79, .86, and .76, respectively, indicating that the measuring device has a degree of reliability in capturing students' attention to different media.

Split-Half Reliability Occasionally, researchers need to use **split-half reliability,** especially when they need to test knowledge. For example, there are many principles about public speaking that can be used as test items after participants are given instruction in public speaking training. If you wanted to test participants' knowledge of these principles at two different points in time, using the same test at the second testing might artificially elevate their scores because participants might remember their responses to the first test.

To avoid this type of bias, the researcher would construct one test. Then he or she would split the test into two parts. For example, the researcher would use half of the items (for example, the odd items) in the first test. The other half of the items, or the remaining even items, would become the second test. Thus, the researcher would have two separate but equal versions of the same information. Computing the correlation, or the split-half reliability, between the two test administrations would indicate the degree of consistency between them.

Improving Reliability   Generally, reliability can be improved. Here are a few ways that can be accomplished:

- Poorly worded or confusing items on a questionnaire can be rewritten.
- Better instructions can be given to respondents.
- Researchers can take steps to make sure that all measurements occur under similar environmental conditions.
- Before working with the data collected for the research project, raters can be trained on similar data until they have achieved consensus on how to unitize, categorize, and evaluate interaction. If similar data are not available and the study generated plenty of data, researchers can select out a small portion of the data to use for training purposes.

Recognize, however, that reliability is subjective. You must decide what is acceptable to you as a consumer of research and as a researcher. When measurements are not reliable, the findings or conclusions based on them are not warranted or defendable.

The Relationship Between Validity and Reliability

Measuring something sounds easy, but developing a measure that is both valid and reliable is difficult. For a measurement to be useful, it must meet two conditions (Hoover & Donovan, 1995). First, the result of the measurement must fit the meaning of what was intended to be measured. If you want to measure the existence of cultural communication norms (for example, greeting and leave-taking behaviors) to capture cultural differences, then differences among cultural norms should be evident when measurements are complete. This is measurement validity. Second, the measurement of variation must be replicable. Thus, the measurements of cultural norms provided by one participant on one day should be very similar to his or her measurements provided the next day. This is measurement reliability.

Although reliability and validity are two separate concepts, they are connected in a fundamental way. This connection is diagrammed in Figure 6.2. You want your measurements and questionnaires to be both reliable and valid. Reliable measurement can be obtained even if the measurement is not valid. For example, a questionnaire could reliably be measuring the wrong thing! Alternately, valid measures are useful only if they are also reliable. When validity is achieved, reliability is presumed. Thus, validity is primary of the two. If you are not measuring what you want to measure, then the consistency of the measurement is pointless. But in developing measurement, validity is more difficult to achieve than reliability. Think of the bathroom scale you use to measure your weight as a metaphor that can help explain this relationship. The scale may weigh

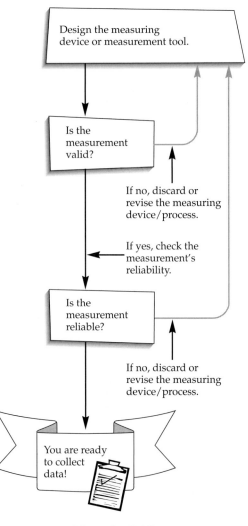

FIGURE 6.2 Validity and Reliability Are Interconnected in a Fundamental Way—Both Must Be Satisfied to Produce Truthful and Consistent Data

you consistently over time at 170 pounds. In other words, it is reliable. But is this reliable measure valid, or accurate? Try your bathroom scale and that of a friend or that at your doctor's office. In no time at all, you will understand the reliability–validity connection!

As you read research reports, you should take careful note of the way in which reliability and validity information is presented. Each researcher makes judgments about the reliability and validity of his or her data. Each consumer must also make judgments: Are the data reliable and valid enough for you to accept the conclusions the researchers offered?

Threats to Validity and Reliability

Should you be concerned about issues of validity and reliability? Yes, if you use research results to make decisions or choices about your communication behavior. And, yes, if you are using research results to answer questions you have about communication issues. Researchers speak of validity and reliability problems as *threats* to validity or reliability. A threat is any data-related problem that could lead you to draw a false conclusion from the data. Both participants and researchers can contribute to these problems. For what kinds of problems should you be on the lookout?

Issues of Data Collection   The use of self-report questionnaires or surveys is very popular in communication research. Unfortunately, they are not always the best instruments for collecting data about how people communicate. Let's say a measuring instrument asks you to think of how you behaved in the past or in a particular communication event. There could be a good deal of difference between how you actually communicated and what you remember about how you communicated (Sypher, 1980). Another type of validity error can occur when researchers use measuring instruments that are dated (Poole & McPhee, 1985), especially instruments that measure communication in relationships that reflect changing social values, like marital relationships. In each of these cases, the threat to internal validity, or the degree to which valid conclusions can be drawn from the data, is caused by the researcher's selection of measuring instruments.

Researchers can cause other threats to internal validity by simply being themselves. Here, the researchers unknowingly influence how participants behave or respond to stimuli because of their sex or communication style. On the surface,

---

**DESIGN
CHECK**

Will These Results Apply to Me?

Students enrolled in communication classes at a large midwestern university were the participants ($n = 401$) in a study that examined how verbal aggressiveness is used in the disengagement phase, or breakup, of dating relationships (Sutter & Martin, 1998). The researchers report three findings. First, participants who were classified as verbally aggressive (based on their scores on a self-report questionnaire) were more likely to be verbally aggressive when ending their dating relationships. Second, some level of reciprocity existed with respect to verbally aggressive messages in this communication context. Participants reported being verbally aggressive while breaking up because their partners used verbal aggression first. Third, verbally aggressive people used a wider variety of disengagement strategies. What arguments could you make for the validity of using this sample and population? What arguments could you make that would threaten the validity of using such a sample and population?

---

using only female research assistants in a study about interpersonal relationships might not seem problematic. But male participants might be more willing to reveal personal information about their relationships to someone of the same sex.

Researchers can unknowingly bias respondents in another way. Continuing with the example of the study about interpersonal relationships, a respondent is describing her interaction in a way that confirms the researcher's expectations. Hearing what she wants to hear from the respondent, the researcher smiles, nods, or gives other confirming behaviors, hoping that the respondent will continue with this type of description. Alternately, when a respondent is providing descriptions contrary to her expectations, the researcher maintains a straight face and provides few other nonverbal cues. To overcome these types of problems, many researchers make sure that the assistants who are collecting data do not know the hypothesis or purpose of the research project.

Researchers also threaten the internal validity of their measurements when they vary their judgments of what they are observing. Researchers coding or observing data over long periods of time can become fatigued, even bored, and are particularly susceptible to this threat to internal validity.

Participants can also threaten the internal validity of a research study. For example, in a study

that follows a team over a long period of time, two things are likely to happen. First, membership of the group may change. Participants drop out of the study simply because they are no longer members of the group being observed. This is known as participant **mortality,** or **attrition.** Attrition can also occur because participants lose interest or lack the motivation to remain with the study. In some cases, participants move away or die.

Second, participants are likely to change, or mature, over the course of the observations. It would be unusual if some level of participation **maturation** did not occur. Participants can become overly familiar with the same questionnaire when it is presented at different points in time. Or maturation can occur simply because participants' attitudes and beliefs change due to some element outside the control of the researcher. When participants leave a quantitative research project, either through mortality or attrition, researchers must deal with this loss of data.

Issues of Sample Representativeness   Some validity concerns are raised by the way in which researchers find and select their samples. This is referred to as a threat to **external validity** because the threat weakens the generalizability of the findings. For example, many researchers use sampling techniques, particularly convenience samples, that are not based on the principles of probability (see Chapter 7). This type of sampling limits the generalizability of the results (Rubin & Perse, 1994). Collecting data only from people who are conveniently available to the researcher and who are willing to participate in the research study creates a problem of external validity. What population would the convenience sample represent? In other words, whose truth would these participants reflect?

Another common threat to external validity can occur when researchers use university students as research participants. Many communication studies are conducted on university students, who do not reflect any population except that of university students. Moreover, many studies are conducted in laboratories. So who is selected to be a research participant and where the study is conducted or how it is controlled can raise serious questions. These are threats to validity because the results for other samples and populations are not known and may be different. This is often referred to as a threat to **ecological validity,** another form of external validity.

Both the degree to which participants are not like those the researcher is really interested in and the degree to which the research setting is artificial and contrived limit the generalizability of the research findings. For example, Kuhn and Poole (2000) wanted to examine if and how organizational teams develop norms about the ways in which conflict from the group setting spills over into the team's decision making. To increase the external validity of the findings, the researchers used established organizational teams comprised of members who regularly worked together on organizational tasks: Studying teams in this naturalistic setting allowed the researchers to follow the teams over a period of time and was more appropriate for the research question than using contrived groups in a laboratory setting.

Alternative Explanations Researchers cannot consider every possible alternative when they design a research study. But they should consider all plausible explanations for the results they find. Researchers hope that the effects they find are due to the communication phenomenon they studied. But they should look for alternative explanations and give the reader arguments and evidence that what they studied is truly responsible for their conclusions. It would be unethical for a research team to not consider alternative explanations.

ISSUES OF DATA INTERPRETATION

Recall from earlier in this chapter the idea that numbers hold no meaning until we assign meaning to them. Researchers who use numbers in their data collection are responsible for collecting data accurately and ethically. They also must interpret and report data responsibly. Why? Because most people who read their research reports will take these actions for granted. In fact, most consumers of research will not question what data collection method was used or why, nor will they question how researchers interpreted the data they collected. This is in spite of the fact that scientific traditions require that researchers report their results and interpretations of the data in separate sections of the research report. For many consumers, these are details that are overlooked. These issues are discussed here for two reasons. First, data interpretation is intimately linked to the data collected. The quality of the interpretation cannot be better than the quality of the data. Second, data are also intimately linked to the theory or premise of the study. As a result, measurement is central to the quality of outcomes produced.

When communication phenomena are measured, they are broken down into their constituent parts. This aspect is data collection. Next, the researcher must interpret the data, or give it meaning, to answer research questions and test hypotheses (Kerlinger, 1986). Thus, there are two areas of concern. First, you might take issue with how the data were collected. The following questions can help you assess the researcher's collection of the data:

- Do you agree on how the variables were operationalized? Were the data collection instruments valid and reliable?

- Did the researcher collect data in such a way that what he or she expected to find became overemphasized and obvious to participants?

- Were the researcher's expectations communicated unknowingly to the participants in any way?
- Were the data collection procedures consistently applied?

In other words, do these data make sense given the research questions or hypotheses presented? These really are issues of technical and procedural adequacy.

The second area of concern is the interpretation of the data (Kerlinger, 1986). Even assuming technical and procedural competence, researchers and consumers can still disagree about what data mean. Interpretations of data are subjective to some degree because researchers' interpretations depend somewhat on their backgrounds (culture, education, language, and experiences) and the context in which the interpretation occurs (Katzer et al., 1978). Some typical problems are

- Drawing sweeping conclusions from nonrepresentative data
- Accepting data results as firm conclusions without examining alternative interpretations
- Not adequately explaining contradictory or unanticipated findings
- Oversimplifying negative or inconclusive results without looking for weakness in the research process (incorrect theory or hypotheses, inappropriate methodology, poor measurement, faulty analysis)

Too often, consumers of research take authors' conclusions for granted. As you learn more about the research process, however, you can make your own evaluation of the research methods and process. You can make these judgments by reading the methods section of the research report. Whether qualitative or quantitative, the researcher should provide you with adequate information about what data were collected, how, and when. Then the analyses of the data should be presented in the results section of the research report. Here is where researchers start to reveal what the data mean. But the conclusions and implications of the data are not fully revealed until the discussion section of the research report.

As a consumer of research, your role is an active one. It is your job to think through the presentation of how the data were collected and analyzed and to test what you believe it means against what the researcher says it means. A series of questions can help:

- What questions did the researchers ask?
- How much confidence do I have in the data collection methods and statistical analyses?
- What did the researchers find?
- What meaning did the researchers infer from the results?
- How does their interpretation fit with the questions asked?
- Do I agree with their conclusions?
- Do their conclusions fit with other known information about the issue or subject?
- Is there anything missing that might be important?
- To whom do the conclusions apply?

By asking and answering these questions you can independently come to your own conclusions about the reliability and validity of the data and the conclusions that come from it.

SUMMARY

1. Research relies on measurement.
2. Measurement allows researchers to make comparisons.
3. Discrete data are known as categorical or nominal data and describe the presence or absence of some characteristic or attribute.
4. For categorical data, each variable is comprised of two or more classes or categories that should be mutually exclusive, exhaustive, and equivalent.
5. Continuous level data can be one of three types: ordinal, interval, or ratio.
6. Ordinal data rank the elements in some logical order, but without knowing the relative difference between ranks.

7. Interval data are more sophisticated in that they represent a specific numerical score and the distance between points is assumed to be equal.

8. Ratio data are the most sophisticated data type; they have the characteristics of interval data and a true zero.

9. Issues of validity and reliability are associated with all types of measurement.

10. Data are valid to the extent that they measure what you want them to measure.

11. Face validity exists when the measurement reflects what we want it to.

12. Content validity exists when the measurement reflects all possible aspects of the construct of interest.

13. Criterion-related validity exists when one measurement can be linked to some other external measurement.

14. Construct validity exists when measurement reflects its theoretical foundations.

15. Reliability is the degree to which measurement is dependable or consistent; it is expressed as a matter of degree.

16. Internal reliability is achieved when multiple items purportedly measuring the same variable are highly related.

17. Test–retest reliability is achieved when measurements at two different times remain stable.

18. Split-half reliability is achieved when two forms of one measuring instrument capture similar results.

19. Measurement of data must be both valid and reliable.

20. Validity and reliability are threatened by the choices researchers make about how they collect data, and whom or what they choose as their sample, as well as alternative explanations that are plausible.

21. Regardless of how data are collected, they must be collected and reported accurately, ethically, and responsibly.

KEY TERMS

attrition	interval
categorical data	interval data
categorizing reliability	Likert-type scale
Cohen's kappa	maturation
concurrent validity	measurement
construct validity	mortality
content validity	mutually exclusive
continuous level data	nominal data
criterion-related validity	ordinal data
	predictive validity
Cronbach's alpha	quantitative data
ecological validity	ratio data
equivalent	reliability
exhaustive	reliability coefficient
external validity	Scott's *pi*
face validity	semantic differential scale
internal reliability	
internal validity	split-half reliability
intercoder reliability	test–retest reliability
interrater agreement	unitizing reliability
interrater reliability	validity

CHAPTER SEVEN

Sampling, Significance Levels, and Hypothesis Testing

Chapter Checklist

After reading this chapter, you should be able to:

1. Identify the population and sampling frame to select an appropriate sample.

2. Argue for how results from a sample are generalizable to its population.

3. Use probability sampling procedures to produce a random sample.

4. Use nonprobability procedures to produce an appropriate sample.

5. Choose an adequate sample size.

6. Choose an appropriate level of significance for each statistical test used in your research project.

7. Make a decision about a hypothesis based on the stated level of significance.

8. Explain the relationship among sampling techniques, significance levels, and hypothesis testing.

9. Identify when an alternative hypothesis is accepted and when a null hypothesis is retained.

This chapter explains three concepts critical to experimental forms of communication research: sampling, significance levels, and hypothesis testing. These scientific traditions are so strong and so widely accepted among communication researchers who use quantitative research designs that they are often applied or adapted to other forms of quantitative communication research, such as surveys. These concepts can be difficult to grasp because you must "trust" commonly held, yet unfamiliar, scientific concepts. In this chapter, we will explore the relationship of a sample to its population and describe sampling techniques most commonly used by communication scholars. Next, the chapter will explore significance levels, or the degree to which scholars accept error for their statistical tests. Finally, the chapter concludes with principles of hypothesis testing.

The material presented in this chapter demonstrates the tension that can exist between generally accepted procedures and procedures that scholars across disciplines have debated. With very minor variations, scholars from many disciplines use the sampling procedures described in this chapter. On the other hand, the procedures associated with significance levels and hypothesis testing vary according to discipline. Although there appears to be a standard, you should know that many question the validity of these techniques and standards. In every case, the researcher, then, must make choices and be able to defend his or her choices. Alternately, a consumer of communication research reports who has a basic understanding of these three concepts can be a more effective critic.

POPULATION AND SAMPLE

A **population** consists of all units, or the universe—people or things—possessing the attributes or characteristics in which the researcher is interested. A **sample** is a subset, or portion, of a popula-tion. Generally, researchers study the sample to make generalizations back to the population. Why not study the entire population?

In most cases, it is impossible, impractical, or both to ask everyone to participate in a research project or even to locate everyone or everything

in the population. When that is possible, the term **census** is used to refer to the complete count of the population. More realistically, there are limitations to your time and other resources. Normally, a **sampling frame,** or the set of people that have a chance to be selected, must be created. Practically, this is the list of the available population in which you are interested and from which participants are selected. Note the slight but important distinction between the population and the sampling frame: The population is all units possessing the attributes or characteristics in which the researcher is interested, whereas the sampling frame is the list of *available* units possessing the attributes or characteristics of interest. It is highly unusual for the sampling frame and the population to be exactly the same.

There are several different ways to select a *sample,* which is a portion, or subset, of the larger group, or population. Regardless of how a sample is selected, researchers collect data from the sample to draw conclusions that are used as representative information about the entire population.

Defining the Population

It is easy to be lulled into believing that a researcher simply selects a sample by identifying a group of people to respond to a questionnaire or by identifying a set of elements to be examined. Such a process, however, would generate results that are unlikely to be relevant to, or representative of, any other group of people or to apply to another set of elements. Even the most ambitious research project cannot be designed to generalize across all possible dimensions. A researcher must choose which dimension or dimensions are most meaningful or important (Katzer et al., 1978). This takes us back to research questions and hypotheses, discussed earlier in the text. The researcher must identify the appropriate population that will best satisfy the expectations presented by the research questions or hypotheses.

Before a sample can be selected, the population must be identified. Researchers begin by identifying the characteristics they want participants or elements to have or contain. There must be at least one common characteristic among all members of a population (Jaeger, 1990). Then care must be taken to make sure that the sample reflects the population in which the researcher is interested. In other words, the sample must contain the same common characteristic that made the researcher interested in the population. Thus, the population of interest is inherently linked to the hypotheses or research questions the researcher wants to answer.

For example, Peterson (1997) wanted to investigate how organizational representatives who conducted job interviews viewed the oral and nonverbal communication skills of job applicants. The population of interest was personnel interviewers. Although other human resource employees would have perceptions or ideas about the communication skills of job applicants, the only individuals who could directly provide answers to the research questions were the personnel interviewers who actually conducted employment interviews. The common characteristic among individuals in this group was that they conducted job interviews and thus would be in a position to make the assessments in which Peterson was interested.

Generally, it is impossible to use all members of a broadly defined population in a research study. For example, it would be nearly impossible to identify and list all students attending universities. As a result, researchers more narrowly define their populations. In the case of university students, it may be more reasonable to identify a population of sophomores at three private colleges or to identify a population of women in one sorority across universities. A researcher would have to decide which dimension is more important. Is the dimension of class level—being a sophomore at a private college—more important? Or are the dimensions of sex and being a member of a sorority more important? The researcher must make this decision based upon the research questions or hypothesis for the study. Does the researcher want to generalize the research findings to sophomores at private colleges or to women in sororities? Identifying the population should be the researcher's primary concern even though the research is actually

done on the participants or elements that constitute the sample.

As you can imagine, availability and access also play a role in which individuals are available to be considered as members of a particular population. The format for collecting data (face-to-face, written questionnaire, phone interview, web-based questionnaire, lab experiment, etc.) will affect who is available to be a participant—not everyone has a telephone, not everyone has electronic access, not everyone will take the time to make a trip to the lab.

The point here is that defining the population for a research project is a necessary first step and must be done before trying to identify and select the sample. Despite the problems caused by limited access or availability, the researcher must define the population on the dimensions most important to the research project and find a way to ensure representative sampling.

Addressing Generalizability

Once your population is identified, it is necessary to select a sample, or subset, of the population. There are a variety of ways for doing so, each with its own advantages and disadvantages. But first the issue of generalizability needs to be addressed.

Most communication research is primarily interested in people—how they communicate, why they communicate, how they perceive communication, and so on. As you search the research literature, you are likely to find one or more studies that address the variables or concepts in which you are interested. For example, to study how students might differentiate between the immediacy behaviors (behaviors that demonstrate closeness) and the sexually harassing behaviors of instructors, Mongeau and Blalock (1994) had students from a midwestern university whose average age was 21 evaluate descriptions of instructor behavior. How would the results they found apply to you? Do you differ from these students with respect to age? With respect to geographical location? Would these differences matter? Of course, other differences may exist with respect to ethnic and racial identity, socioeconomic status, religious affiliation, and so on.

How a sample is selected affects the degree to which the results are generalizable to, or representative of, others. Thus, **generalizability** is the extent to which conclusions developed from data collected from a sample can be extended to the population. A well-defined population and a representative sample diminish generalizability concerns. Theoretically, representative sampling of participants eliminates selection bias. Alternately, having a poorly defined population and nonrepresentative sample raises concerns about generalizability. In this case, a researcher could not be certain that any differences found were truly results from the research study. The differences might have occurred based on how the sample was identified or the population defined.

Choosing people to study—the sample—who are like the larger group or the population in all essential ways helps establish the generalizability of results. Thus, representativeness is the goal in selecting a sample from a population. To the degree that a sample is representative, all elements in the sample had the same chance for being selected and included as part of the research project. Hence, characteristics of the population should appear to the same degree in the sample as in the entire population. To the degree that a sample is not representative, it is said to be **biased,** to favor one attribute or characteristic of the population more than another. In other words, some elements were more likely to be chosen than others. Representativeness can be ensured only in random sampling. Several methods of random sampling are described in the following sections.

Generalizing results from one set of people to another is strengthened when researchers use **replication**—basing their study on other studies that have investigated the same topic. Three types of replication are available (Lyken, 1968). First, a research study can repeat the exact procedures of a previous study. This is known as *literal replication.* This type of replication is unusual. Second, researchers can use *operational replication,* in which they attempt to reconstruct the procedures used previously. This type of replication is more common. Finally, researchers can use *constructive replication,* in which subsequent studies focus on the same constructs or variables but use different sampling techniques, different populations from

which to pull samples, and different research procedures and measures. This type of replication is common in communication research, and it provides strong evidence of generalizability if similar results are found under dissimilar conditions. If several researchers working in different environments, using different populations, employing similar but different methods arrive at the same results, you can be more confident that these results are generalizable to your population. Replication can be powerful. When scholars replicate the findings of previous studies, alternative plausible explanations of outcomes are eliminated—which, in turn, strengthens the generalizability of the findings (Boster, 2002).

Thus, researchers should point out in the written research report how and why their results are similar to or different from earlier but similar studies conducted on different populations. To use this argument for generalizability, however, what you are studying must have a welldeveloped and published research history, and that may not always be the case.

Whether or not replication is used as a basis for designing a research study, generalizability can be improved by using a principled, or theoretical, basis for the research questions or hypotheses (Shapiro, 2002). "Theoretical knowledge gives us much greater power to predict effects with other people, in other settings, at other times, and with other messages" (p. 495). Selecting an appropriate population and sample to study is important. Complementing that selection with a theoretically driven design that cleanly explores underlying communication phenomena increases a study's ability to produce valid findings that can be generalized to others.

Probability Sampling

The best sampling procedures produce a representative sample, or model, of the population. These procedures are known as probability or random sampling. Each technique uses some form of random selection. Although no sampling technique is perfect, researchers agree that the techniques described in the following paragraphs ensure that the selected sample is sufficiently representative of the population for the purposes of research.

Probability sampling is a statistical basis, and the most rigorous way, for identifying whom to include as part of a sample. What is characteristic of and common to probability sampling techniques is that the probability, or chance, of any element being included in the sample is known and equal for everyone or every element in the sample. So, regardless of who you are, your score on any measurement, or where you are in the sampling frame, you have the same chance of being selected as any other person included in the sampling frame. When the probability for selection is equal, selection is said to be **random.** Random selection procedures decrease bias because other potential systematic selection biases brought to the procedure of selecting participants by the researcher are eliminated.

With every member of a population assigned a known and nonzero chance of being selected to participate (Henry, 1990), the sampling error can be calculated. Sometimes referred to as the margin of error, **sampling error** is the degree to which a sample differs from population characteristics on some measurement. Sampling error will always occur because the researcher collects data from the sample, not from all of the elements in the population. However, as sample size increases and becomes a larger proportion of the population, sampling error is reduced.

Sample size, population size, and sampling error are intimately connected. These relationships have been worked out by others and are shown in Table 7.1. The sample sizes are based on the use of random sampling, a population's known size, a 95% **confidence level** (the degree of accuracy in predicting the result for the population from the result of the sample), and a 5% sampling error (Krejcie & Morgan, 1970; Meyer, 1973). Notice how sample size increases less rapidly than population size.

The following example explains how sampling error can affect the generalizability of research results. Asked if they will vote in the upcoming presidential election, 70% of participants indicate that they will vote. With a population of 10,000 and a confidence level of 95%, the convention most researchers use, sampling error would be about 5% in the sample of 370 people. Thus, when inferring the result of the sample—70%

indicating that they will vote—to the population, the researcher could state as a generalization that 65–75% of the population would vote in the upcoming presidential election. The result of the sample, 70%, is adjusted up and down by the amount of the sampling error, 5% in each direction. That range, in this case 65–75%, is known as the **confidence interval.**

Sampling error is dependent upon sample size. Even though there is an equation with which you can calculate specific sample size, the table can help determine sample size for most research projects. If your population size falls in between one of the suggested levels, use the next larger population size and its corresponding sample size. If there is a question or doubt about sample size, it is always best to use a larger rather than smaller sample size.

Although probability sampling is used to ensure the representativeness of the sample selected, there is no guarantee that any one sample selected is representative of its population (Kerlinger, 1986). Each sample selected from a population is unique, and many different samples have an equal chance of being selected from the same population. Scientists rely on the principle that a randomly drawn sample is representative of the population. Using one of four common probability sampling techniques—simple random sampling, systematic sampling, stratified random sampling, and cluster sampling—described in the following paragraphs, researchers can increase the likelihood that their sample is representative of the population of interest.

Simple Random Sampling In **simple random sampling,** every person has an equal chance of being selected to participate in the study. Individuals are selected one at a time and independently. The easiest way to select a random sample is to order the sampling frame and then assign a number to each element, beginning with 1. Then, after deciding on the required sample size, use a random numbers table to generate a set of numbers equal to the number of people you want in the sample. A random numbers table is displayed in Appendix C, and most spreadsheet programs can also produce a table of random numbers. With the random numbers selected or

TABLE 7.1 Sample Size for Different Populations at 95% Confidence Level

	95% Confidence Level 5% Sampling Error		
Population Size	Sample Size	Population Size	Sample Size
50	44	260	155
75	63	280	162
100	80	300	169
120	92	400	196
130	97	500	217
140	103	1,000	278
150	108	1,500	306
160	113	2,000	322
170	118	3,000	341
180	123	4,000	351
190	127	5,000	357
200	132	10,000	370
220	140	50,000	381
240	148	100,000 & over	384

SOURCE: "Determining Sample Size for Research Activities," by R. V. Krejcie and D. W. Morgan, 1970, *Educational and Psychological Measurement, 30,* pp. 607–610. Reprinted by permission of Sage Publications.

generated, simply select the individuals on the numbered list who correspond to the generated random numbers.

Petronio and Bradford (1993) used a simple random sample to identify potential participants for their study of how divorced, absentee fathers use written communication to establish or continue relational bonds with their children. To obtain their sample, the authors contacted a nationwide writing program for noncustodial fathers and were given the names of those who inquired about the program. This list of names constituted the sampling frame for their study, because it would be impossible to construct a population list of all noncustodial fathers. Using a simple random selection procedure, written questionnaires were sent to each of the 148 names selected.

Although simple random sampling is the simplest and quickest technique for selecting a sample, it cannot be used in all situations (Barker & Barker, 1989). Simple random sampling should not be used if there are important subgroups to be represented in a population because the technique lacks the ability to capture distinctions in the population that may be important to the research project. And it cannot be used if it is impossible to generate a complete and accurate sampling frame. This is often a problem if a sample needs to be drawn from a large population for which there is no complete listing (for example, all residents of a city).

Systematic Sampling   A second type of random sampling is **systematic sampling.** To select a systematic sample, you need to determine the number of entries of the population, or the sampling frame, and assign a unique number to each element in the sampling frame. Now decide on the number of entries to be selected for the sample. Divide the population figure by the sample figure (for example, a population of 3,600 and a sample of 351 equals 10.26, or every 10th person). Every 10th person on the list needs to be included in the sample. To ensure randomness, researchers do not start their selection of every 10th person by counting from the top of the population list. Rather, turn to the random numbers table in Appendix C (or use a random numbers–generating program). Starting in the far left column, move down the column until you find the first number between 1 and 351. In this case, it is 65. Count down your population or sampling frame list to the 65th person. Although you will start here, you do not include this person in your sample. Now count to the 10th person from the 65th, and you have your first potential participant. Count to the next 10th person and you have your next potential participant. Continue counting every 10th person, starting over at the top of the list when necessary, until you have identified the total number of participants you are seeking.

The obvious advantage to this technique is that it is simple and unbiased and requires little or no technology. It is a particularly effective sampling technique if the elements of the population are randomly listed (Barker & Barker, 1989). Using a randomly ordered sampling frame, systematic sampling results in a truly random sample. However, not all sampling frames are randomized. Many sampling frames, like phone lists or employment rosters, are ordered in some repetitive cycle (for example, residents are listed in alphabetical order by last and first name; supervisors of each department are listed before hourly workers); in such a case, you will need to carefully analyze how frequently the cycle occurs. Check to see if the random numbers generated to identify the systematic sample can overcome this cycle. Otherwise, you may have to recompile or recompose the list in a random fashion.

Sometimes a systematic random sampling procedure is used to identify the individuals who will participate in the sample. In other cases, a systematic random sampling procedure is used to select the stimuli participants in the study will evaluate. For example, Austin et al. (2002) used this procedure to select magazine advertisements from 72 popular consumer magazines targeted to the young adult market. First, all advertisements for alcohol were flagged. Then magazines were alphabetized by their titles. Next, the research team selected every third alcohol advertisement. Thus, the research team ended up with 40 alcohol advertisements systematically and randomly selected from popular consumer magazines targeted to the population of interest from the same publication month.

Stratified Random Sampling   A third type of random sampling is **stratified random sampling.** In this technique, the population is divided according to subgroups of interest, or homogeneous groups. Then elements are randomly selected from each homogeneous subgroup of the population with respect to its proportion to the whole. This technique is possible because lists of people or elements are available with the stratification information the researcher needs. This sampling technique ensures representativeness for each of the subgroups of interest. The goal of this sampling technique is to first create homogeneous subgroups and then randomly sample from each of them proportionately.

In their study investigating individuals' willingness and intentions to sign organ donor cards, Morgan and Miller (2002) used a stratified random sampling procedure. Wanting to find a sample that was representative of employees at two sites of a large package delivery corporation, the sampling strategy was designed around employees' occupational classification. To accomplish this, the payroll department of the organization used a computer program to create a simple random sample of 10% of employees within each of the following occupational categories: administrators, drivers, managers, mechanics, package handlers, pilot or crew members, and technical occupations. Thus, the sample was stratified by occupation of employees in the organization.

In another example of stratified random sampling (Schmitz, Rogers, Phillips, & Paschal, 1995), users of a citywide computer-based electronic communication network were categorized, or stratified, according to how frequently they logged on to the system during the first 8 months of network operation. Thus, frequent users were distinguished from infrequent users. As with the example above, this method ensures that a random sample with proportional representation is obtained from each of the subgroups that form the total population. This technique is recommended when individuals within strata are believed to be similar to one another, yet different from individuals in another strata. Researchers use this sampling technique because sampling frames are available according to strata, or subgroups, that are believed to be related to the expected outcomes (Fink, 1995b). In other words, the strata must be justified with respect to the research. In this particular example, the researchers believed that frequency of logging on would distinguish different types of users.

Cluster Sampling   Note that the probability sampling techniques described so far require you to obtain a complete listing of the population you want to study. Sometimes, particularly when a population is dispersed over a wide geographical area, that could be difficult or impossible. In that case, cluster sampling can resolve the dilemma. **Cluster sampling** is a two-stage or multistage process. The first stage is accomplished when you can identify the population by groups, or clusters. In the second stage, you use simple random sampling in each cluster to select your sample. There is an inherent strength and weakness to this sampling technique. It captures the diversity of the population, but it also increases sampling error. Usually, cluster sampling is used because it is cheaper and easier than waiting to develop or purchase a full listing of the population (which, of course, is sometimes impossible). A researcher can always compensate for the increased error by increasing the sample size.

Cluster sampling is ideal when it would be impossible to obtain a complete listing of a population because such records do not exist. This was the problem encountered by Kim, Lujan,

and Dixon (1998) in their study of American Indians in Oklahoma. Many Indian communities are maintained through churches and civic organizations. Yet, intermarriages and urban migrations have weakened tribal and community structures, causing some Indians to be without tribal affiliation. Thus, a complete listing of Indians in Oklahoma was not available. Kim and colleagues used cluster sampling because it provided the best method for reflecting the geographical distribution of the Oklahoma Indian population. In selecting interview sites, the research team sought four clusters to balance urban and rural areas as well as geographic regions of the state. The four areas, or clusters, selected had sizable Indian populations as well as tribal organizations and agencies that provide social services to this population.

The sampling strategies just described are commonly used in communication research. Which one you choose is based on practicality, feasibility, and costs. The use of probability sampling is preferred when feasible because it provides greater confidence that the sample is representative of the population.

Nonprobability Sampling

Ideally, all samples would be randomly selected from the populations they represent. The alternative is **nonprobability sampling**, or sampling that does not rely on any form of random selection. Although the use of nonprobability samples weakens the sample in regard to population representativeness, these samples are commonly used in communication research when no other sampling technique will result in an adequate and appropriate sample. Nonprobability sampling is also used when researchers study communication variables that are believed to be generally distributed through a population. As you will see, there are also the obvious benefits of ease and economy—advantages that may induce researchers to use them.

More commonly, though, researchers use nonprobability sampling because they desire research participants with some special experience or communication ability. Using random selection techniques would not guarantee finding these

AN ETHICAL ISSUE

Participant Selection Can Make a Difference

Ethical questions arise when researchers make decisions about the research process, especially in the selection of research participants. Unfortunately, researchers may not always understand the consequences of the participant population they select. For example, much communication research is conducted on undergraduate students. Zakahi and McCroskey (1989) wanted to explore the degree to which a person's communication orientation could impact communication research. They hypothesized that individuals who did not like to interact or who were unwilling to communicate would not participate in such research requests compared to individuals who were willing to communicate. They found that individuals who had a high willingness to communicate were more likely to agree to participate in a study when first contacted and were more likely to show up for the study. One conclusion is that individuals who have a high willingness to communicate are more likely to be used in research studies. As consumers of research, you should ask yourself, "Did the population from which participants were chosen, or the way participants were chosen, make a difference in the results or in the interpretation of the results?"

participants. Finally, sometimes, there simply is no other alternative to nonprobability sampling because there is no practical way to identify all members of a population or to draw a sample if the population can be determined. Methods of nonprobability sampling are explored in the sections that follow.

Convenience Sampling   The easiest way to obtain a sample is to choose those individuals who are convenient to use. In **convenience sampling,** the researcher simply selects those people who are convenient to him or her as respondents. This can be a major disadvantage, particularly if you are seeking individuals who possess traits or characteristics similar to your traits and characteristics. For example, if you want to conduct a survey about alumni support, you may unconsciously select individuals, like you, who have supported their alma mater in the past. The problem, of course, is that a sample selected this way would be biased and not necessarily include individuals who do not provide alumni support. A convenience sample cannot guarantee that all eligible units have an equal chance of being included in the sample. Moreover, this type of

sample makes it more difficult to make inferences because it is impossible to tell to what degree the sample is representative of the population.

Despite these disadvantages, communication research often relies on convenience sampling for several reasons. In some cases, using a convenience sample is the only way to gain access to the desired population. For example, most researchers would agree that getting access to surgical teams is a problem. Cooperation from medical facilities is necessary to gain organizational entry, and then cooperation from physicians is necessary to gain access to the surgical team. To help overcome the limitations of a convenience sample, Lammers and Krikorian (1997) approached several different types of medical facilities and used several different data collection techniques.

Second, most researchers have immediate access to a body of students who can be encouraged to participate in research studies through requiring research participation as a course responsibility or giving extra credit. Thus, the sample is convenient to the researcher, but also accidental in that participants are available to the

DESIGN CHECK

Are Students Too Convenient?

Many researchers continue to use students as their convenience samples. Does that raise any problems or sources of error? It can, depending on how students came to participate in the research project. Some students participate because of course requirements or because they need the extra credit from such participation. Other students participate because they are genuinely curious about the research process or the topic being investigated.

In what ways could a student convenience sample bias the results? Perhaps all of the students come from one course and have just had a unit on compliance gaining, the topic under investigation in the experiment. Or perhaps students participate because they feel pressure from their professor to participate. Could it be possible that students who participate in studies toward the end of the semester are different from those who participate at the beginning of the semester? There could be if extra credit was offered for their participation. Students who desire extra credit as insurance for their grade in the beginning of the semester are likely to be different from students who need extra credit at the end of the semester.

A student sample can be studied to generalize back to a student population, particularly when the research inquiry focuses on instructional practices in the college classroom, or other issues relevant to college students. However, could a convenience sample of students drawn from your university be used to generalize results to the population of working adults in your community? To the population of organizational members who conduct performance evaluations? To the population of moviegoers nationwide? You should carefully assess the conclusions drawn by researchers when a convenience sample of students is used.

researcher by virtue of their selection and schedule of classes. The communication discipline is not unique with respect to this problem. The field of psychology has received the same criticism for using convenience samples of college undergraduates. Some scholars have investigated the extent to which using college students in research differs from using nonstudent participants (Field & Barnett, 1978).

Unfortunately, the results are not clear. Thus, two perspectives on the use of convenience samples exist. The first suggests that researchers should use convenience samples only when resources are not available for probability sampling. The second suggests nonprobability sampling can be used if researchers are not trying to apply findings of a sample directly to a population. Much of communication research is descriptive rather than predictive. Therefore, researchers

are not necessarily trying to infer results from a sample to a population. When this is the case, convenience samples are less problematic (Stanovich, 1986). Of course, using a theoretically driven research design helps counter some of these criticisms (Shapiro, 2002).

Volunteer Sampling   Using volunteers is another form of nonrandom sampling. In **volunteer sampling,** the researcher relies on individuals who express interest in the topic or who willing to participate in research. Initially you may believe that it is best for people to volunteer to be part of your study. Logistically, their volunteering may expedite the research process. However, there is evidence to suggest that people who volunteer to participate in research studies are "better educated, have higher occupational status, [are] higher in the need for approval, score higher on intelligence tests, [are] less authoritarian, and [are] better adjusted than nonvolunteers" (Katzer et al., 1978, p. 52). So if a research study is examining one of these characteristics or a related characteristic, volunteer participants can certainly bias (although unknowingly) the results.

One way in which a volunteer sample can be obtained is through a gatekeeper. McLaurin (1995) approached teachers, principals, and administrators at middle and high schools about using their students in his research project on rap music and pro-social messages directed to African American at-risk students. Targeting schools in ethnically homogeneous communities, McLaurin simply approached these gatekeepers and asked if classes of students could participate in his research project. Classes of students were volunteered for a variety of reasons. Sometimes it was purely coincidental scheduling in that the researchers were available to conduct the sessions when a class had a break in its schedule. Other times, teachers had a "hole" in their lesson plans and were willing to take a break from day-to-day teaching responsibilities. In some cases, a substitute was willing to give the class over to the research project. And, actually, some principals simply volunteered a class.

Even though others volunteered them, the researcher still had to obtain students' consent to participate. Interestingly, all students were eager to participate; no one asked to be excused from the project. Students also had to get their parents' permission to participate in the project. Again, not one parent denied permission.

In this case, gaining volunteers as research participants through gatekeepers worked well because the researcher targeted an appropriate population for his study on rap music. Students were eager to volunteer to participate because they felt that no one had ever asked them their opinions (P. McLaurin, personal communication, February 16, 2000).

Inclusion and Exclusion Criteria   A third way of obtaining a nonprobability sample is to establish an inclusion or exclusion criterion. An **inclusion criterion** identifies the people or elements that meet some specific characteristic. For example, to

study how the role of fatherhood has changed, Morman and Floyd (2002) sought father–son dyads so they could investigate the quality of men's relationships with their fathers as well as their sons. To qualify for the study, men had to have at least one son 12 years old or older, and both father and son had to agree to participate in the study. Thus, three inclusion criteria were used: (1) only men with sons could participate, (2) the son had to be at least 12 years old, and (3) both father and son had to agree to participate.

Alternately, an **exclusion criterion** rules out people or elements from participating in your survey or study based on some specific characteristic. For example, in a study of television advertising geared toward children (Kunkel & Gantz, 1993), researchers videotaped a composite week of children's programming in seven medium-to-large television markets. Certain times of the day were selected for videotaping because some time slots are more likely to broadcast programming for children (an inclusion criterion). There was no guarantee, however, that programs taped during these targeted times met that criterion. Researchers reviewed the taped programming and excluded any program that was originally produced to appeal to general audiences, even though the programming appeared in the selected time slots and children were part of the viewing audience. Thus, the exclusion criterion could be described as any programming produced to appeal to general audiences.

Inclusion and exclusion criteria set boundaries or limits for a sample. This is still a nonprobability sample because you are including or excluding individuals or elements on a case-by-base basis and not ensuring that all potential members of the population have been identified.

Snowball Sampling   In some cases, snowball sampling or network sampling is the only type of sampling to use, particularly when the research topic is controversial or a specific population of participants is difficult to find. **Snowball sampling,** a nonprobability sampling technique, is used when participants help researchers obtain their sample by identifying other similar participants.

For example, to find married couples or domestic partners, Walker and Dickson (2004) used

DESIGN CHECK

Justifying Nonprobability Sampling

Anytime a nonprobability sample is used, you should read the study closely to detect your satisfaction with the way in which the study was conducted and to see if the researcher addresses potential sources of sampling bias. These questions can guide your analysis and acceptance of the findings:

- How does the author use theory as a foundation for the hypotheses or research questions asked?
- Did the author address potential sources of sampling bias?
- Did the researcher use procedures that could compensate for or eliminate potential biases?
- Does the sampling bias (reported or not reported) affect your acceptance of the results of the study?
- In what ways did the researcher justify the use of nonprobability sampling?

snowball sampling. When couples met the selection criteria and participated in the study, the research team gave them flyers and encouraged them to pass along the flyers to other couples. Why? It's common for people to know and associate with others with similar characteristics. Thus, the sample grows, or snowballs, as participants help the researcher identify more participants with the same characteristics.

Network Sampling   Unlike snowball sampling, **network sampling** does not rely on research participants for help in identifying the sample. Rather, the researcher actively solicits individuals who fit a specific profile and asks them to participate in the research study. For example, Ford (2003) asked both traditional and nontraditional students to seek a variety of adults in their personal and professional networks to participate in a study on customers' perceptions of satisfaction with the service provided by their physician, dentist, auto mechanic, or hairdresser. Was using the networks of students a successful strategy for identifying eligible couples? Yes, and by relying on interpersonal networks other than her own, the researcher was more likely to gather data from individuals with broader and more diverse customer service experiences.

Purposive Sampling   When researchers want to select cases that are typical of the population of interest, they use **purposive sampling,** which depends on the judgment of the researcher, who hand-picks the cases to be included in the sample. Purposive sampling is completely dependent on the researcher's ability to know what is typical (Selltiz et al., 1959). To help control the bias in such a process, researchers should spend considerable time developing what is "typical" about the population. From there, the researcher can develop some objective basis for making judgments to include or not include an element in the sample.

Purposive sampling is often used when sensitive topics are of research interest or very specialized populations are sought. For example, Petronio, Reeder, Hecht, and Ros-Mendoza (1996) used purposive sampling techniques to find sexually abused children and adolescents to participate in their research project. With approval from their university's human subjects committee, the research team used a gatekeeper to find appropriate participants. A social service worker who treated sexual abuse survivors identified those children and adolescents under her care who had already voluntarily disclosed their abuse to peers, family, or friends.

Potential participants for the study had to meet two conditions. First, they had to be victims of sexual abuse, and second, they must have already disclosed this information to others. These children became the population for the study. To select the sample, the social worker then contacted the parents of the children; members of the research team followed up with the parents to discuss the nature of the study. Parental permission for each child was obtained. Obviously, the difficulty and restrictions in obtaining this type of sample required that the research team use purposive sampling as well as the assistance of a gatekeeper. Purposive sampling was required because of the desire to find research participants with unique experiences who were willing to talk about those experiences with researchers.

Quota Sampling   In **quota sampling,** the researcher uses the target, or *quota,* as a goal for seeking people or elements that fit the characteristics of the subgroup. Once the researcher meets the quota for each subgroup, data collection is complete. Researchers use the following steps to select a quota sample. As in stratified sampling, the population is divided into subgroups that do not overlap. The subgroups must be mutually exclusive. That is, a person or element should not be a member of more than one subgroup. The number of elements in the subgroup is calculated as a proportion of the total population. Once sample size is decided, then a proportional number of cases or elements from each subgroup becomes a target number of cases to fill.

A study of working women's experiences with sexual harassment (Clair, 1993) illustrates why quota sampling can be the preferred sampling technique. Using figures for four demographic characteristics (occupation, marital status, race, and full-time or part-time employment) from the U.S. Bureau of Labor Statistics as a base, the researcher created a matrix for a sample of 50 to be proportional to the census data. With the matrix as their target, research assistants used a networking and referral system (first asking relatives, friends, and coworkers and eventually asking friends of friends, acquaintances, and strangers) to help identify women who could fulfill the quota sample. This

sampling technique was effective in this case because Clair wanted to interview women who had the same characteristics, and in similar proportions, as reported by the government.

As another example of quota sampling, Webster and Lin (2002) needed to find a way to limit the sample of websites and their users. First, they limited the population to the top 200 websites as reported by Nielsen/NetRatings. Identifying the unit of analysis as pairs of websites, the researchers then had to compare sites based on their content (similar or different; for example, a news site is different than an entertainment site) and structure (similar or different; for example, a website from the same family, or domain, of websites). A 2×2 matrix was developed that represented four types of website pairs: similar content and similar structure; different content and different structure; similar content and different structure; or different content and similar structure. Using the statistics of web use provided to them, the research team could select pairs of websites that met these conditions and their quota of 20 for each condition.

Sample Size

Regardless of which technique is used, the size of the sample must also be determined prior to selecting the sample. **Sample size** is the number of people from whom you need to observe or collect data to obtain precise and reliable findings (Fink, 1995b). Notice that this number would be less than the number of people you ask to participate, or the number of people who sign up to participate. It is common for researchers to oversample to ensure that the sample size needed is met. There are both practical and theoretical issues to be addressed in considering sample size. Practically, the larger the sample, the higher the costs to conduct the survey or experiment. For example, in survey research, a larger sample size would increase the number of people needed to administer the survey; costs associated with paper, copying, and postage; and costs associated with data entry and data processing.

Theoretically, the larger the sample relative to its population, the less error or bias introduced into the study. Hence, a sample representing a

TRY THIS!   **Identifying Populations, Generating Samples**

For each of the types of participants or elements listed below, specify the population and the sampling frame. Then describe how you would select the sample. Be sure to assess any source of potential bias.

Specify the Population	*Specify the Sampling Frame*	*Describe Sample Selection Procedures*	*Potential Biases From How Population Was Defined or How Sample Was Selected*
Example: Children who play more than 20 hours of video games per week	Children under the age of 10 who attend Elm Elementary school whose parents participate in the parent–teacher organization	Use a roster of parents in the organization to generate a systematic random sample	Students are likely to be from the same socio-economic background
Young couples who plan to be married in the next year			
Retired men and women who participate in senior citizen activities			
Manager and employee dyads that have worked together for less than 1 year			
Amateur sports teams that have remained intact despite past losing seasons			
Segments of radio talk-show hosts' interaction with on-air, in-studio guests			

Did you choose probability or nonprobability samples? What arguments could you provide for the choices you made? What are the strengths and weaknesses of your sampling procedures? What procedural or logistical problems would you expect to encounter trying to identify, communicate with, or attract these candidates to participate in a research project?

AN ETHICAL ISSUE

Selected, But Not Required to Participate

In identifying the research population and in selecting the sample, recall that no one can or should be forced to participate in a research project. This ethical principle remains regardless of the difficulty, time, or expense a researcher experiences in locating a sampling frame or in selecting a sample. For many communication research projects, finding enough participants with the characteristics you desire is not a problem. But, for research projects requiring a more specialized type of person or experience, it can be frustrating to find a potential participant who meets your criteria, is asked to participate, and refuses. When interacting with potential participants, courtesy and respect is an utmost consideration. Although someone may refuse your request to participate in a research project, perhaps your respectful acceptance of their refusal will encourage them to consider such a request in the future.

---

larger proportion of the population results in more accurate data (Kerlinger, 1986). This is particularly true with respect to probability sampling. Simply put, larger samples provide greater opportunity for randomization to work.

The following principles can help you in selecting a sample size for a research project (Barker & Barker, 1989; Fowler, 1993). First, estimate the size of the population. Now, look at the subgroups within the total population. Taking the smallest of the subgroups, estimate how large a sample will be required to provide an adequate sample of this subgroup. What you are doing is looking for the minimum sample size that can be tolerated for the smallest subgroups within the population of interest. Recognize, however, that the greater the number of subgroups you are interested in, the larger the sample must be to ensure representativeness of each subgroup.

There is seldom a definitive answer to how large a sample should be, but Table 7.1 (on p. 123) provides guidelines that most researchers accept as the convention for selecting sample size. As you determine your sample size, reflect on its ability to be representative of the population. This is the primary criterion for choosing sample size, whether you are using a probability or a nonprobability sampling technique.

Regardless of how a researcher selects the sample or determines its size, he or she is responsible for justifying both selection and size issues in the written research report. All sampling decisions are subjective and strategic. And most sampling decisions create some type of bias. Thus, sampling decisions should be described and explained in the methods section of a research article (Ryan, 1998).

A Final Word on Sampling

As a researcher conducting a study or as a consumer of research reports, you should include or be aware of five pieces of information about sampling issues that should be available in research reports. If you can answer "yes" to the following questions, then **population validity,** or the degree to which the sample represents and can be generalized to the population, exists (Lowry, 1978):

- Is the population, or the aggregation of persons or objects, under investigation defined?
- Is the sampling frame identified?
- Are the sampling procedures described in detail? Is the type of sampling procedure (probability, nonprobability) described?
- Is the completion, participation, or return rate specified?
- Is the geographic area of the population and sample described?

SIGNIFICANCE LEVELS

In quantitative research, once the sample is selected, the researcher turns to the issue of setting significance levels. Significance levels are based on probability. *Probability* is a scientific term to identify how much error the researcher finds acceptable in a particular statistical test. But you are also familiar with the concept of probability in a less scientific sense. You have made many decisions in your life based on the degree of probability for some event occurring. Did you ever drive to the beach even though rain clouds were approaching from the west? Have you ever gambled that you had enough gas to get you to your destination? Did you ask either your mother or your father for money based on the likelihood of which one would give it to you? In these decisions and others similar to them, you were basing your actions on your informal rules of probability. In other words, you accepted a certain degree of risk, or error, in making these decisions. It probably would not rain, but what if it did? The last time your fuel gauge was close to empty you drove another 50 miles without a problem. And you knew better than to ask your dad. He always said no, while your mom usually said yes.

In scientific research, **probability** is an estimate of "what would happen if the study were actually repeated many times, telling the researcher how wrong the results can be" (Katzer et al., 1978, p. 60). In other words, probability is a calculation about the validity of the results. Researchers could choose to conduct the same survey or experiment many times, but calculating the probability, or significance, of a statistical test for a sample of data has become the accepted manner in which scientists deal with this issue. As a result, the level of probability provides an estimate of the degree to which data from a sample would reflect data from the population the sample was drawn from.

Perhaps you are thinking, "Why wouldn't the results of a study be valid?" Generally, researchers are looking to make inferences from the sample, or people who participated in their particular study, to the population, or larger group from which the sample was pulled.

Besides using an appropriate sampling technique, researchers establish a threshold of acceptance for each statistical test. Accepting the conclusions derived from the sample and assuming that those conclusions are also applicable to the population is known as **statistical inference.** Social scientists base this inference on the probability level computed for each statistical test. However, the principle of statistical inference applies only if probability sampling is used. It is inappropriate to infer conclusions from a sample to a population if researchers choose nonprobability sampling.

The **probability level,** or **significance level,** which is established for each statistical test used prior to computing the statistical test, is the level of error the researcher is willing to accept. You will find this symbolized in written research reports as the letter p or referred to as the **alpha level.** If the probability level of the statistical test is acceptable, or within the traditions of the discipline, then the findings are believed to be real, not random, and the inference can be presumed to be valid. If the probability level is unacceptable, then no conclusion can be drawn (Boster, 2002).

Generally, the probability level of .05 is accepted as the standard in the communication discipline. This means that 5 out of 100 findings that appear to be valid will, in fact, be due to chance. When the probability level of a statistical test is .05 or less, the finding is real, and labeled as statistically significant. Setting the standard as a .05 probability level is arbitrary, and, generally, communication researchers have adopted this standard (.01 and .001 are other common standards). You should note, however, that the selection of a .05 probability level was not based on mathematical, statistical, or substantive theory (Henkel, 1976).

If the probability level of a statistical test is greater than .05 (for example, $p = .15$, $p = .21$), then the finding is labeled nonsignificant. This means that the difference could easily be caused by chance or random error. What causes the probability level to be unacceptable, or higher than .05? Many different things can contribute to high probability levels.

Items on a survey or questionnaire intended to measure one construct may be so poorly written that participants respond inconsistently to them. In instances where many different interviewers are used, open-ended questions are often answered in such widely disparate ways that acceptable probability will not result. The researcher or assistants conducting an experiment can also create bias that generates unacceptable levels of probability. For example, male participants may be treated differently than female participants. Research assistants may unconsciously smile at participants they know and ignore those with whom they are unfamiliar. Of course, research participants also bring their own types of bias with them to the research process and with it the potential for error. What kind of bias or error might you, as a research participant, introduce? Did you get enough sleep last night? Are you hungry? Did you just receive a test back with a poor grade?

It is important to remember that setting the significance level at .05 is arbitrary. There can be good reasons to make the probability level more rigorous, setting it, for example, at .01. In their study of the effectiveness of message strategies for talking about AIDS and condom use, Reel and Thompson (1994) set the level at <.01. Why? The probability level needed to be more rigorous because the results of the study have direct implications for AIDS education efforts. Thus, the researchers had to create greater certainty about the results they achieved. Because a person's health could be at risk, they would not want to recommend strategies as being effective when that effectiveness in the study could have resulted from random chance or error.

Seldom is there a good reason to set the probability level at a more generous level of .10—in doing so the researcher would be allowing more opportunity for research results to support a claim when, in reality, it is not supported.

It is tempting to believe that achieving statistical significance proves something. Recognize, however, that achieving statistical significance does not guarantee **social significance** of the result (Selltiz et al., 1959). Using a very large sample can create statistically significant differences that have little relevance in application. Also recognize that how a researcher interprets a statistical finding is as important as the level of significance the

researcher chooses. The research process is more subjective than objective. Thus, statistical significance must always be interpreted with respect to social and practical significance—or how the results might actually be applied or used in everyday life (Kirk, 1996). Statistical significance must also be interpreted with respect to how the population was defined and to how the sample was selected.

HYPOTHESIS TESTING

Recall from Chapter 3 that hypotheses state the expected relationship or difference between two or more variables. Also recall that whereas scientific tradition privileges the alternative hypothesis in the writing of journal articles, it is technically the null hypothesis that is statistically tested. Hypothesis testing relies on the two scientific techniques you just read about—sampling and significance testing.

Testing the null hypothesis is, in essence, an act of decision making. Do you accept the alternative explanation, or do you retain the null hypothesis? Most researchers rely on the conventions of hypothesis testing because, combined with random sampling and significance testing, they can be effective in separating those hypotheses and their results that deserve additional attention from those that do not (Harlow, 1997). But, as with significance levels, these traditions are not absolute.

Researchers develop an alternative hypothesis, an assertion that states how they believe the variables are related or are different. However, in hypothesis testing, belief in the null hypothesis continues until there is sufficient evidence to make the assertion of the null hypothesis unreasonable. This decision is based on a comparison between the significance level established by the researcher prior to conducting the study, usually .05, and the significance level produced by the calculation of the statistical test. If the significance level computed for the statistical test is .05 or less, the alternative hypothesis is accepted. However, if the significance level computed for the statistical test is greater than .05, the null hypothesis is retained, as no conclusion can be

TABLE 7.2 Relationship Between Type I and Type II Errors

	In Reality, the Null Hypothesis Is True	*In Reality, the Null Hypothesis Is False*
Researcher uses level of significance to reject the null hypothesis.	**Type I Error**—The null hypothesis is rejected even though it is true, OR researcher claims some difference or relationship exists when one does not.	**Decision 1**—The null hypothesis is rejected when it is false (or the alternative hypothesis is accepted), OR researcher claims some difference or relationship exists and that difference or relationship is found.
Researcher uses level of significance to retain the null hypothesis.	**Decision 2**—The null hypothesis is retained (or the researcher fails to reject the null hypothesis) when it is true, OR researcher does not claim a difference or relationship, and one is not identified.	**Type II Error**—The null hypothesis is retained even though it is false, OR researcher misses claiming a difference or relationship that is real.

drawn about the relationship or difference between the variables tested.

In the hypothesis testing process, two types of error can occur. Known as Type I and Type II errors, these represent decision errors in accepting or rejecting the null hypothesis. **Type I error** occurs when the null hypothesis is rejected even when it is true. The level of Type I error is set or controlled by the researcher when he or she chooses the significance level for the statistical test. Often called the alpha level, it is the same as the level of significance described earlier. Thus, if the significance level is set at .05, then there is a 5% chance that the null hypothesis will be rejected even though it is true. This means that you run some risk in accepting the premise of the alternative, or research, hypothesis when in fact the premise would not hold. Another way of interpreting the .05 alpha level is to recognize that this significance level will retain a true null hypothesis 95% of the time. Recognize that anytime hypotheses are tested, some error of this type will occur.

Alternately, **Type II error** occurs in the opposite case. Now the level of significance is not met. Thus, the researchers simultaneously fail to reject, or they accept, the null hypothesis and reject the alternative hypothesis. Type II error results when the alternative hypothesis is rejected even when it is true. One way the researcher can control

the level of Type II error is to increase the sample size.

Table 7.2 can help you see the relationship between Type I and Type II errors. With each hypothesis tested, four outcomes are possible. Obviously, the goal of research is to make good decisions. However, the research process is not perfect, and error and bias can be introduced in many places—for example, errors can occur in selection of sample and in measurement. Hypothesis testing allows the researcher opportunities to control some of the error. Type I error can be controlled in setting a significance level that is appropriate. Type II error can be controlled by increasing the sample size.

You will find both types of decisions about hypotheses—Decision 1 and Decision 2 in Table 7.2—in the research literature. Looking at an example for each will help you apply these decision rules about hypotheses to a research setting. There is a growing literature intended to find strategies to help college students avoid peer pressure for harmful activities, especially drinking alcohol. The purpose of one study (Harrington, 1997) was to identify and investigate the strategies college students use in persuading others to drink alcohol and to determine what strategies are most effective in refusing those offers. Much of the previous research had been conducted using participants' recall, or retrospective

Addressing Issues of Sampling, Significance Levels, and Hypothesis Testing

In reading scholarly reports, you should be able to identify how the researcher addressed sampling, significance levels, and hypothesis testing. The following questions can help you:

- How has the researcher described the population, sampling frame, and sample?
- In your opinion, do the most appropriate people or units comprise the sample? Was the sample appropriately selected?
- Do the characteristics of the sample affect your acceptance of the researcher's conclusions?
- What significance level is reported for each of the statistical tests reported in the research report?
- How does the statistical significance level relate to the practical significance of the study?
- Do you agree with the researcher's decisions about accepting or rejecting the research hypothesis?

accounts, of these situations, so many details of how the offer strategies and refusal strategies work might be concealed.

To explore those interactions, college students participated in interactive laboratory sessions, with each participant assigned to one of eight conditions based on type of resistance strategy to be used by a confederate. Research participants were asked to role-play a party situation and were asked to offer their confederate partner an alcoholic drink. Harrington (1997) hypothesized that "The most common persuasive strategy overall will be a simple offer" (p. 232), something, for example, like "Do you want a drink?" Based on the results of the study, this hypothesis was supported; participants were more likely to use a simple offer than any other type of offer in trying to persuade their confederate partner to drink alcohol. These decisions, like Decision 1 in Table 7.2, are presented in research reports in the following ways:

- The hypothesis is supported.
- The alternative hypothesis is accepted.
- Support was found for this hypothesis.

- The results were statistically significant.
- Results support this prediction.
- Results support this hypothesis.
- The hypothesis is confirmed.

In essence, the researcher is saying that the alternative hypothesis asserted some difference or relationship and that the research succeeded in finding that very difference or relationship. Many researchers do not use phrases like "reject the null hypothesis" because technically, the null hypothesis can never be rejected since there is always some possibility that it is true. This is where the level of significance comes into play. Remember that researchers set the alpha level, usually at .05 and never at .00. Thus, we can never be absolutely certain about the truth of the null hypothesis.

Using the same study, we can also examine Decision 2 from Table 7.2. Recall that researchers are usually interested in the research, or alternative, hypothesis even though they are statistically testing the null hypothesis. It is unusual for researchers to want to confirm the null. So how do researchers describe Decision 2 when their results do not support the alternative hypothesis?

Harrington (1997) also hypothesized that "resistance to a complex offer will more likely be met with additional persuasion than resistance to a simple offer" (p. 232). In other words, a research participant would be more likely to use additional persuasive techniques if he or she initially made a complex drink offer and the confederate refused than if the initial offer was a simple one and the confederate refused. This hypothesis was not supported. In fact, research participants used more persuasive attempts after initially using a simple offer than after initially using a complex one. These decisions, like Decision 2 in Table 7.2, are presented in research reports in the following ways:

- The [alternative] hypothesis was not supported.
- The results were not statistically significant.
- The null hypothesis is accepted.
- Results failed to support the [alternative] hypothesis
- No support emerged for the [alternative] hypothesis.
- The [alternative] hypothesis is rejected.

In essence, the researcher is saying that the alternative hypothesis asserted some difference or relationship and that the research could not confirm that very difference or relationship. Thus, the null hypothesis is retained.

How do significance level and these principles of hypothesis testing apply to research questions? Recall that a research question is used because there is not enough prior evidence from which to develop a position or an assertion for a hypothesis. When a research question is used, the researcher uses the results to answer the question. Whereas hypotheses make assertions that must be responded to with a "yes, you are correct" or "no, you are not correct" type of decision, a research question poses a question that can be answered in a greater variety of ways. Thus, even though researchers set a significance level for their statistical tests associated with research questions, there is no way to "accept" or "reject" a research question.

A FINAL WORD

One of the difficulties in learning about scientific traditions is to recognize that the principles addressed in this chapter are just that, traditions. There is not an absolute or objective set of research procedures that guarantee correct interpretation of results or that can be justified in every case (Abelson, 1997). In fact, the traditions used for setting significance levels and hypothesis testing have been widely disputed by scientists from many disciplines (Boster, 2002; Carver, 1978; Harlow, Mulaik, & Steiger, 1997; Judd, McClelland, & Culhane, 1995; Oakes, 1986).

One way to integrate the use of scientific traditions but still honor the subjective interpretations of researchers is to view these traditions as interpretive tools rather than as absolute decision makers. These traditions invoke strong language—fail to reject the null hypothesis, accept the alternative hypothesis—that overemphasizes an either/or decision. A more contemporary view is that scientific traditions should aid the judgment of the researcher, not dictate it (Abelson, 1995).

SUMMARY

1. A population is all units—people or things—possessing the attributes or characteristics that interest the researcher.

2. A sample, or subset, is selected from the population through probability or nonprobability sampling.

3. Generalizability is the extent to which conclusions drawn from a sample can be extended to a population.

4. Sampling error is the degree to which a sample differs from population characteristics.

5. Probability sampling ensures that the selected sample is sufficiently representative of the population as every person or element has an equal chance of being selected.

6. In a simple random sample, every person or element has an equal chance of being selected for a study.

7. In systematic sampling, every *n*th, for example every 14th, element is selected for the sample.

8. A stratified random sample first groups members according to categories of interest before random techniques are used.

9. Cluster sampling is used when all members of elements of a population cannot be identified and occurs in two stages: (1) the population is identified by its groups, and (2) then random sampling occurs within groups.

10. Nonprobability sampling weakens the representativeness of a sample to the population because it does not rely on random sampling; however, it is used when no other sampling technique will result in an adequate and appropriate sample.

11. Types of nonprobability sampling include convenience, volunteer, inclusion and exclusion, snowball, networking, purposive, and quota samples.

12. Sample size is estimated from the size of the population and the level of error a researcher is willing to tolerate.

13. Significance levels are set for each statistical test used in a research project; generally, the probability level of .05 is accepted as the standard in communication research.

14. Hypothesis testing is based on probability sampling techniques and the stated level of significance.

15. By convention, researchers are interested in the alternative hypothesis but statistically test the null hypothesis.

16. Hypothesis testing is an act of decision making—accepting the alternative hypothesis or retaining the null hypothesis.

17. Type I and Type II errors occur when researchers accept or reject results as valid when the opposite is true.

KEY TERMS

alpha level

biased

census

cluster sampling

confidence interval

confidence level

convenience sampling

exclusion criterion

generalizability

inclusion criterion

network sampling

nonprobability sampling

population

population validity

probability

probability level

probability sampling

purposive sampling

quota sampling

random

replication

sample

sample size

sampling error

sampling frame

significance level

simple random sampling

snowball sampling

social significance

statistical inference

stratified random sampling

systematic sampling

Type I error

Type II error

volunteer sampling

CHAPTER EIGHT

Quantitative Research Designs

Chapter Checklist

After reading this chapter, you should be able to:

1. Select and develop the appropriate research design for your hypotheses or research questions.

2. Understand the strengths and limitations of each design form as it relates to research findings, and argue for your design choices.

3. Explain the benefits of experimental forms over quasi-experimental and descriptive forms.

4. Facilitate appropriate random assignment of participants to treatment and control groups.

5. Manipulate independent variables according to their theoretical foundation.

6. Conduct manipulation checks of independent variables.

7. Interpret findings from experimental and quasi-experimental designs with respect to cause–effect relationships.

8. Appropriately interpret findings from descriptive research designs.

9. Develop a research protocol to limit researcher effects and procedural bias when conducting research studies.

There are three types of quantitative research design: experimental forms, quasi-experimental forms, and descriptive forms. These forms differ in fundamental ways on two characteristics: manipulation of independent variables and random assignment of participants to treatments or conditions (Pedhazur & Schmelkin, 1991). The first characteristic on which quantitative research designs differ—**manipulation** of independent variables—occurs when the researcher intentionally varies or changes how the independent variable is presented to participants. This fundamental characteristic must be satisfied to locate a research study in the classic experimental framework. Manipulation of independent variables also occurs in quasi-experimental research designs but is absent from descriptive forms.

The second characteristic on which quantitative research designs differ—**random assignment** of participants to treatments or conditions—is unique to experimental forms. After being selected to participate in the experiment, the researcher randomly assigns individuals to one of at least two groups. One group is the control group and is not exposed to the independent variable, or the control group receives only the standard level of the independent variable, which serves as a baseline against which the treatment groups are evaluated. Other groups are labeled as experimental groups, or treatment groups, with each group receiving a different treatment or level of the independent

variable. This characteristic is absent from both quasi-experimental and descriptive forms. Figure 8.1 demonstrates how these two characteristics differ for the three quantitative research designs.

Initially developed for study in the physical sciences, experimental forms can be found in all disciplines related to communication education, management, psychology, and sociology. Due to their widespread acceptance, the essential characteristics of the experimental framework have become the standard by which quasi-experimental and descriptive forms of research are evaluated. All three types of quantitative research design are explored and relevant communication examples are presented in this chapter.

THE EXPERIMENTAL FRAMEWORK

When researchers are curious about causes, they often turn to **experimental research,** which has a long tradition in the social sciences, including communication. This type of research is most often conducted in the laboratory or in other simulated environments that are controlled by researchers. Alternately, researchers can conduct experiments in the field, or naturally occurring environments. This type of experiment is very popular with communication scholars who study applied communication problems.

	Experimental forms	Quasi-experimental forms	Descriptive forms
Manipulation of independent variables	Present: researcher controlled	Present: natural variation	Absent
Random assignment of participants to conditions	Present	Absent	Absent

FIGURE 8.1 Three Forms of Quantitative Research Designs

The traditional definition of an *experiment,* one often associated with the physical sciences, would characterize it as the manipulation of the independent variable in a controlled laboratory setting conducted on a randomly selected sample of participants who are randomly assigned to control or treatment groups. A broader definition of **experiment** and one that fits the study of communication phenomena more appropriately is the recording of measurements and observations made by defined procedures and in defined conditions. The data collected or produced by these procedures are then examined by appropriate statistical tests to determine the existence of significant differences between and relationships among variables.

Experimental research is chosen when a researcher wants to determine causation. In other words, a researcher has developed a hypothesis that asserts that one variable, the independent, causes a second variable, the dependent. Experimentation allows a researcher to evaluate hypotheses that have been developed from theories in the literature. In this case, results from previous research studies generate new questions, and the researcher wants to answer the questions "Why?" and "How?" Experimentation is also chosen when researchers want to test a new method or technique. This is especially true of instructional techniques that are believed to have potential application in the classroom. Conducting an experiment allows the researcher to test one technique against another to see if differences between techniques exist. In other cases, experiments are conducted to explore the specific conditions under which a phenomenon occurs. By varying the conditions of the experiment, researchers can identify which environmental conditions, for example, are most likely to make speakers nervous.

When research is identified as experimental, the goal of the researcher is to establish or explain what caused a person's behavior, feelings, or attitudes to change. Because this is the goal, certain characteristics must be satisfied. First, the research design must have a temporal component, with one element occurring before another. For something to cause something else, the causal agent must precede the change

in behavior, feelings, or attitudes. In this way, an experiment provides control of one variable to test its effect on another variable. Second, there are comparisons between at least two groups. Finally, the entire experiment is conducted within a limited time frame, seldom more than 1 hour, with all of the interaction under the control and observation of the researcher.

When the word *experiment* is used, most people think of laboratory experiments. The primary defining characteristic of laboratory experiments is that the researcher structures the environment in which the investigation takes place and in which the data are collected (Miller, 1970). Conducting research in the lab environment serves several purposes. First, it physically isolates the research process from the day-to-day and routine interaction of participants. This isolation gives a researcher greater control over what participants are and are not exposed to. By limiting and controlling exposure in this way, a researcher is attempting to eliminate extraneous variables and influences that are not central to the investigation (Kerlinger, 1986).

Berger and DiBattista's (1993) study of communication failures demonstrates how the lab environment controls for extraneous influences. For example, giving directions is a normal and routine type of communication event, and most people have experienced communication failure as the sender (and receiver) in this type of interaction. Someone (whose first language is different from yours and who appears to you to be visiting your university) asks you for directions, and you provide what you believe is the needed detail. Although you have fulfilled the request and are satisfied with your directions, the other person responds, "I'm sorry, I don't understand English well. I had trouble following your directions. Could you give me the directions again?" (Berger & DiBattista, p. 225). So, you launch into the directions again, maybe emphasizing certain points or including additional information.

Over a long period of time and with a great deal of luck, a researcher might be able to overhear enough of these conversations to use the interaction as data for a study. More realistically, however, Berger and DiBattista created a laboratory experiment to study how people respond when they initially experience communication failure. In the lab, research participants were told that their task would be to give another person—actually, a confederate, someone who pretends to also be participating in the research project but is really helping the researcher—directions from where they were to a nearby train station. By working in the lab environment and using a confederate, the research team could control the type of directions requested and how the person to whom the directions were given would respond, as well as that person's age, race, and sex. The researchers provided further constraints by asking participants not to engage the other person in any dialogue or ask any questions.

Being in the lab controlled the interaction environment. Thus, the results of the study can be assumed to result from the conditions of the study rather than from any number of other influences (such as familiarity with the person receiving directions, outside physical noise that could prevent the conversational partners from hearing one another, research participants' lack of familiarity with the place to which they were giving directions).

Many universities and communication departments have rooms equipped as communication laboratories. Some are set up with one-way mirrors so that researchers can view what is going on, although participants cannot see the researchers. Some are equipped with sophisticated audio- and videotaping equipment, and internet and other communication technologies. Although some labs are relatively sterile in appearance, others are designed to simulate comfortable interaction environments like a living room, waiting area, or computer lab. Researchers without these types of laboratory environments often use traditional classroom space and temporarily transform it into a lab for research purposes.

Using manipulation and random assignment, researchers design and conduct a study, evaluate the evidence, and then develop a causal explanation for what has occurred. Experimental designs are deliberate, standardized, and used as the research protocol in many disciplines. Their strength lies in the control they provide to researchers, which in turn helps them eliminate

rival explanations for the changes they observe and record. Several of the experimental designs more commonly used in communication research are described in the following sections.

The Classical Experiment

Researchers devised the classical, or true, experimental form as a technique to help them in assigning causation. Many researchers believe that the experiment is the most powerful research form for testing cause–effect relationships. The clear logic of its design helps researchers eliminate many of the other explanations that can be given for the results found.

In a **classical experiment,** the researcher controls the treatment or the manipulation of the independent variable by randomly assigning participants to treatment or control groups. A **treatment,** or manipulation, is one of the ways in which the researcher varies the type of stimuli or the amount or level of stimuli presented to research participants. This fundamental characteristic must be satisfied to locate a research study in the classical experimental framework.

Experiments allow researchers to test two types of hypotheses—those that predict differences and those that predict relationships. Recall from Chapter 3 that hypotheses test differences and relationships between and among variables, not the variables themselves (Kerlinger, 1986). For the first type of hypothesis—the difference hypothesis—the experiment is designed so that the independent variable precedes the dependent variable in temporal order. Thus, the corresponding hypothesis predicts that the independent variable causes changes, or effects, in the dependent variable. For the second type of hypothesis—the relational hypothesis—the experiment is designed so that two variables, the independent and dependent, occur close together. The hypothesis predicts that the two variables exist together in some type of relationship where the value of the independent variable is causing a change in the value of the dependent variable. See Chapters 11 and 12, respectively, for the statistical tests that accompany these hypotheses.

The researcher also controls the order of variables in an experiment. One element, the independent variable, cannot be considered the cause of another element, the dependent variable, if the independent variable occurs after the dependent variable (Selltiz et al., 1959). Simply put, the independent variable can be considered the cause of changes in the dependent only if the independent precedes the dependent or if the two occur close together.

With this level of control, experiments are designed to demonstrate a cause–effect relationship. Still, an experiment may not be able to provide a complete explanation of why an effect occurs. Remember that researchers rely upon a theoretical base to provide a foundation for the variables in the study and from which to develop hypotheses. Thus, for the experiment to reflect a causal relationship, the cause, or independent variable, must come before the effect, or dependent variable. The gap between the two variables can vary greatly—from just a few minutes to years—but the variables must have a time order. The dependent variable must also be capable of change. Some variables cannot be changed in experiments. Your sex, for example, will not be changed by a researcher's intervention. But your attitude toward a public relations campaign can be. Finally, the causal relationship between and among the variables must have theoretical plausibility. In other words, the presumed reason for the causal effect must make sense (de Vaus, 2001).

Random Assignment of Participants In any experiment in which the researcher wants to compare two or more groups, the underlying principle is that individuals in the groups are equivalent before the treatment. To achieve equivalency, participants are *randomly assigned* to treatment or control groups. This means that each participant has an equal chance of being assigned to either group. Selecting a random sample from an appropriate population is not the same as randomly assigning individuals to treatment and control groups. The two procedures together help eliminate any true differences between individuals in the groups before the treatment is applied. Thus, the researcher can argue that differences that result after the treatment is applied are caused by the independent variable.

For example, to test the effects of different types of alcohol warning messages, participants 21 to 65 years old who used alcohol a minimum of once a month were recruited for a study (Slater, Karan, Rouner, & Walter, 2002). They were randomly assigned to different visual conditions. Some participants saw car crash scenes like those commonly shown in public service announcements about drinking and driving. Other participants saw drinking scenes in social settings, such as bars and living rooms. The first condition, the threatening visual condition, included an audio track of sirens; the second condition, the nonthreatening visual condition, included an audio track of conversation typical of that found in bar and living room settings. Both scenes were followed by warnings about drinking and driving. In a third plain background condition, participants saw only the warning as white text on a black background. In the control condition, participants were shown the advertisements, but given no warning.

In this experiment, participants were both randomly selected and randomly assigned to different conditions. These procedures maximize the chances that individuals in the treatment and control groups are relatively similar. Thus, any differences between the groups on the dependent variable are said to be caused by the manipulation of the independent variable and not by differences in individual participants. These aspects of the classical experiment give the researcher greater assurance that other alternative explanations for the results are eliminated (Sapsford & Jupp, 1996).

Creating Treatment and Control Groups The **treatment group** is the group of participants who receive a stimulus—anything that the researcher is interested in studying. Alternately, if a participant is assigned to a **control group,** no treatment or stimuli is offered. In the experimental framework, creation of the treatment and control groups provides the opportunity for the manipulation of the independent variable. It is important to note here that identification of what constitutes a treatment, or condition, is driven by theory (Boruch, 1998); not just any treatment will do.

Returning to Berger and DiBattista's (1993) study of communication failure, the research team formulated its hypothesis on the basis of an extensive literature review and analysis of previous research. From this they hypothesized that when individuals attempt social goals, such as giving directions, and fail, they will take the least-demanding option available to them. In this case, it is easier and simpler to just repeat the same directions and do so with a louder voice than to adjust the directions into different words and sentence structures. Type of failure in delivering directions was one of the independent variables manipulated by the research team. The confederate to whom the directions were given replied in one of two ways: "I'm sorry, I don't understand English well. I had trouble following your directions. Could you give me the directions again?" (p. 225) or something like, "I understand your English well, I'm just having difficulty following the directions." In the first condition, or response, the failure was language-based, creating a more complex situation to which the direction-giver needs to respond. In the second response condition, the failure was direction-based, which should require a less complex response. By comparing how participants responded to the type of failure, the research team provided support for the hierarchy hypothesis—that is, when communication action is thwarted, individuals will first modify their message plans, using the least amount of cognitive resources. As you can see, the conditions of the independent variable chosen by the research team were inextricably linked to the theory of interest.

In some communication experiments, multiple treatment groups are used without a control group. Sometimes one group is considered a control group even though participants in it receive some form of the stimulus or treatment. Usually, the more standard, common, or traditional form of the stimulus serves as the control group. In other instances, the treatment groups serve as a control for one another, and the researcher forgoes the use of a pure control group.

Nabi (1998) demonstrates this use of treatment groups in her exploration of how disgust affects attitude change. Participants were randomly assigned to watch one of four videos about the use of animals for experimental medical research. To create the four treatment groups, four different versions of the same video were created. Thus, there was not a pure control group. Although each of the four versions of the video had the same structure, the videos differed in their use of accompanying visuals in two ways. Visuals differed in the intensity of the disgust-evoking images of animals used in experimentation. The visuals were either very graphic, with animals receiving traumatic injuries, or more benign, showing animals in a laboratory setting. The visuals also differed in their portrayal of humans. These visuals accompanied the part of the video that gave the medical community's rebuttal that animal experimentation is humane and necessary. To elicit high emotional responses, visuals depicted sick and deformed people, presumably helped by animal research. To elicit low emotional responses, visuals depicted laboratory workers performing routine lab tasks. Thus, participants saw one of the four treatment videos that manipulated two independent variables—disgust and emotional affect:

- Low disgust animal visuals and low emotional visuals
- Low disgust animal visuals and high emotional visuals
- High disgust animal visuals and low emotional visuals
- High disgust animal visuals and high emotional visuals

The researcher identified the video with both the high disgust and high emotional visuals as the control against which to compare the other treatment groups because these intense visuals were the most emotionally evocative.

Participants, regardless of which video they saw, responded to the same set of dependent measures, including attitude toward the issue of animal experimentation and attitude toward people who support animal experimentation. The expectation was that the video viewed would affect participants' responses to these dependent variables.

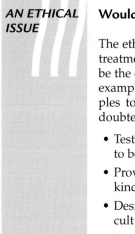

AN ETHICAL
ISSUE

Would You Ask Participants To . . . ?

The ethical issues of experimental design are primarily focused on developing the treatment and control conditions to which participants are assigned. What would be the ethical objections to creating manipulations for the following scenarios? For example, in the first instance, would it be ethical to knowingly assign engaged couples to a treatment group in which they received counseling even though you doubted its effectiveness?

- Testing different types of relational maintenance counseling for couples about to be wed?
- Providing instruction about different discipline strategies to parents of kindergarten-age children before videotaping their interaction with their child?
- Designing different persuasive appeals for nurses to use in dealing with difficult patients?
- Testing different visual strategies for making empathic appeals to solicit donations to a children's charity from television viewers?

Thus, treatment groups are chosen by the researcher based on theory. Researchers must have meaningful reasons for selecting the treatment groups—just trying different things does not uphold the scientific tradition upon which experimentation is based. Withholding treatment or the stimulus creates the control group. In cases in which it would not make sense to have a traditional control group, multiple treatment groups can act as controls for one another, or the researcher may designate one treatment group as the standard against which the other treatments will be evaluated.

Manipulation Checks When an independent variable is manipulated, a researcher should conduct a **manipulation check.** This test, or check, verifies that participants did, in fact, regard the independent variable in the various ways that the researcher intended. This check is conducted prior to statistical analyses of the hypotheses. Why is this necessary? First, researchers need to confirm that participants were sensitive to the different treatments. Second, researchers need to confirm that differences in treatments as perceived by participants were in line with the differences the researcher intended. Without this

confirmation, a researcher might assume that differences in the dependent variable were due to differences in the independent variable when they were, in fact, not.

Returning to the experiment about different types of alcohol warning messages, the research team (Slater et al., 2002) confirmed that participants in the threatening visual did in fact see that visual as more threatening than the nonthreatening condition. As part of the study, participants responded to two items to capture their perceptions of the visuals. As expected, the manipulation check demonstrated a statistically significant difference. Participants who saw the threatening condition had a mean score of 6.74 and participants who saw the nonthreatening condition had a mean score of 3.75 on the two items.

Another type of manipulation check should be used when research designs include a confederate. To examine how participants in a group discussion allow nonverbal cues from other members to influence them, Van Swol (2003) used two confederates posing as participants with one naïve participant. Together, the three individuals, role-playing as managers in a pharmaceutical company, were to decide which cholesterol-lowering drug they would market.

During the discussion, only one confederate mirrored the nonverbal behavior (posture, hand gestures, facial expressions, adaptors, and head movements) of the naïve participant. To assess the confederates' behaviors, two coders unaware of what the confederates were instructed to do and unaware of the study's hypotheses viewed videotapes of the group discussions and evaluated the coders' smiling behavior, friendliness, persuasiveness, talkativeness, and the degree to which the confederates appeared to like the participant. Statistical tests indicated that the confederates' behaviors were not significantly different on these dimensions, suggesting that the confederates were not acting differently except with respect to the mirroring behavior of one. Manipulation checks should be conducted prior to the statistical testing of any hypothesis in which the manipulated variable is used.

Types of Experimental Design

Several types of experimental design meet the fundamental criteria of random assignment of participants and researcher control of the manipulations of the independent variable. Three of the basic designs commonly used in communication research are described here—posttest only, pretest–posttest, and factorial design. More complex experimental designs exist (for example, see Campbell & Stanley, 1963; de Vaus, 2001). Starting with these basic designs, however, will increase your ability to comprehend complex designs, since they are embedded variations of the basic designs presented here.

Posttest Only   After randomly assigning the sample to treatment and control groups, researchers need to measure the dependent variable either during or after the participants' exposure to the independent variable. This type of research design—the **posttest only,** or simple comparison—allows a researcher to conclude that any significant differences found are due to the fact that the treatment group received some stimulus that participants in the control group did not. Thus, this type of design answers the question "Do the two groups differ after the stimulus is presented to only one group?"

This research design is fairly common in communication research. As an example, student participants were randomly assigned to one of two treatments manipulating an instructor's office aesthetic quality (Teven & Comadena, 1996). Students in the first treatment visited an unknown instructor's office that was designed to be aesthetically pleasing. This office was very clean and tidy. Students in the second treatment visited an instructor's office (ostensibly the same person) designed to be of low aesthetic quality, or displeasing. This office was disorganized and unattractive. Students were asked to wait in the instructor's office because they believed that they were to meet with him, although they did not. They were given this instruction to heighten students' interest in observing the office décor. Students assigned to the control group did not visit an office; rather, they simply skipped this aspect of the research design. Thus, the stimulus, the aesthetic quality of the instructor's office, was the independent variable, and it was manipulated in two different ways—high aesthetic quality and low aesthetic quality.

In the next part of the research procedure, students watched a 5-minute videotape of the instructor lecturing in a basic communication course. Students then completed a questionnaire that captured their responses about the professor's credibility and communication style. The research team was interested in discovering how the aesthetic quality of the instructor's office (the independent variable) influenced students' perceptions of the instructor's credibility ratings and his communication style (the dependent variables). This posttest-only design is presented in Figure 8.2. The objective of this type of experimental research is to demonstrate a cause–effect relationship by looking for differences between scores of the treatment and control groups on the dependent variable.

Pretest–Posttestt   By adding one step to the posttest-only design, a researcher achieves the **pretest–posttest** experimental form. Here, a researcher measures the dependent variable before the treatment group is exposed to the stimulus. After the stimulus is given, the dependent variable is measured once again in exactly the

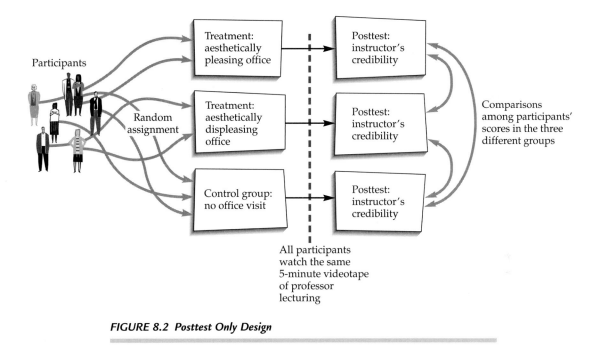

FIGURE 8.2 Posttest Only Design

same way with the same participants. In some written research reports, the researcher will refer to these measurements as Time 1 and Time 2. Time 1 would be the measurement before any stimulus is given to the treatment group, and Time 2 would be the measurement after the stimulus.

The posttest-only design allows a researcher to document no more than that a difference exists between groups. Adding the pretest, or Time 1, measurement allows the researcher to determine the degree of change in the dependent variable from one measurement to the next. Although many researchers agree that this experimental form is more powerful, there is one caveat. Because measurements at Time 1 and Time 2 are conducted in the very same way, there is some danger that participants become overly sensitized to the measurement, especially when data are collected through questionnaires. Two different effects can occur. In the first, participants may try to respond at Time 2 as they responded at Time 1, or, in other words, try to be consistent even though a change has occurred. In the second, participants assume that the researcher is

looking for differences and may try to make sure they answer differently at Time 2 than at Time 1. In either case, the participants' motivations or expectations are confounding the research design.

Students enrolled in general education courses who had already responded to questionnaires about their communication apprehension and who reported high communication apprehension scores were randomly selected to participate in a study to determine whether performance visualization could be helpful in reducing their communication apprehension when giving a speech (Ayres & Sonandre, 2003). First, half of the participants gave a pretest speech on "What I expect to get out of college"; the other half gave a speech on "What I expect to do in the future" (p. 263). Second, immediately following their speech, participants were randomly assigned to one of four treatment conditions: One performance visualization condition featured Barbara Jordan as a model speaker (labeled the *great speech*), whereas a second performance visualization condition featured another student who had previously been

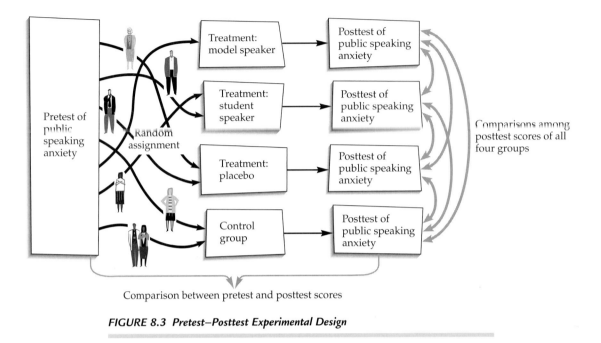

Comparison between pretest and posttest scores

FIGURE 8.3 Pretest–Posttest Experimental Design

judged as an excellent student speaker. The third condition was a placebo condition in which participants read information about communication processes in general. A fourth condition was the control, as participants were left alone for 35 minutes without any specific task or activity. Immediately after these treatments, all participants delivered a second, or posttest, speech on the topic they did not use in the pretest, and completed questionnaires about their communication apprehension.

Using this research design, the researchers could compare the pretest and posttest scores of students' communication apprehension, allowing them to discover that students who were in the treatment groups with the performance visualization reported lower communication apprehension on their posttest speech than those in the placebo or control conditions. However, participants who saw the student speaker reported a greater decrease in communication apprehension than those who saw the great speech, suggesting that students can be useful role models to one another.

This pretest–posttest experimental design is presented in Figure 8.3. The objective of this type of experimental design is to demonstrate a cause–effect relationship by looking for differences from Time 1 to Time 2 in addition to looking for differences among groups at Time 2.

Factorial Design In a **factorial design** experiment, treatment groups are based on two or more independent variables. Researchers use this type of research design to investigate complex cause–effect relationships that cannot be adequately tested with only one independent variable. A factorial design allows the researcher to test for the effects of each independent variable. In addition, he or she can test for the **interaction effect,** or how the independent variables can combine to influence the dependent variable.

Because more than one independent variable is of interest, random assignment is necessary on only one. Natural variation on the personal attributes of participants may create assignment for the other independent variable. This is fairly common in communication research in which

Sex of Supervisor

	Female supervisor sexually harassing male subordinate	Male supervisor sexually harassing female subordinate
Female participant	**1** Female participants watch scene in which female supervisor sexually harasses male subordinate.	**2** Female participants watch scene in which male supervisor sexually harasses female subordinate.
Male participant	**3** Male participants watch scene in which female supervisor sexually harasses male subordinate.	**4** Male participants watch scene in which male supervisor sexually harasses female subordinate.

Sex of Participant

FIGURE 8.4 *Main Effects and Interaction Effects in a Factorial Design*

participants' sex is one of the independent variables of interest. Obviously, a researcher cannot randomly assign sex to participants. Thus, he or she must rely on the participants' natural variation on this independent variable. But then participants must be randomly assigned by the researcher to one of the treatment groups or to the control group on the other independent variable.

Factorial designs allow researchers to test for the treatment effects of each independent variable separately, as well as for the joint effect of the two independent variables together. In research reports, the simple influence of one independent variable by itself is referred to as a **main effect.** In other words, the influence of one independent variable is examined without considering the influence of the other independent variable. A researcher can also examine the interaction effect, or how the dependent variable is jointly affected by the two or more independent variables.

Keyton and Rhodes (1999) used a factorial design to examine the effects of two independent variables—supervisor sex and participant sex—on participants' sexual harassment identification scores. Participants watched videotaped scenes to which they were randomly assigned.

This procedure controlled which supervisor, male or female, they saw sexually harassing a subordinate of the opposite sex. This was the first independent variable. The second independent variable was created through the natural variation in participants' sex. With these two variables, or factors, participants were in one of four treatment conditions, as demonstrated in Figure 8.4.

In this case, the factorial design allowed researchers to test for the main effects of sex in two different ways. In other words, how did participants' sex affect their perceptions of viewing the sexually harassing video scene? Looking at Figure 8.4, significant differences would show up as differences between the rows. Scores for participants in boxes 1 and 2 would be similar to one another, yet different from scores for participants in boxes 3 and 4. This design also allowed researchers to test for the main effects of supervisor sex. Here the question would be "How did supervisor sex affect participants' perceptions of the sexually harassing scene?" Looking at Figure 8.4, significant differences would show up as differences between the columns. Scores for participants in boxes 1 and 3 would be similar to one another, yet different from scores for participants in boxes 2 and 4.

Testing for the interaction effect could answer the question "Did viewing a supervisor of the same sex produce different perceptions of sexual harassment than when participants viewed a supervisor of the other sex?" If an interaction effect existed, differences would not be between rows or columns. Rather, differences would be between, for instance, female participants who viewed the female supervisor sexually harass the male subordinate (participants in box 1) and male participants who viewed the male supervisor sexually harass the female subordinate (participants in box 4). This is called an interaction because the differences are not solely dependent on participants' sex or on the sex of the supervisor.

In a factorial design, the minimum configuration requires two independent variables with at least two levels each. But the design can be extended to consist of several factors with as many levels as necessary and feasible for each one. Generally, no more than four independent variables are built into one factorial design. Likewise, seldom are more than four levels of an independent variable considered. When a factorial design is extended to more than two variables, the number of interactions increases as well.

Longitudinal Designs

When experiments of the types just described are designed so that there are multiple measurements of the dependent variable, the design is also labeled as **longitudinal.** Researchers often call for longitudinal experimental designs as they discuss the limitations of their research in the discussion section of the written journal report.

How much time must there be between measurements for a design to be considered longitudinal? That depends on the nature of the communication phenomenon under study. In other words, it is relative to the topic. Days, weeks, sometimes even years could occur between measurement points. As you might guess, the greater the length of time between measurements, the more likely it is that other factors will influence the dependent variable.

Communication scholars frequently use longitudinal experimental designs to test the influence of message design strategies to identify which strategies are more effective in changing participants' attitudes and behaviors. For example, Harrington et al. (2003) designed a pretest–posttest laboratory experiment over 4 weeks to investigate the cumulative effectiveness of different types of antidrug public service announcements. Students who participated were randomly sampled from a university registrar's list of students. To simulate the type of repeated exposure a participant would have to similar messages on television, participants came to the lab to view the conditions twice a week for 4 weeks. Based upon the condition to which they were randomly assigned, participants saw antidrug messages that had high or low sensation value coupled with many arguments against drug use or few arguments against drug use. By designing the study this way, the research team was able to simulate how participants would typically be exposed to public service announcements and how different message strategies influenced participants' attitudes and behaviors toward drug use.

Longitudinal designs are also particularly helpful in determining the degree to which training has been effective. In one study (Seibold, Kudsi, & Rude, 1993), employees participated in a 2-day public speaking training workshop. All participants received the same training but were randomly assigned to evaluation conditions that differed with respect to the type of evaluation and length of time between their pretraining and posttraining evaluations. By designing the study in this way, the research team conducted a rigorous examination of participants' reactions to public speaking training, knowledge of public speaking principles, and perceptions of their public speaking skills. This longitudinal design allowed the research team to examine both the short- and long-term training effects.

Strengths of Experimentation

The primary advantage of experimentation is that researchers can manipulate the independent variable to observe changes in the dependent variable. Because the researcher controls the manipulation and because participants are randomly assigned to treatment and control groups,

Designing an Experiment

You have likely read about or studied the constructs of communication apprehension and communication competence. If you need information about these communication phenomena, the following articles should provide you with enough background to try this exercise.

- Cole, J. G., & McCroskey, J. C. (2003)
- Hopf, T., Ayres, J., Ayres, F., & Baker, B. (1995)
- Hinton, J. S., & Kramer, M. W. (1998)
- Hutchinson, K. L., & Neuliep, J. W. (1993)

Try your hand at designing an experiment for communication apprehension, communication competence, or both for three different populations. Use the table below to guide you through this primary development process.

	What will you have participants do in the lab?	*What will you, the researcher, manipulate as the independent variable? What are the various treatments or conditions?*	*On what dependent variable do you expect the manipulation to have an effect? Why?*
Children ages 5–7			
Teenagers 16–18			
Young married adults 22–25			

What other literature will you need to become familiar with to finish the experimental designs? What arguments can you give for the research design choices you have made? What are the limitations of your designs at this stage of their development?

any significant difference found is assumed to be the cause of variations in the independent variable (de Vaus, 2001). Other primary advantages of experimentation are that the design and researcher control over variable manipulation allows testing of extremes and multiple replica-tions. Operationalizations and measuring techniques are decided on in advance, and a researcher repeats the procedures and methods in exactly the same way for each participant or each group of participants. This leads to precision (Kerlinger, 1986). A less obvious benefit is that when the lab environment remains static, experimentation can be cost effective and more convenient for the researcher. Once a lab environment is secured and outfitted for a particular experiment, the researcher uses it over and over. Seldom can all participants of an experiment be tested all at the same time.

Limitations of Experimentation

Despite its strengths, there are several limitations to experimentation. Not all communication scholarship can be conducted using one of the experimental forms. In some cases it would be immoral or unethical to conduct the research because subjecting participants in one group to some stimuli could be negative or hurtful (de Vaus, 2001). Legal standards might also make experimentation impossible. Thus, moral, ethical, and legal issues prevent a researcher from assigning participants to some categories or from otherwise manipulating an independent variable. In other cases, it simply is impossible to manipulate the independent variable because these qualities are fixed in the participants. For instance, variables such as sex, socioeconomic class, age, and communication competence cannot be manipulated. These characteristics and attributes are fixed within participants; the researcher has no control over them. Thus, the first limitation is that experimentation by the nature of its design characteristics will be inappropriate or impossible to use in all situations.

The second major limitation is that even with its stringent design, experimental forms cannot guarantee that some factor other than the treatment factor produced the significant effect (Sapsford & Jupp, 1996). Researchers can control or minimize the influence of variables they know about. But researchers can never know if they succeeded completely, and they certainly cannot control the influence of a variable that is unknown to them.

Third, laboratory experiments rely on a researcher's manipulation of the independent variable. In some cases, such pure manipulation may not exist in reality. Thus, participants may react to the artificiality of the lab environment as well as to the potentially artificial manipulation of the independent variable.

Another limitation to experimentation is derived from one of its strengths. Experimentation is hailed because it allows researchers to test several variables or combinations of variables at once. Although the variables can be manipulated and measured in the lab, this activity does not always equate with how those variables exist and interact in natural communication settings.

The most frequent complaint about experimentation is the lack of reality in experimental designs. Conducting research in sterile laboratories, available classrooms, or other environments unusual to participants could influence how participants will respond or react, and that may be different than they would behave in more natural surroundings or environments. In general, then, experimental research, especially that conducted in laboratories, may be investigating communication behaviors that are less complex than they are in the communication environments in which they are found day to day (Miller, 1970). Other scholars, however, suggest that lab experiments should not attempt to re-create natural interaction. Rather, artificiality is necessary to reduce or eliminate all of the confounding variables that exist in the real world (Pedhazur & Schmelkin, 1991).

QUASI-EXPERIMENTS

Because of the limitations mentioned earlier, sometimes researchers rely upon natural variations in the independent variable. Called **quasi-experiments**, or natural experiments, this alternative form of research design is possible because some variation in the independent variable exists naturally. In other words, participants are not assigned randomly to treatment and control groups. Lacking this assignment opportunity, variation in the independent variable is not under the control or direction of the researcher. The three basic designs of posttest only, pretest–posttest, and factorial can still be used as

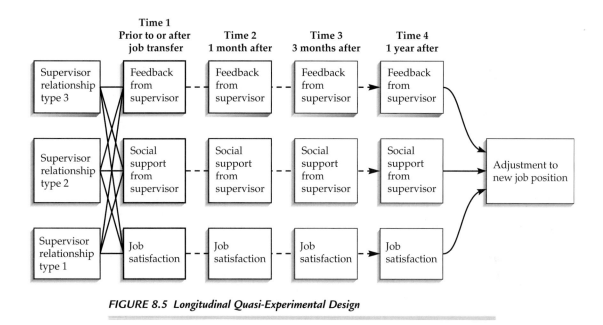

FIGURE 8.5 Longitudinal Quasi-Experimental Design

long as natural variation of the independent variable can be substituted for manipulation of the independent variable.

Longitudinal designs can also be incorporated with quasi-experimentation. Recall that the distinguishing characteristic of this research design is multiple measurements of the dependent variable. For example, Kramer (1995) collected data at four points to examine how well employees adjusted to job transfers. First, data were collected just prior to or just after job transfers. Then, data were collected at 1 month, 3 months, and 1 year after employees transferred jobs. By using a longitudinal design, the researcher could assess the degree to which, and the ways in which, employees adjusted to their new positions over a period of time.

In this design, time was an independent variable as all participants self-reported scores at four time points. Type of supervisor relationship was the other independent variable. For this variable, participants were given three descriptions and asked to identify which one best described their relationship with their supervisor. This study characterizes features of quasi-experimental design as both independent variables were based on natural variation rather than researcher assignment of participants to treatments or conditions. This longitudinal quasi-experimental design is presented in Figure 8.5.

Scholars who study the efficacy of research methods differ in the degree to which they support quasi-experimentation. The primary limitation, of course, stems from the lack of control the researcher has over manipulating the independent variable. Although natural variation can be said to be a substitute for this manipulation, there are some concerns about the quality, or the purity, of the manipulation. For example, in communication research, assignment of participant sex is obviously not under the control of the researcher. Thus, communication researchers rely on individuals to self-identify as females or males. These self-identifications are used to classify participants with respect to sex. It seems simple, but there are inherent problems.

Whereas we could agree that there are obvious differences between women and men, there are also differences among women and among men. And it is these differences within categories that can confuse any results researchers find. Confusion about interpretation also occurs because there are likely to be between-group differences on an assortment of variables that affect the dependent variable but that are not included in the research design. Think of the problem in this way: Just because women and men differ with respect to physical sex does not mean that women and men will differ as distinctly on the communication aspects of gender, such as communicating with feminine, masculine, or androgynous styles.

Thus, the goal for researchers using quasi-experimental forms is to create and communicate clarity about the differences desired in the independent variable (Pedhazur & Schmelkin, 1991). In many quasi-experimental studies, participants assigned to treatment groups by the researcher are assigned to different categories of the independent variable by how they respond to that variable on the questionnaire. For example, participants respond to the questionnaire item that asks them to identify their sex. Males are assigned to the male level of that variable if they check that box on the questionnaire. Likewise, females are assigned to the female level of the variable if they check that box on the questionnaire.

In essence, participants self-select into the category of the independent variable to which they belong by labeling themselves. Other variables on which this type of self-selection is common include marital status, political affiliation, race or ethnicity, and university class level. Although researchers can never completely overcome problems associated with self-selection, they can reduce the potential error by providing full and complete descriptions of any categories used and by making sure categories are exhaustive, mutually exclusive, and equivalent.

When treatment groups are based on natural variation, some researchers refer to these as nonequivalent comparison groups. They are nonequivalent because participants are not randomly assigned. Thus, the way in which researchers use existing natural variation to assign participants to treatment groups should be carefully considered. The goal is to use groups that are as equivalent as possible, and achievement of this goal relies primarily on the procedures chosen by the researcher.

A good example of the way in which quasi-experiments rely on natural variation is demonstrated in a study investigating potential differences between hospice volunteers and hospital volunteers who would offer social support to terminally ill patients (Egbert & Parrott, 2003). Obviously, potential study participants could not be assigned to conditions to realistically portray the roles of hospice volunteer or hospital volunteer. As an alternative, the research team invited individuals who currently volunteer at a hospice or hospital. Thus, the variation on this independent variable—type of volunteer—existed naturally.

How equivalent were these groups? Generally, information presented by the researcher in the methods section can help you make that determination. In this study the two volunteer groups were compared on basic demographic characteristics. There were no statistically significant differences between the two groups relative to ethnicity, sex, marital status, age, and volunteer experience. The groups did differ however, on their religious affiliation. There were a greater number of Jewish hospice volunteers than there were hospital volunteers. The research team explains that one hospice from which participants were recruited was a hospice that specifically served Jewish patients. There were also a greater number of hospice volunteers who reported their religious affiliation as "other." But as the researchers explain, "A difference in spirituality among hospice and hospital volunteers is not surprising, as an earlier study of hospice patients also found differences regarding religion" (Egbert & Parrott, 2003, p. 23). By reviewing this type of information, readers can determine that these volunteers were similar in many ways. As a result, equivalency between the groups is enhanced and the researcher could draw meaningful comparisons between the two groups.

Field Experiments

As the name implies, **field experiments** are like experiments in terms of researcher control over the manipulation of independent variables and

DESIGN
CHECK

Is One Study Ever Enough?

Imagine the following: In doing an assignment for one of your communication courses, you find a journal article that addresses the very constructs in which you are interested. Even though you use several electronic databases to search for more articles like the one you found, you are not successful. So, with one article in hand, you set out to complete the assignment. As you read about the hypotheses and the quasi-experimental design used in the study, several questions arise:

- Is there anything about the way in which the research was conducted that would detract from its findings, even though the study examines exactly the variables in which you are interested?
- To what degree did the researcher's procedures create control over the natural variation in the independent variables?
- Are the research procedures reported in enough detail and to your satisfaction?
- Could there be explanations for the findings other than what the researcher offers?
- Would the results from one study, even if it were an experiment, ever be enough?

random assignment of participants. However, the research environment is realistic and natural. Participants are not asked to come to a laboratory environment that is used exclusively for experimentation. Rather, the research is conducted in environments with which participants already are familiar. This provides another advantage—field experiments are better suited for observing and evaluating complex and unfolding interaction events. But in field experiments researchers also lack the degree of control they have in true experiments.

Clearly, as a researcher moves from the lab into a natural environment, some control is lost. Although researchers can control nearly all outside interferences (for example, people interrupting the research process, intruding noises) in the lab, they will be less likely to control outside interferences in the field because they are not in charge of the environment in which the research is taking place. Although some control is lost, realism is increased (Kerlinger, 1986). When realism is increased, findings have greater generalizability.

Field experiments are particularly effective for studying communication in context. For example,

Krendl, Olson, and Burke (1992) used a field experiment to examine the effectiveness of a communication campaign designed to encourage participation in a publicly funded curbside recycling program. To initiate the recycling program and test its viability, 18 subdivisions in one city were selected for participation and organized into four pickup routes. In an attempt to increase participation, the research team proposed a campaign to boost participation rates. Three of the pickup routes were randomly assigned to one of three treatment conditions, whereas the fourth route served as the control condition. For the treatment groups, three different types of communication appeals were developed. Households on one route, or treatment group, received an interpersonal influence campaign, with individuals going door-to-door to remind their neighbors of the recycling program. Households on the second route, or second treatment group, received educational printed materials. The third received printed materials recounting the economic benefits of recycling. Finally, households on the fourth route served as the control group and were not exposed to any of these influences.

Obviously, the research questions addressed in this study could not have been studied in a laboratory environment. Using a field experiment was practical because the results would be used to encourage citizens in this community to use curbside recycling. By designing the project in this way, the research team could assess the effectiveness of different persuasive appeals on residents' participation in the recycling program. The persuasion attempts were studied in their natural environment without researcher interference, as sanitation workers—who had no knowledge about which treatment their route received or even the details of the campaign—collected the data. Thus, the results from this research design had high generalizability because researcher intrusion was minimized to the greatest extent and the differing message treatments were studied in the environments in which they would actually be used. Recognize, however, that precision in measurement may have decreased when data collection was shifted from trained to untrained data collectors.

DESCRIPTIVE DESIGNS

Descriptive designs, sometimes called, **cross-sectional**, or **non-experimental** designs, differ from experimental and quasi-experimental research designs in three fundamental ways. Although the study is still systematic, the researcher does not have direct control over the independent variables nor are participants randomly assigned. Additionally, data are collected in such a way that temporal order cannot be determined. Despite these differences, the logic is basically the same—researchers want to demonstrate that differences or relationships exist between the independent and dependent variables.

These differences in descriptive designs decrease the degree to which causation can be ensured. Because a researcher has less control, variables other than those selected as independent variables may be responsible for changes in the dependent variable (Kerlinger, 1986). This characteristic makes it difficult for inferences to be made from the independent variables to the dependent variables (Pedhazur & Schmelkin, 1991). Because of this issue, some researchers substitute the terms *predictor variable* and *criterion variable* for *independent variable* and *dependent variable*, respectively. Using these two terms is more appropriate because they do not imply causality. Nevertheless, the tradition of naming variables as independent and dependent is very strong, and many researchers use these terms even when their research design is non-experimental. Although some researchers believe that experimental research is always superior to other research designs (Kerlinger, 1986), descriptive research can paint a picture of a communication phenomenon as it naturally occurs without relying on an intervention or a designed condition (Bickman, Rog, & Hedrick, 1998).

One type of descriptive communication research occurs when researchers want to demonstrate that categorical differences exist on some dependent variable. When a researcher limits interpretation of results from this type of study to a description of differences, descriptive forms can be successful in identifying variables that may later be used to build a theoretical explanation of the relationship between the independent variable and the dependent variable. However, researchers overstep the boundaries of descriptive research if they try to offer the differences they find as an explanation.

For example, finding the answer to the research question "What are the categorical structures of ritual functions in marital relationships?" (Bruess & Pearson, 2002, p. 317) is a question for which a descriptive answer can be found. But knowing the categorical structures does not explain why such a structure exists or how that structure influences other communication variables in marital relationships.

In this descriptive study, over 400 married individuals provided data on rituals in their marriage and how they believed the ritual functioned in that relationship (e.g., Did the ritual bring them closer? Provide fun?). They provided the same information for a friendship. Participants were not randomly assigned to conditions, nor did the researchers manipulate any variables. Rather, participants reported on their communication with their marital partner and with a friend. And, as in most descriptive research, the data were collected simultaneously through written self-report questionnaires.

Data analysis resulted in seven types of marital ritual functions and seven types of friendship ritual functions, with some overlap between the two sets. The research report does not venture beyond description. However, the researchers do suggest that these findings could be used in the development of theoretically grounded explanations of relationship functions, and suggest directions such research could take.

As another example, Benoit (2003) investigated the relationship between the state of the U.S. economy and the topics addressed in presidential TV spots for all presidential elections from 1952 through 2000. He hypothesized that there would be a positive relationship between two economic indicators (i.e., rate of inflation and rate of unemployment) and the frequency of economic terms. Statistics from the Bureau of Labor Statistics to represent the state of the economy were tested for their relationship to the number of economic terms used in a sample of presidential television spots for each of the campaigns. The variables were positively and moderately to strongly related. When there was higher inflation and unemployment, presidential candidates did talk more about the economy in their campaign spots.

"Although finding that two variables are correlated does not establish cause it does mean that a causal explanation is possible" (de Vaus, 2001, p. 178). Thus, it would be inappropriate to claim that the state of the economy *caused* presidential candidates to talk about the economy in their campaign. Benoit (2003), more appropriately, states that "the content of presidential campaign messages appears to be driven in part by the state of the economy" (p. 269) or that "presidential candidates' television spot messages move in concert with recent economic conditions" (p. 274). Clearly, candidates do react to the state of the economy. But, because of the retrospective nature of the study and its descriptive design, it is impossible to know if other factors influenced what candidates included in their campaign messages. However, as Benoit points out, the logic of the study's design eliminates the possibility that the presidential campaign spots caused the economy to suffer, as economic data from the first 6 months of a campaign year were used. Benoit continues, "It seems plausible that the state of the economy would be a ready resource for candidate messages. . . .

Of course, it is impossible that the news media (a third variable) plays a role in this relationship because economic news may influence candidate message design" (pp. 273–274). As in all descriptive research designs, care must be taken in how findings are interpreted. This type of research design cannot explain why relationships or differences occur, but it can describe their occurrence.

Strengths and Limitations of Descriptive Research Designs

Simply, some of the research issues that exist in the study of communication do not lend themselves to experimental or quasi-experimental designs. So, clearly, descriptive research is not without merit. The most obvious advantage is that descriptive studies are most often conducted in more realistic environments with participants who are more like the individuals to whom the researcher wants to generalize. Also important, descriptive studies can be used in an exploratory manner to provide an orientation to a topic (Henry, 1998).

You have already seen that the differences between experimental and descriptive research— inability to manipulate the independent variable and lack of power to randomly assign participants—create two of the fundamental limitations of this type of research design. These two weaknesses lead to a third limitation, and that is the risk of improper interpretation of the research findings. With significant findings, researchers are eager to accept these as meaningful and real despite the possibility that other explanations for the findings may exist. Thus, descriptive research designs can be more powerful when researchers offer several alternative hypotheses as explanations and test each one. When one hypothesis is supported and other alternatives are not, the findings of the significant hypothesis are strengthened (Kerlinger, 1986).

RESEARCHER EFFECTS AND PROCEDURAL BIAS

Regardless of the degree of control offered by experiment and its alternate forms, researchers or other members of the research team can introduce bias and error into the research process through their interaction with research partici-pants. Researchers can influence participants' behaviors during the research session, or they can create effects on the data itself (Brooks, 1970). All types of quantitative research designs—experimental, quasi-experimental, and descriptive forms—are susceptible because each requires a researcher or assistant to conduct or facilitate the process.

It is easy to see that researchers and research participants interact in a social environment. Who the researcher is (for example, age, sex, and race or ethnicity) and how the researcher com-municates with participants or other members of the research team can create influences on participants' responses. Imagine the difference in your reaction as a research participant if you are met warmly and cordially by the researcher as contrasted to being met in a hostile and re-jecting manner. How would you respond if you heard two research assistants arguing over re-search procedures before your experimental session began? Likewise, the degree of experi-ence or expertise demonstrated by a researcher can influence research participants' responses to stimuli.

Researchers' expectations can also create unwanted effects on participants' responses (Abelson, 1995). Remember that researchers develop hypotheses before a study is con-ducted. As a result, a researcher may unknow-ingly encourage participants to respond in the way that supports the predictions. Even subtle nonverbal cues may be perceived by partici-pants and, as a result, influence their responses and measurements. Each of these biases can occur in quasi-experimental designs as well.

One way to overcome researcher expectancy is for the individuals conducting the experiment to be blind to the hypotheses driving the re-search and, if possible, blind to the condition to which participants are assigned (Abelson, 1995). Generally, however, the person who develops the research study conducts the research study. If the researcher is aided by a confederate or by re-search assistants who observe or read accounts of interaction to code it, then these individuals should be blind to, or have no knowledge of, the hypotheses as well as blind to conditions or

treatments to which participants are assigned or which they fulfill.

Expectancy bias can be particularly salient when researchers use participants with whom they are acquainted. This can occur when researchers conduct studies on student popula-tions with whom they are familiar or in field settings where familiarity with potential partici-pants eased their access to the field location. Even if the researcher does not know the stu-dents, it is very likely that students in the same department or university know of, or know something about, the researcher. These types of acquaintanceship between researcher and research participant can influence the way research partici-pants react or respond. As a research participant, would you knowingly or unknowingly alter your behavior if the researcher were your advisor? If you were going to take a class from that professor next semester? If he or she were the department chair?

Students as research participants are also sen-sitive to demand characteristics, a situation that creates a bias based on participants' perceptions and interpretations of the research procedures. Students, particularly those with knowledge of research methods and communication theory, may try to second-guess what the researcher is looking for—the demand—and then try to pro-vide answers to fulfill it.

Demand characteristics are also created when the research topic has some socially desirable el-ement. For example, in conducting research on topics like sexual harassment, date rape, or de-ceptive practices, researchers need to develop procedures that encourage participants to answer honestly. Honesty is encouraged when research procedures do not create the perception for par-ticipants that they can be identified as victims or perpetrators of these socially undesirable acts.

To counter these effects, researchers write **research protocols** detailing each procedural step of the study. Protocols should be prac-ticed with individuals similar to the research participants and evaluated for their effective-ness before data are collected. An example of a research protocol is presented in Appendix D. Standardizing how the researcher and his or her assistants interact with participants and how research procedures are administered ensures more control.

COMPARING RESEARCH DESIGNS

For the study of relationships among and differences between communication phenomena that can be quantified, experimental research designs are the most powerful. However, in many cases they simply are impractical or impossible. Thus, researchers turn to quasi-experimental and descriptive forms for their quantitative research.

Ideally, the authors of research reports would always explicitly describe the research design they used, explain why that design was selected, and then identify the design by name. Figure 8.6 can help you decipher the methods section of a research report when these issues are not made explicit.

Once you have identified the type of quantitative research design, the next step is to identify what was measured. You should be able to identify a specific operationalization of each variable included in the research hypotheses and research questions. This information should be included in the methods section of the research report. Finally, you should examine how the research procedures were carried out, particularly with respect to the temporal order of measurement.

By independently checking these issues, you can critically assess the results the researcher presents and draw your own conclusions. You should be satisfied that the researcher used a design that was appropriate for the communication phenomena, setting, and participants, as well as

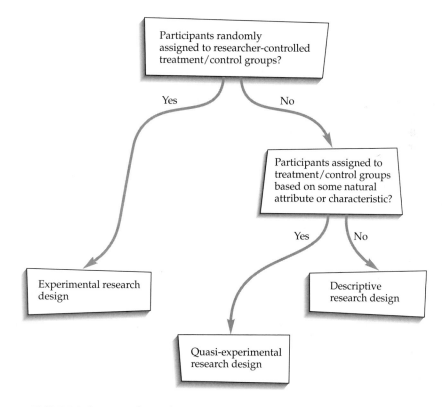

FIGURE 8.6 How Is the Study Designed?

effective in answering the hypotheses and research questions. With a good understanding of the research design and the implications of the choices made, you can make an independent assessment of the researcher's interpretations.

SUMMARY

1. There are three categories of quantitative research design: experimental forms, quasi-experimental forms, and descriptive forms.

2. Experimental research is used to establish cause–effect relationships between or among variables, and is most often conducted in a laboratory.

3. In an experiment, the researcher controls the manipulation of the independent variable by randomly assigning participants to treatment or control groups; this ensures that the treatment and control groups are equivalent before any treatment is applied or withheld.

4. Manipulation checks should be conducted to ensure that participants perceived variation in the independent variable as the researcher intended.

5. In the posttest only design, only individuals in the treatment group are exposed to the stimulus.

6. In the pretest–posttest design, only individuals in the treatment group are exposed to the stimulus; the dependent variable is measured for all participants prior to and after the treatment group receives the stimulus.

7. In the factorial design, treatment groups are based on two or more independent variables, with random assignment occurring on one of the variables.

8. The time between the multiple measurements of the dependent variable in a

longitudinal design is based on the communication phenomena under study and the theoretical foundation of the study.

9. In quasi-experiments, the researcher uses the natural variation that exists on the independent variable to assign participants to treatment and control conditions.

10. Field experiments are a form of quasi-experimental research design conducted in a naturalistic setting.

11. Descriptive designs are those studies that do not use random assignment of participants or researcher manipulation of the independent variable; as a result of lacking these controls, these research designs cannot demonstrate causation.

12. Communication researchers often use descriptive designs when communication phenomena do not lend themselves to experimental or quasi-experimental designs.

13. All research designs can suffer from bias from researcher effects or procedural bias.

KEY TERMS

classical experiment

control group

correlational design

cross-sectional design

descriptive design

experiment

experimental research

factorial design

field experiment

interaction effect

longitudinal design

main effect

manipulation

manipulation check

non-experimental design

posttest only

pretest–posttest

quasi-experiment

random assignment

research protocols

treatment

treatment group

CHAPTER NINE

Surveys and Questionnaires

Chapter Checklist

After reading this chapter, you should be able to:

1. Design a survey or questionnaire to answer a research question or test a hypothesis.

2. Select the survey format (face-to-face, telephone, self-report, web, email) that will best serve the purpose of the survey.

3. Select existing or design appropriate questionnaire items and response sets.

4. Use open and closed questions appropriately.

5. Pretest the method of data collection.

6. Collect the data in an honest and ethical manner.

7. Analyze the data completely and appropriately.

8. Draw conclusions that do not overstate the limitations of your data or sample.

9. Present the data to others in an appropriate fashion.

Surveys and questionnaires are the most common quantitative method for collecting data about communication phenomena. You have probably responded to a questionnaire as part of a research project at your school. Or perhaps you have been asked to answer a survey over the phone or while you were shopping at your local mall. Or maybe you were selected to participate in a political poll conducted by a national news organization. In any of these instances, researchers asked you to respond to questions so that they could obtain information.

Generally, surveys and questionnaires are excellent methodological tools for obtaining information about what people do (for example, how many times a week a person reads a newspaper), identifying what people believe influences their behavior (for example, how a television commercial affects views of a mayoral candidate), and identifying respondents' attitudes or characteristics (for example, identifying a person's level of dogmatism or leadership style). *Survey* is the appropriate term when a questionnaire is the only method of data collection, such as in a mail, phone, face-to-face, web, or email survey. A poll, like a survey, collects data only through a questionnaire, generally addresses issues of national or societal concern, and is conducted with a nationwide or statewide sample. In these instances, the questionnaire is the survey or poll, and is considered a type of descriptive research design. Questionnaires, however, can be used with other data collection methods in many research designs, and are frequently used in experimental, quasi-experimental, and descriptive research designs.

WHAT IS A SURVEY?

A **survey** is a system for collecting information. By asking questions, or having participants respond to stimuli statements, researchers can collect data that can be used to describe, compare, or explain knowledge, attitudes, or behavior (Fink, 1995b). Also known as a questionnaire or a poll, a survey is probably the most commonly used (and perhaps misused) methodological tool and can be used in gathering information about almost any communication concept or topic. Generally, the purpose of asking questions in survey form is to produce comparable information across many people so that data from the sample can be generalized to the population from which respondents were selected.

Types of Surveys

Surveys come in many forms; of course, each has advantages and disadvantages. The most common survey form is one that is self-administered in written form. In a **self-administered survey** individuals read and select a response on their own. Often called **self-reports,** these can be done on-site, as in the research setting, or mailed or electronically sent to individuals at work or home. An advantage of self-reports for the participant is that the survey can be completed more anonymously and at the respondent's own pace. Questions can be revisited; responses can be changed.

This advantage also creates a disadvantage for researchers in that completing a survey may take longer than planned. In a laboratory setting, there is often a set amount of time between research sessions. A person who reads slowly may take longer than the 20 minutes you allowed for participants to complete this part of the research process and might hold up the group as a whole or the next set of participants. If the survey is mailed to a participant's home, the survey may end up on the pile of things to be attended to at the end of the month, which is past your deadline for collecting data. Another disadvantage is that some respondents may have difficulty interpreting the instructions or the questions. Without someone to ask, the respondent is left to his or her own interpretation. One way to overcome this disadvantage is to be specific in the survey instructions.

As an alternative, some researchers use interviewers to facilitate the question-and-response process in a one-on-one interview. The advantages of one-on-one interviewing include the ability to probe for more complete answers as well as the ability to create a personal and trusting relationship with the respondent. However, the presence of the interviewer may create a

social desirability response, or the potential for the participant to respond with answers he or she believes the interviewer will perceive as favorable. Thus, if your topic requires asking a sensitive question or a question that has a socially desirable answer, you should consider embedding the question among less threatening items (Sudman & Bradburn, 1982). Another way to minimize the effects of threatening questions in the face-to-face format is to lead into an open question with a qualifier phrase such as, "We know a lot of people try using drugs when they are teenagers" and then continue with your question, "Can you tell me about your experiences with drugs as a teenager?"

Collecting survey data over the telephone has become popular, particularly for polls, because almost everyone has a telephone, making it the quickest way to reach potential participants. Using random-digit dialing (identifying the three-digit exchanges to be used as targets and then randomly generating four-digit numbers to complete the phone number) as a sampling technique helps overcome the problems associated with unlisted and new numbers and out-of-date directories. If you want to use this form of data collection for your survey, be sure to have all callers, or interviewers, use a standardized introduction that identifies who they are, what the research is about, who is conducting the research, and the purpose for collecting the information. Callers should also verify that the right person, household, or telephone number has been reached, state any conditions of the interview (for example, confidentiality), and then ask for permission to proceed (Frey & Oishi, 1995). Using this type of introduction will distinguish your telephone survey from those phone callers who use a short survey as a way to introduce and market their products or services.

The advantages accrued by the face-to-face and phone methods of data collection are offset, however, by the need to train many interviewers. Interviewers need to be trained so that standardized procedures are followed. Without standardized procedures, multiple interviewers can introduce variance in how they ask or code responses. Training should include the opportunity to watch an experienced person conduct a survey interview and the opportunity to practice before the actual data collection begins.

More recently, researchers have been using computers to assist their data collection activities in three ways. First, the questionnaire is created and posted as a public webpage with a unique URL. Then the researchers advertises for the sample, or survey respondents—often on websites with heavy traffic, newsgroups, webpage banners, or through announcements in other media—by publicizing the URL of the survey. Thus, the respondent comes to the survey rather than the survey coming to the respondent, which is typical in other survey research designs. As a result, the degree to which the survey sample is representative of the population is always in question. Second, the questionnaire is created and posted as a webpage and its URL is given to a specific group of people who were initially recruited for the study in another way. This is especially a good technique if your sample is geographically dispersed making face-to-face surveying difficult; and it is certainly less expensive than a mail survey. Third, the questionnaire can be created as a word document and sent to previously recruited participants as an email attachment. Participants fill out the questionnaire and return it via email or by mail. Obviously, the advantage is improved efficiency and effectiveness in data collection and management. However, not everyone is comfortable using computer technology. Moreover, typing mistakes may create an additional source of response bias.

Will how you collect the survey information affect its results? Yes, as each format tends to have increased nonresponse rates with certain types of respondents (Schwarz, Groves, & Schuman, 1998).

For example, less literate respondents are less likely to complete and return a written, mailed survey. Elderly respondents are less likely to respond to telephone surveys. Surveys mailed to respondents have a higher risk of respondent self-selection. Because respondents have the opportunity to review the survey before answering, it is more likely that they will respond only to topics that interest them. This type of self-selection bias is less prominent in face-to-face and telephone

Are All Polls the Same?

You have probably noticed television stations' use of public opinion polls. Often at the conclusion of news coverage on a controversial issue (for example, gun control, abortion, potential tax increase), a news program will provide one or more phone numbers for viewers to call. For example, calling the first number means you, as the caller, advocate stronger gun control; calling the second number means you do not. How do these types of "instant polls" differ from the more traditional random sampling public opinion poll? Bates and Harmon (1993) found that viewers with strongly held opinions and pro-change or activist attitudes are more likely to respond to phone-in polls. Thus, the results of phone-in polls are likely to differ substantially from those of random phone surveys. If your television station reports the results of a poll, listen carefully for the description of how the poll was conducted.

interviews because the respondent must make the decision to participate very quickly and is unlikely to reverse his or her participation decision once the interviewer starts the interaction. Obviously, each type of survey has advantages and disadvantages. See Table 9.1 for a summary (Fowler, 2002). These issues should be taken into consideration as part of your survey design.

DESIGNING A SURVEY

To be the most effective, surveys should have the following features (Fink, 1995b). First, the survey should be used as part of a sound research design. Second, the questions, or items, in the survey should be straightforward. Third, survey respondents, or the sample, should be chosen to be representative of a population by procedures that are appropriate, given the research question or hypothesis. Fourth, a survey should be both reliable and valid. Fifth, participants' responses to survey questions should be analyzed within the context of the questions asked. Sixth, survey results should be reported accurately and ethically. This includes not using the data out of context.

The research questions or hypotheses developed in the early stages of the research project's design will guide you in developing the survey. Generally, researchers use multiple items to help capture the complexity or depth of the concept

associated with the objective. Of course, if you have multiple objectives for a survey or if a survey needs to capture data about several variables, the survey is likely to need multiple items for each objective or variable. To develop your survey objective, define your information needs. Look at the following example.

Researchers want to know how to construct and target media campaigns for teenagers on the risks of smoking cigarettes. In this case, there are multiple objectives. One objective is to find out which media teenagers use. Another objective would be to find out the degree to which informational messages (as contrasted to entertainment messages) in these media are heard and heeded. A third objective could be to find out what teenagers know (and don't know) about risks associated with smoking. Thus, the survey developed for this example would have multiple items and sections. Survey items can be designed only after the research questions or hypotheses have been developed.

Evaluating Existing Questionnaires or Surveys

Fortunately for communication researchers, there are many established questionnaires that can be adopted. *Communication Research Measures: A Sourcebook*, edited by R. B. Rubin, P. Palmgreen, and H. E. Sypher (2004), is a collection of scales

TABLE 9.1 Comparison of Types of Surveys

Type of Survey	Advantages	Disadvantages
Face-to-face survey	• Effective for encouraging participation, building rapport • Allows probing of responses • Can capture nonverbal cues • Probably best for longer surveys	• Costly in terms of personnel and time • Interviewers must be trained • Impractical for geographically dispersed sample • Interviewer bias or error
Mail survey	• Does not require many personnel • Easy to access geographically dispersed sample • Respondents have time to give thoughtful answers	• Nonresponse rate can be high • Cost of mailing • Need for accurate mailing addresses • Delay in getting surveys returned
Phone survey	• Cost and time efficient • Random-digit dialing can be used for random sampling • Easy to access geographically dispersed sample • Better response rate than mail	• Nonresponse or refusal rate can be high • Not suited for lengthy surveys • Inappropriate for sensitive or personal topics
Webpage and email surveys	• Cost effective • Respondents can return data quickly • Easy to present visual information • Effective for technology topics	• Limited to sample of internet users • Challenging to identify cooperative participants • Concerns of computer security • Must have skills to create webpage • Must have accurate email addresses

that measure communication constructs in the interpersonal, mass, organizational, and instructional communication contexts. Besides providing the scale itself, the book describes scale background, validity, and reliability and also provides primary citations. These scales are available to researchers and may be used for research without gaining additional permission from the authors of the scales.

Although there are many occasions when these questionnaires can be used exactly as they were designed, some contexts may require minimal changes for them to be used effectively. What kinds of modification are appropriate? Minor wording changes may be necessary so that the survey is appropriate for the respondent population. But even this type of change is tricky. Most ques-

tionnaires are developed for adult audiences, and changing the items for teenagers and children, for example, may substantially alter the intent as well as the validity and reliability of the scale. Likewise, translating a questionnaire developed in English into another language version may create similar difficulties.

Are there modifications that are inappropriate and should be avoided if possible? Some instruments are lengthy and it is tempting to use only some of the items. Copyright restrictions may prohibit this type of altering. If the instrument is not copyrighted, you should contact the scale's author and ask his or her advice on selecting only some of the survey items for your particular use. Be aware that making any changes or modifications to an existing questionnaire or

---

TRY THIS!   **Survey Design**

Think of two communication issues on your campus. Perhaps there are problems with the distribution of the campus newspaper, or faculty and students are having discussions about the appropriateness and effectiveness of the current method by which students evaluate faculty. Isolate each problem, and write research questions to guide the design of a survey. Given the focus of your research questions, can you use existing questionnaires or will you need to develop new ones? How would you select an appropriate sample for the survey? Would you use probability or non-probability sampling? What survey technique would you use: face-to-face, mail, phone, webpage, or email? What are the potential challenges in distributing the survey and collecting data to answer your research questions?

---

scale will require that you pilot test, or pretest, the questionnaire once modifications have been made (more on this later in the chapter).

Even with these warnings, it is still recommended that you adopt or adapt questionnaires and scales from other studies whenever possible rather than create your own (Bourque & Fielder, 1995). These scales have undergone extensive testing, refinement, and competitive selection for publication. Using them also creates the opportunity to compare your results with results obtained by others. Moreover, building on the work of others is one way to maximize the clarity of your own research. Remember to document where you obtained the instrument and give credit to the authors of the questionnaire.

Writing Your Own Questionnaire

If you cannot find an appropriate survey instrument or questionnaire, then you will have to develop your own. Start by conducting a literature review of the appropriate research literature to learn what might be included. For example, for her thesis, a student wanted to study the communication competence of members of top management teams (CEO, president, vice presidents, and others who report directly to the CEO or president of the organization). As she explored this literature she found very few studies of top management teams, and none of these directly examined their communication

competence. She had some choices. She could have used one of the existing communication competence questionnaires. She reviewed those options and decided that they were too global or general for her research questions because she wanted her participants to respond to behaviors that constitute communication competence at this organizational level (for example, specific leadership and decision-making communication behaviors).

In reading reports of top management teams, she compiled a list of behaviors that would be described as positive or competent for executives in these positions. Working from that list, she developed a questionnaire that asked respondents to make a judgment about how often they used each particular behavior. And so, working from the literature, she developed a questionnaire about the communication competence of executives. Before using it as part of her thesis, though, she needed to pilot test the questionnaire with a handful of executives to make sure that each item was understood by respondents and that the items generated the types of responses she desired.

Designing Survey Items

A survey or questionnaire is only as good as the items that it includes. What is a good survey question? A good question provides answers that are a reliable and valid measure of something we want to describe (Fowler, 2002). To obtain such results, survey items or questions should be straightforward. An item is straightforward, or concrete, when it is precise and unambiguous. Each item should be one complete thought written in sentence or question format. The sentence, or question, should be written in such a way that the respondent knows how to answer. In some cases, open questions are preferred over closed questions. Both forms are explained later in this chapter.

Regardless of which question form you select, how you word survey or questionnaire items is crucial to obtaining the information you desire. Even small changes in wording can create large differences in participant responses (Sudman & Bradburn, 1982). As a result, there are several issues you should consider as you write survey items (Fink, 1995a; Fowler, 2002). First, respondents must be able to understand the terminology used in questions. Because your interpretation of the data will rely on how easily and accurately respondents can answer the questions, you need to consider the literacy and language-proficiency levels of your respondents. Second, each survey item should have a purpose. If you believe respondents will have a difficult time identifying the purpose of the question, give them a reasonable explanation for asking for that information as a lead-in to the question.

The next two issues are related. Third, all respondents should have access to the information needed to answer your question. You would not want respondents to answer a question if they lacked the knowledge or ability to do so. For example, respondents are unlikely to have the exact figure for the crime rate in their neighborhood. But they will be able to provide answers about their own status as a victim of crime or respond to questions about their perceptions of crime. The fourth issue is one of social desirability. Respondents must be willing to provide answers called for by the question and not feel pressured to give an answer that is socially desirable. For example, in sexual harassment research, the socially desirable answer to "Have you sexually harassed someone where you currently work?" would be "no." It is unlikely that someone would volunteer that

they have, in fact, sexually harassed another employee. As you can see, some types of questions, regardless of how they are asked, may not produce the type of results in which you are interested.

These next issues are practical ones. Fifth, avoid using abbreviations. Rather, use both the abbreviation and the full name or term, at least the first time the abbreviation is used. For example, in collecting data on sexual harassment, a question might include the abbreviation EEOC. Rather than assume that respondents know that EEOC stands for Equal Employment Opportunity Commission, use the full name followed by the abbreviation in parentheses—for example, "Have you read the Equal Employment Opportunity Commission's (EEOC's) guideline on sexual harassment?" Sixth, avoid using slang expressions or jargon. Such expressions change quickly and are used differently by subgroups. This advice is invalid, of course, if you are collecting data about slang or jargon usage. Seventh, shorter questions are better than long questions. Eighth, questions should be administered in a consistent way. Generally, multiple items measuring the same construct use one set of instructions and the same response set.

Finally, remember that all survey questions are asked within some social and cultural context. As an example, Tan, Nelson, Dong, and Tan (1997) surveyed students who were enrolled in three different high schools in the Northwest. They administered their survey in required English, history, and world civilization classes. Using this method, all students in 10th through 12th grades, except those who were absent, had the opportunity to participate. Thus, the social and cultural context of this region of the country at this point in time as well as the ages of participants and attitudes displayed in these particular courses affected participant responses.

You are also more likely to obtain accurate data if you do not ask the respondent to reveal his or her identity. Survey respondents should remain anonymous unless there is some clear and pressing justification for collecting information about their identity. Be sensitive to including too many requests for demographic information. Although it may be interesting to know this information, ask for only the data you will need to answer your research questions or hypotheses. More sensitive questions can be asked if respondents' identities are not known.

Remember that respondents pay close attention and infer meaning from how the question or statement is worded; thus, taking these issues, as well as conversational norms, into account will help you write questions and statements that elicit the type of response you desire (Schwarz et al., 1998). Pretesting survey items with individuals with the same characteristics as potential respondents can help assure you that your question is meaningful and understandable.

Open Questions   There are two question formats. The first is the open question. When respondents use their own words to respond to a question, it is an **open question.** This question form gives you data from a respondent's point of view rather than your own (Fink, 1995a). Open questions are particularly helpful when the topic you are studying is relatively new. For example, a researcher wants to know if, and to what degree, the respondent uses websites to obtain information in making voting selections about candidates. The web is still a relatively new site of political campaigning. Thus, an open question could be a good way to find out how influential websites are after the researcher has asked closed questions (questions that have a few defined answers) about computer availability and web usage. Look at Table 9.2 for examples.

Open questions will create multiple responses. As a result, responses from participants may not be comparable. For example, one respondent can provide the URLs of websites he frequently visits whereas another respondent admits she has trouble distinguishing between webpages sponsored by a candidate's political party and unofficial webpages that describe the candidate and his views. As you can imagine, responses to open questions are often difficult to compare and interpret. If you must use open questions, use them sparingly.

Open questions rely on how people respond. Thus, researchers need to consider what constitutes an adequate answer and build that request into the question. A good open question is one

TABLE 9.2 Examples of Open and Closed Questions

Type of Question	Example
Closed	Do you have access to a personal computer?
Closed	(If the respondent's answer is "yes") Do you ever use the computer to surf the web?
Open	(If the respondent's answer is "yes") What do you look for on the web?
Closed	Do you ever look for information about political candidates or political parties?
Open	(If the respondent's answer is "yes") What types of information are helpful on those sites? Or, What appeals to you about sites with political information?

that is communicated in the same way to all respondents. Simply, if respondents differ in their perceptions of what constitutes an adequate answer, their answers will differ for reasons that have nothing to do with what you are trying to measure. For example, in a study on how students identify with their university, a researcher wanted to ask, "How would you describe the University of Kansas?" Possible answers could include "it's a public university," "it's where I'm getting my degree," "it has a great basketball program," "it's a school with tradition; both my mom and dad graduated from there," and so on. All of these and more are possible and reasonable. A better way to state the question would be to ask, "How would you, as a student, describe the University of Kansas to a potential student?" because it better specifies the kind of answer the researcher was seeking.

In other open formats, participants are directed to recall episodes or past interactions they participated in. Researchers use a **recall cue** to draw participants' attention to the issue they are interested in or to restrict their attention to a particular type of interaction. For example, in a study of rituals in marriages, Bruess and Pearson (1997) used the following recall cue:

> Below, please list and EXPLAIN in DETAIL all of the "routines" (or "rituals") that you and your spouse have developed either presently or have had in the past. Some of these routines might be very silly and trivial (such as regularly tugging on each other's ears to say "I love you") or they might involve elaborate planning (such as taking a "get away weekend" every fall).
>
> We are interested in "routines" (or "rituals") that you and your spouse repeatedly do together, or for one another. For instance, other couples have reported that they regularly called each other during the day, go to particular restaurants or other favorite spots together, have a ritual of eating out on certain nights, take walks together at certain times, or regularly purchase special treats for one another [that have] special meanings.
>
> Another couple reported regularly playing cribbage and drinking a cocktail together which served as a prelude to love making. Another couple regularly planned "adult dinners" after the children were in bed; they explained that no food was on the floor, they ate [slowly], were able to talk with another, and shared a glass of wine.
>
> Please describe ANY routine (or "ritual") shared with your spouse no matter how small or large it is. After explaining each routine (or "ritual") completely, please respond to the questions which follow it. (p. 31)

This recall cue is very specific and should restrict the answers respondents give. When you need to include a recall cue, try it out before administering the survey or questionnaire. Recall cues are effective when they make reference to what happened, where it happened, and who was involved. Recall cues that ask participants to begin with the most recent event are generally more effective unless the material has an inherent temporal or historical order—such as recalling where someone has lived since graduating from high school (Schwarz et al., 1998). Because recalling may take several seconds, give participants plenty of time to respond if you are using recall cues in face-to-face or telephone surveys.

If you are using open questions in an interactive format, capture everything the respondent says in exactly the way he or she says it. Do not try to code or abbreviate responses while the person is talking. Coding procedures are best done after all data have been collected. If you are using open questions in a written survey format, leave more space than you believe respondents will need to write their response. You do not want participants to base their response on the amount of space. Rather, you want them to be motivated to write as much and in as much detail as they would like.

Closed Questions   When respondents are asked a question (or given a statement) and then given a set of responses to select from, the question is **closed.** Questions that require a simple "yes" or "no" answer are closed questions. Likewise, questions that ask for a specific piece of information are closed. For example, "How old are you?" is a closed question because simply answering "I'm 23" answers the question. No other explanation or description is required.

Some closed questions are more difficult to write because the answers must be known in advance and standardized into a response set (Fink, 1995a). However, this difficulty is offset by the ease of comparability, which makes closed questions ideal when surveys or questionnaires are used with large samples.

Closed questions are also ideal for capturing attitudes or perceptions. Generally, constructs (for example, interaction involvement, communication adaptability) will require multiple items. If this is the case, a stimulus statement or stimulus question is also required. For instance, the stimulus statement for the Communicative Adaptability Scale (Duran, 1983) reads:

> The following are statements about communication behaviors. Answer each item as it relates to your general style of communication (the type of communicator you are most often) in social situations. Please indicate the degree to which each statement applies to you by placing the appropriate number (according to the scale below) in the space provided.

As you can see, the stimulus statement directs the respondent's attention to the type of

---

DESIGN CHECK

Racial and Ethnic Group Identification

Many respondents are confused or frustrated when asked to identify their race or ethnicity on a survey or questionnaire. In some cases, the terminology used is unfamiliar to respondents. In other cases, individuals with mixed racial or ethnic backgrounds are uncomfortable when asked "select the category that best describes you." As a result of these and other problems in how people use racial and ethnic identifiers, the Office of Management and Budget (OMB) created standards for maintaining, collecting, and presenting federal data on race and ethnicity. This directive standardized racial and ethnic categories used in the 2000 U.S. census. All other federal programs adopted these standards. The categories used by the OMB are often applied in research projects as well, especially those funded by government agencies. Working from the position that the categories represent a social–political construct for collecting data on race and ethnicity of broad population groups in the United States, the OMB recognizes that the recommended minimum categories are not anthropologically or scientifically based. The OMB recommends that, whenever possible, respondents should self-identify their ethnicity and race using the following two-part question:

Ethnicity (Select one)

- Hispanic or Latino
- Not Hispanic or Latino

Race (Select one or more)

- American Indian or Alaska Native
- Asian
- Black or African American

---

questions he or she will be answering and gives general instructions for completing the questionnaire. If several constructs are measured in your survey, you may need a separate stimulus statement for each section as well as general instructions as an introduction to the survey.

RESPONSE SETS FOR CLOSED QUESTIONS   There are many different types of response sets for closed questions. The most typical response set is *nominal,* or *categorical.* This means that responses in the set do not have a numerical equivalent. In a survey about communication choices at work, the researcher asks

Are you (check the appropriate box):

☐ a member of the clerical staff?

☐ a member of the maintenance team?

☐ a member of the management team?

☐ a member of the production team?

Respondents are being asked to name or categorize themselves. The answers have no natural numerical value. In other words, one answer has no more or no less value than another.

As explained in Chapter 6, nominal or categorical responses are often used to obtain demographic information about respondents (for example, age, sex, marital status, employment status, socioeconomic status, education, income, occupation, religious preference or affiliation, race and ethnic background), and there are special considerations in developing these response sets. Options in a response set should be exhaustive, mutually exclusive, and equivalent. *Exhaustive* means that all possible choices are represented.

- Native Hawaiian or Pacific Islander
- White

Alternately, a combined format can be used, especially when observers collect data on race and ethnicity. For this format, researchers should try to record ethnicity and race or multiple races, but it is acceptable to indicate only one category of the six. For the combined format, the minimum categories are

- American Indian or Alaska Native
- Asian
- Black or African American
- Hispanic or Latino
- Native Hawaiian or Pacific Islander
- White

In presentation of data on race and ethnicity, the OMB indicates that it is inappropriate to identify certain population groups as minority groups or "nonwhite." The OMB recognizes, however, that use of all the categories may not always be the most effective or appropriate manner for describing the racial and ethnic distinctions for certain populations. Thus, after collecting data with the minimum categories, researchers can present their data in the following ways, using collective descriptions of minority races when appropriate:

- White, Black or African American and Other Races, All Other Races
- White, Black or African American, All Other Races
- Whites, All Other Races

Mutually exclusive means that the respondent will view only one of the choices in the response set as the correct or best answer. The response set is not mutually exclusive if a respondent finds two different choices that can represent his or her answer. *Equivalent* means that the response choices are equal to one another.

In the previous example about communication choices at work, it may appear at first glance that all employees will be able to select a response that best identifies them. But, an engineer might not know where he or she fits. Is an engineer with supervisory responsibility a member of the management team or a member of the production team? Thus, the response set is not satisfactory because it is neither exhaustive nor mutually exclusive, although the response choices appear to be equivalent, as each is a choice about job function.

Many times, researchers add the response of "other" to catch the responses they have not considered or identified or to cover categories for which they believe there will be only a few respondents. Relying on this strategy too frequently will produce data that are not interpretable. To develop exhaustive, mutually exclusive, and equivalent response sets, think of the context and the population. Looking at response sets on other closed-question survey items will help you in developing your own. Be careful, however, about including too many demographic items. Some respondents will regard these as sensitive inquiries and may become suspicious. It is best to ask for only the demographic information that you need to answer your research questions or test your hypotheses. If you find that you need to collect demographic data, consider collecting these data at the end of the survey.

LIKERT-TYPE SCALES   The most common response set to closed questions is the **Likert-type scale,** which asks respondents to respond to a survey item with one of these (or similar) choices: strongly agree, agree, disagree, strongly disagree. To treat the data statistically, numerical values are assigned to each of the response choices. Because the numerical values are considered interval level data, the responses to a set of questions can be added together to create a total score for that variable.

Most survey response sets have a 5-point scale as response choices. Sometimes the response sets are expanded to accommodate a 7-point scale. For example, the Organizational Communication Conflict Instrument (Putnam & Wilson, 1982) uses a 7-point scale with the anchors of "always, very often, often, sometimes, seldom, very seldom, never." Typically, larger numerical values are associated with the response choice that represents the most or the largest. For example, 5 is commonly anchored with "very often" or "completely agree." However, you may want to reverse this principle for embarrassing or sensitive items (Fink, 1995a) or if the item is written in the negative rather than positive form. For example, in McCroskey and McCain's (1974) Interpersonal Attraction Scale, the response set for the item "It would be difficult to meet and talk with him (her)" has the highest number anchored with "strongly disagree" rather than "strongly agree."

Although frequently used, any response that contains "strongly" is considered unsuitable by some researchers because the "strongly" acts as an emotional trigger (Fowler, 1995). Alternative phrasing could be "completely agree, generally agree, generally disagree, completely disagree," or "completely true, mostly true, mostly untrue, completely untrue."

These types of response sets generally offer a middle, or neutral, response like "agree and disagree" or "undecided." Although this sometimes accurately captures the respondent's belief or answer, many respondents will use this middle category when they do not have enough information about the question or have not formed an opinion. Table 9.3 can help you identify appropriate

and meaningful response sets for different types of closed questions.

Notice how these response sets are balanced (Fink 1995a). In other words, the two end points mean the opposite of each other. Also notice that the intervals between the choices are about equal. Remember that using the neutral category may capture data different from what you intend or that respondents may use the neutral choice as an excuse for not answering the question. Thus, use a neutral category as a middle point only when it could be a valid response. Beware of sticking "no opinion" or "don't know" in as a neutral choice. Having no opinion is different from having an opinion that is partially favorable *and* partially unfavorable. Do use "no opinion" or "don't know," however, when that response could be appropriate for your questionnaire or survey topic (Schwarz et al., 1998).

Finally, select the word anchors carefully. Although you may clearly discriminate among *usually, sometimes,* and *seldom,* others using the scale may view these three words as synonyms for one another. Use the exercise in the Try This! box ("How Different Are *Usually, Sometimes,* and *Seldom?*") to gauge the type of responses these words evoke.

SEMANTIC DIFFERENTIAL SCALES   Another common response set for closed questions is a **semantic differential scale** (Osgood et al., 1957). For each question or item, a respondent is given a numerical scale anchored by word opposites, or bipolar adjectives. Look at the examples in the next paragraph. Notice how the adjectives in the pairs are complete opposites of each other. The 7-point number continuum between the word anchors represents the degree to which the respondent agrees with one or the other anchor.

| Friendly | 1 \| 2 \| 3 \| 4 \| 5 \| 6 \| 7 | Unfriendly |
| Satisfied | 1 \| 2 \| 3 \| 4 \| 5 \| 6 \| 7 | Not Satisfied |

In the first example, if respondents circle 1, then they are indicating that the person they were asked about is friendly. If the respondents choose 3, then they are indicating that the target person is more friendly than unfriendly. The midpoint of the scale, indicated by the number 4, is used if the respondent is unsure if the target person is

TABLE 9.3 Response Set Alternatives for Likert-Type Scales

Type of Survey Item	Examples of Response Set Alternatives				
Frequency	Very often	Fairly often	Occasionally	Rarely	Never
	Always	Usually	Sometimes	Rarely	Never
Feelings	Very positive	Generally positive	Mixed	Generally negative	Very negative
Evaluation	Excellent	Very good	Good	Fair	Poor
Satisfaction	Completely satisfied	Mostly satisfied	Unsure	Mostly dissatisfied	Completely dissatisfied
Agreement	Completely agree	Generally agree	Unsure	Generally disagree	Completely disagree
Accuracy or endorsement	Completely true	Somewhat true	Unsure	Somewhat untrue	Completely untrue
Intensity	None	Very mild	Mild	Moderate	Severe
Comparison	Much more than others	Somewhat more than others	About the same as others	Somewhat less than others	Much less than others

friendly or unfriendly. In the second example, respondents would circle 7, 6, or 5 to indicate some level of dissatisfaction with their performance on a particular communication behavior.

Notice that only the ends of the continuum are anchored with words. This allows the respondent to select the meaning he or she has for the stimulus or target, which can be an object, a communication practice or process, him- or herself or another person, or even an abstract concept. A continuum and its pair of opposing adjectives captures respondents' evaluations and is commonly used to measure attitudes or predispositions toward the stimulus or target.

Choosing Between Open and Closed Questions
To summarize survey design issues, use open questions if

1. Respondents' own words are important and you want to be able to quote what respondents say
2. Respondents are willing and can answer the question in their own words

3. The set of response choices is unknown
4. You are willing to analyze the text of the responses
5. Your reporting needs are best met by this question form

Alternately, use closed questions if

1. There is agreement on what the response set should be
2. Statistical analysis and reporting of the data is desirable or necessary

Regardless of your choice, remember these caveats. It is easier for respondents to endorse an opinion in a closed-response format. If you rely on an open-response format, the opinion may not be volunteered. On the other hand, if your response set is written in such a way as to omit a potential response, the opinion will not be reported at all (Schwarz & Hippler, 1991). As you can see, both response-set formats have clear and profound implications for data collection.

TRY THIS!   ### How Different Are *Usually, Sometimes,* and *Seldom?*

In developing a questionnaire item, you must carefully consider how to word the statement or question. You should also be careful in choosing the response set for each item. In response to questions that ask about frequency of behaviors, some researchers use *always, usually, sometimes, seldom,* and *never*. Whereas most people would agree that *always* means 100% and *never* means 0%, what percentages would you infer from *usually, sometimes,* and *seldom?* Ask three people to identify the percentages they associate with *usually, sometimes,* and *seldom*. In each of these trials, change the order of word anchors. Compare the responses they provide with the responses others in your class receive. Are the percentages similar enough for you to have confidence in using this terminology to capture participants' responses? Were the percentages given in the same frequency order in which you would have ordered the words?

How the Survey Looks

You can see that there is a great deal to consider when developing or collecting data. Additionally, you should consider the design or layout of the questionnaire (Fink, 1995a). It should be uncluttered and readable. You can easily make it so by using the table function in your word-processing program. Columns should line up neatly. There should be space between survey items. The stimulus question or statement should be prominently displayed. Respondents should be told explicitly how and where to mark their responses. If an interviewer reads the survey to a respondent over the phone or in person, the survey should be designed so that the interviewer can easily distinguish between instructions to him or her and questions or instructions to be read to the respondent.

PRETESTING THE SURVEY OR QUESTIONNAIRE

As you can see, a researcher can spend considerable time and energy either in looking for and adopting an existing questionnaire or in developing a new questionnaire. This energy should not be wasted. Thus, it is a good idea to pretest the instrument. **Pretesting,** sometimes called

pilot testing, occurs when, before data collection actually begins, the researcher tries the survey or questionnaire with a small group of participants who are similar to those individuals who form the population. Note that this form of pretesting is not the same as pretesting as part of experimental or quasi-experimental research designs. Data are not collected when a researcher is pretesting the survey or questionnaire.

There are four approaches to pretesting a survey: cognitive, conventional, behavior coding, and expert panels (Presser & Blair, 1994). The cognitive approach to pretesting helps uncover questions that can stimulate multiple interpretations. For example, your survey includes the question and response set "Do you own your own home?" followed by "yes" and "no." This seems a simple and straightforward question. Researchers would likely expect individuals participating in the survey to be able to answer the question. With **cognitive pretesting,** you would ask questions about the question "Do you own your own home?" When a participant answers "yes" to this question, does that mean personally owning the place where he or she lives, or does it mean owning the home with someone else? In answering "yes," does the person mean that he or she owns the home outright or that there is a mortgage on the home? In answering "yes," does the participant mean a single-family home or a condo, high-rise apartment, or duplex? If these differences are important to your survey, you would need to rephrase the question to be more specific. Thus, cognitive pretesting allows the researcher to test for semantic problems, or problems affecting how easily the questions are understood. As another example, if you were researching the social network of individuals and looking at their living arrangements as a predictor of the breadth of their network, making specific distinctions in living arrangements could make a difference in the interpretation of your results.

Cognitive pretesting is best done face-to-face with a person who is similar to those who will participate. Being face-to-face allows the researcher to watch the nonverbal expressions as individuals try to answer the questions. Probing questions and follow-up questions can be used to capture what the individuals think questions mean. The advantage here, obviously, is that the researcher can ask questions and try rephrasing questions until she is receiving exactly the type of data she wants.

A second type of pretesting is the **conventional pretest.** In this type of pretest, the researcher selects several individuals who are like persons in the population. The survey is completed just as it will be done in the study. This type of pretest allows the researcher to reflect on the survey process and make any changes to the administration of the survey before it is mailed, given, or sent to members of the sample. Conventional pretesting captures the experience of the interviewers, or survey administrators, but it does not capture information from the perspective of those who participate in the survey.

This was the strategy used by Ellis (2000), who developed a questionnaire to assess students' perceptions of teachers' confirmation behaviors. She pretested the questionnaire on a group of 24 students before it was used with the larger sample in the study.

Behavior coding is the third type of pretesting and is used only when the survey is conducted in the face-to-face format. The idea in this type of pretesting is to have a third person monitor the interaction between the interviewer and respondent. The monitors are outside the survey process and, as a result, are more objective in identifying problems. The monitor observes the interaction as it happens. This means that he or she can look for only a few problems at a time. A monitor can look for problems from the perspectives of both the interviewer and the respondent. These include the interviewer changing how a question is read across many participants, interviewer probes for additional answers from some respondents and not others, respondent asking for clarification, and respondent giving uncodable or unexpected answers.

A fourth type of pretesting is the use of **expert panels.** In this type of pretesting, experts in research methodology or in the survey's content read through the questionnaire together and discuss potential problems they see with the survey. Because they are experts, this type of pretesting can point out semantic problems in how questions are worded and interviewer administration techniques, as well as potential problems with analyzing the data after the survey is complete. For example, Mueller and Lee (2002) used graduate communication students with work experience to be an expert panel to examine a questionnaire on leader behavior and communication satisfaction. The panel was asked to identify any unclear wording, evaluate the ease of response, and indicate the time it took them to complete the survey. Based on feedback from the expert panel, the research clarified some terminology and how respondents would mark their answers on the survey. The survey was then used to collect data from full-time employees. Although it is time consuming and sometimes difficult to find experts who are willing to help you out, pretesting with expert panels is the most productive way to identify problems with survey and questionnaire administration.

At the completion of pretesting, make the final changes. Before copying the survey, proofread it one last time. If your survey is mailed to respondents or given to a large group of people as part of a laboratory experiment, be sure that a thank you is the last thing respondents see. If you collect the survey data in person, be sure to thank the respondent for his or her time and cooperation. If respondents must take an additional

TRY THIS!

Does This Questionnaire Need Modification?

Review the questionnaire below. How do its overall design and item design adhere to the principles identified in this chapter? Are there changes or modifications you believe are necessary?

Communicative Adaptability Scale

Instructions: The following are statements about communication behaviors. Answer each item as it relates to your general style of communication (the type of communicator you are most often) in social situations. Please indicate the degree to which each statement applies to you by circling the appropriate number (according to the scale below) for each item.

5	4	3	2	1
Almost always true of me	*Often true of me*	*Sometimes true of me*	*Rarely true of me*	*Never true of me*

		5	4	3	2	1
1.	I feel nervous in social situations.	5	4	3	2	1
2.	People think I am witty.	5	4	3	2	1
3.	When speaking I have problems with grammar.	5	4	3	2	1
4.	I enjoy meeting new people.	5	4	3	2	1
5.	In most social situations I feel tense and constrained.	5	4	3	2	1
6.	When someone makes a negative comment about me, I respond with a witty comeback.	5	4	3	2	1
7.	When I embarrass myself, I often make a joke about it.	5	4	3	2	1
8.	I enjoy socializing with various groups of people.	5	4	3	2	1
9.	I try to make the other person feel important.	5	4	3	2	1
10.	At times I don't use appropriate verb tense.	5	4	3	2	1
11.	I often make jokes when in tense situations.	5	4	3	2	1
12.	While I'm talking I think about how the other person feels.	5	4	3	2	1
13.	When [I am] talking, my posture seems awkward and tense.	5	4	3	2	1
14.	I disclose at the same level that others disclose to me.	5	4	3	2	1
15.	I find it easy to get along with new people.	5	4	3	2	1

16.	I sometimes use words incorrectly.	5	4	3	2	1
17.	When I self-disclose I know what I am revealing.	5	4	3	2	1
18.	I try to be warm when communicating with another.	5	4	3	2	1
19.	I am relaxed when talking with others.	5	4	3	2	1
20.	When I am anxious, I often make jokes.	5	4	3	2	1
21.	I sometimes use one word when I mean to use another.	5	4	3	2	1
22.	I do not "mix" well at social functions.	5	4	3	2	1
23.	I am aware of how intimate the disclosures of others are.	5	4	3	2	1
24.	I am verbally and nonverbally supportive of other people.	5	4	3	2	1
25.	I sometimes use words incorrectly.	5	4	3	2	1
26.	I have difficulty pronouncing some words.	5	4	3	2	1
27.	I like to be active in different social groups.	5	4	3	2	1
28.	I am aware of how intimate my disclosures are.	5	4	3	2	1
29.	My voice sounds nervous when I talk with others.	5	4	3	2	1
30.	I try to make the other person feel good.	5	4	3	2	1

Circle the appropriate response for each of the following items:

31.	I am a college: freshman sophomore junior senior
32.	I currently attend college: full time part time
33.	I am: a Communication major not a Communication major undecided or have not declared my major
34.	I am: female male

Thank you. Please return this survey to the session facilitator.
You may leave when you are finished.

SOURCE: Duran, R.L. "Communicative Adaptability: A Review of Conceptualization and Measurement," *Communication Quarterly, 40,* pp. 253–268. Used by permission of Eastern Communication Association.

AN ETHICAL ISSUE

Would You Participate?

Survey research relies on the extent to which people are willing to respond to and answer the questions presented them. This self-selection bias on the part of participants creates a tension with researchers' desire to obtain responses from all members of a selected sample. Obviously, researchers cannot require, threaten, or force individuals to participate or respond. As a result, a tension exists between the scientific needs of a survey study and the rights of people to decline to participate partially or in total. Are there survey topics that would cause you to decline to participate? Is there anything the researcher or interviewer could say or do to make you change your mind? Think of at least three sensitive survey topics. How would you design the survey and its administration to increase the likelihood of participation?

step to return the survey by mail or fax, be sure to give specific instructions and a reasonable deadline for doing so. Also consider using preaddressed and stamped envelopes to increase the response rate for mailed surveys.

SAMPLING ISSUES FOR SURVEYS

In addition to the sampling issues presented in Chapter 7, using surveys requires the researcher to consider some unique issues.

Response Rate

A common error is to confuse sample size with response rate. They are not the same. **Response rate,** or return rate, is the number of people who respond after they have been contacted as part of the sample and asked to participate. An easy way to calculate response rate is to divide the number of people who responded by the number of respondents identified as part of the sample. For example, if you identified 300 potential individuals as the sample for your survey and 175 responded, your response rate would be 58.33% (175 divided by 300 equals 0.5833).

Although researchers wish for a high response rate, there is no standard, and response rates vary by survey technique, the interest your survey topic generates, and the type of respondent you are seeking. How will you know what an acceptable response rate is? A study of journal articles in the managerial and behavioral sciences found a median response rate of 60% and a standard deviation of 20%. Thus, a response rate of 40 to 80% could be considered normal (Baruch, 1999). If you believe that the response rate will be low, you could choose to oversample. By increasing your sample size, you might also increase your response rate—but this is no guarantee.

Unfortunately, all surveys will suffer from **nonresponse,** or the failure to obtain data from individuals in the sample. Perhaps people are ill, too busy, or reluctant, or they do not have the time your survey would take. If you rely on mail or email to distribute your surveys, you will discover that people move or change addresses. If your response rate is low, you can use a second, or follow-up, mailing or phone call to increase your response rate. Following up with nonrespondents is important because distinct demographic differences are often found between groups of respondents and non-respondents (Erickson, Cheatham, & Jordan, 1978). Thus, researchers should be sensitive to the differences that may exist between those who choose to respond and those who do not. These differences could create a potential bias in the data and, subsequently, the results.

Unfortunately, yet another problem exists: Some questionnaires or surveys are returned in an unusable form. In most of these cases, participants fail to fill out the survey in its entirety.

Sometimes, participants write in remarks instead of using the response categories provided. When calculating the response rate, be sure to identify the number of usable surveys returned.

Using Census as an Alternative to Sampling

Finally, there are some situations in which sampling from the population is not advisable (Henry, 1990). Specifically, two situations would require that the researcher survey everyone in the population rather than use a subset of the population as a sample. This is known as a **census.** The first is when the population of interest consists of fewer than 50 members. In this case, collecting data on the entire population improves both the reliability and the credibility of the data.

The second situation is when there is some overriding reason to include everyone. For example, when there is a single unique or extreme case, sampling is not appropriate because there is a chance that the unique case may be left out and invalidate results. Or there may be a political reason to include everyone. For example, leaving out some of an organization's executives from a survey on employee practices may create a situation in which those left out would not support the recommendations based on the findings. Regardless of the reason, if all members of the population are surveyed, you have achieved a census design.

SURVEY RELIABILITY AND VALIDITY

The most common form of reliability for questionnaires and surveys is internal reliability, because they contain multiple items to measure one construct. As you recall from Chapter 6, *reliability* means consistency. For example, the Communicative Adaptability Scale contains 30 items. Of the 30 items, five are associated with each of the six following subconstructs: social composure, social confirmation, social experience, appropriate disclosure, articulation, and wit.

Internal reliability is the degree to which each set of five items was consistent in measuring the subconstruct. Referred to as Cronbach's alpha, the measurement of internal reliability is expressed in value from 0 to 1.00, with 0 indicating that the five items had no internal consistency and 1.00 indicating that respondents answered each of the five questions for a particular construct in a similar way. Perfect internal reliability is rare. Generally, an internal reliability of .70 or greater is considered adequate and acceptable in communication research. This level of reliability means that, in most cases, respondents gave the same response or a similar response to most items in that particular construct. Most statistical programs can compute a scale's or subscale's internal reliability using Cronbach's alpha. Recall from Chapter 6 that other forms of reliability are also important to consider when using questionnaires. These include test–retest and split-half reliability.

Also recall that *validity* means accuracy, or that the survey or questionnaire assesses what it purports to measure. Surveys should have high *content validity.* This means that the survey instrument or items measure thoroughly and appropriately what they are intended to measure. For example, a questionnaire investigating the construct of marital conflict should include items about arguments over household and childcare responsibilities, as well as items about the influence of third parties (e.g., in-laws) in creating tension between husband and wife. Another type of validity typically found in survey questions is *face validity.* A good way to establish face validity is to ask yourself the question "Does this item (or items) ask all the needed questions in language that is appropriate?" For example, in measuring sexual harassment, a researcher would achieve face validity by including items that address actions frequently associated with sexual harassment, such as telling sexual jokes or inappropriate touching.

With respect to surveys, *construct validity* is established when a survey in fact does distinguish between people who do and do not have certain characteristics. Researchers use surveys to establish or identify levels or types of communication behavior. For example, a survey might ask about a respondent's media usage. The survey has construct validity to the extent that it distinguishes between people who are heavy and light media users.

ANALYZING AND REPORTING SURVEY DATA

Once data are collected, a survey or questionnaire still cannot be useful until the data are interpreted. Researchers collect survey data from a sample of many individuals so the results can be generalized to the population from which the sample was selected. This is an important point! The researcher should not be interested in the responses of any individual, or even a set of individuals. Data are interpreted as a whole. In other words, the data of all participants are combined to create a picture of the population.

One of the weaknesses of using questionnaires or surveys as the only data collection method is that the data produced are largely descriptive and can only describe relationships between variables (see correlation as one test of variable relationships in Chapter 12). Because the data are collected at one point in time on all variables, it is difficult to demonstrate that one variable caused a change in another variable (Schwarz et al., 1998).

One way to overcome this weakness is to use a panel survey design. **Panels** are longitudinal research designs. Data are collected through survey techniques at more than one point in time. In this case, a sample of persons is repeatedly measured over time. If the same individuals participate in each survey, or wave, then the panel is fixed. If some of the same individuals participate, and in addition, new participants are added, the panel design is rotating. Still, problems exist. One is with participants who leave the panel survey because of some reason connected with the survey variables (for example, a married couple participates in the first wave but separates before the second wave of questioning). There is also some evidence that measuring a variable at time 1 causes changes in how the variable is measured at time 2 (Schwarz et al., 1998).

Although panel surveys allow the researcher to draw causal inferences and to assess change over time, panel surveys are also subject to practical problems as well as measurement error. For example, Johnson and Chang (2000) used a panel survey design to investigate the internal and external communication among a confederation of contractors who provided service to a geographically dispersed organization. Self-report questionnaires were mailed to all members of the confederation at three points. To encourage questionnaire completion, the research team emailed participants three times: (1) to notify them that the questionnaire was coming, (2) to remind them that it was time to begin recording their data, and (3) to remind them to return their questionnaire.

Communication scholars can also overcome this weakness by testing data on models developed from theory. For example, Mueller and Lee (2002) used a survey to collect data at one point in time. The design of the survey was based on the research literature and a well-developed theory allowing them to advance and test hypotheses.

Generally, the data produced by closed questions can be interpreted using conventional statistical tools. These data can be organized and described using the descriptive statistics explained in Chapter 10. These tools assist the researcher in developing basic reports and explanations of the data. More complex interpretations can be made by using the statistical tools that test for differences and relationships (Chapter 11 and Chapter 12, respectively). Responses to open questions first need to be categorized or content analyzed, as described in Chapter 13. Once this is done, frequency counts are useful tools for organizing and reporting data.

Once analyzed, the results are written as a research report. Chapter 17 describes, in detail, how to write a quantitative research report. If survey data will be presented to respondents, charts, tables, and graphs are effective ways to present survey data. By viewing the data in a graphic form, most people will be able to make sense of the information, even without having a background in research or statistics. If you entered the data on a spreadsheet or statistics program, graphic functions available there will produce a variety of visual displays.

Regardless of their use, the data and their results should never be reported out of context or without describing the respondents or context of the survey or questionnaire. If you used graphics, data reports should be appropriately labeled to allow others to make their own interpretation of the data at a glance. This does not mean that you should refrain from interpreting the data first.

Rather, whoever reads or uses the report of the data should be able to come, independently, to the same conclusions that you have drawn. Forcing the data or results to fit your need or to satisfy a survey objective when it does not is unethical.

SUMMARY

1. Surveys and questionnaires are the most common quantitative method used in communication research.

2. Often self-administered, surveys can be distributed in written format through the mail, web, or email, or interviewers can ask questions face-to-face or over the phone.

3. Research questions or hypotheses drive the survey or questionnaire design.

4. Existing and established questionnaires can be used in some instances; otherwise, the researcher has to develop the questionnaire.

5. Recall cues, or stimulus statements, are needed to direct or restrict participants' responses.

6. Open questions allow the respondent to use his or her own words in responding to a question or statement.

7. Closed questions are complete with standardized response sets; respondents choose from the responses provided by the researcher.

8. Many closed questions can be adequately responded to using a 5-point or 7-point Likert-type response scale, and must be exhaustive as well as mutually exclusive.

9. How the survey looks can affect if and how respondents will answer; it should be uncluttered and readable and respondents should be told explicitly how and where to mark their responses.

10. Before using the survey in a research project, it should be pilot tested, or pretested.

11. Response rate, or the number of people who respond after they have been contacted to participate, should not be confused with sample size.

12. An aspect of reliability central to questionnaires is internal reliability, or the degree to which multiple questions or items consistently measure the same construct.

13. Once collected, the researcher must analyze and interpret the data as a whole, rather than focusing on the responses of any individual.

14. Survey data are collected at one point in time, which weakens their predictive ability unless theoretical models have been developed before the survey data are collected.

KEY TERMS

behavior coding
census
closed question
cognitive pretesting
conventional pretesting
expert panel
Likert-type scale
nonresponse
open question
panel
pilot testing

pretesting
recall cue
response rate
self-administered survey
semantic differential scale
self-reports
social desirability response
survey

CHAPTER TEN

Descriptive Statistics

Chapter Checklist

After reading this chapter, you should be able to:

1. Explain the concept of the normal curve.

2. Assess the data you collected for its distribution and compare it to the normal curve.

3. Create a frequency distribution and polygon for each variable in a dataset.

4. Compute and interpret the mean, median, and mode for each variable in a dataset.

5. Compute the range and standard deviation for each variable in a dataset.

6. Explain the relationship between the mean and standard deviation for scores on a variable.

7. Use frequencies and percentages to provide a summary description of nominal data.

8. Accurately calculate descriptive statistics.

9. Accurately report descriptive statistics.

Numbers are just one tool researchers can use to collect **data,** or information about communication phenomena. In their most basic function, numbers can capture the quality, intensity, value, or degree of the variables used in quantitative communication studies. Recall from Chapter 6 on measurement that numbers have no inherent value. Rather, a numerical value is meaningful and can be interpreted only within the context in which the number was collected. Also recall that each variable must be operationalized, meaning that the researcher must specify exactly what data were collected and how. These processes are valuable to scholarly research because they help researchers say precisely what is being studied and what is not.

The numerical data, or **raw data,** collected from each participant is compiled into a **dataset** or collection of the raw data for the same variables for a sample of participants. A dataset is shown in Figure 10.1. Using the numbers in the dataset, researchers compute another set of numbers. These are called **descriptive statistics,** and they convey essential basic information about the dataset as a whole.

Look at the data in Figure 10.1. From the raw data, a researcher can compute four numbers to summarize and represent variables in the dataset regardless of its size. The mean, standard deviation, range, and number of cases are commonly used to provide a summary interpretation of the data. Each of these is discussed in detail in this chapter.

Besides their descriptive, or summarizing, function, numbers are also used in more complex ways to provide information about the relationships between or among variables in the study and to help researchers draw conclusions about a population by examining the data of the sample. This use of numbers is known as **inferential statistics;** several types of inferential statistics, or statistical tests, are covered in Chapters 11 and 12.

Regardless of which statistical test may be called for by a hypothesis or research question, you should be able to interpret and report, or read and interpret, basic information about the participants and each variable in a research study. Having a basic understanding of how researchers

use numbers as a tool in collecting and interpreting data can help you make an independent assessment of a researcher's conclusion.

But before we can turn to those summary descriptive statistics, we need to introduce the properties of the normal curve. Descriptive statistics and their interpretation are inextricably linked to it.

NORMAL CURVE

Generally, it is not meaningful to analyze or interpret a score on one variable from one individual. One participant's score (for example, a participant's leadership score) is just raw data. Without other data to compare the score to, the researcher would be left with an isolated data point. Interpreting and reporting individual scores is not practical, for it would make the research report too long. Besides, researchers are generally not interested in the results of one individual.

More interesting, and useful, is the comparison of data collected from many individuals on one variable. Knowing how individuals in one sample scored on a leadership assessment provides the opportunity to examine any one score against other scores in the sample and the opportunity to examine the set of scores as a whole. As scientists over time and across disciplines have collected data from natural sources, they have discovered that frequency distributions of datasets tend to have one particular shape (Jaeger, 1990). This shape is the normal curve and represents one of the primary principles of statistics.

The **normal curve,** or bell curve, is a theoretical distribution of scores or other numerical values. Figure 10.2 illustrates the normal curve. The majority of cases are distributed around the peak in the middle, with progressively fewer cases as one moves away from the middle of the distribution. The normal curve is recognizable because of its distinct bell shape and symmetry—one side of the curve is a mirror image of the other side.

The horizontal axis represents all possible values of a variable, whereas the vertical axis represents the relative frequency with which those values occur. In a normal curve—and remember that it is a theoretical model—the mean (the average score), median (the score in the

Participant
identification
number   Variable names

id	train	tolerate	livesup	type1	type2	beh1	beh2	beh3
703	1	0	5	3	3	0	0	1
704	1	0	3	3	3	0	0	0
706	1	0	1	1	2	0	0	0
707	1	0	2	3	3	1	1	1
708	1	0	4	3	3	1	1	1
709	1	0	4	1	4	1	1	1
710	1	0	3	1	2	1	1	1
711	1	0	4	3	3	1	1	1
712	1	0	2	1	2	1	0	1
713	1	1	3	3	0	1	1	1
714	1	0	3	0	2	0	0	1
715	1	0	4	3	2	1	1	1
716	1	0	4	1	2	1	1	1
717	1	0	5	3	3	1	1	0
901	1	0	4	1	2	0	1	1

Raw data

Descriptive statistics for the variable *livesup*:
N (or number of cases) = 15
mean = 3.6 (sum of 54 divided by 15, the number of cases)
standard deviation = 0.91
range = 2 to 5, or 3

FIGURE 10.1   Example of a Dataset

middle of the distribution), and mode (the score that occurs most frequently) would have the same value and would divide the curve into two equal halves. Although it is highly unlikely that data for a variable could be represented as a true normal curve, scientists look for the normality of their data and the degree to which the distribution of their data deviates from the normal curve.

Skewed Distributions

When a distribution of scores is not normal, it is referred to as a **skewed distribution.** One side is not a mirror image of the other. Rather, the curve is asymmetrical; one side is different from the other. Thus, the mean, median, and mode will not be at the same point. Skewness, or the degree to which the distribution of data is bunched to one side or the other, is a direct reflection of the variability, or dispersion, of the scores.

A **positively skewed curve** represents a distribution in which there are very few scores on the right side of the distribution (see Figure 10.2). Thus, there are very few very high scores. The long tail pointing to the right indicates this. In a positively skewed curve, most of the scores are lumped together on the left side of the curve, below the mean. For example, students from a communication department with a strong focus on communication skills would likely have a positively skewed distribution of communication apprehension scores. Why? The department's curriculum requires each course to include a communication skill or performance element. As students take communication classes, they become more comfortable communicating, and their communication apprehension decreases significantly. As a result, very few students in the department have very high communication apprehension scores.

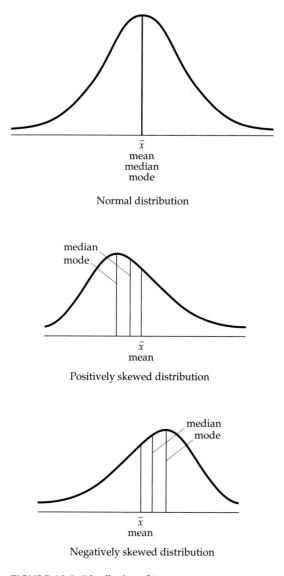

FIGURE 10.2 **Distribution of Scores**

Alternately, a **negatively skewed curve** represents a distribution in which there are very few scores on the left side of the distribution (see Figure 10.2). Thus, there are very few very low scores. The long tail pointing to the left indicates this. In a negatively skewed curve, most of the scores are lumped together on the right side of the curve, above the mean. If we return to the

example of communication students, this sample of students is also likely to have a negatively skewed distribution of communication competence scores. As students complete the skill or performance element in each class, they become more competent in their interactions. As a result, very few students in the department would have very low communication competence scores.

Notice the relative positions of the mean, median, and mode on the skewed distributions. The mean is always pulled to the skewed side (or side with the tail) of the distribution. Thus, the mean will always be the largest value of the three measures of central tendency in a positively skewed distribution and the smallest in a negatively skewed distribution. When distributions are skewed, the median is a better measure of central tendency than the mean.

Distributions of Data

Anytime you collect data, your first step should be to develop a frequency distribution and polygon for each variable in the dataset for which you have collected quantitative data.

Creating a frequency distribution is simple. Simply list the scores in order, from highest to lowest, and then identify the number of times each score occurs (Figure 10.3). With these steps completed, you can create a polygon. In this type of diagram, the range of possible scores for the variable is displayed on the horizontal axis. The frequencies with which those scores occur are listed on the vertical axis. With the axes defined, simply plot each data point according to its frequency of occurrence. Now, draw a line to connect each of the points you plotted. How would you interpret the polygon in Figure 10.3 for this dataset? Is it normal? Or is it skewed positively or negatively?

DESCRIPTIVE STATISTICS

Descriptive statistics are those numbers that supply information about the sample or those that supply information about variables. They simply describe what is found. Having this information, researchers and consumers of research reports can make value judgments or inferences about what the data mean.

Data as they were collected	Data ordered from highest to lowest	Scores x	Frequency f
73	83	83	1
82	82	82	1
76	81	81	1
75	80	80	2
83	80	79	3
79	79	78	4
77	79	77	4
76	79	76	4
69	78	75	3
78	78	74	3
71	78	73	1
78	78	72	1
80	77	71	1
77	77	70	1
74	77	69	1
81	77		
74	76		
79	76		
80	76		
78	76		
78	75		
77	75		
77	75		
74	74		
76	74		
79	74		
75	73		
76	72		
70	71		
72	70		
75	69		

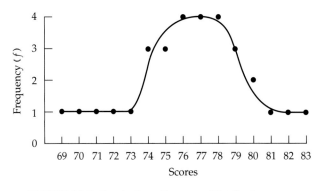

FIGURE 10.3 *Developing a Frequency Distribution*

TRY THIS!   **Are the Data Normal or Skewed?**

One of the best ways to learn about the normal curve is to demonstrate to yourself that this phenomenon exists naturally in many places. Collect data from at least two of the following populations (admittedly, you will not be conducting a random sample) and plot the data as a frequency distribution. Try to get at least 50 cases in your sample.

- Shoe sizes of other students (do not mix men and women)
- Amount of money other students have on them (convert to pennies)
- Number of pets other students have
- Number of times other students have been issued a traffic violation ticket

After plotting your data on a frequency distribution, assess the normalcy of the curve. Does it look more like the normal curve or like a skewed distribution? If it is skewed, what could account for that type of distribution? (Hint: If you collected the data about the amount of money people have on them, collecting data before or after lunch will affect their responses.)

Researchers describe data for each quantitative variable in three different ways. These are the number of cases or data points, central tendency, and dispersion or variability. Each of these descriptions provides information about the frequency of scores. The number of cases simply indicates the number of sources from which data were collected. Measures of central tendency describe how the majority of participants responded to a variable. Dispersion describes the spread of scores from the point of central tendency. Each of these concepts is described in the following sections. Figure 10.4 shows abbreviations commonly used in descriptive statistics.

Descriptive statistics provide a standardized method and procedure for summarizing and organizing all of the cases of one quantitative variable. In a research study, descriptive statistics are computed for each variable. When this step is complete, researchers use this information to assess differences and relationships between variables.

Recall from Chapter 6 on measurement that data can be captured in four different levels: nominal, ordinal, interval, and ratio. Data must be collected at interval or ratio levels for the mean and median to be computed. Of course, the

number of cases and the mode can be computed for data at any level.

Number of Cases

Generally, the greater the number of cases, or data points, the more reliable the data. One way for consumers of research to make this determination is to look for this information in the methods or results section of the written research report. The number of cases for which data are reported is represented by the letter n or N (for example, $n = 231$). Although styles vary by journals, generally N refers to the total number in a sample while n refers to a subsample, or a group of cases drawn from the sample.

Remember that the number of cases may not always be people. Rather, cases may be the number of speaking turns, arguments, conflict episodes, or commercials—virtually any type of communicator or communication phenomenon that a researcher has identified as being worthy of study.

Measures of Central Tendency

Measures of **central tendency** are the primary summary form for data. One of the most common summaries is the average. One number, the

Number of cases	n	N	
Frequency	f		
Mean	M	$\bar{x}$	
Median	Mdn	Md	
Mode	Mo		
Standard deviation	sd	SD	S

FIGURE 10.4 Symbols Used to Represent Descriptive Statistics

average, can represent the sample of data on one variable. In other words, this one number acts as a summary of all the scores on one variable. Research reports would not have the space to report the raw data, or the data collected for every case on every variable. Instead, researchers report summary statistics for each variable. But there are several measures of central tendency in statistics. In research, we must specify which one we're using.

Mean   The arithmetic mean, or simply the **mean,** is the most common measure of central tendency. Commonly referred to as the **average,** the mean is computed by adding up all the scores on one variable and then dividing by the number of cases, or n for that variable. In this and other statistics, the mean should be calculated to include two decimal points. Because all of the scores are added together, the mean depends upon each and every score available. If one score is changed, the mean will also change. The mean is the most sensitive to extremely high or extremely low values of the distribution. Still, it is the most commonly reported measure of central tendency.

Median   Another measure of central tendency is the median. The **median** is the middle of all the scores on one variable. To compute the median, the data must be arranged in order from smallest to largest score. If there is an uneven number of cases, the median is the score exactly in the middle of the distribution. If there is an even number of scores, the median is found by counting equally from the smallest and largest numbers to the midpoint where no

number exists. Take the numbers above and below this midpoint, add them together, and divide by 2. This calculation is the median. It may or may not be the same as the mean for a set of scores. Because the median is always in the middle, scores in the dataset can change without the median being affected.

Look at Figure 10.5. Notice the line between 76 and 75 on the numbers in the ordered list. This is the midpoint of the dataset. Because a researcher cannot report the midpoint as "between 76 and 75," he or she adds the two numbers together (76 + 75 = 151). This total is divided by 2 (151 ÷ 2 = 75.5) to find the median of the dataset, or 75.5.

Mode   A third measure of central tendency is the mode. The **mode** is the score that appears most often in a dataset. If datasets are large, then it is common for the dataset to be bimodal or multimodal, which means that more than one score has the largest frequency of occurrence. In fact, most distributions of scores are bimodal or multimodal, making it impossible for a researcher to use the mode to represent the average in later statistical calculations.

Looking at the dataset in Figure 10.5, you can see that the value of 78 is the most frequent score. Thus, 78 is the mode for this dataset.

If a distribution of scores is normal, or completely symmetrical, then the mean, median, and mode will be the same number. But data are seldom this perfect. It is far more likely that a distribution of scores will be somewhat asymmetrical. Thus, the mean, median, and mode will be different.

Data in its raw order form	Data in order from highest to lowest
73	83
83	83
75	80
83	80
79	79
69	78
78	78
71	78
62	78
78	76
80	75
74	75
73	74
80	73
78	73
56	71
78	69
64	64
76	62
75	56

Descriptive statistics for the dataset:
mean = 74.25
standard deviation = 7.00
median = 75.5 (the two middle scores of 76 and 75 are averaged)
mode = 78
range = 27, from 56 to 83
$N = 20$

FIGURE 10.5 The Data From a Measure of Communication Competence

Most researchers report and use the mean in describing the data for a variable. It is an appropriate choice if the distribution is relatively normal. But if a set of scores is skewed, then it may be better to report the median and use it in later calculations because it better reflects the middle of the distribution. Computing the variability in the scores can help you determine if the mean or median is most appropriate. Mode scores are infrequently reported. When they are, the mean or median scores accompany them as well.

Measures of Dispersion

To fully describe a distribution of data, a measure of dispersion, or variability, is also needed. Two distributions can have the same mean but different spreads of scores. Whenever a measure of central tendency is used, a measure of dispersion should also be reported. The two most commonly reported are the range and the standard deviation; both provide information about the variability of the dataset.

Range   The simplest measure of dispersion is the **range,** or the value calculated by subtracting the lowest score from the highest score. Generally, the range is used to report the high and low scores on questionnaires. For example, for the data shown in Figure 10.5, the range of 27 is the result of subtracting 56, the lowest score, from 83, the highest score. The range is a crude measure of dispersion because changing any values between the highest and lowest score will have no effect on it.

The range can also be used to describe demographic characteristics of the research participants. In these instances, however, the lowest value is not subtracted from the highest value. Rather, the researcher simply reports the highest and lowest values. For example, Erbert and Floyd (2004) describe their participants in the following way:

> Participants were 235 adults (64% female) who were recruited from communication courses at a medium-sized university in the Midwest. Participants ranged in age from 16 to 63, with a mean age of 24.33 years (SD = 8.10). (p. 259)

Some scholars might report the range in age here simply as a range of 47 years (for example, 63 − 16 = 47). However, reporting just the distance between the smallest and largest value does not tell us what part of the age continuum participants represent. It is more effective to report the smallest and largest value, as Erbert and Floyd demonstrate.

Standard Deviation   Even when the range is reported, it is impossible to determine how close or how far apart the scores are from one another. Thus, researchers use **standard deviation** as the standard calculation and representation of the variability of a dataset. The formula for computing a standard deviation is shown in Appendix B. Of course, you can use any spreadsheet or statistical software program to calculate the standard deviation as well. Both the mean and standard deviation are commonly reported; see the example above. In fact, the mean reported by itself is not interpretable. For instance, the larger the standard deviation, the more the scores differ from the mean. Alternately, if the standard deviation is small, this indicates that the scores were very similar or close to one another. Or, if the standard deviation is zero, all of the scores are the same.

Notice the vertical markers in the normal distribution in Figure 10.6. The middle marker is the point at which the mean exists. Now notice the two points on either side of the mean where the curve changes direction from convex to concave. These are the inflection points at which the +1 and −1 standard deviations are

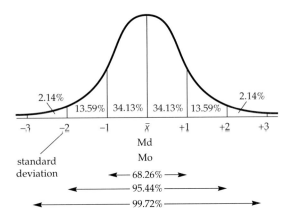

FIGURE 10.6 Standard Deviations of the Normal Curve

placed. The perpendicular lines to the right of the mean are positive standards of +1, +2, and +3. The perpendicular lines to the left of the mean are negative standards of −1, −2, and −3. The distances between the perpendicular lines are equal and, in turn, divide the horizontal axis into standard deviations.

Regardless of what your data are measuring or the range of scores in your dataset, the normal curve and this set of standards are always the same. This is a property of the theoretical normal curve. The more normal a distribution of scores, the more this property, or rule, applies. The less normal the distribution, the less accurate this rule. Using the normal curve as a base and the standard deviation for a set of scores, the distribution of scores for a variable can be compared to the normal curve. Thus, researchers use the theoretical normal curve to assess the distribution of the data they obtained. When a distribution is not normal, researchers should provide some explanation for this phenomenon.

The area of the curve between the +1 and −1 standards is identified in a variety of ways, including "within one standard deviation of the mean" and "one standard deviation above and below the mean." According to the theoretical normal curve, 68.26% of the cases in a dataset will fall within the +1 to −1 standards (see Figure 10.6).

To find the range of scores from a dataset that would fall within the +1 to −1 standard deviations, simply add (or subtract) the standard deviation to the mean. When researchers refer to the typical participant or typical score, they are referring to the range of scores within this area. For example, if your score on some measure of communication apprehension fell within these standards, you would be considered as average, or someone for whom apprehension is not exceptional in either direction.

For the set of scores used in Figure 10.5 (mean = 74.25; standard deviation = 7.00), the following would represent the range of scores within the +1 to −1 standard deviations:

Mean = 74.25: Add the standard deviation of 7.00 to equal 81.25, or the score at the +1 standard deviation.

Mean = 74.25: Subtract the standard deviation of 7.00 to equal 67.25, or the score at the −1 standard deviation.

Thus, in this case, scores from 67 to 81 would be within the +1 to −1 standards and considered typical for this sample. Now to check, count the frequency of scores with values from 67 to 81. That count should be 15 out of 20, or 75% of total number of cases. When the curve is normal, about 68% of the cases should lie between these two values. The remaining cases are above and below these values.

The further out a score on the distribution, the more extreme the score. The area between the +2 and −2 standard deviations would contain 95.44% of the scores in that dataset. The area between +3 and −3 standards would contain 99.72% of the scores in the dataset. Notice that the normal curve does not touch the horizontal axis. Rather, it extends infinitely to the right and the left. Remember that the normal curve is theoretical and must allow for the most extreme cases, even those that fall outside +3 or −3 standard deviations.

APPLICATION OF DESCRIPTIVE STATISTICS

One reason the mean, median, and standard deviation are reported in the methods section of a written research report is so the reader can assess the normalcy of the data.

The following excerpt from a research report characterizes one way researchers (Mendelson & Thorson, 2004) report this information:

> Participants in the study had a mean visualizer score of 23.67 (*SD* = 8.35) on a scale that varied from 10 to 70, with 10 being most visual. The *most visual* person in the samples scored a 10 and the *least visual* scored a 53. Cronbach's α for the 10 items on the visual scale was .71. (p. 482)

With this information, the mean and standard deviation can be interpreted to reveal the normalcy of the scores for the visualizer variable. In this case, it is easy to see that the variable had a positively skewed distribution, or very few very high scores.

Alternately, when the distribution of scores appears normal, researchers indicate this by phrases such as "The distribution of scores approximated the normal curve" or "The distribution of scores appeared normal."

Frequencies and percentages are also commonly used to provide summaries of nominal data. Examples of each will demonstrate their utility.

Frequencies

A commonly used descriptive statistic is **frequency,** or the number of times a particular value of a variable occurs. Communication researchers often use frequency data to report on the occurrence of communication events. This type of data is actually at the nominal level, because the researcher is making a decision for each occurrence—did this communication phenomenon occur or did it not?

For example, researchers investigating how employees use email at work to shape and facilitate workplace romance (Hovick et al., 2003) asked participants to indicate how they used email in this type of relationship. The research team coded participants' responses to an open-ended question and reported the findings as frequencies, as shown in Table 10.1.

The table provides basic descriptive information about what the research team found. Of the 83 employees participating in the study, 3 never used email, so the frequencies are interpreted from a base of 80 employees—this is an important point. Sixty-two used email to ask questions

DESIGN CHECK

Describing Variables

When reading a research report, look for the descriptive statistics for each variable in the methods section. Here you should find

1. The mean or median
2. The standard deviation
3. The range of scores possible or the range of scores obtained

With this information you can make a determination of the normalcy of the data even if the researcher omits this description.

of their workplace romantic partner, 58 used email as small talk, and 57 used email to talk about work. Examining the frequencies indicates how employees in romantic relationships at work use email to communicate and allows us to identify the most typical use of email for these participants.

Percentages

Most commonly, we think of a percentage as being a number that represents some part of 100.

But not all variable scores use 100 as the base or foundation. Thus, it is more accurate to describe a **percentage** as a comparison between the base, which can be any number, and a second number that is compared to the base. Look again at the previous example for the frequencies and percentages reported in Table 10.1. The frequencies and the number of responses in each category (in this case, 80) are the bases from which the percentages are calculated.

Percentages are also frequently used to describe characteristics or attributes of the participants.

TABLE 10.1 Email Use in Workplace Romantic Relationships

Type of Use	Frequency	Percentage
Ask Questions	62	78
Small Talk	58	73
Talk About Work	57	71
Flirting	52	65
Express Intimacy	32	40
Start a Relationship	21	26
Gain More Information	15	23
Other	11	14
Conflict	9	11

SOURCE: "E-mail Communication in Workplace Romantic Relationships," by R. A. Hovick, R. A. Meyers, and C. E. Timmerman, 2003, *Communication Studies, 54*, pp. 468–482. Used by permission of Central States Communication Association.

AN ETHICAL ISSUE

Mistakes in Calculations

Whether you collect data by yourself or with the help of others, whether you calculate by hand or with a spreadsheet or statistical program, and whether you interpret data by yourself or with the help of an expert, as the researcher who reports the data, you are ultimately responsible for all aspects of data collection. Why? Because the researcher is the author of the research report. Thus, double-checking the procedures for data collection, the validity of the data as it is entered, and the results are all responsibilities of the researcher—no one else. Failing to take the time to double-check and failing to correct mistakes when they are found are ethical violations of scientific standards. People trust what they read to be accurate. In fact, they may use reported results to develop a communication training program to help others or to alter their own communication behaviors. A researcher's credibility—past, present, and future—rests on the extent to which consumers trust what they read. If you are collecting data for a project, please double-check everything.

For the same study, the participants are reported as follows:

> Seventy-four percent ($n = 61$) of subjects who participated in this study were involved in a workplace romantic relationship with a fellow co-worker, 13% ($n = 11$) with a superior, 7% ($n = 6$) with a subordinate, and 5% ($n = 5$) with an immediate supervisor. (p. 472)

By putting the nominal or demographic information about the study's participants in percentage form, the researchers make it easy for the reader to get an idea of what is typical or whom the data represent.

CRUNCHING THE NUMBERS: CALCULATOR OR COMPUTER?

In research, enough data are collected that computing statistics by hand is generally out of the question. Few of us have the patience to add, subtract, multiply, or divide a long list of numbers, let alone do it accurately. For many small datasets, you will be able to perform the needed calculations with a calculator. Any calculator will do as long as it has a square root function—that is, the calculator can find the square root of a

number. The square root function is indicated by the symbol $\sqrt{}$.

With medium or large datasets, you will need to use a spreadsheet program (such as Excel) or a statistics program (such as SAS, SPSS, SYSTAT). A spreadsheet program works just fine for many data analysis projects and is easy to use. Programs specifically designed for statistical use require a more specialized knowledge of statistics and programming.

One caution, however, about using any program to help compute statistics is that although programs like Excel can run most statistical tests, the program relies on you to request the appropriate test and to make the appropriate interpretation of the outcome. Likewise, the program relies on you to indicate which data should be included in the test. If you specify the wrong test or indicate the wrong data, Excel will still do the calculation and provide a result—but it will be the wrong result or a noninterpretable result! If you are going to use any of these programs, you will need basic instruction on how to set up the spreadsheet or statistical program, how to enter data, and how to appropriately run and interpret the statistical tests.

Despite the obvious advantages, the use of spreadsheet or statistical software can create a false sense of security. There are five issues that you should consider if you use these programs for data entry and statistical computation (Pedhazur & Schmelkin, 1991). First, computers can fail. Programs can stall. Never trust all of your data to one file on a hard drive or a disk. Second, results can only be as good as the data entered. Whereas a spreadsheet or statistical package may decrease the number of computational errors, data-entry errors are still likely to occur. Errors such as entering the wrong value or omitting a value are common. Because your conclusions and interpretations rest on the validity of the data, it is wise to double-check all data entered.

Third, researchers—even experienced ones—tend to limit their thinking to statistical procedures they know they can do on the computer. Researchers always need to be mindful of this and periodically stretch their statistical knowledge and expertise. Fourth, the power of personal computing makes it possible to create an abundance of analyses. Do not be tempted to "see what will happen" by running any and all statistics. Rather, the techniques and statistics chosen should be driven by your research questions and hypotheses. Finally, you will find it difficult to thoroughly understand a statistical procedure or technique until you have mastered it by hand and grappled with the data and interpretation yourself. As the researcher, you are the person responsible for the results and their interpretations, even if someone else does your statistical programming.

SUMMARY

1. Numbers are one of many tools researchers use to collect data.

2. From the raw data collected, researchers compute the descriptive statistics that convey essential summary data of the dataset as a whole.

3. The normal curve is a theoretical distribution in which the majority of cases peak in the middle of the distribution, with progressively fewer cases as one moves away from the middle of the curve.

4. In normal distributions, one side mirrors the other; the curve is symmetrical.

5. In positively or negatively skewed distributions, the curve is asymmetrical.

6. Frequency distributions and polygons are the first step in analyzing a set of scores for one variable.

7. Descriptive statistics—number of cases, central tendency, and dispersion—are summary information about the dataset for one variable.

8. The number of cases is the number of data points.

9. Measures of central tendency—mean, median, or mode—reflect different types of average or typical data.

10. Measures of dispersion—range and standard deviation—provide a description of the variability of the data.

11. Researchers also use frequencies and percentages to describe their data.

12. Data may be calculated by hand, or with the help of a spreadsheet or statistical program.

13. Researchers are responsible for the results and their interpretations, even if an expert helps them in this aspect of the research process.

KEY TERMS

average

central tendency

data

dataset

descriptive statistics

frequency

inferential statistics

mean

median

mode

negatively skewed curve

normal curve

percentage

positively skewed curve

range

raw data

skewed distribution

standard deviation

CHAPTER ELEVEN

Testing for Differences

Chapter Checklist

After reading this chapter, you should be able to:

1. Explain the difference between descriptive and inferential statistics.

2. Use the four analytical steps to design and evaluate research designs and statistical findings.

3. Develop a hypothesis or research question and select the appropriate statistical test of difference (chi-square, *t*-test, ANOVA).

4. Differentiate among the assumptions and functions of chi-squares, *t*-tests, and ANOVAs.

5. Interpret research findings developed from results of chi-squares, *t*-tests, and ANOVAs.

Whether the research design is experimental, quasi-experimental, or descriptive, many researchers develop their studies to look for differences. Recall from earlier chapters that some hypotheses and research questions contain independent or predictor variables for which the data are nominal or categorical. When this is the case, communication researchers can hypothesize that differences in the independent or predictor variable will result in differences in the dependent variable. In these instances, researchers are looking for differences between or among the groups or categories of the independent variable in relationship to the dependent variable.

In a study of the effectiveness of public speaking training, Stitt, Simonds, and Hunt (2003) hypothesized that instructors who provided their students with training in using a specific speech evaluation form would have higher instructor–student agreement than instructors who did not train their students using the form. Here the independent variable would be instructors' training of students: Some instructors provided the training (the treatment condition); some instructors did not (the control condition). The dependent variable would be the degree of instructor–student agreement about the evaluation of the speech. In other words, does it matter which *group* the instructor belonged to? Does the group the instructor is randomly assigned to in this field experiment create a difference in instructor–student agreement about the student's speech?

Another example of communication research is a study that investigated differences between married men and women (Xu & Burleson, 2001). The research question asked, "Do men and women differ with regard to the amount of support they reportedly (a) experience and (b) desire from their spouses?" (p. 541). A statistical test of difference would ask, "Is the amount of spousal support experienced and desired statistically different with respect to how participants are categorized?" In other words, does sex have an influence on the dependent variable?

In either of these cases, it is likely that there are real numerical differences in the data. We could look at the scores in the dataset to see if the mean scores for these dependent variables were different based on how the participants were categorized on the independent variables. But knowing that a simple difference exists in mean scores is not enough. Rather, researchers use inferential statistics to ask, Are those differences big enough to make a real difference—are they statistically significant? In other words, are the differences observed greater than the differences that might occur due to chance? Before we discuss three types of tests for differences—chi-square, *t*-test, and analysis of variance (ANOVA)—a brief explanation of inferential statistics is in order.

INFERENTIAL STATISTICS

In contrast to descriptive statistics described in Chapter 10, **inferential statistics** are used to draw conclusions about a population by examining the sample. On a more basic level, inferential statistics help researchers test hypotheses and answer research questions, and derive meaning from the results. With these steps complete, the results or findings from a sample on a statistical test can be used to make inferences about the population. A result found to be statistically significant by testing the sample is assumed to also hold for the population from which the sample was drawn. The ability to make such an inference is based on the principle of probability. Recall from Chapter 7 that researchers set the significance level for each statistical test they conduct. By using probability theory as a basis for their tests, researchers can assess how likely it is that the difference they find is real, not due to chance.

Two other assumptions accompany inferential statistics. The first is that the populations from which samples are drawn are normally distributed on the dependent variable. Let's say that the dependent variable is communication competence. If the population is normally distributed, and the sample is randomly selected, then the communication competence scores for this sample would also be expected to be normally distributed. When a normal distribution is not known or cannot be assumed, a statistical test can only provide approximations of the differences.

The second assumption is that participants are randomly assigned to categories or groups of the independent variable. Recall that random assignment occurs when participants have an equal chance of being assigned to any one of the treatment or control groups. Researchers use random assignment to help ensure that groups are similar to one another. In other words, the random assignment procedure is used to reduce bias. When participants are randomly assigned to treatment or control groups, differences found between these groups are presumed to be due to the effects of the treatments of the independent variables. This assumption is often violated, particularly in communication research in which naturally occurring groups are used as the independent variable.

Many researchers use chi-squares, *t*-tests, and ANOVAs when their research designs do not meet the basic assumptions upon which inferential statistics are based—the principles of probability, normal distribution, and random assignment. Generally, meeting these assumptions would require that all communication scholarship be based on experimental designs, and that is not possible when studying some communication phenomena. Some scholars (Lacy & Riffe, 1993; de Vaus, 2001) argue that using inferential statistics when the assumptions cannot be met is inexcusable. Other scholars—by virtue of the many published articles using quasi-experimental and descriptive research designs and inferential statistics without meeting these assumptions—take a more liberal view. Even when all of the conditions mentioned are not met, if the researcher selects the appropriate statistic to match the research design and the data collected, inferential statistics can provide information about a particular dataset (Tabachnick & Fidell, 2001). In such a case, however, researchers have to be careful not to overgeneralize their results.

It is also important to remember that inferential statistics examine the patterns of scores or the patterns across categories. Examining data at this more holistic level allows a researcher to make inferences from the sample to the population. Thus, any significant differences found are not differences between individuals; they are differences between groups of individuals.

Alternative and Null Hypotheses

Inferential statistics test the likelihood that the alternative, or research, hypothesis is true and the null hypothesis is not. In testing differences, the alternative, or research, hypothesis would predict that differences would be found, whereas the null hypothesis would predict no differences. By setting the significance level (generally at .05), the researcher has a criterion for making this decision. If the .05 level is achieved (*p* is equal to or less than .05), then a researcher rejects the null hypothesis and accepts its alternative hypothesis. If the .05 significance level is not achieved, then the null hypothesis is retained. Recall from Chapter 7 that the null hypothesis is retained until there is sufficient statistical support for accepting the research hypothesis.

Degrees of Freedom

Degrees of freedom are the way in which the scientific tradition accounts for variation due to error. Represented by the abbreviation *df*, it specifies how many values vary within a statistical test. In other words, scientists recognize that collecting data can never be error-free. Each piece of data collected can vary, or carry error that we cannot account for. By including degrees of freedom in statistical computations, scientists help account for this error.

Another way of looking at degrees of freedom is as the latitude of variation within a statistical test (Kerlinger, 1986). For nominal or categorical variables, the general rule is that degrees of freedom will be the number of categories for the variable minus 1. So, if a variable has six categories representing choices the participant could make, the degrees of freedom associated with that variable are 5 (*df* = number of categories −1). A participant had the opportunity to select five options other than the one chosen.

Although the concept of degrees of freedom can be difficult to comprehend (and such an explanation certainly is beyond the objective of this introduction to statistics), there are clear rules for how to calculate the degrees of freedom for each statistical test. These rules will be explained as each test is discussed.

Four Analytical Steps

With inferential statistical tests, there are four major steps to any statistical analysis the researcher undertakes (Simon, 1969). First, the statistical test is applied to determine whether differences or relationships exist. This chapter describes statistical tests of difference (used when data for the independent variable is categorical, or nominal). Chapter 12 describes statistical tests for relationships. In this step, the researcher selects the appropriate statistical test as indicated by the hypothesis or research question. The hypothesis and the statistical test must be parallel. If the hypothesis makes a presumption about differences, then a statistical test designed to capture differences must be used. Moreover, which statistical test is used will depend on the type of data collected by the researcher (such as nominal or continuous level data).

The second analytical step characterizes the type of difference or relationship. Sometimes, the difference that appears in the data may not be the difference the researcher predicted. For example, Guerrero (1996) examined how individuals with different attachment styles displayed intimacy and nonverbal involvement with their romantic partners. Specifically, she hypothesized that individuals who reflected low levels of self-sufficiency and high need for external self-validation would convey greater social anxiety (as characterized by random body movements) than would individuals without these characteristics. Differences in body movements were found between the two groups of people, but opposite to those that were predicted. Rather than having more random body movements, those with low levels of self-sufficiency and high need for external self-validation had fewer random body movements. Thus, researchers must check to make sure that the differences they find are indeed the differences they predicted.

The third analytical step assesses the statistical importance of the difference or relationship. Recall from Chapter 7 that a probability level, or significance level, is established for each statistical test used. Knowing that a difference exists and whether it is the difference that is expected is not enough. A researcher must go one step further. Using the significance level, usually set at .05, a researcher can determine if the size of the differences he or she finds can be accepted as real, not random. Alternately, if the probability level is not achieved, then any differences found are not statistically significant, and no conclusion can be drawn.

Finally, researchers want to move beyond the data tested into the future. Thus, the fourth analytical step evaluates the importance of the observed differences or relationships and then generalizes the findings. To make this evaluation, researchers must assess all the steps in the research process:

- How was the sample obtained?
- Were participants randomly selected?
- Were participants randomly assigned to treatment or control groups?
- To what extent does the sample represent the population in which the researchers are interested?
- Was the research design appropriate for the hypothesis and research question?
- Were the data collected in reliable and valid ways?

By asking and answering these questions, researchers can determine the extent to which they can generalize from the findings of the sample to the population.

Each of these four steps must be completed for each statistical test conducted. Recognize, however, that even with the most effectively designed research study, there is never a guarantee that results from the sample will reflect what happens in the population (Simon, 1969).

How do these analytical steps apply when experimental assumptions are violated? The four steps should be thought of as an ideal practice and should be followed for quasi-experimental and descriptive research designs as well. Obviously, in these cases, the fourth step is most jeopardized and is the one with which researchers must take the most caution.

CHI-SQUARE

Researchers choose **chi-square,** or χ^2, as the statistical test when they want to determine if differences among categories are statistically significant. Thus, a chi-square is the appropriate test when data for one or more variables are nominal, or categorical. In principle, a chi-square examines the data to see if the categorical differences that occurred are the same as would occur by chance. Researchers compare the **observed frequency,** or the number of times the category actually appears, with the **expected frequency,** or the number of times the category was expected to appear. If the observed frequency exactly matches the expected frequency, then χ^2 is zero. The greater the difference between the observed and expected frequency distributions, the larger the value of χ^2. And, the larger the value of χ^2, the more likely that the difference will be statistically significant.

Researchers obtain observed frequencies from the collected data, but how are expected frequencies obtained? Generally, researchers work from a no-differences model specifying that frequencies for each category of a variable are equal. In this model, an expected frequency is calculated by dividing the number of observations by the number of categories, or cells, for that variable. This results in the same expected frequency value for each cell or category. As an alternative to the no-differences model, researchers can use the published research literature to establish expected frequencies that favor one category over another.

Recall from Chapter 6 that nominal variables do not have a numerical value. Rather, in a chi-square, the frequency for each category is used as the numerical value. As an example, for the nominal variable sex, the frequencies of females and males were 57 and 83, respectively. Each number represents the number of times, or the frequency with which, participants identified themselves as female or male. These values are used to calculate the chi-square. Both types of chi-squares—one-dimensional chi-square and the contingency analysis—rely on frequency data. Each is detailed below.

One-Dimensional Chi-Square

A **one-dimensional,** or **one-way, chi-square** is the statistical test for determining if differences in how the cases are distributed across the categories of one categorical, or nominal, variable are significant. In this case, the chi-square allows the researcher to test the question "Are the differences found real or due to chance?" In an experiment designed to examine which persuasive strategies students use to get other students to drink alcohol, chi-square was selected as the statistical test for the hypothesis "The most common persuasive strategy overall will be a simple offer" (Harrington, 1997, p. 232). As is the tradition, the null hypothesis is unstated. If it were stated, it would be something like "The persuasive strategies will be equally offered," or "There will be no differences in the frequencies with which strategies are offered."

For this study, the researcher used six types of persuasive strategies as different categories of the variable persuasive strategy. Student participants in a simulation tried to persuade other students to drink alcohol. Their interactions were taped and coded according to the six categories. But just coding what was said into the six categories and examining their frequency differences would not reveal if there were statistically significant differences for which strategy college students were most likely to use. These differences could have occurred by chance. The chi-square is used to demonstrate that the differences in frequencies, or in which strategies were used, are real by comparing the observed frequencies to expected frequencies.

If the null hypothesis states that all persuasive strategies will be equally offered, then the expected frequencies for the six persuasive strategies should be equal. For the null hypothesis to be retained, the 532 strategies coded for this hypothesis must be distributed equally. Each strategy should have been used about 89 times. But, look at Table 11.1, which displays the frequencies and percentages of the data. You can see that strategy use was not equally distributed across the six categories. The observed frequencies were not the same as the expected frequency of 89.

In this case, the chi-square was statistically significant, and the research hypothesis is accepted. College students are more likely to use a simple offer (for example, "You want a drink?") than other types of strategies (those that give the benefits of drinking, address the availability of alcohol, minimize the risk associated with drinking, and use peer pressure and group norms, and those in which the offerer intervenes or facilitates, perhaps by offering to take the other student home after he

TABLE 11.1 Frequency Chart for College Drinking Study

			Types of Persuasive Strategies			
Simple Offers	Statement of Benefits	Availability of Alcohol	Appeal to Group Minimization	Norms	Facilitation	Total N = 532
46.4%	14.7%	17.3%	7.3%	11.5%	2.8%	100%
n = 247	n = 78	n = 92	n = 39	n = 61	n = 15	

or she drinks). Of the 532 strategies used, 46.4% were simple offers. The next most frequently used strategy addressed the availability of alcohol, and it was used 17.3% of the time. The significant chi-square demonstrates that this variation in strategy use did not occur by chance.

Now, take a look at how this chi-square was reported by the authors in the journal article.

> The first hypothesis predicted that the most common persuasive strategy would be a simple offer. This hypothesis was supported ($\chi^2 = 329.86$, $df = 5$, $p < .001$). (Harrington, 1997, p. 234)

The calculated chi-square value of 329.86 results from the statistical computation of the test. The formula and steps for this calculation are shown in Appendix B. The degrees of freedom, or df, of 5 indicates that six coding categories were used. For one-way chi-squares, df is equal to number of categories minus 1, or in this case, $6 - 1 = 5$. You know that the chi-square was statistically significant by the reported significance level of $p < .001$. This means that the significance level of the computed chi-square was smaller than .001, which is less than the generally set standard of .05. Thus, the researchers could reject the null hypothesis (that the six strategies will be equally used) and accept the research hypothesis (that a simple offer will be the most frequently used strategy to get peers to drink alcohol).

You should note, however, that obtaining a significant χ^2 value is not enough to provide total support for the research hypothesis. A chi-square cannot tell researchers where the significant difference occurred—only that one exists. In this case, the significant difference could have potentially occurred between any of the six persuasive

strategies. With chi-square, researchers must visually inspect the frequencies and percentages to determine if the significant difference is, in fact, the difference they predicted.

Contingency Analysis

Obviously the chi-square just presented is fairly simple. The researcher was looking at the frequency distribution on only one nominal variable. The chi-square can also be used for examining the association between two nominal variables. In this case, participants are classified on two variables in relationship to each other. This statistic is also known as a **contingency analysis, two-way chi-square,** or **two-dimensional chi-square.** The two nominal variables are arranged in a table where rows represent one nominal variable and columns represent a second nominal variable. The display of frequency data in this type of table is called a **contingency table.** Such an arrangement makes it easy to see how frequencies for one variable are contingent on, or relative to, frequencies for the other variable.

The simplest form of a two-dimensional chi-square would be composed of two nominal variables, each with two levels. This would be a 2 × 2 chi-square. But in reality, this chi-square design is not often used because most nominal variables have more than two categories. More frequently used are contingency analyses of two variables with multiple categories. The formula for calculating a contingency analysis is shown in Appendix B.

Bruess and Pearson (1997) used this type of contingency analysis, or chi-square, to determine if types of rituals differed across friendships and marital relationships (see Table 11.2).

TABLE 11.2 Contingency Analysis Table

| Ritual Type | Relationship Type | | Totals |
	Marital Relationships	Friendships	
Enjoyable activities	154	150	304
Escape	31	17	48
Communication	50	43	93
Patterns/habits/mannerisms	38	6	44
Idiosyncratic/symbolic favorites	48	7	55
Play rituals	27	16	43
Celebration	13	22	35
Totals	361	261	622

SOURCE: "Interpersonal Rituals in Marriage and Adult Friendship," by C. J. S. Bruess and J. C. Pearson, 1997, *Communication Monographs, 64,* pp. 25–46. Used by permission of the National Communication Association.

This 2 × 7 chi-square—two relationship types and seven ritual types—was significant, χ^2 $(df = 6) = 46.77, p < .001$. Thus, the researchers could conclude that frequency of occurrence of rituals is contingent upon relationship type. As a consumer of research, you can tell the chi-square was significant by looking at the significance level, or *p*. When it is .05 or less, it is considered significant and the alternative hypothesis is accepted.

Degrees of freedom, or *df*, for a contingency analysis depend on the number of rows and columns in the contingency table. Specifically, degrees of freedom equal the number of rows minus 1 times the number of columns minus 1 [(no. of rows − 1) × (no. of columns − 1)]. In the example in Table 11.2, relationship type is represented by the columns (2 − 1 = 1) and ritual type is represented by the rows (7 − 1 = 6). Multiplying those two (1 × 6 = 6) together results in $df = 6$.

Limitations of Chi-Square

Besides being limited to variables of nominal data, the chi-square also has other limitations. One limitation is that the chi-square is a test of frequencies.

As a result, when the observed frequency is zero in any cell or when the expected frequency is less than 5 in any cell, the test may not be accurate. The second limitation addresses the number of variables the chi-square can test. Although the chi-square is not limited to testing only two variables, the results from chi-squares with more than three variables can be very difficult to interpret (Kerlinger, 1986). A more sophisticated statistical test, log-linear analysis, is available when three or more nominal level variables need to be simultaneously examined.

Finally, the primary design limitation is that the test cannot directly determine causal relationships. It would be inappropriate to say that categorization on one variable caused categorization on another variable. However, logical interpretation of the variables in a contingency table analysis can help a researcher make causal statements about the data. Even so, causation is not absolute because the variables are not independent and dependent in the truest sense.

As a result, it is easy for both researchers and consumers to overextend the results from chi-square analyses. Most commonly, overgeneralization of the findings would be found in the

Interpreting Chi-Squares

1. Identify the research hypothesis or research question. Develop the related null hypothesis or statement of no differences.

2. From information presented in the methods section, verify that each variable in the chi-square hypothesis is at the nominal or categorical level. Identify the categories or groups for each variable.

3. In the results section, look for the specific test results. You must find the χ^2 and the significance level, or p.

4. If the p of the χ^2 is .05 or less, accept the differences in the chi-square test. The differences found are statistically significant. Determine if the differences found are the differences predicted by the hypothesis.

5. If the p of the χ^2 is greater than .05, retain the null hypothesis. Any differences reported are due to chance or are not different enough to be statistically significant.

6. In the discussion section, look for the researcher's interpretation of the chi-square. To what degree are the statistically significant results practical or relevant to the issue being studied? Independently come to your own conclusion. Do you agree or disagree with the researcher?

discussion and implication sections of a research report. Clearly, there are limitations to the extent to which researchers should use findings from chi-squares to draw conclusions about the population from which participants are drawn. However, this does not mean that findings from chi-square analyses have no utility.

THE *t*-TEST

The *t*-test, represented by the symbol *t*, is used to test hypotheses that expect to find differences between two groupings of the independent variable on a continuous level dependent variable. First, participants or elements are categorized according to one of two levels of the independent variable. Second, the dependent variable is measured for all participants. Then, the dependent-variable scores of one group are compared to the dependent-variable scores from the other group.

In experimental research designs, the *t*-test is used to test the significance of difference between the means of two populations, based upon the means and distributions of two samples. However, the *t*-test is also regularly used in quasi-experimental and descriptive research designs.

In a *t*-test, the independent variable must be a nominal variable composed of only two groups. Only one independent variable can be tested. For example, sex could be an independent variable because it is composed of two groups, females and males. Just as the *t*-test is restricted to one independent variable, the test is also restricted to one dependent variable. The dependent variable must be of continuous level data at the interval or ratio level.

Referring back to the four analytical steps introduced earlier in this chapter, the *t*-test asks, Are the sample means different from each other? If the answer is "yes," then, as suggested earlier, the researcher must continue with the other three analytical steps. A researcher must determine if the difference was in the direction it was expected. The statistical significance of the *t*-test must be determined. Finally, the difference must be interpreted for what it means or how it is to be applied.

Common Forms of *t*-Test

Several common forms of the *t*-test are used in communication research. The first investigates differences between the means of two independent samples. The formula and steps are shown in Appendix B. This type of *t*-test is commonly used because researchers want to compare the mean scores of the dependent variable for two different groups of people.

For the **independent sample *t*-test,** degrees of freedom are calculated according to the sample size for each of two categories of the independent variable. Thus, if the *t*-test is calculated for 100 cases, 50 of which are assigned to one category of the independent variable and 50 assigned to the other category of the independent variable, the equation for calculating degrees of freedom would be $df = (n_1) + (n_2) - 2$. In this case, the calculation is $df = (50 + 50 - 2) = 98$.

For example, in testing the efficacy of computer training for students, Downing and Garmon (2001) found that men and women differed significantly in their confidence using PowerPoint on their posttraining scores: $t(66) = -2.27$, $p < .05$; Female $M = 10.07$, $SD = 8.83$; Male $M = 5.52$, $SD = 7.63$. Females and males are the two categories of the independent variable sex. Confidence using computers is the dependent variable. Because participants are in one category of the independent variable or the other, the samples are independent. A participant cannot be identified with both categories of the independent variable.

A second type of *t*-test is known as a **paired comparison** because it compares two paired or matched scores. In this case, scores on the dependent variable are not independent. One participant provides two scores that can be compared. For example, in the same study testing the efficacy of computer training, students' scores before training were the pretest; students' scores after training were the posttest. In this instance, the pretest is one category and the posttest score is the other category of the independent variable. The difference between the two scores is used as the dependent variable. In this study, there was a statistically significant difference between students' pretest ($M = 31.67$, $SD = 11.17$) and students' posttest scores ($M = 39.93$, $SD = 7.32$), $t(72) = -8.19$, $p < .001$.

The formula and steps for calculating a paired comparison *t*-test are shown in Appendix B. For the paired sample *t*-test, degrees of freedom are calculated for the total number of cases. Thus, if the *t*-test is calculated for 50 paired cases, the equation for calculating degrees of freedom would be $df = (n - 1)$, or $df = (50 - 1) = 49$.

To summarize, the *t*-test examines the data for significant differences. The mean and standard deviation of the dependent variable are calculated for both groups of the independent variable. The test compares the two sets of descriptive statistics to determine if differences between them are statistically different. Without a statistical test, you can compare the means and interpret one as higher or lower than another. But you will not know if the difference is real or simply due to chance.

With these principles in mind, the *t*-test can be further distinguished by the extent to which its hypothesis or research question specifies the difference the test is intended to find. Two-tailed *t*-tests are used when differences are not specified. One-tailed *t*-tests are used when differences are specifically identified in the hypothesis or research question. Both are described in the sections that follow.

Two-Tailed *t*-Test

When a researcher asks a research question or states a hypothesis for which a difference in either direction is acceptable, the *t*-test is called a **two-tailed test.** Using this form of hypothesis or research question to guide the examination of the data, it would not matter which group had the higher or lower score on the dependent variable. Researchers use the two-tailed *t*-test when they presume a difference exists but they cannot predict the direction of the difference.

For example, in a study of how emotions that exist after an organizational conflict alter future organizational relationships, Gayle and Preiss (1998) asked, "Will the reported emotional intensity vary according to the respondent's attribution of blame?" (p. 287). In reviewing the literature, the research team did not find earlier reports that agreed on how emotions employees expressed varied according to whom employees blamed.

Thus, their question does not suggest which type of conflict attribution, self-blame, or other-blame would result in the most emotional intensity. The t-test must be two-tailed so it can capture differences that exist in either direction. Will emotional intensity be higher for those who blame themselves for the conflict? Or will emotional intensity be higher for those who blame someone else for the conflict?

The authors report that degree of emotional intensity did not differ between the two groups—those who blamed themselves, and those who blamed someone else, $t(142) = 2.00$, $p > .13$. The t value of 2.00 did not achieve statistical significance, as the p value was .13, greater than the common standard of .05. In this case the nondirectional research question cannot be answered because the researchers could not determine from these data if emotional intensity differed according to who was blamed for the organizational conflict.

One-Tailed t-Test

Alternately, a t-test is said to be **one-tailed,** or directional, if a specific difference is identified in the research question or hypothesis. For example, the research question "Do students perceive professors to be more powerful than graduate teaching assistants?" (Golish, 1999, p. 17) presumes that one group, professors, will be perceived more powerfully than the other group, graduate teaching assistants (GTAs). This stated, or expected, difference requires a one-tailed t-test.

Golish (1999) reports the findings as follows:

Results of the overall analysis revealed that students perceived professors as more powerful than GTAs ($t(231) = 4.97$, $p = .001$). (p. 22)

The t value is significant because the significance level, or p, is less than the standard of .05. Given the direction of the hypothesis, the t-test answers the research question in the affirmative. Yes, students perceive professors as more powerful than graduate teaching assistants.

But for a moment assume that the t statistic was -4.97 instead of 4.97. The t-test would still be significant, but the difference would be in the opposite direction. In this case, the result would indicate that students perceive graduate teaching

assistants as more powerful than professors—a finding in opposition to the direction supposed by the research question. When this happens, researchers have still found a statistically significant difference, but the difference is the opposite of the one they predicted.

Limitations of the t-Test

The primary limitation of the t-test is that it is designed to examine the differences on one dependent variable according to two groupings, or categories, of the independent variable. Thus, researchers cannot use the t-test to examine more complex communication phenomena. See An Ethical Issue, "Are Two Categories Fully Representative?" for some of the issues related to this limitation.

ANALYSIS OF VARIANCE

Analysis of variance is generally referred to with the acronym **ANOVA.** This statistical test compares the influence of two or more groups (the independent variable) on the dependent variable and is represented by the symbol F. **Variance** is the dispersion of the distribution of scores on the dependent variable. The greater the variance, the more the scores deviate from the mean. Alternately, the smaller the variance, the closer the scores are to the mean. ANOVA examines the degree to which categories of the independent variable can explain the variance of the dependent variable.

As with the t-test, the independent variable must be nominal data and the dependent variable must be continuous level data. But ANOVA extends the t-test in two ways. First, ANOVA can accommodate more than two categories of the independent variable. Second, the test can accommodate more than one independent variable. Thus, the difference between the t-test and ANOVA is the number of categories of the independent variable that can be tested and the number of independent variables that can be tested.

Researchers have long noticed that testing one independent variable and one dependent variable cannot capture the complexity of communication

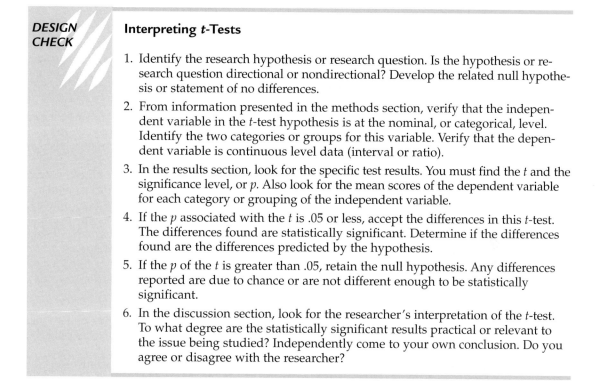

Interpreting *t*-Tests

1. Identify the research hypothesis or research question. Is the hypothesis or research question directional or nondirectional? Develop the related null hypothesis or statement of no differences.

2. From information presented in the methods section, verify that the independent variable in the *t*-test hypothesis is at the nominal, or categorical, level. Identify the two categories or groups for this variable. Verify that the dependent variable is continuous level data (interval or ratio).

3. In the results section, look for the specific test results. You must find the *t* and the significance level, or *p*. Also look for the mean scores of the dependent variable for each category or grouping of the independent variable.

4. If the *p* associated with the *t* is .05 or less, accept the differences in this *t*-test. The differences found are statistically significant. Determine if the differences found are the differences predicted by the hypothesis.

5. If the *p* of the *t* is greater than .05, retain the null hypothesis. Any differences reported are due to chance or are not different enough to be statistically significant.

6. In the discussion section, look for the researcher's interpretation of the *t*-test. To what degree are the statistically significant results practical or relevant to the issue being studied? Independently come to your own conclusion. Do you agree or disagree with the researcher?

phenomena. They have also noticed that variables do not always act independently (Kerlinger, 1986). Being restricted to using *t*-tests would mean that researchers could test only one independent variable at a time and thus lose the ability to test for the complexity of most communication phenomena. In its simplest form, ANOVA can test one independent with more than two categorical levels (for example, school standing: freshman, sophomore, junior, senior). In its more complex form, ANOVA can test two or more independent variables simultaneously. These ANOVAs are known as one-way and two-way ANOVAs, respectively.

ANOVA Basics

Because ANOVA can deal with greater complexity in testing for differences, several other basic issues must be addressed. These issues—planned or unplanned comparisons, between-groups and within-groups variance, degrees of freedom, between-subjects and within-subject designs—are described in the sections that follow.

In either form, ANOVA allows the researcher to compare individuals' scores on the dependent variable according to the groups or categories they belong to for the independent variable. These comparisons can be planned or unplanned. **Planned comparisons** are those comparisons among groups that are indicated in the research hypothesis. These comparisons are specified before the data are gathered. Alternately, unplanned comparisons, called **post hoc comparisons,** are conducted after the researcher finds that a significant ANOVA exists. Post hoc comparisons are not predicted by the research hypothesis. Thus, when used they are considered exploratory. After finding a significant *F* value, the researcher realizes that some statistically significant difference or differences exist. Then the researcher must use post hoc comparisons to find what differences exist

AN ETHICAL ISSUE

Are Two Categories Fully Representative?

Using a *t*-test is a good statistical choice for simple comparisons. But can two categories really represent the characteristics or attributes of individuals? Suppose for a moment that handedness, or the dominance of your right or left hand, is a characteristic you want to study with respect to how people greet one another and shake hands (see Provine, 1997). The independent variable would be handedness; right or left would be its two categories. The dependent variable would be comfort in extending the right hand for a handshake. Is the *t*-test an appropriate statistical test if it limits the independent variable to two categorical levels? Besides right-handedness and left-handedness, what other hand-dominance attribute could be important? Did you consider someone who is truly ambidextrous? What about sex (female, male), marital status (married, single), or hierarchical status (subordinate, superior)? Can two categorical levels accurately represent these as independent variables? What ethical issues would the researcher need to address when using variables with only two categories like these that capture most, but not all, of the differentiation on a characteristic?

among which groups or categories of the independent variable.

Although ANOVAs are commonly referred to as looking for differences between groups of the independent variable, ANOVA actually tests differences between and among means. When differences are found, there is **between-groups variance.** The groups vary enough to distinguish themselves from one another. To be significant, the between-groups variance must be greater than **within-groups variance,** or the variation among individuals within any category or level.

The difference between these two types of variance can be explained with Gayle and Preiss's (1998) study of organizational conflicts. Their research question asks, "Will the reported emotional intensity vary across conflict topics?" (p. 286). Five conflict topics were reported: work tasks, interpersonal problems, work climate, organizational policies, and authority issues. Variation in emotional intensity among participants reporting on different conflict topics would be between-groups variance. The variance between groups is what the researcher is interested in testing. Alternately, variation in emotional intensity among participants reporting on any one type of organizational conflict

(for example, work task conflict) would be within-groups variance.

For ANOVA, degrees of freedom are computed for each independent variable and for the number of participants. Between-groups degrees of freedom are based on the number of categories in an independent variable. The number of categories minus 1 equals the degrees of freedom and is calculated for each independent variable. Thus, sex as an independent variable would result in one degree of freedom (2 categories—female and male—minus 1). An independent variable with five categorical levels, like the conflict topic example just mentioned, would have four degrees of freedom, and so on.

Within-groups degrees of freedom are based on the number of participants and the between-groups degrees of freedom. There are several steps to calculate the within-groups degrees of freedom. For an ANOVA research design with one independent variable with 3 categorical levels and 200 participants, the within-groups degrees of freedom would be calculated as follows. First, subtract 1 from the number of participants (or, $n - 1$). Second, calculate the between-groups degrees of freedom. For this ANOVA with one independent variable with three categorical levels, this *df* would be 2 (*df* = no. of categories − 1). Third, subtract the between-groups degrees of freedom from the number computed in step 1.

Number of participants providing data for this *F* test	*n* = 200
1. *n* − 1	200 − 1 = 199
2. Between-groups degrees of freedom or number of categories − 1	3 − 1 = 2
3. Within-groups degrees of freedom	199 − 2 = 197

Both degrees of freedom are reported with the *F* value. Between-groups degrees of freedom are reported first, followed by the within-groups degrees of freedom. Thus, the *F*(2, 197) notation indicates that the independent variable has three categorical levels. The notation also indicates that data from 200 participants were included in this ANOVA.

The researcher must calculate the *F* statistic to determine if differences between groups exist and if those differences are statistically significant, or not due to chance. Although a researcher can simply compare the means for each group, which are likely to be different, the statistical test is precise and takes into account each group's mean and variation (standard deviation) on the dependent variable.

The *F* is really a measure of how well the categories of the independent variable explain the variation in scores of the dependent variable. If the categories explain no variation, *F* is zero. The better the categories of the independent variable explain variation in the dependent variable, the larger *F* becomes. When the *F* statistic is statistically significant, researchers can interpret the differences of the means between groups as real. In other words, the differences are not due to chance. If the *F* statistic is not significant, then the null hypothesis is retained, indicating no differences between or among means for the groups.

There are two alternatives to the null hypothesis. First, the research hypothesis could predict specific differences between groups, indicating which group would be higher or lower than another. This would be a directional hypothesis, and planned comparisons would be built into the statistical test. For example, Frymier and Wanzer (2003) investigated how students with and without disabilities differ in their communication with their instructors. The hypothesis is "Students with disabilities will report significantly less willingness to communicate with professors than students without disabilities" (p. 178). In this hypothesis, one specific comparison is planned: Students with disabilities will be compared to students without disabilities. One group is predicted to be less willing to communicate with professors than the other group.

Second, the research hypothesis could predict differences between groups but not specify which group will be larger or smaller. This would be a nondirectional hypothesis. Post hoc comparisons would be required if the overall ANOVA is significant. Using the study above, the hypothesis could be restated in this nondirectional form: Students with disabilities will differ from students without disabilities in their willingness to communicate with professors. Stated in this form, there is no prediction as to which group will be more willing to communicate with their professors. In this case, comparisons between the two groups would be computed post hoc only if the *F* statistic proved to be significant.

ANOVAs also differ with respect to another design feature—between-subjects design or within-subject design. **Between-subjects design** is one where each participant is measured at only one group or category, or under only one condition. The ANOVA design is called between-subjects because the researcher wants to examine differences across individuals in the study. The study described above is a between-subjects design because participants self-identified as having or not having a physical or learning disability. Between-subjects comparisons occurred on the independent variable—presence or absence of a disability. Thus, participants' scores on the dependent variable were independent of one another.

Alternately, a **within-subject design** measures each participant more than once, usually at different levels or for different conditions. Researchers often use the term **repeated measures** to describe a within-subject design. To test presentation skills training, Seibold et al. (1993)

used a repeated measures design as they tested participants' perceptions of their presentation skills prior to the training, after the first day of training, after the second day of training, and one month after the training. The design is within-subject because participants were measured multiple times on the same dependent variable after being exposed to different stimuli.

One-Way ANOVA

A **one-way ANOVA** (or one-way analysis of variance) tests for significant differences in the dependent variable based on categorical differences on one independent variable. For this test, there is one independent variable measured at a nominal, or categorical, level. There must be at least two different categories for the independent variable, but there can be many more. Because only one independent variable is tested, a between-subjects design must be used.

The statistical test, F, examines the distributions by comparing the means and standard deviations of the dependent variable for each group, category, or level of the independent variable. If the difference between groups is larger than the difference within groups, the ANOVA is significant. In this case, the researcher would reject the null hypothesis and accept the research hypothesis.

In its original formulation, the ANOVA was designed to make comparisons of roughly equal size. In communication research, in which many comparisons are among naturally occurring groups, meeting this assumption is often impossible and impractical. Computer programs used today to compute ANOVA can overcome this problem by making programmatic adjustments. In most statistical software packages, there will be one statistical test for comparing groups of equal size (usually called ANOVA) and another statistical test for comparing groups of unequal size (usually called general linear model).

Refer again to the study of how students with and without disabilities differ in their communication with their instructors. For one hypothesis, "Students with disabilities will report significantly less willingness to communicate with professors than students without disabilities" (p. 178), the F statistic was not significant, $F(1, 133) = .09, p = .76$. In other words, these data could not support the predicted difference. The mean score for students with disabilities ($M = 69.62, SD = 17.64$) was not statistically different than the mean score for students without disabilities ($M = 70.62, SD = 20.05$).

However, the F statistic for a second hypothesis, "Students with disabilities will report feeling less understood by their professors than students without disabilities" (Frymier & Wanzer, 2003, p. 178), was statistically significant, $F(1, 128) = 5.64, \eta^2 = .04, p < .05$. The mean score for students with disabilities ($M = 12.03, SD = 12.44$) was statistically different than the mean score for students without disabilities ($M = 16.81, SD = 10.36$). Each of these tests was a one-way ANOVA, as each tested the influence of categorical differences of one independent variable on one continuous level dependent variable. In this study, the independent variable for both F tests had only two categories, but ANOVA can be used with an independent variable comprised of two, three, four, even five categories.

You probably noticed the report of $\eta^2 = .04$ in this example. **Eta squared,** or η^2, is an assessment of the proportion of variance in the dependent variable, students' feelings of being understood by their professors, associated with the categories of the independent variable, students' (dis)ability. When you see this symbol, it is an indication of the degree of that association, which in this case is minimal. Whereas the F test indicates that a statistically significant difference exists, η^2 allows the researcher to determine if this statistical difference is practically or socially meaningful. That, of course, depends upon the hypothesis or research question asked and the setting of the research study.

Two-Way ANOVA

In a **two-way ANOVA,** there are two categorical independent variables and one continuous level dependent variable. In testing the effects or influence of two independent variables, ANOVA can determine the relative contributions of each

TABLE 11.3 Two-Way ANOVA for Age Group Identification Study

| | Sex | |
Culture	Female	Male
Australia	Australian females	Australian males
Laos	Laotian females	Laotian males
Spain	Spanish females	Spanish males
Thailand	Thai females	Thai males
United States	American females	American males

independent variable, or a *main effect,* to the distribution of the dependent variable. Additionally, ANOVA can test for the *interaction effect,* or the combined influences that can occur from both independent variables simultaneously.

For example, a research study that investigates how important individuals perceive their membership in their age group demonstrates how a two-way ANOVA is used in communication research (McCann, Kellermann, Giles, Gallois, & Viladot, 2004). The research team used a survey to collect data from 544 young adults ($M = 20.9$, $SD = 2.66$) from five cultures (Australia, Laos, Spain, Thailand, and the United States). Thus, culture was one of the categorical independent variables. The other independent variable was sex of participant (382 females, 162 males). As part of the survey, participants responded to a questionnaire to capture their age identity. For example, one of the items of that scale was "I value being a member of my age group."

A two-way ANOVA was used to test for the effects of two independent variables—culture with five categories and sex with two categories—on the dependent variable, age identification (see Table 11.3). With a two-way ANOVA, the research team could test for the main effects of each independent variable. A main effect occurs when one independent variable influences scores on the dependent variable, and this effect is uninfluenced by the other independent variable. In other words, are young adults' perceptions of age identity

different due to cultural influences, one main effect? Or are differences in age identity due to participants' sex, another main effect?

For the hypothesis "Young adults' age identity is highest in the USA and Australia, moderate in Catalonia, Spain, and lowest in Thailand and Laos" (McCann et al., 2004, p. 93), the F statistic revealed a main effect for culture, $F(4, 522) = 4.87$, $p < .001$, $\omega^2 = .03$. Notice that the hypothesis does not specify which cultural group would have a higher age identity. Thus, when the statistic resulted in a significant finding, post hoc tests were used to determine where those differences were. In this case, young adults in the United States and Laos were more age identified than young adults in Australia, Thailand, and Spain.

Notice the ω^2 in the report of the statistical finding. This is **omega squared,** another measure of the strength of the association between the independent and dependent variable. Thus, age identity varied by culture, but not as the research team predicted. As the research team notes, "Surprisingly, culture had very little effect (3%) on participants' age identity. . . . These results suggest the effect of culture on age identity may be quite modest, at least for student samples" (McCann et al., 2004, p. 98).

The main effect of the other independent variable, age, was different. For the hypothesis "Women are more age identified than men" (McCann et al., 2004, p. 93), no main effect was found, $F(1, 522) = .12$, *ns.* Thus, the hypothesis

---

TRY THIS!   **Should Differences Be Significant or Practical?**

Communication researchers explore a variety of applied communication problems and issues. In some cases, differences on the dependent variable would need to be large to persuade policy makers to change their practices or procedures. In other cases, differences—even small ones—could positively benefit people. Take a look at each of the situations below. How much of a difference would be enough to persuade you that a policy needs to be developed and implemented or that a procedure needs to be changed? Does the difference need to be statistically significant? Even if testing a hypothesis produces statistical significance, policy makers must also consider practical significance. Assess both the advantages and disadvantages of basing policy or procedure changes on statistically significant differences.

Situation	Communication Phenomena	Questions
Police responding to domestic violence calls	Assertiveness and sex of police officers in talking with victim	How assertive should officers be in persuading victims to file complaints against their attackers? Would the impact of assertiveness differ if female officers talked with female victims and male officers talked with male victims?
Elementary school teacher controlling students in classroom	Loudness of teacher's voice and directness of eye contact in talking with students	How loudly should the teacher talk when the classroom is unruly? Should his or her eye contact be directed at all of the students or at only those who are disruptive?

---

was not supported. Notice here the use of the symbol *ns*. Researchers use this to indicate that the statistical was not significant.

Because two independent variables are used in a two-way ANOVA, researchers can also test for an interaction effect. An interaction effect occurs when the results of one main effect cannot be interpreted without acknowledging the results of the other main effect. In this study, the research team hypothesized an interaction effect, "Age identity is most elevated among American female adults (vs. American male adults and female adults from the other four cultures)" (McCann et al., 2004, p. 93). The *F* statistic supported this hypothesis, $F(1, 529) = 33.28$, $p < .001$, $\omega^2 = .06$.

Young adult American females were more age group identified than all other respondents. Although the effect is modest, it is stronger than the more modest main effect of culture. Recall that sex had no effect on participants' age identification. Generally, when a significant interaction is discovered, the main effects are ignored.

Factorial ANOVA

ANOVA is not limited to a two-way design. Rather, it can also be used for more complicated *factorial* designs with three or even four independent variables. At a minimum, a factorial design would include at least two categorical

TABLE 11.4 Factorial ANOVA for Television-Reality Study

First Independent Variable	Second Independent Variable	Third Independent Variable	Fourth Independent Variable
Age (3 categories) 1. Students in 2nd grade 2. Students in 12th grade 3. Elderly adults	Visual manipulation (2 categories) 1. Visually distinct 2. Visually similar	Time of testing (2 categories) 1. Immediate 2. One week later	Order of stimuli (2 categories) 1. Trailer first 2. News story first

independent variables, each with at least two levels. The effects of these variables would be tested on one continuous level dependent variable.

For example, a $3 \times 2 \times 2 \times 2$ between-subjects ANOVA was used to examine how individuals confuse what they see on television with reality (Mares, 1996). Table 11.4 graphs the four independent variables that the researcher tested for their influence on the dependent variable, source confusions between news and fiction programming.

This complex ANOVA addresses another issue—that is, in complex designs with multiple independent variables of nominal data, researchers will often choose regression over ANOVA as their statistical test. Although traditionally reserved for examining the effects of a continuous level independent variable on a continuous level dependent variable, the regression test can accommodate nominal level independent variables. Some statisticians have argued that regression is preferred over ANOVA because the regression test is more comprehensive and can be applied equally to experimental and descriptive research designs (Pedhazur & Schmelkin, 1991). Regression is described in more detail in Chapter 12.

Limitations of ANOVA

The obvious limitation of ANOVA is that it is restricted to testing independent variables made up of nominal, or categorical, data. The other limitation is really one of complexity. When researchers use three or four independent variables, differences found can be significant, but confusing and difficult to interpret.

ASKING FOR STATISTICAL HELP

The statistics presented in this chapter allow a researcher to test for differences between groups or categories. Figure 11.1 can help you determine the appropriate test of difference by identifying the number and types of variables in the research questions or hypotheses. Having a basic understanding of chi-squares, t-tests, and ANOVAs can help you interpret the research literature, making the results more meaningful for you. And with the help of spreadsheet and statistical programs, you can also collect and interpret data using these tests.

After you enter the raw data, you must select which data are to be used for the test and select the appropriate statistic. For t-tests and ANOVAs, the spreadsheet or statistical program will calculate the statistic, the significance level, or p, and the degrees of freedom and will provide the mean scores and standard deviations for each category of the independent variable.

However, the use of these and other statistics is subjective because there are many variations for each of the tests described. I strongly suggest that you ask someone with statistical expertise to look over your research plan and that you seek help at any confusing point in the research process (for example, when generating hypotheses, developing method and procedure of data collection, developing statistical programming or spreadsheets, interpreting statistical tests). Although researchers tend to follow a generally accepted series of steps in the research process and in using statistics, even professors benefit from expert advice. Most universities have statistical experts available to both students and faculty to help them with their research activities.

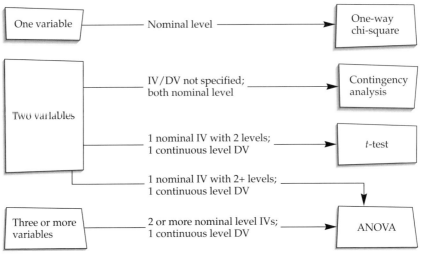

FIGURE 11.1 Identifying the Appropriate Statistical Test of Difference:
IV = Independent Variable; DV = Dependent Variable

SUMMARY

1. Chi-square, *t*-test, and ANOVA are statistical tests of difference.

2. The function of inferential statistics is to draw conclusions about a population by examining the sample.

3. Inferential statistics rely on several assumptions: the use of probability in establishing significance levels, normal distribution of populations and samples, and random assignment of participants to groups.

4. Meeting these assumptions may not always be possible; thus, some scholars use these tests of differences outside the experimental design framework.

5. Four analytical steps assist the researcher through statistical interpretation of tests of differences: (1) conducting the statistical test to determine if differences exist; (2) characterizing the differences found as expected or not expected; (3) assessing differences for statistical significance; and (4) interpreting differences found with respect

to the population from which the sample was drawn.

6. A one-way chi-square looks for statistically significant differences in categories within one nominal variable; contingency analysis looks for categorical differences between two or more nominal variables.

7. The *t*-test is used to test hypotheses that expect to find a difference between two groupings of the independent variable on a continuous level dependent variable.

8. A *t*-test can be two-tailed, in which any difference found is accepted, or one-tailed, in which the direction of the difference is specified by the research question or hypothesis.

9. Analysis of variance, or ANOVA, compares the influence of two or more groups of the independent variable on the dependent variable.

10. Design issues to consider in using ANOVA include planned or post hoc comparisons, and between-subjects and within-subject forms.

11. One-way ANOVA tests for significant differences in the continuous level dependent

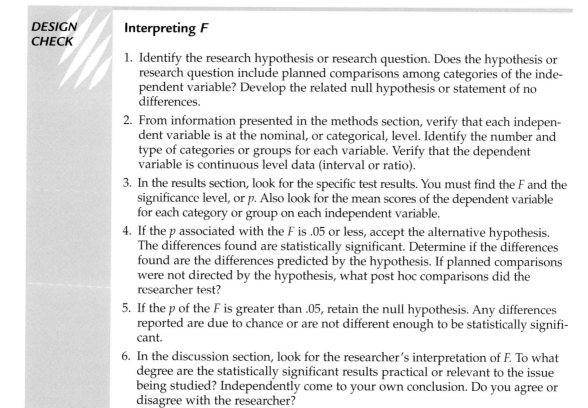

DESIGN CHECK

Interpreting *F*

1. Identify the research hypothesis or research question. Does the hypothesis or research question include planned comparisons among categories of the independent variable? Develop the related null hypothesis or statement of no differences.

2. From information presented in the methods section, verify that each independent variable is at the nominal, or categorical, level. Identify the number and type of categories or groups for each variable. Verify that the dependent variable is continuous level data (interval or ratio).

3. In the results section, look for the specific test results. You must find the *F* and the significance level, or *p*. Also look for the mean scores of the dependent variable for each category or group on each independent variable.

4. If the *p* associated with the *F* is .05 or less, accept the alternative hypothesis. The differences found are statistically significant. Determine if the differences found are the differences predicted by the hypothesis. If planned comparisons were not directed by the hypothesis, what post hoc comparisons did the researcher test?

5. If the *p* of the *F* is greater than .05, retain the null hypothesis. Any differences reported are due to chance or are not different enough to be statistically significant.

6. In the discussion section, look for the researcher's interpretation of *F*. To what degree are the statistically significant results practical or relevant to the issue being studied? Independently come to your own conclusion. Do you agree or disagree with the researcher?

variable based on categorical differences of one independent variable.

12. A two-way ANOVA tests for the effects of two categorical independent variables on a continuous level dependent variable.

13. Both main effects and interaction effects are possible in a two-way ANOVA.

14. Factorial ANOVA can accommodate three or four independent variables.

KEY TERMS

analysis of variance

ANOVA

between-groups variance

between-subjects design

chi-square

contingency analysis

contingency table

degrees of freedom

eta squared

expected frequency

independent sample *t*-test

inferential statistics

observed frequency

omega squared

one-dimensional chi-square

one-tailed *t*-test

one-way ANOVA

one-way chi-square

paired comparison *t*-test

planned comparisons

post hoc comparisons

repeated measures *t*-test

two-dimensional chi-square

two-tailed *t*-test

two-way ANOVA

two-way chi-square

variance

within-groups variance

within-subject design

CHAPTER TWELVE

Testing for Relationships

Chapter Checklist

After reading this chapter, you should be able to:

1. Explain the difference between tests of differences and tests of relationships.

2. Use the four analytical steps to design and interpret research designs and statistical findings.

3. Know which assumptions of inferential statistics your research project meets and which assumptions it does not meet.

4. Develop a hypothesis or research question and select the appropriate statistical test of relationship (correlation or regression).

5. Differentiate among the assumptions and functions of correlation and regression.

6. Interpret research findings developed from results of correlation and regression.

Besides looking for statistically significant differences, researchers are also interested in looking for statistically significant relationships between and among variables. There are two statistical tests for examining relationships between and among continuous level variables—correlation and regression.

Correlation, a statistical test that describes the type of relationship between two continuous variables, is the simpler of the two. Do the scores on both variables increase? Decrease? Does one score increase while the other score decreases? Or is there no relationship between the two variables?

For example, Wrench and Richmond (2004) predict a relationship between two constructs with the hypothesis, "There will be a positive relationship between a teacher's perceived humor assessment and a student's perception of teacher credibility" (p. 97). The null hypothesis or statement of no relationship would be: There is no relationship between a teacher's perceived humor assessment and a student's perception of teacher credibility.

In other studies, researchers use a research question to explore a relationship without predicting how the variables will be related. For example, Schrodt (2002) asked, "What is the relationship between employee perceptions of organizational culture (i.e., teamwork, morale, information flow, involvement, supervision, and meetings) and employee perceptions of organizational identification?" (p. 193). At first glance, this research question might seem complex. But, in essence, the researcher is asking how are employee perceptions of teamwork related to organizational identification, how are employee perceptions of morale related to organizational identification, and so on. In each of these cases, the relationship to be examined is simple and straightforward; only two variables are included. The correlation statistic is used to test these types of relationships.

Of course, not all relationships are this simple. Some communication phenomena are more complex, and researchers need to develop hypotheses and research questions to examine more than just the nature of the relationship between two variables. It is not unusual for three or more independent variables to be hypothesized as influencing a dependent variable; in such a case, regression is the appropriate statistic. Although correlation is restricted to describing the nature of the relationship, the regression statistic allows researchers to examine causal or predictive relationships among continuous level variables.

As an example of the type of complexity regression can handle, Cayanus and Booth-Butterfield (2004) explored how evoking jealousy was used as a communication strategy in romantic relationships. Participants' scores on four independent variables were used to predict the likelihood that they would activate jealous responses in their romantic partners. Thus, the research question, "Do exchange orientation, communal orientation, positive responses to jealousy, and length of relationship influence evoking jealousy?" (p. 244) was answered with regression. Based upon the literature, the research team considered four different constructs as influencing the use of jealousy as a communication strategy. Using regression, the unique influence of each variable could be identified.

In their simplest form, tests of relationship look for **linear** relationships. This means that a one-unit change in one variable is associated with a constant change in the other variable. Because this discussion is an introduction to statistics, the examples and methods described here are restricted to tests of relationships for two or more continuous level variables. Restricting the discussion this way will help you grasp the basic principles behind the statistical tests. Realize, however, that various forms of both correlation and regression can address categorical variables. And, of course, not all relationships are linear. Some are **curvilinear,** representing a U-shaped curve (both concave and convex forms). The regression statistic can be useful in testing for curvilinear relationships, but that discussion is beyond the scope of this chapter.

Why do researchers need to turn to statistics to look for these patterns or relationships? Without statistical tests, researchers would have to visually examine the raw data for patterns, which can be elusive and difficult, depending on the size of the dataset and the number of related variables. Even if a pattern were detected, knowing that a relationship exists is not enough. Researchers use

Paying Attention to Details

A correlation or regression is only as meaningful as the theoretical model or basic assumptions about the relationships for which the researchers can argue. Thus, selection of the correlation or regression statistic should be based on a theory or on the findings of previous research studies. Spreadsheet and statistical programs can determine the relationship between and among sets of variables—even nonsensical relationships. As you read a research report, the authors should persuade you that they have selected the most appropriate set of variables to be studied. As a consumer, you should always be asking yourself if the variables for which a relationship is tested make sense.

statistics to ask, "Is the relationship strong enough to be real—is it statistically significant?" In other words, is the relationship observed in the data stronger than the relationship that might occur due to chance? The two statistics this chapter addresses share a common logic.

BASIC ASSUMPTIONS

Before describing these two tests, however, we need to return to the discussion of inferential statistics, alternative and null hypotheses, degrees of freedom, and the four analytical steps introduced in Chapter 11. Just as with the statistical tests for differences, the tests for relationships are used to draw conclusions about a population by examining the sample. In claiming that a finding from a sample holds true for its population, the researcher must meet four assumptions. Just as in difference tests, researchers set the significance level for each statistical test they conduct to assess how likely it is that the relationship found is real and not due to chance. Second, the data assumption must be met. Data are assumed to come from a normally distributed population. If not, a statistical test can provide only an approximation of the relationship.

The third assumption, very important to tests of relationships, is that the appropriate variables are selected to be tested. Thus, the theoretical model researchers use to specify which variables are to be included in a hypothesis and to specify which variable influences another is essential.

Excluding influential variables is problematic. Finally, individuals participating in the research project should be selected through probability sampling. Violating this assumption restricts the result to a purely descriptive form.

Recall from Chapter 11 that these principles are the ideal from which statistical tests were developed. And, if at all possible, all of these assumptions should be addressed and met in the research design phase of the research project. However, not all research meets these assumptions. As with the limitations and cautions for statistical tests of differences, violating these assumptions means that researchers need to be careful to not overextend research findings.

Remember that tests of relationships are not pertinent to the scores of any one participant in the research project. It would not be appropriate to investigate or report the relationship of variables for any one person. Rather, it is the pattern of scores across the sample that is of interest. When the basic assumptions listed earlier are met, examining the data at this holistic level allows a researcher to make inferences from the sample to the population. Thus, any significant relationship found is not significant for any participant, but representative of the population from which participants were selected.

Alternative and Null Hypotheses

Tests of relationships, just like tests of differences, test the likelihood that the alternative hypothesis is true and the null hypothesis is not.

The alternative, or research, hypothesis would predict that a relationship will be found, whereas the null hypothesis predicts that no relationship will be evident. The significance level is usually set at .05 to provide a criterion for making this decision. If the .05 level (or a lower one) is achieved, then a researcher rejects the null hypothesis and accepts its alternative hypothesis. If the .05 significance level is not achieved, then the null hypothesis is retained.

Degrees of Freedom

As with statistical tests of differences, correlations and regressions require that degrees of freedom be calculated. Represented by the abbreviation *df,* degrees of freedom specify how many values vary within a statistical test. Once again, there are clear rules for calculating the degrees of freedom for each statistical test. These rules will be explained in the sections that follow.

Four Analytical Steps

The four analytical steps introduced in Chapter 11 can also be applied to statistical tests of relationships. First, the statistical test is applied to determine if a relationship exists between or among variables. Here, the researcher selects the appropriate statistical test—correlation or regression—as indicated by the hypothesis or research question. The hypothesis and the statistical test must be parallel.

The second analytical step characterizes the type of relationship found. Sometimes the relationship that appears in the data may not be the relationship predicted. Thus, researchers and consumers must check to make sure that the relationship found is indeed the relationship predicted.

The third analytical step assesses the statistical importance of the relationship. A researcher, generally using the significance level set at .05, determines if the strength and direction of the relationship found can be accepted as real, not random. If the probability level is not achieved, then any relationship found is not significant and no conclusion can be drawn.

Finally, the researcher wants to move beyond the data tested into the future. Thus, this fourth analytical step evaluates the importance of the observed relationships in the sample and then generalizes the findings to the population. Once again, the researcher must make an assessment of all the steps in the research process:

- How was the sample obtained?
- Were participants selected through probability sampling?
- To what extent does the sample represent the population in which the researcher is interested?
- Was the research design appropriate for the hypothesis and research question?
- Were the data collected in reliable and valid ways?

Only by asking and answering these questions can a researcher determine the extent to which he or she can generalize from the findings of the sample to the population.

CORRELATION

Correlation, also known as the **Pearson product-moment correlation coefficient,** is represented by the symbol *r.* It is a statistical test that examines the linear relationship between two continuous level variables. Generally, a correlation can answer one of the following questions about the type of relationship between two variables:

- Do the scores on both variables increase?
- Do the scores on both variables decrease?
- Does one score increase at the same time the other score decreases?

The correlation coefficient indicates the degree to which two variables are related. To use a correlation as a statistical test, each participant must have provided measurements on two separate variables; that is, data on one variable must be paired with data on another variable. It is the pattern of the relationships between these two variables across all participants that correlation examines. If a correlation is statistically significant, then some type of relationship exists between the two variables. If a correlation is not significant,

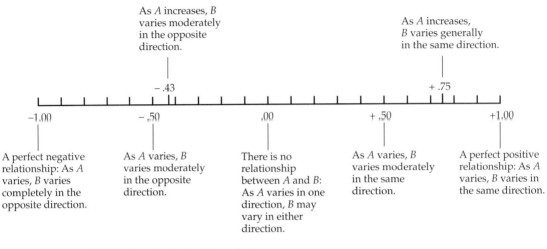

FIGURE 12.1 The Scale of Correlation

then no conclusion can be drawn about the relationship between the two variables. The formula and steps for calculating the correlation coefficient are shown in Appendix B.

The degrees of freedom in a correlation are based on the number of variables in the test. A correlation tests for the relationship between two variables, X and Y. So, degrees of freedom for correlation are calculated as $df = n - 2$, with n referring to the pairs of data, not the individual data points. In a study with 100 participants providing scores on two continuous variables, the df would be 98 ($n - 2$, or $100 - 2 = 98$).

The one thing that a correlation cannot do is determine causation. Even when a correlation is significant, the statistical test does not provide any information about the cause-and-effect relationship between the two variables. The first variable could cause the second. Or vice versa; the second could cause the first. But, most important, a third variable could be the cause of both.

When two variables are statistically correlated, but not causally linked, a third variable creates the spurious relationship. A **spurious correlation,** or *spurious relationship,* is one in which a third variable—sometimes identified, at other times unknown—is influencing the variables tested. The correlation coefficient does not test for the existence of this third variable.

Interpreting the Coefficient

Once the coefficient, or r value, is calculated, its interpretation requires two steps. The first addresses the direction of the relationship. The second deals with the strength of the relationship. Look at Figure 12.1 to see how these two interpretive steps work together.

Relationships can be positive or negative. In a positive relationship, values on one variable increase as values on the other variable increase. Alternately, you could interpret a positive relationship as one in which values on one variable decrease as values on the other variable decrease as well. Either way, the principle behind a positive correlation is that the relationship is linear and both variables change in the same direction. A positive correlation coefficient is expressed as a positive number; some researchers will include a plus sign to emphasize the positive nature of the relationship. Thus, both .79 and +.79 represent the same positive correlation.

In a negative relationship, the relationship is still linear, but now the variables change in directions opposite to each other. Thus, values on one variable increase whereas values on the other variable decrease. A negative correlation coefficient is expressed as a negative number (for example, −.79).

Therefore, the direction of the correlation coefficient represents how the two variables change with respect to one another. The positive or negative symbol of the *r* value is the indicator that the correlation is positive or negative.

The second interpretive step is an interpretation of the strength, magnitude, or size of the correlation. A simple principle aids the interpretation. The greater the absolute value of a correlation coefficient, or *r*, the stronger the relationship between the two variables. The numerical value of a correlation coefficient is restricted in range from −1.00 to +1.00. If you calculate a correlation and get a number less than −1.00 or greater than +1.00, there is an error in computation.

Interpreting the absolute value of the correlation in this step, the positive or negative nature of the *r* value is ignored. A perfect linear relationship would have an *r* value of +1.00 or −1.00. In this type of relationship, for every unit one variable increased, the other variable would also increase a unit. Or for every unit one variable increased, the other variable would decrease a unit. These are extreme cases and seldom found in communication research. The other extreme is a correlation coefficient of zero. In this case, there is no relationship between the two variables. In other words, no pattern can be discerned between the two distributions.

Practically, interpreting *r* values is subjective. Other than for the extreme values described, interpreting the magnitude of the correlation depends on what is being studied. There are, however, some general rules researchers use to begin the process. Communication scholars, like other social scientists, generally follow these rules for interpreting the magnitude or strength of a correlation coefficient (Guilford, 1956; Williams, 1968):

< .20	Slight, almost negligible relationship
.20 – .40	Low correlation; definite but small relationship
.40 – .70	Moderate correlation; substantial relationship
.70 – .90	High correlation; marked relationship
> .90	Very high correlation; very dependable relationship

These rules apply whether the correlation is positive or negative. So, a correlation of +.63 is of the same strength as a correlation of −.63.

Recognize, however, that these are rules; and there are often exceptions to rules. For example, a statistically significant correlation coefficient may have little practical relevance. The only way to tell if a correlation coefficient is large or small is to know what is typical for similar measures of the same variables (Jaeger, 1990). Thus, the practical significance of the relationship must be determined not only by obtaining a statistically significant *r* but also by reading the scholarly literature.

Finally, in comparing one *r* value with another, it is inappropriate to compare their relative size. A correlation of .40 is not twice the relationship of a correlation of .20 (Williams, 1968). The *r* value is simply an index, not a measurement in and of itself.

Amount of Shared Variance   Because of this interpretation problem, researchers use r^2 to represent the percentage of variance two variables have in common. Transforming *r* to r^2 allows comparisons between and among different correlated variables. Also known as the **coefficient of determination,** r^2 is found by simply squaring the *r* value. Researchers frequently do not report this calculation because it is easy for consumers of research to calculate themselves. Take a look at Table 12.1. Notice how little variance is accounted for by low values of *r*. Alternately, the amount of variance accounted for is closer to the *r* value when *r* is large.

When a correlation is presented as a statistical result, you should always mentally calculate r^2. Why? A correlation, or *r*, of .40 can be interpreted as a moderately positive result. But when you recognize that this *r* value accounts for only 16% of the variance, you must also acknowledge that the correlation did not account for 84% of the variance between the two variables. Simply stated, other variables, not the ones tested, were influencing the relationship. Thus, both researchers and consumers must be cautious in interpreting correlation coefficients and not confuse correlation with causation.

Notice that both positive and negative correlation coefficients result in the same level of r^2. A negative correlation of −.63 would account for

TABLE 12.1 Determining Variance Accounted For

r Correlation Coefficient	r^2 Amount of Variance Accounted For
.2 or −.2	.04
.3 or −.3	.09
.4 or −.4	.16
.5 or −.5	.25
.6 or −.6	.36
.7 or −.7	.49
.8 or −.8	.64
.9 or −.9	.81

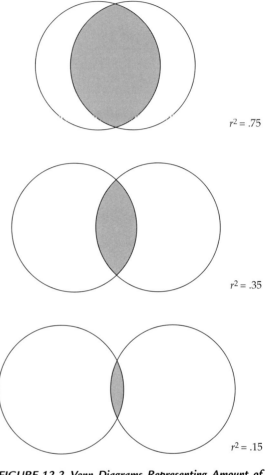

$r^2 = .75$

$r^2 = .35$

$r^2 = .15$

FIGURE 12.2 Venn Diagrams Representing Amount of Shared Variance in Correlations

40% (.3969 rounded) of the variance, just as the positive correlation of +.63 would. The Venn diagrams in Figure 12.2 demonstrate several different sizes of correlations. The shaded and overlapping parts of the circles represent the variance accounted for, or the common variance between the two variables.

Plotting the Data   As a researcher, you should first plot out the data on a scattergram to verify that a linear relationship exists between the variables. A correlation is not a suitable test if the relationship is not linear. You can plot data for the two variables on a graph, or scattergram. The Excel spreadsheet program can do this for you: Using the Chart Wizard function, select the X Y (or Scatter) design, and data entered on a spreadsheet are automatically transformed into a scattergram. Statistical software can also provide this same function.

To check for linearity, draw a straight line through the middle of the data points. If a straight line "fits" the data, then there is some linearity to the relationship between the variables, and you can continue with calculating and interpreting the correlation coefficient. If a straight line cannot be drawn among the data points, the relationship is likely to be curvilinear and the correlation coefficient is an inappropriate

test. Some statistical software packages can draw and fit the line for a relationship between two variables.

Examples of Correlation

A correlation provides descriptive information about the relationship between two variables. Recall the hypothesis presented at the beginning of the chapter: There will be a positive relationship between a teacher's perceived humor assessment and a student's perception of teacher credibility. Over 400 undergraduate students responding to a written survey were instructed to think of the instructor they had for the class immediately before their communication class, in which the data were collected. The survey included a questionnaire that captured students' perceptions of teacher humor. For example, one item was "My teacher regularly communicates with others using humor." The survey also included a questionnaire that captured students' perceptions of their teachers' credibility, which was measured by the three subconstructs of competence, goodwill, and trustworthiness.

Using the scores for these variables, the research team used correlation to test if the relationship they predicted was true for this sample. Wrench and Richmond (2004) report:

> The fifth hypothesis predicted that there would be a positive relationship between a teacher's perceived humor assessment and a teacher's perceived credibility (competence, caring/goodwill, and trustworthiness). This hypothesis was supported in this study, (competence) r (432) = .39, $p < .0001$, (goodwill) r (432) = .37, $p < .0001$, and (trustworthiness) r (434) = .28, $p < .0001$. (p. 100)

The number in parentheses behind r is the degrees of freedom for that test of correlation; the significance level of the test is also given. Notice that all of the relationships are positive. Students' perceptions of their teachers' humor increase while students' perceptions of teachers' competence, goodwill, and trustworthiness increase. Also notice that the strongest correlation is between humor assessment and competence.

This use of correlation is fairly simple and straightforward. The researchers hypothesized a correlation between two constructs; reported their findings, which confirmed their hypothesis; and described the findings from the tests of correlation in the discussion section of the research report.

Return to the research question that asked if there were relationships between employees' perceptions of organizational culture and organizational identification. For this research question, six components of organizational culture—teamwork, morale, information flow, involvement, supervision, and meetings—were tested for their relationship to employees' perceptions of organizational identification. Written surveys were used to collect data from employees of a retail sales organization to answer the research question. Here's how the researcher described the findings:

> To answer the first research question, which explored the relationship between employee perceptions of organizational culture (i.e., teamwork, morale, information flow, involvement, supervision, and meetings) and employee perceptions of organizational identification, a Pearson product-moment correlation matrix was obtained. The correlation matrix revealed significant relationships among each of the six dimensions of organizational culture and employee perceptions of identification. (Schrodt, 2002, p. 198)

The correlation matrix is displayed in Table 12.2.

When correlations are displayed in a table like this, it is called a **correlation matrix** because it is possible to see how every variable is correlated with every other variable. Notice how the variable names are numbered and in the same order across the top row of the table as well as down the far left column of the table. With this type of table, you can select any two variables and determine the correlation between them.

For example, find the variable morale in the far left column in Table 12.2 and follow that row until you have reached the column identified as 1 to represent OIQ, or organizational identification. Here you should find the correlation between the two variables represented as $r = .75$. Do the same for information flow. Locate it in the far left column and follow that row until you reach the column for organizational identification. Here you should find the correlation between the two variables represented as $r = .60$. Also notice that the significance level for all of the correlations is presented as a note to the table.

You have probably also noted that the matrix is incomplete—that values are not presented in the top right triangle of the table. A matrix repeats all of the variables across the top and down the left column. A fully completed matrix would mean that correlations are reported twice. This is unnecessary because the correlation between

TABLE 12.2 Correlations and Descriptive Statistics for Organizational Culture and Organizational Identification Study

Variables	M	SD	α	1	2	3	4	5	6	7
1 OIQ	113.36	18.55	.95	—						
OCS Subscales										
2 Teamwork	32.58	5.72	.93	.41	—					
3 Morale	27.44	5.69	.93	.75	.61	—				
4 Information flow	15.19	2.92	.81	.60	.54	.76	—			
5 Involvement	14.41	3.86	.91	.54	.57	.75	.69	—		
6 Supervision	31.54	7.20	.94	.36	.65	.60	.53	.72	—	
7 Meetings	18.55	3.91	.83	.51	.45	.66	.64	.66	.63	—

NOTE: All correlations are significant at $p < .0001$.
SOURCE: "The Relationship Between Organizational Identification and Organizational Culture: Employee Perceptions of Culture and Identifications in a Retail Sales Organization," by P. Schrodt, 2002, *Communication Studies, 53,* pp. 189–202. Used by permission of the Central States Communication Association.

organizational identification and morale is exactly the same as the correlation between morale and organizational identification.

Finally, notice in the table that columns provide the mean, standard deviation, and Cronbach's alpha for each variable. With this additional information, you can fully interpret the variables and their relationships to one another.

Other Forms of Correlation

The correlations described in the previous section are the most common, because the Pearson product-moment correlation requires that data for both variables be at the interval or ratio level. Less frequently, researchers will need to compute a correlation for other types of data. For example, a **point biserial correlation** is used to examine the relationship between two variables when one variable is measured at the continuous level and the other is **dichotomous,** or measured at one of two nominal levels. Point biserial correlation is used, as an example, when researchers need to use a variable like sex (identified as female or male) as one variable in a correlation.

A **Spearman correlation coefficient,** or **rho,** is the appropriate correlation statistic to use to examine the relationship between two variables, both with data captured on ordinal scales. Recall that data at the ordinal level of measurement are ranked. These correlations are interpreted in the same manner as Pearson product-moment correlations. Both point biserial correlation and Spearman correlation coefficient are interpreted for their direction (positive or negative) and the strength of the relationship.

Limitations of Correlation

Although data used in a correlation are generally measured at the interval or ratio level, this is usually not seen as a limitation, as other forms of the correlation statistic exist to handle data gathered at the nominal or ordinal level. The test is limited, however, to finding a relationship for two variables, and the relationship between the variables is presumed to be linear, another limitation. These limitations severely restrict the development of hypotheses and research questions.

Interpreting Correlations

1. Identify the research hypothesis or research question. Develop the related null hypothesis or statement of no relationship.
2. From information presented in the methods section, verify that each variable in the correlation hypothesis is measured continuously.
3. In the results section, look for the specific test results. You must find the r and the significance level, or p.
4. If the p of the r is .05 or less, accept the relationship in the test of correlation. The relationship found is statistically significant. Determine if the relationship found is the relationship predicted by the hypothesis.
5. If the p of the r is greater than .05, retain the null hypothesis. Any relationship reported is due to chance, or the variables are not related enough to be statistically significant.
6. In the discussion section, look for the researcher's interpretation of the correlation. To what degree are the statistically significant results practical or relevant to the issue being studied? Independently come to your own conclusion. Do you agree or disagree with the researcher?

But the primary limitation is the degree to which inferences can be made from correlations. Even when all of the assumptions described at the beginning of this chapter are met, correlation does not *necessarily* equal causation (Vogt, 1999). The strength and direction of the correlation coefficient do not speak to the likelihood that one variable caused the other variable to increase or decrease in the way that it did. Rather, causality would be more directly inferred from the theoretical foundation for testing the two variables.

When two variables are known to be causally linked, the correlation coefficient can provide some evidence of that link. Still, it is important to remember that "statistics do not establish causation; *causation depends on the logic of relationships*" (Hoover & Donovan, 1995, p. 118). This logic is established by providing evidence from previous research studies and from practical knowledge of the sequence of events. As a researcher and consumer, you should be careful not to overextend findings about correlations as evidence of causation. Interpretation of the causal aspect of the relationship between two variables

should be based on the foundation presented in the literature review, not just on the size of the correlation coefficient.

REGRESSION

Whereas correlations describe the relationship between two variables, predicting relationships among continuous variables is the task of regression. **Regression**—actually, a set of statistical techniques that predict some variables by knowing others—is a highly flexible statistical procedure that allows researchers to address many different types of research questions and hypotheses and different types of data. The most common use of regression is to assess the influence of several continuous level predictor, or independent, variables on a single continuous criterion, or dependent, variable. But to understand the concept behind regression, we will begin with a model of simple linear regression with just two variables. One variable will serve as the independent variable; one will serve as the dependent variable. Both are measured at the continuous level.

It is worth mentioning here that even though regression is used to test for causation, it does not necessarily rely on an experimental research design. Regression is particularly well suited for testing the relationship between naturally occurring variables. In other words, the researcher does not manipulate anything. It is this characteristic of regression that is of particular advantage to communication researchers, because regression allows researchers to study variables that cannot be experimentally manipulated.

For example, to study the influence of social and emotional support on attributional confidence, or the ability to predict another's behavior, Avtgis (2003) asked men with brothers to respond to questionnaires to capture their perceptions on these variables and test these relationships. As you can imagine, it would be impractical and probably impossible to manipulate one brother's perception of another brother in an experimental design. Thus, the research question "How do each of the social support styles and emotional support contribute to attributional confidence in the brother-brother relationship?" (p. 343) was answered using regression in a descriptive research design. Many concepts of interest to communication scholars would be difficult to manipulate experimentally. Thus, regression is an attractive alternative for testing naturally occurring phenomena.

As in correlation, "variance accounted for" is a phrase commonly associated with regression. In using this phrase, a researcher is describing the percentage of variance in the criterion variable accounted for by the predictor variable. In research reports, you are likely to find many different ways of interpreting regression. Phrases that researchers use include

- It is the proportion of variance due to regression.
- It is the proportion of variance predicted by the independent variable.
- It is the proportion of variance accounted for by the independent variable.
- It is the proportion of variance explained by the independent variable.

The one chosen is based upon researcher preference, and that selection should be based upon the research context, the design of the research project, and the theoretical foundation for the regression model (Pedhazur & Schmelkin, 1991).

Linear Regression

Linear regression is a form of regression in which the values of a dependent, or criterion, variable are attributed to one independent, or predictor, variable. Without getting too technical, this statistical technique finds the **regression line,** a line drawn through the data points on a scattergram that best summarizes the relationship between the independent and dependent variables (or the predictor and criterion variables). Of course, unless there is a perfect one-to-one relationship between the two variables, the line can only represent a best fit. The regression line of best fit is the one that minimizes the distances of the data points from the line (Cader, 1996). The better the fit of the regression line, the higher the correlation. In regression, this value is identified by the symbol R.

As in correlation, squaring R provides the proportion of variance explained or accounted for on the dependent variable by the independent variable. It is symbolized by R^2. Statistical software provides an adjusted R^2 that is often preferred by researchers, because the nonadjusted R^2 can be an inappropriately high estimate of the variance accounted for (Wright, 1997).

The value of R ranges from -1.00 through $.00$ to 1.00. Values close to zero indicate a very weak relationship between the predictor and criterion variables. As R values become larger and approach 1.00, they indicate stronger relationships between the variables. Researchers consider R^2, the squared multiple correlation coefficient, to be more meaningful. An R^2 value of $.48$ indicates that 48% of the variance of the dependent variable is accounted for, or determined, by the combination of the independent variables. As in correlation, R^2 is called the coefficient of determination.

In most cases, the independent (predictor) variables in a regression will not be based on the same unit of measurement. Even when all measures of the variables are based on a 5-point response set of a Likert-type scale (strongly agree to strongly disagree), variables are likely to be composed of different numbers of items, making direct comparisons among mean scores problematic. Statistical software transforms each of the measurements for each variable into standard deviations. In this form, the variables can be compared more easily. Variables, despite their original measurement scales, with high variability will have large standard deviations. Conversely, variables with low variability will have much smaller standard deviations.

These standardized scores are referred to as **beta coefficients,** also known as **beta weights.** The greater the beta coefficient, or β, the greater the variability of that variable. Thus, β can be interpreted as the effect of the independent variable on the dependent variable. As with correlation coefficients, beta coefficients range from +1.00 to −1.00. A beta coefficient of +1.00 would indicate that a change of one standard deviation in the predictor variable is associated with a change of one standard deviation in the criterion variable and that the changes are both in the same direction. Of course, if the beta coefficient were −1.00, the changes would be in the opposite direction.

To summarize, you will need to look for several different symbols or descriptions as you read research for which the hypotheses or research questions have been tested with regression. Identify the R, R^2, and β. Looking at the examples later in this chapter will help make this clearer.

Multiple Regression

Of course, most communication phenomena are more complicated than can be tested by the simple linear regression model with one independent and one dependent variable; thus, our need for multiple regression. **Multiple regression** allows a researcher to test for a significant relationship between the dependent variable and multiple independent variables separately and as a group. The test is symbolized by R, which is known as the **multiple correlational coefficient.** This is the type of regression most commonly seen in the communication literature. Like a correlation coefficient, it is an index of the magnitude of the relationship among the variables.

Theoretically, there is no limit to the number of independent, or predictor, variables tested. But, practically, communication researchers seldom

test more than four in any one regression model. With the ability to test multiple independent, or predictor, variables, we need to consider another set of Venn diagrams (Figure 12.3). Diagram I demonstrates how the three predictor variables— A, B, and C—are correlated with each other and together influence the criterion variable as a group. Diagram II shows that predictor variable A is not correlated with predictor variables B and C and that B and C are correlated with each other. This diagram demonstrates how A influences the criterion variable separately from the B and C variable combination. Finally, Diagram III demonstrates the degree to which predictor variables A and C influence the criterion variable, whereas B has no influence on it. This diagram also shows how predictor variables can be unrelated to one another yet still influence the criterion variable.

By looking at the amount of overlap, or the degree to which the predictor variables influence the criterion variable, you can estimate the amount of variance accounted for, independently or in combination with one another. By diagramming regression relationships in this way, you should be able to get a feeling for the relative importance of each variable to the regression relationship.

Degrees of freedom, df, for regression are calculated by first identifying the number of independent variables in the full multiple regression equation. If there are three predictor variables, the first degree of freedom is 3. Then use the formula $n - k - 1$, where n equals the number of observations for the statistical test and k equals the number of independent variables in the test. So for 200 observations and a regression with three predictor variables, the second degree of freedom is 196 ($n - k - 1$, or $200 - 3 - 1$). In the results section, df is reported as 3, 196 after the F value.

Interpreting Multiple Regressions Because multiple regressions allow a researcher to test both the separate and common influences of predictor variables on the criterion variable, interpreting multiple regressions can get a little tricky. First, the calculated F ratio indicates whether the squared multiple correlation coefficient, R^2, is significant. If the significance level is .05 or less, then at least one of the relationships among the variables is significant.

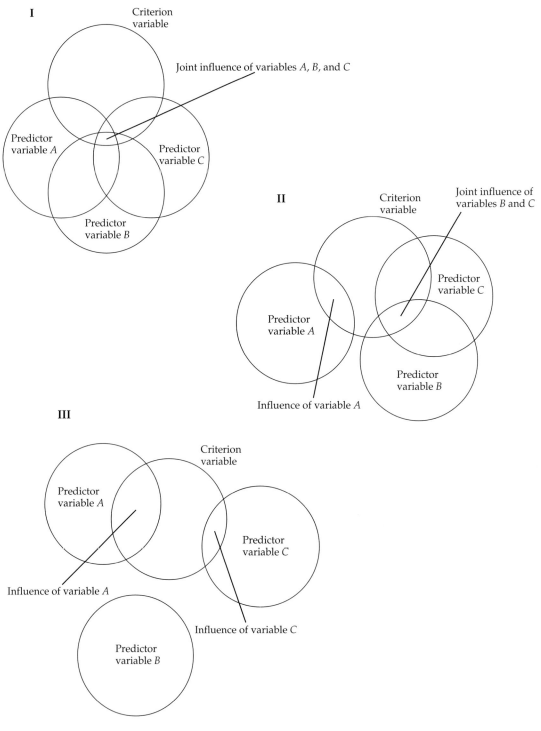

FIGURE 12.3 Venn Diagrams of Multiple Regression

Researchers rely on the beta weights, or β, to interpret the relative contributions of each independent, or predictor, variable. But this interpretation is not absolute because independent variables are often correlated with one another. The ideal predictive situation is when the correlations between independent variables and dependent variable are high, and the correlations among the independent variables are low (Kerlinger, 1986). Thus, the greater the correlations among the independent variables, the more difficulty in establishing the unique contribution of each independent variable.

Interpretations of multiple regression are also more difficult when independent variables can both positively and negatively influence the dependent variable in the same model. Thus, whereas increases in one independent variable are related to increases in the dependent variable, decreases in another independent variable may be related to increases in the dependent variable. Given the objectives of this introduction to statistical methods, know that the researcher, guided by β, is ultimately responsible for interpreting the influence of individual independent variables.

Regression Examples

Return to the research question for the study of brothers' relationships at the beginning of this section. Avtgis (2003) wanted to examine if, and how, social and emotional support would influence how men predict the behavior of their brothers. To answer the research question, four independent variables (three types of social support and emotion support) were tested with regression to determine the influence of these variables on one dependent variable, attributional confidence. The results are explained this way:

> The research question asked if each of the social support styles and emotional support contribute to explaining attributional confidence in the brother-brother relationship. The results of the regression analysis [$F(4, 191) = 23.28, p < .001$] accounted for 33% of the variance. Interpersonal depth ($\beta = .29$), relational support ($\beta = .28$), and relational conflict ($\beta = -.19$) significantly contributed to the equation. Emotional support ($\beta = .05$) did not significantly contribute to the equation. (p. 343)

An accompanying table provides more information:

Variables	B	SE B	β
Interpersonal depth	7.34	2.17	.29
Relational support	6.12	2.33	.28
Relational conflict	−2.90	1.18	−.19
Emotional closeness	.41	.80	.05

NOTE: ($N = 196$); $R^2 = .33$.
SOURCE: "Male Sibling Social and Emotional Support as a Function of Attributional Confidence," by T. A. Avtgis, 2003, *Communication Research Reports, 20*, pp. 341–347. Used by permission of the Eastern Communication Association.

Notice how the researcher provides you the test results. First, the F value is presented. The overall test of the influence of the four independent variables on the dependent variable was statistically significant and accounted for 33% of the variance. When the regression test is significant, that signals the researcher to look for which independent variables contributed to that finding. Next, the beta weights, or β, are given to indicate the amount of variance accounted for each of the independent variables. As you can see, the first two social support types (interpersonal depth and relational support) had positive influences on attributional confidence. As interpersonal depth and relational support increased, so did attributional confidence. Conversely, the third social support type (relational conflict) had a negative influence on attributional confidence. As relational conflict decreased, attributional confidence increased. The emotional support variable had no relationship with attributional confidence. Thus, the result of the regression test could be interpreted this way: When brothers perceive social support from their brothers in terms of interpersonal depth and relational support, and do not perceive relational conflict, they have greater confidence in predicting their brothers' behaviors.

In another example, regression is used to test five predictor variables in explaining crime as the most important problem facing the United States over a 21-year time span (Lowry, Nio, & Leitner, 2003). In this study, the research team used data from existing sources. Data for the criterion variable—What is the most important problem facing this country today?—came from responses to Gallup Poll questions. Data for the predictor variables were evaluations of the importance of crime stories on TV news (story length, story position, and number of stories), and crime rates (rate of all violent crimes, rate of all other crimes) from the *FBI Uniform Crime Reports*. Theorizing from the premise that media images shape public attitudes more than facts, the research team hypothesized that network TV news predictor variables account for more variance in crime as the most important problem in the country than do actual crime rates.

Indeed, the regression was significant [$F(5, 19) = 15.01, p < .001$)]. This statistic resulted in an overall R^2 of .80 (adjusted $R^2 = .75$). And, as predicted, the TV variables explained .34 of the variance in the criterion variable, crime as the most important problem facing the country, whereas the crime statistic variables accounted for only .09. Thus, the research hypothesis was supported.

Regression tests the influence of multiple independent or predictor variables on one dependent or criterion variable. If the overall F statistic is significant, then each predictor variable should be examined for the degree to which it influences the criterion variable. As with any statistical test, be sure to examine the degree of variance explained or accounted for by the predictor or independent variables. Although the overall F statistic is significant, that will not ensure that all of the predictor variables significantly contribute to predicting the criterion variable. Statistical significance may be accounted for, but practical or social significance is also important in interpreting results.

Other Forms of Multiple Regression   Multiple regression is a flexible and sophisticated test, and there are many other types of regression analyses that are beyond the scope of this introductory chapter. Although the discussion here has focused on the use of continuous level variables, regression can also accommodate nominal variables. This introduction also focused on linear relationships. Yet, multiple regression can detect curvilinear relationships as well.

Hierarchical regression is commonly used in communication research. This regression form allows the researcher to enter independent variables

in the order or sequence in which the variables are presumed to influence the dependent variable. Researchers rely on the theoretical connections among the variables to determine which variables are first, second, and so on. For example, demographic variables might be entered first because they do not change over the life of participants and thus are perceived to have more influence than attitudes or beliefs.

Stepwise regression is a similar form of regression in that independent variables are entered in some sequence or order. But in this case, the order of variables is determined by the statistical program (in essence, the computer), not the researcher. Generally, the steps of entry are based on the degree of influence the independent variables have on the dependent variables.

Limitations of Regression

Because regression is based on correlations between and among variables, it is inappropriate, even when significant relationships are found, to unequivocally state that the relationship is evidence of cause-and-effect relationships. Although a certain asymmetry is established by the hypotheses and research questions tested, it is often more appropriate to indicate that significant relationships found are consistent with what the researcher hypothesized or expected to find. It would be overextending the results to suggest an absolute cause-and-effect relationship; however, regression is an excellent statistical tool for determining if one or more independent (predictor) variables explain the variation in the dependent (criterion) variable.

Scientists use regression to continue to confirm their beliefs about the causal links among variables. Cause-and-effect relationships are never proven with one study. Rather, consistent results over a period of time combined with practical reasoning provide the cumulative evidence and logic needed to establish causal links.

CAUTIONS IN USING STATISTICS

The statistics presented in this chapter allow a researcher to test for relationships between and among variables. Having a basic understanding

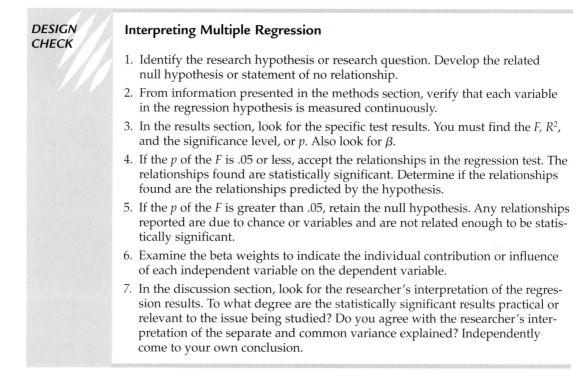

DESIGN CHECK

Interpreting Multiple Regression

1. Identify the research hypothesis or research question. Develop the related null hypothesis or statement of no relationship.

2. From information presented in the methods section, verify that each variable in the regression hypothesis is measured continuously.

3. In the results section, look for the specific test results. You must find the F, R^2, and the significance level, or p. Also look for β.

4. If the p of the F is .05 or less, accept the relationships in the regression test. The relationships found are statistically significant. Determine if the relationships found are the relationships predicted by the hypothesis.

5. If the p of the F is greater than .05, retain the null hypothesis. Any relationships reported are due to chance or variables and are not related enough to be statistically significant.

6. Examine the beta weights to indicate the individual contribution or influence of each independent variable on the dependent variable.

7. In the discussion section, look for the researcher's interpretation of the regression results. To what degree are the statistically significant results practical or relevant to the issue being studied? Do you agree with the researcher's interpretation of the separate and common variance explained? Independently come to your own conclusion.

of correlations and regressions can help you understand the research literature, making the results more meaningful for you. With the help of spreadsheet and statistical programs, you can also collect and interpret data using these tests. However, just as with the statistical tests for differences, use of these statistical tests is subjective, and there are many variations for each of the tests described. Thus, the advice given at the end of Chapter 11 is repeated here.

If you assume the role of the researcher, I strongly suggest that you ask someone with statistical expertise to look over your research plan and seek help at any point in the research process that includes the use of statistics (for example, in generating hypotheses, determining method and procedure of data collection, developing statistical programming or spreadsheets, and interpreting statistical tests). A statistical expert can help you use these statistics in an appropriate and valid way. Seek expert advice anytime you have a question. Consult your university's statistical

expert when you need assistance with your research activities.

Beyond this general recommendation for seeking statistical help, there are three questions that can help you assess the use of statistics (Katzer et al., 1978). First, are the results worth interpreting statistically? You have probably heard the phrase "garbage in, garbage out." With respect to statistics this means that despite the sophistication of any statistical test or procedure, if the data used are invalid (for example, collected in an ambiguous or suspect manner), then any result, even a significant one, is invalid. A sophisticated statistical test cannot cure a bad dataset or provide meaning to unmeaningful data. Statistics are a tool, not a panacea.

If you can argue for the use of statistics, then ask the next questions: Are the results statistically significant? Was the appropriate statistical procedure selected and then used appropriately? If not, then the statistical significance of the test is called into question. Remember, too, that if the

TRY THIS!

Identifying Independent Variables for Multiple Regression

The primary advantage of multiple regression for communication research is that it allows researchers to measure relationships among variables that cannot be manipulated by the researcher, as some forms of experimental designs would require. For the four dependent variables listed, identify the accompanying independent variables you believe communication researchers should investigate, explaining the reasoning for capturing the independent variables in their naturally occurring form without manipulation. To start, consider the following combination of variables:

Dependent Variable	Independent Variables	Reasoning
Marital satisfaction	Amount of time talking with partner about the relationship	It would be unethical for researchers to require participants to stop talking to their spouse.
	Quality of marital communication	Quality of conversation cannot be practically or logistically controlled by researcher.
Intercultural assimilation		
Political cynicism		
Belief in televised news		
Adopting practices promoted on television public service announcements		

results were nonsignificant, there are multiple reasons for this outcome. A nonsignificant finding for one cause or relationship does not suggest that another causal factor or relationship is valid. Rather, a nonsignificant finding means that the cause or relationship tested could not be verified in this particular examination. If you believe the appropriate statistical test was effectively used, error could have been introduced into the process at many different junctures (for example, in how the sample was selected, how the variables were operationalized, or how data were collected). And you must not dismiss the possibility that the assumption presumed by the researcher may have been wrong or not well founded.

The third question is more personal: Are the results meaningful to you? Statistical significance does not always equal social significance. Thus, you, the consumer of research, must decide if the results have meaning and utility within the context in which you will use the information.

SUMMARY

1. The degree to which the following assumptions are met determine the degree to which findings from the tests can be generalized from the sample to the population: (a) significance level of the test is based on probability theory, (b) data are assumed to come from a normally distributed population, (c) the appropriate variables are included in the test, and (d) individuals participating in the research project should be selected through probability sampling.

2. A correlation is a simple description of the degree to which two variables are related.

3. Causation cannot necessarily be established with correlation.

4. A correlation coefficient must be interpreted for its direction and its strength or magnitude.

5. Researchers rely on r^2 to describe the amount of variance shared between the two variables.

6. Regression is an extension of correlation; however, multiple regression can test for the influence of multiple independent or predictor variables on the dependent or criterion variable.

7. Regression is particularly well suited for communication research as it tests the relationship among naturally occurring variables.

8. R^2 provides information about the amount of variance of the dependent variable explained by the independent variables separately or in common.

9. The beta weight, or β, provides information about the direction and strength of influence for each independent variable.

KEY TERMS

beta coefficients
beta weights
coefficient of determination
correlation
correlation matrix
curvilinear
dichotomous
hierarchical regression
linear
linear regression
multiple regression
multiple correlational coefficient

Pearson product-moment correlation coefficient
point biserial correlation
regression
regression line
rho
Spearman correlation coefficient
spurious correlation
stepwise regression

CHAPTER THIRTEEN

Quantitative Analysis of Text

Chapter Checklist

After reading this chapter, you should be able to:

1. Differentiate between manifest and latent content in content analysis.

2. Explain the basic processes for conducting a content analysis.

3. Identify appropriate uses of interaction analysis.

4. Explain the basic processes for conducting a research study using interaction analysis.

5. Assess the appropriateness and adequacy of a category scheme.

6. Identify suitable texts or messages to be coded and analyzed.

7. Reliably identify units of analysis.

8. Reliably apply the coding scheme.

9. Assess the validity of a coding scheme.

10. Assess the utility of the coding results with respect to the research questions and hypotheses.

Despite the wide variety of communication phenomena and contexts available for examination, most researchers would agree that the study of messages or message content is central to the communication discipline. As a result, what constitutes message content, or the text of messages, is broadly defined. Some communication scholars use the terms *content* and *text* only as a referent for spoken discourse, such as discourse that occurs in a group's interaction, a couple's conversation, or a speaker's public presentation. Other scholars use the terms *content* and *text* more broadly to include any form of discourse (written, spoken, or visual) that can be captured in some form with which the researcher can work.

The methods for coding and analyzing messages presented in this chapter—content analysis and interaction analysis—are two ways in which researchers can analyze content. These methods allow researchers the opportunity to analyze the content of messages, or what participants actually say in interaction. In contrast, communication research designed as experimental, quasi-experimental, or descriptive research projects often rely on participants' perceptions of their interaction. This distinction can be crucial to the practical significance of research, especially when senders' own words or interactions are crucial to the investigation.

Content analysis is the most basic method of analyzing message content. In addition to providing researchers with a quantitative method for examining what people say, content analysis can also be used to examine emerging themes in participants' retrospective accounts of interaction situations, what participants believe they might say in hypothetical interaction settings, and mediated communication (for example, song lyrics, political advertisements). Like content analysis, interaction analysis is a quantitative method of coding communication into categories. However, interaction analysis is restricted to examining the ongoing communication between two or more individuals, and its focus is on identifying the features or functions of the stream of conversational elements.

CONTENT ANALYSIS

Content analysis integrates both data collection method and analytical technique as a research design to measure the occurrence of some identifiable element in a complete text or set of messages. Neuendorf (2002) defines content analysis as the "summarizing, quantitative analysis of messages that relies on the scientific method and is not limited as to the types of variables that may be measured or the context in which the messages are created or presented" (p. 10). Thus, content analysis can answer research questions such as How often are older adults shown in television commercials? How much violence are children exposed to by watching television? What kinds of conflicts do adults have with their friends? Each of these questions, and others like them, can be answered through content analysis. As a technique, content analysis helps researchers make inferences by identifying specific characteristics of messages.

Researchers agree that content analysis should be objective and systematic and meet the requirement of generality (Berleson, 1952; Holsti, 1969). This method can be used to provide a description of the characteristics of the content itself—the **manifest content.** Or content analysis can be used to study the **latent content**—interpretations about the content that imply something about the nature of the communicators or effects on communicators. An example will help clarify the difference.

In a study of how older adults are portrayed in commercials (Roy & Harwood, 1997), coders looked for direct mentions of chronological age (manifest content), references to being retired or being a grandparent (latent), or adjectives or nonverbal indications that would identify the person as being an older adult (latent). In the commercial, if an actor was directly identified as being 65, that is manifest content because this element is physically present in the data, countable, and easily verified (Gray & Densten, 1998). But the other two distinctions—mention of being retired or being a grandparent, and adjectives or nonverbal symbols indicating one as an older adult—are more subjective, requiring the coder to infer the age of the actor from what was said or how the person acted. Being retired or a grandparent does not necessarily classify a person as an older adult. Thus, being categorized as an older adult is an inference constituting latent categorization.

Restricting content analysis to manifest content would not always be interesting or perhaps even meaningful unless the content's latent value were also analyzed. If a researcher addresses the latent content, he or she is assuming that the behaviors, attitudes, and values found in the text reflect the behaviors, attitudes, and values of the people who create the material. Thus, content analysis is an indirect way to make inferences about people (Berger, 1998).

But for such inferences to have value, content analysis must be objective. That is, each step must be carried out according to specified rules and procedures. This differentiates content analysis from literary criticism or rhetorical criticism. Having objective codes and procedures for coding established before the coding is conducted helps decrease coders' subjective analysis. If a coding is objective, then another coder should be able to use the same procedures with the same data and arrive at similar conclusions (Holsti, 1969).

Likewise, content analysis must be systematic in both identifying content and interpreting it (Kaid & Wadsworth, 1989). In other words, what is to be included or excluded for coding is decided systematically, making it more difficult for researchers to include only those elements that support the research question or hypothesis.

Finally, *generality* means that findings must have theoretical relevance (Holsti, 1969). Simply put, coding text for its content is of little value unless the results of the coding are related to other attributes of the text or characteristics of the message senders or receivers. So researchers would not code the content of something simply because the technique could be applied. Rather, content analysis is used because the results it produces can answer a sufficiently interesting research question or hypothesis.

Procedurally, the central idea behind content analysis is that regardless of the size of text or the number of messages, meaning can be classified into many fewer categories (Weber, 1990). Thus, content analysis is one type of data reduction technique, used in much the same way researchers use numbers and statistics to represent participants' actions and perceptions about communication.

The assumption here is that elements classified together have similar meanings.

An example of how content analysis serves as a data reduction technique will help clarify this. In a study of how and why individuals use home email, researchers conducted telephone interviews with 112 individuals (Stafford, Kline, & Dimmick, 1999). Interviewers asked participants to describe the reasons they sent and received email. Responses to this open-ended question resulted in 203 different reasons for using email. Using analytic induction procedures, these statements were content analyzed for the kinds of reasons given for home use of email. One coder initially segmented the transcripts into idea units, or independent clauses; these were then grouped based upon their semantic similarities into 20 categories. These categories were then collapsed into 15 larger thematic categories. After coding the responses, the 15 categories were then collapsed into 4 superordinate categories for analysis. Thus, data from 112 people were reduced from 203 units to 20, and then 15, and finally 4 categories, allowing the researchers to make more meaningful analyses.

Researchers use content analysis to produce frequency counts for each coded element so that comparison can be made among them. However, restricting content analysis to a simple analysis of frequencies would dilute some interesting findings and perhaps place undue emphasis on frequency of occurrence. Consider this: Just because an element occurs many times, does it necessarily have greater value than one essential element mentioned only once? In addition to using the frequency counts generated by the content coding, a researcher should also address the relevance of the frequencies to the theoretical propositions supporting the study.

What Content Can Be Analyzed?

What constitutes appropriate content to be analyzed? Literally, any message, or aspect of a message, that can be captured in some permanent form, such as in writing or on audio- or videotape, can be content analyzed. The messages may exist naturally, such as in newspaper comic strips, or the messages may be created in response to a researcher's request. Content that can be analyzed

---

DESIGN CHECK

Content Analyzing Media Messages

Content analysis is often used on media messages. Media content can easily be captured, and comparative studies can be completed because content captured in one year can be compared with content captured from an earlier or subsequent year. The website of the Center for Media and Public Affairs at http://www.cmpa.com is an excellent source for consumer-oriented analyses of media content. This site has links to research studies of the news, the entertainment media, profanity in popular entertainment, and even late-night political jokes. As you learn about content analysis, return to this website to read the summary reports posted. How would you assess the design features of the content analytic studies? What features of the studies can you point to that would allow you to argue that the findings can be generalized?

---

includes the following (Holsti, Loomba, & North, 1968; Neuendorf, 2002):

- Sources or senders of messages
- Reasons for sending messages
- The channels messages are sent through
- Actual content of the message
- Message effects
- Recipients of messages
- Visual images
- Nonverbal cues or behaviors
- Sounds

Regardless of what is analyzed, content analysis achieves its best results when the researcher has a well-developed research design with hypotheses or research questions.

The Content Analysis Process

Once the researcher has identified the hypotheses or research questions that call for a content analysis research design the steps of content analysis consist of the same initial steps of any sound quantitative research design. That is, the researcher should identify a problem, review theory and research, and then pose research questions or hypotheses. Then specific to content analysis, the process continues with (1) selecting the text or messages to be analyzed, (2) selecting categories and units by which to analyze the text

or messages, (3) developing procedures for resolving differences of opinion in coding, (4) selecting a sample for analysis if all the messages cannot be analyzed, (5) coding the messages, (6) interpreting the coding, and (7) reporting the results relative to the research questions or hypotheses (Kaid & Wadsworth, 1989; Riffe, Lacy, & Fico, 1998).

Selecting What to Code First, the researcher must identify the universe of messages to which the hypotheses or research questions apply. Second, the researcher must ask, "Do the messages I am interested in exist?" If no, then they must be created. Once text or messages are available for coding, the next question to answer is "Do I need to code all of the messages in the dataset?" In some cases, the answer will be yes, particularly when a researcher is using stories or stimulated-recall accounts as the dataset. Generally, in these instances, the entire text or set of messages is coded. In other cases, far too many data exist to practically code each message or piece of data. Thus, the text or messages must be narrowed to a reasonable and practical sample.

The first narrowing technique is to cull the dataset for the element of interest. For example, if the research question directs you to code arguments, then it is not necessary to code statements or messages that are not arguments. If this produces a reasonable number of messages to be coded (for example, 500 or fewer), then the researcher codes all of the arguments. But, for sake of example, let us assume that even after eliminating all other elements, more than 5,000 arguments still exist. Now the researcher can turn to the sampling techniques described in Chapter 7. However, content analysis presents some special considerations with respect to sampling.

One consideration in sampling is to remember that even moderately long exchanges of interaction generally have a beginning, middle, and end. Certain types of statements (greetings, for example) may appear at the beginning of exchanges and not at the end. In group discussions evidence is likely to be presented in the middle, whereas arguments for selecting a solution are more frequently given toward the end of the discussion. Thus, for any dataset in which there a cycle to the data (e.g., Sunday newspapers have different sections than do newspapers published other days of the week; a public relations or political campaign in which issues or language may change), random sampling may weight the dataset in an unfavorable manner. Stratified random sampling may be the best choice—so that the selected data to code are proportional to the entire dataset (Riffe, Lacy, & Fico, 1998).

Developing Content Categories Content categories are the useful distinctions a researcher makes and are often based on previously reported research. At the same time, the categories must represent the phenomenon the research question or hypothesis calls on to be examined (Kaid & Wadsworth, 1989). Some categorical schemes might call for the researcher to content analyze *what* was said. Other schemes might call for the researcher to content analyze *how* the messages were said (or visualized). As with responses to questions in survey research, content categories must be exhaustive, equivalent, and mutually exclusive. Thus, the categories must cover all possible occurrences and be of the same type. Moreover, a unit cannot be coded into multiple categories. There are, however, rare exceptions to the mutual exclusion criterion.

It is not uncommon to see coding schemes with one category identified as "other." This category typically represents those elements that could not be coded according to one of the specific categories. In essence, then, the "other" category

reflects a failure of the classification scheme (Kumar, 1996). Using the "other" category too often usually means that the category system is not as developed as it should be (Krippendorff, 2004). As a general rule, if more than 5% of the coded elements fall into the "other" category, the category system needs to be revised, or coding procedures need to be reexamined.

For example, in coding memorable messages for their valence, or tone, regarding aging, Holladay (2002) initially conceptualized the coding categories for this variable as positive, negative, or neutral. However, in coding the data a fourth category was added to code messages that contained both positive and negative elements. Because the coding unit was an entire message, it was possible, of course, for some messages to be of such a length or complexity that both positive and negative tone could be detected by the coders.

It is common to have a set of theoretical or practical categories established before the coding work begins. But to avoid having too many units coded in the "other" category, it is common for researchers to find units that do not fit into an existing category. Usually, these are set aside and later examined for commonalities, oftentimes resulting in additional categories being added to the coding scheme.

Alternately, content categories can also emerge from the data in what is known as the grounded theory approach of constant comparison (Glaser & Strauss, 1967; Strauss & Corbin, 1998). The relevant categories are derived directly from the data. Such was the case in Sabourin and Stamp's (1995) study of abusive and nonabusive couples. In repeated listening to the couples' taped conversations, the researchers made notes about themes, issues, and patterns. More listening and analysis of their notes led to identifying similarities and differences between the two types of couples. As a result, the authors found seven communication categories and identified relevant quotes and segments of conversation that were typical to the categories.

Units of Analysis The **unit of analysis** is the discrete thing that is coded and counted. It is an observable and measurable unit that provides a standard way of dissecting the text into elements to be analyzed. Without a standard or uniform unit, the analysis will be flawed because comparisons will be either impossible or meaningless (Berger, 1998).

In some cases, the unit of analysis is obvious. Often, these are physical units, such as a website. For example, Cai and colleagues (2003) examined children's websites to see how many collected personal information from children, included privacy statements, and required parental permission for children to participate or give personal information. The website was the unit of analysis regardless of the number of links or subpages it had. Coders aggregated their codings across a website's various pages to create one coding sheet per site. Even so, the rules for identifying the unit should be explicit.

In other cases, the unit of analysis is dependent on the context of the interaction. For example, for a study of impression management strategies used in spoken and written corporate discourse, Allen and Caillouet (1994) used the statement as the unit of analysis. They defined a statement as "a sentence or set of sentences which expressed a complete thought interpretable as a strategic act (i.e., influencing or describing the corporate actor's public image)" (p. 50). With this definition, some statements were as short as one sentence, whereas over half of the statements were longer.

Some typical units of analysis in communication research include

- Words or phrases. For example, Malkin, Wornian, and Chrisler (1999) analyzed the content of headlines ("Walk Your Way to Thin") on men's and women's magazine covers for evidence of their gendered influence.

- Complete thoughts or sentences. As an example of the most common unit of analysis, one research team (Pratt, Wiseman, Cody, & Wendt, 1999) examined how questions were used to develop relationships between senior citizens and youngsters over email. Normally, a question is easily identified by the question mark at the end of a sentence. However, in email format, where speed is valued and grammatical accuracy is not, question marks do not always appear. Thus, the research team had to more closely assess the emails for instances when requests for information and implicit pressure to respond were made.

- Themes, or a single assertion about some subject. For example, Clayman and Heritage (2002) coded the themes embedded in the questions or questioning sequences used by journalists at presidential press conferences.

- Paragraphs or short whole texts. As an example, Hickson, Scott, and Vogel (1995) content coded whole television news stories according to 12 local news standards.

- Characters or speakers. For example, Harwood and Anderson (2002) content analyzed speaking characters in prime time dramas and sitcoms.

- Communication acts, behaviors, or processes. As an example, Borzekowski and Robinson (1999) recorded family members while they were watching television. For every 5 minutes the television was on, coders identified who was in the room and whether the person was looking at the TV, participating in other activities, and eating or drinking.

- Advertisements. Stephenson (2002) examined antidrug public service announcements directed toward parents to evaluate the preventive behaviors they advocated.

- Television programs, films, or scenes. To study the differences in films that had both R-rated versions and NC-17 rated versions, Leone (2002) analyzed sequences present in the former, but not the latter. For this study, a sequence was defined relative to the context from which it was removed. For example, sequences were the "uninterrupted shots in a film's scenes. A shot ended when an edit occurred and a different point of view (an alternate character or neutral) was presented" (p. 945). The coding unit was the scene from which the sequence or sequences were removed.

Besides making decisions about what to code, researchers conducting content analyses must also establish how they will quantify the coded content. Codes could be simply counted for frequency—the most common unit of enumeration. But others

TRY THIS!   **Identifying Themes of Freshman Socialization**

Try this as a class exercise in collecting and coding content data. Following a study conducted by Jorgensen-Earp and Staton (1993), ask 10 of your peers (but not class members) to finish the statement "Being a university freshman is like _____" on an index card. Combine the responses you collect with those of another member of your class. Individually, each of you should read each index card. Now, working in pairs, examine the cards and identify the evident themes. When you find cards that are similar, start a stack. Continue this until every card is in a stack. If a card is truly distinct from the others, it is okay for that one card to be in a stack by itself. Now look at the stacks you created. Do the stacks need refining? The next step is to begin creating labels for the stacks. After this step, examine each card in each stack to verify that the card is representative of the stack label. Adjust stacks and labels as necessary. To what extent did you and your coding partner agree on identifying the themes? How did you resolve any disagreements? Were there disagreements that could not be resolved? Did you find themes beyond those identified by Jorgensen-Earp and Staton, which are presented below?

Themes of Newness	*Themes of Status*	*Themes of Engagement*	*Themes of Satisfaction*
New environment	Back to square one	Cut adrift	Rude awakening
New experience	Low prestige	Stranger in a strange land	Prison
New chapter	Accomplishment	Lost	Unpleasant experience
New beginning	Moving up	Isolated	Survival
Clean slate		Small	Ordeal
Metamorphosis	*Themes of Control*	Freedom	Self-discovery
Adult	Overwhelmed	Breaking away	Enlightenment
Rebirth	Pressure	Journey	Challenge
Freshness	Confusion	Explorer	Contented
	Competition	Belonging	Supportive
	Struggle		Learning
	Command		
	Self-discipline		
	Poised on the brink		
	Receptive		

are possible. For example, seconds and minutes or inches and pages could quantify media messages. Recognize the assumptions accompanying both units of enumeration (Holsti, 1969). With these, the researcher is assuming that frequency, length of interaction, and message size are valid indicators of concern, focus, intensity, value, importance, and so on.

Training Coders   Because content coding should be systematic and objective, all coders, including the researchers who develop the coding system, must be trained. Research has demonstrated that training can increase agreement among coders. But to achieve increased agreement, training must be more than a simple discussion of the coding categories (Kaid & Wadsworth, 1989).

The coding system should be committed to paper so that all coders are trained from the same category scheme and so that coders can return to it at any time. Many researchers prepare a codebook to identify coding content, coding units, and rules for coding. As part of their training, coders generally practice on text or messages similar to those that must be coded. Once a sufficient degree of reliability is established among coders, coders then work by themselves.

Coding Reliability There are several reliability issues with respect to content analysis. These issues were first introduced in Chapter 6. In content analysis reliability is identified as intercoder or interrater reliability, and it must be calculated for two different sets of coding decisions. First, intercoder reliability is established for coders' ability to identify and agree upon the unit of coding. This is known as *unitizing reliability.* If the unit to be coded is a sentence, then agreement should not be too much of a problem. Natural units, like complete sentences, have standardized identifiers for marking their beginning and ending. But if the text is naturally occurring conversation, and speakers do not speak in complete sentences, then identifying the unit to be coded is far more difficult. Coding units, like themes or stories, are more abstract, and it will generally take more time to train coders to identify the unit.

After the units to be coded have been identified, each coder decides independently into which category the unit will be placed. The more frequently coders choose the same category, the greater their degree of coding or *categorizing reliability.*

There are several formulas for determining the degree of **intercoder** or **interrater reliability** in coding content. **Scott's *pi*** is commonly used in communication research when two coders are used, because it accounts for the number of categories in the coding scheme as well as for the probable frequency for each category. This formula and steps for calculating intercoder reliability are shown in Appendix B.

Calculating intercoder reliability is fairly straightforward; identifying an acceptable level of intercoder reliability is far more subjective. Generally, researchers must make this judgment based upon the research question or hypothesis and the context of the coding. As number of categories increases or as the coding process becomes more complex, lower levels of reliability can be acceptable. In general, intercoder reliability of .90 is nearly always acceptable and .80 is acceptable in most situations. Intercoder reliability of .70 is appropriate in some exploratory studies and the lower end limit for acceptable coding decisions (Lombard, Snyder-Duch, & Bracken, 2002). The degree of intercoder reliability and the procedures used to obtain it should be reported in the research study.

Validity In content analysis, *validity* refers to the appropriateness and adequacy of the coding scheme for the text or messages being coded. Researchers increase the validity of their coding schemes by examining previous research on the same and similar issues and by basing their coding schemes on theory (Potter & Levine-Donnerstein, 1999). At a minimum, any categorical coding scheme must have face validity. Recall, however, that face validity is generally weak in establishing the accuracy or truthfulness of what is being measured. Researchers using content analysis produce the most valid results when content coding schemes are examined for construct validity by comparing the results of coding with another external measure (Weber, 1990). Return to Chapter 6 to review issues of construct validity.

Krippendorff (2004) also recommends that researchers using content analysis should be concerned about **semantic validity.** That is, to what degree do the analytical categories of the content coded have meaning for individuals in a particular context? Content coding of messages and symbols depends upon both denotative and connotative meaning. Considering semantic validity reminds researchers to code content and interpret those codings within the context from which the texts were selected.

Interpreting the Coding Results

Once the coding is complete, the researcher must interpret what was coded. Just like any other research method, content analysis must be relative to the initial research question or hypothesis and interpreted back to the context from which the

How Did the Researcher Perform the Content Analysis?

1. How did the researcher define the coding unit?
2. How did the researcher define the categories for coding the units? Are the categories exhaustive, mutually exclusive, and equivalent?
3. Was the coding system tested before being used to answer the research question or hypothesis?
4. What steps were taken to train coders? Was coder training adequate?
5. How reliable were coders?
6. How was the coding conducted?
7. How well did the coding scheme relate to the issues posed by the research question or hypothesis?
8. Do you agree with the researcher's interpretation of the coding results?

data were selected. There are several ways researchers can analyze content coded data. The simplest, and most common, method of analysis is to simply look for the frequency of categorical occurrences. Remember, however, that the underlying assumption here is that frequency can be interpreted as a measure of importance or value. A closely related, but more sophisticated interpretive approach is to look for differences in the application of categories. Researchers using these interpretive frames often use chi-squares to determine if there are significant differences in the frequencies of the categories.

Trends, patterns, and structures of communication phenomena can also be revealed through content analysis (Krippendorff, 2004). These types of analysis seek to identify which elements precede or succeed other elements. Finally, a researcher can evaluate the coded content against some previously established set of standards. An example of each is described in the paragraphs that follow.

A study of sex-role stereotyping in children's television shows is an example of the most common type of content analysis—which looks for frequency of occurrences and differences. Barner (1999) hypothesized about several of these: Males will be represented more than females, male characters will exhibit more stereotypical male behavior, female characters will exhibit

more stereotypical female behavior, and male characters will be granted more positive consequences for behaving like males and more negative consequences for behaving like females (and the female equivalent). Looking for frequency of occurrence and differences by gender was appropriate because the study was designed to test the effects of FCC programming mandates.

When researchers look for trends, they examine how the data move or change over time, or they look for the way in which data are sequenced by categories. For example, Potter and Warren (1996) examined prime-time television programming for displays of violence. Early evening hours have been designated as family viewing time. At the time of the study, proposed industry regulation suggested that no violent acts should occur during that time period. To test the effects of this proposed industry regulation, the research team captured television programming from 6 P.M. until midnight. Using acts of aggression as their coding unit, the research team found that nearly half of a night's television aggression happened during the hours when children were watching in the highest numbers. Thus, the expected trend—that violent acts would diminish during family viewing hours—did not exist.

A study of email usage between older adults and children demonstrates how content analysis can be used to illuminate communication patterns. The research team (Pratt et al., 1999) hypothesized that politeness in questions would be greater during earlier stages of email conversation. Based on the number of messages sent, four stages were identified, and messages per stage were counted. Using ANOVA, the research team found that there was a statistically significant difference in the use of politeness between stages. As expected, politeness was highest in the first stage and then tapered off across the three remaining stages.

Coding content according to a set of standards occurs much less frequently. A good example of this type of content coding is a study of television news stories (Hickson et al., 1995). The research team identified 12 criteria (timeliness, hard news, local story, fairness, contextual frame, opinion, difficulty, research, exclusivity, nonsensational, overproduction, staff quantity) that had appeared in the broadcast literature as standards that local television news stories should meet. Each news story was coded on each criterion to create an index of journalism excellence in local television news.

Neuendorf (2002) recommends that researchers consider the **first-order linkages** among components as they develop the research design for a content analysis study. Doing so moves content analysis beyond a simple coding of messages. Using Cai and associates' (2003) study of children's websites as a prototype, a first-order linkage would be to link their findings (information they coded and counted from the websites, such as requests for personal information from children, privacy statements, and required parental permission) to survey results from children's use of these websites. Although the unit of analysis is the same (the children's websites), the data collection unit is different. The websites are the data in the former; children provide data for the latter. Thus, this first-order link investigates a relationship between message and receiver. A first-order link could be designed to investigate the relationship between source and message by linking a survey data from the marketing executives of the companies with findings from a content analysis of their websites for children. Neuendorf encourages researchers to add source or receiver data to their content analysis research designs whenever possible to create first-order linkages.

Computers and Content Analysis

As with most processes, computers and content analysis software programs can be invaluable tools. Although computers can speed up the mechanical process, there are limitations to what they can do. Generally speaking, if your unit of analysis is a discrete unit (for example, a word or phrase), and you have a large quantity of messages or text to examine, then a computer—even the use of the search or find function in a word processing program—will speed up identifying these units for analysis. Some researchers use more sophisticated software programs as an aid in their coding and analytical tasks. But even these programs do not allow the researcher to turn over the entire coding and interpretation process to the computer.

Furthermore, computers will not decrease the need for developing the coding scheme. In fact, using a computer will force you to identify coding units more explicitly because all judgments must be built into the computer program. As a result, coding reliability will increase as long as the researcher has programmed the software with all of the needed assumptions. Once the categories and assumptions are prescribed, the computer is capable of using them over and over without variation. This could certainly be an advantage over human coders. Recognize, however, that if the categories and assumptions built into the program are in error, then the results obtained will contain those same errors.

Strengths of Content Analysis Research

Clearly, a strength of content analysis is that the data are close to the communicator. In some cases, communicators naturally generate text or messages prior to the researcher's involvement. Written texts are also available widely in libraries (for example, magazines, newspapers, books) and over the internet (for example, chat room discussions, webpages, archived materials). Audio- and videotapes can be made of broadcast materials with home equipment (for research purposes only), or researchers can ask people to participate in a study to create or develop texts or messages to be coded. In either

AN ETHICAL
ISSUE

Taking Content Out of Context

Content analysis is a useful method for finding themes in a great number of messages. Because the sample is generally several hundred or more, a researcher typically presents the category scheme, a few examples for each category, and the frequencies and percentages of themes for each category. Thus, a consumer must trust that the researcher is not interpreting the findings out of the context in which participants provided them. For example, a researcher asks participants to write a brief description about what they would consider to be unethical communication practices. From these descriptions, the researcher identifies a handful of themes to include, for example, dishonesty in representing one's self, telling a small lie to protect someone else, telling a small lie to be polite, and so on. It would be unethical for the researcher to interpret these results as unethical communication practices *committed* by participants. They are only the communication practices participants consider to be unethical. Because participants wrote about these themes does not mean they are guilty of the practices. Researchers using content analysis want to make inferences from their findings, but they must retain the contextuality participants used in providing the descriptions.

case, the communicators themselves generate text or messages to be coded. As a result of this closeness, it is easy for the researcher to argue that the messages produced are valid and representative and that inferences drawn from the categorical analysis of these texts and messages are plausible.

This method is also unobtrusive. After texts or messages are captured, researchers can pore over and analyze the messages without participants' awareness. Some texts are available without the knowledge or approval of the message creator. Thus, a researcher can study the texts of a person whom they would likely never meet or be granted the opportunity to interview. Finally, the method is applicable to texts or messages of any structure. This advantage increases the scope of research as content analysis can be used on nearly any type of message in any form.

Limitations of Content Analysis Research

Despite these strengths, content analysis also has its limitations. First, if text or messages cannot be captured, the content cannot be coded. Second,

coding schemes can contain too few or too many categories, decreasing the likelihood that nuances of the text or messages will surface.

Third, and as in other quantitative research designs, how researchers obtain participants for their sample can be a limitation of content analysis. Usually, researchers can take steps to overcome these problems. For example, Pruitt, Koermer, and Goldstein (1995) conducted an exploratory investigation of how clergy used communication to create immediacy with their parishioners. To enhance the representativeness and, hence, validity of their findings, the research team sought participants from seven religious denominations. Had they selected participants from one or two denominations, their conclusions would have been less generalizable.

INTERACTION ANALYSIS

Like content analysis, **interaction analysis** codes communication into categories. However, interaction analysis codes the content of *ongoing* communication between two or more individuals. Thus, the focus of interaction analysis is to identify the verbal or nonverbal features or functions of the stream of conversational elements. Using a standard set of rules for coding the interaction, researchers can conduct more complex analyses, including analyzing the intent and function of messages, determining the effects of messages, and examining messages for their relationship to one another over time (Tucker, Weaver, & Berryman-Fink, 1981).

The most effective coding schemes are those based on theories. Much time and energy is involved in developing coding schemes, and they are usually refined and revised over time as researchers—those who originated the coding scheme and others—work with the coding scheme, apply it to different types of interaction, and ask different research questions. Thus, most scholars would agree that interaction coding schemes are always in some stage of development.

There are several interaction analysis coding schemes available for your use in research projects, especially for the study of interpersonal and group communication. Interaction coding is frequently used in interpersonal communication research to analyze which partner has control of the conversation and of the relationship. Rogers and Farace's (1975) relational communication coding scheme identifies the direction of control in relational transactions. Interactions within conversation can be coded as being controlling, accepting of or seeking control, or neutralizing control. By combining speaking turns into a series of contiguous pairs, the researcher can examine the overall pattern or structure of the interactions. Sabourin (1995) demonstrates the use of this coding scheme in her study of the conversations of abusive and nonabusive couples.

Interaction analysis is also a good choice for studying the complexity of interaction that occurs between and among group members. Bales's (1950) Interaction Process Analysis (IPA) has long been used to study the task and relational elements of group interaction. The coding scheme identifies interaction as task or relational based on the function the interaction serves in the group members' conversations. More recently, the Conversational Argument Coding Scheme (Canary, Brossman, & Seibold, 1987; Meyers, Seibold, & Brashers, 1991) was developed to code the structure of arguments in group decision making. This scheme is used in an example later in this chapter (see Table 13.1).

Gathering and Preparing the Interaction for Coding

Interaction coding schemes require that researchers listen to the conversation and determine how elements "fit" the coding scheme relative to what happens before and after. This type of coding complexity is easier to handle when researchers transcribe the interaction from audio- or video-tapes before they begin the process of unitizing and then coding the interaction. As with content analysis procedures described earlier, the data to be coded must first be unitized. This means that independently two or more judges identify the units of analysis to be coded. Unitizing reliability is computed to determine the degree of consistency in how the judges are unitizing the conversation. Disagreements about their choices must be resolved before coding the interaction by categories can begin. Obviously, judges or coders must be trained as to what constitutes the unit of analysis before they begin this phase of the analysis. Often, judges are trained on conversations that are similar to but not part of the dataset for the research project.

One of the most frequently used units of analysis in interaction analysis is the "complete thought." This means that any statement that functions as a complete thought or change of thought is considered one unit. This is an intermediate position between coding words or phrases at a more microlevel and coding complete speaking turns or utterances at a more macrolevel. Look at the example in Table 13.1, drawn from Meyers et al. (1991) to understand how complete thoughts are captured and coded.

Coding the Interaction

As with unitizing, coders must be trained in the specific coding scheme for the research project. For the project from which Table 13.1 was selected, Meyers and colleagues (1991) reported that two pairs of two coders were trained over a period of 5 weeks for more than 40 hours of

TABLE 13.1 Example of Interaction Analysis Coding

Unit #	Speaker	Complete Thought	Coding of Complete Thought
329	Larry	Is not getting a degree from there, is getting the degree from (a less prestigious university) better than going four years and not getting a degree from Harvard?	Proposition
330	Tom	(Better than) Let's say a 90% chance of getting a degree from the (less prestigious university).	Assertion
331	Larry	Is better than a 10% chance?	Proposition
332	Tom	A 10% chance from Harvard.	Assertion
333a	Larry	You say yes.	Assertion
333b	Larry	I say no way.	Objection
334	Kathy	I say no way.	Objection
335	Tom	I say it's better to go to Harvard.	Proposition
336a	Terry	You guys really think if he goes to school and he flunks out he can't go for a degree anywhere?	Proposition
336b	Terry	He can.	Assertion
336c	Terry	He can still go to the other place and still get his degree there.	Elaboration
337a	Tom	Oh good point.	Agreement
337b	Tom	I mean, why not go for it?	Proposition

SOURCE: "Argument in Initial Group Decision-Making Discussions: Refinement of a Coding Scheme and a Descriptive Quantitative Analysis," by R. A. Meyers, D. R. Seibold, and D. Brashers, 1991, *Western Journal of Speech Communication, 55,* pp. 47–68. Used by permission of the Western States Communication Association.

training and practice coding sessions. The four coders worked until their coding decisions achieved 80% agreement. From then on, each pair of coders independently coded half of the transcripts. Although coders worked primarily from the typed transcripts, they could refer to groups' videotaped interaction at any time. Even with this training, independent coding of the transcript resulted in differences between coders. To reduce these differences, teams of coders discussed and clarified each of these instances. Once again, the coding reliability between coders was computed.

Disagreements between coders were discussed until coders could agree on a coding selection. Although specifics may differ slightly from research project to research project, the procedures described here are fairly common.

Analyzing and Interpreting the Coding

Once the interaction is coded, it is time to analyze the codings. Again, the researcher returns to the research question or hypothesis that provides a foundation for the study. In the example from Meyers et al. (1991), the researchers asked, "What is the distribution of argument acts across all group discussions?" (p. 52). Thus, researchers were examining group conversations to discover the ways in which argument is used in group decision making.

In a common type of analysis, researchers conduct frequency analyses for each of the coding categories. At that point, a researcher has summarized the raw data and can now analyze these results against the theoretical position posited in the literature review. But researchers also examine the coded transcripts for evidence of patterns that simple frequency analyses cannot illuminate. Meyers and colleagues (1991) examined the coded transcripts to determine how argumentative elements were placed or sequenced relative to one another.

More sophisticated analyses can also be conducted on coded interaction units. For example, Ellis and Maoz (2002) also used the Conversational Argument Coding Scheme. In this study, the research team coded group conversations from a series of workshops designed to promote the coexistence and peace building among Israeli Jews and Palestinians. After carefully reading the transcripts to distinguish arguments from nonarguments, trained coders identified 232 coded arguments. Using ANCOVA (analysis of covariance, a statistical test similar to ANOVA), the researchers discovered that political dialogues among members of these two groups did not clearly follow cultural communication style predictions. In these group conversations, Palestinians developed more points during argument and Israeli Jews prompted more disagreement but also sought to delimit the arguments. By using the frequency of interaction codes as dependent variables and ethnicity as an independent variable, the research team was able to identify these cultural differences.

Strengths of Interaction Analysis

An obvious strength of interaction analysis is that elements preceding and subsequent to the element being coded are considered in placing conversational elements into categories. Thus, most interaction coding schemes place considerable emphasis on the relative position of any category

to the context and the entirety of the conversation. Although interaction coding schemes can be developed for virtually any communication phenomenon, communication scholars have continued to use and develop several coding schemes that are fundamental to our understanding of communication. This type of scholarship development encourages theoretical insight, a quality missed by developing novel coding schemes for specific research projects.

Limitations of Interaction Analysis

Of course, interaction analysis is limited to the degree the coding scheme is valid and representative of the communication phenomenon being explored. Therefore, the development of the coding scheme is critical to the success of its results.

Unitizing conversation into elements that can be coded is generally a greater problem in interaction analysis than in content analysis because interaction analysis relies solely on ongoing streams of conversation, which are not always neat and tidy. Thus, researchers must train coders to select and identify units consistently. The other limitation is that coding in interaction analysis generally takes longer because it is a more laborious process.

DESIGN CONSIDERATIONS

Whether your research design calls for content analysis or interaction analysis, several criteria are important for designing an effective study (Waitzkin, 1993). First, there should be a balance between method and meaning. Although procedures for validity and reliability should be used, these and the procedures used for data coding and analysis should not overwhelm or distort the meaning of the text. Second, texts should be selected through some type of sampling procedure to ensure the representativeness of the analysis. Third, selected texts should be available to others so that researchers can question or build upon what was found. Fourth, if it is necessary to transcribe audio or video data into written text, standardized rules for transcribing text from spoken or visual form to written form should be developed and applied, and the reliability of the transcription process should be assessed. Fifth, procedures for interpreting the text should be decided in advance and in consideration of the content and structure of the text, as well as in consideration of the research question or hypothesis. Most important, the interpretation procedures should be designed in accordance with the theory or perspective providing the foundation for the analysis.

If you use one of the quantitative methods for analyzing content, you need to consider four general limitations (Street, 1993; Waitzkin, 1993). First, quantifying codes of a text cannot capture the complexity of discourse. Regardless of how discrete a coding scheme appears, some information about the conversation is lost when it is coded quantitatively. Second, quantitative coding cannot capture the contextuality of conversation. In fact, much of the context from which the text is taken or captured cannot be retained. Third, regardless of the technical sophistication of quantitative techniques, they cannot replace interpretations made by people. Likewise, coding interaction into categories cannot represent the quality of messages (for example, meaningfulness, appropriateness).

SUMMARY

1. Content analysis and interaction analysis are two quantitative methods for analyzing communication texts.

2. Content analysis is the most basic methodology for analyzing message content; it integrates data collection method and analytical technique in a research design to reveal the occurrence of some identifiable element in a text or set of messages.

3. Category schemes allow researchers to code the manifest and latent meanings to text.

4. Content analyses are often reported and analyzed using frequency counts and chi-square.

5. Coding schemes can be developed from existing theory or other published research

findings, or coding schemes can emerge from the data.

6. Virtually any communication phenomena can be content analyzed; codable elements include words or phrases, complete thoughts or sentences, themes, paragraphs or short whole texts, characters or speakers, communicative acts or behaviors, advertisements, and entire television programs.

7. At least two trained coders code the selected content; interrater reliability must be calculated for both unitizing and coding decisions.

8. Validity issues for content coding rest primarily with the appropriateness and adequacy of the coding scheme.

9. Content analysis can be used to identify frequencies of occurrence, differences, trends, patterns, and standards; first-order linkages should also be considered in the research design.

10. Computer software is available to assist the researcher in the coding process.

11. Interaction analysis, especially suitable for interpersonal and group communication, codes the ongoing conversation between two or more individuals into categories.

12. Interaction analysis focuses on the features or functions of the stream of conversational elements.

13. Coding of interaction elements is based on the element itself, and what happens before and after it.

KEY TERMS

content analysis	manifest content
first-order linkage	Scott's *pi*
interaction analysis	semantic validity
intercoder reliability	unitizing reliability
interrater reliability	unit of analysis
latent content	

CHAPTER FOURTEEN

Designing Qualitative Research

Chapter Checklist

After reading this chapter, you should be able to:

1. Identify the role of the researcher in qualitative research designs and explain the potential effects of different researcher roles on the research process.

2. Select, and argue for, an appropriate researcher role for a specific research project.

3. Develop a purpose statement and research question for a qualitative research project.

4. Create a research design for a qualitative study.

5. Develop a technique for gaining entry to a research site.

6. Use sampling strategies to identify potential participants or other sampling units.

7. Select effective and appropriate data observation strategies.

8. Document data as evidence in complete and detailed notes.

9. Consider, and, if appropriate, moderate your impact as researcher on participants and the research process.

This chapter explores the process of designing and conducting qualitative research. Just as *quantitative research* is a broad term for many design issues and statistical techniques, the term *qualitative research* also represents a wide variety of methodologies for data collection and data analysis. Recall from earlier chapters that the primary distinction between quantitative and qualitative research is the role the researcher assumes in collecting data. In quantitative methodologies, the researcher assumes the role of a third-party observer, collecting data from participants in as objective a manner as possible. In qualitative methodologies, the researcher as the primary data collection instrument assumes a more active, fluid, and subjective role. As a result, participation and observation are integrated (Lincoln & Guba, 1985).

This objective–subjective difference is often highlighted as the distinction between quantitative and qualitative methodologies. Be careful, however, about extending this relationship to the extreme. All forms of data collection are subjective to some degree. Likewise, all forms of data collection have some degree of objectivity. Whereas more traditional social scientists believe that good research is objective, it may be more productive to think of good research as being well planned using credible methods, effectively carried out, and subject to the scrutiny of others (Phillips, 1992). These criteria can be extended to all studies regardless of methodology.

The subjective nature of qualitative research is easier to identify because of the data collection role of the researcher and the focus on specific interaction cases. But qualitative methodologies can produce data with objective characteristics (Kvale, 1996). First, objectivity can be freedom from bias, which means that knowledge obtained has been checked or controlled and is not distorted by personal bias and prejudices. In qualitative research, freedom from bias means that the researcher is skilled in the methodologies used and has verified the information obtained. Second, objectivity can be intersubjective, which means that the data are testable and reproducible. Repeated observations of the same phenomenon by different observers help qualitative researchers achieve this standard. Finally, objectivity can be achieved by adequately describing the object investigated.

This means that the real nature of the person or the interaction studied is expressed through expanded description and examples or by letting the individual speak for him- or herself. Certainly more so than quantitative methodologies, qualitative approaches are able to capture and report on the complete and complex social world in which interaction occurs. Viewed in this way, qualitative methodologies are as capable as quantitative approaches of generating knowledge and contributing to theory development.

Although it is true that qualitative methodologies are more subjective and initially less structured than quantitative methodologies, this does not mean the researcher fails to address design issues prior to collecting data. Refer back to the qualitative model of research design presented in Chapter 4. Recall that qualitative research design is a process, more cyclical than linear. Still, a researcher needs to develop a research design before entering the field to collect data.

Although the internal structure of qualitative research may be less apparent to outsiders and more flexible than the structure of quantitative research, the process of conducting qualitative research does have standards by which it is evaluated. This chapter will explain the preparations a researcher should make and describe the standards that have been accepted by qualitative researchers across disciplines.

THE RESEARCHER'S ROLE IN QUALITATIVE METHODOLOGIES

Qualitative methodologies are used by communication researchers to study the performance, process, and practice of communication. Because the qualitative researcher is *in* the communication context being studied or is interacting directly with research participants, the researcher takes on roles different from those of the quantitative researcher. In qualitative practices, the role of the researcher is integrated within the context of the individuals who are being observed. Gold (1958) explains:

Every field work role is at once a social interaction device for securing information for scientific purposes and a set of behaviors in which an observer's self is involved. . . . He [sic] continually introspects, raising endless questions about the informant and the developing field relationship, with a view to playing the field work role as successfully as possible. (p. 218)

Rather than collecting data in one laboratory experiment or at multiple points in time through surveys or questionnaires, qualitative researchers are in the research context for extended periods of time—days, weeks, months, even years—giving them the opportunity to sequentially examine in depth the experiences and insights of participants. As a result, researchers observe the communication firsthand rather than through secondhand verbal or written reports of participants. This type of researcher involvement is labeled **participant observation.** Its various forms are described in the sections that follow.

Forms of Participant Observation

As a qualitative researcher, you may take a passive role, only observing what is going on. This would be the case if you observed your city council in action. For example, you would take a seat in the audience, would not identify yourself as a researcher, and would not talk to those around you. Your activity would consist of taking notes about the meeting, detailing who said what and how. Alternately, your role could become active. You could participate in the debate before the council by raising your hand and asking a question. Now you would be participating in the interaction. There are four types of roles researchers assume with respect to observing and participating (Adler & Adler, 1987; Gold, 1958; Lindlof & Taylor, 2002).

Complete Participant   In the **complete participant** role, you are fully functioning as a member of the scene, but you do not reveal to others that you are simultaneously observing and assessing their actions. In other words, you disguise your role as researcher through your role as participant. Permission to observe is legitimated through your role as participant. In this way, you are using yourself as a participant to understand the interaction behavior. And in your role as a

complete participant, you are affecting what happens in the interaction.

In this role, the researcher observes from a perspective of full membership. Full membership is achieved when researchers choose to study a group with which they have prior membership (for example, their family) or by seeking and obtaining membership in a group (for example, joining the Chamber of Commerce in their position as business owner).

What risks are involved if you take on this research role? First, others in the interaction setting will see you as a full participant and create expectations for you in that role. As a result, you cannot whip out your notebook and make notes during the interaction. You must maintain your role as a complete participant. Second, you are likely to receive or hear information that is not intended for outsiders. The private information you receive is given to you based on the nature of your personal relationship with others. You must react to this information as an insider, not as an outsider. Doing otherwise can reveal your identity as a researcher and will encourage others to negatively assess you and the research role when it is uncovered. Third, you can only observe the actions and interactions available to someone in your role. It is impossible to temporarily step outside your role as a participant to ask questions. Fourth, because you are involved in the interaction, it may be more difficult for you to detach yourself to analyze it. It may also be difficult to identify the effects of your participation on the group's interaction. Would the group have taken a certain step if you had not been there? These risks raise ethical questions about the role of complete participant.

Participant-as-Observer   In the **participant-as-observer** role, the researcher is both participant and observer. While openly acknowledging the research purpose, the researcher also takes an active role in the interaction. In this way, the researcher is viewing the interaction as someone inside the system even though others know and accept that research is being conducted.

As an active member, the researcher participates in the core activities of the group and in some ways is the same as any other individual being observed. At the same time, the researcher retains his or her research focus and refrains from committing totally to the group.

Helmer (1993) took on this type of researcher role as he examined how organizational tensions emerged in organizational member storytelling. He conducted his observations at one racetrack over 7 months. Initially the director of public relations and stable superintendent introduced him to others; later he circulated freely and initiated contacts on his own. In his participant-as-observer role, he talked to management, racing officials, security officers, horse trainers, caretakers or grooms, and blacksmiths. Although he was never employed at the racetrack, he did obtain his groom's license and worked alongside participants while he talked with them.

As another example of participant observation, Edley (2000) spent 6 months, or about 350 hours, as an unpaid employee in an interior design firm. Working 12 to 20 hours per week alongside designers, office workers, the owners, and warehouse workers, she was able to immerse herself into the culture. She had many of the same job duties as other organizational members: She answered telephones, filed papers, helped with inventory, waited on customers, sat in on staff meetings and meetings with clients, helped select wallpaper and fabric, and went with designers to some clients' homes. Edley admits, "In working alongside the designers and office staff, I not only learned how to do interior design work, but I also learned the everyday organizing practices of the firm" (p. 283). In this participant observation role, Edley collected observational data in field notes, and interviewed employees and owners. Additionally, information she gleaned from informal work sessions with the owners was included in the field notes. The biggest risk of the participant-as-observer role stems from the extra demands it places on the researcher, who is both team member and researcher. As with the complete participant, not fulfilling an interaction role or fulfilling it ineffectively will ultimately affect the interaction under study.

Observer-as-Participant   Still being both participant and observer, the primary focus in the **observer-as-participant** role shifts to the role of observer. In other words, the researcher has negotiated entrance into an interaction setting to observe with the intention of allowing the interaction to proceed as it naturally would.

In this role, the researcher participates but does not take on a central role in the group being observed. For example, the researcher might fulfill a secondary role within a group—perhaps helping a baseball team keep score or keep their playing equipment organized, for example. However, the researcher would not offer or agree to a request to play in one of the team's key positions. Engagement with participants in the interaction scene is possible, but the interaction is not driven or motivated by the researcher being an actor within the interaction scene.

In such a role, you would not interrupt the roles and interactions of those observed because your participation would be limited to observing or asking questions. The risk of such an arrangement is that your minimal participation may make it more difficult to complete full observations or valid assessments of the interaction. This researcher role is easy to negotiate and carry out but may blind you to the complexity of the interaction.

For example, Palmer (2003), who is a media history professor, describes his observer participant role with Reuters news agency prior to and during the first 21 days of the U.S.- and U.K.-led invasion of Iraq in March–April 2003. Using a case study approach, Palmer observed newsroom operations and analyzed editorial logs to show how this news agency monitored its performance and the performance of other news agencies with the goal of improving its performance on writing style, paragraph order, and news priorities. By being a journalist in the setting, Palmer could observe firsthand how style preferences changed quickly in response to the events being covered and in reaction to how other news agencies were covering the same events.

Complete Observer   In the **complete observer** role, the researcher enacts only the observer role. As a result, the researcher is hidden completely from the interactants in the scene. Thus, data are limited to what one can see or hear. In this role, the researcher does not engage interactants in any fashion. Interviews are not conducted; questions are not posed; people are not asked to explain their comments. Interactants in the setting may

AN ETHICAL
ISSUE

One Role? Or Two?

In qualitative research, the roles of participant and observer can blend together, and this blending can pose significant ethical issues, especially when the researcher collects data via the internet. For example, Sharf (1997) identified the ethical issues of public–private communication in her study of a breast cancer listserv. Sharf began her study by

> "lurking" or just listening in to the interchanges on the List. [Later] when I occasionally posted messages, I introduced myself both as a communication researcher and a person with a personal interest in this disease. . . . Five months into my task, my self-perceived ethos of mere investigator was shattered.

Sharf describes her feelings of sadness in reaction to reading a moving eulogy of someone she did not know except through a listserv member's postings. Sharf writes,

> [I] realized fully for the first time what it meant to be a member of this disembodied, yet strongly connected, community. From that point on, I struggled to maintain a dual consciousness about both the information I was gathering and my personal responses to it, as I proceeded with my analysis.

In her research report, Sharf notes,

> the sensitive nature of the conversations impelled me to secure specific permission to quote from each author/poster. Following completion of the initial draft, I contacted each individual quoted via e-mail with a description of my research, the particular passages I wished to quote, and an offer to review the manuscript. Every person granted me permission, several did read the draft, and many provided me with feedback that has been incorporated in this version.

What is your reaction to how Sharf handled her dual role of participant and observer?

not even know the researcher is there as he or she blends into, but does not interact with, the scene and its participants. Of course, the greatest risk is that the researcher's interpretations of what is observed are totally reliant on what is personally observed. The complete observer does not verify or check interpretations with others because doing so would expose this covert role.

For example, Smith and Keyton (2001) reported and interpreted data collected when, in the role of complete observer, I (Keyton) visited the production of one episode of the television series *Designing Women*. With approval of the show's producer, I observed all rehearsals of the show, the filming of the show before a studio audience, and

some postproduction activities. Although the producer was aware of my research role and knew that I was there to observe and takes notes, we did not meet or have any electronic communication during my visit to the set. Nor did I have any conversations with cast and crew members. Rather, I sat alone in the stands, and from this vantage point, had visual and auditory access to cast and crew interactions during the rehearsals and filming. Thus, the job-related interactions and some informal interactions among the cast, directing staff, and crew could be observed and recorded.

In some qualitative studies, it is necessary (and even desirable) to move among the different researcher roles. Lange (1993) did just this as

---

TRY THIS!   **Assuming Researcher Roles**

Over the next few days, identify interaction settings in which you can assume each of the four roles just described: complete participant, participant-as-observer, observer-as-participant, and complete observer. Stay within the interaction setting only long enough to experience the differences in the four roles. After you have had these experiences, answer the following questions: (1) which role was most comfortable for you? Least uncomfortable? Why? (2) In which role do you believe you could most effectively collect data? Why? (3) To what extent do you believe research participants were aware of your roles?

---

he studied both environmentalist and counter-environmentalist groups. He immersed himself in the timber-industry culture by observing more than 300 hours of interaction, hanging out at local environmental and timber-industry offices, attending government hearings, and acting as a moderator at a public debate. At one point, he was even hired by a federal agency to analyze one aspect of a failed experiment in collaborative forest management. As you can see, Lange moved among the different types of qualitative researcher roles, each affording him a different perspective from which to address his research needs. Regardless of which research role you assume, remember that you are conducting research. The role exists because of your research objective.

IDENTIFYING THE RESEARCH FOCUS

How does a researcher plan for a qualitative study? After the researcher identifies a general research problem or topic, the next step is to articulate a compelling and researchable question that is salient to one or more audiences. Recall the inductive research model presented in Chapter 2. These two steps are the paths through which the qualitative researcher enters the research process.

Practically, then, the researcher is the first audience for the research study. If the question is not personally interesting or compelling, you may lack the stamina or motivation to finish the project or to conduct the project in an effective manner.

As the researcher enters the field to investigate, however, the question may change as evidence of the problem is observed (or not observed). Even though the question is likely to change, the researcher must still have a question with which to begin. With that question in mind, researchers expecting to use qualitative methods can then use the qualitative model of research design, discussed in Chapter 4, developed specifically for projects using qualitative methods.

Because qualitative research is contextually bound to specific interaction and specific interactants, each research project will result in a unique design solution (Lindlof & Taylor, 2002). Often, researchers cannot determine which method or methods will be best until they spend some time in the interaction context. If researchers are not familiar with the interaction setting, they need time to become familiar with the parameters of the interaction. What might initially seem confusing might be a regular part of ongoing interaction to the interactants. Alternately, if the interaction setting is very familiar to the researcher, time is needed within the interaction context to develop some distance from the interaction. In either case, researchers might choose methods to be used even before the observation and participation begins, but they must ask if these methods are best once they are in the interaction setting. Thus, methodological solutions must be both unique and flexible.

At this point in designing the qualitative study, it is helpful to develop a purpose statement as a road map for your project (Creswell, 1998).

You may even use this later when you write your research report. But its purpose now is to make sure you are ready to collect data. By filling in the blanks in the following sentences, you can articulate what you are investigating and how:

> The purpose of this _____ (type of qualitative method) study will be to _____ (describe? understand? discover?) the _____ (communication phenomenon you are interested in studying) for _____ (the unit of analysis: a person? a group of people? a process? a site?). At this stage in the research project, the _____ (communication phenomenon you are interested in studying) is generally defined as _____ (provide a general definition of the central concept).

Consider this completed purpose statement:

> The purpose of these face-to-face interviews and focus groups will be to discover the way in which employees of Organization ABC express acceptance or rejection of the organization's family leave policy. At this stage in the research project, the acceptance or rejection of the policy is generally defined as the acceptance or rejection expressed in the stories or accounts employees give about the policy, expected changes that employees relate about their future use of family leave, and employees' abilities to repeat or paraphrase the policy.

Obviously, in a project of this scope, it is likely that many researchers will be conducting interviews and focus groups. Thus, it is important that all members of the research team have the same road map by which to conduct their research activities. After the first round of interviews and focus groups, research team members will want to meet to consider their ability to fulfill this purpose statement. A rephrasing of the statement may occur. Rephrasing, or revisiting, the initial research problem or research question is a natural part of qualitative research because collecting data continually informs or reinforms the researcher about the subject of the research. This reflexive nature of qualitative research is, in part, what distinguishes it from quantitative approaches.

Another aspect of the planning process is to consider one's flexibility as a researcher (Lindlof & Taylor, 2002). The researcher will not have control over what happens in the field. This means that the researcher must be able to fit in with events, people, and interaction with which he or she is unfamiliar. No longer can the researcher operate or evaluate others by personal rules or standards of conduct. In qualitative research, these come from individuals in the interaction situation, not from the researcher. As a result, the researcher needs to develop a sense of knowing what constitutes important information or actions that should be documented: Events may erupt or develop in a monotonous drone. The researcher must be able to decipher which events and interactions are important and when development (or lack of development) of the interaction creates new questions.

Consulting the Literature

Planning for qualitative research is somewhat different from planning for a quantitative project—but just as critical. Actually, planning may be more critical because some events, once they are over, are not accessible for long periods of time (for example, fan behavior at the Indianapolis 500). In addition to resolving issues about gaining access, the researcher should simultaneously become involved with the research literature as it relates to the content area as well as the qualitative method about to be undertaken.

By searching the research literature, the researcher can become familiar with terminology or practices used in a particular interaction setting and can identify theories that can support observations or be refuted with observations. By reading other qualitative research reports, the researcher can become familiar with these techniques before gaining access. Do not assume that this library search is restricted only to research conducted from a qualitative perspective. Studies conducted with quantitative methodologies can provide highly detailed information about a very specific event or context.

Asking or Stating the Research Objective

Recall that qualitative research tends to emphasize description and explanation more frequently than prediction (Fitch, 1994). Research questions, or a series of research questions, specify the expectations of what the researcher will describe and explain (Lindlof & Taylor, 2002). Different forms of research questions for qualitative studies can be found in Chapter 4.

Alternately, the research purpose or objective can be stated in a declarative sentence. For example, in her ethnographic study of the bonfire collapse at Texas A&M University, Miller (2002) states her purpose as follows:

> This article will consider the immediate aftermath of the collapse within the classroom and offices of the A&M campus. Specifically, it is a consideration of how academic professionals are performers and processors of emotion in the workplace and how an event such as the bonfire collapse can put issues regarding *emotion work* into sharp relief. In short, it asks the research question, "How do we 'profess' in the midst of tragedy?" (p. 575)

Although Miller does provide a research question, note how the research question makes sense only by reading the purpose of the article.

Developing a case study drawn from transcribed 911 calls, participant observation data, and interviews, Tracy (2002) describes the research purpose:

> Understanding how face implications play a role in the interactional (a)synchrony of the 911 interrogation sequence can assist emergency communications employees in reflecting upon and improving their everyday questioning practices. (p. 136)

Whether a research question or statement of the research purpose is used, the researcher should include enough contextual information to help the reader understand the context of the study.

SAMPLING IN QUALITATIVE DESIGNS

Although qualitative researchers are in the field and want to capture the complexity of communication events, the reality is that one researcher, not even a team of researchers, cannot capture the totality of the experience. Thus, qualitative designs require a sampling strategy to guide researcher choices about what to observe or whom to interview (Lindlof & Taylor, 2002). As with other communication research designs, people (or research participants) are the most likely sampling unit. Several sampling strategies can be used.

Just as with quantitative research designs, snowball or network sampling is often employed. Recall from Chapter 7 that **snowball sampling** is accomplished by getting referrals from individuals who already are participating in the research. Because it is common for people to know and interact with people like themselves, research participants are a good source of additional participants. **Network sampling** is a similar strategy. In this case, the researcher does not rely on other research participants. Rather, the researcher actively seeks individuals who fit the profile or characteristics central to the study.

Purposive sampling is often used in qualitative research designs when the researcher is seeking people or other sampling units. As for quantitative research designs, a researcher selects a person or site to be included in the study because the person or site is thought to be typical of the communication being investigated. Usually working from inclusion criteria, researchers purposively seek some people or sites over others. For example, to study social support in support groups it makes sense to go to those sites where social support is most likely to occur, or where people believe they are receiving social support. Choosing a breast cancer support group that has met weekly for a number of years is a purposeful choice, and likely to yield the interaction of interest.

Maximum variation sampling (Lincoln & Guba, 1985) is based on informational redundancy. In this technique, the researcher continues to seek additional participants until the data received are redundant with, or the same as, previously collected data. In other words, the data are saturated with the same information. This is the sampling technique Clark (2002) employed to explore how teenagers use stories about the afterlife, supernatural, and paranormal in the entertainment media as a vehicle for understanding their religious beliefs. The researcher interviewed families with young people expecting that each interview would produce contrasting information.

Sampling, or interviewing, stopped when additional interviews did not reveal new information.

With these types of sampling procedures, what constitutes an acceptable sample size for a qualitative study? Lindlof and Taylor (2002) explain that sample size usually cannot be predetermined. Rather, qualitative researchers should sample until a "critical threshold of interpretation has been reached" (p. 129), or when new information is not being added or existing information is unchallenged.

Special Considerations for Sampling in Qualitative Research

To make sense of what you see or hear you must employ some type of strategy for making comparable observations or notes. Thus, the question is "Of all the interactions available to you, what do you sample?" In the field, the choices can be overwhelming, and over a period of time you may want to sample different units or things. But, initially, you will want to determine the sample in terms of settings, persons, activities, events, and time (Lindlof & Taylor, 2002).

The setting in which the interaction occurs is more narrowly defined than the context. For example, in my study of resident physicians (Keyton, 1995), the context was a medical teaching hospital, whereas the setting was resident interaction with attending physicians and nurses in the intensive and critical care units. Limiting observations to this setting provided one of many focuses available in this context. Residents' interactions over lunch or coffee breaks were excluded, as were residents' conversations with patients and their families. Identifying the setting is important because it defines the physical, social, and cultural parameters of what is being observed.

The persons who were investigated in this study were the resident physicians. Although I also observed attending physicians and nurses, my primary focus was on the resident physicians and their relationships with people in these two other groups. Thus, who is being observed must be salient and related to your research question. By identifying the setting and persons, as a researcher I could also identify the activity in which I was interested. My primary focus was on their

decision-making interactions. Although other communication functions were intertwined with decision-making activities, I was interested in them only to the extent that they informed or provided information about decision making.

Specific events, of course, are related to the settings, persons, and activities previously described. Yet, generally, there are three types of events (Schatzman & Strauss, 1973). The first type includes routine events. These happen regularly or are a regular feature of the interaction. The people involved expect this activity to occur in this setting with these interaction partners. A second type of event is a special event, or an event that does not occur regularly, but when it does is not surprising. For example, celebrating a physician's birthday in the setting of the intensive or critical care unit is a special event. It does not occur every day. Although it may seem odd to an outsider, this setting was the only place the medical staff could gather to celebrate. The third type of event is an untoward event, or an event that results from an emergency. It is unexpected by the people in the setting.

Caution should be exercised in determining what is a routine, special, or untoward event. For example, in my first few days observing in the intensive and critical care units, I did not see physicians yelling and screaming at nurses. Thus, the first time I observed such an event, I coded it as an untoward event. But over time, I came to realize that screaming and yelling regularly occurred and being civil to one another (what I observed in my first few days of observation) was really the anomaly (and probably caused by my presence).

Time is the last sampling unit. Usually, this is not very useful except when the interaction setting is highly repetitive or routine. A good example of this would be in observing the call-receiving behavior of phone reservationists. Because the downtime between calls is controlled by a computer, what reservationists do or say during this time period can be a valuable indicator of employee mood and commitment. Alternately, time can be helpful for analyzing rhythm and pace of interactions. For example, what does your instructor do in the 10 minutes immediately preceding the class for which you are reading this

**DESIGN
CHECK**

Why Was the Researcher There?

Sometimes researchers and field settings coincide, and the researcher is able to take advantage of the opportunity to collect data. At other times, the researcher actively searches for a specific type of setting in which to collect data to answer a research question. Sometimes someone inside the interaction setting wants the interaction diagnosed or wants help in managing the interaction environment and so invites the researcher to collect data. As you read qualitative research reports, it should be clear how the researcher came to this particular research setting. The motivation for being in a particular setting can influence what the researcher sees and how he or she analyzes and reports the data. Information about how the researcher gained access to the interaction studied is usually presented in the methods section of the written research report. Knowing how the researcher gained access and the motivation for conducting the study will help you assess the researcher's claims.

book? How do his or her activities in that time period compare or contrast to how other instructors spend their 10 minutes before class?

By altering when you observe, you are more likely to observe different aspects of routine behavior. Morning rituals are different from evening rituals. This same strategy also applies to other cycles of times. For example, observing college students at the end of the semester would certainly leave a researcher with one impression, whereas observing them at the beginning of a semester would likely create a completely different impression.

Yet another way to sample is to make observations at irregular time points. For example, if courses at your university started on the hour and finished at 50 minutes past the hour, you might select every 7 minutes as your time point for making observations about the interaction activities in the main lobby of your student center. Finally, you can randomly select the days and times of your observations.

Which sampling unit should be used? Most researchers use several in the same study or use several to define a specific event in which they are interested. When sampling units are consistent, data are more easily compared. Also, by having identified the sampling units of your observations, you are more likely to identify anomalies when they occur.

GAINING ACCESS

Gaining access to, or getting into, the research setting is not always easy. For example, you want to study family interaction at dinnertime. To assess some of the difficulties of gaining access to such interaction, think about your family's dining experiences. What does your family talk about at dinnertime? Are the topics always friendly? Are they suitable for a nonfamily audience? How would the presence of an outsider (not at the dinner table, but in close proximity to view and hear the conversation) affect family members' conversation?

Now, reflect on how you would approach others with a request to study their family dinnertime interactions. How would you ask friends if you could observe their family dinnertime conversations? How would you approach strangers and make this same request?

In qualitative research, what seems easy and doable often requires finesse to accomplish. Before you approach anyone to ask for access to collect data, you should consider the following questions: What would you tell the people you approach that you wanted to study? What if they asked why you wanted to study them? Finally, you should consider alternative ways of gaining access to dinnertime conversations of family members. A research project can start out with a great topic or question but be impossible to complete because access to the interaction event is not practical or is difficult—even denied.

In practice, gaining access includes making the initial contact, negotiating access, establishing entry and operational parameters, becoming known to the participants, and observing the interaction. Returning to the family dinnertime-conversation project, you could begin to negotiate access and establish entry by getting yourself invited to dinner at the homes of friends and relatives. With these invitations, you could "case the scene," or become familiar with interactions in this setting. By casing the scene (Lindlof & Taylor, 2002), you can develop a better awareness of the interaction you want to study and can refine the research question. More important, observing these interactions may provide you with clues to the best way to ask others to let you observe their dinnertime conversations.

Of course, if your research question takes you to a public setting, gaining access and casing the scene is all that much easier. In the role of visitor, you can hang out and do what visitors do in this public space. You can engage others in conversation, ask questions, and get directions or advice. Of course, it is still difficult to observe all interactions, even in public spaces. Some people will feel as if you are invading their personal space if you try to get too close to their private conversations in public spaces. As an example, how would you hang out at a bus stop to collect data about the function of nonverbal behavior in such settings? What difficulties would you expect to encounter observing in this public space?

As discussed earlier, gaining access to some settings may require that you assume a research role of participant or member. If you take on one of the covert roles, your acceptance by others as a participant or member is dependent on your ability and willingness to play the part (Foster, 1996). Thus, your physical appearance, your impression management skills, and your communication competence may need some adjustment to give you the credibility needed to gain access to some settings.

In some settings, particularly organizational ones, you may need to gain the permission of a **gatekeeper,** or a person who has authority with the group or organization. Alternately, someone already in the group or organization can act as your **sponsor.** A sponsor can vouch for you to others who will be observed as well as validate and legitimize your presence. Even with such an advocate, the process of gaining access to an organization can be a lengthy one. For example, Muto (1993) describes the process she endured over 6 months to gain entry to an organization.

Gaining access can also be a result of your other roles or activities. For example, James (1995) spent an academic year in Hungary as a Fulbright lecturer. Upon her arrival, several people asked if she would tutor them in English. She agreed with the caveat that she also wanted to practice her Hungarian. Soon James found herself in several language circles that became her entry into the local community. Throughout the year she established friendships with a half-dozen Hungarian families and soon found herself adopted as a member of the families and included in meals, celebrations, excursions, and trips to the market. As her relationships developed, she found that conversations often centered on the profound changes Hungarians were experiencing as a result of the economic transformation of post-Communist East–Central Europe. Soon she developed a research interest in understanding how these individuals were making the transition into a consumer culture. Thus, James moved from the role of a passive participant to the role of an active member when she returned to Hungary for 5 weeks of systematic investigation.

Part of gaining access is also figuring out if this setting and your observations here will provide you with the data you need. You should ask yourself, (1) Is this setting suitable? (2) Can I observe what I want to observe? (3) Will my observations be feasible? and (4) Can I observe in such a way that my tactics will not be suspect to others? (Schatzman & Strauss, 1973). In fact, during the process of gaining access, the researcher is actively negotiating a role regardless of which level of participant observation he or she plans to use.

Becoming Familiar With People and Places

Because the researcher is always the guest, he or she must take all responsibility for becoming familiar with the setting and the interactants.

There are several techniques for doing so. One way to familiarize yourself with the setting is to draw a map. By sketching out the physical nature of the interaction context, you orient yourself to the place in which the interaction occurs. Taking a tour through the interaction setting is another way to observe, ask questions, and learn information about the communication environment. A tour is a good idea even if the interaction setting is familiar to you. By asking one of the individuals you want to observe or interview to take you on a tour, you are seeing the interaction context from the participant's unique perspective.

Another way is to ask for relevant background information. In organizations this might include copies of annual reports or newsletters, public relations or other marketing materials, or reprints of feature stories about the organization or its key members. If you are observing a formally organized group, you could ask for copies of minutes or reports the group has produced. For families or individuals, you might look at scrapbooks or pictures.

Developing Trust

Due to the nature of the researcher's role in qualitative research, trust must be attended to from the first contact with research participants (Lincoln & Guba, 1985). In this situation, trust has some critical characteristics. First, trust is person-specific. This means that the researcher will have to develop trust with each person individually. Second, trust is established developmentally and slowly over time. Moreover, trust is fragile and must always be nurtured. Third, trust—even when it has been steadily growing—can be destroyed with one untoward action.

Trust between participants and researcher is paramount, and researchers can establish trust in a variety of ways. For her study of a witches' coven, Lesch (1994) describes how she attended regular open meetings of the coven to give participants a chance to know her before she attended to take notes with a tape recorder. Witmer (1997) studied the interaction of an Alcoholics Anonymous group, but only after seeking and gaining permission from the group's founder and informal leaders. Even though the meetings she observed were open to anyone, she felt that getting permission was needed as a matter of both ethics and courtesy.

Developing Rapport   In addition to developing trust with others and facilitating participants' trust with the research process, you must also develop rapport with those whom you will be observing and interacting with.

Often, asking simple questions is a good way to start. Most people are eager to answer questions because it gives them the opportunity to demonstrate their expertise or skill. This technique has several benefits. Asking questions yields basic information you will need to avoid making assumptions. Additionally, it provides a cover for your research role, as it minimizes your role as an observer and heightens your role as a participant. Individuals may feel threatened if some stranger (you in the role of researcher) suddenly shows up without explanation to observe them. People are usually more open to your observations if they have some one-on-one contact with you.

When it is not possible to talk with everyone, maintaining a pleasant conversational posture with the person you are speaking with is important. The tone of the conversation carries over into your nonverbal behavior, which can be interpreted by anyone who is looking on.

If your research role allows it, learn the names and titles of people with whom you will be interacting. In some cases you can ask for a list of names and titles ahead of time. Asking for someone by name is an immediate conversation starter even if that person is not available.

Another way in which researchers can build rapport with participants is to help with tasks and activities that participants are doing as a normal part of the interaction setting. These types of **commitment acts** (Feldman, Bell, & Berger, 2003) require an investment of time and energy on the part of the researcher but can yield considerable information in learning about the routine and mundane tasks of the setting. For example, Rudd (2000) studied a symphony to explore the relationship and tension between its creative and business activities. The researcher collected data in the symphony's offices and at symphony functions including rehearsals, performances, board meetings, and social gatherings. In the office setting, he was able to collect additional data while he worked with symphony personnel in creating advertising and promotional materials. Not only did he learn about their work tasks, but he was also able to work alongside symphony staff members to collect data from the informal conversations that occurred while they were completing the tasks. Doing these tasks with participants in the research setting demonstrates interest and humanizes the researcher. As Feldman and colleagues (2003) point out, the tasks do not need to be dramatic. Rather, engaging in mundane or routine tasks can demonstrate a researcher's willingness to listen and trustworthiness.

Locating Key Informants   In some qualitative research settings, there will be one or a few people without whom your project could not be completed. These are your **key informants.** You can identify key informants by asking about the interaction environment beforehand. In an organizational setting you might ask, "Who has worked here the longest? To whom do others turn when they need help? Who always knows the latest rumors?"

Another way to identify a key informant is through your observations. As you watch the interaction, does one person seem more central to the interaction than others? If you are observing a formal setting, who seems to be at the center of the informal conversations? In informal settings, who talks the most or the longest? To whom do others direct their questions? Who tells the jokes? Although you certainly cannot rely solely on one, or even two, key informants, their position in the interaction setting is likely to be essential to your research project.

Key informants are valuable for a variety of reasons. As Rudd (2000) explained, his informants at the symphony were from three groups: musicians, board members, and administrators. "These individuals explained 'native' terms to me, gave me guidance regarding how to pursue

additional information and sources, and assisted me in confirming or disconfirming initial interpretations" (p. 121).

Stumbling Onto Something Interesting

Sometimes, of course, and despite the research plan, the researcher will stumble onto something unexpected or unusual. When this happens, the researcher must make a decision to continue with the original project and look for ways the new situation influences what is being observed or to be flexible enough to change course and pursue the new activity, particularly when it replaces or overshadows routine interaction.

For example, something unexpected happened while I was observing the preproduction and production activities of the television show *Designing Women* (Keyton, 1994; Smith & Keyton, 2001). I had asked to observe the rehearsals, taping, and postproduction of the last episode of the 1989–1990 season. My research purpose was to observe the group interaction necessary to produce a television show. The day I arrived on the show's set to begin observations, rehearsals and all other preproduction activities were halted as one of the show's actresses made public what had been a private show-business feud.

This event overtly influenced all of the activities leading up to and including the production of the show. How the various production teams worked together no longer seemed very interesting. Rather, my attention shifted to how the producer/writer spoke to the actress via the script because the interaction on the set among cast and crew had shifted to that issue. Events of 2 days of rehearsals and the night of filming were captured using extensive field notes. I was also able to capture each revision of the script and later compared how the characters' interaction was scripted and filmed with the final aired version. After I returned home, I found additional information about the relationships among the ensemble's actresses and the producer/writer in media reports and additional factual information about the show in organizational reports. Had I not been able to redesign the study spontaneously, I would have lost the opportunity to capture this crisis that eventually prompted the demise of the production company that produced the series.

Given that qualitative research focuses on the specifics of the here and now, is it possible to plan for a qualitative research project? Broadly, yes (Lincoln & Guba, 1985). Qualitative researchers start with a focus but are open to the possibility that the focus might change as they observe the interaction. Second, qualitative researchers can plan to use certain qualitative methods, depending upon the initial focus. Here, too, they must recognize that the research method or procedure might change if the focus changes or if the research technique is inadequate or inappropriate once in the interaction setting. Third, theory tends to emerge from the inquiry or observation. Questions can be posed before observation begins, but researchers must be flexible and develop theory from what is observed regardless of their initial assumptions. This is an important point, because the data cannot be specified at the beginning of the project in the way in which quantitative data can. Thus, the form of analysis is inductive rather than deductive.

Recall the discussion of many of these concepts in Chapter 2 and Chapter 4. You can see, then, that a researcher cannot lay out or specify all the details of a qualitative inquiry in advance. Rather, some design issues must be decided as the interaction unfolds. This aspect of qualitative research illuminates its reflexive nature.

COLLECTING QUALITATIVE DATA

What makes for successful data collection and observation? It should be becoming clear that simply observing what is going on, as you would do in your normal day-to-day activities, is not the same as observing in the role of a researcher. The qualitative researcher must employ systematic observation (Lindlof & Taylor, 2002; Weick, 1985). This means that the researcher observes and is aware of the interdependence among the people observed, the social situation, and the context in which the interaction occurs. Moreover, the researcher is engaged in the interaction for prolonged periods of time, is conscious and observant of his or her observing ability and activities, and analyzes the

interaction within the complexity of the situation. Thus, when done by a researcher, observing is purposeful, not accidental.

Observation Strategies

Regardless of which qualitative method you use, you will be making observations of interaction. Some methods are more dependent upon observation than others. Even in conducting field interviews, you should practice observation before, during, and after each interview. Doing so engages you with the interaction setting. There are several different methods for making successful observations. A few are explained here. Your instructor is likely to have other observation techniques to share with you. If you propose and conduct a qualitative study, you, too, are likely to develop a strategy that works well. Remember, however, that each qualitative problem requires a unique solution. Do not become too reliant on one or two methods.

The Seamless Container   One way to structure your observations is to conceptualize the setting and context before you as a seamless container. Think of the interaction setting as being round or oval. Starting to your left, describe what you see and what you hear. When you feel as if you cannot add any other detail to this observation, slowly scan your eyes further to the left, stopping at the next detail that catches your attention (for example, someone walks into the room, a noise from a vending machine, a brightly colored poster on the wall). Once again, make as many detailed observations as you can. When finished, once again slowly scan your eyes further to the left and up to the top of the circle until something else catches your attention. Repeat this process until you have scanned the entire container from your near left, up to the top of the circle, down to the right, and back down to your near right. Now you must include yourself in the observation. How is your presence part of the setting?

A container is a good metaphor for making observations because it can help you describe how things enter or leave the setting. How do people enter the setting—quickly, slowly, or hesitantly? Where do sound and noises come from—inside or outside the space? Are interactions spread

TRY THIS!   **Your Classroom as a Seamless Container**

Sitting in your classroom, start to describe the room according to the seamless container metaphor. Be sure to follow the pattern from your near left, up through the left and to the top of the circle, and to the right and down to your near right. Do not forget to include yourself. Compare your description with that of your colleagues. In what ways do your descriptions differ? Do descriptions differ based on where your seat is located in the room? Do your descriptions differ based on your comfort level in the class? If you were training others to make this type of description, what advice would you give them?

throughout or concentrated in one part of the space? Using the container metaphor can help you isolate the setting and interaction but also can make you cognizant of what is outside the setting and how what is outside becomes part of or affects what is going on inside the setting.

Ask Questions   Restricting your role as researcher to one of asking questions and not providing answers is another way to make observations. When researchers use observation in a qualitative study, they are often entering unfamiliar territory. In such a situation, it is natural to ask questions. It is also natural (and often satisfying) to try to answer those questions too quickly. Your first answer may not be the best or correct answer. One way to overcome this natural tendency is to restrict yourself to asking questions about the people, the setting, and the context.

As an example, assume you are in a doctor's waiting room. You are seated in the area where patients wait to be called back to the examining rooms. To your right is a glass panel that divides the waiting area from the office area. Behind the glass you see a woman who appears to be in her mid-30s. She is a tall brunette and wears a white coat over street clothes. You can see her interact with others in the office, but it is difficult to hear entire conversations. Occasionally, she slides back the glass partition and calls someone to the window to talk with her. After these very short conversations, the person either leaves the doctor's office or returns to wait some more. What questions would you ask about these people, the setting, and the context?

After you jot down your questions, look at them for underlying assumptions you hold. Who is the tall brunette? What is her role in this interaction? What type of interaction is she having with those who appear to be patients? What kind of patients are they? If they are not patients, who are they? What are they doing in this setting? What is the context of the setting? If you have provided answers to these questions or if you restricted your questioning to a particular line of questioning, you may be assuming too much. When you ask questions, your attention is on finding answers. Just be sure that you allow the answers to emerge from the interaction setting and context. Do not assume answers to questions prematurely. If you do so, you are limiting your ability to observe the interaction from a perspective other than your own.

Describing and Analyzing   Describing and analyzing are two different activities. Describing means that you are identifying *what* is going on with *whom*. What are you doing right now? Can you describe your actions and the actions of those around you? Once description is complete, you can begin to analyze *why* or *how* the interaction occurred. Why are you doing what you are doing? How are you doing it?

One good way to capture both description and analysis is to draw a vertical line down the middle of a piece of paper. On the left, describe the activities as they occur. You should regularly note the time so that you can create a timeline of action as well. Do not write anything in the right column of your paper until the action is over and the description is complete. Once it is, go back to the top of your descriptions column. Directly opposite in the right column, analyze what happened by asking "Why?" and "How?" When you are finished with the analysis step, go back to the top and ask if alternative explanations could exist. See Figure 14.1 for an example. This process of describing–analyzing–providing alternative explanations is particularly effective when the interaction or activity is ongoing, making it difficult to stop for periodic assessments and analyses. Practice this technique by watching a situation comedy on television. Remember to describe first, then analyze, and then look for alternative explanations.

Taking Notes

How does a qualitative researcher capture what is seen or heard? Many researchers take **field notes,** or notes that are created on the spot while the interaction occurs. Field notes create a continuous, or sequential, record of what was observed. Be sure to read through and reflect on your notes immediately after you leave the interaction setting. At this point you will want to add detail or jot down questions to consider. Also remember to number and date each page of notes. If your observations are made while moving from one interaction scene to another, be sure to identify the place and people you are observing.

In taking notes, it is better to take more than fewer. Because the interaction is unfolding before you, you never know what detail will become important later on. What may seem trivial initially may become an important link to understanding interaction occurring hours, even days or weeks, in the future. How many notes does qualitative research typically generate? In a 10-month study of call-takers at a 911 center, the researchers' observations resulted in 200 pages of single-spaced typed field notes, whereas one-on-one interviews generated 71 pages of single-spaced text (Tracy & Tracy, 1998). Not all qualitative research will generate this many pages of notes. But the number of pages of notes that resulted should give a clear indication that researchers must take full advantage of capturing their observations.

Whenever possible when taking field notes, it is important to move from generalized descriptions of observations to capturing *participants'* words, phrases, or comments. To represent the participants' meaning, it is essential to capture the words they use and to note the context or situation in which the words were spoken (Emerson, Fretz, & Shaw, 1995). For example, in observing a workshop on facilitation skills, I took the following notes:

Carl did an excellent debrief. He described— To get people's attention: "If you can hear my voice, clap one time; if you can hear my voice, clap two times; if you can hear my voice, clap three times."

Carl modeled excellent facilitation skills and process

- Modeled way to get attention (see above)
- Defined nonprofit
- Described importance of board participation
- Then used discussion questions about these ↑ issues to create interaction with large audience
- Related own experiences
- Described legal obligation of board members

I successfully captured Carl's technique for getting people's attention at meetings. Notice how I set it off with quotations? I failed, however, by describing Carl's debriefing and facilitation skills as "excellent." Who thought they were excellent? Me! I have no idea how the people in the workshop evaluated his skills. Certainly, they did clap when they heard Carl's voice (eventually), and then quieted down to participate in the group activity. However, they might have done so out of a politeness norm, not because they believed Carl's facilitation skills were effective. Thus, in these field notes I made two errors. First, I collapsed description with analysis. Second, I failed to take any notes that could be used as evidence of how the group evaluated or responded to Carl.

Field notes should be completed for all qualitative research designs, even when the primary method of data collection is interviews or focus

Information/Facts/Quotes	Questions/Analyses
8:50　　I arrived 10 minutes early and signed in on the sign-in sheet. Staff members sign in as well when they arrive. Overall, area is quiet. Employees speak to each other when they walk in, but not much. Receptionist does not know where meeting will be held; has to ask someone else.	Wonder why staff signs in and out? This is a regularly scheduled staff meeting; why wouldn't the receptionist know where it is to be held?
9:10　　Meeting is supposed to start at 9; meeting leader still not arrived. I ask the receptionist what might be happening and she said, "Shirley is sometimes late and the meeting does not start until 9:30."	I am feeling frustrated. Staff members do not appear to be upset that the meeting has not started. They appear quite calm and nonchalant. No one mentions or gives any other indication that the meeting is late.
9:25　　Several employees walk into Richard's office as if it is time for the meeting. I go in as well. Chris indicates to me that he is going to run the meeting in Shirley's absence.	This appears to be planned. No one acts as if the meeting is late. Does Chris always lead the meeting when Shirley is absent?
9:30　　Staff members sit around the conference table in Richard's office; Richard takes a seat at the head of the table. There is not room for everyone to sit around the table; some staff members sit in a second row behind the people at the table.	Are meetings always held in Richard's office? Although Richard's office is neat and clean, the room has a temporary feeling. The room is not conducive for the entire group to meet and discuss issues.
9:35　　Chris excuses himself and leaves the meeting. He gives no explanation. While he's gone, Candace asks Julianna to start.	Wonder why Candace took over Chris's role as leader?
9:37　　Julianna starts to give her report when Chris comes back in the room.	Difficult to tell if Julianna waited on purpose for Chris to come back in to the meeting, or if this was just coincidence.
9:38　　Julianna's report is interrupted by other staff members as they request answers to questions. During her report, Verna came in and sat in the second row of chairs.	Julianna spoke loudly with strength, but others do not appear to be overly interested in her report. Julianna makes eye contact with all other staff members sitting around the table.
9:48　　After Julianna finishes, Chris asks Richard to give his report next.	Is there some pattern to the reports? Where is Shirley?

FIGURE 14.1 Capturing Description and Analysis

groups and the interaction will be audio- or video-recorded. Why? As a researcher entering the setting, you need to capture information about the setting and people so you can effectively interpret data collected through other methods. Lindlof and Taylor (2002) recommend that field notes contain enough description so you can write answers to the following questions, for example, after you leave the interaction setting:

Who are these people?

What are their roles and their relationships with each other?

What is this activity they are performing?

How, when, and where is it performed?

What artifacts are usually involved?

What uses these artifacts and how is their use determined? (p. 162)

If you are taking field notes for the first time, notice how the questions begin: Who? What? How? When? Where? Just keeping these simple questions in mind will help you take effective field notes. As Lindlof and Taylor remind us, nothing is so trivial or obvious that it should not be noticed and documented.

Is it ever possible to take your notes with audio or video recording? Yes, but it depends on the situation and your role as researcher. It is unethical to audio- or video-record others without their permission. In some of these cases (for example, a city council meeting), audio, video, or written records of the interaction are likely to exist as part of the public record.

If you do take audio- or video-recording notes, be aware of the following issues. First, some people are uncomfortable talking with recording devices on. They may be afraid of telling you the complete story, or they may be afraid of how they will sound when you play the recording back. Second, if you do make audio or video recordings, offer participants the right to turn off the recording device. Always honor their request and do not resume recording until you have cleared it with them.

Third, you are ethically responsible for maintaining recordings you make and playing them only for those on the research team who must hear or see the recording to complete their data collection or interpretation. There is a distinct difference between making recordings as a researcher and making recordings as a member of the news media. Fourth, do not forget that even the best audio recordings cannot capture the full spectrum of accompanying nonverbal behavior. Likewise, the best video recordings leave out interaction that occurs outside its lens direction and focus. Finally, remember that technical problems can accompany use of these devices (for example, low battery power, missing outlets, equipment failure, and so on).

What about taking notes on your laptop computer? This is not recommended unless you can take notes in a place where using a laptop would be considered a routine feature of the interaction space and where you would not disturb others by tapping on the keyboard. Technical breakdowns and human error here too can destroy hours of detailed observation notes.

Transcribing Notes

Of course, any recorded notes need to be transcribed into written form to make these data easier to analyze and compare with other data. The goal of transcription is to create a verbatim record of the interaction. Whether you do your transcribing or have someone do it for you, the first rule is: Do not "tidy up" the transcripts (Poland, 1995). In other words, do not turn spoken language into conventional or traditional written form. People speak differently than they write. One of the unique contributions of communication scholars is that we capture and analyze data as people produce it, not as it is edited.

After an audio or video recording is transcribed, you should listen to the tape and verify the transcription. This may take two or three passes through the data. However, even an accurate transcription will miss important nonverbal cues from an audio or video recording. Whenever possible, take the extra steps to ensure that written transcripts include the following conversational elements: pauses, laughing, coughing, interruptions, overlapping speech, garbled speech, emphasis, held sounds, and paraphrasing or quoting others.

What If You Cannot Take Notes?

Some interaction settings would make it difficult to take notes. At a wedding, for example, your note-taking behavior would seem strange and inappropriate to others, as well as focus unwanted attention on you. In situations like this, you must retreat to a suitable setting (for example, a break room, a private office, your car) for note taking. Take frequent breaks during observations so that you do not overload your memory. Then, when you leave the interaction setting completely, take additional time to review your notes and add to or clarify them.

What Constitutes Data in Qualitative Research?

The concept of data is broadly cast in qualitative research. Generally, qualitative data are continuous rather than discrete (Fitch, 1994); thus, data often represent a stream or unfolding of events or interactions. Obviously, the notes you take that reflect your observations are data. Recordings of interviews in written, audio, or video form are also data. Written documents—including letters, reports, magazine articles, emails, journals, and minutes—are data. Visual documents that you collect or draw are data. Artifacts can also be collected or captured as data (I once took a photo of the toys on an executive's desk and used it as data). Thus, if you can collect, record, or capture it in some way, then it can be used as data.

Qualitative data exist on a continuum from public to private. Some data represent private or personal phenomena (such as a family scrapbook), available to you only because participants willingly provide you access to them. Other data represent more public phenomena, such as an interaction that occurs in an open and public space or a document from an organization's webpage. Some communication scholars (Fitch, 1994; Tompkins, 1994) argue that at least some of the qualitative data used by researchers should be drawn from public or publicly accessible sources or records. The obvious advantage is that others can verify such data, which adds to the credibility of the research and its findings.

Your Impact as a Researcher

The usefulness of your data will depend to some degree on your ability to acknowledge that who you are will affect what you observe and how you observe it. For example, how does your sex, age, or ethnicity affect your observations? In my observations of a corrections facility (Keyton & Rhodes, 1999), I was made very aware of my sex even though female prisoners were incarcerated and many female officers were present. The severity and controlled structure of the environment confronted me, making me feel uncomfortable dressed in a business suit. I felt more comfortable dressed in a blazer, shirt, and slacks because, in this outfit, I was dressed more like the officers. The point here is that on that first day I was uncomfortable, and those feelings affected my observations.

One way to address these issues is to keep a separate personal journal of your research experience (Lindlof & Taylor, 2002). A private journal, or diary, of your experiences can be a place to capture emotions, acknowledged prejudices, doubts about the research process, and reflections on your role as a researcher. Although it is impossible for researchers to completely remove themselves from the notes they are taking, having a place to vent can be used as a tool for learning about yourself in the researcher role and improving your researcher performance.

There is another impact you have as a researcher, and that is the amount of similarity between your physical and cultural attributes and those of the people whom you are observing will also affect your comfort level.

It may also positively affect your ability to gain access. Being similar can even enhance the quality of the data you collect because you possess some degree of insider knowledge or have some familiarity with the interaction event. But there are also drawbacks. Being similar to the people you are observing may make you blind to differences that exist between you and them. Similarities may make it less likely that you evaluate them or their interactions negatively. Because you look alike, or place yourself in the same or similar categories, you believe you have a common grounding with others. Thus, making harsh evaluations of them is

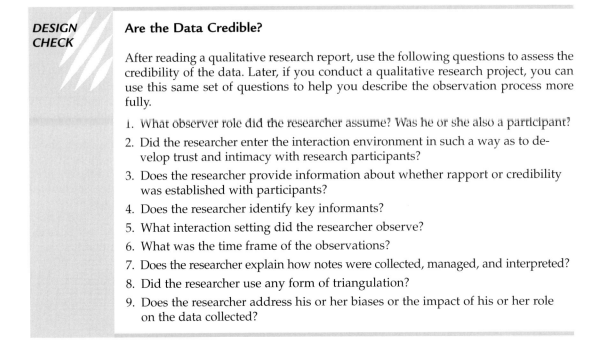

DESIGN CHECK

Are the Data Credible?

After reading a qualitative research report, use the following questions to assess the credibility of the data. Later, if you conduct a qualitative research project, you can use this same set of questions to help you describe the observation process more fully.

1. What observer role did the researcher assume? Was he or she also a participant?
2. Did the researcher enter the interaction environment in such a way as to develop trust and intimacy with research participants?
3. Does the researcher provide information about whether rapport or credibility was established with participants?
4. Does the researcher identify key informants?
5. What interaction setting did the researcher observe?
6. What was the time frame of the observations?
7. Does the researcher explain how notes were collected, managed, and interpreted?
8. Did the researcher use any form of triangulation?
9. Does the researcher address his or her biases or the impact of his or her role on the data collected?

likely to be perceived as an evaluation of yourself. Thus, researchers must be aware of the possible consequences of their identities on the ethics and politics of conducting research (Lindlof & Taylor, 2002).

Qualitative researchers often report their similarities and differences as part of the methodological description in research reports. In that way, readers can also make their own analysis of the degree to which the identity of the observer affected the collection of data and the interpretation of the results. For example, McLaurin (1995) reports on a qualitative study designed to develop prosocial messages for dissemination to African American youth. In the published article, McLaurin describes his racial identity as it relates to his research participants and the steps he took to successfully negotiate the "checking out period" the research participants put him through.

In other settings, using research teams composed of male and female investigators of different ages, races, or cultural groups can help researchers gain broader perspectives on research issues. Because researchers bring their backgrounds,

personal experiences, and demographic characteristics to the collection and interpretation of data, having a diversified research team can help researchers overcome inherent biases.

FINALIZING THE RESEARCH DESIGN

Many decisions must be made before you enter the interaction field. The following list of questions can help you determine if you are ready to conduct a qualitative study (Janesick, 1994):

1. What questions guide your study?
2. Have you identified a site and participants?
3. Have you negotiated access and entry to the site and participants?
4. Have you considered potential ethical issues associated with your study?
5. Do you need informed consent?
6. What is the time frame for your study?
7. Have you selected one or more qualitative techniques for collecting data?

8. Have you addressed credibility issues?

9. Have you considered how theory informs your study? Are you working from an established theory? Or are you attempting to contribute to theory development?

10. Have you identified and acknowledged the biases you bring to the research process?

If you cannot answer one or more of these questions, you are not adequately prepared to enter the field. Collecting data without adequate preparation can waste your (and participants') time. More important, without adequate preparation you may unknowingly engage in activities that are unethical or that can physically or psychologically harm participants.

SUMMARY

1. The role of the researcher is a primary consideration in qualitative research as the researcher is the primary data collection instrument.

2. Researchers can use various roles (complete participant, participant-as-observer, observer-as-participant, or complete observer) to immerse themselves in the interaction setting to collect firsthand data.

3. Developing the purpose for the research project will create a road map for a qualitative study.

4. The focus of a qualitative research study is a broadly stated research question or statement of the researcher's expectations.

5. Although less structured than quantitative research designs, qualitative researchers should still plan and design their study recognizing that flexibility in the field will likely be required.

6. To find their samples, qualitative researchers use snowball, network, purposive, or maximum variation sampling.

7. Gaining access, or getting in, to the research setting includes making the initial contact, negotiating access, establishing entry and operational parameters, and becoming known to the participants.

8. Qualitative data is collected through observation and note taking.

9. The researcher must become immersed in the interaction setting, utilize a variety of observation strategies, and take complete and detailed notes.

10. What counts as data in qualitative research is broadly defined.

11. Who the researcher is—his or her qualities and attributes—will affect what and how he or she observes.

KEY TERMS

commitment acts
complete observer
complete participant
field notes
gatekeeper
key informant
maximum variation sampling
network sampling
observer-as-participant
participant-as-observer
participant observation
purposive sampling
snowball sampling
sponsor

CHAPTER FIFTEEN

Qualitative Methods of Data Collection

Chapter Checklist

After reading this chapter, you should be able to:

1. Distinguish among the various forms of qualitative research methods.

2. Select the most appropriate qualitative research method for your research purpose or research question.

3. Identify the basic steps or process the researcher uses to collect qualitative data.

4. Evaluate the method used for its ability to collect data that is credible.

5. Conceptualize and plan for a field interview.

6. Use open questions in conducting a field interview.

7. Conceptualize and plan for a focus group.

8. Find and select appropriate focus group participants.

9. Develop a focus group outline.

10. Conduct a focus group.

11. Identify several ways to collect narratives.

12. Describe the benefits of ethnographic research.

13. Explain the researcher's role in ethnography.

Just as with quantitative methods, there are a variety of methods for collecting qualitative data. Recall from Chapter 14 the various relationships researchers can create with participants and their interaction environments. The qualitative methods described in this chapter—interviews, focus groups, narratives, and ethnography—are common ways of collecting qualitative data. Although they differ with respect to how the relationship between researcher and participant is constructed and formalized, each requires design and planning before the researcher enters the interaction environment. Just as researchers follow a general process for conducting quantitative research, researchers follow a general process for qualitative research.

Obviously, a researcher using quantitative methods needs theoretical, analytical, and numerical skills. But what skills do researchers working with these qualitative methods need? First, to work effectively with qualitative methods, a researcher needs both theoretical knowledge and social sensitivity (Strauss & Corbin, 1998). This means that the researcher must balance what is being observed with what he or she knows or can draw upon from the scholarly literature. The qualitative researcher must know and understand the literature and the research process and, at the same time, be immersed in the interaction environment. This characteristic allows the researcher to maintain the distance necessary to complete the data analysis.

Second, a researcher must be able to recognize his or her subjective role in the research experience (Strauss & Corbin, 1998). Some qualitative methods create greater distance between the researcher and participants. Even so, in collecting qualitative data, the researcher is always part of the interaction environment. For example, in focus groups, researchers need to be able to avoid asking questions that lead participants toward a particular answer. Without the ability to recognize and avoid this type of bias, it would be impossible for the researcher to gather valid and reliable data. On the other hand, some qualitative methods, like ethnography, create very little distinction between the researcher and the researched. In this case, the researcher's bias and point of view are central to interpretation of the observations, but they still must be recognized and acknowledged.

Finally, a researcher needs to be able to think abstractly (Strauss & Corbin, 1998). This ability allows the researcher to make connections among the collected data, even though no relationships are obvious at first glance. Drawing upon his or her ability to view the world in conceptual terms, the qualitative researcher can uncover meanings and relationships that were hidden or obscured.

As you might expect, many communication researchers can and do use several different techniques in one study. Being familiar with a number of these broadens your skills as a researcher. This chapter provides guidance in planning and conducting field interviews and focus groups and in collecting stories for narrative analysis. Next, the chapter describes ethnography and how the researcher collects data while immersed in the field. The focus of this chapter is on methods of collecting qualitative data. These techniques produce textual data in the form of participants' transcribed or researchers' descriptive accounts. Several methods of qualitative data analysis will be described in Chapter 16.

FIELD INTERVIEWING

Interviews are a practical qualitative method for discovering how people think and feel about their communication practices. But an interview is more than a simple linear process of asking questions and getting answers. **Field interviewing** as a qualitative research method is a semidirected form of discourse or conversation with the goal of uncovering the participant's point of view. Thus, field interviewing goes beyond simply asking questions to obtain factual information.

Field interviews can be challenging because they are minimally structured and conducted in an unstructured environment (Mason, 1993). The interviewer has a general idea of what topics to cover but, at the same time, must draw on terminology, issues, and themes introduced into the conversation by the respondent. Thus, to get the data needed to answer his or her research question, the researcher must have both theoretical and contextual knowledge as well as possess and be comfortable with a wide variety of communication skills.

Sometimes referred to as the "long interview" (McCracken, 1988) or the "depth interview" (Berger, 1998), face-to-face interviewing is a powerful method for understanding how people order and assess their world (Peterson et al., 1994). In conducting an interview, the researcher is trying to meet at least one of the following objectives (Lindlof & Taylor, 2002):

1. Learn about events and interactions that cannot be directly observed.

2. Gain an understanding of a communication event or process from the participant's perspective.

3. Develop a relationship with the participant to infer communication properties and processes.

4. Verify or validate data obtained from other sources.

5. Uncover the distinctive language and communication style used by participants in their natural communication environments.

6. Inquire about occurrences in the past.

To these ends, interviews can be formal or informal. Researchers often use both types, as the different types of information produced by each complement the other. In a study of cultural themes in U.S.-owned companies in Mexico, Lindsley (1999) conducted formal interviews, some lasting as long as 4 hours. To start the interview, she began by asking questions about participants' backgrounds—work experience, work roles, and work responsibilities. Next, she posed a "grand tour" question. In this case, the grand tour question took the form of asking participants to describe a typical workday. The purpose of such introductory questions is to gain background information the researcher will need to analyze and understand subsequent responses and to help the respondent become comfortable with the interviewing process. After these introductory questions, Lindsley focused her questions on the intercultural and cultural interaction issues in which she was interested. To conclude the formal interviews, she asked participants what advice they would give others about intercultural interactions.

In addition to 20 formal interviews, Lindsley (1999) also conducted 30 informal interviews by having conversations with company employees. These informal interviews were unplanned and occurred spontaneously on the job site as well as at other off-site locations. Due to these logistics, Lindsley did not tape-record the informal interviews, as she did the formal interviews. Rather, she completed field notes after she left the interaction setting.

Electronic Interviewing

Although most researchers prefer to conduct interviews in face-to-face settings, there is a trend for collecting interview data through email, websites, and faxes (Fontana & Frey, 2000). Obviously, one advantage is that it is low cost to send and receive emails with participants, or to set up a website with a list of questions on a web form to which participants reply and click to send. These alternatives may be especially relevant if the topic of the study is electronic communication. Another advantage is that electronic interviewing is a way to collect data from participants who are geographically dispersed or unable to meet with researchers.

But a number of disadvantages also exist. Electronic forms of interviewing make it particularly difficult to develop rapport and relationships with participants. Moreover, participant commitment may be difficult to develop or sustain. Markham (1998) describes another disadvantage: Online interviewing can result in fictional social realities. Without the face-to-face interaction and the corresponding nonverbal cues, the opportunity is missed to check out participant sincerity or confusion. Markham's experience with online interviewing suggests that this form can take longer than face-to-face interviews, and result in cryptic responses and less depth. As Fontana and Frey (2000) note, "Asking questions and getting answers is a much harder task than it may seem at first" (p. 645).

The Interview Process

Research investigations that rely on interviewing are composed of seven steps (Kvale, 1996). First, the researcher must conceptualize the study and design the research questions. Second, the researcher must design the interviews, so that the research questions can be addressed. Next, the researcher conducts the interviews. In the fourth step, the interviews, if they were recorded, need to be transcribed. Fifth, the researcher analyzes the data produced by the interviews. Verification is the sixth step; and finally, the description and analyses of the interviews are reported. Thus, interviewing, as a research methodology, is systematic and planned.

Conceptualizing the Interview Study As with most qualitative methods, there are few standards or rules for conducting research interviews. However, there are many points in the interview investigation that require thoughtful selection of alternatives by the researcher. Your objective as a researcher should be to make choices from the methodological options available based on knowledge of the topic (Kvale, 1996). And these choices should be made while not losing sight of the whole—the entirety of the interview as a research process. Because the interview as a research technique is so flexible, the researcher should be able to prepare in advance and argue for the choices made.

In this first stage, the why and what of the research study must be clarified before methodological choices can be made. As with any other research project, the qualitative project begins by examining the published literature.

With this foundation, you should be ready to clarify the purpose of your study. For example, is your study exploratory, seeking to describe or understand a communication phenomenon for which little background research exists? If so, then your interviews will likely be more open and less structured, allowing you to seek new information and create new ways of looking at the topic. Alternately, if your study builds on a substantial foundation of knowledge, then your interviews are likely to be more structured. This structure allows you to compare interview responses from different participants to make comparisons to previously published results. In either case, you cannot design an interview without specifying the research questions that guide your study.

Designing the Interview With the purpose clarified and research questions developed, you are ready to make specific methodological choices. At a minimum, you will need to decide how to find and select your interview participants and then decide on how many participants you will need.

SELECTING RESPONDENTS Often, the focus and context of a qualitative study is so narrowly or specifically defined that not just any participant will do. Generally, researchers are looking for participants with knowledge of a specialized communication environment or for participants representing a certain demographic group. Recall the description of snowball sampling in Chapter 14. This sampling procedure is frequently used to identify participants for interview studies. For example, Braithwaite and Eckstein (2003) used snowball sampling to find individuals with physical disabilities to participate in a study about how disabled initiated assistance and managed unsolicited help from others. The research team made announcements at the office for students with disabilities at a university. They also used their own personal contacts with individuals who had disabilities. Alternately, French (2003) used network sampling to identify potential participants for her study of how victims of acquaintance rape frame their experiences. In this case, the researcher asked a rape crisis center for help in identifying individuals. She also posted fliers at the center and at a college campus. In each of these examples, inclusion criteria, or participant characteristics, were developed by the researchers as an aid to identifying appropriate study participants.

HOW MANY INTERVIEWS ARE ENOUGH? For some research projects, the number of respondents might be limited by the number of people you can identify who have knowledge about your topic or who interact in a particular role you are studying.

In other research projects, the number of respondents is less limited. For example, one research team gained access to four junior high schools in a major metropolitan area (Hecht, Trost, Bator, & MacKinnon, 1997). They were able to recruit students to participate in interviews by means of an announcement over the school's

Where Did the Interviews Occur?

When you read research reports in which interviewing is the primary data collection method, identify where the interviews occurred. Think of yourself in your professional or career role, being asked to participate in a research study about a work topic. Where would be the most likely place for that interview to occur? Would that location give you and the interviewer the privacy you needed? If not, what other locations would be appropriate? If the only office with a closed door were your boss's office, would you feel comfortable being interviewed there? What other locations would hinder truthful responses to the interviewer's questions? As a consumer of research literature, you can make your own assessments of data credibility by putting yourself in the participant's role.

public address system. Using cash and movie tickets as incentives, the research team recruited more than 200 students. In larger schools, the research team randomly selected participants from those students who indicated they wanted to participate. Ultimately, 191 students were interviewed. The research team purposely sought a large number of respondents to reflect the ethnic and gender characteristics of the population.

When finding enough respondents is not a problem, researchers sometimes stop interviewing when the interviews are producing essentially the same data or when they are able to answer their research questions. Recall the concept of maximum variation sampling from Chapter 14. If the data you collect are redundant, you have two choices: You may decide that your interviewing is complete, or you may want to revise your interview schedule, taking into consideration what you have learned from participants thus far.

Conducting the Interview

In an interview, the researcher needs to quickly establish a context for the questioning. Often it helps to frame the interview for the participant. The researcher should define the situation, briefly tell about the purpose of the interview, ask about taping the interview, and ask if the participant has any questions before beginning (Kvale, 1996).

It is also important to select locations and times that are comfortable and accessible for

respondents. In Peterson and associates' (1994) study of equipment safety in farm operations, research assistants conducted interviews in the farmers' home counties in private offices, coffee shops, and farmyards. Conducting the interviews in settings comfortable for and known to the participants helps create a more secure interpersonal setting. Making participants comfortable might require other steps as well. For example, the interview teams in Braithwaite and Eckstein's (2003) study of individuals with disabilities consisted of one interviewer and an informant with a disability. In Buzzanell and Turner's (2003) study of families in which the father had recently lost his job, interviews were conducted with both parents and children. However, each family member was interviewed separately and in private to get each family member's perspective on the experience. Because interviews are neither neutral nor anonymous (for the researcher at least), creating comfortable settings allows the interview to develop as a conversation. This encourages the researcher–participant dyad to move beyond polite conversation between two strangers.

Interviews generally last between 30 minutes and 1 hour. Unless there is an important reason for not doing so, researchers often find that interviewing is best done in pairs. In the team approach, one team member serves as the interviewer, while the other team member is responsible for tape recording or note taking. After the interview is complete and the research team has left the interview site, the team of researchers can discuss and compare their observations and interpretations.

Asking Questions Conducting an interview is more complex than simply asking questions. Rather, the interviewer must carefully construct questions to obtain the needed information or to prompt discussion of the topic of interest. This means that the researcher has thoroughly reviewed the literature for help in defining, narrowing, or extending the area of questioning. It will be difficult to construct a meaningful list of questions, or an **interview guide,** without this preparation. The interview guide may not be followed in exactly the same way in each interview, but it does remind the researcher of which topics to cover. The interview guide for Witmer's (1997) investigation of Alcoholics Anonymous follows.

Orientation and Sample of Guiding Questions for In-Depth Interviews

ORIENTATION

a) *Explanation of this as an organizational culture study*

b) *Assurance that personal anonymity will be preserved in the reporting*

c) *Big Al's permission has been secured for the study*

d) *Permission to use tape recorder*

e) *Results of the completed study available upon request*

QUESTIONS

1. *Tell me a little of your story. What brought you to AA? How did you feel? What was your first experience like in the program? How does it compare with your experience of the program today? How does it compare with your feelings about yourself today?*

2. *What first brought you to the Friendship Group? Why did you stay? If you no longer attend Friendship Group meetings regularly, when did you quit going? Why did you leave?*

3. *How do other meetings compare to the Friendship Group? Are there differences? If so, what are the major differences, in your opinion?*

4. *Can you give an example of the Friendship Group at its best?*

5. *Can you give an example of the Friendship Group at its worst?*

6. *What is your best experience in Alcoholics Anonymous?*

7. *What is your worst experience in Alcoholics Anonymous?*

8. *How do you work the 12 steps? Do you work them differently within the Friendship Group than you have or might outside the Friendship Group? Why? Can you think of an example?*

9. *Have you ever had a Friendship Group sponsor? Have you ever had a sponsor outside the Friendship Group? Do your experiences of being sponsored differ in or out of the Friendship Group? In what ways?*

10. *What adjectives best describe Alcoholics Anonymous for you?*

11. *What adjectives best describe the Friendship Group for you?*

SOURCE: "Communication and Recovery: Structuration as an Ontological Approach to Organizational Culture," by D. F. Witmer, 1997, *Communication Monographs, 64*, pp. 324–349. Used by permission of the National Communication Association.

Regardless of the interview topic, you may want to ask some biographical questions (McCracken, 1988) to help you understand the contextual nature of the interaction you are studying. Depending on the focus of the research study, biographical questions could include

For a study on organizational climate:
- How long have your worked for this employer?
- What is your job title?

For a study on marital communication:
- How long have you been married?
- How long did you date your partner before you married?

For a study on assimilation into American culture:
- How long have you been a resident of the United States?

- Did other family members come with you or follow you to the United States?
- Had you visited the United States before coming here to live?

The respondent's answers to these questions serve two purposes. First, they can help develop rapport between you and your respondent. Second, these responses provide background and clues to interpreting responses more central to your interview topic.

As you construct the interview guide, be sure to include questions that allow the respondent to tell his or her own story (McCracken, 1988). Refer back to the interview guide. Notice how Witmer's questions allowed participants' stories about their experiences with Alcoholics Anonymous to emerge. Thus, questions must be posed in a general and nondirective way. Your questions should encourage respondents to provide their point of view without biasing their response.

Open questions are better than closed questions for initiating dialogue and obtaining fuller descriptions and answers. An open question does not suggest or imply any particular answer. Alternately, a closed question suggests a certain type of answer based on how the question is constructed. Take a look at some examples:

Open Questions	Closed Questions
How would you describe your conflict management style?	Do you always succeed in getting your point across during a conflict?
Why do you believe you are a competent communicator?	Are you a competent communicator?
Why do you watch police dramas on television?	Do you watch police dramas on television because of the suspense in the plot?

Open questions specify the topic or issue you want the respondent to cover. Yet they do not overly restrict how the respondent addresses the issue. Alternately, notice how the questions in the "closed" column suggest one or two alternative answers to the respondent. In each case, the question implies that a "yes" or "no" response is appropriate.

Open questions can help a researcher probe for more detail. Here are ways in which open questions invite respondents to talk about their experiences (Janesick, 2004):

Type of Open Question	Examples
Descriptive question	How would you describe your relationship with your father after you went away to college? Tell me how your relationship with your father changed after you went away to college.
Follow-up question	You mentioned that "winning your way" is important to you. How would you describe "winning your way"?
Experience/ example question	You indicated that you believe you were a competent communicator. How would you describe a competent communicator?
Clarification question	You used the term "democratic leader." How would you define that term? You used the term "democratic leader." Can you describe someone who has those characteristics? You used the term "democratic leader." What do you mean by that term?
Structural/ paradigmatic question	You indicated that you had difficulty talking with your sister. What would you describe as the cause of this problem?

| Comparison/ contrast question | You described several different decisions made by your council. How would you describe the differences in the decisions? |

Regardless of which type of question you are using, be careful not to introduce new language or terminology into the interview. Rather, be sensitive to the terminology used by the respondent. If you are unsure of what is meant, ask probing questions to gain clarity and definition.

Listening   Using interviews to collect data, the researcher, obviously, asks questions. Also crucial is the researcher's ability to listen (Lindlof & Taylor, 2002). Being a good listener will encourage participants to talk. In listening to participants, pay attention by looking at the participant and displaying pleasant and inviting nonverbal cues. Actively listen by asking yourself these questions as the conversation unfolds: "What am I learning now? What else should I learn? What can I do to help the participants to express themselves?" (p. 193).

The Interview Guide   An interview guide indicates the topics to be covered and sequence to be followed in the interview. The interview guide can be highly structured, with the researcher adhering strictly to it. Or the interview guide can be less structured and used as a memory aid as topics are discussed. The nature of the research questions guiding the study directs the structure and formality of the interview guide.

Concluding the Interview   At the conclusion of the interview, the researcher needs to debrief the participant (Kvale, 1996). A good way to conclude the interview and start the debriefing segment is to summarize the main points gleaned from the interaction. The researcher should also summarize any information he or she has heard for the first time (when a series of interviews is being conducted). And because the participant has been polite in responding to the researcher's questions, the researcher should ask if the participant has any questions. If yes, the researcher answers. If not, this is where the researcher thanks the

participant, the interview is concluded, and the tape recorder is turned off.

Recall from Chapter 5 that researchers also use the debriefing segment to explain the purpose of the study, what is known about the problem or topic and the hypotheses tested or questions asked, why the study is important, and what they hope to find. If information was withheld from participants before the interview, now is the time to share it.

Although the researcher will later transcribe the recorded interaction, many researchers find it both necessary and helpful to spend a few minutes reflecting on what was said. Capturing your immediate reactions to the interview, the participant, or the setting in field notes can be helpful later in the analytical steps of the research project.

Transcribing the Interview   In most situations, tape-recording the interview is recommended. Review information in Chapter 5 on obtaining participants' consent before turning on the tape recorder. Taping interviews allows the researcher to concentrate on the interview interaction instead of taking notes. Professional typists or transcriptionists can prepare transcripts, or a member of the research team can prepare the transcript. Recent advances in voice recognition and computer technology also provide a mechanism for transcribing spoken words from a recording into a text document. Still, many researchers prepare their own transcripts because it provides an opportunity to become familiar with the data. Regardless of how it is produced, the written record should be a verbatim account of what was said by both the interviewer and the respondent. Regardless of who types the transcript, the interaction should be captured as given, not corrected or standardized. And the transcript should be verified against the tape recording.

Strengths and Limitations of Interview Research

One obvious advantage of interview research is that the research participant is in front of you for an extended period of time. During your conversations, you can probe more deeply, follow up on a response, or pursue a topic that you did not expect to address. A second advantage is that interviews often provide the only opportunity to collect data on communication that cannot be directly observed.

Because of the strengths noted, interviews often produce an enormous amount of material to be reviewed and analyzed. For example, Braithwaite and Eckstein's (2003) interviews with 30 participants resulted in 310 single-spaced pages of text-based data. Thus, you must have some method for analyzing the data once it is collected.

As with any conversation, the interviewing method can replicate many problems found in other dyadic interactions. It is easy to stray off course, particularly if the respondent is talking. If your respondent strays, you must carefully and politely refocus the conversation (Mason, 1993). However, be careful of cutting off your respondents too quickly. They might be telling you about other events as background to help you understand the point they are trying to make.

The alternate problem occurs when a respondent consents to be interviewed but is hesitant to talk. Two techniques can help. First, be able to ask each question in multiple ways. Although you may prefer one wording of the question, it may not make sense to the respondent. Second, if the respondent has difficulty responding to direct questions, use broadly based questions (for example, "Tell about your day yesterday") to get the respondent talking, and then use follow-up questions to guide the respondent toward the areas of your research study.

FOCUS GROUPS

Another qualitative method that depends on developing conversations with others is the focus group. You may know that focus groups are frequently used in marketing research. But they are also used as a qualitative method in the communication discipline. A **focus group** is a facilitator-led group discussion used for collecting data from a group of participants about a particular topic in a limited amount of time.

Although there are many variations, a focus group is typically a facilitator-led group discussion of 5 to 10 people (Krueger & Casey, 2000). The group meets for 60 to 90 minutes to give participants the opportunity to respond to the facilitator's questions.

The facilitator (who may or may not be the researcher) coordinates the focus group interaction by using a discussion guideline. Like the interview guide described earlier, the discussion guideline is a series of questions to help the facilitator prompt participant interaction. It provides a semistructured interaction experience but is flexible enough to allow the facilitator to take advantage of unexpected twists and turns in the group's conversation.

Respondents are encouraged to interact with one another, not just respond to the facilitator's questions. In fact, one of the advantages of using the focus group methodology is the opportunity it provides to listen to participants talk about the topic among themselves without direction or input from the facilitator. This is an important goal for the facilitator to achieve, as there should be no pressure for the participants to reach any type of consensus. A focus group is not a decision-making group.

Focus groups are an especially good way to capture the ideas and perceptions of difficult-to-reach populations. As an example, Chapel, Peterson, and Joseph (1999) conducted focus groups with youth assigned by courts to rehabilitative programs. All of the participants had committed felony offenses and were at risk of being removed from their families and placed in correctional facilities. To stimulate their discussions, participants viewed seven anti-gang television announcements. A moderator then led them through a discussion of seven questions designed to capture their ideas about how to create effective anti-gang ads, how to decrease gang membership, and what, if any, were the unintended consequences of anti-gang advertising.

The unique advantage of using focus groups to collect data is that it allows participants to offer their viewpoints relative to the viewpoints of others. For example, Dougherty (2001) investigated the different ways men and women used sexually laden interaction in a stressful hospital setting. Specifically, the researcher was interested in discovering how male and female employees differed in their labeling such interaction as sexual harassment. Look at the excerpt on the next page. Dougherty used this segment of interaction from the focus group to demonstrate how men perceived sexual behavior as functional rather than as sexual harassment.

Jack (the moderator): Let me ask you this. What is your definition of sexual harassment?

Male B: I think it's more of a, something personal to person. You know?

Male C: Yeah.

Male B: You do something to that person. Um, I tell a dirty joke out loud, I don't think that's sexual harassment. I don't think a funny joke posted on a board is sexual harassment. If I do something either physical or directly toward, directed toward you. If I make a comment about you, or I tell a joke maybe strictly toward you, or I physically touch you in a [sexual] way, yeah, that is. But I think something. I think like [Male C] said, that stress reliever. That's how our department runs. I mean boy.

Jack: Talk about that stress reliever.

Male B: Oh, telling dirty jokes.

Male C: Yeah.

Male A: Something to lighten up the mood. (p. 381)

Notice how participants in the group develop an explanation for how sexually laden interaction is not sexual harassment in their work setting. In a focus group, participants have the opportunity to refer to other participants' comments, and confirm or challenge what someone else says. Most important, participants are stimulated by the ideas of others, often resulting in a chaining or cascading of information, as in the example above.

Thus, this focus group interaction and others like it succeed in exploiting the *group effect* (Carey, 1994). In other words, the group setting provides an opportunity for participants to create insights about a topic that otherwise would not be easily discovered or easily accessible.

Planning Focus Group Research

It may seem relatively easy to invite a group of people to meet together and discuss a topic. Yet, to conduct focus group research, a more systematic process is required. The researcher must identify selection criteria for the type of participant desired and then figure out where to find enough of these individuals for three to five focus groups. The researcher must develop a discussion guide and then train or practice for this specialized form of group interaction.

Selecting Participants Like research designs that use interviews to collect data, focus group participants are usually solicited through snowball, network, or purposive sampling.

In addition to finding appropriate participants, researchers must also be concerned with how participants are grouped together. Generally, it is best to select individuals who possess similar characteristics and meet your selection criteria but who are also strangers. Ideally, the selection goal is to create a group of participants with homogeneous backgrounds but dissimilar attitudes and perspectives. The homogeneity among participants encourages free-flowing conversation (Morgan, 1997).

Alternately, when the focus group topic is sensitive or controversial, it is best to invite respondents who are familiar with one another and who hold similar attitudes. This is the strategy employed by Press and Cole (1995) in their focus group investigation of the abortion debate. They argue that semistructured focus group interviews provided a casual and intimate setting, which was also supportive and nonconfrontive. They believe that such a setting was optimal for gathering data about the personal, controversial, and potentially emotional issue of abortion. Although this level of familiarity may be beneficial in such cases, the moderator must be aware that participants familiar with one another may avoid talking frankly about the most intimate, personal, or controversial topics (Morgan, 1997).

Whether you use participants who are strangers or who are familiar with one another, potential participants should be screened before the focus group meets. Using a few well-selected questions during a phone call provides assurance that participants meet your inclusion criteria.

Once the researcher has found appropriate participants, they must be motivated to actually attend the focus group discussion. You are more likely to secure their agreement if you provide participants with a few details. They should be informed of the location, time, date, duration, and general topic of the focus group. Because many marketing firms conduct focus groups, be sure to indicate that your focus group is part of a research project and not associated with the marketing or selling of any product. A follow-up phone call a day or two before the focus group event will help maintain participants' interest and motivate their attendance.

Most focus groups range in size from 5 to 10 participants. With fewer than 5 participants, the facilitator may have difficulty sustaining a conversation. With more than 10 participants, it may be difficult for the facilitator to control the discussion or for every participant to have the opportunity to talk. As a practical matter, the researcher should overrecruit by 20% for each group, because it is likely that some participants will not follow through on their commitment to participate (Morgan, 1997).

Most researchers follow the general rule of scheduling three to five focus groups for a research study (Morgan, 1997). Research and experience have demonstrated that conducting more groups does not usually result in additional meaningful insights. But conducting fewer than three increases the likelihood that the researcher will miss an important aspect of discussion. Practically, researchers should plan to conduct three to five focus groups, with the possibility of holding more if the last scheduled focus group is still producing new and helpful data.

Conducting Focus Group Research

The group discussion to which you have invited participants is not a freewheeling conversation, nor is it rigidly controlled or structured. The researcher makes decisions about how much structure the discussion will require and how conversation among participants will be encouraged. More-structured focus group discussions use a standardized set of questions for every group. Less-structured discussions may be stimulated by just a few questions and rely more heavily on group dynamics that develop among participants. You may choose one strategy over another or combine the two.

Most focus group discussions require 90 minutes. In that length of time, the moderator can facilitate introduction of the participants, serve refreshments, conduct the discussion according to the outline, and summarize what he or she heard to receive feedback from the participants. In recruiting participants, it is wise to identify their expected time commitment as 2 hours. This provides the moderator with a cushion of time and some flexibility. A good moderator will never run over the time commitment expected by participants.

Guiding and Maintaining the Conversation

Choosing an appropriate and effective moderator, or facilitator, for a particular focus group situation is critical. Ideally, the focus group moderator is someone with whom participants can identify. It is also important to select a moderator the participants will perceive as credible. In most cases, this means that the moderator should share important characteristics with participants. For example, to study sexual harassment, Dougherty (2001) used a male facilitator to conduct a focus group with men while she conducted a focus group with women. Both facilitators conducted the focus group when participants of both sexes were included.

Likewise, it is important for the moderator to have the communication skills to gently guide a group during its discussion (Herndon, 1993). Obviously, the moderator must communicate in a style that encourages participants to talk. The moderator must also be able to identify when probing questions are required to gain clarity and depth. The moderator is not an interviewer. Thus, he or she needs skill to avoid the spoke-and-wheel pattern of communication, in which participants talk only to the moderator. The moderator sometimes must remain silent to encourage participants to respond to one another. Another interactive technique is for the moderator to ask one participant about his or her reaction to something said by another participant.

The Focus Group Outline   Although some focus group facilitators prefer to strictly follow a **focus group outline** or topic guide, other facilitators use the outline for themselves to identify which topics have or have not been covered. Depending on the context and participants, some focus group discussions can evolve very quickly into dynamic discussions. Thus, the facilitator may need only to start the discussion with a series of opening questions and then let the discussion among participants develop from there. During the group's discussion, however, the facilitator should be checking to determine if all of the desired topics have been covered. If not, introducing questions may be necessary.

As with any research design, a search of the published research literature will provide you with ideas for developing questions or topics for your outline. In particular, look for research suggestions at the end of the discussion section after the results have been interpreted. Some research reports identify a special section of the report for future research considerations. These can be valuable sources for focus group questions and topics.

Generally, the discussion outline is planned as a funnel to take advantage of the types of responses both structured and less-structured discussions provide (Morgan, 1997). With this strategy, opening questions are broad to encourage free discussion among participants. A good opening question to start discussion follows the form of "One of the things we are especially interested in is_____. What can each of you tell us about that?" (Morgan). All participants should be able to respond to this question because they were invited to participate based on their expertise, knowledge, or experience with the issue. Although it is critical that each participant have the opportunity to talk, this type of broad opening question also allows you to identify what other topics or issues participants associate with the issue of the focus group.

As participants become comfortable hearing themselves talk and comfortable discussing the issues, the moderator can move to a more structured phase of the discussion and ask specific questions. This strategy allows the researcher to capture participants' more spontaneous ideas and comments early in the discussion as well as participants' responses to more specific questions. Here is the focus group topic guide for Dougherty's (2001) study of sexual harassment:

1. Discuss each of your stories about sexual harassment. What would you do if you were the victim in this story?

2. What is your definition of sexual harassment?

3. What is the biggest problem with sexual harassment in organizations today? At HCO?

4. Describe your greatest fear related to sexual harassment. What do you think are men's [women's] greatest fears related to sexual harassment?

5. Why does sexual harassment occur?

6. Why do some men sexually harass women?

7. How can people effectively respond to sexual harassment?

8. Describe an ideal sexual harassment policy. (p. 402)

Data From Focus Group Discussions

The data collected in this method are the audiotaped or transcribed group interactions. In addition to taping and transcribing, the moderator should also make field notes immediately after each session. The moderator should identify what issues or topics were talked about most, what issues or topics appeared to be most salient for participants, what issues or topics participants appeared to avoid, even after direct questioning, and any contradictory information participants provided. These elements should be reviewed later in conjunction with analysis of the transcribed group interaction.

As with individual interviews, focus groups can produce a large amount of data—data that are useless unless they are analyzed in some fashion. As with interviews, the analytical process should stem from the research literature and the research questions that prompted the study.

Focus Group Strengths and Limitations

Probably the greatest strength of focus group research is that it directly stimulates interaction among participants on the topic in which the

TRY THIS!   **Motivating Attendance at Focus Groups**

Press and Cole (1995) sought their focus group participants through newspaper advertisements and announcements at local PTA meetings. For each of the focus group topics below, what ideas do you have for finding focus group participants?

Focus Group Topic	What Type of Participants Would You Seek?	How/Where Would You Seek Them?
Investigation commissioned by the humane shelter in your community for developing persuasive messages to spay and neuter dogs and cats.		
Proprietary research for the local committee of the Republican Party who want to develop a campaign to increase voter turnout at local elections		
Scholarly investigation to discover why parents allow their children to watch programming of which they disapprove		
Scholarly investigation for developing more effective methods of doctor–patient interaction		

Compare your ideas for finding focus group participants with those of others in your class. What would motivate individuals to participate in these focus groups?

researcher is interested. Although a facilitator directs the interaction, the group discussion format provides views and opinions in the participants' own words. Moreover, the discussion format allows consensus or conflict among participants to emerge, and these interactions could not occur if participants were interviewed separately (Morgan & Krueger, 1993). Thus, a focus group

Research or Selling?

Many consumers are familiar with focus groups because they are a popular technique for companies to learn how to better market their products and services. Even political candidates use focus groups to test how campaign messages and slogans will be received. Because of the widespread popularity of focus groups as a marketing or public relations tool, individuals selected to participate may be hesitant to agree even if the focus group is for a research project because they question the ethics (and motivation) of the person who invites them to participate.

To counter this hesitancy, researchers must develop carefully planned invitations to participate. Think of yourself as an individual receiving a phone call and being asked to participate in a focus group for a research project. What information would you want to know before you agree to participate? What clues would you use to distinguish between an invitation to participate in a marketing focus group and an invitation to participate in a research focus group? Are there any persuasive strategies that could convince you to participate in a focus group research project? What could the researcher offer as an incentive to encourage your participation?

can produce concentrated amounts of information on a specific topic. The discussion format also allows the moderator to follow conversation paths that were not expected.

Focus groups are a good research method to select for the following situations (Janesick, 2004). If you are new to an area or topic of research or new to studying communication of a particular target group, a focus group can help you orient yourself to the area. Information from participants can help you identify issues that need to be addressed as well as identify areas that you need to learn more about before conducting additional research. Focus groups can also help you become familiar with the language and behavior of people with whom you have little familiarity.

Focus group methodology is extremely flexible. In some cases, researchers enter with a broad research question with the intent to discover the themes that emerge naturally from the interaction. From the emergent themes research questions and hypotheses can be generated for future studies. Alternately, focus groups can be used to help researchers become familiar with a research setting before using other data collection methods. For example, Ballard and Seibold (2004) conducted a focus group with employees in the

organization in which they planned to conduct a subsequent research project. Their goal was to learn more about the nature of the work performed, the challenges and rewards employees encountered in conducting their work, and their experiences surrounding the specific topic of the subsequent research project. Using a focus group first, the research team was able to gain a better understanding of the environment in which employees worked and interacted.

Another strength of focus groups is their ability to generate information about the same topic from different types of people. For example, if you are interested in how children make media choices, you could conduct focus groups with a variety of people who can give you that information. Conducting focus groups separately with parents from two-parent households, parents from one-parent households, children, elementary school teachers, and babysitters would provide different perspectives on the same topic. Thus, focus groups are an excellent choice for gathering comparative data about complex behaviors.

The advantages of the focus group method occur through participants' interaction. Likewise, so do the disadvantages. Depending on the mix of focus group participants, a talkative or opinionated member of the group can dominate the discussion, inhibiting others' contributions. Another risk is that participants in the group will come to a quick consensus because some participants are hesitant to express opinions that are the opposite of the opinions held by other participants (Morgan, 1997). Both of these limitations artificially restrict individual input, hence, generalizability of the data.

Because a focus group is stimulated by the moderator's questions, the interaction that results is not completely natural. Thus, there is always some concern that the moderator has overly influenced participants and their reactions (Morgan, 1997). Some researchers avoid this bias by asking someone else to assume the moderator role. When this is the case, the researcher maintains the research focus by generating the focus group outline for the moderator to use and by observing (if possible) all focus group interactions. There is a certain amount of skill needed to conduct a focus group. Researchers need to honestly assess this skill set before making a decision about who will moderate the groups.

Another risk of focus groups is that it is easy for researchers to overgeneralize focus group findings. After having listened to participants' interaction and having facilitated several focus groups, researchers find that the issues participants talk about seem real and valid. Researchers must balance their findings, however, with respect to how focus group participants were found, selected, and even encouraged to participate. How widely was the net cast for participants? Thus, researchers must carefully assess the degree to which their focus group results can be applicable to others from the same or similar populations.

COLLECTING STORIES

Many communication scholars look to the stories, or **narratives,** people tell as a way of knowing, understanding, and explaining their lives. Stories are a natural part of interaction in many contexts because people create and tell stories to organize and interpret their experiences. As a result, narratives can be a reliable guide to the storyteller's beliefs, attitudes, values, and actions.

By their very nature, stories are subjective because participants relate their conceptualization and understanding of events. Collecting and analyzing stories, or narratives, can provide a method for uncovering how seemingly isolated events are actually part of a larger interaction environment, identifying the explanations and justifications people give for their past actions, and determining how participants make sense of particular events.

Sources for Stories

Stories can be captured in several ways (Brown & Kreps, 1993; Query & Kreps, 1993). First, stories can be collected from one-on-one interviews. Often, a simple question like "Can you tell me a story about _____?" will generate the narratives a researcher is seeking on a particular topic. Or a set of questions can be used as a loosely structured interview, with questions phrased so that members will likely tell stories in answering the questions (Meyer, 1997). Note, however, that using this technique will not necessarily generate stories for which participants have firsthand knowledge.

Second, stories can be collected through the critical incident technique (Flanagan, 1954). **Critical incidents** are those events in an individual's life that stand out as being memorable, positively or negatively. For example, participants are asked to focus on a specific relationship (such as their relationship with their first-grade teacher) or reflect on a specific event (such as their last birthday) or behavior (such as their last disagreement with their supervisor). By focusing the respondent's attention in this way, the story told is the individual's firsthand account of events, not a story he or she has heard from others. The researcher then uses probing open-ended questions to elicit detailed accounts, or stories, about a specific interaction context.

Critical incidents can also be collected about mega-events that generate extraordinary social concern (Carter, Kang, & Taggart, 1999). Through media coverage, incidents like the September 11, 2001, terrorist attacks on the World Trade Center in New York City and the Pentagon in Washington, DC, generate socially critical incidents. Researchers can ask participants to tell their story about the incident to capture their interpretation and understanding of the event.

Critical incidents can also be collected through questionnaires. For example, Miller-Day and Dodd (2004) asked participants to "complete an online questionnaire that will ask you to share a story about a time when your parents talked with you about alcohol, tobacco, or other drugs" (pp. 73–74). Although this questionnaire was online, researcher follow-up was embedded in the questionnaire. After giving space for participants to record their stories, the researchers asked a series of follow-up questions, including: "Who initiated or started the conversation? How was the conversation initiated or started? How old were you at the time of this conversation?" (p. 75). Thus, the initial open-ended and follow-up questions gave participants the opportunity to share their stories with salient or memorable aspects emerging.

Third, and less directly, stories can exist naturally in the course of everyday conversation. These can be collected through the various levels of participant observation. Witmer (1997) collected 60 narratives by attending open meetings held by the world's largest and most successful Alcoholics Anonymous group. As a regular feature of the open meeting, the group's secretary would select "ten-minute" speakers shortly before each meeting. Thus, the stories Witmer collected were those told spontaneously to all who attended the open meetings.

Naturally occurring stories were collected for Coopman and Meidlinger's (2000) study of how stories in a Roman Catholic parish confirmed or challenged the organization's power structure. At the time of the study, Meidlinger was an active member of the parish and had also been employed by the parish. Thus, she was engaged in the participant observer research role. To collect stories, she ate lunch with parish staff members over a period of 6 months. Immediately, or as soon as possible, after lunch, Meidlinger created field notes to capture the stories, responses to the stories, and general topics discussed.

Fourth, narratives can also be found in many print forms. For example, Bunton (1998) used newspaper articles, photographs, editorials, letters to the editor, and advertisements about the largest hog-producing corporation in the United States. The researcher compiled a chronological narrative from these sources over a 4-year period from two competing local newspapers. In comparing the stories from the two chronological narratives about the controversial hog farm, Bunton analyzed the ability of the two papers to perform their ethical responsibility to their communities.

Collecting multiple narratives from multiple sources about one event allows the researcher to explore the relationships among the different stories told. How do stories differ? What elements are the same? Using this technique, O'Connor (1997) examined how different people accounted for the same decision-making event in one organization. Having access to one key individual, O'Connor collected the different narrative accounts through letters, memos, newspaper articles, other documentation, and one in-depth interview.

In this case, the narrative starts with the very lengthy memo that Scott, a midlevel manager, sends to a colleague about personnel practices in their organization. This memo addresses decisions that certainly deserve a response. But Scott does not receive a response from the person to whom he sent the memo. Rather, Scott's memo is referred to the vice president of human resources, who then responds by memo to Scott. Although the primary story was established in the two initial memos, O'Connor was able to continue to follow the story through five more memos and letters, one public statement, and two newspaper articles. Thus, a more macrolevel story—how this organization handles personnel decisions—was available in the rich network of narratives.

A researcher can also collect stories from many individuals about the same type of event. In the November 1992 issue of *Journal of Applied Communication*, the journal's editor printed 20 narratives about sexual harassment, each written from the viewpoint of a victim of harassment. Stamp and Sabourin (1995) collected stories from abusive men. The research team asked participants, who were identified abusers enrolled in a treatment program, to describe their most recent violent episode with their relational partner. In most cases, participants told of the violence that led to their placement in the treatment program. The stories revealed participants' beliefs about why the abuse occurred, as well as descriptions of the nature and severity of the abuse. The point is: Stories, or narratives, can be found in many places, may have more than one storyteller, and can be interpreted from multiple perspectives.

DESIGN CHECK

Finding Participants

Finding the stories a researcher wants often means finding people who can tell that particular type of story. This was Ana Garner's (1999) predicament when she wanted to examine how reading fiction as adolescents influenced the way in which women constructed their identities. To find women willing to tell their stories about this period of their life, Garner searched internet sites that had women as their primary members. the sites she searched were devoted to content areas such as engineering, education, history, law, science and technology, theology, journalism, and theater. To be representative of all women, she also contacted sites devoted to women of color, lesbians, feminists, and women with disabilities. After gaining permission to post a message at each site, she asked women to contact her if they were interested in telling her their stories about reading as young girls. Within days, Garner received over 125 email responses. what other specialized populations could you reach by searching the web that might otherwise be difficult to locate?

Strengths and Limitations of Narrative Research

One of the advantages of collecting narratives is the richness and depth of the data collected. Moreover, stories can be collected about communication events that would be difficult or impossible to observe. There are, of course, risks when researchers ask participants to remember some types of stories. In collecting stories that are potentially troubling or negative, participants may recreate past trauma in their retelling (Clair, Chapman, & Kunkel, 1996). Researchers must also be concerned about the extent to which the story told is real or embellished.

Whereas collecting stories can create a rich qualitative database, some narratives can be very long, and not all story elements are equally important. Part of your job as the researcher in analyzing the narratives is to draw the readers' attention to the most compelling parts of the story.

ETHNOGRAPHY

Ethnography is the study and representation of people and their interaction. Usually, it is the holistic description of interactants in their cultural or subcultural group (Lindlof & Taylor, 2002). In conducting ethnographic studies, researchers immerse themselves in the interaction field for long periods of time—often, but not necessarily, becoming one of the interactants. This immersion allows the researcher to observe and understand how communication is generated and responded to in a particular context (Braithwaite, 1997a). Thus, ethnography relies on some form of participant observation. But ethnographers may also use other strategies for collecting data. Here are the details of Braithwaite's participation and observation experiences at Navajo Community College, a bilingual, bicultural college:

> Eight months of participant/observation began by arranging to live in the dormitory at Navajo Community College with students. When at the college, I ate in the cafeteria, and used the library and computer center in order to spend as much time as possible in context. I also sat in on Department Head meetings, planning meetings of Navajo Language and Culture Faculty, campus meetings, and celebrations such as graduation ceremonies and Tribal Sovereignty Day. I participated in many off-campus activities such as overnight hikes through Canyon De Chelly and Pow Wows through the Navajo Nation. Systematic data collection involved observing over 100 hours of classroom interaction. . . . Additionally, I developed and taught a summer course at Navajo Community College. (pp. 222–223)

During these experiences Braithwaite collected over 300 pages of field notes in which he identified specific verbal and nonverbal speech events. He also collected documents published by the college as well as textbooks used in courses and conducted semistructured interviews with students and faculty.

You will also see the label **ethnography of communication** to describe some ethnographic accounts. Ethnography of communication is a theoretically driven method of ethnography in which researchers focus on language or speech communities to produce highly detailed analyses of how symbolic practices are expressed in a particular social structure (Lindlof & Taylor, 2002). Three key assumptions provide a foundation for ethnographic studies from the ethnography of communication tradition (Phillipsen, 1992). First, "speaking is structured" (p. 9) and rules guide the structure. An ethnographer seeks to identify the code, or rules, of communication that a speech community uses. Second, "speaking is distinctive" (p. 10). Each speech community differs in its code of community. Thus, communication can only be understood by studying it in its cultural setting. Third, "speaking is social" (p. 13). As members of a speech community communicate with one another they are constructing their social lives and social identities.

Scholars who do the fieldwork to produce such data are called ethnographers. As an ethnographer, the scholar shares the environment of those he or she is studying. The ethnographer experiences firsthand the environment, problems, background, language, rituals, and social relations of a specified group of people. In becoming intimate with the communication, the ethnographer should then be equipped to develop a rich, complex, yet truthful account of the social world being studied (Van Maanen, 1988).

Communication scholars use ethnography to investigate a wide variety of interaction contexts that are impossible to simulate. For example, Miller (2002) was already a member of her university community when the bonfire collapsed at Texas A&M University. Hearing the news of the bonfire collapse on the radio created first an emotional response, and then urgency and need to understand what was happening and how it affected routine events at the university. "After the bonfire collapse, I realized very quickly that I would want to write—in some form—about my experiences on those days" (p. 577). Capturing her own experiences in a journal, Miller monitored and collected media reports, collected internal university communication, attended special bonfire events, and talked formally and informally with others about their experiences.

This type of ethnography is an **autoethnography** because it is autobiographical; the researcher is also a participant. Autoethnography "zooms backward and forward, inward and outward, distinctions between the personal and cultural become blurred, sometimes beyond distinct recognition" (Ellis & Bochner, 2000, p. 739). This type of research is embodied in its writing, and is highly personal and emotional. Because the writing is personal, autoethnography often but not always has the same structure as other research articles.

As another example of ethnography, Kramer (2002) gained entrance to a community theater group by auditioning and being selected for a part in an upcoming production. Being cast in one of the play's main roles immersed the researcher in the interaction scene and provided him with the opportunity to both interact with others in the scene and observe others. In this case, Kramer wanted to examine "How do members of a community theatre group communicate to construct, maintain, and negotiate their roles in the group given their memberships in other groups?" (p. 154). By attending all group functions, such as auditions, rehearsals, performances, and cast parties, he was able to collect data on 75 of the approximately 82 hours the group was assembled. Taking notes was made easier for him, as he was cast as a lawyer and carried a legal pad in the part of his character. Thus, he was able to take some notes during the interaction and then expanded them into field notes later.

Depending on the interaction context, time spent in the field varies dramatically. Minimally, researchers would need to collect data from their own interaction or the interaction they observe over several days. At the other extreme, researchers may relocate themselves into the neighborhoods they study, as Conquergood (1994) did for his study of gang communication. Whatever the time frame, researchers must be in the interaction field long enough to gain understanding of the interaction around them. To prepare themselves for such lengthy stays, many ethnographers spend considerable time reading, making preliminary visits, and talking with others who interact in the field of interest.

Practically, ethnography is the label applied to research with the following features (Atkinson & Hammersley, 1994):

1. There is a strong interest in exploring a particular social phenomenon. Researchers are unlikely to have well-developed research questions from which to begin the study because the phenomenon has been unexplored or underexplored.

2. Because the field is underexplored, the researcher must work with data that are unstructured or data that do not fit neatly into categories.

3. Research is focused on a small number of cases—even one case in detail can be sufficient.

4. Analysis of the data produces deep, thick descriptions and explanation of meanings and functions of communication behavior.

Investigating the Here and Now

One of the strengths of ethnography is the opportunity it provides for the researcher to capture interaction as it occurs in its natural context. As an example, Braithwaite (1997b) captured the public interaction of members of a Vietnam veterans' group as he participated in over 100 meetings with the veterans; these ranged in length from 15 minutes to 48-hour-long weekend activities. Besides being a member, he also served the group by being its secretary, vice president, and president. In addition to being a complete participant, Braithwaite conducted unstructured interviews with members of the group to check the accuracy of his observations and interpretations. Thus, Braithwaite was able to capture what was said, by whom, to whom, and in what environmental and situational context. As a result, he had the opportunity to capture and interpret communal themes

as they developed naturally within and across the interaction events of the group.

One of those themes centered on veterans returning from the war. In the "coming home" theme, veterans' stories focused on the intense public criticism of the war that was directed toward them by virtue of their role in it. Braithwaite explains:

> Although few veterans expressed feeling ashamed that they fought in the war, the public criticism resulted in many telling stories about feeling they that they had to hide the fact that they were Vietnam veterans. The following interaction during an informal meeting illustrates one "coming home" theme:
>
>> Two veterans were talking to an employment counselor, also a Vietnam veteran, about their attempts to get work. When the counselor pointed out that certain jobs were supposed to have hiring preference for veterans, one of the men replied, "I never put down I was a vet on any job application, it just wouldn't done any good for me. They see that and, bang, you are out . . . another psycho vet." The other veteran added, "You know that's the way it is. It got so I didn't want anyone to know I was a 'Nam vet. What good would that have done?" The employment counselor nodded in apparent agreement as the men spoke. (field notes, informal meeting) (p. 434)

Entering the Scene

Generally, researchers do not go through a formal process to gain entry to the research setting. Rather, ethnographers become part of the interaction environment, even if they only observe the interaction. If researchers are already natural actors in that environment, others may not know that they are also researchers. If researchers are entering a new interaction context, then they must join the interaction in a presumably normal way and gain the confidence of those they are observing. Thus, the researchers become integrated within the interaction and the surroundings so that others interact with and toward the researchers as if they are normally a part of that interaction environment.

DESIGN
CHECK

Reading Ethnography

1. Does the author give details about how he or she entered the scene?
2. Does the author describe the type and length of involvement and interaction with participants?
3. How does the author describe the method of data collection?
4. Is the description of the researcher's experience detailed enough for you to feel as if "you are there"?
5. Are the details of the methodology sufficient to warrant the claims made by the researcher?
6. Are there plausible explanations for the communication described other than the ones presented by the ethnographer?

In some cases where physical characteristics or formal rules of membership would exclude a researcher from joining the interaction without notice, the researchers declare their research status, negotiate permission to do research, and then assimilate themselves into the interaction setting. Thus, with respect to the participation–observation roles of qualitative research described in Chapter 14, ethnographers assume a role more influenced by participation than observation. As a result, researchers are often unable to take field notes while participating. They must find time and space away from the environment's interactants to write down or audiotape their observations.

Recording Observations

From an ethnographic viewpoint, almost anything can count as data. Thus, the ethnographer must be immersed in the field and notice everything—informal and formal talk, posted written messages, written reports and letters, as well as the design, layout, and use of the interaction space. But most important, ethnographers take voluminous notes.

What type of notes do ethnographers take? Some researchers keep detailed written journals; others audiotape their notes. In either case, the notes are generally made away from the interaction environment. When multiple researchers collect data, it is important to provide some structure for note taking so that comparisons can be made. In the study of advice, Goldsmith and Fitch (1997) report that all research team members made field notes on each advice-giving episode as soon as possible after the interaction. To provide structure to their notes, each team member used a protocol to describe the setting, the participants and their relationship, the perceived purposes and outcomes of the interaction, the sequence and organization of actions, the tone and mood of the conversation, through what channel the advice was given, norms or background knowledge necessary to understand the advice-giving event, and a label or phrase that could be used to describe the event to someone else. These notes were presumably made after and away from the advice-giving setting, although the authors do not state this explicitly in the description of their methods.

Strengths and Limitations of Ethnographic Research

An obvious benefit to ethnography is the rich, deep description that it offers. Reading ethnography is often like being inside the communication environment, rather than being an outsider. Because the researcher is immersed in the cultural and social context where the communication occurs, he or she is able to develop an intimacy with both the communication context and its interactants in a way not possible through other methods.

The most obvious limitation of ethnographic research is the time researchers must commit to the project. Conducting ethnography requires first learning and then understanding the language, concepts, categories, practices, rules, beliefs, and values of those being studied (Van Maanen, 1988). Only after researchers are saturated in the data can they write the research report that does descriptive and analytical justice to the communication environment observed. Thus, ethnographers must commit the time and energy necessary to become more than just familiar with their research surroundings—they must become intimate with the communication environment. As a result of such intense involvement, researchers can overidentify with the participants and lose distance and analytical objectivity.

SUMMARY

1. Different qualitative research methods create different relationships between researcher and participants.

2. Interactions with participants and observations of their interactions with others are captured as textual data.

3. Field interviewing is an informal or practical qualitative method for discovering how people think and feel about communication practices.

4. Researchers use an interview guide composed mostly of open questions to encourage the respondent to tell his or her own story.

5. Most interviews are audiotaped, transcribed, and verified back to the tape.

6. Guided by a facilitator, a focus group is comprised of 5 to 10 people who respond to the facilitator's question in a group discussion format.

7. Focus groups are a practical method for addressing applied communication problems, and capturing the ideas of difficult-to-reach populations.

8. Focus groups take advantage of the chaining or cascading of conversation among participants.

9. Narratives, or stories, can be collected in interviews, as critical incidents, from questionnaires, from the course of everyday conversation, and in many forms of printed communication.

10. Ethnography is a qualitative research method in which the researcher immerses him- or herself in the communication environment for a long time, often becoming one of the interactants.

11. Autoethnography is autobiographical, reveals the author's emotions, and is often written in first person.

12. Ethnography of communication is a theoretically driven method in which researchers focus on language or speech communities to produce highly detailed analyses of how symbolic practices are expressed in a particular social structure.

13. The advantage of ethnography is that it allows researchers to collect communication in its natural state.

14. Ethnographers rely on extensive field notes, often written outside of the view of participants.

KEY TERMS

autoethnography	focus group
critical incidents	focus group outline
ethnography	interview guide
ethnography of communication	narratives
field interviewing	

CHAPTER SIXTEEN

Analyzing Qualitative Data

Chapter Checklist

After reading this chapter, you should be able to:

1. Distinguish between the analysis and interpretation of qualitative data.

2. Write an analytical memo while collecting qualitative data.

3. Search textual data for relevant codes to be analyzed.

4. Create a coding scheme for qualitative data.

5. Use grounded theory, or constant-comparative method, to analyze qualitative data.

6. Use recurrence, repetition, and forcefulness to analyze qualitative data.

7. Recognize when qualitative data analysis is theoretically saturated.

8. Decide whether or not a computer program will be helpful in the data analysis process.

9. Create an interpretation for categorized qualitative data.

10. Enhance the credibility of a qualitative research design.

11. Conduct a member check or member validation.

12. Use triangulation to strengthen data analysis and interpretation.

Marshall and Rossman (1999) explain that qualitative "data analysis is the process of bringing order, structure, and interpretation to the mass of collected data. It is a messy, ambiguous, time-consuming, creative, and fascinating process. It does not proceed in a linear fashion; it is not neat" (p. 150). Simply said, qualitative data are complex because participants do not talk or behave in standardized or comparable units. Thus, even a well-thought-out qualitative research design will need strategies to order and structure data. There are various techniques for analyzing qualitative data. Several of the more common methods will be described in this chapter.

AN OVERVIEW

For qualitative researchers, analyzing data is the process of identifying themes (Bouma & Atkinson, 1995). The analytical process often begins just after the first data collection session. Remember that one advantage of qualitative research is its reflexive nature. Thus, the researcher can move back and forth between stages of data collection and data analysis. This allows the researcher to facilitate the emerging design of the qualitative study as well as tease out the structure of future observations (Lincoln & Guba, 1985). Remember, too, that qualitative research is inductive, which means that the researcher is working from the specific to the general. The collection of data and generation of tentative conclusions makes the inductive process cyclical and evolutionary.

Most researchers start by reading through every note or other piece of data they have acquired to get a sense of the overall data and to start a list of the broad themes that exist. Ideally, you should read the entire database several times to immerse yourself in the details. You are likely to discover something new each time you read through your notes. It's important to have a sense of the whole before you begin to break down the data into more manageable parts. Once broad themes are identified, read your notes again, now looking for relationships among themes or other salient issues that do not fit easily within the themes identified earlier.

Another technique for analyzing qualitative data is to start by rereading the literature that initially prompted or guided your study. This body of literature should suggest themes or broad categories that should be evident in your data. Then examine the data to see if the categories suggested by the literature can be confirmed or rejected.

A good standard to apply in analyzing qualitative data is to spend as much time analyzing data as collecting data in the field (Janesick, 1998). Time spent in examining the data will allow you to move beyond simply describing what happened to an analytical or theoretical level. Where should the analysis start? One place to begin is with points of conflict, tension, or contradiction. These are often fruitful points of departure for analysis or for developing theoretical premises.

CHOOSING AN ANALYTIC METHOD

As suggested, the initial process of analyzing qualitative data begins when the data are being collected. But a more holistic analytical process begins when the researcher can examine the whole of the dataset. Because so much data can be produced using qualitative data collection methods, the choice of analytical method for a quantitative research design must be made carefully (Lindlof & Taylor, 2002). First, the quantity of data that the researcher will sort through is more difficult to reduce to a coherent or meaningful representation. Second, multiple plausible interpretations can exist. Third, the research question that initiated the study may have changed during data collection as the researcher became more involved in the communication setting and more knowledgeable about the communication problem or issue being investigated. Fourth, the researcher's interpretation of the data must remain true to participants' localized meanings; that is, the interpretation must make sense to the participants who provided the data.

Regardless of which analytical technique you use, Lindlof and Taylor (2002) suggest that researchers think of the process as two distinct steps: analysis and interpretation. **Analysis** is the process of labeling and breaking down raw data to find patterns, themes, concepts, and propositions that exist in the dataset. **Interpretation** is making sense of or giving meaning to those patterns, themes, concepts, and propositions.

THE PROCESS OF ANALYSIS

One of the first steps in analyzing qualitative data is to capture your reactions to and impressions of the people, setting, and interactions. Researchers use analytical memos to separate out their analysis from data collection. The second step is the process of categorizing the data into meaningful units.

Analytical Memos

Although the researcher enters the communication setting with a design in mind, recall that qualitative design is more flexible due to its reflexive nature. Thus, what the researcher encounters in the field may not be what he or she had in mind before entering the setting. Even when a researcher's expectations and experience in the setting are similar, it is a good practice to begin the analytical process as data are collected. Thus, researchers use **analytical memos** to capture their first impressions and reflections about the setting, people, and interactions.

Written as memos to yourself, analytical memos are informal. They capture first impressions, tentative conclusions, and descriptions of communication events with which you are not familiar. It is important to point out that analytical memos are not part of the data. Rather, they are accompaniments to the data and your first attempt at analyzing what is going on in a particular interaction scene. Look at the two segments of an analytical memo in Figure 16.1 and compare them to the field notes. These are taken from a project in which the researcher was a complete observer; she was visible to the group she was observing and they were aware they were being observed. The notes are taken from the first day of observation—the first of 8 full days of training.

While observing and taking field notes, the researcher was struck by two statements that she believed deserved further attention. But the pace of the interaction did not allow her to stop and make these analytical comments and develop these questions in the field. Nor was it appropriate for her to make this type of analytical note during short breaks in the training, as the room in which the training was being held was not large enough for her to find a more private space to work. Written immediately after the training session, the analytical memo provided her the opportunity to capture reactions and ask questions that could be explored when collecting other observational data from this same group and through other methods. Whereas field notes are written in the field, analytical memos are more commonly written after the researcher leaves the research setting field.

However you develop analytical memos, it is important to remember that they are not part of the data. They are initial reactions to and impressions of the data. Thus, analytical memos can suggest potential avenues of additional data collection, the beginning of categorizing or analytical scheme, and tentative conclusions, as well as biases that you should be aware of in data collection and data analysis. It is clear in the analytical memo in Figure 16.1 that the researcher questions the credibility of the training program and the trainers. This is the *researcher's* evaluation, not that of the participants. By capturing her reactions and impressions in memo form, the researcher can remind herself that she needs to pay close attention to how participants in the training sessions are responding to the training and to how her biases are influencing what she observes and takes note of. The analytical memo in Figure 16.1 can also be a springboard for a relevant line of investigation.

Diagramming the Data

At this point, some researchers reduce their data by transforming it into graphical form (Creswell, 1998). By placing data in tables, diagrams, or graphs, researchers make relationships among data become more evident. In this form, data can be displayed by case, subject, theme, or interaction event. Clearly at this point, the researcher will confirm that he or she has more data than can possibly be used. Yet, it is essential that no data be discarded. Rather, continue to use the data sorting and reduction strategies already described to

Field Notes

Donna took over, listing all of the towns they've worked in, claiming "resident status." She was very complimentary of the state and its people, saying "you are cutting edge." She explained her role as to set the stage and provide simple instructions and rules. She encouraged people to talk with one another and keep their hands busy with the toys on the tables. She continued to affirm participants, saying they were the "future of [the state]." She gave more background of why the foundation sponsors such leadership training and parallels to programs in other states. Said that the foundation came to her and Barbara to answer the questions:

- What is it that groups need to be like?
- What do leaders need to be like/do?

Additional comments from Barbara:

- Communities (2 or more people) that work/are effective have visions, strategic actions, they are leader-full
- Leaders don't have to all wear different hats
- The goal of the foundation is to transform community leadership programs in the state
- During these 2 days: workshops that model ways to create leaders who create leaders who create leaders . . .
- You'll leave with processes/practices/materials from participatory workshops
- Our Philosophy: Serve one another, we do this as we work together

Corresponding Segments of an Analytical Memo

1. In the introduction, Barbara and Donna were touted as having extensive experience in leadership training, but no single organization was listed other than the foundation sponsoring the training. This left me wondering about their credentials.

2. Donna said that the foundation served to transform leadership programs in the state. From my understanding then, every leadership program is "transformed" in the exact same way, through their training program. Is this wise to have every community working in the same way, or would the state benefit from communities working from a variety of perspectives? Who is to say that their [the trainers'] perspective is the "right" one? Is there ever any evaluation of or follow-up on these techniques?

FIGURE 16.1 Field Notes and Corresponding Analytical Memos

begin isolating the data that will answer your research questions or hypotheses.

Using Computers

Recently, several computer programs, known as computer-assisted qualitative data analysis programs, have been developed to aid qualitative researchers in their analytical tasks. Researchers wanting to use such a program should examine several different ones because programs vary widely in what data management and data analysis steps they can provide. (Data management includes data entry, searching and retrieving data, and coding data; data analysis includes analyzing data codes, linking data, and analyzing links.) Clearly, researchers should assess a program and its capabilities based on its goodness of fit with the research project. Before deciding to use a computer program, other scholars' evaluation of their use and experiences with computer-assisted qualitative data analysis will be helpful. Fielding (2002), Kelle (2004), and Weitzman (2000) provide comprehensive overviews that will help you select the computer program most compatible with your qualitative research design.

Despite the advantages such programs can offer, seasoned researchers acknowledge that the hard work of analyzing qualitative data remains because the work is intellectual, not mechanical (Dohan & Sanchez-Jankowski, 1998). Computer programs are probably most effective in helping researchers manage the large volume of data produced by qualitative studies.

Coding and Categorizing Data

For qualitative research designs, the data will consist of pages and pages of notes, or written text or transcripts. The text can be your field notes from observing participants in the field. The text might be transcriptions of audiotapes from interviews and focus groups. Or, the text could be participants' written narratives. For example, Jameson's (2004) study of how anesthesiologists and certified registered nurse anesthetists manage organizational conflict yielded 280 pages of single-spaced notes from observations and interviews. As another example, 29 interviews with medical students resulted in over 600 double-spaced pages of transcription (Harter & Krone, 2001).

In almost every case, a qualitative researcher will have the need to categorize and code data. Doing so helps the researcher reduce the data into a manageable size from which an interpretation can be made. Some researchers start this process as soon as data are collected; other researchers wait until all of the data are collected. The larger the potential dataset, the more practical it will be to begin categorizing the data at intermediate points during data collection.

As you observe participants in their interaction settings and listen to participants in interviews and focus groups, you will naturally start to link together statements and behaviors and distinguish those from other statements and behaviors.

This is the beginning of the categorizing process. A **category** is a label for a set of excerpts, examples, or themes that are similar. Categories may be drawn from the literature used to build a foundation for the qualitative research design. For example, Martin (2004) used existing categories of humor to begin her categorization of how humor was used in an organizational setting. She describes the process of using existing categories in this way:

> It is important to note that humor categories fundamental to extant theories served only as initial categories. For example, the idea of humor as play and lightness does emerge from the data as an important nuance not usually distinct among humor typology. Holding extant humor labels lightly, as guiding constructs rather than final categories, served to fulfill the communicative approach to organizational studies suggested by Pacanowsky and O'Donnell-Trujillo (1982). (p. 155)

Notice that Martin used the existing categories, but used them as a reference point and not as an absolute. Even when categories are determined beforehand, researchers are wise to let unique or novel categories emerge. As a result, a category scheme may be revised or reformulated.

On the other hand, categories may emerge from the data. Following the inductive model used in most qualitative research (see Chapter 2), researchers inductively derive the categories as representative of the phenomenon they are investigating. At the first attempt, these are likely to be "fuzzy categories due to a certain degree of ambiguity in their definition" (Lindlof & Taylor, 2002, p. 215). They are not distinct, nor are they conceptually clear. But they are a starting point for the analysis. Most likely the initial categories will be somewhat different than the final categories used to develop an interpretation of the data.

If you are having trouble identifying categories, try the following steps. First, return to your research question. Does your research question ask (Lofland & Lofland, 1995):

- If something exists, what are its types?
- How often something occurs?
- How big, strong, or intense something is?

- Is there a process, a cycle, or phases to the interaction?
- Does one thing influence another?
- If the consequences follow an event or interaction?
- How people use interaction in a specific way?

For example, If your research question asks the first question, you can search data for evidence of the existence and the types of interaction in which you are interested. Ellingson's (2003) research question "What are the communication processes among team members in the clinic backstage?" (p. 96) is this type of question. Thus, she looked for "similarities and differences in content and structure of interactions among team members as they communicated in the clinic backstage" (p. 98). Her analyses resulted in 7 categories of backstage communication processes, each with two or more subtypes.

Another strategy is to have a set of questions to reflect on as you read through the data. Lofland and Lofland (1995, p. 186) suggest asking:

1. What is this? What does it represent?
2. What is this an example of?
3. What do I see going on here? What are people doing? What is happening? What kind of events are at issue here?

As categories emerge, you should begin labeling with a code, one word or a short phrase. For example, two of Ellingson's codes are "training students" and "handling interruptions." These codes represent the categories, which are more fully described by the examples within them.

As categories are identified, researchers should test the category system being discovered by looking for the opposite or negative cases and searching for other plausible explanations. "Alternative explanations *always* exist" (Marshall & Rossman, 1999, p. 157). Thus, the researcher must explain why a particular set of categories are the most plausible of all.

If the dataset consists of notes from separate meetings or as transcripts from multiple interviews, a researcher will need to decide how best to analyze the data. Depending on the research question guiding the investigation, a researcher might decide to treat the data as a whole. When

the data are collected from a homogeneous sample, this can be an effective strategy. But, more frequently, a researcher will want to retain the uniqueness of each interaction event or each individual. Thus, most researchers analyze notes for each meeting or each interview in its entirety and then compare and contrast findings across the dataset. In this way, researchers can isolate any unique circumstances (e.g., comparison of categories in first meeting to second and subsequent meetings) or characteristics (e.g., sex, race, ethnicity, hierarchical status) to create a more sophisticated and integrated analysis.

Categorizing and coding data, however, is the most elementary of qualitative analytical techniques. Most communication scholars use one of the two following perspectives for analyzing qualitative data.

GROUNDED THEORY

Many qualitative researchers use **grounded theory,** introduced by Glaser and Strauss (1967) and modified by Charmaz (2000), as an iterative approach for coding their data. Also known as the **constant-comparative method,** the grounded theory approach is based on the notions that "(1) Theory is grounded in the relationships between data and the categories into which they are coded; and (2) Codes and categories are mutable until late in the project" (Lindlof & Taylor, 2002, p. 218). Categories are mutable, or can be changed, because the researcher is constantly identifying new categories and comparing them to the existing categories as the researcher continues to analyze the data or collects new data. Thus, grounded theory can be used to analyze textual data regardless of its type of data collection method.

One caution must be given here. Grounded theory is not simply a method for identifying categories. Rather, grounded theory requires that researchers examine the relationships between the data and its category, and the relationships among categories.

The first step using this approach is to become very familiar with the data. Often researchers do not try to code on their first pass through the data. The second step is to code the data. A typical approach would be to use a highlighting pen to identify parts of the transcript or field notes that are relevant to the research questions. The third pass is then made to identify the initial categories that emerge from the data. The fourth and subsequent passes through the data are used to compare and contrast the categories that emerge. Harter (2004) explains her emergent categorizing process using grounded theory in this way:

> I read all transcripts and documents in their entirety to develop a sense of these data as a whole. I re-read the transcripts while playing the original tapes to ensure accuracy of transcriptions in and to note special emphases or cues that might affect interpretation but did not appear on the transcripts. After gaining a holistic sense of the discourse, I started the actual analysis. A constant comparative method allowed themes representing recurring patterns of behavior and meaning to emerge from subjects' own words. The process began with manually coding the data on the actually transcripts. By engaging in a constant comparative analysis of data I continually compared specific incidents in the data, refined concepts, and identified their properties. (p. 98)

The process is iterative, meaning that the process is repeated until the researcher believes all relevant categories have been identified. Barge and Loges (2003) describe how their multiple member research team used grounded theory:

> The qualitative information from the focus groups was analyzed in three stages. First, following the completion of each focus group, the facilitator and two recorders who conducted the focus group read over the field notes and identified themes of parental involvement based on the answers provided to the two primary questions tapping into perceptions of high-quality parental involvement. Using a grounded theory approach (Glaser & Strauss, 1967), the facilitator and the two recorders generated themes by clustering parent responses and observations using an iterative inductive method. Once the themes had been articulated, the field notes were searched for verbatim quotes, stories, examples, and metaphors illustrating each theme. This process created a set of themes constituting high-quality parental involvement along with relevant examples, quotes, and metaphors for each theme. Second, the primary researcher and one facilitator examined the list of themes for each focus group and identified similarities and differences among the groups. A list of common themes was generated that characterized the parental focus groups. In order to count as a theme, it had to be mentioned by at least five of the focus groups. (p. 144)

Their description demonstrates the multiple steps taken to identify and justify themes of high-quality parental involvement across the nine parent and seven student focus groups.

The steps of grounded theory, or the constant-comparative method, are coding data, developing inductive categories, revising categories, and writing memos to explore preliminary and tentative ideas. Throughout the process, the researcher is continually comparing parts of the data to other parts and the research literature.

In the grounded theory process, researchers use two types of categories. The first is **open coding,** or unrestricted coding, and is the first pass through the data. Open coding is unrestricted because the researcher is not looking for data that fit a set number or type of categories. Nor is the researcher interested in how categories fit together. Rather, the researcher is "open" to all possibilities of categories. In later passes, the researcher uses **axial coding,** or the process of linking together categories in a meaningful way. It is in the process of axial coding that categories are collapsed or relabeled into fewer categories.

When all of the data relevant to the research question can be coded into a category, researchers label the data as being **theoretically saturated** (Glaser & Strauss, 1967). New categories are not emerging, and the existing category structure appears stable. Once the categories are stable, the researcher explores the relationships among the categories. How are the categories similar? Different?

THEMATIC ANALYSIS

Thematic analysis, sometimes identified as thematic interpretation (Owen, 1984), is based on participants' conceptions of actual communication episodes. A theme is a conceptualization of an interaction, a relationship, or an event. Themes are identified in textual data based on three criteria: recurrence, repetition, and force-fulness. Recurrence is present when at least two parts of a report have the same thread of meaning. Recurrence is not simply repetition of the same words or phrase; different wording may result in the same meaning. Thus, this criterion focuses on salient meaning.

The second criterion, repetition, is the explicit repetition of key words, phrases, or sentences. The third criterion, forcefulness, is present when the data reveal

> vocal inflection, volume, or dramatic pause which serve to stress and subordinate some utterances from other[s] . . . it also refers to the underlining of words and phrases, the increased size of print or use of colored marks circling or otherwise focusing on passages in the written reports. (Owen, 1984, pp. 275–276)

The three criteria—recurrence, repetition, and forcefulness—are found in participants' vocal or written records. Thus, when used they identify what the salient issues are and demonstrate the degree of salience for participants.

Hoppe-Nagao and Ting-Toomey (2002) used Owen's recurrence and repetition to analyze interviews of husbands and wives. The research team examined the 40 interview transcripts for occurrences of recurrence and repetition within interviews as well as across interviews, which resulted in identifying an autonomy–connection dialectic represented by four themes, and an openness–closedness dialect represented by three themes. Buzzanell and Turner (2003) also used Owen's three criteria to identify themes in interview data from family members in which the father had lost his job. To be included as a theme, the research team required that each theme meet all three criteria.

THE PROCESS OF INTERPRETATION

No matter now much time is spent coding and categorizing, these steps do not "guarantee a sensitive reading of a life, a social ritual, or a cultural scene" (Lindlof & Taylor, 2002, p. 232). Thus, interpretation is critical in analyzing qualitative data. As described earlier in this chapter, interpretation is making sense of or giving meaning

to patterns, themes, concepts, and propositions. It is the act of translating categories into a meaningful whole by switching from a micro frame, which consists of the coding and categorizing, to a macro frame, which analyzes the data as a whole. Three of these macro frames—metaphoric, dramatistic, and theoretical—are described below (Lindlof & Taylor)

One of the holistic frames is the **metaphoric frame.** For example, Ellingson (2003) uses the theater metaphor to interpret health care professionals' communication in the clinical setting. She describes what part of the interaction environment is backstage (e.g., the desks, hallway, and other areas in which patients are not typically allowed) and how that interaction differs from the onstage interaction, or the interaction with and in front of patients in the treatment rooms. Each of the seven emergent categories is explained relative to the onstage–backstage distinction. But, she takes the metaphor a step further by explaining how the backstage interaction prepares the health care professionals for their onstage performance with patients. Thus, the metaphor of actors preparing backstage for their onstage performance is complete. Metaphors can be powerfully used to create new meanings because they fuse together two concepts that are dissimilar (Lindlof & Taylor, 2002). Certainly, you would not normally describe health care professionals' interaction the way you describe what happens in the theater. Thus, the unknown (the interaction setting of the health care professionals) becomes more salient as the metaphor draws relationships between the two interaction scenes.

Another macro framing device is a **dramatistic frame.** Here, the attention is focused on the roles, settings, and scripts necessary to telling a story. In some studies, participants are asked to provide an account, which is often revealed in storylike fashion. For example, Kassing (2002) asked participants to:

> Recall a time when you disagreed with workplace policies and practices and you decided to discuss your concerns with someone above you in the chain of command (e.g., supervisor, manager). Please be as specific as you can when describing what you did and said when discussing your disagreement. (pp. 193–194)

In other instances, researchers look for naturally occurring stories. For example, in Coopman and Meidlinger's (2000) study of a Catholic parish, one researcher observed stories being told and later recounted them in field notes.

The focus on the story in these two studies is easily matched with a dramatistic frame because the researchers used data collection techniques that directly solicited stories. However, a dramatistic frame can also be used when data collected are not initially found in story fashion. A researcher in the field for an extended period of time is likely to see stories played out and become able to identify data that represent the story, its characters, plot, and setting. For example, an ethnography in a heart catheterization unit (Morgan & Krone, 2001) revealed "patterns of performance" such that the researchers organized their data "around a set of dramatic performances involving the playing of roles, writing of scripts, descriptions of settings, and audience reactions" (p. 325).

Theory can also provide a macro frame from which to bring together analytical categories. A **theoretical frame** exists when a researcher uses two or more theories to provide tension in how the data might be interpreted. Miller (2002), for example, first used a theory about emotional labor to examine data and then used the theory of concertive control to examine the same data for evidence of organizational identity. Although researchers often cast rationality and emotion as thesis and antithesis, Miller's analysis demonstrates that rationality and emotion were "contradictory parts of a unified whole that could not be understood independently of each other" (p. 594). Thus, as Lindlof and Taylor (2002) suggest, theoretical framing can help researchers "stretch their imaginations and validate claims about the data they have generated" (p. 238).

With coding completed and stable categories chosen, researchers once again turn to memos as an "intermediate step between coding and the first draft of the completed analysis" (Charmaz, 2000, p. 517). Researchers use the **memo writing** step to "elaborate processes, assumptions, and actions that are presumed" in the coding and categorizing process (p. 517). Memo writing encourages researchers to detail the properties of each category and to suggest how each category fits with others. Quotes from participants or phrases from field notes are used in memo writing first to test the specificity of the analysis, and then later as exemplars of the category. These memos are used as the basis for organizing the research report, and often they become drafts of the results section of the research report.

When the categories are finalized, the researcher then selects exemplars of each category to use in the research report. How many exemplars are needed? There is no standard here, but three is a number that allows you to express the nuances of the category and use as a basis for the conclusions that you advance.

Evaluating Interpretation

How does the researcher evaluate his or her results once the coding, categorizing, and interpretations are completed? What cues can a consumer use in reading a research report to assess the soundness of a qualitative study and its claims? Participant quotes, credibility, member validation, and triangulation are the primary tools qualitative researchers use to enhance the quality of their findings.

Participant Quotes   The initial test of the researcher's ability to analyze and interpret qualitative data is the degree to which participant quotes illuminate the analysis and interpretation. In other words, quotes from participants must be provided in the research report as evidence that the analysis and interpretation are plausible. By reading the examples provided, it should be obvious to the reader of the report that the categories described are based on the qualitative data collected. Thus, qualitative researchers often use quotes from several participants or segments of field notes from different parts of a meeting to document the existence of a category and to distinguish this category from others.

How many examples are needed? Generally, researchers need to give enough examples to demonstrate the breadth and depth of a category. Many times, three examples are enough to convey the researchers' analysis and interpretation of a category. Overall, researchers should work for balance between the presentation of the categories and the presentation of data as examples (Lofland & Lofland, 1995).

Credibility   **Credibility** is the criterion used to assess the effectiveness and accuracy of a qualitative research design and findings drawn from its data. How does a qualitative researcher enhance credibility? First, the researcher must plan for and carry out the inquiry in such a way that the findings are believable to others. How can this be achieved? With prolonged and persistent engagement with the interactants and the interaction setting, you have the opportunity to develop a real sense of the interaction culture as well as test for any misinformation introduced through distortion or bias. And, as a result of prolonged interaction, the researcher has additional opportunities to build trust.

Second, credibility is enhanced when the findings are agreeable to those who were research participants. Recall that member validation is the process of asking those observed to respond to your observation summaries. Besides giving you the opportunity to correct errors, participants can also challenge your interpretations and provide insight from their point of view. By providing participants with the details or interpretation of the interaction, you might also stimulate their recall of additional information or insight. This is what Pierce and Dougherty (2002) did to enhance the credibility of their findings. By taking their findings back to the pilots who provided the data, they were able to assess how well they had captured the pilots' experiences. Besides these opportunities to correct or gain information, your willingness to share what you found with participants strengthens the researcher–participant bond. These activities inherently enhance your credibility as a researcher and the credibility of your findings.

Triangulation   Qualitative researchers often rely on **triangulation** to increase the credibility of their research. Refer to the initial discussion of triangulation in Chapter 4. The most common form is data triangulation, in which a variety of qualitative methods are used to produce different types of data. The validity of a finding is enhanced if the researcher comes to similar or complementary conclusions using two or more different methods. For example, Miller (1995) used participant journals, interviews, and participant observation to capture data about mother–daughter relationships to explain how suicide is a social construction of family culture.

Investigator triangulation is another form of triangulation. Two researchers observing the same interaction are likely to capture a more complete view of what happened in the interaction than would one observer, due to differing vantage points or differing perspectives. Their interpretations may blend into one as they talk about what happened, or their interpretations may remain separate and distinct accounts of what transpired. Researchers have even studied the extent to which multiple coders agree on the thematic analysis of focus group interaction. Armstrong, Gosling, Weinman, and Martaeu (1997) found that even though researchers have their own views, which are part of the subjective nature of qualitative research, the themes that the coders found were similar. Divergence among the coders occurred as they packaged or bound the themes together in different frameworks. Two or more researchers are likely to provide alternative frameworks from which the data can be interpreted.

Another way to triangulate findings is to observe at different times. Recall the information on representative sampling presented earlier in this chapter. Capturing data across time and at different intervals or times of day provides a greater variety of data from which to draw conclusions and, as a result, creates greater reliability.

Triangulation is especially important in overcoming threats to external validity. One of the most frequent criticisms of qualitative research is that the qualitative method creates an overreliance on one case or a series of cases (Denzin, 1970a). By observing multiple parties over a period of time, qualitative researchers can overcome biases believed to exist either because the individuals studied have unique properties or characteristics or because there is instability in the population under observation. Thus, qualitative researchers must demonstrate that the individuals or cases studied are representative of the class of units to which generalizations are made. To avoid a threat to external validity, qualitative researchers should become familiar with the social and personal characteristics of individuals observed and be sensitive to any biasing features they possess.

Although the practice of triangulation can be planned for, it is actually carried out as the research is being conducted (Hickson & Jennings, 1993). Thus, triangulation practices can also be added to a research project once it is underway. This points to the greater flexibility of qualitative methods over quantitative methods. As you can see, the role of the researcher (or research team members) can be enhanced or expanded to meet the demands of the interaction situation as it occurs.

SUMMARY

1. Analysis of qualitative data, or identifying patterns and themes, is distinct from interpreting, or making sense of the patterns and themes.

2. Because qualitative research is inductive, data collection and analysis can be cyclical and evolutionary.

3. Generally, a researcher spends as much time analyzing qualitative data as collecting data.

4. Researchers write analytical memos to capture their first impressions and reflections of the data.

5. Diagramming the data, or putting the data into some graphical form, can help a researcher find relationships among the data.

6. Coding and categorizing qualitative data reduces it to a manageable size.

7. Categories may be drawn from the literature or emerge from the data.

8. Grounded theory, or the constant-comparative method, is an iterative process that guides a researcher through identifying categories and identifying relationships among categories.

9. Data are saturated theoretically when all data can be coded into a category.

10. Thematic analysis of data is based on the criteria of recurrence, repetition, and forcefulness.

11. Once data are analyzed, or categorized, a researcher must develop an interpretation of the patterns, themes, and concepts.

12. Researchers use participant quotes, credibility, member validation, and triangulation to affirm the quality of their findings.

KEY TERMS

analysis

analytical memo

axial coding

category

constant-comparative method

credibility

dramatistic frame

grounded theory

interpretation

memo writing

metaphoric frame

open coding

thematic analysis

theoretical frame

theoretical saturation

triangulation

CHAPTER SEVENTEEN

Reading and Writing the Quantitative Research Report

Chapter Checklist

After reading this chapter, you should be able to:

1. Construct a literature review that situates your research study in the historical context of research similar to yours.

2. Develop a compelling problem statement.

3. Find and integrate empirical research reports, theory articles, and literature review articles in your literature review.

4. Organize your literature review to make the best presentation of research questions and hypotheses.

5. Write a methods section describing the participants, research procedures, and variables.

6. Write a results section that presents the findings in a straightforward manner.

7. Write a discussion section that provides interpretations and implications of the research findings.

8. Identify the limitations of your study and interpret the limitations with respect to your findings.

9. Recommend future research ideas and methods.

10. Finish the research report with an appropriate title, title page, abstract, and list of references.

11. Use APA style for direct and indirect citations and for developing the reference list.

12. Use the revision process to enhance the quality of the written research report.

13. Submit your paper for review to a communication association convention.

No study is complete until the researcher writes the research report to communicate the findings to others. Just as researchers draw from previously presented and published research, they are also responsible for preparing a research report for use by others. Thus, the typical audience for a research report is other researchers and scholars, including students like you.

Following one of the traditions of science, disciplines that study human behavior (such as communication, management, psychology, sociology) and the physical world (such as biology and chemistry) rely upon the same basic format for presenting research results. This chapter focuses on the four basic sections of a quantitative research paper written to be published in communication journals: literature review, methods, results, and discussion.

THE LITERATURE REVIEW

The **literature review** is the framework, of the research investigation (Katzer et al., 1978). It includes a summary of the literature the researcher sought and studied to design and develop his or her research study. Thus, it provides the structure and orientation for the research project and the rest of the written research report. Although there are many ways in which to organize a literature review, this section has one objective, and that is to provide a foundation for the present study by putting it into the context of the applicable and appropriate research history and theoretical development (Katzer et al.). With this objective, the literature review reports on previous articles that both support and contradict the researcher's position. Both types of information should be reported with explanations and justifications.

A literature review should provide a historical account of the variables and concepts used in the study. In some cases, this history can be substantial. It can always be succinctly summarized; it should never be excluded. A good literature review also includes the latest research, generally including publications within the past 6 to 12 months. Now that libraries provide access to electronic databases, it is much easier to locate the most current material.

But a good literature review goes beyond a simple description of previously published work to include analysis, synthesis, and a critique of this work (Ryan, 1998). It should provide an assessment of previous efforts and suggest why these issues should be explored again or in new ways. The literature review is also the place to point out gaps in previous research.

In addition to acknowledging themes and gaps in the literature, a good literature review seeks to identify and establish relationships among previously published work and the study presented. The writer should address the major assumptions that have guided earlier work and address how the current study accepts or rejects those assumptions. Finally, the literature review should state clearly how the current study contributes to the understanding of theory or theoretical assertions (Ryan, 1998).

Thinking of a literature review as describing the relationships among previous studies helps authors avoid long strings of references or quotations, which could lead readers to miss the trends or themes that the researcher found in the literature. In essence, the literature review is effective to the degree that the researcher helps the reader see and understand relationships that the researcher saw in the initial development of the research project.

The Problem Statement

The problem statement is usually positioned near or at the beginning of the literature review. It identifies the research objectives. Although the exact research question or hypotheses are not stated directly here, they are suggested. The problem statement answers the questions "What precisely is the problem?" and "Why is this problem worthy of study?" In other words, the problem statement explains why the researchers conducted the study and why you, as a consumer, should be interested. The problem statement presents the primary objective of the study and introduces several subobjectives, which identify the specific issues to be examined (Kumar, 1996).

Look at how Myers (1998) presents the problem statement for a study on the assimilation and socialization of graduate teaching assistants.

> The use of graduate teaching assistant (TA) as an instructor in the college classroom has become a common practice (Anderson, 1992). Researchers have found that universities rely heavily on the use of GTAs as classroom instructors (e.g., Buerkel-Rothfuss & Gray, 1990; Nyquist & Wulff, 1987; Zimpher & Yessayan, 1987); yet, GTAs are often left to perform a task for which they are unprepared (Anderson, 1992). Over half of all GTAs in noncommunication departments do not receive any training (Buerkel-Rothfuss & Gray, 1990) and even less receive any type of supervision on a regular basis (Prieto, 1995). A national survey of 1400 GTAs has discovered that at least 25% are not trained in fundamental tasks such as grading, lecturing, and facilitating discussion (Diamond & Gray, 1987). Although considerable research has been conducted on the benefits of GTA training (see Buerkel-Rothfuss & Gray, 1990; Carroll, 1980), little research has been conducted on how GTAs become socialized into the academic community. (p. 54)

From this paragraph, a reader would know what the problem is and how severe the problem is perceived to be. This type of problem statement presents a compelling argument for the study that follows.

Types of Material to Include in the Literature Review

Researchers can include three types of articles in their literature review (Galvan, 1999). First are empirical research reports, articles that present findings from research studies. Second are articles that evaluate a theory or propose a theory. In this type of article, data are not collected. Rather, the author is concerned with the conceptual development of the theory. Third are literature review articles that review and summarize an expanse of literature on one topic, issue, or theory. In this case, the author organizes and evaluates the relevant literature to make evaluative statements about the "state" of the topic, issue, or theory. Often, the author offers suggestions for future research.

The first two types of articles can be found in the communication journals. Some literature reviews can be found there as well. *Communication Yearbook* is a good source of literature review articles. Likewise, many handbooks published for communication contexts include substantial literature reviews (see Chapter 2).

How many articles should be included in a literature review? Most students ask this question, and it is a difficult one to answer. Most instructors will require student scholars to have an adequate background in the theory, issue, and variables needed for your research project. But it is unlikely that your instructor will require you to locate every article ever written. Your knowledge will be less incomplete, however, if you locate a literature review central to your study. Using the keywords "handbook" and "communication" on your library's electronic catalog, you should be able to identify any of the communication handbooks your library has in its holdings. *Communication Yearbook* is published annually, each year addressing new topics. Many libraries have the complete series in their holdings.

Articles can also be found on the many web-based databases. Your instructor and reference librarian can offer guidance in searching the databases most central to your needs.

As you select articles for your literature review, you are likely to see certain authors, or even one article, cited over and over. This is an indication that the author is central to the discussion of this research issue or that this one article is considered a landmark or classic study (Galvan, 1999). Another way to identify noted authors or classic studies is to turn to a textbook in the area of your research study. These authors and studies are often highlighted there. If at all possible, locate the published article so you can read it in its original form and in its entirety. Otherwise, you will have to rely on others' summaries and evaluations.

Finally, as you read the work of other researchers, be careful to distinguish between assertions made in the literature review and conclusions supported with evidence in the discussion section (Galvan, 1999). It is easy to confuse the two. In the literature review, researchers often make predictions or claims as they set up their research questions and hypotheses. But these claims

TABLE 17.1 Ways of Organizing a Literature Review

Organizing Framework	Description and Uses
Chronological order	In temporal order based on publication dates. Especially good for tracing the development of an issue, concept, or theory.
General to specific	Information about the broadest issue is presented first, followed by research that deals with more narrow aspects of the issue.
Contrast-comparison	Research that is similar is separated into sections to highlight differences among the types or topics of studies.
Trend identification	Research is separated into identifiable trends. Trends are placed in order of importance to the study.
Methodological focus	Studies using the same methodology are grouped together and compared to other methodologies.
Problem-cause-solution	Description of the problem is followed by description of its cause and suggestion of a solution.
Topical order	All information about a topic is presented in separate sections. Topics are introduced sequentially in order of importance or in order of appearance in research questions or hypotheses.

can be categorically different from conclusions found in the discussion section. Claims made in the discussion section are based on data from the research study. So, even though a researcher may hypothesize something in the literature review, support for that claim is not known until the study is completed and the data analyzed and interpreted.

Organizing the Literature Review

There are several different forms for organizing a literature review. Table 17.1 reviews several of the most common approaches.

Writing a literature review is no small task. Actually, it is much like writing a paper or essay for a class that does not require you to collect data to support your claims. Many of the writing techniques useful for that type of paper are also helpful in research reports.

For example, the first paragraph of the literature review should be a road map for the rest of the literature review. Specify what you are going to cover and what you hope to accomplish. Use headings and subheadings to structure the review and to distinguish between its major and minor sections. Use internal summaries to signal the end of one section and transitions to signal that another section of the literature review is beginning. Within sections, major points can be enumerated with "first," "second," "third," and so on. Finally, remember that a literature review is not a long string of quoted material. Your evaluations and summaries of the literature are important elements of the literature review because your opinions and arguments shape the research project.

Most quantitative research reports are written in the third person. This form is preferred for two reasons. First, it distances researchers, allowing them to make a more objective presentation, a characteristic of quantitative research. Second, use of the third person shifts the focus from the researcher to the content of what is being written about (Galvan, 1999). Some communication scholars use the first person, although the third person still appears to be more preferred.

Because research reports are considered formal writing, some other advice includes

- Spell out acronyms the first time they are used.
- Avoid contractions; instead write out both words completely.
- Avoid slang expressions (for example, "you know").
- Eliminate bias in your writing with respect to sex, sexual orientation, racial or ethnic group, disability, or age.

Presenting the Research Questions and Hypotheses

There are two general forms for presenting research questions and hypotheses. The first is to display the questions and hypotheses as they emerge from the literature review. In this form of presentation, these elements are interspersed throughout the literature review, and the literature review has a repetitive broad-to-narrow structure as each hypothesis or research question flows from the narrative before the next broad-to-narrow section begins. The alternative is to present the research questions and hypotheses together as a summary to the literature review.

Regardless of which form you use, each hypothesis or research question should be separately stated as a simple sentence or simple question. And each hypothesis or research question should be identified as such, usually with the notations H_1, H_2, or RQ_1, RQ_2, and so on. Besides helping to identify specific questions and hypotheses, this notation form creates a shortcut in the results section as the researcher can simply refer to H_1, or the first hypothesis, without restating it again. Null hypotheses are not provided.

THE METHODS SECTION

The **methods section** describes how the research study was executed. By describing the research procedures, the researcher allows readers to make a determination about the appropriateness and adequacy of the methods for meeting the purpose of the study. At a minimum, the methods section should include descriptions of the research participants and the research procedures, as well as descriptive information for each of the variables included in the study.

Describing Participants

Until recently, most published research reports described the setting and the participants of the research project in an anonymous fashion. Given the topic or focus of some studies, some scholars now recognize that the political, historical, legal, economic, social, and cultural environment of the population, organization, or geographic area studied are important to the research process and the interpretation of data (Ryan, 1998). Although you should not report the identity of participants or organizations without their consent, you can probably provide a description that goes beyond "working adults in the mid-South." This remains, however, an individual or journal-specific editorial preference.

As a general rule, researchers report demographic information about participants in this section of the research report even when the categories of information (sex, ethnicity, age) form independent variables in the research study. Sunwolf and Leets (2004) provide an example of the way in which demographic information can be reported:

> In the study, 682 adolescents (377 males, 301 females, and 4 undeclared) from one private ($n = 139$), two public ($n = 481$), and two continuation ($n = 50$) high schools (grades 9–12), from large urban school districts in northern California, comprised a convenience sample. The high schools were located in diverse communities having residents with various linguistic, cultural, and socioeconomic backgrounds. The sample ranged in age from 13 to 19 ($Mdn = 14$). From self-reported ethnic identities, 41.3% were Caucasian/White, 18.8% Asian American, 24.2% Hispanic American, 5.7% African American, and 10.0% other. Some participants did not report demographic information. (p. 204)

This type of description paints a picture of the participants and helps consumers of research evaluate the study's outcomes as relevant to a particular group or type of individual.

This subsection should also include any information about the sampling techniques used to select participants. Researchers also report the size of the sample here. Finally, this subsection should also present any special conditions regarding informed consent, confidentiality, or anonymity.

Describing the Research Procedure

In the second part of the methods section, the researcher should describe in sufficient detail what was done in the research study. The research design should be fully described. In other words, after reading this subsection, the consumer should know what the researcher did to collect the data. The research design should be evident, as should all of the research procedures.

What kinds of detail are necessary? Stimuli used to create experimental conditions need to be completely explained. If confederates were used, the role of the confederate should be explained in detail. The researcher should also note whether interactions were audio- or videotaped. If other equipment or technologies were used to collect data, this should be described as well.

The scientific ideal requires that researchers describe their research procedures with enough detail that other researchers could easily replicate the research design. In practice, however, a methods section with that much detail would be too cumbersome. Most scholars take a more moderate approach by describing the basic procedures for each aspect of the research design. This should give consumers enough information on which to evaluate the adequacy and appropriateness of the research procedures. If you decide to replicate a study, you will probably need to contact the researcher directly. Contact information for authors is usually provided on the first or last page of the journal article.

Describing the Variables

The third element of the methods section is devoted to describing the variables used in the study. An operationalization, or specific way in which the variable is observed or measured, must be provided for each variable. A variable's operationalization specifies the concrete steps or processes for creating and measuring the variable.

When data are collected through a previously developed questionnaire, the researcher should provide a brief description of the questionnaire, including the number of items, an example of an item, the type of response scale, and a citation where readers can locate the scale. Information about the questionnaire's reliability and validity should also be included.

If a questionnaire is developed specifically for a study, then the researchers should describe the essential steps in constructing the scale, indicate if and how the scale was pilot tested, and provide information about the steps the researcher took to address issues of reliability and validity. In this case, most researchers will include the entire instrument as an appendix to the research report.

If data were collected through content or interaction analysis, then the researcher should provide description of how the category scheme was developed and pilot tested, as well as information about how coders were trained and how intercoder reliability was established. Also important in this description would be how disagreements between coders were resolved.

Each category of a nominal variable should be described by the percentage of respondents. Continuous level variables should each be described by the mean, standard deviation, range of scores, and, if appropriate, internal reliability. If several continuous variables are used in the study, then researchers should consider adding a correlation matrix to describe the relationships among them and for presenting this descriptive information. Refer back to Table 12.2 for a typical correlation matrix. In some cases, researchers add rows or columns to the matrix so that the mean, standard deviation, and internal reliability of each variable can be included.

Finally, each variable should also be identified as an independent (predictor) or dependent (criterion) variable. Readers should not have to guess how the researcher situated or sequenced the variables in the study.

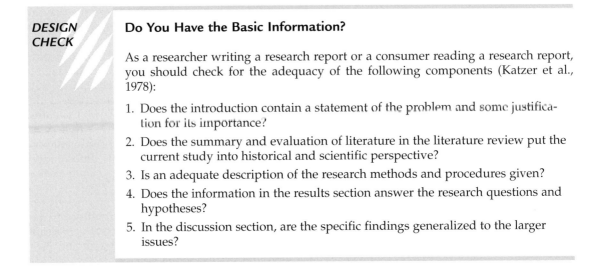

DESIGN CHECK

Do You Have the Basic Information?

As a researcher writing a research report or a consumer reading a research report, you should check for the adequacy of the following components (Katzer et al., 1978):

1. Does the introduction contain a statement of the problem and some justification for its importance?

2. Does the summary and evaluation of literature in the literature review put the current study into historical and scientific perspective?

3. Is an adequate description of the research methods and procedures given?

4. Does the information in the results section answer the research questions and hypotheses?

5. In the discussion section, are the specific findings generalized to the larger issues?

THE RESULTS SECTION

Traditionally, results are presented in the order of the research questions and hypotheses. In the **results section,** results are presented as information without interpretation. Thus, accuracy of reporting is critical. All numbers used as results should be double-checked. And there should be complete consistency between the numerical report and textual description of the numbers.

At a minimum, several pieces of information need to be presented for each hypothesis or question:

- The statistical test used
- The results of the test
- The significance level of the test
- A written description connecting the result of the statistical test as support for or rejection of the research hypothesis, or connecting the result of the statistical test to the answer of the research question

The scientific tradition also requires researchers to report all results, even if they do not support the researcher's expectations. If a hypothesis or research question is provided, the results from the associated test must be reported. It would be unethical not to do so.

Using Tables and Graphs

Tables are used to graphically display numerical data. As a consumer, you should be able to easily interpret a table because it is well identified and labeled. But even with complete identification, a table never stands alone. A researcher should briefly describe the important elements of the table in the accompanying written text. Of course, information in the text should coincide with the tabular presentation. Figures and graphs are used sparingly in research reports, but they are useful when striking or important data could be otherwise overlooked.

THE DISCUSSION SECTION

In the **discussion section** of the written research report, researchers provide an interpretation of the results. In this section the researcher tries to answer the question "What do these results mean?" As a researcher, you need to provide a full, fair, and detailed account of the implications of the data. As a consumer, you need to make an assessment of the results independently of what is written.

The discussion section is the place for the author to interpret the results. Although interpretations are linked to data results, the discussion section should not be a simple restatement of significant and nonsignificant findings. Rather, the discussion section indicates what the results mean and why the results are important or meaningful. Conclusions presented in this section should be linked to the literature review. Furthermore, the author should describe how the conclusions of this study contribute to theory development (Ryan, 1998). The discussion section also includes brief subsections on the limitations of the research methodology and suggestions for future research.

As you read or write a discussion section, three questions can guide you. We will look at each question first from the consumer point of view and then from the researcher's point of view. First, do you know how the author arrived at the interpretation or summary (Katzer et al., 1978)? It should be clear to you what observations, measurements, or data were used to draw the stated conclusions. If you are not sure how the researcher came to the conclusions, then you need to refer back to the methods section of the document. As the researcher writing the discussion section, you should be sure to expand on any procedural or descriptive details that will help readers agree with your conclusions.

Second, as a consumer, be aware. Does the conclusion given make sense (Katzer et al., 1978)? Are there alternative interpretations of the data that the author ignores or dismisses? Seldom is there a "correct" or single interpretation of the data. Rather, the author has formed his or her conclusions based on the framework established in the literature review and in response to the research questions or hypotheses. As a consumer, can you follow the path (literature review to hypotheses to data collection) that leads the author to this particular conclusion? Are the results linked to the theory presented in the literature review? Is the interpretation of results consistent with other research findings presented in the literature review? If not, does the author provide a sufficient explanation for why these results might be different?

In making the transition from consumer to writer, you can use this same logic as you develop the discussion section. Remember that as the researcher and author of the research report, you are inherently more familiar with why and how the

data were collected. These elements influence the conclusions you present. You must remember that anyone reading your report will not be as familiar with the research setting. Develop and describe your interpretations and conclusions with enough detail to make them credible.

Third, can you think of anything that could have been left out (Katzer et al., 1978)? Rereading the methods section again can help you identify potential gaps between data collected and data interpreted. Check to see if each hypothesis or research question was answered. If any were eliminated, what reason was given for doing so? Was any part of the data reported and published elsewhere? As a researcher and writer of a research report, remember that a conscientious researcher will account for everything that was assumed from the beginning. Give honest and fair explanations if data were not meaningful, if variables did not predict as hypothesized, or if questions were dropped from your study.

Developing Interpretations From Results

It is not always straightforward or easy to explain what the results mean. But you must. You cannot assume that the brief conclusion and description of statistical tests in the results section eliminates the need for you to describe in writing the results found.

Most research projects seek to answer a set of research questions or hypotheses, and the answers to these are not always consistent. So not only must a researcher interpret findings for each question or hypothesis, but he or she must also be able to reconcile the findings as a whole.

One way to do so is to return to the study's main objective (Bouma & Atkinson, 1995). What did the study seek to find? Starting with the answer to this question can help a researcher frame the discussion section. If the results are the answers the researcher expected, writing the discussion section will be more straightforward. But if the results do not answer the main objective directly or if findings contradict one another, the researcher must address these inconsistencies or unexpected findings.

As part of interpreting the results, the researcher should address to whom the research findings apply (Bouma & Atkinson, 1995). In the

AN ETHICAL
ISSUE

Dealing With Unexpected Results

Imagine yourself as a researcher who has just spent several months designing and conducting a study. When you get the printout of your statistical calculations, you see several alarming results. One hypothesized difference is not significant, and one hypothesized relationship runs in the direction opposite to your expectation. Now what? Before you panic, consider the following:

- Are you certain that the data were entered accurately and in the required format?
- Is the statistical programming correct and appropriate?

If the data and programming are not suspect, you have several alternatives:

- Consider alternative explanations for the findings. Reread everything you can find about your topic and methodology.
- Reexamine the methods and procedures of the previous studies to determine the extent to which differences in methodologies would create different results.
- Talk to others with expertise in your research topic and research methodology. They may provide useful insight.
- Determine the damage of these unexpected results to the overall worth and conclusion of your study.

After taking these steps, you will have to decide whether to continue with your plan to write the research report. If you decide to continue, taking these steps should help you write about the unexpected results with more confidence. Although researchers are not fond of unexpected results, the scientific process allows for them. never hide a result, even if it is not the result you expected. You and other scholars will benefit from your straightforward and realistic description and assessment of them.

---

strictest sense, research findings are limited to the participants who were part of the research project. However, most researchers want to extend the application of their findings to larger issues and individuals beyond the sample of participants. Findings can be stated firmly with respect to the sample, but when researchers make broader generalizations, they should be tentative.

Manner of Presentation

There are several forms for providing interpretation of research results in the discussion section. One way is to simply interpret the results for each research question and hypothesis in order. Another way is discuss the most important result first and then continue the discussion with the interpretations of results that are secondary. Yet a third way is to respond to the study's primary objective and then provide detail about each research question and hypothesis.

However the discussion section is organized, this section usually starts with a one-paragraph summary of the overall results. An example of this type of summary is provided by Gross, Guerrero, and Alberts (2004):

Given the contextual nature of competence, one cannot assume that behavior assessed as appropriate and effective in one context or type of relationship will be evaluated similarly in another. Therefore, findings on the relationship between conflict strategies and perceptions of competence in personal relationships cannot be applied automatically to other contexts (such as task-oriented situations involving temporary dyads). This study examined whether the competence model of interpersonal conflict generalizes to a context in which temporary task partners have little or no relational history. Overall, findings suggest that a modified version of the competence model may be applied fruitfully to task-oriented situations involving temporary dyads or small groups, such as students working together on a project, ad hoc committee members determining a university policy for downsizing faculty, or realtors trying to find a compromise between the seller's and buyers' positions. (p. 262)

This one paragraph generally summarizes the results before the researcher addresses the findings more specifically.

One other feature of a discussion section is consistent regardless of how it is organized—the researcher should link the findings back to the literature described in the literature review. Doing this completes the research cycle by demonstrating how new results are consistent or inconsistent with previous findings. Researchers should avoid presenting new citations in the discussion section. All of the relevant literature should appear in the literature review.

Presenting the Limitations

It is also customary for the researcher to acknowledge any methodological limitations that may affect the results or interpretation of the results. Sometimes researchers present a limitations subsection; in other cases, limitations will be presented near the end of the discussion section.

All research designs and all methodologies have limitations. Although the point in this section is not to address each and every potential limitation, researchers should draw readers' attention to those that are most likely to influence the research results and implications drawn from the findings. Frymier and Wanzer (2003) describe the limitations of their study on students' perceptions of communication with their professors:

A limitation of this study is that our data only reflects the perceptions of students and not those of faculty, nor did we examine actual behavior. Future research also needs to examine the impact of OCC [out-of-class communication] between instructors and disabled students on learning and related outcomes. (p. 189)

By acknowledging this limitation, the authors are engaging in the type of self-reflexive criticism that is part of the scientific tradition.

Recommending Future Research

Recommendations about future research may be presented as a separate subsection or as a conclusion to the discussion section. In the future research subsection, authors give advice about what they believe should be studied next or how they believe the next study should be carried out. These recommendations should be specific, rather than a vague statement to the effect of "Future research is needed." An example of how researchers can address future research issues is provided by Henningsen, Henningsen, Cruz, and Morrill (2003):

Two features of the experiment present opportunities for future study. First, the task was judgmental (i.e., there was no observably correct answer), and therefore, precluded an examination of the connection between group performance and influence behavior or interaction goals. In other words, because there was no right answer to the decision task, the relationship between decision performance and influence cannot be examined in this study. Thus, it remains an important direction for future research.

Second, RFT [relational framing theory] has enjoyed initial support in the context of social influence in groups. A more rigorous test, however, should include an induction to vary the context of interaction to determine if the dominance and affiliation frames are differentially salient. (p. 195)

In this paragraph, the authors address issues that limited the scope of their findings and offer a recommendation that they or others can use in the design of a similar future research project.

TRY THIS!   **How to Read a Research Report**

In reading research reports, the consumer must be a critic. This means that you should bring a healthy level of skepticism as well as an open mind to reading research reports. The following recommendations will help you become a better consumer of research (Katzer et al., 1978; Tucker et al., 1981):

1. Read the entire article.
2. Do not evaluate the research as good or bad because of one aspect of the research that you liked or disliked.
3. Do not be easily impressed, positively or negatively.
4. Recognize that something can be learned from every study. Even if you discount a study's results, you should be able to learn something about how to conduct, or not conduct, research from reading the research report.
5. Acknowledge that all research has limitations.
6. Seek to identify the assumptions that are unwritten but at the foundation of the research report. Ask if these assumptions are acceptable to you.

FINISHING THE QUANTITATIVE RESEARCH REPORT

After the major sections of the research report are written, the researcher must complete several more elements that help introduce the manuscript and make it appealing for readers.

Title

Researchers generally have a tentative, working title even before they start writing the research report. But now, with the report essentially finished, that title must be checked to see if it is still representative of what was written. The guidelines below can help you create an effective title (Pyrczak & Bruce, 2000):

1. If your study has just a few variables, these should be identified in the title.
2. Indicate what was studied in the title, not the results or conclusions of the study.
3. If the population is important, identify it in the title (for example, adolescent internet users).

With your title written according to these guidelines, examine it more closely. Is the title as concise and succinct as possible? Is it consistent with the research questions or hypotheses in your study? The title provides readers with a framework for engaging what you have written. And, many times, readers make a decision to read or not read a research report by examining the title. Make sure yours reflects the study you completed.

Title Page

Obviously, the title goes on the title page. Other information that goes here includes the author's name, contact information, and date the report was written or submitted. The title page is also the place to acknowledge and thank anyone who helped during the research process. Almost all researchers get help from others in data collection. The rule is, if someone helped on your project and is not one of the report's authors, then this person should be thanked in an acknowledgment sentence at the bottom of the title page.

Abstract

An abstract is not always required. If it is, it can be written only after the research manuscript is complete. Generally, an abstract is very short, 75 to

150 words, and has three objectives (Bouma & Atkinson, 1995). First, the abstract states the aim or overall objective of the research. Second, the abstract gives a brief explanation of the research method. Finally, the abstract briefly summarizes the results of the study. Researchers should write the abstract carefully as it is potentially the first—and perhaps the last—element a consumer will read. The abstract should help a reader find the potential value of the study for his or her research project.

References

The **reference list** is an alphabetical listing by author's last name of all materials cited in the research report. It must be complete and without error because it is the mechanism by which readers trace backward from your document to other research reports. It should not include materials you examined or consulted but did not use to write your research report. A reference list must follow an academic style. The information you need is provided in the next section of this chapter.

USING APA STYLE

The scientific tradition requires that researchers use one of many standardized styles for citing the work of others and for providing a list of material used in writing the research report. Typically, in the communication discipline, the preferred style is that of the style book of the American Psychological Association (APA style). Its formal title is *Publication Manual of the American Psychological Association* (5th ed., 2001). More commonly it is referred to as the APA style book.

Citing Others' Work

Citing the work of others is essential. It would be unethical not to give other researchers credit for their ideas or conclusions. Recall from Chapters 2 and 5 that there are two types of citations with which you need to be familiar.

The first is the direct citation. Here, you are using word-for-word what others have written.

The phrases or sentences of others that you want to use must be indicated with opening and closing quotation marks or by block indent. The author or authors, the year of the publication, and the page number are also required. With this information, a reader of your report can turn to the reference list and find the original source of the material.

The second is the indirect citation. Here, you are paraphrasing the words, phrases, and sentences of other researchers. In this case, quotation marks and page numbers are not required. Refer back to Chapter 2 for a complete description of how to use both direct and indirect citations. Also check with the writing center at your university for additional resources.

Creating the Reference List

When you are ready to create the reference list for your research article, you can turn to several resources to guide you through the process. Obviously, you should check your library or writing center for a copy of the APA style manual. Your writing center will likely have handouts to help you master this style for creating reference lists and placing citations in the text of your manuscript.

Given the pace of technological change, a consistent format for references from web-based sources does not exist. But in general, this format provides all the necessary information for someone to identify your source and find it again. For example, if you accessed the website of the Center for Media and Public Affairs, you would create this reference:

> Center for Media and Public Affairs. Retrieved September 6, 2004, from http://www.cmpa.com/

Note that no date follows the title of the website, as no date appears on the website. For a website that is dated, the following type of reference would be created:

> The Annenberg Public Policy Center of the University of Pennsylvania. (2003). Retrieved September 6, 2004, from http://www.annenbergpublicpolicycenter.org/

TRY THIS!   **Submit Your Research Paper to a Communication Convention**

You may write a research paper for your research methods class or some other class, or even as a senior project. Given your hard work, why not submit your paper to be reviewed and considered for presentation at a conference or convention of one of the communication associations? Although the dates do vary, the table below lists several of the communication associations, a general time frame for their submission deadlines and convention dates, and websites so you can check out their submission requirements. Some associations have sections or units especially for students (for example, see the Undergraduate Honors Conference at the SSCA website). Another outlet for your research is your state communication association.

Convention	General Time Frame for Submission Deadlines & Convention Dates	Association Website
Association for Education in Journalism and Mass Communication	Submissions are due early April for the next August's convention.	http://www.aejmc.org
Broadcast Education Association	Submissions are due early December for the next April's convention.	http://www.beaweb.org
Central States Communication Association	Submissions are due mid-September for the next April's convention.	http://www.csca-net.org
Eastern Communication Association	Submissions are due mid-October for the next April's convention.	http://www.ecasite.org
International Communication Association	Submissions are due in November for the next May/June convention.	http://www.icahdq.org
National Communication Association	Submissions are due early to mid-February for the next November's convention.	http://www.natcom.org
Southern States Communication Association	Submissions are due mid-September for the next April's convention.	http://www.ssca.net
Western States Communication Association	Submissions are due early September for the next February's convention.	http://www.westcomm.org

If you submit your paper, it will be reviewed by several evaluators and judged for its quality. If the quality of your paper is acceptable and competitive with other submissions, your paper will be programmed on a panel with other papers. At the convention, each presenter on a panel has 10 to 15 minutes to present the major ideas of his or her paper. After all paper presentations are complete, a respondent will provide constructive feedback about the papers. Good luck!

If you access a page within or a document from a website, then the following type of reference is needed:

> Name of website. (date if available). Name of webpage or report. Retrieved month and date, year, from complete URL.

ISSUES IN WRITING

The writer's presentation of his or her efforts is crucial to how the written report is received. Unfortunately, writers call negative attention to their writing when they fail to recognize some common writing problems. Several of these common to writing research reports are described here (Ryan, 1998).

The first common problem is carelessness. Although you have heard this advice before, it is repeated here as well—proofread your document. Use the spelling checker on your word-processing program and then read your manuscript to double-check for problems the computer will not find. Manuscripts should be error-free—no typographical errors, spelling mistakes, and grammatical problems. Errors like these cause readers to doubt the credibility of your findings. After all, if you are not careful with the written manuscript and make noticeable mistakes, readers will wonder to what extent you were careful with data collection and interpretation.

Beyond being error-free writing, your research report should not include rambling, ambiguous, or wordy phrases. Simple, basic sentences are better than complex ones. Carelessness can also extend to the style in which citations and references are included. When you follow a style, the implication is that you can follow procedures in other aspects of the research process as well.

The second common problem is making unspecified assumptions. Remember that the written research report is the only "conversation" you will have with readers. Thus, your major assumptions should be specified. Do not expect the reader to piece together your assumptions based on your literature review, hypotheses, and methodology. The best way to help a reader understand your point of view is to describe it and its supporting framework.

A third type of common problem with written research reports is the authors' failure to place their study within the context of published research. You should describe the literature on which your study is based. If special circumstances prevailed at the time of data collection, you should contextualize your research with respect to these events. For example, if you are collecting data on employee perceptions of corporate scandals and a high-profile case is featured prominently in the news immediately preceding or during your data collection, you should include this information in the methods section and consider its influence in the interpretation of the findings.

The fourth writing problem is lack of clarity of the research questions and hypotheses. If you can answer "yes" to each of the following, you have succeeded in avoiding this common problem:

- Do your research questions or hypotheses provide a clear focus and direction for the research?
- Do your hypotheses predict relationships between or among variables?
- Do your research questions and hypotheses suggest how the relationships will be tested?

These questions can be used as criteria to test the clarity of research questions and hypotheses regardless of a study's methodological approach or research design.

The fifth common problem is the use of vague and undefined terms. Dictionary definitions are generally not suitable for scholarly writing. All concepts, constructs, and variables should have clear definitions that flow from prior research or from the theoretical perspective guiding the study. These definitions should be provided in the literature review, with the operationalizations described in the methods section.

The Revision Process

Finally, be prepared to revise and rewrite your manuscript. It is unlikely that you will be able to create the most effective presentation of information in the first draft. Effective writing is achieved through rewriting. As you review the manuscript, check for writing clarity, and look for spelling, punctuation, and grammar errors.

You should also check that every citation in the text of your paper is listed in the reference section. Likewise, every item in the reference list should be found somewhere in the paper. Finally, every item in the reference list should have complete information.

Most important to the revision process is to look for the clarity and strength of your arguments. Ask others, even if they are not experts on your topic or method, to read your research report. Responding to the questions they have is likely to make your report clearer and more succinct. Every claim should be based on evidence, and you should not make claims that overstate the findings.

SUMMARY

1. A study is not complete until the researcher writes a research report to communicate his or her findings with others.

2. Following the scientific tradition of many disciplines, there are four major parts to the written quantitative research report: literature review, methods section, results section, and discussion.

3. The literature review is comprised of the literature the researcher sought and studied to design the research project; provides a brief historical background of the variables, issues, and topics studied; and goes beyond simple description of previous work to analyze and integrate this work into a coherent whole.

4. Literature reviews usually begin with a problem statement, can be organized in several ways, are written in third person,

and present research questions and hypotheses.

5. The methods section describes how the research study was executed, and includes descriptions of the participants, the research procedures, and the research variables.

6. The results section presents the findings as information without interpretation.

7. In the discussion section, the researcher provides the interpretation and implications of the results to answer the question, "What do these results mean?"

8. Researchers include subsections on the limitations of their research design and methodology as well as recommendations for future research in the discussion section.

9. To complete a research report, the researcher must develop a title, finalize the title page, develop an abstract, and develop the reference list.

10. Most quantitative research reports are written in the APA style.

11. Researchers need to be very careful in their written work as their level of carelessness translates to lack of credibility for readers.

12. Researchers should be prepared to spend time in the revision process.

KEY TERMS

discussion section	reference list
literature review	results section
methods section	

CHAPTER EIGHTEEN

Reading and Writing the Qualitative Research Report

Chapter Checklist

After reading this chapter, you should be able to:

1. Select the story you want to tell.

2. Read through all of the data collected before you begin writing.

3. Decide whose voice will be the primary storyteller and select an appropriate writing style.

4. Identify the core ideas you want to present in the story.

5. Write a description about how the data were collected.

6. Make (and then honor) decisions about revealing the identity of participants.

7. Include both description and analysis in the written report.

8. Select the most appropriate quotes from participants to support your analysis.

9. Write a discussion section that reviews what was attempted, what has been learned, and identifies new questions.

10. Refine your written report through several revisions.

11. Write a title that accurately introduces your study in an interesting way.

12. Write an abstract for the written report.

13. Develop a complete and accurate list of references used in the report in the preferred style.

As with other research designs, a qualitative study is not complete until the researcher writes the research report to communicate findings to others. Although there are some similarities between qualitative and quantitative research reports, there are significant differences. The primary difference is that a qualitative researcher usually analyzes the data and writes about the analysis in back-and-forth reflective steps. Contrast this approach to that of the quantitative researcher, who bases his or her analyses on the results of statistical tests. Clearly, the two writing processes are different. The quantitative researcher completes the research report after determining what the data mean. The qualitative researcher drafts the research report as part of figuring out the interpretation of the data.

As a result, in any report of qualitative research, legitimacy is at stake. The writer's job is to convince readers that the description is authentic and significant. In some sense, the writer of a qualitative research report becomes a guide helping the reader move through unfamiliar interaction (Lindlof & Taylor, 2002). If the interaction being reported belongs to the familiar and everyday, then the writer's objective is to help the reader see it in a new way or to expose some aspect that is often overlooked. Whether the interaction is new or familiar, researchers using qualitative methods can increase our understanding about how humans construct and share meanings (Potter, 1996). Therefore, the researcher-now-writer must pay special attention to what is written and how it is written.

Generally, writing qualitative research reports is more difficult than writing quantitative research reports. Why? First, there are fewer conventions or traditions for writing the qualitative research report. So the researcher has more decisions to make about what to present as data and how to present data to support conclusions. Second, qualitative research by its very nature is more difficult to report, because data or evidence is not necessarily categorized into discrete units the way it is in quantitative reports. For example, researchers using qualitative methods cannot rely on descriptive statistics to summarize and represent a group of data. Given these problems, one evaluative criterion to use at each stage of the qualitative writing process is to ask yourself how your description and analysis is increasing the reader's understanding of how humans construct messages and share meaning.

PARTS OF THE QUALITATIVE RESEARCH REPORT

Qualitative research reports vary considerably in their structure and writing style. But minimally, a qualitative research report should include an introduction, a summary of the literature that provided a foundation for the study, a description of data collection and analytic techniques, and a report of the interpretation and analyses. In addition to these sections, many qualitative reports include sections on implications of the findings and research questions that remain to be explored or research questions that develop as a result of the study.

PRESENTING THE CORE IDEA OR QUESTION

Most qualitative studies begin with an introductory premise that serves as a frame for the descriptions and analyses that follow. One way to begin is for the author to explain why he or she was in this particular setting. For example, students studying the entertainment center described earlier begin their study with

> Our research started out like any other team ethnography. Eight of us had received permission to study an interesting cultural site—a large "entertainment center" in the middle of an urban shopping mall that, at the beginning of the project, employed more than 300 people, and served up to 10,000 customers each week. (Communication Studies 298, 1997, p. 251)

With information about why the research team was there and who was part of the research team, readers very quickly can make several assumptions. Assumption 1: Students were conducting the study as part of some class project. Assumption 2: These student researchers were similar in age to the customers of such an establishment.

Another introductory premise explains why a particular setting is important or interesting. For example, examine how Mayer (2003) uses the introduction to create relevance for and interest in her study:

> Telenovelas, or Latin-American soap operas, may not be the most popular programs among Latinos in the United States, but they are certainly the programs most targeted toward a Latino audience. Airing mornings, afternoons, and during prime time, telenovelas generate public discussions simply by virtue of their omnipresence on Spanish-language network leaders, Univision and Telemundo. The genre's dominance proceeds from a market strategy to accrue advertising revenues from Spanish speakers in the United States, but this hardly explains the subtle context in which a Latino might find a telenovela engaging enough to watch daily, talk about with friends, and identify with. This study examines the complexities of telenovela viewing over time for a small sample of young Mexican-American viewers. (p. 479)

Or, the manuscript can begin more dramatically with an excerpt from field notes or a quote from a participant. For example, Tracy (2002) presents data from her field notes to set the scene and create interest for the reader:

> *Incident*
>
> A woman calls 911 to report a drive-by shooting. She sounds panicked, hysterical. Call-taker Christy asks, "Did anyone get shot?" The caller says, "I don't care whether someone got shot." Christy yells, "We have to ask these questions!" The caller says "I've lived in this neighborhood for a long time and the police never come." Christy tries to ask several more questions, but the caller resists, saying, "Just don't come," before she hangs up. When Christy gets off the phone, her face is bright red, and she exclaims, "I couldn't help it, she wasn't answering my questions." (p. 129)

The incident continues for several more lines before the researcher declares, "Asking questions and taking down information is one of the most important, yet problematic, parts of a 911 call-taker's job"

(p. 130). By starting with the excerpt from her field notes, Tracy foreshadows the emotional and problematic interaction she presents and analyzes in the article.

Of course, your manuscript can begin with the more traditional approach of situating the study in the literature. In this case, you would use the opening paragraphs to demonstrate your familiarity with similar studies or to position your study in opposition to what has been previously studied. These and the techniques described earlier give you an idea of how you might begin to write your qualitative report.

Many introductory techniques will work. The one that works best will depend upon the subject matter and the audience. Regardless of how you begin, your goal is to draw the reader into your experiences of being in and with the participants in the communication environment you studied. One piece of writing advice that many qualitative researchers share is that to begin writing you must know the story you want to tell. This is why the introduction is so important: It frames the rest of the manuscript. In fact, it is likely that you will write the introductory paragraphs several times, perhaps even revising them after the rest of the manuscript is complete.

After the introduction, qualitative research reports generally then transition into the literature review. Ethnographies are one type of qualitative research report that most often break with this tradition. The same general guidelines given for literature reviews in quantitative research reports in Chapter 16 can also be used to develop a literature review section for a qualitative research report.

WRITING ABOUT THE METHOD

Some qualitative researchers write about the methods and practices used to collect data separately from writing up the data. This separation in the writing process has an advantage. Primarily, it allows you to focus on the substance of what you found, not how you found it. The section about your method can be drafted early on in the process and later blended into the essay. As qualitative research methods are increasingly acknowledged, it is no longer necessary to write about the method as if you have discovered it or to give the complete history of the method you used. Nor is there a need to defend the selection of qualitative methods.

At the same time, the writer should not make gross assumptions for the reader. Someone reading a qualitative research study should know, at a minimum, (1) when the fieldwork was conducted, (2) the extent or length of your involvement in the interaction environment, (3) information about the participants and the communication context and scene, (4) the steps and methods for analyzing the data, and (5) to what extent the data was triangulated, or cross-checked (Kvale, 1996; Wolcott, 2001). Information about research methods and procedures should always be included in the written research report.

For example, after her literature review, Tracy (2002) presents a section titled "Background, Data and Method" consisting of several paragraphs. The first paragraph describes the emergency call center and its location, the work shifts of 911 call-takers, and the number of calls made to this emergency call center. A second paragraph explains the process an emergency call follows from when the call is received, how it is processed by call-takers, and how it is transferred to emergency responders.

Next, Tracy describes the data. She describes the number of hours she observed and where, and the number of pages of field notes produced from those observations. She describes the interviews she conducted, including who was interviewed and about what topics. She describes the documents she obtained and analyzed. Last, she describes the transcripts of the emergency calls that she downloaded from the call center's audio archive, and how she transcribed and cataloged those calls.

Finally, Tracy describes her analytical method. This is about one fourth of her description of the research design and methods she used:

> I focused my analysis of data on matters that caused problems or disruptions in the 911 sequence. I analyzed data using a version of Glaser and Strauss's (1967) constant comparative method, an iterative, circular method characterized by multiple readings of data, identification

of emergent themes and evaluation (and reevaluation) of data (see Charmaz, 2000; Lindlof, 1995 for reviews of this method). In initial readings, I examined data for organizational issues that call-takers found to be problematic.

Revealing the Identity of Participants

In writing about participants, the researcher must keep his or her agreement about confidentiality and anonymity with participants. If participants' privacy is to be maintained, you must develop fictitious names to refer to participants. There are several ways to do this. One method is to develop a set of substitute names that maintain the sex and ethnicity of participants. For example, Janice would be an appropriate substitute for Joann. But Joan or Joanne would be too similar to use. Changing Joann to Juanita or Juana would not be appropriate as it invokes a change in ethnicity. Another method is to refer to participants as Physician 1, Physician 2, and so on. Your readers will probably appreciate the first approach as it personalizes the description and makes the report more readable. Other ideas for protecting the identity of participants are given in Chapter 5.

In some cases, you must go beyond simply changing the name. If a description of a participant is so unique as to allow the person to be identified, you should also change some of the participant's nonessential characteristics. In no case should you camouflage an identity so that it is misleading. You would not want readers to accept the actions of a female as those of a male. Nor would you want readers to believe a participant was a child when he or she was an adult. Researchers report that these name and identity changes have been made either by stating so in the methods section or by adding an endnote to the report.

PRESENTING THE DATA

In qualitative research, data are textual. Whether the researcher audio- or videotaped the interaction or observed the interaction firsthand, the observations end up in a written or textual form. Thus, once the qualitative data collection process of the research study is complete, the major problem is not having sufficient data, but judiciously editing the data to a manageable amount (Wolcott, 1990). This is often a difficult process: The researcher has painstakingly collected the data and is reluctant to not include all the written data in the final research report. Besides reducing the amount of data to be presented, the researcher must also select data that provide a meaningful frame for interpretation. In other words, decisions must be made about what to tell and how to tell it (Van Maanen, 1988). Thus, Wolcott (1990) suggests that in planning to write the qualitative research report, you determine "the basic story you are going to tell, who is to do the telling, and what representational style you will follow for joining observer and observed" (p. 18). To help your readers understand your points, you will need to take extra care in presenting your analytical process in a clear way to your readers.

Authorial Voice

In qualitative research reports, the writer must make a decision about **authorial voice**—or who will tell the story. This question is critical in qualitative research (Wolcott, 2001). Because qualitative research is conducted among participants in the field, many scholars allow participants to tell the story in their voice. Interweaving the participants' voices with that of the writer (in the role of narrator) can be a successful approach.

This writing style is common in reporting ethnographies. For example, students in Communication Studies 298 at California State University, Sacramento describe their experiences in an entertainment center that included a brew pub, a sports bar, a dance bar, a piano bar, a country-western bar, a comedy club, a game arcade, and two restaurants. The manuscript, team-written, flows effortlessly between their impressions and their interaction with the center's employees and customers. An excerpt demonstrates:

> The dance bar is quiet now, the sweaty bodies gone. Steely energy lingers, pressing in on me from all sides. The man is here, leaning against the bar. He is wearing a name tag on his shirt that reads "Manager, Dance."
>
> "It's the edge in the room," he whispers, moving closer. "You can feel it. Have you ever been outside just before a thunderstorm, and it's in the air?"
>
> He snaps his fingers and the music, a primal heartbeat begins. It pulses around and through my body. It pierces my ears and throat. "These short, sharp pulses spread across the spectrum of sound our ears pick up," the man explains proudly, "overloading our hearing, inducing trance." He offers a beguiling smile. "Why don't you dance?" (Communication Studies 298, 1997, p. 261)

This approach interweaves multiple voices, acknowledging the roles of researchers and participants.

Descriptive accounts are generally written in the first person, although third-person language can be used. Be cautious, however. The impersonality of the third-person approach can make it appear that you are representing an objective truth (Wolcott, 2001)—an idea opposed in qualitative research.

Another common technique is to alternate between third person for the analysis and first person for the presentation of the data. Reporting on issues of a perceived generational curse in a study of intergenerational suicide and mother–daughter communication, Miller (1995) demonstrates this technique:

> The theme of differentiation was driven by the perception that the family was victim to a generational curse that all the women in the family lack respect for their mothers. It was perceived by most of the women that their mothers mistreat or have a conflictual relationship with their own mothers. *I think that there can be generational curses handed down. You know the Bible speaks of them in the Old Testament and stuff. Grandma Rose would talk bad about her mother and then my mother started being verbally abusive to her mother . . . we are all verbally abusive, it's strong in our family. Now we're doing it with Mom.* (pp. 253–254)

To make her arguments, Miller alternates between analysis, written in the third person, and the italicized presentation of data, presented in the first person. This structure allows the voice of participants to be heard. Additionally, it integrates the data or evidence with the researcher's assessment of the data in a larger framework.

Adopting a Writing Style

Certain traditions have developed about the writing style presented in qualitative research reports. These traditions differ in the degree to which they hide or acknowledge the researcher's presence. Researchers can adopt the writing style of the realist, the confessional, or the impressionist when they write about the setting, the participants, and the interaction they observed (Van Maanen, 1988). Although developed originally for the writing of ethnographies, each style can be adapted to writing about the data collected with other qualitative methods.

The Writing Style of the Realist   When the author takes the **realist** position, he or she narrates the story in a dispassionate, third-person voice. Four characteristics are central to the realist label.

First, the author is almost absent. Only the people who were studied are visible in the text. The author must work on good faith. That is, readers hold the author responsible for observing and reporting what any good researcher would see and report. To achieve this characteristic, the author refrains from using "I," or first-person voice, to describe the setting, the participants, or the interaction.

The second characteristic of the realist tradition is focus on the minute, maybe even mundane, details of everyday life. Such details are used systematically to demonstrate a point the author wants to make. This level of detail forces the author to be as concrete as possible. For example, "a dog is not simply a dog, but a 'large, brown-and-white dog who jumps on people and answers to the name of Blue'" (Van Maanen, 1988, p. 49).

The third characteristic is close editing of the work by the author to convey the point of view of the persons who were observed rather than the point of view of the researcher. Thus, the reader should know what the observed person

said, did, thought, saw, and felt—not what the author said, did, thought, saw, and felt.

The final characteristic of the realist tradition is interpretive omnipotence. This means that the author has the final word on the participants and how their interaction is interpreted and presented. Adhering to this writing style raises certain questions: Did the author get it right? Are there other interpretations possible? Thus, in the realist tradition, the author is all-powerful. He or she must demonstrate confidence in that power through careful and detailed description.

The realist style is often used when the researcher has collected narratives, or stories, as the qualitative data. Using interviews to stimulate the collection of 19 narratives at a day care center, Meyer (1997) then needed to present an organized analysis in the research report. First, he read the stories to identify the dominant themes throughout the set of narratives. Next, he categorized the narratives according to thematic groups based on similarities of statements and meaning, repetition of keywords, and descriptions of analogous events. Using the thematic groups as evidence of expressed organizational values, he used the themes to organize the written research report.

Meyer (1997) uses the realist writing style to present the descriptions and analyses of the narratives in the following way. First, an organizational value is introduced with a third-person description. Then, a narrative, in the words of the participant, is given to illustrate the value. Meyer continues with his analysis of how the narrative embodies the value. This pattern is repeated throughout until each value is fully explored. The following excerpt will demonstrate his technique:

Teaching Children. The third most common value associated with humorous narratives involved teaching children; here the humor stemmed from mistakes the children made as they learned. This suggests that when some individuals know what others do not, their naïve errors are funny to those in the superior position of knowing. One member's account illustrates the point:

Just this morning, uh, our, uh, little Tommy in our class, he's a Ninja Turtle nut (Laugh), and he was talking to two of the other little boys, and they were talking about, uh, "That's radical, dude, that's radical!" And, I asked him what "radical" means; he said, "I don't know, I just like to say it." (Laughter).

Here, a child using a word without knowing its meaning sparked humor, as the teachers recounting the story were in the superior position of knowing what the word meant, which provided the humorous incongruity. (p. 199)

The Writing Style of the Confessional   Whereas the style of the realist hides the researcher, the style of the **confessional** reveals everything. The motivation to reveal is driven by the author's need for the reader to validate and verify both what was discovered and how it was discovered. Three conventions characterize the confessional writing style.

The first convention of the confessional is use of the first person: The author makes himself or herself visible with liberal references to "I." By doing so, the author hopes to establish intimacy with the reader. Writing in the confessional style, authors often reveal their personal biases. They also attempt to establish themselves in the role of newcomer to the interaction setting. Such a strategy positions the writer in a role similar to that of the reader—both are trying to make sense of the interaction for the first time.

The second characteristic of the confessional is presentation of the point of view of the researcher. Thus, how the researcher's point of view develops and changes is part of the story to be told. The researcher moves back and forth between being an insider, experiencing the interaction in the same way that participants do, and being an outsider, seeing interaction for the first time. The confessional style often makes frequent references to being shocked and surprised as intimacies of the interaction are discovered.

Naturalness is the third convention of the confessional writing style. Because the confessional tells all, including the flaws and problems in the observations, the researcher must reclaim or reestablish the position that the work is still adequate or is representative of the natural interaction observed. This is accomplished, in part, by describing how the participants accepted the researcher. It is also accomplished by using moderation in describing attitudes and emotions toward the participants. "The exotic is downplayed, the theatrical is understated, [and] intense feelings are left out" (Van Maanen, 1988, p. 80).

In telling his story of being a Peace Corps volunteer in Ethiopia, Crawford (1996) uses the confessional writing style first to explain how his interest in ethnographic research was stimulated, second to convey what it is like to experience ethnography, and third to respond to ethnographic dilemmas. The following excerpt is from the second part of his essay.

> The game became hypnotic. The heat. The humidity. The brown water. Hypnotic. Each cycle of the game deepened the spell. The constant sound of rushing water was like the white noise of sensory deprivation. Our casual conversations became strangely disembodied. The natives watching us with interest shimmered on the shore. We were out there. In the sun. On a rock. Hypnotic.
>
> The trance was broken when someone suggested that we swim to a sandbar. We were all together and resting on the upstream rock before beginning another ride downstream in the current. We liked the idea. It was time to change the game. The sandbar was upstream. I silently wondered if I could make it. (p. 160)

The Writing Style of the Impressionist   The style of the **impressionist** is intended to startle the reader. By using metaphors, phrasings, imagery, and expansive recall, a researcher writing as an impressionist creates striking stories. Four conventions, or characteristics, describe this writing style.

Dramatic recall is the first characteristic of the impressionist writing style. The researcher draws the reader into the unfamiliar story by retelling the story in chronological order with as much detail as possible. The researcher holds back on interpreting what was observed in favor of making the observations real for the reader. In effect, this strategy transfers the reader into the observed world because the reader relives the story with the writer.

Fragmented knowledge is the second characteristic. The reader's knowledge of how the observations were collected and what problems

AN ETHICAL ISSUE

Creating Something From Nothing

In writing qualitative research reports, researchers cannot be tempted to create quoted material from notes that are not in the direct words of participants. For example, your field notes indicate, "Jerry was upset and seemed angry at Lisa's interpretation of their disagreement." That is how you, the researcher, described the interaction you observed. These are your words, not the words of Jerry, the participant. It would be unethical to turn those field notes into the following description and quote in the written research report: "Jerry seemed upset at Lisa. 'I can't believe that's how you interpreted our disagreement.'" The rule here: Use only what you have captured as the direct words of participants as quoted material. Besides the prohibition against creating something from nothing, what other ethical concerns should researchers be aware of when they use quotes from research participants?

were encountered is fragmented because the writer's primary purpose is the telling of the story. Necessary bits of information about methodological process are revealed along the way, but not in such a way as to detract from the story.

The way in which researchers characterize the primary interactants is the third convention of the impressionist writing style. People in the story are given names, faces, and motives. Thus, this style would favor descriptions of individuals rather than descriptions of groups of people.

The fourth characteristic of the impressionist style is dramatic control. Researchers use present tense to invoke the feeling that the reader is there too. Another way to increase dramatic control is for the researcher not to reveal the ending of the story. A degree of dramatic tension is developed and only released at the end. In this way, the researcher keeps the reader alert and interested.

Taylor (1997) uses the impressionist style as he presents his ethnographic fieldwork at the Los Alamos National Laboratory. An excerpt reveals the dramatic tone and imagery:

I have, however, also suffered losses, and I believe that they have led me to enter this field in order to ask questions about violence, fear, and discourse. Here, as always, I find myself wanting to write another kind of sentence. But the sentence that I have is the one where I tell you my family—my original home—was sometimes a violent place. Is *falling* the natural path of

violence? I think it is (until it rises). In our home, angry shouts fell, flying hands fell, whistling belts fell (decades later, it is the sounds I remember). Tears fell. I am thirty-five years old, and am learning anew—consciously—how to *stand*, how to correct the habitual falling of my head and shoulders, a cringe learned from the anticipation of blows. I am seeking, of course, to lose these losses. To no longer need them. (pp. 224–225)

The Writing Style of the Critical Scholar   The style of the **critical scholar** is concerned with drawing out and foregrounding the perspective of disadvantaged or marginalized groups. As a result, this type of writing also exposes inequalities and injustices.

For example, Martin (2004) investigated how women in middle management positions at a zoo used humor to negotiate the paradoxes of being women in a masculine work structure and being members of middle management, caught between supervising subordinates and being supervised by executives. In reporting her findings that organizational paradox is also gendered paradox, Martin described and illustrated with examples how these women used humor. To illustrate the power structure and its inherent differential, one theme drawn from the observations and interviews was that when women "initiated playful discourse about serious topics, they often immediately checked with the director [all were men] to see if they had overstepped relational bounds" (p. 156).

Martin (2004) presents evidence of another power-laden theme in the paradox of power-(lessness):

> In one case, male staff members teased a manager, Carole, about her blonde hair and hair coloring, speculation about the manager's personal hair care activities in a disparaging way. The excerpt below occurred in the middle of a three-hour meeting, just as the group was returning from a coffee break:
>
> Bob: I don't put any color in my hair, or Grecian formula, so get that smile off your face [to another male staff member].
>
> Manny: What kind does she [indicating Carole, the manager] have?
>
> Bob: We'll go to your house and steal the blond, [pause] I'm joking, Carole.
>
> Manny: You are playing her too close, man.
>
> Bob: I know.
>
> Manny: You'll get probation.
>
> Bob: I'm going back on grave [overnight shift]. Then I only have to see her on Tuesdays for about 5 min.
>
> [long pause]
>
> Carole: Now Barry [the assistant manager] is late; he has the next agenda. (p. 157)

Martin goes on to explain that Carole, the only blonde in the room, was most certainly the target of the humor. She analyzes how Carole's male subordinates assume power by making her, their supervisor, the target of the teasing humor. By combining description and analysis and documenting both with a cogent example, Martin explores the disadvantages of being a female middle manager at this organization.

In another example of this type of writing, Zoller (2003) explores how employees of an automobile manufacturing plant contribute to hazardous health and working conditions by sharing and affirming the organization's construction of health and safety norms. The researcher first describes in detail two contradictions evident in the organization: organizational rhetoric that it was a safe place to work *and* associates having or knowing someone with work-related health issues; and low injury rates as measured by OSHA *and* employee experiences of being discouraged from reporting health problems and requesting alternative work. Zoller explores the way in which employees contribute to their own injustice:

> I would argue that this proof represents a deeper contradiction, because, without coaxing, the Associates I interviewed provided insight into the multiple cultural and structural processes that excluded employees' experiences from official reports of ill-health and injury. They told me explicitly about practices by line Associates, team leaders, and company doctors that discouraged or prevented them from reporting health problems and requesting job redesigns. These practices prevented Associates' lived experience from gaining *official* status in OSHA reports. (p. 126)

Although the employees, or Associates, did not see the contradiction even as they discussed these issues with the researcher, Zoller did and could make that contradiction visible by writing about it.

Regardless of which writing style you choose as most appropriate, the following criteria, adapted from Lindlof and Taylor (2002), can be used to evaluate your writing:

- Is your manuscript written well? Does it engage the reader emotionally and intellectually? Does it evoke shared experiences or frames of reference?

- Does your manuscript effectively address multiple audiences?

- Are data in your manuscript credible and interesting?

- Did you reflect on your role in producing the interpretation of the data?

- Is your manuscript ethically produced and politically accountable?

- Did you balance the tension between coming to conclusions or resolutions and remaining open to other alternatives?

- Does your writing invite readers to actively participate in the interpretation?

Who Did What? How? When?

When you read a qualitative research report, consider asking these analytical questions: Who did the observations? How did their background, training, expectations, or attitudes affect their collection and interpretation of the data? Was the context and manner in which the observations were made suitable and acceptable to you? Did the researcher use other data collection methods to account for or control for observer distortion? Are the interpretations acceptable to you? Are other interpretations of the data possible?

- Does your writing alternate between the personal and the social, or the individual and the larger group?
- Does your manuscript contribute to our understanding of social life?
- Is your writing generalizable? Does the detail of a person, scene, or setting belong to a broader group or class?

Qualitative scholars generally agree on these criteria. However, the primary objectives of reporting qualitative data are to find your own voice and remain true to your data.

RESULTS AND DISCUSSION

In contrast to writers of quantitative reports, researchers using qualitative methods have greater flexibility in reporting their results and interpretation. It would be impossible for the researcher to present all of the research data from a qualitative study. Thus, the researcher has to select and condense data in relationship to the analyses of the data. In addition to finding the appropriate balance between description and analysis, researchers need to address two other issues in writing the results and discussion sections—an organizing scheme for presenting the material and decisions about how to use participants' quoted material.

Balancing Description and Analysis

If you have trouble starting the qualitative research report, describe the interaction by answering the question "What happened?" Because analysis is based on description, the descriptive

account of who, what, when, and where may be the most important contribution made in the research report. To begin descriptively, the writer takes on the role of the storyteller. In this role, the writer invites readers to see what he or she has observed or heard. A natural place to start is to begin with the details of the settings and events. These should be revealed in a fairly straightforward and journalistic manner.

What is enough detail? Being familiar with the research setting may cause you to omit important details readers unfamiliar with the setting will need to make sense of the description. Ask people unfamiliar with your research setting to read the description. If they need to ask questions after reading it, pay close attention to the types of questions they ask. These will guide you in adding detail that makes sense to readers.

Another way to gauge the adequacy of your descriptive passages is to shift between writing description and analytic passages. If the analysis or interpretation does not make sense without additional descriptive detail, then you know more description is needed. On the other hand, descriptive detail not referenced by the analysis is extraneous and can be edited—or else it needs to be explained.

It can be difficult to separate descriptive from analytical writing, especially when writing the qualitative manuscript. One way to make this distinction is to change the authorial voice mentioned earlier in this chapter. For example, Taylor (1996) first presents three episodes from one 3-month study of the Bradbury Science Museum located at Los Alamos National Laboratory, a nuclear weapons facility. Each episode is his description of different voices and the accompanying political

TRY THIS!   ## Describe, Then Analyze

Find a place where you can take notes freely and observe the interaction of two to four people. You might want to takes notes on the nonverbal behavior of the mother and her two children sitting across the aisle from you on the bus. You could take a seat in the entryway of the library and watch students interact with members of the library staff as they ask for information or check out books. For at least 15 minutes, take notes describing the interaction environment, the interactants, and the interaction. When you are through, review your notes to distinguish between notes that describe and notes that analyze. Descriptive notes answer "What?" "Who?" "When?" and "Where?" Analytical notes answer "Why?" and "How?" Try writing first a description of what you observed and then an analysis of those interactions. What could you do differently in how you took notes to improve both the description and the analysis?

interests found in three different interaction environments in and around the museum. To signal that the descriptive part of the manuscript is finished, Taylor identifies the subsequent section as "Reflection." Here, he reemphasizes his role as a coparticipant in the production of the episodes. Then he moves the reader into his analyses of the episodes as well as an analysis of his methods by identifying specific themes revealed in his study.

Identifying and Presenting Organizing Patterns

Qualitative researchers collect a great deal of data. Finding the thread of the story you want to present is an important first step. Next, as you tell the story of your research, it can be helpful to find an organizing scheme so your readers can see the same patterns and themes that you saw so clearly.

The most obvious pattern for presentation of ideas in qualitative research is the sequence of events, especially for ethnographies. Telling the story in this way treats the research in sequential, or chronological, order—what happened first, what happened next, and so on. This is the strategy Miller (2002) uses to present her analysis of the bonfire collapse at Texas A&M University. The article starts when she first hears about the crisis from the clock radio when the alarm wakes her. After setting the context and providing information about her methods and analytical approach, Miller begins again with the sequence of

events of making sense of the tragedy. Another approach would be to relate the story as you learned about it and recorded it, which is not necessarily in chronological order. In this case, revelation of important elements can provide the analytical scheme for the research report.

Another type of organization relies on presentation of critical points regardless of the order of events. This approach can be effective if you are observing a series of similar events or if your data were collected from interviews or focus groups. The order of events is usually meaningless if your observations are spread across enough cases.

A similar and related way to organize patterns is to present a series of problems in order of importance (from major to minor, from minor to major). In this case, the research report is organized in three-part sets that identify a problem, describe the interaction attributed to the problem, and then analyze the interaction with respect to the problem. This type of organization works better if your observations come from many similar events or from many similar people rather than from one long stream of interaction of a confined set of participants, as might be the case in an ethnographic study. Other strategies to consider include using the study's research questions as a structure for presenting the data, or using the themes drawn from the data and presenting them in order of importance.

To help you find a pattern that is compelling and revealing, write a few words about each major event or each major issue revealed in a field interview—on a note card, for example. This is a practical way to sort and organize your data. Try arranging the note cards differently—first in sequential order, then in order of importance, and so on. As you read the layout of note cards, one of these organizing patterns should make more sense than the others, and that is the organizing scheme you should use to start writing your research report.

Using Participants' Quoted Material

Researchers strengthen their reporting and analysis of qualitative data by using the directly quoted interaction of participants. Several guidelines can help you in selecting and reporting this type of material (Kvale, 1996). First, provide a frame of reference or the interaction context for quoted material. Readers should not have questions about who said what, when, or where. Second, interpret all material quoted from participants. The researcher should clearly state what a quotation illuminates, illustrates, proves, or disproves. Third, find an appropriate balance between use of quoted material and your descriptions and interpretations. One standard for evaluating this balance is that quoted material should not be more than half of the results and discussion.

Fourth, short quotations are better than long ones. If longer passages are necessary, consider breaking them up by interspersing them with your description and analysis. The fifth criterion is to use only the best quotations. In making choices about which of two similar quotations is better, ask which one is most extensive, illuminating, or well formulated. Finally, if participants' quoted material is edited, include a note about this fact. If symbols are used to note omissions, those should be included in a note as well.

DRAWING AND SUPPORTING CONCLUSIONS

Qualitative research does not produce the same types of conclusions that quantitative research does. Trying to work toward a conclusion, something that must be proved or disproved, which is common in quantitative research reports, is not appropriate for qualitative research and could lead to overgeneralization. Instead of thinking in terms of a conclusion, portray the ending of your research report as being decision-oriented (Wolcott, 2001). In other words, what decisions can be made given the descriptions and analyses that have been presented? By its very nature, qualitative research is less generalizable than quantitative research, and writers should avoid the urge to draw conclusions larger than their findings.

By all means, a qualitative research report should finish with closing paragraphs that review what has been attempted, what has been learned, and what new questions have been raised. Rather than conclusions, include summaries, recommendations, or implications—even a statement of personal reflections (Wolcott, 2001).

There are several different closing techniques you can use to complete the inductive argument. Taylor (1996) moves the reader from specific events at the nuclear weapons facility he studied to broader questions surrounding the study of nuclear weapons. He ends his account by raising several questions about the way politics are integrated with ethnographic study. Lange (1990) concludes his study of Earth First! with summary comments about the way in which conflict and compromise in this case study align with societal views of conflict. Although both researchers move from the specific to the general, they do not make claims that their findings would apply to interactions in all nuclear facilities or in all environmental conflicts.

Alternately, a more traditional closure can be developed. Summarizing and integrating the results of the research according to the research questions can be followed by limitations and suggestions for future research. However, it is important to end with a statement that reflects the specific research setting investigated in the study.

Revisiting Your Analysis

A qualitative research report will likely require more revisions than will a quantitative study. Why? Simply because you, as the researcher, are the analyst. There are no objective statistical tests on which to rely. There are likely no hypotheses to defend. Rather, your analytical skills are constrained by your writing ability as you explore the assertions and research questions that guided your study.

Once your report is written, use the following seven criteria to judge the adequacy of what you have written (McCracken, 1988). Revisiting your written analysis will help you sharpen your conclusions and extend the usefulness of your research.

The first step in revisiting your description and analysis of the data is to consider its accuracy and exactness. It must be so complete that ambiguity does not exist. Second, your writing must be economical so that it forces the reader to make the minimum number of assumptions. Third, the analysis you expose through your writing must be consistent, or reliable. The conclusions that you draw should not contradict or interfere with one another. Moreover, the analysis must also be detailed enough to allow the reader to develop his or her conclusions.

The fourth criterion, being externally consistent, is tricky. Your descriptions and analyses should be consistent, or ring true, with what others have reported or with what is commonly known about a communication event. This does not mean that you ignore new or novel information or explanations. Rather, such novelty must be explained in relationship to more commonly held knowledge and assumptions. If you ignore what your reader would hold as true or expected, you risk the reader's not believing your description and analysis.

Fifth, you should scrutinize your writing for its unification and organization. Rather than presenting one conclusion after another, are your ideas organized in a framework that is, or becomes, apparent to the reader? Have you addressed relationships among the conclusions? Providing a clear and harmonious structure encourages your readers to accept your analyses.

The sixth criterion examines the power of your explanation. Does your written report explain as much of the data as possible? Your explanation should be complete and comprehensive. Alternately, it should not compromise any of the data you presented. Finally, your description and analysis should be both heuristic and fertile.

Your explanations and conclusions should suggest new opportunities and insights. At the same time, they should give readers a new way to explain this interaction phenomenon.

Evaluating your written description and analysis using these criteria is one way to judge the credibility and utility of your work. Asking a colleague whose opinion you trust to read your written work is also advisable. The more subjective nature of qualitative research demands that you pay careful attention to both the level of detail in your descriptions and the quality of explanations. These two elements are central to creating validity for your conclusions.

FINISHING THE QUALITATIVE RESEARCH REPORT

Generally, as the written research report begins to look like a complete report, authors pay attention to three other details: the title, the abstract, and the references. Although these three elements are considered earlier, the author now puts together all of the pieces of the research report to see how the entire document looks.

Title

Titles are important to the final written research report because they are the readers' first introduction to what you have to say about a particular communication phenomenon. Thus, the title should reflect the content of your essay and not misguide readers into developing false expectations.

Some researchers draft a working title (Creswell, 1994) to help them develop the direction of the manuscript. Doing so helps you position the central ideas at an early stage of writing. It is unrealistic to think, however, that the working title will not change. It almost always does as your description and analysis become clearer throughout the writing and revising process.

Some title-writing advice follows (Creswell, 1994; Wilkinson, 1991):

1. Be brief.
2. Avoid wasting words.

3. Eliminate unnecessary words (for example, "A Qualitative Study of . . .").

4. Avoid long titles (more than 12 words).

5. Decrease rather than increase the number of articles and prepositions.

6. Include the focus of the study.

With that advice in mind, remember that titles remain a very individual choice. Because the title is the first thing your reader sees, it sets up expectations and provides an entry into your writing.

If you are submitting your written report to a conference or to be reviewed for publication, the title plays another important role. Your work will be indexed and referenced primarily by its title. So if you want someone to find your work on men's anger groups, then the phrase "men's anger groups" should be in the title. Alternately, you could use the phrase "counseling groups." But if your title uses only the keywords "empathy" and "understanding," it is likely that students and other scholars will miss your work on men's anger groups. Although they are short and often the last element to be determined, the importance of titles should not be downplayed.

Abstract   Like the abstract written for a quantitative report, the abstract for a qualitative report has three objectives (Bouma & Atkinson, 1995). First, the abstract states the aim or overall objective of the research. Second, the abstract gives a brief explanation of the research method. Finally, the abstract briefly summarizes the results of the study. But the elements are not necessarily in any specific order.

Two different examples illustrate how these elements can be presented in qualitative research abstracts. This first example is the abstract of a qualitative study of married couples (Hoppe-Nagao & Ting-Toomey, 2002):

> This study explores dialectical contradictions in marriage and identifies the communication strategies used to manage the dialectical tensions. Qualitative analyses of transcripts from separate semi-structured interviews with husbands and wives focused on two dialectical contradictions: autonomy-connection and openness-closedness. (p. 142)

The abstract continues with specific themes within each contradiction. The first sentence of this abstract describes the overall objective of the research project and the second sentence identifies the research method.

The abstract written for a qualitative case study (Lange, 1990) gives greater attention to the contextual setting of the study:

> This qualitative case study examines Earth First!, a radical environmental group whose motto is "No Compromise in the Defense of Mother Earth!" The group creates controversy by engaging in guerilla theater, civil disobedience, and specific acts of private property destruction, variously labeled "monkeywrenching," "ecotage," or "ecodefense." Earth First! texts use paradox, satire, contradiction, parody, and irony to desecrate or recontextualize unfavorable contexts. This larger environmental movement suffers and benefits as a result. Compromise is shown to be a matter of context and perspective.

Notice that the author starts by stating the method he used and then gives a detailed description of the organization studied. This was necessary because not all readers will be familiar with Earth First! The abstract concludes with the primary result of the study.

Using the APA Style Manual

Generally, scholars who conduct communication research from the social science perspective use the *Publication Manual of the American Psychological Association*. Commonly referred to as the APA style book, the manual's 5th edition (2001) shows the reference and citation style preferred by most communication journals that publish quantitative and qualitative research.

Not only does the manual provide guidance in how to prepare your in-text citations and end-of-manuscript references, but it also provides invaluable advice for writing research reports. Although psychological research is primarily quantitative, the manual's advice on how to type a research manuscript and its many sections on punctuation, spelling, abbreviations, capitalization, headings, and so on are also valuable to writers of qualitative research.

For class projects, you should always check with your instructor to determine which style manual he or she prefers. Learning a style requires discipline. However, learning to use a standardized writing style helps you communicate your research ideas more clearly.

Probably the part of the style manual you will find most helpful is the information for using in-text citations and information for creating the reference list at the end of your written report. Your library and writing center will have a copy of the APA style manual.

SUMMARY

1. There are few conventions or traditions associated with the qualitative research report.

2. One way to check on your writing process is to ask how the description or analysis is increasing the reader's understanding.

3. At a minimum, qualitative research reports should include an introduction; a summary of the literature; a description of data collection and analysis; and a report of the findings, interpretation, and analysis.

4. Qualitative research projects create too much rather than not enough data.

5. The researcher must also decide whether he or she, or the participants will have the responsibilities of authorial voice.

6. A good way to begin a qualitative research report is to explain why the setting was important or interesting.

7. In writing about data collection, the reader should know when the fieldwork was conducted, how long and in what way the researcher was involved with participants, descriptive information about the participants and their communication environment, steps taken in data collection and analysis, and if data collection was triangulated.

8. If the researcher has agreed to maintain the anonymity of participants, a system for referencing participants will need to be created.

KEY TERMS

authorial voice

confessional

critical scholar

impressionist

realist

Personal Report of Communication Apprehension

INSTRUCTIONS

This instrument is composed of 24 statements concerning your feelings about communication with other people. Please indicate the degree to which each statement applies to you by marking whether you (1) strongly agree, (2) agree, (3) are undecided, (4) disagree, or (5) strongly disagree with each statement. There are no right or wrong answers. Many of the statements are similar to other statements. Do not be concerned about this. Work quickly; just record your first impression.

1	I dislike participating in group discussions.	1	2	3	4	5
2	Generally, I am comfortable while participating in a group discussion.	1	2	3	4	5
3	I am tense and nervous while participating in group discussions.	1	2	3	4	5
4	I like to get involved in group discussions.	1	2	3	4	5
5	Engaging in a group discussion with new people makes me tense and nervous.	1	2	3	4	5
6	I am calm and relaxed while participating in group.	1	2	3	4	5
7	Generally, I am nervous when I have to participate in a meeting.	1	2	3	4	5
8	Usually I am calm and relaxed while participating in meetings.	1	2	3	4	5
9	I am very calm and relaxed when I am called upon to express an opinion at a meeting.	1	2	3	4	5
10	I am afraid to express myself at meetings.	1	2	3	4	5
11	Communicating at meetings usually makes me uncomfortable.	1	2	3	4	5
12	I am very relaxed when answering questions at a meeting.	1	2	3	4	5
13	While participating in a conversation with a new acquaintance, I feel very nervous.	1	2	3	4	5
14	I have no fear of speaking up in conversations.	1	2	3	4	5
15	Ordinarily I am very tense and nervous in conversations.	1	2	3	4	5
16	Ordinarily I am very calm and relaxed in conversations.	1	2	3	4	5
17	While conversing with a new acquaintance, I feel very relaxed.	1	2	3	4	5

(continued)

18	I'm afraid to speak up in conversations.	1 2 3 4 5
19	I have no fear of giving a speech.	1 2 3 4 5
20	Certain parts of my body feel very tense and rigid while [I am] giving a speech.	1 2 3 4 5
21	I feel relaxed while [I am] giving a speech.	1 2 3 4 5
22	My thoughts become confused and jumbled when I am giving a speech.	1 2 3 4 5
23	I face the prospect of giving a speech with confidence.	1 2 3 4 5
24	While giving a speech I get so nervous, I forget facts I really know.	1 2 3 4 5

SCORING

Group apprehension = 18 − (1) + (2) − (3) + (4) − (5) + (6)

Meeting apprehension = 18 − (7) + (8) + (9) − (10) − (11) + (12)

Dyadic apprehension = 18 − (13) + (14) − (15) + (16) + (17) − (18)

Public speaking apprehension = 18 + (19) − (20) + (21) − (22) + (23) − (24)

Overall communication apprehension = group + meeting + dyadic + public

Each subscale starts with a score of 18. Subtract and add your scores for the items indicated in parentheses.

SOURCE: "The Content Validity of the PRCA-24 as a Measure of Communication Apprehension Across Communication Contexts," by J. C. McCroskey, M. J. Beatty, P. Kearney, and T. G. Plax, 1985, *Communication Quarterly, 33,* pp. 165–173. Used by permission of the Eastern Communication Association.

Formulas and Steps for Statistical Calculations

COEFFICIENT OF RELIABILITY

The coefficient of reliability (C.R.) is a simple way to calculate coding reliability for unitizing or categorizing decisions. This formula bases reliability on the ratio of decisions coders agreed upon to the total number of coding decisions made by each coder.

$$C.R. = \frac{2M}{N_1 + N_2}$$

M = Number of coding decisions agreed upon

N = Total number of coding decisions made by each coder

Step 1: Identify the number of coding decisions made by coder number 1.

Step 2: Identify the number of coding decisions made by coder number 2.

Step 3: Identify the number of coding decisions agreed upon by the coders.

Step 4: Compute C.R.

$$C.R. = \frac{2M}{N_1 + N_2}$$

$$C.R. = \frac{2(76)}{79 + 81} \quad C.R. = \frac{152}{160}$$

$$C.R. = .95 \text{ or } 95\%$$

SCOTT'S *pi*

Scott's *pi* is used as an index of categorizing reliability for content coding, accounting for the number of categories in the coding scheme and the frequency with which each category is used. This reliability formula can accommodate any number of coders and any number of categories. Moreover, it accounts for the rate of agreement that would occur by chance alone.

$$pi = \frac{\% \text{ observed agreement} - \% \text{ expected agreement}}{1 - \% \text{ expected agreement}}$$

Step 1: Determine the coefficient of reliability (C.R.), which is the ratio of coding agreements to the total number of coding decisions, as demonstrated on page 334; this value is the percentage of observed agreement to be used in Scott's *pi*.

Step 2: Set up three columns as shown, and list the frequency with which each category was used in column 1.

Step 3: Determine the percentage of expected agreement by dividing the frequency for each category by the total number of codings. Enter in column 2.

Step 4: Compute the squared percentages of expected agreement for column 3 by squaring the values in column 2.

Step 5: Sum the values in column 3; this number is the percentage of expected agreement.

Step 6: Compute Scott's *pi*.

Category	Column 1 *Frequency* *n = 160*	Column 2 *Percentage of* *Expected Agreement*	Column 3 *Squared Percentage* *of Expected Agreement*
A	60	.375	.141
B	48	.300	.09
C	36	.225	.051
D	16	.100	.01
			.292

$$pi = \frac{\% \text{ observed agreement} - \% \text{ expected agreement}}{1 - \% \text{ expected agreement}}$$

$$pi = \frac{.95 - .292}{1 - .292} \qquad pi = \frac{.658}{.708} \qquad pi = .93$$

STANDARD DEVIATION

Deviation score method:

$$SD = \sqrt{\frac{\Sigma x^2}{n}}$$

Step 1: Set up columns as shown, and list the scores in column 1 (can be in any order).

Step 2: Obtain n by counting the cases in the distribution.

Step 3: Find $\overline{X}$ for the distribution of scores; put this value in column 2.

Step 4: Obtain x (the deviation score) in column 3 by subtracting column 2 from column 1.

Step 5: Obtain x^2 (the squared deviation score) in column 4 by squaring the values in column 3.

Step 6: Obtain Σx^2 by adding the values in column 4.

Step 7: Enter Σx^2 and n in the formula and solve.

Column 1 Scores (X)	Minus	Column 2 Mean	Equals	Column 3 Deviation Scores (x)	Column 4 Squared Deviation Scores (x²)
15	−	9	=	6	36
12	−	9	=	3	9
10	−	9	=	1	1
9	−	9	=	0	0
7	−	9	=	−2	4
7	−	9	=	−2	4
3	−	9	=	−6	36
					90

$$SD = \sqrt{\frac{\Sigma x^2}{n}} \qquad SD = \sqrt{\frac{90}{7}} \qquad SD = \sqrt{12.86} \qquad SD = 3.59$$

Raw score method:

$$SD = \sqrt{\frac{\Sigma x^2}{n}}$$

Step 1: Set up two columns and list the scores in column 1 (can be in any order).

Step 2: Obtain n by counting the number of cases in the distribution.

Step 3: Obtain X^2 (the squared score) for column 2 for each score (X) by squaring the score in column 1.

Step 4: Obtain ΣX by adding the scores in column 1.

Step 5: Obtain ΣX^2 by adding the values in column 2.

Step 6: Obtain Σx^2 using the formula $\Sigma x^2 = \Sigma X^2 - \dfrac{(\Sigma X)^2}{n}$

Step 7: Enter Σx^2 and n in the formula for SD and solve.

Column 1 *Scores* (X)	*Column 2* *Squared Score* (X^2)
15	225
12	144
10	100
9	81
7	49
7	49
3	9
63	657

$$\Sigma x^2 = \Sigma X^2 - \frac{(\Sigma X)^2}{n} \qquad \Sigma x^2 = 657 - \frac{(63)^2}{7} \qquad \Sigma x^2 = 657 - \frac{3,969}{7}$$

$$\Sigma x^2 = 657 - 567 \qquad \Sigma x^2 = 90$$

$$SD = \sqrt{\frac{\Sigma x^2}{n}} \qquad SD = \sqrt{\frac{90}{7}} \qquad SD\sqrt{12.86} \qquad SD = 3.59$$

ONE-WAY CHI-SQUARE

$$\chi^2 = \Sigma \frac{(\text{observed frequency} - \text{expected frequency})^2}{\text{expected frequency}} \quad \text{or} \quad \chi^2 = \Sigma \frac{(Q - E)^2}{E}$$

Step 1: Graph the categories for the variable; set up five columns and list the observed frequency for each category or cell in column 1.

Step 2: Calculate the expected frequency for each category (unless previous research suggests otherwise, simply divide the number of cases by the number of categories); use this value as the expected frequency for each category; list in column 2.

Step 3: Obtain the value for column 3 for each cell by subtracting the expected frequency from the observed frequency.

Step 4: Obtain the value for column 4 for each cell by squaring the value found in step 3.

Step 5: Obtain the value for column 5 by dividing the value in column 4 by the expected frequency.

Step 6: Obtain χ^2 by summing the values in column 5.

Step 7: Calculate the degrees of freedom (number of categories minus 1).

Step 8: Identify critical value of χ^2 at .05 significance level corresponding to the degrees of freedom in Table B.1.

Step 9: Interpret χ^2: If calculated χ^2 meets or exceeds the critical value, results are statistically significant; accept the research hypothesis. If calculated χ^2 is less than the critical value, retain the null hypothesis.

	Column 1 *Observed* *Frequency*	*Minus*	*Column 2* *Expected* *Frequency*	*Equals*	*Column 3* $(O - E)$	*Column 4* $(O - E)^2$	*Column 5* $\frac{(O - E)^2}{E}$
Single	8	—	10	=	−2	4	.4
Dating	8	—	10	=	−2	4	.4
Married	14	—	10	—	4	16	1.6
							2.4

$\chi^2 = 2.4$

$df = (3 - 1) \quad df = 2$

Critical $\chi^2 = 5.991$

Interpretation: Results are not statistically significant; retain the null hypothesis.

TABLE B.1 Critical Values of Chi-Square

Degrees of Freedom	Significance Level		
	.10	*.05*	*.01*
1	2.706	3.841	6.635
2	4.605	5.991	9.210
3	6.251	7.815	11.345
4	7.779	9.488	13.227
5	9.236	11.070	15.086
6	10.645	12.592	16.812
7	12.017	14.067	18.475
8	13.362	15.507	20.090
9	14.684	16.919	21.666
10	15.987	18.307	23.209
11	17.275	19.675	24.725
12	18.549	21.026	26.217
13	19.812	22.362	27.688
14	21.064	23.685	29.141
15	22.307	24.996	30.578
16	23.542	26.296	32.000
17	24.769	27.587	33.409
18	25.989	28.869	34.805
19	27.204	30.144	36.191
20	28.412	31.410	37.566

SOURCE: Adapted from *Statistical Tables for Biological, Agricultural, and Medical Research,* 6th edition, by R. A. Fisher and F. Yates, 1963. London: Hafner. © 1963 R. A. Fisher and F. Yates. Reprinted by permission of Pearson Education Limited.

CONTINGENCY ANALYSIS

$$\chi^2 = \Sigma \frac{(\text{observed frequency} - \text{expected frequency})^2}{\text{expected frequency}} \qquad \text{or} \qquad \chi^2 = \Sigma \frac{(O - E)^2}{E}$$

Step 1:   Graph the categories for the variables in a contingency table.

Step 2:   Set up five columns as shown, and list the observed frequency for each cell in column 1.

Step 3:   Compute the row marginals for the contingency table by adding the observed frequencies across each row.

Step 4:   Compute the column marginals for the contingency table by adding the observed frequencies down each column.

Step 5:   Confirm that the row marginals and column marginals in the contingency table equal the grand sum, or n.

Step 6:   Calculate the expected frequency for each cell by multiplying the row marginal by the column marginal for each respective cell; divide that value by the grand sum.

Step 7:   List the expected frequency for each cell in column 2 and in the contingency table.

Step 8:   Obtain the value for column 3 for each cell by subtracting the expected frequency from the observed frequency.

Step 9:   Obtain the value for column 4 for each cell by squaring the value found in step 3.

Step 10: Obtain the value for column 5 by dividing the value in column 4 by the expected frequency.

Step 11: Obtain χ^2 by summing the values in column 5.

Step 12: Using the contingency table, calculate the degrees of freedom; multiply (number of columns minus 1) by (number of rows minus 1).

Step 13: Identify critical value of χ^2 at .05 significance level corresponding to the degrees of freedom (calculated in step 12) in Table B.1.

Step 14: Interpret χ^2: If calculated χ^2 meets or exceeds the critical value, the results are statistically significant; accept the research hypothesis. If calculated χ^2 is less than the critical value, retain the null hypothesis.

CONTINGENCY TABLE

	Females	Males	Row Marginals
Target of Sexual Harassment	E = 25.15 **44**	E = 30.85 **12**	56
Not a Target of Sexual Harassment	E = 49.85 **31**	E = 61.15 **80**	111
Column Marginals	75	92	**Grand sum = 167**

	Column 1 Observed Frequency	Minus	Column 2 Expected Frequency	Equals	Column 3 $(O - E)$	Column 4 $(O - E)^2$	Column 5 $\dfrac{(O - E)^2}{E}$
Female Target	44	−	25.15	=	18.85	355.32	14.13
Male Target	12	−	30.85	=	−18.85	355.32	11.52
Female Not a Target	31	−	49.85	=	−18.85	355.32	7.13
Male Not a Target	80	−	61.15	=	18.85	355.32	<u>5.81</u>
							38.59

$\chi^2 = 38.59$

$df = (2 - 1) \times (2 - 1) \qquad df = 1 \times 1 \qquad df = 1$

Critical $\chi^2 = 3.841$

Interpretation: Results are statistically significant; accept the research hypothesis.

t-TEST FOR INDEPENDENT MEANS

$$t = \frac{(\overline{X}_1 - \overline{X}_2) - 0}{s_{\overline{X}_1 - \overline{X}_2}}$$

Step 1:   Set up four columns and list the dependent variable scores for one category of the independent variable in column 1; list dependent variable scores for the other category of the independent variable in column 3.

Step 2:   Square each score by multiplying the score by itself to create values for column 2 (X_1^2) and column 4 (X_2^2).

Step 3:   Sum each column to find values for ΣX_1, ΣX_1^2, ΣX_2, and ΣX_2^2.

Step 4:   Calculate the mean scores for both column 1 ($\overline{X}_1$) and column 3 ($\overline{X}_2$).

Step 5:   Calculate Σx_1^2 and Σx_2^2.

Step 6:   Calculate s_p^2.

Step 7:   Calculate $s_{\overline{X}_1 - \overline{X}_2}$.

Step 8:   Calculate *t*.

Step 9:   Calculate the degrees of freedom ($n_1 + n_2 - 2$).

Step 10: Identify critical value of *t* at .05 significance level corresponding to the degrees of freedom (calculated in step 9) in Table B.2.

Step 11: Interpret *t*: If calculated *t* meets or exceeds the critical value, the results are statistically significant; accept the research hypothesis. If calculated *t* is less than the critical value, retain the null hypothesis.

Column 1 Married Men (X_1)	Column 2 X_1^2	Column 3 Married Women (X_2)	Column 4 X_2^2
19	361	16	256
24	576	22	484
21	441	20	400
23	529	15	225
14	196	13	169
15	225	16	256
17	289	14	196
16	256	18	324
19	361	15	225
21	441	20	400
24	576	17	289
23	529	18	324
$\Sigma X_1 = 236$	$\Sigma X_1^2 = 4{,}780$	$\Sigma X_2 = 204$	$\Sigma X_2^2 = 3{,}548$

(*Step 4*) $\overline{X}_1 = \dfrac{236}{12}$ $\overline{X}_1 = 19.67$ $\overline{X}_2 = \dfrac{204}{12}$ $\overline{X}_2 = 17$

(*Step 5*) $\Sigma x_1{}^2 = \Sigma X_1{}^2 - \dfrac{(\Sigma X_1)^2}{n_1}$ $\Sigma x_1{}^2 = 4{,}780 - \dfrac{(236)^2}{12}$

$\Sigma x_1{}^2 = 4{,}780 - \dfrac{55{,}696}{12}$ $\Sigma x_1{}^2 = 4{,}780 - 4{,}641.33$ $\Sigma x_1{}^2 = 138.67$

$\Sigma x_2{}^2 = \Sigma X_2{}^2 - \dfrac{(\Sigma X_2)^2}{n_2}$ $\Sigma x_2{}^2 = 3{,}548 - \dfrac{(204)^2}{12}$ $\Sigma x_2{}^2 = 3{,}548 - \dfrac{41{,}616}{12}$

$\Sigma x_2{}^2 = 3{,}548 - 3{,}468$ $\Sigma x_2{}^2 = 80$

(*Step 6*) $s_p{}^2 = \dfrac{\Sigma x_1{}^2 + \Sigma x_2{}^2}{n_1 + n_2 - 2}$ $s_p{}^2 = \dfrac{138.67 + 80}{12 + 12 - 2}$ $s_p{}^2 = \dfrac{218.67}{22}$ $s_p{}^2 = 9.94$

(*Step 7*) $s_{\overline{X}_1 - \overline{X}_2} = \sqrt{\dfrac{s_p{}^2}{n_1} + \dfrac{s_p{}^2}{n_2}}$ $s_{\overline{X}_1 - \overline{X}_2} = \sqrt{\dfrac{9.94}{12} + \dfrac{9.94}{12}}$

$s_{\overline{X}_1 - \overline{X}_2} = \sqrt{.83 + .83}$ $s_{\overline{X}_1 - \overline{X}_2} = \sqrt{1.66}$ $s_{\overline{X}_1 - \overline{X}_2} = 1.29$

(*Step 8*) $t = \dfrac{(\overline{X}_1 - \overline{X}_2) - 0}{s_{\overline{X}_1 - \overline{X}_2}}$ $t = \dfrac{(19.67 - 17) - 0}{1.29}$ $t = \dfrac{2.67}{1.29}$ $t = 2.07$

(*Step 9*) $df = n_1 + n_2 - 2$ $df = 12 + 12 - 2$ $df = 22$

(*Step 10*)   Critical $t = 1.717$

(*Step 11*)   Interpretation: Results are statistically significant (for a one-tailed test); accept the research hypothesis.

PAIRED SAMPLE *t*-TEST

$$t = \frac{\overline{D} - \mu_{D(hyp)}}{s_{\overline{D}}}$$

Step 1:   Set up four columns, and list the paired or matched scores for the dependent variable in column 1 and column 2.

Step 2:   Compute the difference score for column 3 by subtracting X_2 from X_1.

Step 3:   Compute the squared difference score for column 4 by squaring the value in column 3.

Step 4:   Find the sum of the difference scores by adding the values in column 3.

Step 5:   Find the sum of the squared difference scores by adding the values in column 4.

Step 6:   Compute the average difference score ($\overline{D}$).

Step 7:   Compute Σd^2.

Step 8:   Compute s_D.

Step 9:   Compute $s_{\overline{D}}$.

Step 10:   Compute *t*.

Step 11:   Calculate degrees of freedom (number of pairs minus 1).

Step 12:   Identify critical value of *t* at .05 significance level corresponding to the degrees of freedom (calculated in step 11) in Table B.2.

Step 13:   Interpret *t*: If calculated *t* meets or exceeds the critical value, the results are statistically significant; accept the research hypothesis. If calculated *t* is less than the critical value, retain the null hypothesis.

Pair	Column 1 X_1	Column 2 X_2	Column 3 Difference Score (D)	Column 4 Difference Score Square (D²)
1	150	145	5	25
2	145	147	−2	4
3	188	141	47	2,209
4	125	120	5	25
5	135	128	7	49
6	171	176	−5	25
7	148	156	−8	64
8	168	147	21	441
9	143	124	19	361
10	131	154	−23	529
			$\Sigma D = 66$	$\Sigma D^2 = 3{,}732$

(*Step 6*) $\overline{D} = \dfrac{\Sigma D}{n}$ $\overline{D} = \dfrac{66}{10}$ $\overline{D} = 6.6$

(*Step 7*) $\Sigma d^2 = \Sigma D^2 - \dfrac{(\Sigma D)^2}{n}$ $\Sigma d^2 = 3{,}732 - \dfrac{(66)^2}{10}$

$\Sigma d^2 = 3{,}732 - \dfrac{4{,}356}{10}$ $\Sigma d^2 = 3{,}732 - 435.6$ $\Sigma d^2 = 3{,}296.4$

(*Step 8*) $s_D = \sqrt{\dfrac{\Sigma d^2}{n-1}}$ $s_D = \sqrt{\dfrac{3{,}296.4}{9}}$ $s_D = \sqrt{366.27}$ $s_D = 19.14$

(*Step 9*) $s_{\overline{D}} = \dfrac{s_D}{\sqrt{n}}$ $s_{\overline{D}} = \dfrac{19.14}{\sqrt{10}}$ $s_{\overline{D}} = \dfrac{19.14}{3.16}$ $s_{\overline{D}} = 6.06$

(*Step 10*) $t = \dfrac{\overline{D} - 0}{s_{\overline{D}}}$ $t = \dfrac{6.6 - 0}{6.06}$ $t = 1.09$

(*Step 11*) $df = n - 1$ $df = 10 - 1$ $df = 9$

(*Step 12*) t critical $= 1.833$

(*Step 13*)   Interpretation: Results are not statistically significant (for a one-tailed test); retain the null hypothesis.

TABLE B.2 Critical Values of *t*

One-Tailed Tests →	.05	.025	.005
Two-Tailed Tests →	.10	.05	.01
df			
1	6.314	12.706	63.657
2	2.920	4.303	9.925
3	2.353	3.182	5.841
4	2.132	2.776	4.604
5	2.015	2.571	4.032
6	1.943	2.447	3.707
7	1.895	2.365	3.499
8	1.860	2.306	3.355
9	1.833	2.262	3.250
10	1.812	2.228	3.169
11	1.796	2.201	3.106
12	1.782	2.179	3.055
13	1.771	2.160	3.012
14	1.761	2.145	2.977
15	1.753	2.131	2.947
16	1.746	2.120	2.921
17	1.740	2.110	2.898
18	1.734	2.101	2.878
19	1.729	2.093	2.861
20	1.725	2.086	2.845
21	1.721	2.080	2.831
22	1.717	2.074	2.819
23	1.714	2.069	2.807
24	1.711	2.064	2.797
25	1.708	2.060	2.787
26	1.706	2.056	2.779
27	1.703	2.052	2.771
28	1.701	2.048	2.763
29	1.699	2.045	2.756
30	1.697	2.042	2.750
40	1.684	2.021	2.704
60	1.671	2.000	2.660
120	1.658	1.980	2.617
∞	1.645	1.960	2.576

- If the *df* for your test falls in between levels, use the level with fewer *df*.
- Use the significance level for one-tailed tests in the top row if the hypothesis predicted a specific directional difference.
- Use the significance level for two-tailed tests in the bottom row if the hypothesis predicted a difference without specifying the direction of the difference.

SOURCE: Adapted from *Statistical Tables for Biological, Agricultural, and Medical Research*, 6th edition, by R. A. Fisher and F. Yates, 1963. London: Hafner. © 1963 R. A. Fisher and F. Yates. Reprinted by permission of Pearson Education Limited.

CORRELATION

$$r = \frac{\Sigma xy}{\sqrt{(\Sigma x_2)(\Sigma y_2)}}$$

Step 1:   Set up five columns and list data for variable X in column 1 and data for variable Y in column 2.

Step 2:   Compute X^2 for column 3 by squaring scores in column 1.

Step 3:   Compute Y^2 for column 4 by squaring scores in column 2.

Step 4:   Compute XY for column 5 by multiplying scores (X) in column 1 by scores (Y) in column 2.

Step 5:   Find ΣX, ΣY, ΣX^2, ΣY^2, and ΣXY by computing the sums for columns 1 through 5.

Step 6:   Compute Σx_2.

Step 7:   Compute Σy_2.

Step 8:   Compute Σxy.

Step 9:   Compute r.

Step 10: Calculate degrees of freedom (number of pairs minus 2).

Step 11: Identify critical value of r at .05 significance level corresponding to the degrees of freedom (calculated in step 10) in Table B.3.

Step 12: Interpret r: If calculated r meets or exceeds the critical value, the results are statistically significant; accept the research hypothesis. If calculated r is less than the critical value, retain the null hypothesis.

ID number	Column 1 X	Column 2 Y	Column 3 X^2	Column 4 Y^2	Column 5 XY
101	14	15	196	225	210
102	12	10	144	100	120
103	8	12	64	144	96
104	6	7	36	49	42
105	10	10	100	100	100
	$\Sigma X = 50$	$\Sigma Y = 54$	$\Sigma X^2 = 540$	$\Sigma Y^2 = 618$	$\Sigma XY = 568$

(Step 6) $\Sigma x_2 = \Sigma X^2 - \dfrac{(\Sigma X)^2}{n}$ $\Sigma x_2 = 540 - \dfrac{(50)^2}{5}$ $\Sigma x_2 = 540 - \dfrac{2,500}{5}$

$\Sigma x_2 = 540 - 500$ $\Sigma x_2 = 40$

(Step 7) $\Sigma y_2 = \Sigma Y^2 - \dfrac{(\Sigma Y)^2}{n}$ $\Sigma y_2 = 618 - \dfrac{(54)^2}{5}$ $\Sigma y_2 = 617 - \dfrac{2,916}{5}$

$\Sigma y_2 = 618 - 583.2$ $\Sigma y_2 = 34.8$

(*Step 8*) $\Sigma xy = \Sigma XY - \dfrac{(\Sigma X)(\Sigma Y)}{n}$ $\qquad \Sigma xy = 568 - \dfrac{(50)(54)}{5}$

$\Sigma xy = 568 - \dfrac{2{,}700}{5}$ $\qquad \Sigma xy = 568 - 540 \qquad \Sigma xy = 28$

(*Step 9*) $r = \dfrac{\Sigma xy}{\sqrt{(\Sigma x_2)(\Sigma y_2)}}$ $\qquad r = \dfrac{28}{\sqrt{(40)(34.8)}}$ $\qquad r = \dfrac{28}{\sqrt{1392}}$ $\qquad r = \dfrac{28}{37.31}$

$r = .75$

(*Step 10*) $df = n - 2 \qquad df = 5 - 2 \qquad df = 3$

(*Step 11*) Critical $r = .805$ (one-tailed test)

(*Step 12*) Interpretation: Results are not statistically significant (for a one-tailed test); retain the null hypothesis.

TABLE B.3 Critical Values of _r_

One-Tailed Tests →	.05	.025	.005
Two-Tailed Tests →	.10	.05	.01
df			
1	.988	.997	.9999
2	.900	.950	.990
3	.805	.878	.959
4	.729	.811	.917
5	.669	.754	.874
6	.622	.707	.834
7	.582	.666	.798
8	.549	.632	.765
9	.521	.602	.735
10	.497	.576	.708
11	.476	.553	.684
12	.458	.532	.661
13	.441	.514	.641
14	.426	.497	.623
15	.412	.482	.606
16	.400	.468	.590
17	.389	.456	.575
18	.378	.444	.561
19	.369	.433	.549
20	.360	.423	.537
25	.323	.381	.487
30	.296	.349	.449
35	.275	.325	.418
40	.257	.304	.393
45	.243	.288	.372
50	.231	.273	.354
60	.211	.250	.325
70	.195	.232	.302
80	.183	.217	.283
90	.173	.205	.267
100	.164	.195	.254

- If the *df* for your test falls in between levels, use the level with fewer *df*.
- Use the significance level for one-tailed tests in the top row if the hypothesis predicted a specific directional relationship.
- Use the significance level for two-tailed tests in the bottom row if the hypothesis predicted a relationship without specifying the direction of the relationship.

SOURCE: Adapted from *Statistical Tables for Biological, Agricultural, and Medical Research*, 6th edition, by R. A. Fisher and F. Yates, 1963. London: Hafner. © 1963 R. A. Fisher and F. Yates. Reprinted by permission of Pearson Education Limited.

Random
Numbers Table

INSTRUCTIONS

You can enter the table at any point—at any row or any column. First decide if you will move row-to-row or column-to-column. Select a point to enter the table. Now, move to the next row or column to identify the number of the first randomly selected element. Continue moving row-to-row or column-to-column until you have identified random numbers for the size of your sample. If your sample is less than 100, use the last two digits. If your sample is less than 1,000, use the last three digits. If you find that the next number is a repeat of one already selected or larger than your sample size, ignore it and move on to the next number. Now, use this set of randomly generated numbers and select the corresponding numbered elements from your population to identify your sample.

4558	6962	3593	2613	9157	7512	5937	6834	6301	2949
4905	7384	8538	5764	6799	9528	4263	3704	5790	8120
2964	3434	3883	5222	8061	2862	8251	2196	6137	4135
7917	2558	1962	4807	5334	7434	2826	6210	4444	6155
0065	2795	0981	8998	7210	2800	6546	0257	2007	5769
7779	2493	5681	2450	9229	9613	6599	7376	7073	2091
4230	7444	8523	5789	8550	5531	4853	1803	9440	6871
4333	8465	0406	7263	5045	8268	1075	6460	6535	1820
3283	7081	3583	8148	6294	9304	4981	5694	7719	4197
5141	1127	8056	4064	6589	3789	8379	6480	6986	1983
2727	9746	5159	3607	8950	1475	6814	7704	4443	8678
2106	5366	5991	7342	4031	8141	6275	1757	8752	9620
3030	9080	6359	1150	0712	2593	3359	5810	8705	7858
6200	5717	4521	9641	8545	6457	5235	3843	3659	9053
5523	7922	7276	4255	5993	5346	5653	6099	1304	4432
8066	3503	9645	3015	2452	2429	3851	2581	5903	1620
3354	9994	4177	5167	3644	1282	8199	2659	3096	0479
1302	0161	5293	5129	7041	6298	8639	7710	5024	9831
5149	6474	0386	6630	5697	9492	2061	9579	0510	5775
6634	5786	9857	8057	2930	0015	4070	3545	3201	5298
5084	7717	1293	8953	6750	3749	9572	4980	9875	4837
1386	2870	1613	3799	2263	3478	1687	5661	8533	2829
8546	0619	0335	0294	6978	6673	7075	8451	5006	3588
7360	8099	1940	2324	2084	3425	1340	7074	8943	9095
2362	0190	9013	3196	0447	3840	7336	3643	6076	7846
8023	3998	3114	7558	1427	4390	4127	0856	7052	9922
9609	5759	4512	9456	5593	1574	8412	2297	5341	0976
1949	3369	7178	8133	6148	4192	3535	1751	1976	3682
6523	4653	0998	6975	5869	2663	0965	5201	3560	5231
1894	6716	2366	2730	2174	7896	7107	1780	1120	9496
2086	1812	9081	2791	5444	3176	8745	8219	1394	9540
1568	8138	4221	5073	1423	4392	3784	9939	3507	0894
0793	6051	0270	1186	1619	8641	7756	1039	6572	8266
6532	2638	2132	7019	8792	1531	3256	4593	7577	6577
0916	1541	7243	7409	6075	4976	0263	9766	1035	7144
5453	8779	3423	1396	0326	8044	0838	9550	9559	3525
3915	9739	4518	0841	2435	3487	1921	6873	8325	3314
1792	9728	7539	5549	2965	1779	8914	3726	7452	8235
5924	1178	1800	1817	4825	8373	8124	9341	6579	4524
2165	5807	3665	6327	4826	4679	8610	7329	9473	3950
2239	6497	9778	6127	7455	3341	1004	8810	9767	4186
8381	8378	3997	3608	6163	9529	3534	5329	3082	1975

(continued)

3426	4463	6451	6157	2642	0055	0480	9451	8698	9197
0035	8370	3921	2144	4092	0104	0722	6924	8876	9720
9254	1496	9326	7792	4531	1187	8916	6815	1679	9317
2095	3862	7413	9245	0655	1148	2960	6833	5192	5854
8704	3333	5472	5474	3661	9024	5163	3476	7668	5542
9175	9141	5526	5801	9312	4852	7516	7699	9484	7494
4998	7008	2177	9082	4093	8031	7868	8366	0674	6639
4751	1532	4997	4586	0187	8119	7827	1374	3381	4923
2434	9702	9909	6541	4454	0349	9260	2294	2397	6932
2098	7439	3767	1054	3684	4190	9677	8125	7780	8742
9843	5856	6027	9183	3366	2735	5176	8957	8617	4138
5404	4441	6279	0069	9614	6594	0082	0652	5262	1521
5458	2694	9277	2571	0868	0694	3281	7560	2039	6920
8169	9549	6883	4528	6453	5734	8262	8257	8453	7170
3037	7991	8807	9443	9893	6515	7120	6345	6179	2250
6855	5324	5062	2151	5837	8480	6712	4284	1112	0940
1463	2305	3384	1044	2276	8544	0628	0106	3515	0782
0155	1180	6519	1249	3623	7165	2152	1723	7854	5617
5236	6009	3787	8571	0583	0363	2739	7614	9993	5577
1543	6530	7162	8035	3267	1327	2695	0804	8222	0124
4605	0046	0728	3518	0621	6479	0742	9337	7345	6358
5851	4440	7930	1581	8358	0149	4293	3906	4243	7288
3966	5621	1331	6681	6004	8159	6193	2054	6156	3263
3293	7379	0904	0725	8540	0125	4641	0558	4787	3812
0606	3670	5718	4520	4396	4091	7533	6140	7540	1586
5464	9300	0451	6142	8746	8021	9714	2586	6107	6617
5768	4990	7177	6320	8085	8272	0011	7709	4882	3981
1389	1117	5533	6595	1449	5432	2926	3119	1326	9339
3833	2697	0855	7380	2877	4559	8385	2101	3637	5133
0006	9708	4881	2269	9834	4767	7720	7389	7929	4753
8491	4658	6902	7212	6792	3795	0654	2482	8751	6399
0892	8949	1832	7730	7738	9929	1559	1690	9768	2824
3273	4769	6848	2208	6429	8386	2555	7202	3746	5425
1598	0111	2617	6019	1689	7640	1570	9666	8595	8269
0297	5632	7734	9279	7775	1223	5608	4849	9372	8038
9603	2199	0446	9564	5261	6243	0928	9594	5962	4461
2669	1184	2770	8872	7097	5964	0068	2889	3898	3820
5904	0008	1552	8936	6982	3161	3455	7726	7879	3646
9438	9199	6821	9908	6350	0341	3299	0873	7003	4996
7049	3084	1211	1621	8143	5372	1886	1964	1157	2443
0225	9673	4527	0113	2214	7137	3526	1456	3845	4511
5103	6028	6582	6302	1979	8868	8499	2541	2235	0530
6868	7665	2728	4643	5643	7256	4367	6090	2241	7953
2810	9447	1390	9979	0519	4604	4544	6983	3685	1688
7563	0957	1942	2866	4118	5120	0426	8110	3155	0458
4959	0531	2589	9756	1324	5080	7818	3533	7523	0130
8841	5463	1138	8201	1666	5738	6259	9927	0507	9063
2890	4571	7260	5501	7502	6937	9306	5550	5351	9173
0816	6368	3873	2743	6906	9116	8455	8583	1460	5648
4720	9592	3074	6790	8997	8411	1939	4742	4277	8022
8437	0871	4458	2293	3447	6542	1597	9511	6094	9223
2190	8496	5364	7148	0737	8296	2615	1607	7940	3658
7625	7884	2417	4412	4831	0064	5322	6896	1468	9562
4086	9249	9211	5772	3027	6097	3714	9709	9543	4707
8430	3938	2575	6851	6823	4754	2369	7599	0450	9792
9171	1659	8211	1251	0634	9790	1925	7197	6116	7338
9718	7789	2505	6844	9793	8932	0005	8880	3335	7698
9743	1274	2272	6041	0427	6074	5815	1638	7423	9757

Sample Protocol for Experimental Study

PROTOCOL FOR SEXUAL HARASSMENT
FOLLOW-UP STUDY

All manager sessions meet at 8:30, 9:30, and 10:30

- November 2, 1999—Commission Chambers Participants; 26 in each session
- November 3, 1999—Health Dept. Auditorium; 20 in each session
- November 5, 1999—Road Dept. Conference Rm.; 26, 27, and 25, respectively

Call contacts the day before session:

- Shanita Kelley   555-xxxx (General contact)
- Ron Summers   555-xxxx (Commission Chambers contact)
- Julie Kennedy   555-xxxx (Health Dept. contact)
- Ray Harris   555-xxxx (Road Dept. contact)

Before group arrives, ensure that video equipment is working properly and video is cued; ensure that all materials are available for the session; meet contacts at location at 8:15 A.M.

- Name tag(s) for facilitators
- Videos/backups
- Answer sheets for videos
- Red and green pens
- Pencils
- Clipboards (Commission Chambers only; Ron Summers will supply)
- Paper clips and/or stapler
- Box

Handouts: (Pick up first day from Ron Summers)

- Post-video handouts
- Pre-video handouts
- Agreement to Participate forms
- Master copies of all forms
- Signs for door

Welcome/greeting

- Welcome the group and thank them for coming to the session—create an inviting climate.
- Introduce facilitator(s) and build credibility for the study.

Explain purpose of the study and gain their interest in helping.

- To provide _____ with follow-up information regarding sexual harassment process to enable them to ensure a harassment-free environment to all _____ employees
- To provide follow-up data to the research project that was conducted at _____ in 1993–94 regarding sexual harassment in the workplace

Explain the study process in general to assist participants in becoming more comfortable with the process and the study as a whole.

Hand out the Agreement to Participate form and discuss; tell that it is required by the University of _____ any time research is conducted; inform participants that by completing the questionnaire they are agreeing to participate; make sure participants understand that participation is voluntary; ask them to keep the Agreement to Participate form for their records.

- Confidentiality/anonymity; ask them please to not identify themselves in any way on the forms; ask them to keep the form for their files; let them know that we are interested in their opinions as a group not as an individual, and data will be reported only in aggregate form; reassure that their supervisor does not get to see; at least 200 people participating and only average scores are reported back to management.
- Discuss how long it will take—approximately 30 minutes.
- Hold all forms until the end of the session and turn them in to the research facilitator as you leave.

Discuss and complete the pre-video questions

- Pre-video questions will provide helpful data to _____ so that management can better understand how to provide a harassment-free workplace and understand how to better provide training that works for the employee population.
- Hand out pre-video questions; explain how to complete each section; and monitor room to see if anyone needs assistance; when everyone has completed this section begin the video.

Video process

- Discuss that they are really short and they will need to focus on the video and then look at the answer sheet; four vignettes that show different scenes of flirting and sexual harassment and how to use red and green pens to highlight what they perceive to be flirting vs. sexual harassment. Red pen is used to underline sexual harassment and the green pen is used to underline flirting behaviors. They may underline with both pens if they believe it is both. There is a reminder about the pens on the answer sheet in the box.
- Hand out the answer sheets for vignettes 1–4; remind how to complete using the red and green pens; ask group to keep all forms until the end of the full session.

  > Announce vignette 1
  > Announce vignette 2
  > Announce vignette 3
  > Announce vignette 4

Post-video questionnaire

- Hand out the post-video questionnaire; explain how to complete each section, with the participants turning to the pages as discussed.
- Monitor the room to see if anyone needs assistance; explain that they may leave when they complete this last section (they do not have to wait until all

have completed); ask them to leave all of their forms with the research facilitator as they leave the room.

End of session

- Stand at the back of the room; give eye contact, shake hands; take forms and criss-cross, upside-down on table
- Completion of administration
  Code with code # and subject # (both starting with 01)
  Complete log
  Put forms in order by pre; post; video sheets
  Paper clip/staple together

Log for _____ Sexual Harassment Follow-Up Study (Managers Only)

Date	Time	Tape	Code #	# Participants Males	Females
November 2, 1999	8:30		01		
November 2, 1999	9:30		02		
November 2, 1999	10:30		03		
November 3, 1999	8:30		04		
November 3, 1999	9:30		05		
November 3, 1999	10:30		06		
November 5, 1999	8:30		07		
November 5, 1999	9:30		08		
November 5, 1999	10:30		09		
Total					

GLOSSARY

alpha level The significance or probability level set by the researcher for each statistical test prior to conducting the study; in communication research, most often set at .05; represented by the symbol p.

analysis In qualitative research, the process of labeling and breaking down raw data to find patterns, themes, concepts, and propositions.

analysis of variance Statistical test compares the influence of two or more groups of one or more nominal independent variables on a continuous level dependent variable; represented by the symbol F; also referred to as *ANOVA*.

analytical memo Used in qualitative research to capture first impressions and reflections about the setting, people, and interactions; informal writing to distinguish the analysis from the data.

anonymity Protection of names and other pieces of information that can identify participants; researchers do not ask participants to reveal information that would aid the researcher in identifying participants' individual data.

ANOVA Statistical test that compares the influence of two or more groups of one or more nominal independent variables on a continuous level dependent variable; represented by the symbol F; also referred to as *analysis of variance*.

antecedent variable Variable manipulated by the researcher; presumably, this manipulation, or variation, is the cause of change in other variables; also referred to as *independent variable, experimental variable, treatment variable,* and *causal variable.*

attrition Threat to the internal validity of research when participants can no longer be observed or used for data collection because they have dropped out of the research project; also known as *mortality.*

authorial voice The person(s), researcher or the participants, who tells the story in a qualitative research report.

autoethnography A type of ethnography in which the researcher is also a participant; the research report is highly personal and emotional.

average See *mean.*

axial coding Used in coding qualitative data after open coding, this coding pass links categories together in a meaningful way.

behavior coding Type of questionnaire pretesting for face-to-face surveys; a third person monitors the interaction between the interviewer and respondent to look for problems in the questionnaire or its administration.

beneficence Protection of the well-being of participants; the researcher must meet the obligation to maximize possible benefits while minimizing possible harms.

beta coefficients Unit of standardized scores in regression; indicates the difference in a dependent variable associated with an independent variable; also known as *beta weights.*

beta weights Unit of standardized scores in regression; indicates the difference in a dependent variable associated with an independent variable; also known as *beta coefficients.*

between-groups variance Variation of scores between categories or groupings of independent variable sufficient to distinguish themselves from one another.

between-subjects design Design feature of ANOVA in which each participant is measured at only one level, group, or category, or under only one condition; designed to examine differences across individuals in the study.

biased Favoring one attribute or characteristic more than another.

categorical data Form of discrete data; describes the presence or absence of some characteristic or attribute; also known as *nominal data.*

categorizing reliability Degree to which multiple coders make similar distinctions among the data to be coded in assigning data to categories; used in content analysis.

category In qualitative research, a label for a set of excerpts, examples, or themes that are similar;

may be drawn from the literature or emerge from the data.

causal variable   Variable manipulated by the researcher; presumably, this manipulation, or variation, is the cause of change in other variables; also referred to as *antecedent variable, experimental variable, treatment variable,* and *independent variable.*

census   Situation where every element of a population is included in a research project.

central tendency   Term applied to any of several measures that summarize a distribution of scores; mean, median, and mode are common measures of central tendency; this one number acts as a summary of all the scores on one variable.

chi-square   Represented by the symbol χ^2; statistical test used to determine if differences among nominal, or categorical, level data are statistically significant; examines the observed frequencies in comparison to the expected frequencies to determine if the categorical differences that occurred are the same as would occur by chance.

classical experiment   Research design in which participants are randomly selected and the researcher controls the treatment or the manipulation of the independent variable by randomly assigning participants to treatment or control groups.

closed question   Question form in which respondents are asked a question (or given a statement) and then given a set of responses to select from.

cluster sampling   Form of random, or probability, sampling used when researchers do not have access to a complete list of population members; a two-stage or multistage process; in the first stage, groups, or clusters, of the population are selected; then simple random sampling is used in each cluster to select the research sample.

coefficient of determination   The percentage of variance two variables have in common; represented by the symbol r^2; found by simply squaring the r value.

cognitive pretesting   Type of questionnaire pretesting in which researcher asks questions about the stimulus question to eliminate alternative meanings.

Cohen's kappa   Measure of interrater reliability for categorical data; ranges from perfect agreement (1.00) to agreement that is no better than would be expected by chance (0).

commitment acts   In qualitative research, helping participants with routine tasks and activities to acquaint one's self with the research setting and to gain information.

complete observer   Form of participant observation; the researcher enacts only the observer role; the researcher is hidden completely from the interactants.

complete participant   Form of participant observation; researcher is a fully functioning member of the scene; the research role is disguised through the role as participant.

concept   Abstract idea or way of thinking about something that helps us distinguish it from other elements; can be an object, event, relationship, or process.

conceptual scheme   A set of concepts connected together to form an integrated whole that specifies and clarifies the relationships among them; individually, each concept describes a unique process; as a group, the concepts still retain common characteristics.

concurrent validity   Method for establishing criterion-related validity of a new measurement; demonstrates that the new measuring instrument and the established measuring instrument—both measuring the same or similar things—are related.

confederate   Someone who pretends to also be participating in the research project but is really helping the researcher; a deceptive practice because research participants do not know that an individual is playing the confederate role; used when the researcher needs to create a certain type of interaction context or to provide a certain type of interaction to which an unknowing research participant responds.

confessional   Writing style of the author of a qualitative research report; the author reveals everything; allows the reader to validate and verify both what was discovered and how it was discovered.

confidence level   Degree of accuracy in predicting the result for a population from the result found by testing the sample.

confidentiality   Protection of research participant; any information the participant provides is controlled in such a way that others do not have access to it.

confounding variable   Variable that confuses or obscures the effect of one variable on another; when present, it is often difficult to isolate the effects of independent variables.

constant-comparative method   See *grounded theory.*

construct   Theoretical definition of a concept; not directly observable.

construct validity   Extent to which measuring device measures the core concept that was intended to be measured and not something else; researchers use a different, but theoretically related, measure of the same or a similar phenomenon to establish construct validity.

content analysis   Quantitative research method that integrates both data collection method and analytical technique to measure the occurrence of some identifiable element in a complete text or set of messages.

content validity   Degree to which the measurement items are representative of all of the potentially items available for measuring the construct of interest.

contingency analysis   Form of chi-square in which frequency distributions are created simultaneously on two nominal variables; cases are classified on two variables in relationship to each other; also referred to as *two-way chi-square* or *two-dimensional chi-square.*

contingency table   Table in which two nominal variables are arranged; rows represent one nominal variable, and columns represent a second nominal variable; used to display data for contingency analyses.

contingent accuracy   Way to interpret meaning in qualitative research; relies on tangible artifacts, which are believed to be accurate representations of the phenomenon; most objective of the three interpretive positions.

continuous level data   Data for which values can differ in degree, amount, or frequency and for which these differences can be ordered on a continuum; also referred to as *quantitative data.*

control group   Group in which assigned participants receive no treatment or stimuli or receive the standard form of the treatment.

convenience sampling   Sampling technique not based on random selection or probability; the researcher simply selects those who are convenient as respondents; no guarantee that all eligible units have an equal chance of being included in the sample; also referred to as *opportunity sampling.*

conventional pretesting   Type of questionnaire pretest in which a researcher selects several individuals who are like persons in the population; the survey is completed just as it will be done in the study.

correlation   Statistical test that examines the linear relationship between two continuous level variables; represented by the symbol r; also known as *Pearson product-moment correlation coefficient.*

correlation matrix   Display of variables in a table; makes it possible to see how every variable is correlated with every other variable.

correlational design   See *descriptive design.*

credibility   The criterion used in qualitative research to assess the effectiveness and accuracy of the research design and findings drawn from its data.

criterion-related validity   Determination of whether one measurement can be linked to some other external measurement; achieved through two procedures—predictive validity and concurrent validity.

criterion variable   Variable that is influenced or changed by the predictor variable.

critical incidents   Positive or negative events remembered by participants.

critical scholar   A qualitative writing style in which the researcher identifies the perspective of disadvantaged or marginalized groups, or exposes inequalities and injustices.

Cronbach's alpha   Measure of internal reliability for a series of items across all respondents; also referred to as *internal reliability* or *internal consistency;* also known as *coefficient alpha.*

cross-sectional design   See *descriptive design.*

curvilinear   Type of relationship between two variables represented by a U-shaped curve (either concave or convex).

data   Quantitative or qualitative information about any communication phenomenon.

dataset   Entirety of the data from each participant or about each element compiled by variables or by cases; also referred to as a *database.*

data triangulation   Method of triangulation in which a variety of data sources are used in one study.

debriefing   Interaction between researcher and participants immediately following the research activity; researcher explains the purpose of the study and what he or she hopes to find; any information that was withheld from participants before the research activity is shared at this time.

deception   Situation where researcher purposely misleads participants; should be used only if there is no other way to collect the data and the deception does not harm participants.

deductive   Reasoning process in which researcher begins with a theory and then gathers evidence, or data, to assess whether the theory is correct; generally used with quantitative research methods.

degrees of freedom   Number of values that vary within a statistical test; represented by the symbol *df;* accounts for variation due to error.

dependent variable   Variable that is influenced or changed by the independent variable.

descriptive design   Type of research design in which a researcher lacks direct control over variation in the independent variables and temporal order of variables; participants are not randomly assigned to conditions; also called *correlational, cross-sectional,* or *non-experimental design.*

descriptive statistics   Numbers that summarize essential and basic information about the dataset as a whole.

dichotomous   Data measured at one of two nominal levels.

directional hypothesis   A precise statement indicating the nature and direction of the relationship or difference between the variables.

discourse   Set of naturally occurring messages that serve as data in qualitative methodologies.

discrete data   Data classified by the presence or absence of some characteristic or attribute; based on distinct categorical characteristics; also known as *nominal data* or *categorical data.*

discussion section   Section of the written research report in which the authors provide an interpretation of the results.

dramatistic frame   A frame of interpretation for qualitative data based on the roles, settings, and scripts necessary to telling a story.

ecological validity   Form of external validity; the degree to which participants are like those the researcher is really interested in and the degree to which the research setting is natural.

empirical   Refers to observations or experiences; empirical methodologies in communication are based on or are derived from experiences with observable phenomena.

equivalent   Characteristic of nominal or categorical response set; responses must be equal to one another or of the same type.

eta²   The amount of variance in the dependent variable that can be accounted for by the independent variable; also represented by the symbol r^2.

ethnography   Detailed study and representation of people and their interaction; the holistic description of interactants in their cultural or subcultural group.

ethnography of communication   A theoretically driven method of ethnography; researchers focus on language or speech communities; the research report is detailed analyses of how symbolic practices are expressed in a particular social structure.

exclusion criterion   A standard or guideline that, if met, excludes participants from being selected as part of a nonprobability sample.

exhaustive   Characteristic of nominal, or categorical, response set; responses must represent the entirety of the variety of characteristics of the people or element being measured.

expected frequency   The number of times a category was expected to appear in a test of chi-square.

experiment   Research design used to determine causation; the recording of observations made by defined procedures and in defined conditions; researcher must have control over manipulation of the independent variables and random assignment of participants to conditions.

experimental research   Type of research most often conducted in the laboratory or other simulated environments controlled by researchers.

experimental variable   Variable manipulated by the researcher; presumably, this manipulation, or variation, is the cause of change in other variables; also referred to as *antecedent variable, independent variable, treatment variable,* and *causal variable.*

expert panels   Form of questionnaire pretesting in which experts in research methodology or in the survey's content read through the questionnaire together and discuss potential problems with the survey.

external validity   Degree to which the findings of a research project can be extended to participants and settings beyond those studied.

face validity   Extent to which the items reference the construct intended to be measured; exists if the measurement looks and feels as if it will capture the intended construct.

factorial design   Type of ANOVA design based on two or more categorical independent variables, each with at least two levels; allows the researcher to test for the effects of each independent variable and the interaction effect on the continuous level dependent variable.

field experiment   Form of a quasi-experimental design; like an experiment in that researcher controls the manipulation of independent variables and random assignment of participants; the research environment is realistic and natural, so researcher lacks the degree of control found in classical experiments.

field interviewing   Qualitative research method; a semidirected form of discourse or conversation with the goal of uncovering the participant's point of view.

field notes   Notes about observations made in the field, in the interaction setting or while interaction occurs.

first-order linkage   The link between the findings from content analysis and other relevant data.

focus group   Qualitative research method; facilitator-led group discussion used for collecting data from a group of participants about a particular topic in a limited amount of time.

focus group outline   A question or topic guide used to facilitate a focus group, usually structured as a funnel from broad to more specific questions or topics.

frequency   Number of times a particular value or category of a variable occurs.

gatekeeper   Person who has authority to allow the researcher into an environment to collect data.

generalizability   Extent to which conclusions developed from data collected from a sample can be extended to the population; the extension of the findings to similar situations or to similar others.

grounded theory   An iterative approach for coding qualitative data into categories; requires that researchers examine the relationships between the data and its category as well as the relationships among categories.

heuristic   Characteristic of research; results of one study lead to more questions.

hierarchical regression   Form of regression in which the researcher determines the order or sequence in which the independent variables are presumed to influence the dependent variable.

human subjects review committee   University committee that uses a formal process for considering the soundness and reasonableness of research proposals; also known as *institutional review board (IRB)*.

hypothesis   Tentative, educated guess or proposition about the relationship between two or more variables; often, hypotheses take the form of statements like "If x occurs, then y will follow," or "As x increases, so will y."

impressionist   Writing style of the author of a qualitative research report; intended to startle the reader; uses metaphors, phrasings, imagery, and expansive recall.

inclusion criterion   A standard or guideline participants must meet to be included in a nonprobability sample.

independent sample *t*-test   Statistic used to compare means of two sets of scores, each set collected from a different set of people or collected about a different set of stimuli.

independent variable   Variable manipulated by the researcher; presumably, this manipulation, or variation, is the cause of change in the dependent variable; also referred to as *antecedent variable, experimental variable, treatment variable,* and *causal variable.*

inductive   Reasoning process in which data are gathered and examined, hypotheses are formulated, and eventually theories are developed in response to what the data reveal; generally used with qualitative research methods.

inductive analysis   Reasoning process in which researchers work from what emerges from the data to formulate hypotheses and eventually develop theories; generally used with qualitative research methods.

inferential statistics   Statistical tests that provide information about the relationships between or among variables in the study; used to draw conclusions about a population by examining the sample.

informed consent   Agreement participant gives to researcher to participate in the research project after having been given some basic information about the research process.

institutional review board (IRB)   University committee charged with the formal process of considering the soundness and reasonableness of research proposals; also known as *human subjects review committee.*

interaction analysis   Quantitative research method; codes the content of ongoing communication between two or more individuals; identifies the verbal or nonverbal features or functions of the stream of conversational elements.

interaction effect   Combined and simultaneous influence of two or more independent variables on the dependent variable.

intercoder reliability   See *interrater reliability.*

interdisciplinary triangulation   Form of triangulation in which researchers from a variety of disciplines work together on a research project.

internal reliability   Degree to which multiple items invoke the same response from a participant; expressed in value from 0 (no internal consistency) to 1.00 (complete internal consistency).

internal validity   Extent to which one can draw valid conclusions about the effects of one variable on another; depends upon how the research is designed and the data collected; addresses the relationship between the concept being measured and the process for measuring it.

interpretation   In qualitative research, making sense of or giving meaning to the identified patterns, themes, concepts, and propositions.

interrater agreement   See *interrater reliability.*

interrater reliability   Degree to which two or more coders assign communication behaviors to the same categories or to which two or more raters similarly evaluate a communication act on a scale or index; also referred to as *interrater agreement* or *intercoder reliability.*

intersubjectivity   How people jointly construct their social lives through interactions with others and their rules for doing so.

interval   The distance between any two adjacent, or contiguous, data points.

interval data   Data measured based on specific numerical scores or values in which the distance between any two adjacent, or contiguous, data points is equal; scale without a meaningful zero.

intervening variable   Element that is presumed to explain or provide a link between other variables.

interview guide   List of questions or topics used in interview research.

investigator triangulation   Method of triangulation in which several different researchers or evaluators are used.

justice   Issue of fairness in conducting research; addresses who should receive the benefits of research and who should bear its burdens.

key informant   Individual from whom data must be collected for a research project to be complete.

latent content   Type of content coded in content analysis; inferences or interpretations about the content that imply something about the nature of the senders or producers of the content or effects on senders.

Likert-type scale   Type of interval scale measurement widely used in communication research; participants are given a statement and then asked to respond, indicating the degree to which they agree or disagree with the statement; the response set is something like "strongly disagree, disagree, undecided, agree, strongly agree."

linear   Type of relationship between variables in which a one-unit change in one variable is associated with a constant change in the other variable in the same or opposite direction; when plotted forms a straight line.

linear regression   Form of regression in which the values of a dependent or criterion variable are attributed to one independent, or predictor, variable.

literature review   Section of the written research report that provides the framework of the research investigation; summarizes the literature the researcher sought and studied to design and develop the research study.

longitudinal design   Type of research design that allows for multiple measurements of the dependent variable over time.

main effect   Simple influence of independent variable on the dependent variable; the influence of one independent variable is examined without considering the influence of other independent variables.

manifest content   Type of content coded in content analysis; a description of the characteristics of the content itself.

manipulation   One of the ways in which the researcher varies the type of stimuli or the amount or level of stimuli presented to research participants; also referred to as *treatment.*

manipulation check   Verification that participants did, in fact, regard the independent variable in the various ways that the researcher intended; conducted prior to statistical analyses of the hypotheses.

maturation   Threat to the internal validity of research as participants change, or mature, over the course of the observations.

maximum variation sampling   Sampling technique used in qualitative research; based on informational redundancy; a researcher continues to seek additional participants until the data received are redundant with, or the same as, previously collected data.

mean   Most common measure of central tendency; commonly referred to as the *average;* computed by adding up all the scores on one variable and then dividing by the number of cases, or n, for that variable.

measurement   Use of numbers to represent a communication phenomenon; more broadly, a process that includes everything the researcher does to arrive at the numerical estimates, including the measuring device or instrument, how the device or instrument is used, the skill of the person using the device or instrument, and the attribute or characteristic being measured.

median   Measure of central tendency indicating the middle of all the scores on one variable; the point or score that divides a distribution of scores in half.

member check   *See* member validation.

member validation   The process of asking individuals from whom data were collected to verify the interpretation of the data.

memo writing   In qualitative research, a writing process that serves as an intermediate step between coding and the first draft of the analysis; used as the basis for organizing the research report.

metaphoric frame   A frame of interpretation for qualitative data in which the unknown becomes salient because it is linked or described as something that is commonly known.

methods section   Section of the written research report that describes how the research study was executed.

mode   Measure of central tendency indicating the score that appears most often in a dataset.

mortality   Threat to the internal validity of research when participants can no longer be observed or used for data collection because they have dropped out of the research project; also known as *attrition*.

multiple correlational coefficient   Represented by the symbol R; an index of the magnitude of the relationship among the variables in a multiple regression.

multiple regression   Statistic to test for the significant relationships between the dependent variable and multiple independent variables separately and as a group.

mutually exclusive   Characteristic of choices in a response set; categories should present only one option for which a person is able to identify him- or herself.

mutual simultaneous shaping   Belief that everything influences everything else in the here and now; with so much going on at once, identifying specific causality is difficult, if not impossible; used in qualitative research.

narratives   Stories people tell as a way of knowing, understanding, and explaining their lives.

negatively skewed curve   Distribution in which there are very few scores on the left side of the curve; there are very few very low scores; most of the scores are lumped together on the right side of the curve, above the mean.

network sampling   Form of nonprobability sampling in which researcher actively solicits individuals who fit a specific profile and asks them to participate in the research study.

nominal data   Discrete data that describe the presence or absence of some characteristic or attribute; data that name a characteristic without any regard to the value of the characteristic; also referred to as *categorical data*.

nondirectional hypothesis   Statement that a difference or relationship between variables will occur; does not specify the direction of the difference or the nature of the relationship.

non-experimental design   See *descriptive design*.

nonprobability sampling   Sampling technique that does not rely on any form of random selection.

nonresponse   Failure to obtain data from individuals in the sample.

normal curve   Theoretical distribution of scores, or other numerical values, in which the majority of cases are distributed around the peak in the middle with progressively fewer cases as one moves away from the middle of the distribution; has a distinct bell shape and symmetry—one side of the curve is a mirror image of the other side; the mean, median, and mode for the distribution are at the same point; also referred to as the *bell curve.*

null hypothesis   Implicit complementary statement to the research hypothesis that states that no relationship, except one due to chance, exists between the variables.

observed frequency   Used in chi-square; the number of times the category actually appears; is compared to the expected frequency.

observer-as-participant   Form of participant observation; researcher in both participant and observer roles, but the primary focus shifts to the role of observer, although the researcher has negotiated entrance into an interaction setting with the intention to allow the interaction to proceed as it naturally would.

omega squared   A measure of the strength of the association between the independent and dependent variable.

one-dimensional chi-square   Statistical test to determine if differences in how the cases are distributed across the categories of one categorical, or nominal, variable are significant; also referred to as *one-way chi-square.*

one-tailed *t*-test   Statistic used to test for a specific difference on a continuous level dependent variable relative to one of two categories of a nominal level variable.

one-way ANOVA   One-way analysis of variance; statistical test to identify significant differences in the dependent variable based on categorical differences on one independent variable.

one-way chi-square   Statistical test to determine if differences in how cases are distributed across the categories of one categorical, or nominal, variable are significant; also referred to as *one-dimensional chi-square.*

open coding   The first and unrestrictive pass in coding qualitative data.

open question   Question for which respondents use their own words to formulate a response.

operationalization   Statement that denotes how the variable is observed and measured in a specific way; most variables can be operationalized in multiple ways.

ordinal data   Data measured based on the rank order of concepts or variables; differences among ranks need not be equal.

outcome variable   Variable that is influenced or changed by the independent, or predictor, variable.

paired comparison *t*-test   Statistic used to compare two paired or matched scores.

panels   Longitudinal design for a survey in which data are collected from the same participants at more than one point in time.

participant-as-observer   Form of participant observation; the researcher is both participant and observer; researcher openly acknowledges the research purpose, but also takes an active role in the interaction.

participant observation   Data collection method used with qualitative methods; allows researchers to observe communication firsthand.

Pearson product-moment correlation coefficient   Statistical test that examines the linear relationship between two continuous level variables; represented by the symbol r; also known as *correlation.*

percentage   Comparison between the base number and a second number; represented by the symbol %.

pilot testing   Researcher's trial of a survey or questionnaire with a small group of participants who are similar to those individuals who constitute the population before data collection actually begins; also referred to as *pretesting.*

planned comparisons   Hypothesized statistical comparisons used with ANOVA to compare individuals' scores on the dependent variable according to the groups or categories of the independent variable.

point biserial correlation   Form of the correlation statistic used to examine the relationship between two variables; one variable is measured at the continuous level; the other is dichotomous, or measured at one of two nominal levels.

population   All units or the universe—people or things—possessing the attributes or characteristics in which the researcher is interested.

population validity   Degree to which the sample represents the population of interest.

positively skewed curve   Distribution in which there are very few scores on the right side of the distribution or very few very high scores; most of the scores are lumped together on the left side of the curve, below the mean.

post hoc comparisons   Unplanned statistical comparisons used with ANOVA to compare individuals' scores on the dependent variable according to the groups or categories of the independent variable; conducted after the researcher finds a significant ANOVA.

posttest only   Type of research design in which participants are assigned to treatment or control groups; the simple comparison between groups allows a researcher to conclude that any significant differences found are due to the fact that the treatment group received some stimulus that participants in the control group did not.

predictive validity   Method for establishing criterion-related validity; exists when measurement predicts performance or behavior.

predictor variable   Variable that causes change in the dependent, or criterion, variable; used in nonexperimental research designs because the researcher cannot directly control manipulation of the independent variable.

pretesting   Trial of a survey or questionnaire with a small group of participants who are similar to those individuals who constitute the population before data collection actually begins; also referred to as *pilot testing.*

pretest–posttest   Type of research design in which the dependent variable is measured before the treatment group is exposed to the stimuli; after the stimulus is given, the dependent variable is measured once again in exactly the same way with the same participants.

probability   Degree to which a particular event or relationship will occur.

probability level   Level of error the researcher is willing to accept; established for each statistical test; symbolized as p or referred to as the *alpha level;* also referred to as *significance level.*

probability sampling   Most rigorous way for identifying whom to include as part of a sample; the probability, or chance, of any element being included in the sample is known and equal for everyone or every element in the sample; also referred to as *random sampling.*

proprietary research   Research that is commissioned by an individual or organization for its private use.

purposive sampling   Form of nonprobability sampling; depends on the judgment of the researcher who hand-picks the cases to be included in the sample; used when researcher wants to select cases that are typical of the population of interest and when sensitive topics are of research interest or when very specialized populations are sought.

qualitative methods   Research in which the researcher is the primary observer, or data collector.

quantitative data   Data that represent the values (degree, amount, or frequency) that can be ordered on a continuum; also known as *continuous level data.*

quantitative methods   Research that relies on numerical measurement.

quasi-experiment   Research design in which variation in the independent variable is natural, or not manipulated by the researcher; participants are not assigned randomly to treatment and control groups; also referred to as *natural experiment.*

questionnaire   A method of data collection, such as in a mail, phone, face-to-face, web, or email questionnaire; can be used by itself or with other data collection methods in many research designs.

questions of fact   Questions that ask for definitions for phenomena in which we are interested.

questions of policy   Questions that ask for evaluation of procedures or programs.

questions of value   Questions that ask for individuals' subjective evaluations on issues and phenomena, usually about the aesthetic or normative features of communication.

questions of variable relations   Questions that examine if, how, and the degree to which phenomena are related.

quota sampling   Form of nonprobability sampling in which a researcher uses a target, or quota, as a goal for seeking people or elements that fit the characteristics of the subgroup; when the quota for each subgroup is met, data collection is complete.

random   Characteristic of a sample in which probability for selection is equal; decreases bias.

random assignment   Procedure in which each participant or element has an equal chance of being assigned to any one of the treatment or control groups of the independent variable.

range   Simplest measure of dispersion; the value calculated by subtracting the lowest score from the highest score.

ratio data   Measurement for which intervals between data points are equal; a true zero exists; if the score is zero, there is a complete absence of the variable.

raw data   Data in the form in which they are collected from each participant or about each element; compiled with data from all participants into a dataset.

realist   Writing style for a qualitative research report; author narrates the story in a dispassionate, third-person voice.

recall cue   Statement preceding a survey or questionnaire designed to direct participants to recall episodes or past interactions in which they participated.

reference list   Section of the written research report that provides an alphabetical listing by authors' last names of all materials cited or referenced in the research report.

regression   Set of statistical techniques that predict some variables by knowing others; the most common use of regression is to assess the influence of several continuous level predictor, or independent, variables on a single continuous criterion, or dependent, variable.

regression line   Line drawn through the data points on a scattergram that best summarizes the relationship between the independent and dependent variables (or the predictor and criterion variables).

reliability   Achieved when researchers are consistent in their use of data collection procedures and when participants react similarly to them; other researchers using the same measure in another project with comparable participants would produce similar results; measurement is stable, trustworthy, or dependable; a reliable measure is one that is consistent or gives very similar results each time it is used.

reliability coefficient   Number between 0 and 1 to express the degree of consistency in measurement; 1.00 represents complete consistency or reliability; a score of 0 indicates that consistency or reliability was no better than would be due to chance.

repeated measures   Form of ANOVA design in which each participant is measured more than once, usually at different levels or for different conditions; also referred to as *within-subject design.*

replication   Design of current study to follow the procedures of other studies that have investigated the same topic, often using the same methods or procedures.

research   The discovery of answers to questions through the application of scientific and systematic procedures.

researcher construction   Way in which researcher interprets meaning in qualitative research; interpretation from researcher's personal, subjective position or perspective on the experience; evidence is fully the construction of the researcher.

research protocol   Written detailed procedures for conducting the research study and collecting data.

research question   Question that asks what the tentative relationship among variables might be or asks about the state or nature of some communication phenomenon.

respect for persons   Two separate principles: treating individuals as capable of making decisions and protecting those who are not capable of making their own decisions.

response rate   Number of people who respond after they have been contacted as part of the sample and asked to participate; divide the number of people who responded by the number of respondents identified as part of the sample; also referred to as *return rate.*

results section   Section of the written research report that provides the results of the study without interpretation.

rho   The statistic for Spearman correlation coefficient; examines the relationship between two variables, both with data captured on ordinal scales.

sample   A subset, or portion, of a population; data are collected from a sample to make generalizations back to a population.

sample size   Number of people or elements from whom or on which data are collected.

sampling error   Degree to which a sample differs from population characteristics on some measurement; as sample size increases and becomes a larger proportion of the population, sampling error is reduced; also referred to as *margin of error.*

sampling frame   Set of people or elements that are available to be selected as part of the sample; the list of the available population from which participants are selected.

Scott's *pi*   A measure of interrater reliability for coding categorical data; ranges from perfect agreement (1.0) to agreement that is no better than would be expected by chance (0); accounts for the number of categories in the coding scheme and the frequency with which each category is used.

self-administered survey   Data collection method in which a participant reads and selects a response without the researcher's aid; also called *self-report.*

self-report   Type of survey, questionnaire, or poll in which respondents read the question and select a response by themselves without researcher interference.

semantic differential scale   Form of interval measurement; using a stimulus statement, participants are asked to locate the meaning they ascribe to the stimulus on a response scale anchored by two opposites, usually bipolar adjectives.

semantic validity   The degree to which the analytical categories of a content analysis design have meaning for individuals in a particular context.

significance level   Level of error the researcher is willing to accept; established for each statistical test; symbolized as p or referred to as the *alpha level;* also referred to as *probability level.*

simple random sampling   Sampling technique in which every person or unit—selected one at a time and independently—has an equal chance of being selected to participate in the study.

skewed distribution   Shape of a distribution of scores that is not normal; the curve is asymmetrical; the mean, median, and mode will not be at the same point.

snowball sampling   Nonprobability sampling technique in which participants help the researcher identify other similar participants; used when the research topic is controversial or a specific population of participants is difficult to find.

social desirability response   Response for which there is the potential for participants to respond with answers they believe the interviewer will perceive as favorable.

social science research   Research conducted through the use of scientific and systematic methods; based on the assumption that research can uncover patterns in the lives of people.

social significance   The practical relevance of a statistically significant finding, or how the results might actually be applied.

Spearman correlation coefficient   A statistic, rho, used to examine the relationship between two variables, both with data captured on ordinal scales.

split-half reliability   Expression of internal consistency between two separate but equal versions of the same test or questionnaire.

sponsor   Someone to vouch for person in the role of researcher; also validates and legitimizes researcher's presence.

spurious correlation   Relationship between two variables in which a third variable—sometimes identified, at other times unknown—is influencing the variables tested. Also called *spurious relationship.*

standard deviation   Representation of the variability or spread of the dataset; the amount the scores in a distribution deviate from the mean.

statistical inference   Accepting the conclusions derived from the sample and assuming that those conclusions are also applicable to the population; based on the probability level computed for each statistical test.

stepwise regression   Form of regression in which independent variables are entered in sequence or order as determined by the statistical program based on the degree of influence the independent variables have on the dependent variables.

stratified random sampling   Form of random or probability sampling in which the population is divided according to subgroups of interest, or homogeneous groups; then elements are randomly selected from each homogeneous subgroup of the population with respect to its proportion to the whole.

subjective valuing   Way in which researcher interprets meaning in qualitative research; interpretation relies on a mix of both objective and subjective elements; the researcher mixes his or her interpretations with interpretations received directly from participants.

subjectivity   Approach to research in which researcher uses interpretive research processes to make the subject of the interpretation meaningful.

survey   System for collecting information to describe, compare, or explain knowledge, attitudes, and behavior; also known as questionnaire or poll.

systematic sampling   Form of random or probability sampling in which every *n*th element is chosen after starting at a random point.

test–retest reliability   The expression of the relationship, or correlation between scores at two administrations of the same test, or measurement, to the same participants; 1.00 would indicate that the same participants evaluated the stimulus the second time exactly as they did the first time; a score of 0 would indicate that the two measurements were no better related than they would be by chance.

thematic analysis   A method of qualitative analysis based on participants' conceptions of actual communication episodes; a theme is identified based on recurrence, repetition, and forcefulness.

theoretical frame   A method of qualitative analysis based on the use of two or more theories to explain how the data might be interpreted.

theoretical saturation   The point at which all data can be coded into a category; new categories are not emerging, and the existing category structure appears stable.

theory   Related set of ideas that explains how or why something happens; present a systematic view of the phenomenon; and specifies the relationships among the concepts with the objective of describing, explaining, and predicting the phenomenon.

treatment   One of the ways in which the researcher varies the type of stimuli, or the amount or level of stimuli, presented to research participants; also referred to as *manipulation.*

treatment group   The group of participants who receive a stimulus, or one manipulation of the independent variable.

treatment variable   Variable manipulated by the researcher; presumably, this manipulation, or variation, is the cause of change in the dependent variable; also referred to as *antecedent variable, experimental variable, independent variable,* and *causal variable.*

triangulation   Use of several kinds of methods or data to further validate research outcomes and results.

t-test   Statistic used to find differences between two groupings of the independent variable on a continuous level dependent variable.

two-dimensional chi-square   Form of chi-square in which frequency distributions are created on two nominal variables; cases are classified on two variables in relationship to each other; also referred to as *contingency analysis* or *two-way chi-square.*

two-tailed t-test   Statistic used to test for differences on a continuous level dependent variable relative to one of two categories of a nominal level variable; no specific difference identified in hypothesis or research question.

two-way ANOVA   Statistical test to examine the influence of two categorical independent variables on one continuous level dependent variable; can determine the main effect of contributions of each independent variable and the interaction effect.

two-way chi-square   Form of chi-square in which frequency distributions are created on two nominal variables; cases are classified on two variables in relationship to each other; also referred to as *contingency analysis* or *two-dimensional chi-square.*

Type I error   Error in hypothesis testing that occurs when the null hypothesis is rejected even when it is true; set or controlled by the researcher when choosing the significance level for the statistical test.

Type II error   Error in hypothesis testing that occurs when the alternative hypothesis is rejected even when it is true.

unitizing reliability   Degree to which two or more observers agree that communication action has taken place and can identify the interaction in the stream of interaction; used in content analysis.

unit of analysis   Discrete element coded and counted in content analysis; an observable and measurable unit that provides a standard way of dissecting the text or content into elements to be analyzed.

validity   Achieved when the measurement does what it is intended to do; related to truthfulness or accuracy in measurement.

variable   Element that is specifically identified in the research hypotheses or questions; must be able to be expressed as more than one value or in various categories.

variance   Dispersion of the distribution of scores.

volunteer sampling   Type of nonprobability sampling; research participants offer to participate.

within-groups variance   Variation among scores within any category or level of an independent variable.

within-subject design   Form of ANOVA design is which each participant is measured more than once, usually at different levels or for different conditions; also referred to as *repeated measures design.*

REFERENCES

Abelson, R. P. (1995). *Statistics as principled argument.* Hillsdale, NJ: Erlbaum.

Abelson, R. P. (1997). The significance test ban of 1999. In L. L. Harlow, S. A. Mulaik, & J. H. Steiger (Eds.), *What if there were no significance tests?* (pp. 117–141). Mahwah, NJ: Erlbaum.

Adams, R. J., & Parrott, R. (1994). Pediatric nurses' communication of role expectations to parents of hospitalized children. *Journal of Applied Communication Research, 22,* 36–47.

Adler, P. A., & Adler, P. (1987). *Membership roles in field research.* Newbury Park, CA: Sage.

Allen, M. W., & Caillouet, R. H. (1994). Legitimation endeavors: Impression management strategies used by an organization in crisis. *Communication Monographs, 61,* 44–62.

Altheide, D. L., & Johnson, J. (1994). Criteria for assessing interpretive validity in qualitative research. In N. K. Denzin & Y. Lincoln (Eds.), *Handbook of qualitative methodology* (pp. 485–499). Thousand Oaks, CA: Sage.

American Psychological Association. (2001). *The publication manual of the American Psychological Association* (5th ed.). Washington, DC: Author.

Andersen, P. A. (1989). Philosophy of science. In P. Emmert & L. L. Barker (Eds.), *Measurement of communication behavior* (pp. 3–17). New York: Longman.

Anderson, J. A. (1996). Thinking qualitatively: Hermeneutics in science. In M. B. Salwen & D. W. Stacks (Eds.), *An integrated approach to communication theory and research* (pp. 45–59). Mahwah, NJ: Erlbaum.

Apker, J. (2002). Front-line nurse manager roles, job stressors, and coping strategies in a managed care hospital. *Qualitative Research Reports in Communication, 4,* 75–81.

Armstrong, D., Gosling, A., Weinman, J., & Martaeu, T. (1997). The place of inter-rater reliability in qualitative research: An empirical study. *Sociology, 31,* 597–606.

Arpan, L. M., & Pompper, D. (2003). Stormy weather: Testing "stealing thunder" as a crisis communication strategy to improve communication flow between organizations and journalists. *Public Relations Review, 29,* 291–308.

Atkinson, P., & Hammersley, M. (1994). Ethnography and participant observation. In N. K. Denzin & Y. S. Lincoln (Eds.), *Handbook of qualitative research* (pp. 248–261). Thousand Oaks, CA: Sage.

Austin, E. W., Miller, A. C., Silva, J., Guerra, P., Geisler, N., Gamboa, L., et al. (2002). The effects of increased cognitive involvement on college students' interpretations of magazine advertisements for alcohol. *Communication Research, 29,* 155–179.

Avtgis, T. A. (2003). Male sibling social and emotional support as a function of attributional confidence. *Communication Research Reports, 20,* 341–347.

Ayres, J., & Sonandre, D. M. (2003). Performance visualization: Does the nature of the speech model matter? *Communication Research Reports, 20,* 260–268.

Bales, R. F. (1950). *Interaction process analysis: A method for the study of small groups.* Cambridge, MA: Addison-Wesley.

Ballard, D. I., & Seibold, D. R. (2004). Organizational members' communication and temporal experience: Scale development and validation. *Communication Research, 31,* 135–172.

Barge, J. K., & Loges, W. E. (2003). Parent, student, and teacher perceptions of parental involvement. *Journal of Applied Communication Research, 31,* 140–163.

Barker, D. A., & Barker, L. L. (1989). Survey research. In P. Emmert & L. L. Barker (Eds.), *Measurement of communication behavior* (pp. 168–196). New York: Longman.

Barner, M. R. (1999). Sex-role stereotyping in FCC-mandated children's educational television. *Journal of Broadcasting & Electronic Media, 43,* 551–564.

Bartoo, H., & Sias, P. M. (2004). When enough is too much: Communication apprehension and employee information experiences. *Communication Quarterly, 52,* 15–26.

Baruch, Y. (1999). Response rate in academic studies: A comparative analysis. *Human Relations, 52,* 421–438.

Bates, B., & Harmon, M. (1993). Do "instant polls" hit the spot? Phone-in vs. random sampling of public opinion. *Journalism Quarterly, 70,* 369–380.

Beach, W. A. (1990). Orienting to the phenomenon. In J. A. Anderson (Ed.), *Communication yearbook 13* (pp. 216–244). Newbury Park, CA: Sage.

Beach, W. A., & Metzger, T. R. (1997). Claiming insufficient knowledge. *Human Communication Research, 23,* 562–588.

Beatty, M. J. (1987). Communication apprehension as a determinate of avoidance, withdrawal, and performance anxiety. *Communication Quarterly, 35,* 202–217.

Beatty, M. J. (1988). Situational and predispositional correlates of public speaking anxiety. *Communication Education, 37,* 28–39.

Beatty, M. J., & Andriate, G. S. (1985). Communication apprehension and general anxiety in the prediction of public speaking anxiety. *Communication Quarterly, 33,* 174–184.

Beatty, M. J., Balfantz, G. L., & Kuwabara, A. Y. (1989). Trait-like qualities of selected variables assumed to be transient causes of performance state anxiety. *Communication Education, 38,* 277–289.

Beatty, M. J., & Friedland, M. H. (1990). Public speaking state anxiety as a function of selected situational and predispositional variables. *Communication Education, 39,* 142–147.

Benoit, W. L. (2003). State of the economy and presidential television spots. *Communication Research Reports, 20,* 269–276.

Berger, A. A. (1998). *Media research techniques* (2nd ed.). Thousand Oaks, CA: Sage.

Berger, C. R., & DiBattista, P. (1993). Communication failure and plan adaptation: If at first you don't succeed, say it louder and slower. *Communication Monographs, 60,* 220–238.

Berleson, B. (1952). *Content analysis in communication research.* New York: Free Press.

Bickman, L., Rog, D. J., & Hedrick, T. E. (1998). Applied research design: A practical approach. In L. Bickman & D. J. Rog (Eds.), *Handbook of applied social research methods* (pp. 5–37). Thousand Oaks, CA: Sage.

Booth-Butterfield, S., & Gould, M. (1986). The communication anxiety inventory: Validation of state- and context-communication apprehension. *Communication Quarterly, 34,* 194–205.

Boruch, R. F. (1998). Randomized controlled experiments for evaluation and planning. In L. Bickman & D. J. Rog (Eds.), *Handbook of applied social research methods* (pp. 161–191). Thousand Oaks, CA: Sage.

Borzekowski, D. L. G., & Robinson, T. N. (1999). Viewing the viewers: Ten video cases of children's television viewing behaviors. *Journal of Broadcasting & Electronic Media, 43,* 506–528.

Boster, F. J. (2002). On making progress in communication science. *Human Communication Research, 28,* 473–490.

Bostrom, R. N. (2003). Theories, data, and communication research. *Communication Monographs, 70,* 275–294.

Bouma, G. D., & Atkinson, G. B. J. (1995). *A handbook of social science research* (2nd ed.). New York: Oxford University Press.

Bourque, L. B., & Fielder, E. P. (1995). How to conduct self-administered and mail surveys. Thousand Oaks, CA: Sage.

Braithwaite, C. A. (1997a). Sa'ah Naagháí Bik'eh Hózhóón: An ethnography of Navajo educational communication practices. *Communication Education, 46,* 219–234.

Braithwaite, C. A. (1997b). "Were YOU there?" A ritual of legitimacy among Vietnam veterans. *Western Journal of Communication, 61,* 423–447.

Braithwaite, D. O., & Eckstein, N. J. (2003). How people with disabilities communicatively manage assistance: Helping as instrumental social support. *Journal of Applied Communication Research, 31,* 1–26.

Brannen, J. (2004). Working qualitative and quantitatively. In C. Seale, G. Gobo, J. F. Gubrium, & D. Silverman (Eds.), *Qualitative research practice* (pp. 312–326). London: Sage.

Brooks, W. D. (1970). Perspectives on communication research. In P. Emmert & W. D. Brooks (Eds.), *Methods of research in communication* (pp. 3–8). New York: Houghton Mifflin.

Brown, M. H., & Kreps, G. L. (1993). Narrative analysis and organizational development. In S. L. Herndon & G. L. Kreps (Eds.), *Qualitative research: Applications in organizational communication* (pp. 47–62). Cresskill, NJ: Hampton Press.

Bruess, C. J. S., & Pearson, J. C. (1997). Interpersonal rituals in marriage and adult friendship. *Communication Monographs, 64,* 25–46.

Bruess, C. J., & Pearson, J. C. (2002). The function of mundane ritualizing in adult friendship and marriage. *Communication Research Reports, 19,* 314–216.

Bunton, K. (1998). Social responsibility in covering community: A narrative case analysis. *Journal of Mass Media Ethics, 13,* 232–246.

Burgoon, J. K. (1976). The unwillingness-to-communicate scale: Development and validation. *Communication Monographs, 43,* 60–69.

Buttny, R. (1997). Reported speech in talking race on campus. *Human Communication Research, 23,* 477–506.

Buzzanell, P. M., & Turner, L. H. (2003). Emotion work revealed by job loss discourse: Backgrounding-foregrounding of feelings, construction of normalcy, and (re)instituting of traditional masculinities. *Journal of Applied Communication Research, 31,* 27–57.

Cader, S. (1996). Statistical techniques. In R. Sapsford & V. Jupp (Eds.), *Data collection and analysis* (pp. 225–261). Thousand Oaks, CA: Sage.

Cai, X., Gantz, W., Schwartz, N., & Wang, X. (2003). Children's website adherence to the FTC's online privacy protection rule. *Journal of Applied Communication Research, 31,* 346–362.

Campbell, D., & Stanley, J. (1963). *Experimental and quasi-experimental designs for research.* Chicago: Rand McNally.

Campbell, S. W., & Russo, T. C. (2003). The social construction of mobile telephony: An application of the social influence model to perceptions and uses of mobile phones within personal communication networks. *Communication Monographs, 70,* 317–334.

Canary, D. J., Brossman, B. G., & Seibold, D. R. (1987). Argument structures in decision-making groups. *Southern Speech Communication Journal, 53,* 18–37.

Cappella, J. N. (1977). Research methodology in communication: Review and commentary. In B. D. Ruben (Ed.), *Communication yearbook 1* (pp. 37–53). New Brunswick, NJ: Transaction Books.

Cappella, J. N. (1987). Interpersonal communication: Definitions and fundamental questions. In C. R. Berger & S. H. Chaffee (Eds.), *Handbook of communication science* (pp. 184–238). Newbury Park, CA: Sage.

Cappella, J. N. (1990). The method of proof by example in interaction analysis. *Communication Monographs, 57,* 236–242.

Carey, M. A. (1994). The group effect in focus groups: Planning, implementing and interpreting focus group research. In J. Morse (Ed.), *Critical issues in qualitative research methods* (pp. 225–241). Thousand Oaks, CA: Sage.

Carmines, E. G., & Zeller, R. A. (1979). *Reliability and validity assessment.* Beverly Hills: Sage.

Carter, S., Kang, M., & Taggart, R. (1999). An interdisciplinary approach to a critical incident course. *Journalism & Mass Communication Educator, 54,* 4–23.

Carver, R. P. (1978). The case against statistical significance testing. *Harvard Educational Review, 48,* 378–399.

Caughlin, J. P. (2003). Family communication standards: What counts as excellent family communication and how are such standards associated with family satisfaction? *Human Communication Research, 29,* 5–40.

Cayanus, J. L., Booth-Butterfield, M. (2004). Relationship orientation, jealousy, and equity: An examination of jealousy evoking and positive communicative responses. *Communication Quarterly, 52,* 237–250.

Chapel, G., Peterson, K. M., & Joseph, R. (1999). Exploring anti-gang advertisements: Focus group discussions with gang members and at-risk youth. *Journal of Applied Communication Research, 27,* 237–257.

Charmaz, K. (2000). Grounded theory: Objectivist and constructivist methods. In N. K. Denzin & Y. S. Lincoln (Eds.), *Handbook of qualitative research* (2nd ed., pp. 509–535). Thousand Oaks, CA: Sage.

Chiles, A. M., & Zorn, T. E. (1995). Empowerment in organizations: Employees' perceptions of the influences on empowerment. *Journal of Applied Communication Research, 23,* 1–25.

Clair, R. P. (1993). The use of framing devices to sequester organizational narratives: Hegemony and harassment. *Communication Monographs, 60,* 113–136.

Clair, R. P., Chapman, P. A., & Kunkel, A. W. (1996). Narrative approaches to raising consciousness about sexual harassment: From research to pedagogy and back again. *Journal of Applied Communication Research, 24,* 241–259.

Clark, L. S. (2002). U.S. adolescent religious identity, the media, and the "funky" side of religion. *Journal of Communication, 52,* 794–812.

Clark, R. A. (1990). Teaching research methods. In J. A. Daly, G. W. Friedrich, & A. L. Vangelisti (Eds.), *Teaching communication: Theory, research, and methods* (pp. 181–191). Hillsdale, NJ: Erlbaum.

Clayman, S. E., & Heritage, J. (2002). Questioning presidents: Journalistic deference and adversarialness in the press conferences of U.S. presidents Eisenhower and Reagan. *Journal of Communication, 52,* 749–775.

Cole, J. G., & McCroskey, J. C. (2003). The association of perceived communication apprehension, shyness, and verbal aggression with perceptions of source credibility and affect in organizational and interpersonal contexts. *Communication Quarterly, 51,* 101–110.

Communication Studies 298, California State University, Sacramento. (1997). Fragments of self at the postmodern bar. *Journal of Contemporary Ethnography, 26,* 251–292.

Conquergood, D. (1994). Homeboys and hoods: Gang communication and cultural space. In L. R. Frey (Ed.), *Group communication in context: Studies of natural groups* (pp. 23–55). Hillsdale, NJ: Erlbaum.

Coopman, S. J., & Meidlinger, K. B. (2000). Power, hierarchy, and change: The stories of a Catholic parish staff. *Management Communication Quarterly, 13,* 567–625.

Craig, R. T. (1993). Why are there so many communication theories? *Journal of Communication, 43,* 26–33.

Craig, R. T. (1995). Applied communication research in a practical discipline. In K. N. Cissna (Ed.), *Applied communication in the 21st century* (pp. 147–155). Mahwah, NJ: Erlbaum.

Craig, R. T. (1999). Communication theory as a field. *Communication Theory, 6,* 119–161.

Crawford, L. (1996). Personal ethnography. *Communication Monographs, 63,* 158–170.

Creswell, J. W. (1994). *Research design: Qualitative & quantitative approaches.* Thousand Oaks, CA: Sage.

Creswell, J. W. (1998). *Qualitative inquiry and research design: Choosing among five traditions.* Thousand Oaks, CA: Sage.

Cronbach, L. J. (1951). Coefficient alpha and the internal structure of tests. *Psychometrika, 16,* 297–334.

Cushman, D. P. (1998). Visions of order in human communication theory. In J. S. Trent (Ed.), *Communication: Views from the helm for the 21st century* (pp. 8–12). Boston: Allyn Bacon.

Dainton, M. (2003). Equity and uncertainty in relational maintenance. *Western Journal of Communication, 67,* 164–186.

Deetz, S. A. (1992). *Democracy in an age of corporate colonization: Developments in communication and the politics of everyday life.* Albany, NY: SUNY Press.

Denzin, N. K. (1970). *The research act: A theoretical introduction to sociological methods.* Chicago: Aldine.

Denzin, N. K. (1978). *The research act. A theoretical introduction to sociological methods* (2nd ed.). New York: McGraw-Hill.

Denzin, N. K., & Lincoln, Y. S. (1994). Introduction: Entering the field of qualitative research. In N. K. Denzin & Y. S. Lincoln (Eds.), *Handbook of qualitative research* (pp. 1–17). Thousand Oaks, CA: Sage.

Denzin, N. K., & Lincoln, Y. S. (2000). Introduction: The discipline and practice of qualitative research. In N. K. Denzin & Y. S. Lincoln (Eds.), *Handbook of qualitative research* (2nd ed., pp. 1–28). Thousand Oaks, CA: Sage.

de Vaus, D. A. (2001). *Research design in social research.* Thousand Oaks, CA: Sage.

Dixon, T. L., & Linz, D. G. (1997). Obscenity law and sexually explicit rap music: Understanding the effects of sex, attitudes, and beliefs. *Journal of Applied Communication Research, 25,* 217–241.

Dochartaigh, N. O. (2002). *The internet research handbook: A practical guide for students and researchers in the social sciences.* Thousand Oaks, CA: Sage.

Dohan, D., & Sanchez-Jankowski, M. (1998). Using computers to analyze ethnographic field data:

Theoretical and practical considerations. *Annual Review of Sociology, 24,* 477–498.

Dougherty, D. S. (2001). Sexual harassment as [dys]functional process: A feminist standpoint analysis. *Journal of Applied Communication Research, 29,* 372–402.

Downing, J., & Garmon, C. (2001). Teaching students in the basic course how to use presentation software. *Communication Education, 50,* 218–229.

Duran, R. L. (1983). Communicative adaptability: A measure of social communicative competence. *Communication Quarterly, 31,* 320–326.

Eastman, S. T., Newton, G. D., & Bolls, P. D. (2003). How promotional content changes ratings: The impact of appeals, humor, and presentations. *Journal of Applied Communication Research, 31,* 238–259.

Edley, P. P. (2000). Discursive essentializing in a woman-owned business: Gendered stereotype and strategic subordination. *Management Communication Quarterly, 14,* 271–306.

Egbert, N., & Parrott, R. (2003). Empathy and social support for the terminally ill: Implications for recruiting and retaining hospice and hospital volunteers. *Communication Studies, 54,* 18–34.

Eisner, E. (1991). *The enlightened eye.* New York: Macmillan.

Elgesem, D. (1996). Privacy, respect for persons, and risk. In C. Ess (Ed.), *Philosophical perspectives on computer-mediated communication* (pp. 45–66). Albany: State University of New York Press.

Ellingson, L. L. (2003). Interdisciplinary health care teamwork in the clinic backstage. *Journal of Applied Communication Research, 31,* 93–117.

Ellis, C., & Bochner, A. P. (2000). Autoethnography, personal narrative, reflexivity: Researcher as subject. In N. K. Denzin & Y. S. Lincoln (Eds.), *Handbook of qualitative research* (2nd ed., pp. 733–768). Thousand Oaks, CA: Sage.

Ellis, D. G., & Maoz, I. (2002). Cross-cultural argument interactions between Israeli-Jews and Palestinians. *Journal of Applied Communication Research, 30,* 181–194.

Ellis, J. B., & Smith, S. W. (2004). Memorable messages as guides to self-assessment of behavior: A replication and extension diary study. *Communication Monographs, 71,* 97–119.

Ellis, K. (2000). Perceived teacher confirmation: The development and validation of an instrument and two studies of the relationship to cognitive and affective learning. *Human Communication Research, 26,* 264–291.

Emerson, R. B., Fretz, R. I., & Shaw, L. L. (1995). *Writing ethnographic fieldnotes.* Chicago: University of Chicago Press.

Emmert, P. (1989). Philosophy of measurement. In P. Emmert & L. L. Barker (Eds.), *Measurement of communication behavior* (pp. 87–116). New York: Longman.

Erbert, L. A., & Floyd, K. (2004). Affectionate expressions as face-threatening acts: Receiver assessments. *Communication Studies, 55,* 254–270.

Erbert, L. A., Perez, F. G., & Gareis, E. (2003). Turning points and dialectical interpretations of immigrant experiences in the United States. *Western Journal of Communication, 67,* 113–137.

Erickson, F. (1986). Qualitative methods in research on teaching. In M. C. Wittrock (Ed.), *Handbook of research on teaching* (3rd ed., pp. 119–161). New York: Macmillan.

Erickson, K. V., Cheatham, T. R., & Jordan, W. J. (1978). Demographic characteristics of nonrespondents to speech communication survey research. *Communication Quarterly, 26,* 35–40.

Fairhurst, G. T. (1993). The leader-member exchange patterns of women leaders in industry: A discourse analysis. *Communication Monographs, 60,* 321–351.

Feldman, M. S., Bell, J., & Berger, M. T. (2003). *Gaining access: A practical and theoretical guide for qualitative researchers.* Walnut Creek, CA: AltaMira.

Field, H. S., & Barnett, N. J. (1978). Students vs. "real" people as jurors. *Journal of Social Psychology, 104,* 287–293.

Fielding, N. (2002). Computer applications in qualitative research. In P. Atkinson, A. Coffey, S. Delamont, J. Lofland, & L. Lofland (Eds.), *Handbook of ethnography* (pp. 453–467). Thousand Oaks, CA: Sage.

Fink, A. (1995a). *How to ask survey questions* (Vol. 2). Thousand Oaks, CA: Sage.

Fink, A. (1995b). *The survey handbook* (Vol. 1). Thousand Oaks, CA: Sage.

Fisher, C. B., & Fryberg, D. (1994). Participant partners: College students weigh the costs and benefits of deceptive research. *American Psychologist, 49,* 417–427.

Fitch, K. L. (1994). Criteria for evidence in qualitative research. *Western Journal of Communication, 58,* 32–38.

Flanagan, J. C. (1954). The critical incident technique. *Psychological Bulletin, 51,* 327–357.

Floyd, K., & Ray, G. B. (2003). Human affection exchange: IV. Vocalic predictors of perceived affection in initial interactions. *Western Journal of Communication, 67,* 56–73.

Fontana, A., & Frey, J. H. (2000). The interview: From structured questions to negotiated text. In N. K. Denzin & Y. S. Lincoln (Eds.), *Handbook of qualitative research* (2nd ed.), (pp. 645–672). Thousand Oaks, CA: Sage.

Ford, W. S. (2003). Communication practices of professional service providers: Predicting customer satisfaction and loyalty. *Journal of Applied Communication Research, 31,* 189–211.

Foster, P. (1996). Observational research. In R. Sapsford & V. Jupp (Eds.), *Data collection and analysis* (pp. 57–93). Thousand Oaks, CA: Sage.

Fowler, F. J., Jr. (1993). *Survey research methods* (2nd ed.). Newbury Park, CA: Sage

Fowler, F. J., Jr. (1995). *Improving survey questions: Design and evaluation.* Thousand Oaks, CA: Sage.

Fowler, F. J., Jr. (2002). *Survey research methods* (3rd ed.). Thousand Oaks, CA: Sage.

French, S. L. (2003). Reflections on healing: Framing strategies utilized by acquaintance rape survivors. *Journal of Applied Communication Research, 31,* 298–319.

Frey, J. H., & Oishi, S. M. (1995). *How to conduct interviews by telephone and in person.* Thousand Oaks, CA: Sage.

Frymier, A. B., & Wanzer, M. B. (2003). Examining differences in perceptions of students' communication with professors: A comparison of students with and without disabilities. *Communication Quarterly, 51,* 174–191.

Galvan, J. L. (1999). *Writing literature review: A guide for students of the social and behavioral sciences.* Los Angeles: Pyrczak.

Garner, A. C. (1999). Negotiating our positions in culture: Popular adolescent fiction and the self-constructions of women. *Women's Studies in Communication, 22,* 85–111.

Gayle, B. M., & Preiss, R. W. (1998). Assessing emotionality in organizational conflicts. *Management Communication Quarterly, 12,* 280–302.

Glaser, B. G., & Strauss, A. L. (1967). *The discovery of grounded theory: Strategies for qualitative research.* New York: Aldine.

Glaser, B., & Strauss, B. (1967). *The discovery of grounded theory: Strategies for qualitative research.* Chicago: Aldine.

Gold, R. L. (1958). Roles in sociological field observations. *Social Forces, 36,* 217–223.

Goldsmith, D. J., & Fitch, K. (1997). The normative context of advice as social support. *Human Communication Research, 23,* 454–476.

Golish, T. D. (1999). Students' use of compliance gaining strategies with graduate teaching assistants: Examining the other end of the power spectrum. *Communication Quarterly, 47,* 12–32.

Gossett, L. M. (2002). Kept at arm's length: Questioning the organizational desirability of member identification. *Communication Monographs, 69*, 385–404.

Gray, J. H., & Densten, I. L. (1998). Integrating quantitative and qualitative analysis using latent and manifest variables. *Quality & Quantity, 32*, 419–431.

Gross, M. A., Guerrero, L. K., & Alberts, J. K. (2004). Perceptions of conflict strategies and communication competence in task-oriented dyads. *Journal of Applied Communication Research, 32*, 249–270.

Gubrium, J. F., & Holstein, J. A. (2000). Introduction: The discipline and practice of qualitative research. In N. K. Denzin & Y. S. Lincoln (Eds.), *Handbook of qualitative research* (2nd ed., pp. 487–508). Thousand Oaks, CA: Sage.

Guerrero, L. K. (1996). Attachment-style differences in intimacy and involvement: A test of the four-category model. *Communication Monographs, 63*, 269–292.

Guilford, J. P. (1956). *Fundamental statistics in psychology and education.* New York: McGraw-Hill.

Hackman, J. R. (1992). Commentary: Time and transitions. In P. J. Frost & R. E. Stablein (Eds.), *Doing exemplary research* (pp. 73–76). Newbury Park, CA: Sage.

Harlow, L. L. (1997). Significance testing introduction and overview. In L. L. Harlow, S. A. Mulaik, & J. H. Steiger (Eds.), *What if there were no significance tests?* (pp. 1–17). Mahwah, NJ: Erlbaum.

Harlow, L. L., Mulaik, S. A., & Steiger, J. H. (1997). *What if there were no significance tests?* Mahwah, NJ: Erlbaum.

Harrington, N. G. (1997). Strategies used by college students to persuade peers to drink. *Southern Communication Journal, 62*, 229–242.

Harrington, N. G., Lane, D. R., Donohew, L., Zimmerman, R. S., Norling, G. R., Jeong-Hyun, A., et al. (2003). Persuasive strategies for effective anti-drug messages. *Communication Monographs, 70*, 16–38.

Harter, L. M. (2004). Masculinity(s), the agrarian frontier myth, and cooperative ways of organizing: Contradictions and tensions in the experience and enactment of democracy. *Journal of Applied Communication Research, 32*, 89–118.

Harter, L. M., & Krone, K. J. (2001). Exploring the emergent identities of future physicians: Toward an understanding of the ideological socialization of osteopathic medical students. *Southern Communication Journal, 67*, 66–83.

Harwood, J., & Anderson, K. (2002). The presence and portrayal of social groups on prime-time television. *Communication Reports, 15*, 81–97.

Hawes, L. C. (1975). *Pragmatics of analoguing: Theory and model construction in communication.* Reading, MA: Addison-Wesley.

Hecht, M., Trost, M. R., Bator, R. J., & MacKinnon, D. (1997). Ethnicity and sex similarities and differences in drug resistance. *Journal of Applied Communication Research, 25*, 75–97.

Helmer, J. (1993). Storytelling in the creation and maintenance of organizational tension and stratification. *Southern Communication Journal, 59*, 34–44.

Henkel, R. E. (1976). *Tests of significance.* Beverly Hills: Sage.

Henningsen, M. L., Henningsen, D. D., Cruz, M. G., & Morrill, J. (2003). Social influence in groups: A comparative application of relational framing theory and the elaboration likelihood mode of persuasion. *Communication Monographs, 70*, 175–197.

Henry, G. T. (1990). *Practical sampling.* Newbury Park, CA: Sage.

Henry, G. T. (1998). Practical sampling. In L. Bickman & D. J. Rog (Eds.), *Handbook of applied social research methods* (pp. 101–126). Thousand Oaks, CA: Sage.

Heritage, J., & Atkinson, J. M. (1984). Introduction. In J. M. Atkinson & J. Heritage (Eds.), *Structures of social action: Studies in conversation analysis* (pp. 1–15). New York: Cambridge University Press.

Herndon, S. L. (1993). Using focus group interviews for preliminary investigation. In S. L. Herndon & G. L. Kreps (Eds.), *Qualitative research: Applications in organizational communication* (pp. 39–45). Cresskill, NJ: Hampton Press.

Hickson, M., III, & Jennings, R. W. (1993). Compatible theory and applied research: Systems theory and triangulation. In S. L. Herndon & G. L. Kreps (Eds.), *Qualitative research: Applications in organizational communication* (pp. 139–157). Cresskill, NJ: Hampton Press.

Hickson, M., III, Scott, R. K., & Vogel, R. (1995). A content analysis of local television news in a top 50 market. *Communication Research Reports, 12*, 71–79.

Hinton, J. S., & Kramer, M. W. (1998). The impact of self-directed videotape feedback on students' self-reported levels of communication competence and apprehension. *Communication Education, 47*, 151–161.

Holbert, R. L., Benoit, W. L., Hansen, G. J., & Wen, W-C. (2002). The role of communication in the formation of an issue-based citizenry. *Communication Monographs, 69*, 296–310.

Holladay, S. J. (2002). "Have fun while you can," "you're only as old as you feel," and "don't ever get old!": An examination of memorable messages about aging. *Journal of Communication, 52*, 681–697.

Holsti, O. R. (1969). *Content analysis for the social sciences and humanities.* Reading, MA: Addison-Wesley.

Holsti, O. R., Loomba, J. K., & North, R. C. (1968). Content analysis. In G. Lindzey & E. Aronson (Eds.), *The handbook of social psychology* (Vol. 2, pp. 596–692). Reading, MA: Addison-Wesley.

Hoover, K., & Donovan, T. (1995). *The elements of social scientific thinking* (6th ed.). New York: St. Martin's Press.

Hopf, T., Ayres, J., Ayres, F., & Baker, B. (1995). Does self-help material work? Testing a manual designed to help trainers construct public speaking apprehension reduction workshops. *Communication Research Reports, 12,* 34–38.

Hoppe-Nagao, A., & Ting-Toomey, S. (2002). Relational dialectics and management strategies in marital couples. *Southern Communication Journal, 67,* 142–159.

Hopper, R. (1990). Describing speech phenomena. In J. A. Anderson (Ed.), *Communication yearbook 13* (pp. 245–254). Newbury Park, CA: Sage.

Hovick, S., Meyers, R. A., & Timmerman, C. E. (2003). E-mail communication in workplace romantic relationships. *Communication Studies, 54,* 468–482.

Hullett, C. R. (2002). Charting the process underlying the chance of value-expressive attitudes: The importance of value-relevance in predicting the matching effect. *Communication Monographs, 69,* 158–178.

Hutchinson, K. L., & Neuliep, J. W. (1993). The influence of parent and peer modeling on the development of communication apprehension in elementary school children. *Communication Quarterly, 41,* 16–25.

Jacobs, S. (1990). On the especially nice fit between qualitative analysis and the known properties of conversation. *Communication Monographs, 57,* 243–249.

Jaeger, R. M. (1990). *Statistics: A spectator sport* (2nd ed.). Newbury Park, CA: Sage.

James, B. (1995). Learning to consume: An ethnographic study of cultural change in Hungary. *Critical Studies in Mass Communication, 12,* 287–305.

Jameson, J. K. (2004). Negotiating autonomy and connection through politeness: A dialectical approach to organizational conflict management. *Western Journal of Communication, 68,* 257–277.

Janesick, V. J. (1994). The dance of qualitative research designs: Metaphor, methodolatry, and meaning. In N. K. Denzin & Y. S. Lincoln (Eds.), *Handbook of qualitative research* (pp. 209–219). Thousand Oaks, CA: Sage.

Janesick, V. J. (1998). *"Stretching" exercises for qualitative researchers.* Thousand Oaks, CA: Sage.

Janesick, V. J. (2000). The choreography of qualitative research design. In N. K. Denzin & Y. S. Lincoln (Eds.), *Handbook of qualitative research* (2nd ed., pp. 379–399). Thousand Oaks, CA: Sage.

Janesick, V. J. (2004). *"Stretching" exercises for qualitative researchers* (2nd ed.). Thousand Oaks, CA: Sage.

Johnson, J. D., & Chang, H. (2000). Internal and external communication, boundary spanning, and innovation adoption: An over-time comparison of three explanations of internal and external innovation communication in a new organizational form. *The Journal of Business Communication, 37,* 238–263.

Jones, S. M., & Guerrero, L. K. (2001). The effects of nonverbal immediacy and verbal person centeredness in the emotional support process. *Human Communication Research, 27,* 567–596.

Jorgensen-Earp, C. R., & Staton, A. Q. (1993). Student metaphors for the college freshman experience. *Communication Education, 42,* 123–141.

Judd, C. M., & McClelland, G. H. (1998). Measurement. In D. T. Gilbert, S. T. Fiske, & G. Lindzey (Eds.), *The handbook of social psychology* (Vol. I, 4th ed., pp. 180–232). Boston: McGraw-Hill.

Judd, C. M., McClelland, G. H., & Culhane, S. E. (1995). Data analysis: Continuing issues in the everyday analysis of psychological data. In J. T. Spence, J. M. Darley, & D. J. Foss (Eds.), *Annual review of psychology* (Vol. 46, pp. 433–465). Palo Alto, CA: Annual Reviews.

Kaid, L. L., & Wadsworth, A. J. (1989). Content analysis. In P. Emmert & L. L. Barker (Eds.), *Measurement of communication behavior* (pp. 197–217). New York: Longman.

Kaplan, A. (1964). *The conduct of inquiry.* San Francisco: Chandler.

Kassing, J. W. (2002). Speaking up: Identifying employees' upward dissent strategies. *Management Communication Quarterly, 16,* 187–209.

Katzer, J., Cook, K. H., & Crouch, W. W. (1978). *Evaluating information: A guide for users of social science research.* Reading, MA: Addison-Wesley.

Kelle, U. (2004). Computer-assisted qualitative data analysis. In C. Seale, G. Gobo, J. F. Gubrium, & D. Silverman (Eds.), *Qualitative research practice* (pp. 473–489). Thousand Oaks, CA: Sage.

Kerlinger, F. N. (1986). *Foundations of behavioral research* (3rd ed.). New York: Holt, Rinehart and Winston.

Keyton, J. (1994). Designing a look at women. *The Mid-Atlantic Almanack, 3,* 126–141.

Keyton, J. (1995). Using SYMLOG as a self-analytical group facilitation technique. In L. R. Frey (Ed.), *Innovations in group facilitation: Applications in natural settings* (pp. 148–174). Cresskill, NJ: Hampton Press.

Keyton, J. (2005). *Communication and organizational culture: A key to understanding work experiences.* Thousand Oaks, CA: Sage.

Keyton, J., Ferguson, P. R., & Rhodes, S. C. (2001). Cultural indicators of sexual harassment. *Southern Communication Journal, 67,* 33–50.

Keyton, J., & Rhodes, S. C. (1997). Sexual harassment: A matter of individual ethics, legal definitions, or organizational policy? *Journal of Business Ethics, 16,* 129–146.

Keyton, J., & Rhodes, S. C. (1999). Organizational sexual harassment: Translating research into application. *Journal of Applied Communication Research, 27,* 158–173.

Kibler, R. J. (1970). Basic communication research considerations. In P. Emmert & W. D. Brooks (Eds.), *Methods of research in communication* (pp. 9–49). New York: Houghton Mifflin.

Kim, Y. Y., Lujan, P., & Dixon, L. D. (1998). "I can walk both ways": Identity integration of American Indians in Oklahoma. *Human Communication Research, 25,* 252–274.

Kirk, R. E. (1996). Practical significance: A concept whose time has come. *Educational and Psychological Measurement, 56,* 746–759.

Kramer, M. W. (1995). A longitudinal study of superior-subordinate communication during job transfers. *Human Communication Research, 22,* 39–64.

Kramer, M. W. (2002). Communication in a community theatre group: Managing multiple group roles. *Communication Studies, 53,* 151–170.

Krejcie, R. V., & Morgan, D. W. (1970). Determining sample size for research activities. *Educational and Psychological Measurement, 30,* 607–610.

Krendl, K. A., Olson, B., & Burke, R. (1992). Preparing for the environmental decade: A field experiment on recycling behavior. *Journal of Applied Communication Research, 20,* 19–36.

Krippendorff, K. (2004). *Content analysis: An introduction to its methodology* (2nd ed.). Thousand Oaks, CA: Sage.

Krueger, R. A., & Casey, M. A. (2000). *Focus groups: A practical guide for applied research* (3rd ed.). Thousand Oaks, CA: Sage.

Kuhn, T., & Nelson, N. (2002). Reengineering identity: A case study of multiplicity and duality in organizational identification. *Management Communication Quarterly, 16,* 5–38.

Kuhn, T., & Poole, M. S. (2000). Do conflict management styles affect group decision making? Evidence from a longitudinal field study. *Human Communication Research, 26,* 558–590.

Kumar, R. (1996). *Research methodology: A step-by-step guide for beginners.* Thousand Oaks, CA: Sage.

Kunkel, D., & Gantz, W. (1993). Assessing compliance with industry self-regulation of television advertising to children. *Journal of Applied Communication Research, 21,* 148–162.

Kvale, S. (1996). *InterViews: An introduction to qualitative research interviewing.* Thousand Oaks, CA: Sage.

Lacy, S. R., & Riffe, D. (1993). Sins of omission and commission in mass communication quantitative research. *Journalism Quarterly, 70,* 126–132.

Lammers, J. C., & Krikorian, D. H. (1997). Theoretical extension and operationalization of the bona fide group construct with an application to surgical teams. *Journal of Applied Communication Research, 25,* 17–38.

Lange, J. I. (1990). Refusal to compromise: The case of Earth First! *Western Journal of Speech Communication, 54,* 473–494.

Lange, J. I. (1993). The logic of competing information campaigns: Conflict over old growth and the spotted owl. *Communication Monographs, 60,* 1993.

Lee, E. (2004). Effects of visual representation on social influence in computer-mediated communication: Experimental tests of the social identity model of deindividuation effects. *Human Communication Research, 30,* 234–259.

Leonardi, P. M. (2003). Problematizing "new media": Culturally based perceptions of cell phones, computers, and the internet among United States Latinos. *Critical Studies in Media Communication, 20,* 160–179.

Leone, R. (2002). Contemplating ratings: An examination of what the MPAA considers "too far for R" and why. *Journal of Communication, 52,* 938–954.

Lesch, C. L. (1994). Observing theory in practice: Sustaining consciousness in a coven. In L. R. Frey (Ed.), *Group communication in context: Studies of natural groups* (pp. 57–84.). Hillsdale, NJ: Erlbaum.

Lett, M. D., DiPietro, A. L., & Johnson, D. I. (2004). Examining effects of television news violence on college students through cultivation theory. *Communication Research Reports, 21,* 39–46.

Lim, T. S., & Bowers, J. (1991). Facework: Solidarity, approbation, and tact. *Human Communication Research, 17,* 415–450.

Lincoln, Y. S., & Guba, E. G. (1985). *Naturalistic inquiry.* Beverly Hills: Sage.

Lindlof, T. R. (1991). The qualitative study of media audiences. *Journal of Broadcasting & Electronic Media, 35,* 23–42.

Lindlof, T. R. (1995). *Qualitative communication research methods.* Thousand Oaks, CA: Sage.

Lindlof, T. R., & Taylor, B. C. (2002). *Qualitative communication research methods* (2nd ed.). Thousand Oaks, CA: Sage.

Lindsley, S. L. (1999). Communication and "the Mexican way": Stability and trust as core symbols in maquiladoras. *Western Journal of Communication, 63,* 1–31.

Littlejohn, S. W. (1991). Deception in communication research. *Communication Reports, 4,* 51–54.

Littlejohn, S. W. (1999). *Theories of human communication* (6th ed.). Belmont, CA: Wadsworth.

Lofland, J., & Lofland, L. H. (1995). *Analyzing social settings: A guide to qualitative observation and analysis* (3rd ed.). Belmont, CA: Wadsworth.

Lombard, M., Snyder-Duch, J., & Bracken, C. C. (2002). Content analysis in mass communication: Assessment and reporting of intercoder reliability. *Human Communication Research, 28,* 587–604.

Lowry, D. T. (1978). Population validity of communication research: Sampling the samples. *Journalism Quarterly, 55,* 62–68, 76.

Lowry, D. T., Nio, T. C., & Leitner, D. W. (2003). Setting the public fear agenda: A longitudinal analysis of network TV crime reporting, public perceptions of crime, and FBI crime statistics. *Journal of Communication, 53,* 61–73.

Lustig, M. W. (1986). Theorizing about human communication. *Communication Quarterly, 34,* 451–459.

Lyken, D. E. (1968). Statistical significance in psychological research. *Psychological Bulletin, 70,* 151–159.

Malkin, A. R., Wornian, K., & Chrisler, J. C. (1999). Women and weight: Gendered messages on magazine covers. *Sex Roles: A Journal of Research, 40,* 647–655.

Mandelbaum, J. (1990). Communication phenomena as solutions to interactional problems. In J. A. Anderson (Ed.), *Communication yearbook 13* (pp. 255–267). Newbury Park, CA: Sage.

Manusov, V., Trees, A. R., Reddick, L. A., Rowe, A. M. C., & Easley, J. M. (1998). Explanations and impressions: Investigating attributions and their effects on judgments for friends and strangers. *Communication Studies, 49,* 209–223.

Mares, M. (1996). The role of source confusion in television's cultivation of social reality judgments. *Human Communication Research, 23,* 278–297.

Markham, A. N. (1998). *Life online: Researching real experience in virtual space.* Walnut Creek, CA: AltaMira.

Markham, A. N. (2004). The internet as research context. In C. Seale, G. Gobo, J. F. Gubrium, & D. Silverman (Eds.), *Qualitative research practice* (pp. 358–374). London: Sage.

Marshall, C., & Rossman, G. B. (1999). *Designing qualitative research* (3rd ed.). Thousand Oaks, CA: Sage.

Martin, D. M. (2004). Humor in middle management: Women negotiating the paradoxes of organizational life? *Journal of Applied Communication Research, 32,* 147–170.

Mason, S. A. (1993). Communication processes in the field research interview setting. In S. L. Herndon & G. L. Kreps (Eds.), *Qualitative research: Applications in organizational communication* (pp. 29–38). Cresskill, NJ: Hampton Press.

Mastro, D. E., & Stern, S. R. (2003). Representations of race in television commercials: A content analysis of prime-time advertising. *Journal of Broadcasting & Electronic Media, 47,* 638–647.

Maxwell, J. A. (1996). *Qualitative research design: An interactive approach.* Thousand Oaks, CA: Sage.

Mayer, V. (2003). Living telenovelas/telenovelizing life: Mexican American girls' identities and transnational telenovelas. *Journal of Communication, 53,* 479–495.

McCann, R. M., Kellermann, K., Giles, H., Gallois, C., & Viladot, M. W. (2004). Cultural and gender influences on age identification. *Communication Studies, 55,* 88–105.

McCracken, G. (1988). *The long interview.* Newbury Park, CA: Sage.

McCroskey, J. C. (1970). Measures of communication-bound anxiety. *Speech Monographs, 37,* 269–277.

McCroskey, J. C., Beatty, M. J., Kearney, P., & Plax, T. G. (1985). The content validity of the PRCA-24 as a measure of communication apprehension across communication contexts. *Communication Quarterly, 33,* 165–173.

McCroskey, J. C., & McCain, T. A. (1974). The measurement of interpersonal attraction. *Speech Monographs, 41,* 261–266.

McCroskey, J. C., Richmond, V. P., Johnson, A. D., & Smith, H. T. (2004). Organizational orientations theory and measurement: Development of measures and preliminary investigations. *Communication Quarterly, 52,* 1–14.

McGee, D. S., & Cegala, D. J. (1998). Patient communication skills training for improved communication competence in the primary care medical consultation. *Journal of Applied Communication Research, 26,* 412–430.

McLaurin, P. (1995). An examination of the effect of culture on pro-social messages directed at African-American at-risk youth. *Communication Monographs, 62,* 301–326.

McPherson, M. B., Kearney, P., & Plax, T. G. (2003). The dark side of instruction: Teacher anger as classroom norm violations. *Journal of Applied Communication Research, 312,* 76–90.

Meares, M. M., Oetzel, J. G., Torres, A., Derkacs, D., & Ginossar, T. (2004). Employee mistreatment and muted voice in the culturally diverse workplace.

Journal of Applied Communication Research, 32, 4–27.

Mendelson, A. L., & Thorson, E. (2004). How verbalizers and visualizers process the newspaper environment. *Journal of Communication, 54,* 474–491.

Metzger, M. J., & Flanagin, A. J. (2002). Audience orientations toward new media. *Communication Research Reports, 19,* 338–351.

Meyer, J. C. (1997). Humor in member narratives: Uniting and dividing at work. *Western Journal of Communication, 61,* 188–208.

Meyer, P. (1973). *Precision journalism.* Bloomington, IN: University Press.

Meyers, R. A., Seibold, D. R., & Brashers, D. (1991). Argument in initial group decision-making discussions: Refinement of a coding scheme and a descriptive quantitative analysis. *Western Journal of Speech Communication, 55,* 47–68.

Miller, G. R. (1970). Research setting: Laboratory studies. In P. Emmert & W. D. Brooks (Eds.), *Methods of research in communication* (pp. 77–104). New York: Houghton Mifflin.

Miller, G. R., & Nicholson, H. E. (1976). *Communication inquiry: A perspective on a process.* Reading, MA: Addison-Wesley.

Miller, K. (2002). The experience of emotion in the workplace: Professing in the midst of tragedy. *Management Communication Quarterly, 15,* 571–600.

Miller, M. (1995). An intergenerational case study of suicidal tradition and mother-daughter communication. *Journal of Applied Communication Research, 23,* 247–270.

Miller-Day, M., & Dodd, A. H. (2004). Toward a descriptive model of parent-offspring communication about alcohol and other drugs. *Journal of Social and Personal Relationships, 21,* 69–91.

Monahan, J. L., & Lannutti, P. J. (2000). Alcohol as social lubricant: Alcohol myopia theory, social self-esteem, and social interaction. *Human Communication Research, 26,* 175–202.

Mongeau, P. A., & Blalock, J. (1994). Student evaluations of instructor immediacy and sexually harassing behaviors: An experimental investigation. *Journal of Applied Communication Research, 22,* 256–272.

Morgan, D. L. (1997). *Focus groups as qualitative research* (2nd ed.). Thousand Oaks, CA: Sage.

Morgan, D. L., & Krueger, R. A. (1993). When to use focus groups and why. In D. L. Morgan (Ed.), *Successful focus groups: Advancing the state of the art* (pp. 3–19). Newbury Park, CA: Sage.

Morgan, J. M., & Krone, K. J. (2001). Bending the rules of "professional" display: Emotional improvisation in caregiver performances. *Journal of Applied Communication Research, 29,* 317–340.

Morgan, S. E., & Miller, J. K. (2002). Communicating about gifts of life: The effect of knowledge, attitudes, and altruism on behavior and behavioral intensions regarding organ donation. *Journal of Applied Communication Research, 30,* 163–178.

Morgan, S. E., Miller, J., & Arasaratnam, L. A. (2002). Signing cards, saving lives: An evaluation of the worksite organ donation promotion project. *Communication Monographs, 69,* 253–273.

Morman, M. T., & Floyd, K. (2002). A "changing culture of fatherhood": Effects of affectionate communication, closeness, and satisfaction in men's relationships with their fathers and their sons. *Western Journal of Communication, 66,* 395–411.

Mueller, B. H., & Lee, J. (2002). Leader-member exchange and organizational communication satisfaction in multiple contexts. *The Journal of Business Communication, 39,* 220–244.

Muto, J. (1993). "Who's that in my bed?" The strange bedfellows made by the politics of applied qualitative organizational research. In S. L. Herndon & G. L. Kreps (Eds.), *Qualitative research: Applications in organizational communication* (pp. 19–28). Cresskill, NJ: Hampton Press.

Myers, S. A. (1998). GTAs as organizational newcomers: The association between supportive communication relationships and information seeking. *Western Journal of Communication, 60,* 54–73.

Nabi, R. L. (1998). The effect of disgust-eliciting visuals on attitudes toward animal experimentation. *Communication Quarterly, 46,* 472–484.

Nabi, R. L. (2003). Exploring the framing effects of emotion: Do discrete emotions differentially influence information accessibility, information seeking, and policy preference? *Communication Research, 30,* 224–247.

National Commission for the Protection of Human Subjects of Biomedical and Behavioral Research. (1979). *The Belmont report: Ethical principles and guidelines for the protection of human subjects of research* (Y 3.H 88:2 B 41). Washington, DC: U.S. Government Printing Office.

Neuendorf, K. A. (2002). *The content analysis guidebook.* Thousand Oaks, CA: Sage.

Nofsinger, R. E. (1991). *Everyday conversation.* Newbury Park, CA: Sage.

Oakes, M. (1986). *Statistical inference: A commentary for the social and behavioural sciences.* New York: Wiley.

O'Connor, E. S. (1997). Discourse at our disposal: Stories in and around the garbage can. *Management Communication Quarterly, 10,* 395–432.

Olson, L. N., & Golish, T. D. (2002). Topics of conflict and patterns of aggression in romantic relationships. *Southern Communication Journal, 67,* 180–200.

Osgood, C. E., Suci, C. J., & Tannenbaum, P. H. (1957). *The measurement of meaning.* Urbana: University of Illinois Press.

Owen, W. F. (1984). Interpretive themes in relational communication. *Quarterly Journal of Speech, 70,* 274–287.

Palmer, M. (2003). News: ephemera, data, artifacts and . . . quality control—Iraq now and then. *Journalism, 4,* 459–476.

Patterson, B. R., Neupauer, N. C., Burant, P. A., Koehn, S. C., & Reed, A. T. (1996). A preliminary examination of conversation analytic techniques: Rates of inter-transcriber reliability. *Western Journal of Communication, 60,* 76–91.

Pedhazur, E. J., & Schmelkin, L. P. (1991). *Measurement, design, and analysis: An integrated approach.* Hillsdale, NJ: Erlbaum.

Peterson, M. S. (1997). Personnel interviewers' perceptions of the importance and adequacy of applicants' communication skills. *Communication Education, 46,* 287–291.

Peterson, T. R., Witte, K., Enkerlin-Hoeflich, E., Espericueta, L., Flora, J. T., Florey, N., Loughran, T., & Stuart, R. (1994). Using informant directed interviews to discover risk orientation: How formative evaluations based in interpretive analysis can improve persuasive safety campaigns. *Journal of Applied Communication Research, 22,* 199–215.

Petronio, S., & Bradford, L. (1993). Issues interfering with the use of written communication as a means of relational bonding between absentee, divorced fathers and their children. *Journal of Applied Communication Research, 21,* 163–175.

Petronio, S., Reeder, H. M., Hecht, M. L., & Ros-Mendoza, T. M. (1996). Disclosure of sexual abuse by children and adolescents. *Journal of Applied Communication Research, 24,* 181–189.

Phillips, D. C. (1992). *The social scientist's bestiary: A guide to fabled threats to, and defenses of, naturalistic social science.* Oxford: Pergamon Press.

Phillipsen, G. (1992). *Speaking culturally: Explorations in social communication.* Albany: State University of New York Press.

Pierce, T., & Dougherty, D. S. (2002). The construction, enactment, and maintenance of power-as-domination through an acquisition: The case of TWA and Ozark Airlines. *Management Communication Quarterly, 16,* 129–164.

Pittam, J., & Gallois, C. (2000). Malevolence, stigma, and social distance: Maximizing intergroup differences in HIV/AIDS discourse. *Journal of Applied Communication Research, 28,* 24–43.

Poland, B. D. (1995). Transcription quality as an aspect of rigor in qualitative research. *Qualitative Inquiry, 1,* 290–310.

Pomerantz, A., Fehr, B. J., & Ende, J. (1997). When supervising physicians see patients: Strategies used in difficult situations. *Human Communication Research, 23,* 589–615.

Pool, M. M., Koolstra, C. M., & van der Voort, T. H. (2003). The impact of background radio and television on high school students' homework performance. *Journal of Communication, 53,* 74–87.

Poole, M. S., & McPhee, R. D. (1985). Methodology in interpersonal communication research. In M. L. Knapp & G. R. Miller (Eds.), *Handbook of interpersonal communication* (pp. 100–170). Beverly Hills: Sage.

Potter, W. J. (1996). *An analysis of thinking and research about qualitative methods.* Mahwah, NJ: Erlbaum.

Potter, W. J., & Levine-Donnerstein, D. (1999). Rethinking validity and reliability in content analysis. *Journal of Applied Communication Research, 27,* 258–284.

Potter, W. J., & Warren, R. (1996). Considering policies to protect children from TV violence. *Journal of Communication, 46,* 116–138.

Pratt, L., Wiseman, R. L., Cody, M. J., & Wendt, P. F. (1999). Interrogative strategies and information exchange in computer-mediated communication. *Communication Quarterly, 47,* 46–66.

Press, A. L., & Cole, E. R. (1995). Reconciling faith and fact: Pro-life women discuss media, science and the abortion debate. *Critical Studies in Mass Communication, 12,* 380–402.

Presser, S., & Blair, J. (1994). Survey pretesting: Do different methods produce different results? In P. V. Marsden (Ed.), *Sociological methodology* (Vol. 24, pp. 73–104). Washington, DC: American Sociological Association.

Provins, K. A. (1997). Handedness and speech: A critical reappraisal of the role of genetic and environmental factors in the cerebral lateralization of function. *Psychological Review, 104,* 554–571.

Pruitt, W., Koermer, C., & Goldstein, M. (1995). How the clergy conveys immediacy to parishioners: An exploratory qualitative study. *The Journal of Communication and Religion, 18*(1), 35–47.

Pudlinski, C. (1998). Giving advice on a consumer-run warm line: Implicit and dilemmatic practices. *Communication Studies, 49,* 322–341.

Pudlinski, C. (2003). The multiplicity of response options in social support situations. *Qualitative Research Reports in Communication, 4,* 23–30.

Punch, M. (1994). Politics and ethics in qualitative research. In N. K. Denzin & Y. S. Lincoln (Eds.),

Handbook of qualitative research (pp. 83–97). Thousand Oaks, CA: Sage.

Putnam, L. L., & Wilson, C. E. (1982). Communicative strategies in organizational conflicts: Reliability and validity of a measurement scale. In M. Burgoon (Ed.), *Communication yearbook 6* (pp. 629–652). Beverly Hills: Sage.

Pyrczak, F., & Bruce, R. R. (2000). *Writing empirical research reports: A basic guide for students of the social and behavioral sciences* (3rd ed.). Los Angeles: Pyrczak.

Query, J. L., Jr., & Kreps, G. L. (1993). Using the critical incident method to evaluate and enhance organizational effectiveness. In S. L. Herndon & G. L. Kreps (Eds.), *Qualitative research: Applications in organizational communication* (pp. 63–77). Cresskill, NJ: Hampton Press.

Reel, B. W., & Thompson, T. L. (1994). A test of the effectiveness of strategies for talking about AIDS and condom use. *Journal of Applied Communication Research, 22,* 127–140.

Reel, B., & Thompson, T. L. (2004). Is it a matter of politeness? Face and effectiveness of messages about condom use. *Southern Communication Journal, 69,* 99–120.

Richmond, V. P., Smith, Jr., R. S., Heisel, A. D., & McCroskey, J. C. (2002). The association of physician socio-communicative style with physician credibility and patient satisfaction. *Communication Research Reports, 19,* 207–215.

Riffe, D., Lacy, S., & Fico, F. G. (1998). *Analyzing media messages: Using quantitative content analysis in research.* Mahwah, NJ: Erlbaum.

Roberto, A. J., Meyer, G., Boster, F. J., & Roberto, H. L. (2003). Adolescents' decisions about verbal and physical aggression: An application of the theory of reasoned action. *Human Communication Research, 29,* 135–147.

Robinson, J. D. (1998). Getting down to business: Talk, gaze, and body orientation during openings of doctor-patient consultations. *Human Communication Research, 25,* 97–123.

Rogan, R. G., & Hammer, M. R. (1994). Crisis negotiations: A preliminary investigation of facework in naturalistic conflict discourse. *Journal of Applied Communication Research, 22,* 216–231.

Rogers, L. E., & Farace, R. V. (1975). Analysis of relational communication in dyads: New measurement procedures. *Human Communication Research, 1,* 222–239.

Roskos-Ewoldsen, D. R., Yu, H. J., & Rhodes, N. (2004). Fear appeal messages affect accessibility of attitudes toward the threat and adaptive behaviors. *Communication Monographs, 71,* 49–69.

Roy, A., & Harwood, J. (1997). Underrepresented, positively portrayed: Older adults in television commercials. *Journal of Applied Communication Research, 25,* 39–56.

Rubin, A. M., & Perse, E. M. (1994). Measures of mass communication. In R. B. Rubin, P. Palmgreen, & H. E. Sypher (Eds.), *Communication research measures: A sourcebook* (pp. 37–56). New York: Guilford Press.

Rubin, R. B., Palmgreen, P., & Sypher, H. E. (Eds.). (2004). *Communication research measures: A sourcebook.* Mahwah, NJ: Erlbaum.

Rudd, G. (2000). The symphony: Organizational discourse and the symbolic tensions between artistic and business ideologies. *Journal of Applied Communication Research, 28,* 117–143.

Ryan, M. (1998). Pitfalls to avoid in conducting and describing scholarly research. *Journalism & Mass Communication Educator, 52*(4), 72–79.

Sabourin, T. C. (1995). The role of negative reciprocity in spouse abuse: A relational control analysis. *Journal of Applied Communication Research, 23,* 271–283.

Sabourin, T. C., & Stamp, G. H. (1995). Communication and the experience of dialectical tensions in family life: An examination of abusive and nonabusive families. *Communication Monographs, 62,* 213–242.

Sapsford, R., & Abbott, P. (1996). Ethics, politics, and research. In R. Sapsford & V. Jupp (Eds.), *Data collection and analysis* (pp. 317–342). Thousand Oaks, CA: Sage.

Sapsford, R., & Jupp, V. (1996). Validating evidence. In R. Sapsford & V. Jupp (Eds.), *Data collection and analysis* (pp. 1–24). Thousand Oaks, CA: Sage.

Schatzman, L., & Strauss, A. L. (1973). *Field research: Strategies for a natural sociology.* Englewood Cliffs, NJ: Prentice-Hall.

Schmitz, J., Rogers, E. M., Phillips, K., & Paschal, D. (1995). The Public Electronic Network (PEN) and the homeless in Santa Monica. *Journal of Applied Communication Research, 23,* 26–43.

Schneider, D. E., & Beaubien, R. A. (1996). A naturalistic investigation of compliance-gaining strategies employed by doctors in medical interviews. *Southern Communication Journal, 61,* 332–341.

Schneider, E. F., Lang, A., Shin, M., & Bradley, S. D. (2004). Death with a story: How story impacts emotional, motivational, and physiological responses to first-person shooter video games. *Human Communication Research, 30,* 361–375.

Schrodt, P. (2002). The relationship between organizational identification and organizational culture: Employee perceptions of culture and identifications in a retail sales organization. *Communication Studies, 53*, 189–202.

Schwarz, N., Groves, R. M., & Schuman, H. (1998). Survey methods. In D. T. Gilbert, S. T. Fiske, & G. Lindzey (Eds.), *The handbook of social psychology* (4th ed., Vol. 1, pp. 143–179). New York: McGraw-Hill.

Schwarz, N., & Hippler, H. (1991). Response alternatives: The impact of their choice and presentation order. In P. P. Biemer, R. M. Groves, L. E. Lyberg, N. A. Mathiowetz, & S. Sudman (Eds.), *Measurement errors in surveys* (pp. 41–56). New York: Wiley.

Scott, C. R., & Rockwell, S. C. (1997). The effect of communication, writing, and technology apprehension on likelihood to use new communication technologies. *Communication Education, 46*, 44–62.

Seibold, D. R., Kudsi, S., & Rude, M. (1993). Does communication training make a difference?: Evidence for the effectiveness of a presentation skills program. *Journal of Applied Communication Research, 21*, 111–131.

Selltiz, C., Jahoda, M., Deutsch, M., & Cook, S. W. (1959). *Research methods in social relations* (Rev. ed., one vol.). New York: Holt, Rinehart and Winston.

Shapiro, M. A. (2002). Generalizability in communication research. *Human Communication Research, 28*, 491–500.

Sharf, B. F. (1997). Communicating breast cancer on-line: Support and empowerment on the internet. *Women & Health, 26*, 65–84.

Sharf, B. F. (1999). Beyond netiquette: The ethics of doing naturalistic discourse research on the internet. In S. Jones (Ed.), *Doing internet research: Critical issues and methods for examining the net* (pp. 243–256). Thousand Oaks, CA: Sage.

Sieber, J. E. (1992). *Planning ethically responsible research: A guide for students and internal review boards.* Newbury Park, CA: Sage.

Sieber, J. E. (1994). Will the new code help researchers to be more ethical? *Professional Psychology: Research and Practice, 25*, 369–375.

Sieber, J. E. (1998). Planning ethically responsible research. In L. Bickman & D. J. Rog (Eds.), *Handbook of applied social research methods* (pp. 127–156). Thousand Oaks, CA: Sage.

Simon, J. L. (1969). *Basic research methods in social science.* New York: Random House.

Sirkin, R. M. (1995). *Statistics for the social sciences.* Thousand Oaks, CA: Sage.

Slater, M. D., Karan, D. N., Rouner, D., & Walters, D. (2002). Effects of threatening visuals and announcer differences on responses to televised alcohol warnings. *Journal of Applied Communication Research, 30*, 27–49.

Smith, F. L., & Keyton, J. (2001). Organizational storytelling: Metaphors for relational power and identity struggles. *Management Communication Quarterly, 15*, 149–182.

Soliz, J., & Harwood, J. (2003). Perceptions of communication in a family relationship and the reduction of intergroup prejudice. *Journal of Applied Communication Research, 31*, 320–345.

Sparks, G. C., Pellechia, M., & Irvine, C. (1998). Does television news about UFOs affect viewers' UFO beliefs?: An experimental investigation. *Communication Quarterly, 46*, 284–294.

Stacks, D. W., & Salwen, M. B. (1996). Integrating theory and research: Starting with questions. In M. B. Salwen & D. W. Stacks (Eds.), *An integrated approach to communication theory and research* (pp. 3–14). Mahwah, NJ: Erlbaum.

Stafford, L., Kline, S. L., & Dimmick, J. (1999). Home e-mail: Relational maintenance and gratification opportunities. *Journal of Broadcasting & Electronic Media, 43*, 659–669.

Stamp, G. H., & Sabourin, T. C. (1995). Accounting for violence: An analysis of male spousal abuse narratives. *Journal of Applied Communication Research, 23*, 284–307.

Stanovich, K. E. (1986). *How to think straight about psychology.* Glenview, IL: Scott Foresman.

Stephenson, M. T. (2002). Anti-drug public service announcements targeting parents: An analysis and evaluation. *Southern Communication Journal, 67*, 335–350.

Stitt, J. K., Simonds, C. J., & Hunt, S. K. (2003). Evaluation fidelity: An examination of criterion-based assessment and rater training in the speech communication classroom. *Communication Studies, 54*, 341–353.

Strauss, A. L. (1987). *Qualitative analysis for social scientists.* New York: Cambridge University Press.

Strauss, A. L. & Corbin, J. (1998). *Basics of qualitative research: Techniques and procedures for developing grounded theory.* Thousand Oaks, CA: Sage.

Street, R. L., Jr. (1993). Analyzing messages and their outcomes: Questionable assumptions, possible solutions. *Southern Communication Journal, 58*, 85–90.

Sudman, S., & Bradburn, N. M. (1982). *Asking questions.* San Francisco: Jossey-Bass.

Sunwolf, & Leets, L. (2004). Being left out: Rejecting outsiders and communicating group boundaries in childhood and adolescent peer groups. *Journal of Applied Communication Research, 32*, 195–223.

Sutter, D. L., & Martin, M. M. (1998). Verbal aggression during disengagement of dating relationships. *Communication Research Reports, 15*, 318–326.

Swazey, J. P., Anderson, M. S., & Lewis, K. S. (1993). Ethical problems in academic research. *American Scientist, 81*, 542–553.

Sypher, H. E. (1980). Illusory correlation in communication research. *Human Communication Research, 7*, 83–87.

Tabachnick, B. G., & Fidell, L. S. (2001). *Using multivariate statistics* (4th ed.). Boston: Allyn & Bacon.

Tan, A., Nelson, L., Dong, Q., & Tan, G. (1997). Value acceptance in adolescent socialization: A test of a cognitive-functional theory of television effects. *Communication Monographs, 64*, 82–97.

Taylor, B. C. (1996). Make bomb, save world: Reflections on dialogic nuclear ethnography. *Journal of Contemporary Ethnography, 25*, 120–143.

Taylor, B. C. (1997). Home zero: Images of home and field in nuclear-cultural studies. *Western Journal of Communication, 61*, 209–234.

Teven, J. J., & Comadena, M. E. (1996). The effects of office aesthetic quality on students' perceptions of teacher credibility and communicator style. *Communication Research Reports, 13*, 101–108.

Tidwell, L. C., & Walther, J. B. (2002). Computer-mediated communication effects on disclosure, impressions, and interpersonal evaluations: Getting to know one another a bit at a time. *Human Communication Research, 28*, 317–348.

Tompkins, P. K. (1994). Principles of rigor for assessing evidence in "qualitative" communication research. *Western Journal of Communication, 58*, 44–50.

Tracy, S. J. (2002). When questioning turns to face threat: An interactional sensitivity in 911 call-taking. *Western Journal of Communication, 66*, 129–157.

Tracy, S. J., & Tracy, K. (1998). Emotion labor at 911: A case study and theoretical critique. *Journal of Applied Communication Research, 26*, 390–411.

Treadwell, D. F., & Harrison, T. M. (1994). Conceptualizing and assessing organizational image: Model images, commitment, and communication. *Communication Monographs, 61*, 63–85.

Tucker, R. K., Weaver, R. L., & Berryman-Fink, C. (1981). *Research in speech communication.* Englewood Cliffs, NJ: Prentice-Hall.

Vanderpool, H. Y. (1996). Introduction to part I. In H. Y. Vanderpool (Ed.), *The ethics of research involving human subjects: Facing the 21st century* (pp. 33–44). Frederick, MD: University Publishing Group.

Van Swol, L. M. (2003). The effects of nonverbal mirroring on perceived persuasiveness, agreement with an imitator, and reciprocity in a group discussion. *Communication Research, 30*, 461–480.

Van Maanen, J. (1988). *Tales of the field: On writing ethnography.* Chicago: University of Chicago Press.

Vogt, W. P. (1999). *Dictionary of statistics & methodology: A nontechnical guide for the social sciences* (2nd ed.). Thousand Oaks, CA: Sage.

Waitzkin, H. (1993). Interpretive analysis of spoken discourse: Dealing with the limitations of quantitative and qualitative methods. *Southern Communication Journal, 58, 128–146.*

Walker, K. L., & Dickson, F. C. (2004). An exploration of illness-related narratives in marriage: The identification of illness-identity scripts. *Journal of Social and Personal Relationships, 21*, 527–544.

Weber, R. P. (1990). *Basic content analysis* (2nd ed.). Newbury Park, CA: Sage.

Webster, J. G., & Lin, S. (2002). The internet audience: Web use as mass behavior. *Journal of Broadcasting & Electronic Media, 46*, 1–12.

Weick, K. (1985). Systematic observation methods. In G. Lindzey & E. Aronson (Eds.), *Handbook of social psychology: Theory and method* (3rd ed., pp. 567–634). New York: Random House.

Weitzman, E. A. (2000). Software and qualitative research. In N. K. Denzin & Y. S. Lincoln (Eds.), *Handbook of qualitative research* (2nd ed., pp. 803–820). Thousand Oaks, CA: Sage.

Wigley, C. J., III. (1999). Verbal aggressiveness and communicator style characteristics of summoned jurors as predictors of actual jury selection. *Communication Monographs, 66*, 266–275.

Wilkinson, A. M. (1991). *The scientist's handbook for writing papers and dissertations.* Englewood Cliffs, NJ: Prentice-Hall.

Williams, F. (1968). *Reasoning with statistics: Simplified examples in communication research.* New York: Holt, Rinehart and Winston.

Witmer, D. F. (1997). Communication and recovery: Structuration as an ontological approach to organizational culture. *Communication Monographs, 64*, 324–349.

Wolcott, H. F. (1990). *Writing up qualitative research.* Newbury Park, CA: Sage.

Wolcott, H. F. (2001). *Writing up qualitative research* (2nd ed.). Thousand Oaks, CA: Sage.

Wrench, J. S., & Richmond, V. P. (2004). Understanding the psychometric properties of the humor assessment instrument through an analysis of the relationships between teacher humor assessment and instructional communication variables in the college classroom. *Communication Research Reports, 21*, 92–103.

Wright, D. B. (1997). *Understanding statistics: An introduction for the social sciences.* Thousand Oaks, CA: Sage.

Wrobbel, E. D. (1998). A conversation analyst's response to Patterson, Neupauer, Burant, Koehn, and Reed. *Western Journal of Communication, 62,* 209–216.

Xu, Y., & Burleson, B. R. (2001). Effects of sex, culture, and support type on perceptions of spousal social support: An assessment of the "support gap" hypothesis in early marriage. *Human Communication Research, 27,* 535–566.

Zakahi, W. R., & McCroskey, J. C. (1989). Willingness to communicate: A potential confounding variable in communication research. *Communication Reports, 2,* 96–104.

Zimmerman, D. H. (1988). On conversation: The conversation analytic perspective. In J. A. Anderson (Ed.), *Communication yearbook 11* (pp. 406–432). Newbury Park, CA: Sage.

Zoller, H. M. (2003). Health on the line: Identity and disciplinary control in employee occupational health and safety discourse. *Journal of Applied Communication Research, 31,* 118–139.

AUTHOR INDEX

SUBJECT INDEX